THE HISTORY OF PHOTOGRAPHY

AS SEEN THROUGH THE SPIRA COLLECTION

THE HISTORY OF

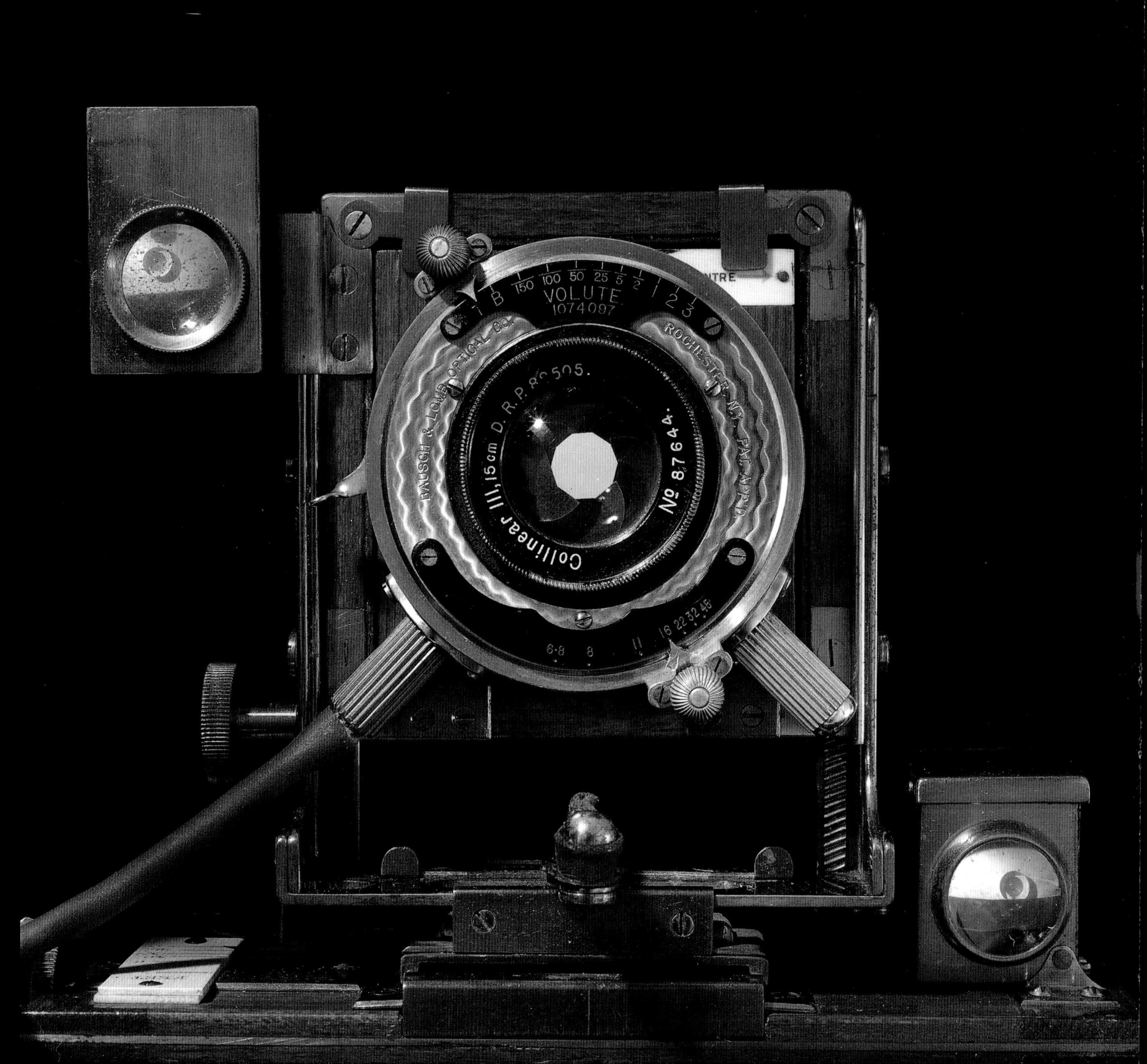

PHOTOGRAPHY

AS SEEN THROUGH THE SPIRA COLLECTION

S. F. SPIRA

WITH EATON S. LOTHROP, JR.

AND JONATHAN B. SPIRA

PREFACE BY HEINZ K. HENISCH

APERTURE

Table of Contents

Frontispiece: Volute shutter, Improved Model, Bausch & Lomb Optical Co., ca. 1905. The Volute shutter was constructed so that its blades also operated as the diaphragm. While the top speed of 1/150 second was not as fast as some other shutters, the Volute's speeds were nearly one hundred percent reliable.

Foreword

My father has been writing the history of photography for over thirty years. He started collecting photographica in the 1960s through a rather indirect route. Although he is known as founder of Spiratone, having opened up the U.S. market to low-cost, quality Japanese photographic goods and conceived of and designed many now-standard photographic accessories, when he turned to an avocation, it was the collecting of Habsburg autographs. He later became interested in autographs from the photographic world; one of his first acquisitions in this category was a framed autograph of Daguerre, something my mother discovered in a B. Altman's advertisement in the Sunday *New York Times*. This still hangs over the desk in his study. It was a natural progression for him to move from autographs to the equipment and images created by these same people.

In fact, the *New York Times* referred to my father as "a pioneer" and "one of the nation's leading collectors of photography equipment." As noted editor John Durniak wrote in *infinity*, "Henry Ford did not invent the automobile and Fred Spira did not invent photography, yet, both these men have had almost as much influence on their respective fields as the original inventors."

It is a hallmark of my father's style that his collection was not to be a historical curiosity but a living phenomenon. At every opportunity, he has sought to bring contemporary meaning and significance to his collection. My father built his home as a showplace of technology (remote control panels abounded, controlling everything from aerials to draperies to lighting to oversized stereo speakers coming out of walls) and of art (built into yet another wall was a huge Lumia, a piece of kinetic art of his own commission).

My father followed his own philosophy of collecting. He was alternately participant and historian, not just a collector who amassed thousands of objects. His desire was not to collect dozens of Leicas with different screws, but rather to show how each was developed as the result of a previous thought or design. He showed the connection between one phase of photographic development and the next and the connection between photography and other disciplines. Not only did he acquire the rare Sutton Camera, but found an interesting aside in the novels that Thomas Sutton himself wrote, which feature his unique panoramic camera as well as a daguerreotyping protagonist. The Spira Collection came to hold, almost in equal measure, hardware (largely, cameras), images, books, and ephemera. Usually the ephemera told the story of a particular camera or technology and helped place it in a larger historical context.

The world is richer for the time and effort he put into his work. It has been indeed a labor of love for photography which represents his life.

But today, I am writing the Foreword, not he. Illness has prevented him from participating in these last phases of the book. His encouragement to me as I complete this project has been the source of my energy and inspiration.

—JONATHAN B. SPIRA

Preface

To photo-enthusiasts of my generation, the name "Spiratone" remains a ringing symbol of service to the photographic community. It was the trade name of the company which, in the pre-digital days of blessed memory, supplied every conceivable camera accessory to eager clients. Its advertisements kept the community informed of recent technical developments and helped sustain public interest in the field. "Spiratone" was a name to be reckoned with.

To create such a company was a considerable achievement in itself, but its founder did not stop there; he went on to establish his own private Spira Collection, a treasure chest of photographica of lasting value and fame. No aspect of photography escaped his attention; the emphasis was not on selective specifics, but on the total impact of the invention. The Spira Collection grew to be one of the largest, most comprehensive, and most distinguished collections of photographic equipment and literature in the world. It has long served the needs of authors everywhere, thanks to the liberal generosity with which Fred Spira has always been willing to meet requests for the use of his material in the books and journal articles of other scholars. Over the years, Mr. Spira came to be in demand as a highly valued contributor to the literature of photography and as a lecturer at conventions. The variety of uncommon themes he explored on such occasions (e.g., "Photographs in Early Employment Contracts," "Graves and Graven Images," "The Photo-Rebus," "Daguerreotypes as a Selling Tool") reflects the enormous range of his interests.

From 1980–81, "Selections from the Spira Collection" was exhibited at George Eastman House, Rochester. The present book represents an attempt to share the collection with a wider circle of photo-historians and with the general public. Because the emphasis of the collection is "social" in the broadest sense, its benefits will be felt in fields as diverse as photo-technology, historical record keeping, photo-journalism, advertising and propaganda, war photography, studio photography, stereo photography, stage photography, medical photography, archaeological and architectural photography, photo-jewelry, photography-and-painting, photography-and-humor, and photography-and-music. We have good reason to be grateful for the work that brought this volume, with its superbly useful illustrations, into being. I feel certain that it will stand the test of time as an important document in its own right, and as a monument to the spirit Fred Spira brought to his enterprise.

—HEINZ K. HENISCH

Professor Emeritus of the History of Photography, Pennsylvania State University

Founding Editor (1977–1991) of the international quarterly *History of Photography*

CHAPTER ONE:

PHOTOGRAPHY'S PRECURSORS

Scioptric ball (ox eye), English, ca. 1785.

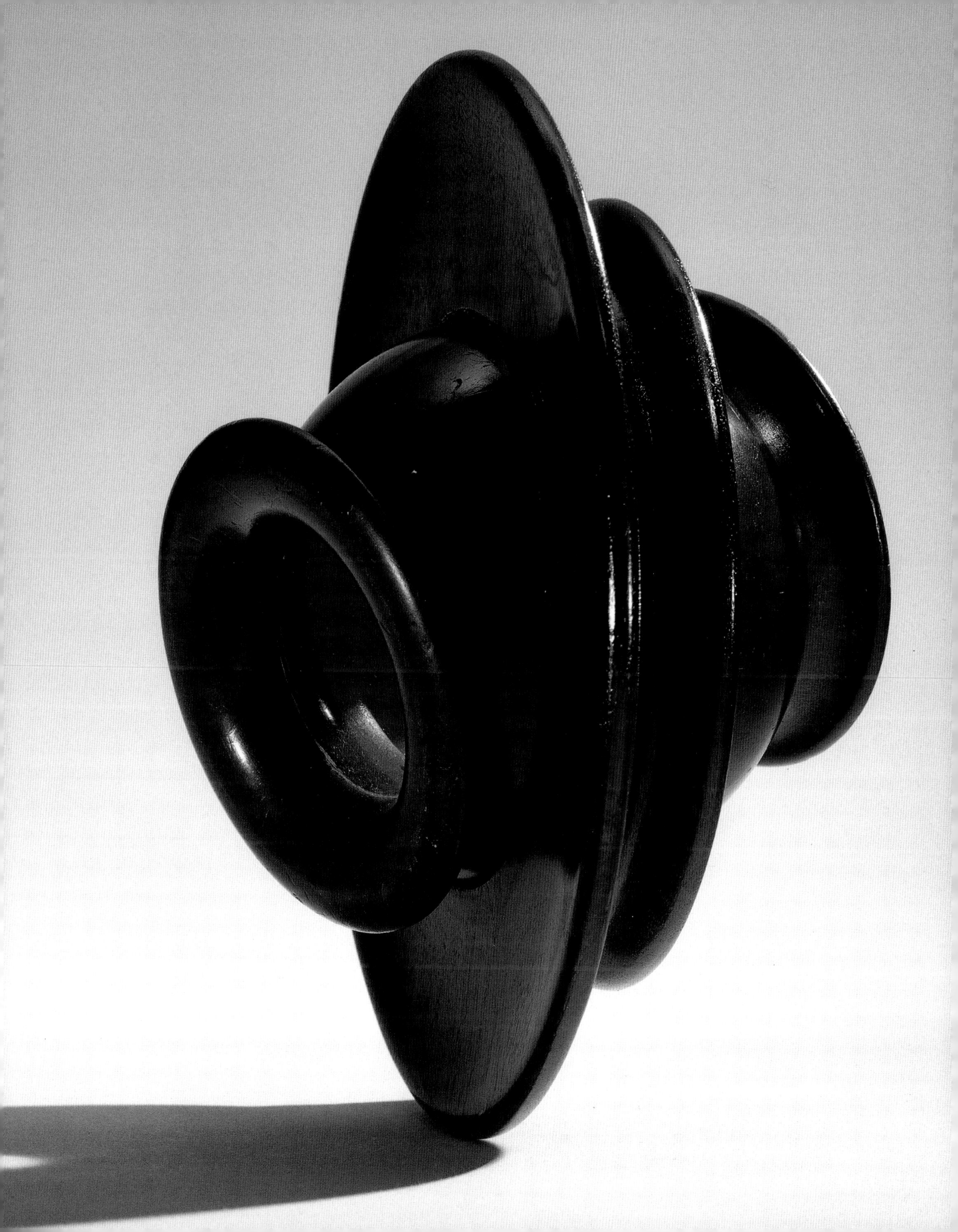

For ages, human beings have had the impulse to depict themselves and their surroundings. Since the first marks were made on cave walls more than 35,000 years ago, people have drawn, painted, and carved representations of their lives, observations, ideas, and beliefs. But it is only very recently that humankind has been able to enlist light, the very energy that illuminates all that is seen, to this end.

The process of photography relies on the confluence and interaction of three components: light, a closed chamber with an opening through which the light can pass, and a light-sensitive medium. Louis Jacques Mandé Daguerre and William Henry Fox Talbot separately announced processes in 1839 that united these three elements. Their discoveries were made possible by earlier optical innovations and tools for the facilitation of representation.

Man's early photographic training perhaps began, then, with the observation of the behavior of shadows. In most cases, an object illuminated by a light source casts a distorted shadow. However, when a light source is positioned directly in line with an object and intersects the surface plane behind the object at exactly 90 degrees, the object will cast a shadow that accurately retains its proportions. The distance of the illuminated object from the light source, as well as from the surface upon which the shadow is cast, determines the degree to which a shadow is enlarged.

This principle was first used as a drawing tool in the silhouette. Made by tracing the shadow of an object or person cast on a piece of cloth or paper, the silhouette is an accurate two-dimensional representation of form. Shadow silhouettes have long been known, but only received their modern name in the mid-1700s, when Étienne de Silhouette, one of King Louis XV's financial controllers, became a public advocate for this type of shadow drawing as a cheaper alternative to the painted portrait.

L'expérience du professeur Charles, woodcut, from *Les merveilles de la photographie*, Gaston Tissandier, 1874. The purported making of photographic silhouettes by Jacques Charles, prior to the invention of photography.

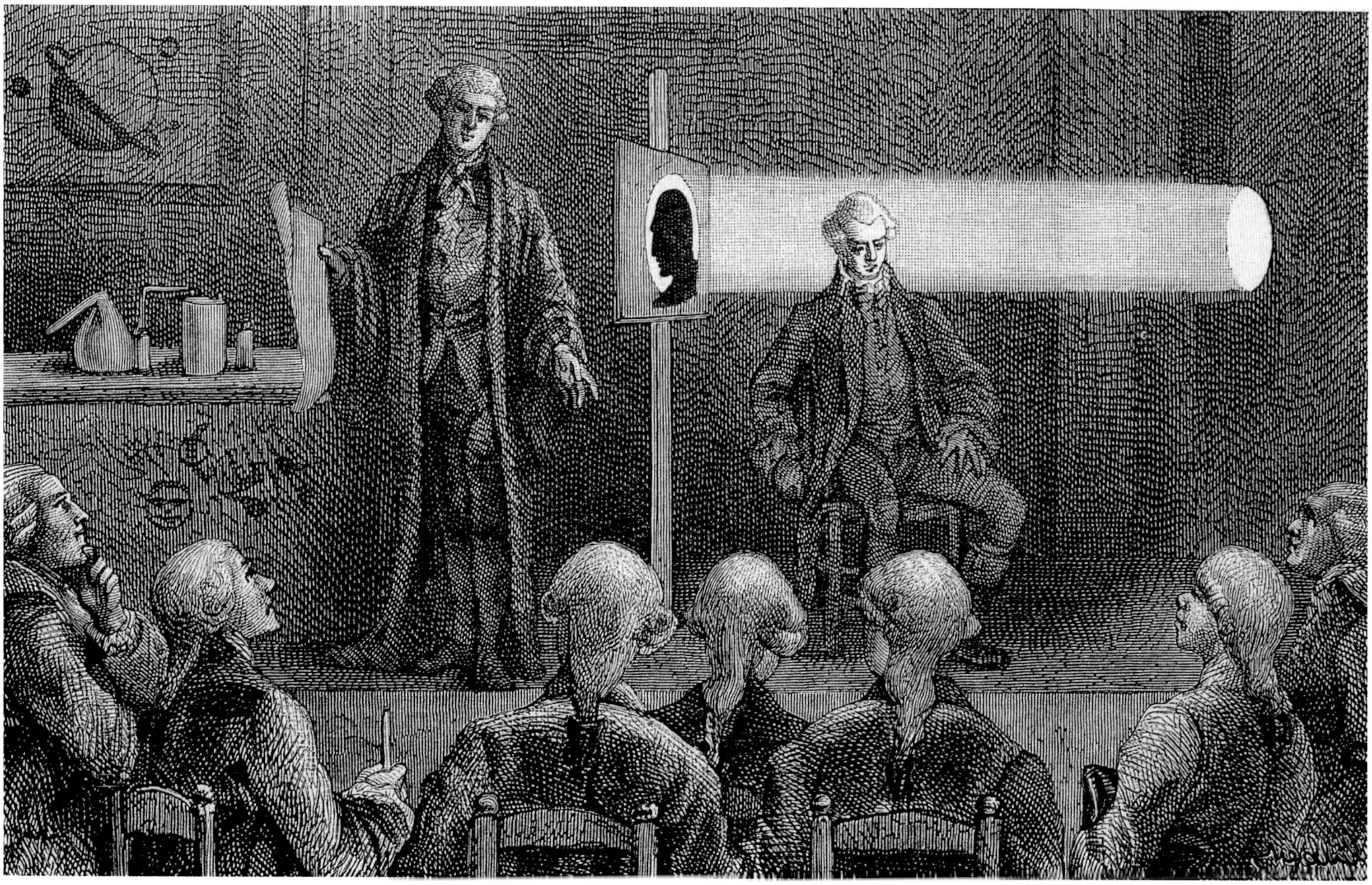

Silhouettes were also an ideal method for preserving likenesses of Europe's expanding middle classes. By the end of the eighteenth century, silhouettes were produced using profile machines, which employed a pantograph, a drawing tool invented in 1743, to reduce the scale of the outline to an acceptable size. Either the sun or a lantern served as the light source.

As a by-product of silhouette production, several inroads were made into our understanding of the behavior of light and its photographic potential. For example, Jacques Charles, who invented the hydrogen balloon, was reputed to have made silhouettes on silver-salt-coated paper in the early 1800s.

The consideration of the camera lucida in regard to the history of photography is somewhat problematic. Though the word *camera* is part of its name, the camera lucida is an open optical instrument; there is no "room" (*camera* is Latin for "chamber" or "enclosed area") involved. The term *camera lucida* was first applied by Robert Hook, in the 1600s, to an instrument corresponding in some respects to a microscope. However, the camera lucida referred to in most histories of photography bears no resemblance to that earlier instrument. The more familiar instrument was invented by William H. Wollaston and introduced in 1807.

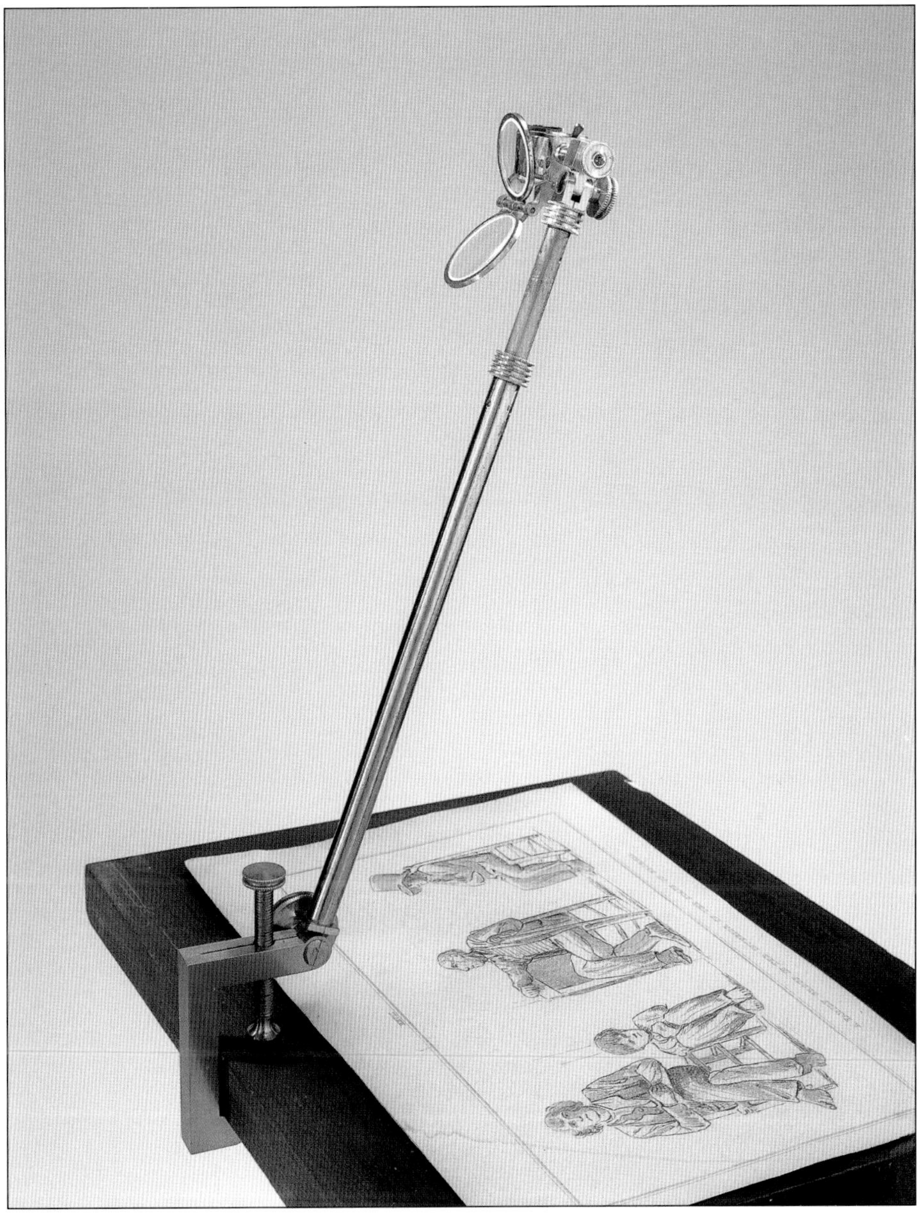

Camera lucida, English, ca. 1835.

Wollaston's camera lucida was a small, portable instrument, made of brass. Resembling a large magnifying glass, it consisted of a clamp that could be affixed to a surface, such as a drawing table. By looking through a prism attached to the same rod, the user of the camera lucida could see both his drawing paper and the object or scene directly in front of the camera lucida at the same time. By tracing the faint, superimposed image onto the drawing paper, an accurate rendition could be obtained. It should be noted, however, that the camera lucida required much skill at drawing in order to achieve successful results.

The camera lucida was used by both professional and amateur artists. One such amateur was William Henry Fox Talbot, who employed the device to make sketches of the shore while vacationing at Lake Como, Italy, in 1833. As he later wrote, in 1844 in *The Pencil of Nature*, "I should say, attempting to take [pictures]: but with the smallest possible amount of success." After "fruitless attempts," Talbot abandoned the camera lucida and turned to another artist's aid, the camera obscura. While using that instrument, he got the idea to capture and fix these images on paper.

The principle of the camera obscura (literally, "dark room") has been known for centuries. Prior to the sixteenth century, references to the camera obscura were limited to the observation of its principle: light passing through a tiny hole in the wall or shutter of a darkened room forms an inverted image on the surface located opposite the opening. This axiom of optics was recognized in the fourth century B.C. by Aristotle, in regard to observing eclipses, and was probably known in China around the same time. Other references to the camera obscura appeared in subsequent years. In the tenth century, the Arabian scholar Alhazen described the camera obscura. Roger Bacon, in his writings in the thirteenth century, seems to have been familiar with the camera obscura as a device for observing eclipses. In the fifteenth century, Leonardo da Vinci clearly described the camera obscura in one of his notebooks.

Although knowledge of the concept preceded him by some centuries, Giovanni Battista Della Porta is credited as the first to suggest an instrument using the principle of the camera obscura as an artist's aid. His book *Magiae naturalis*, published in 1558, described the camera obscura more fully than any previous work. It was particularly effective in spreading knowledge about the instrument, which quickly became indispensable to artists in mastering the new style of rendering perspective realistically in painting.

The employment of a lens to produce a more brilliant image seems to be attributable to the Italian physician and mathematician Girolamo Cardano. The image formed when light enters a camera obscura through a tiny hole is always in focus but somewhat dim. Its size varies with the distance between the hole and the surface on which it is projected. The introduction of lenses to the camera obscura brought the necessity of focusing the image. In 1636, one Daniel Schwenter described an unusual device for viewing the exterior of a room. Called the "globus" or "scioptric ball," and later "ox-eye," it consisted of a ball with a hole through its center and a lens at either end of the hole. By placing the ball in a mount in the camera obscura's opening, it was possible to vary the field of view.

As the camera obscura's popularity grew among artists and scientists, it became more compact. In the late 1500s, Friedrich Risner, a German mathematician, recommended the building of a light, portable wooden hut to be used as a camera obscura. In the mid-1600s, the Jesuit scholar Athanesius Kircher described a cube-shaped lightweight box fitted with horizontal bars for sedan chair-like portability. Lenses in each side wall focused images on the walls of an inner cube of paper. The artist entered the box from beneath and then drew the image on the paper. In addition to the room- and sedan chair-like portable cameras obscura, a number of other forms were developed over the years. Johannes Kepler, the astronomer, used a tent camera obscura to survey areas in the Austrian kingdom. In *Magia universalis*, in 1657, Kaspar Schott published the first account of a small, portable camera obscura. Of box-in-box construction, to allow focusing, this device had a small hole in the side affording a view into the box's interior so the user could see the image.

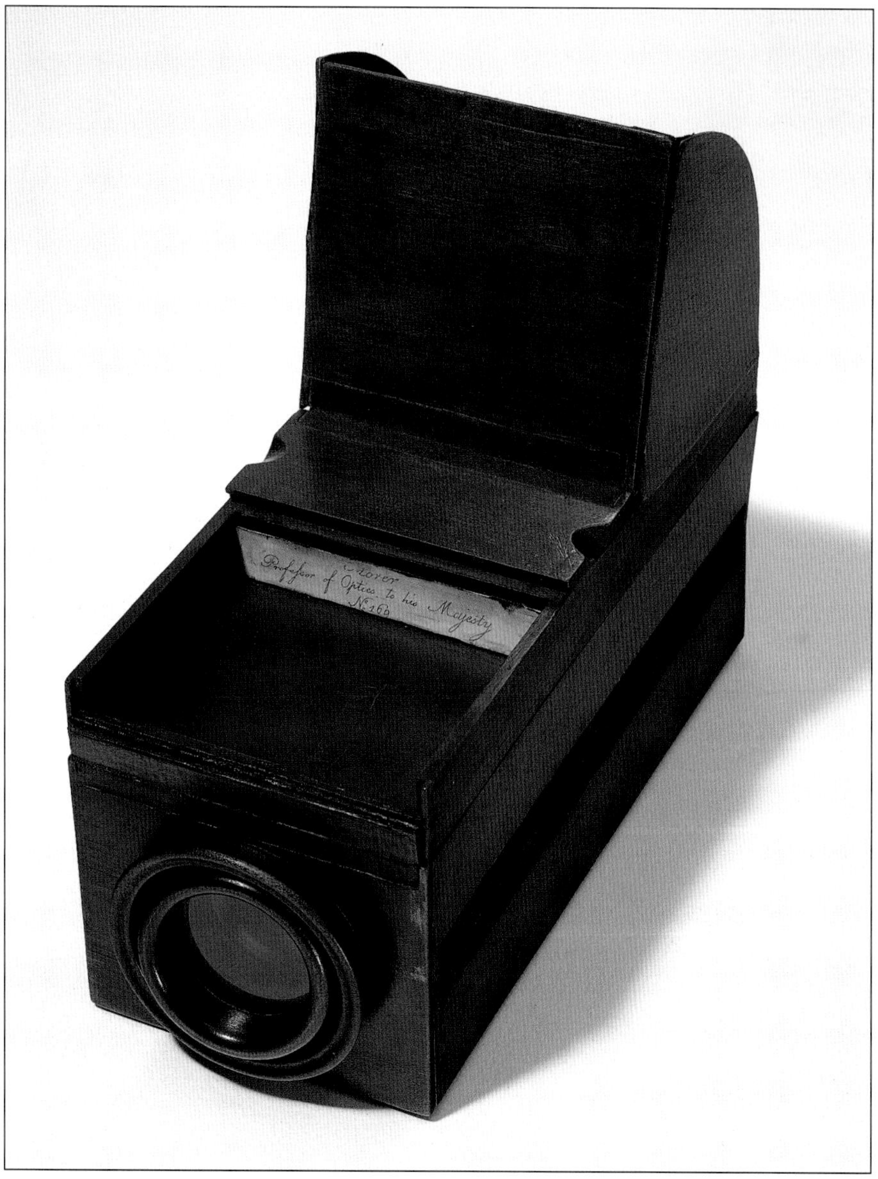

Reflex camera obscura, English, ca. 1790. This instrument is fitted with a scioptric ball.

Opposite: Book-form camera obscura, Robert Sayer, ca. 1765, 4 1/4" x 15 1/4" x 22 1/2" collapsible camera obscura.

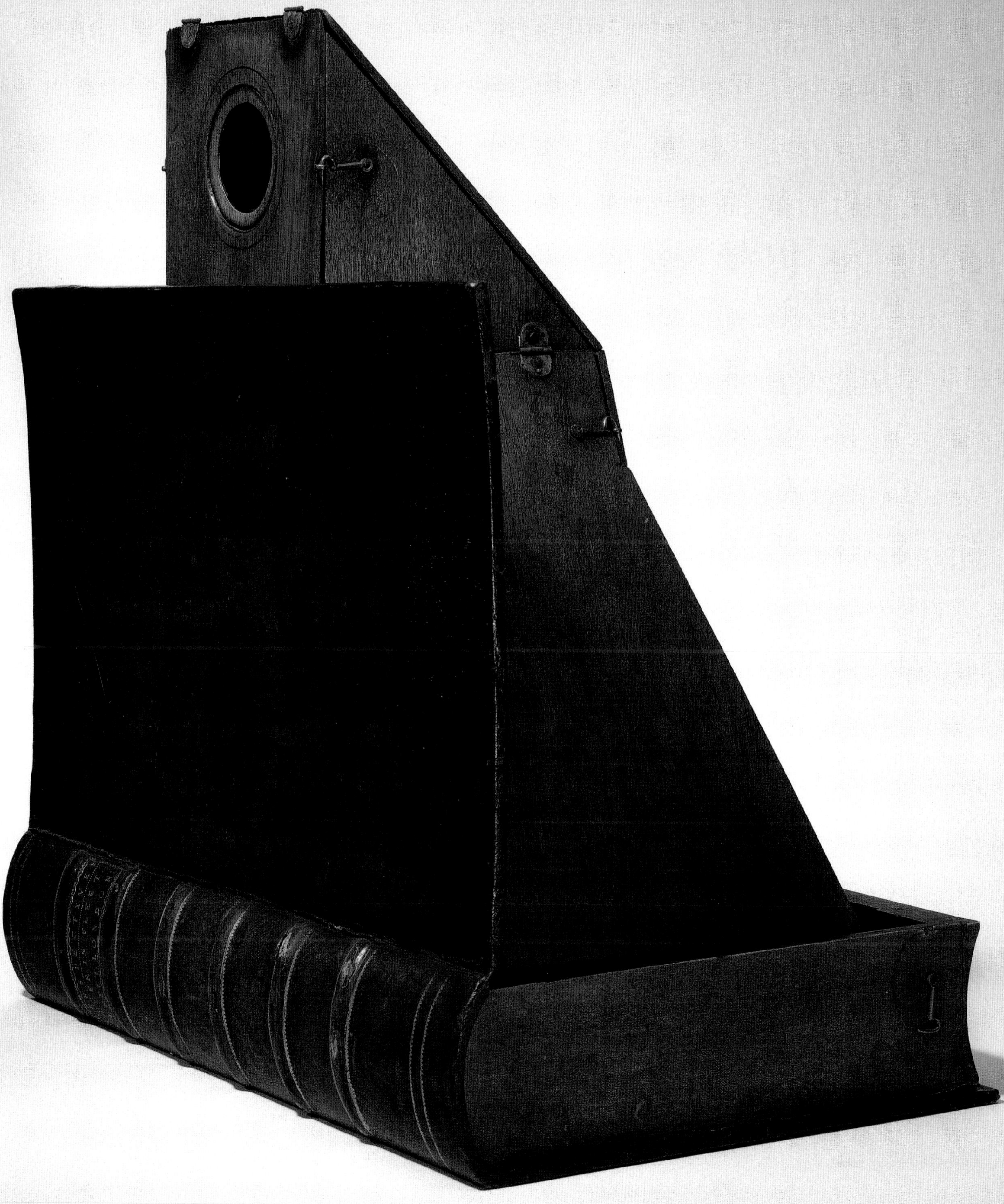

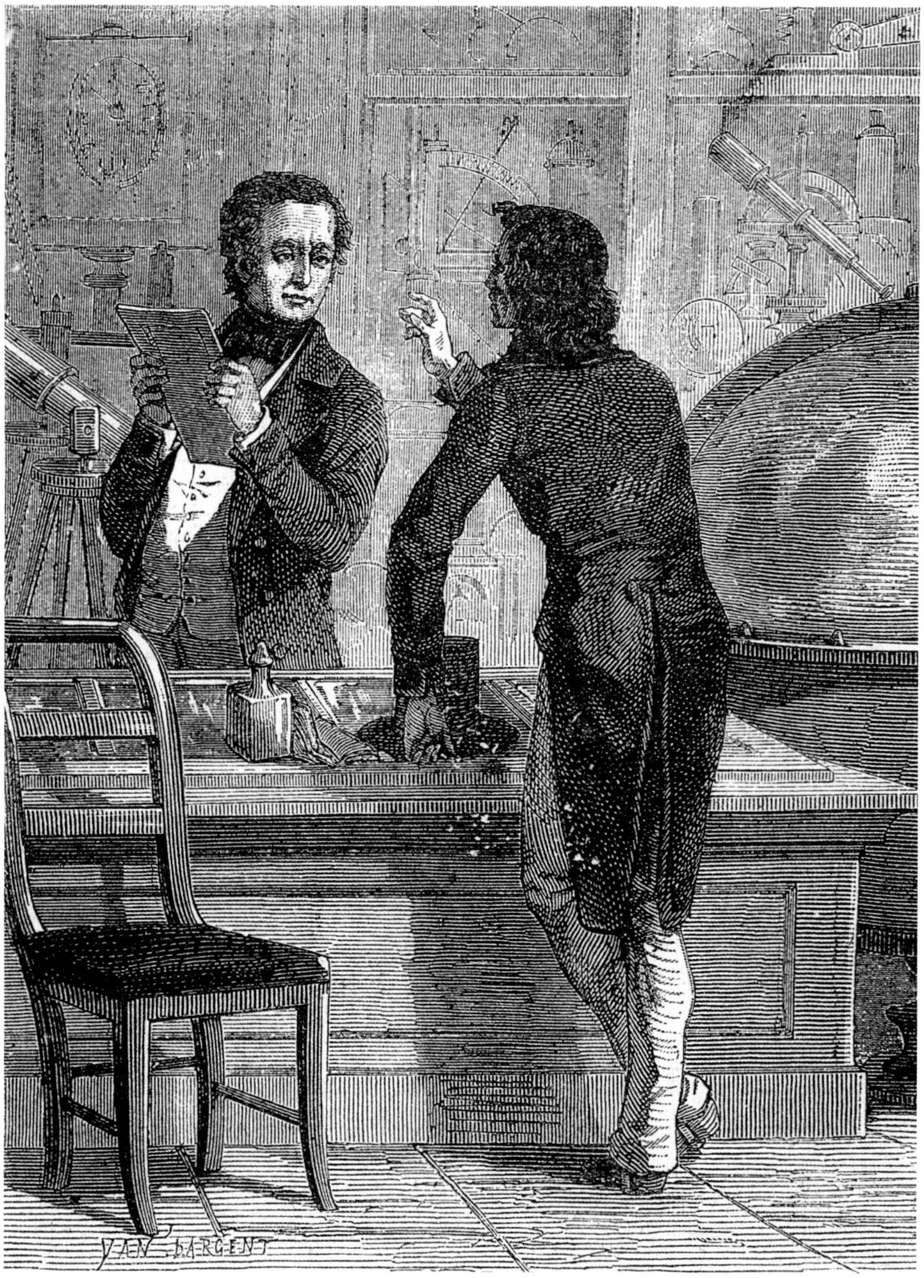

Yan Dargent, Nicéphore Niépce exhibiting his prints to Charles Chevalier, December, 1825, woodcut, from Frank Leslie's *Popular Monthly*, July 1876.

While all cameras obscura projected an image onto the surface opposite the opening, the image was an inverted one. The problem could be corrected, however, by placing a mirror at a 45-degree angle to the path of the light coming through the lens. This reflected the image upward onto a surface placed at a right angle to the plane at which the light entered. Described and illustrated in 1676 by Johann Sturm, a German engraver, this construction anticipated—and informed—the form of the single-lens reflex camera, introduced almost two centuries later.

During the eighteenth century, the camera obscura came into increased use among artists and travelers alike. The Italian artist Canaletto, noted for his landscapes of Venice, used the camera obscura to attain perspective in his sweeping scenes. Count Francesco Algarotti, in his 1764 *Essay in Painting*, devoted an entire chapter to the camera obscura and its use. Portability was one of the key elements that contributed to the increased popularity of cameras obscura. In 1769 Georg Bander illustrated a "table model" camera obscura that looked more like a cumbersome writing desk, with telescoping wooden segments beneath it, toward the front. Another, more delicate, table-model camera obscura was designed by A. Guyot in 1770. Collapsible cameras obscura were popular as well. Some were cloth, tentlike in form, and could be placed on a table for use, while others were equipped with folding wooden sides. All of these were carried in chests, sometimes with the appearance of folio books. Large, room-type cameras obscura, popular as tourist attractions in cities and seaside towns, often had a mirror mounted on top, outside, that could be rotated 360 degrees. The image was then projected onto a table in the middle of the room. A number of these devices built in the nineteenth century are still in operation today.

With the perfection of the small camera obscura, two of the three components for photography had been established: light and the closed, dark chamber. All that remained to enable the discovery of photography was for the chemical component to be harnessed. As early as the thirteenth century, Albertus Magnus was reputed to have noticed that salts of silver were turned black by the action of light. Angelo Sala in the early 1600s and William Homberg in the late 1600s observed this same reaction in silver nitrate, although both attributed the blackening to the sun's heat rather than its light.

In 1725 Johann Schulze of Nuremberg performed a series of experiments involving the action of sunlight on silver nitrate. Filling a bottle with chalk that was saturated with nitric acid and a small amount of silver, Schulze placed a paper stencil, with words cut out of it, over the bottle.

Where the words had been cut out, the chalk turned black. When the stencil was removed, the remaining material also turned black. Through further experimentation, Schulze isolated silver nitrate as the crucial reactive agent. Although he never developed any practical application of this discovery, in a literal sense Schulze's work with the stencil and the silver nitrate-soaked chalk was impermanent photography.

Giacomo Beccaria was the first to discover a similar reaction to light with silver chloride. Carl Wilhelm Scheele also experimented with silver chloride and light's action upon it. He discovered that silver chloride was soluble in ammonia, but not after it was exposed to sunlight. While this was a form of fixing, rendering the darkened portion of the silver chloride powder placed on paper permanent, Scheele failed to recognize its significance.

In 1773 Josiah Wedgwood sought to use a camera obscura to copy ornamental pictures onto china produced in his family's factory. In the late 1700s, Thomas Wedgwood, one of Josiah's sons, began various photographic experiments. He employed silver nitrate in making contact prints of insects' wings and plant fibers, but was unable to fix the images permanently. Humphrey Davy, an acquaintance of Thomas Wedgwood's, repeated some of Wedgwood's experiments, perhaps even working with him. But the ability to fix images continued to elude them both.

It was in the 1820s and 1830s that the elements necessary for photography to be born began to come together. Three individuals, each working independently, developed photographic processes in which a stable, relatively permanent image was formed. These individuals were Joseph Nicéphore Niépce and Louis Jacques Mandé Daguerre, both Frenchmen, and William Henry Fox Talbot, an Englishman.

The first of these three to experiment with photography and the first to produce stable results was Niépce, an inventor from Chalon-sur-Saône who began his work in the field in 1816. He gained familiarity with the camera obscura by using it to project images onto lithographic limestone. No light-sensitive chemicals were employed in this process. In the 1820s, Niépce began experimenting with bitumen of Judea—a form of asphalt—in the reproduction of prints, trying glass, stone, and copper, in succession, as a base, until in 1826 he finally settled on pewter. While bitumen of Judea could normally be dissolved in oil of lavender, when the bitumen hardened as a result of the action of light, it became insoluble. From 1816 to 1820, Niépce also carried out photographic experiments

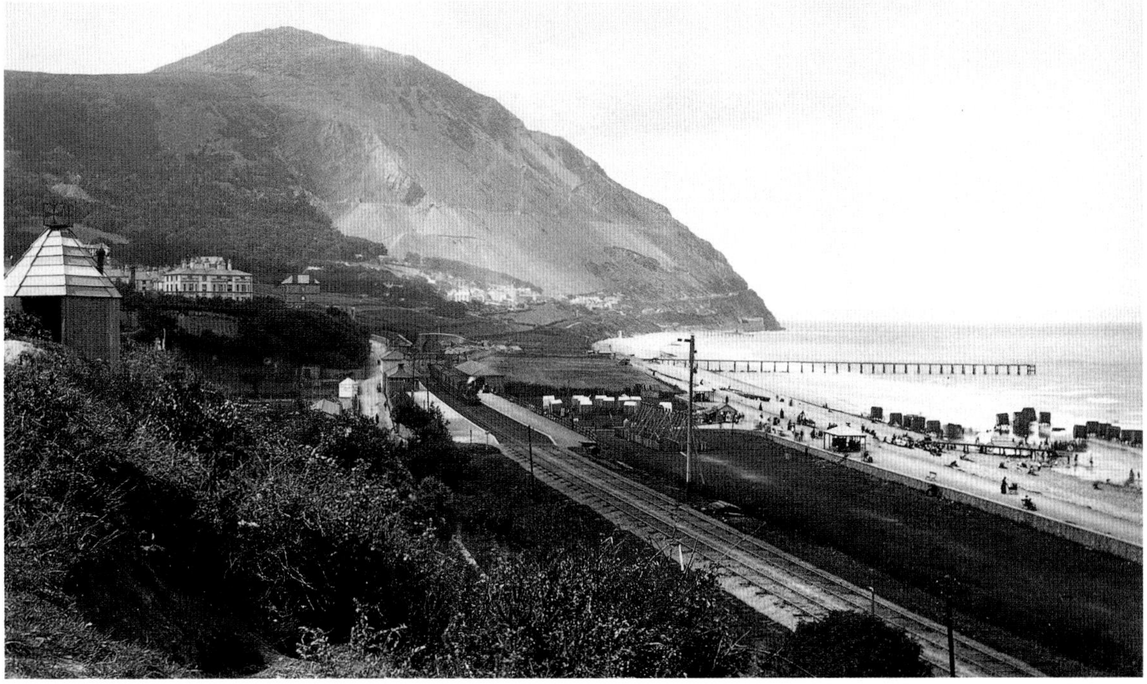

Francis Bedford, Penmaenmawr from the camera obscura, ca. 1875, albumen print, 5" x 7 3/4". Welsh seaside resort, with camera obscura at left.

FOCUS: *The Diorama*

Prior to his photographic endeavors, Louis Jacques Mandé Daguerre was a well-known figure in the artistic community of Paris. After displaying talent at an early age, Daguerre was apprenticed to an architect when just thirteen years old. Three years later, he became a pupil of Eugene-Marie Degotti, a painter of scenery at the Paris Opera, commencing a long relationship with theater.

In the early 1800s, Daguerre assisted Pierre Prevost, a painter of scenery for the Paris Panorama. Housed in a circular building, the Panorama gave its audience, seated on a round platform before a 16-by-45-foot semicircular painted canvas, the illusion of all-round vision. The Panorama was created in the early 1790s by Robert Barker. Following the popularity of the original location in London's Leicester Square, Panoramas were opened in major cities throughout Europe and America.

Through his involvement with the Panorama, Daguerre came into contact with another painter, Charles-Marie Bouton. Together they developed an improved form of the Panorama, which they named the Diorama. In this theater without actors, light was reflected onto or transmitted through a gigantic screen of transparent muslin, painted on both sides. The paintings were two depictions of the same scene, usually day and night. Variations in lighting gave two different effects. The audience was seated on a circular, moving platform and while they rotated, the Diorama produced the sensation of being inside a turning world.

Daguerre's Diorama opened in Paris in July 1822, to immediate success. His talent for drawing and painting, aided by use of the camera obscura, created an enticing, realistic effect for the Parisians and tourists who visited the Diorama. Nicéphore Niépce, another photographic pioneer, saw the Diorama in 1827 and was duly impressed. Writing to his son, he told of a scene depicting a Swiss village "facing a mountain of tremendous height." He commented, "The illusion is even so great that one attempts to leave one's box in order to wander out into the open and climb to the summit of the mountain. . . . I have seen nothing here [in Paris] that impressed me more, that gave me more pleasure, than the Diorama."

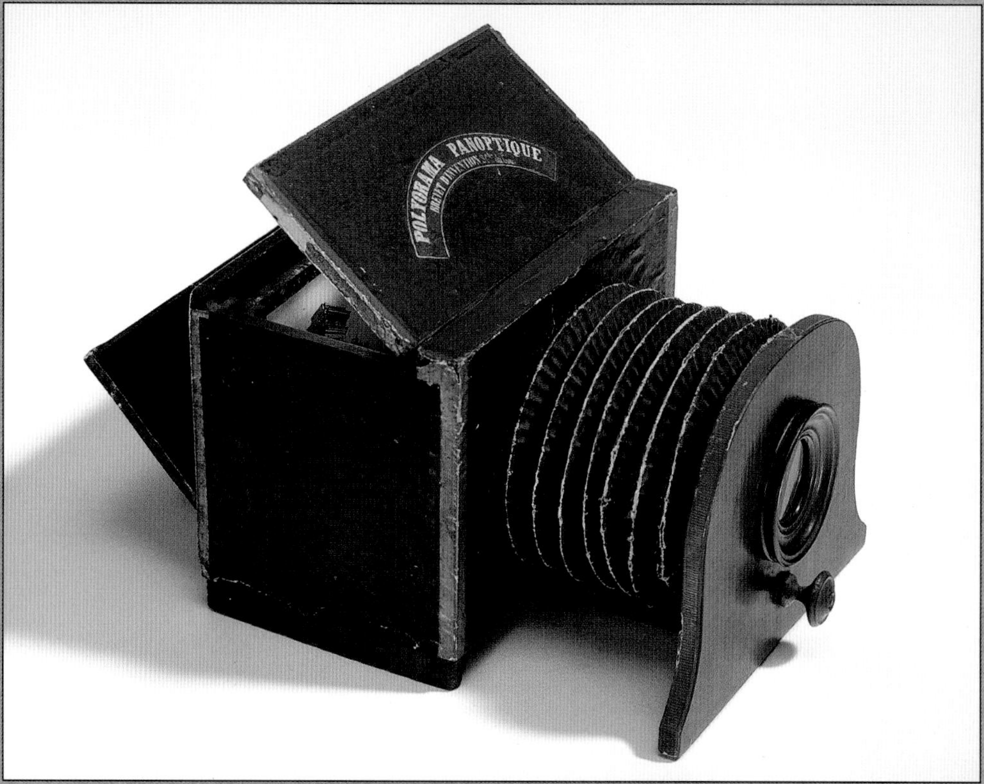

Polyorama Panoptique, France, ca. 1859.

In painting the scenes for the Diorama, Daguerre and Bouton had many assistants, including Hippolyte Sebron and Charles Arrowsmith (the latter whose sister Daguerre later married). Together they painted church interiors, including Canterbury Cathedral, as well as church ruins, the Italian volcano Vesuvius, Napoleon's tomb, and other famous sights. A second Diorama was opened on London's Regent Street in 1823. Over the ensuing years, additional theaters were opened in Wroclaw, Poland; Berlin; Stockholm; Quebec; and Birmingham, England. While pamphlets from these theaters claimed to feature scenes painted "in the style of Daguerre," it is doubtful that the artists had much involvement with them.

The Paris Diorama was destroyed by fire in 1839. Although Bouton rebuilt it in 1843, Daguerre's interest by then had shifted to the photographic process that was to earn him lasting fame.

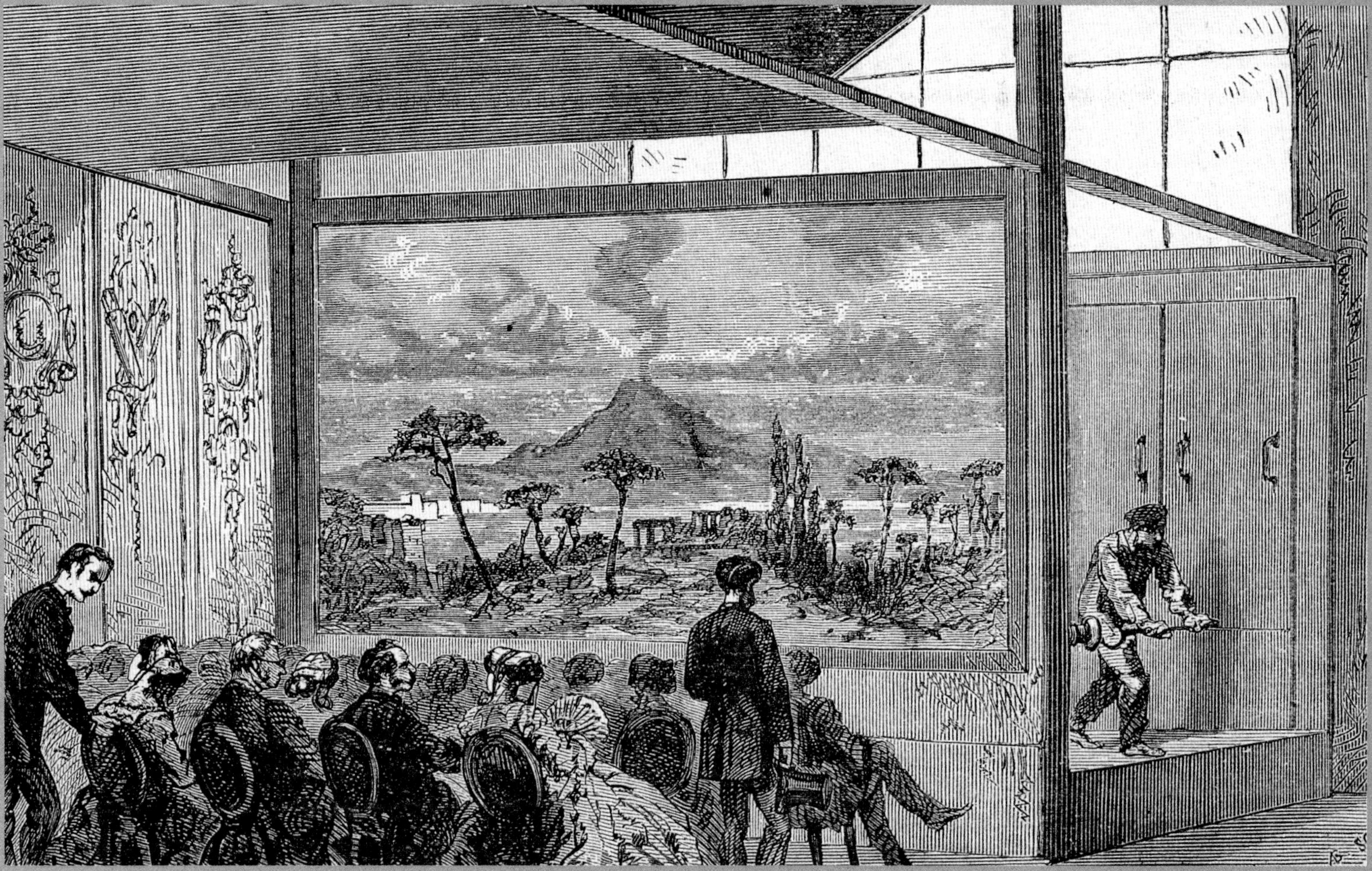

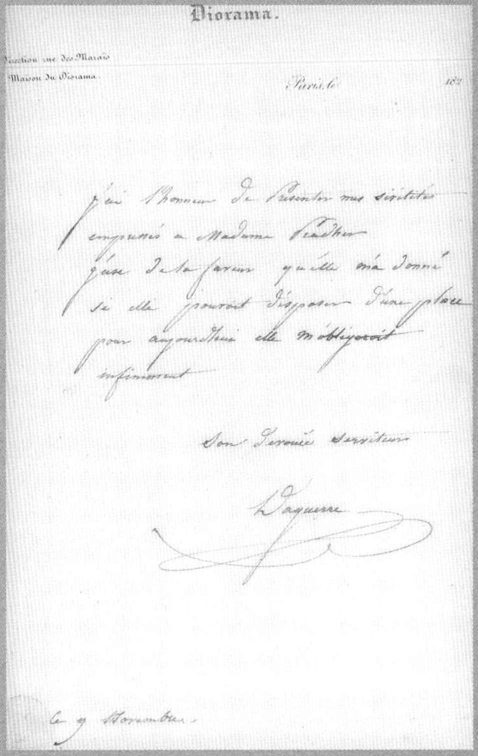

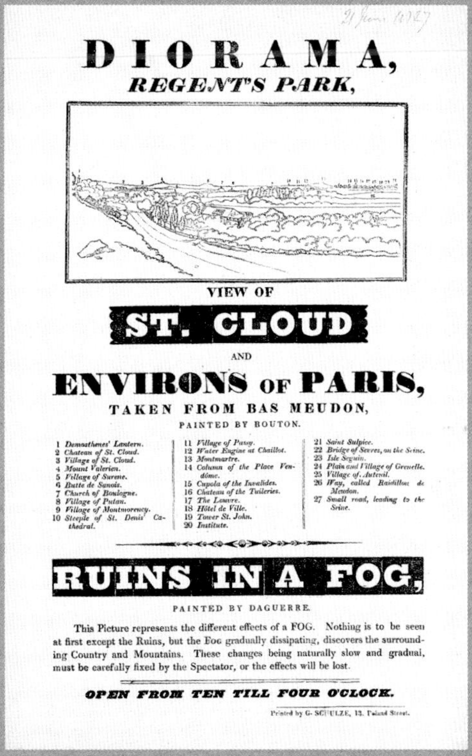

Le Diorama de Daguerre, woodcut, from *Les merveilles de la photographie*, Gaston Tissandier, 1874. Bay of Naples Diorama, Mt. Vesuvius in background, Diorama mechanism at right.

Left: Note from Louis Jacques Mandé Daguerre requesting admission for a lady to the Diorama, ca. 1828. The note, written on Diorama stationery, requests "a place for today."

Right: Broadside for London's Regent's Park Diorama, G. Schulze, printer, June 1827, 8 1/4" x 13 1/4".

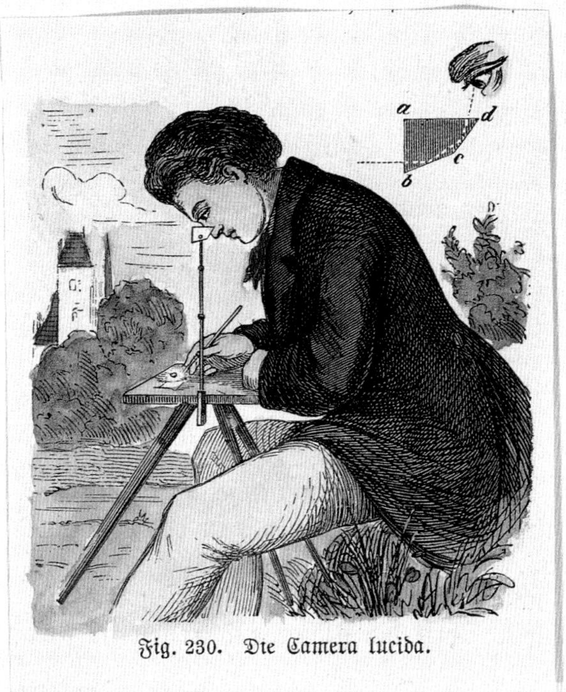

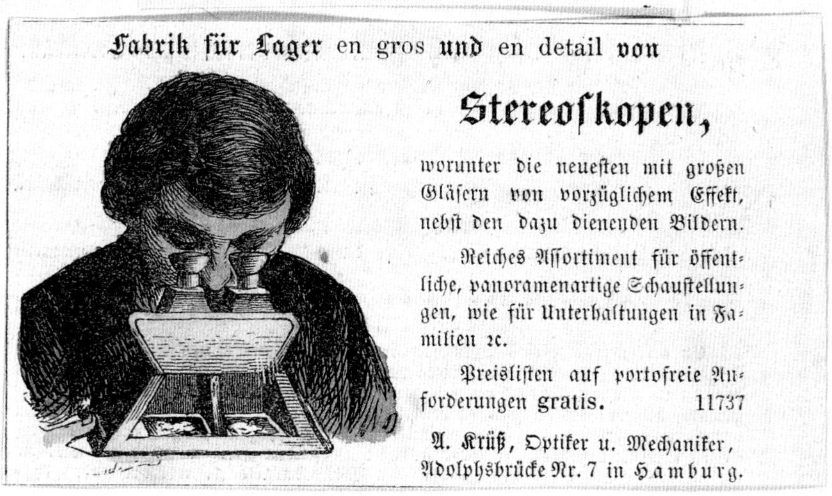

Advertisements for camera lucida and Brewster-type stereoscope, tinted woodcuts, Germany, ca. 1860.

using the camera obscura. While he had obtained results—albeit negatives—using paper sensitized with silver chloride, these were but fleeting and in time were lost, as he had no way of fixing the images. Using bitumen of Judea again in 1826–1827, this time in the camera obscura, Niépce obtained a photograph possessing a range of tones, as opposed to the line illustrations he produced by contact printing. That first photograph—which still exists—was taken from an upstairs window of his estate and required an exposure on the order of eight hours.

In 1826 Charles Chevalier, from whom Niépce obtained lenses, made a comment to Daguerre about the field in which Niépce was experimenting. This brought about a meeting of the two that soon led to a partnership. Daguerre was a prominent French artist specializing in the painting of realistic scenery, as well as the creator and proprietor of the Diorama in Paris.

The partnership benefited Daguerre more than Niépce. For a year prior to their meeting, Daguerre had been trying to produce permanent photographs using the camera obscura. At the time the partnership was formed, however, Daguerre had yet to produce a single, unfixed image—much less a permanent one. In 1829 Niépce had used iodine fumes to blacken the bare parts of silver-coated copper plates that he had begun to use with his bitumen-of-Judea process. Daguerre went on to find that exposing the plates to iodine fumes made them sensitive to light. But they were still not sensitive enough for an image to form.

In 1835, two years after Niépce's death, Daguerre accidentally hit upon how to bring out the image on exposed plates. He had put an exposed plate—as usual, with no visible image—into his chemical cupboard, intending to prepare it for reuse at a later date. A few days after, he went to the cupboard and discovered a fully visible image on the plate. Subsequent tests revealed that the mercury fumes from a broken thermometer had been responsible for the unexpected result. Still, the image was not a permanent one. It wasn't until 1837 that Daguerre found he could fix his images by soaking them in a solution of hot water containing ordinary salt. His first successful image, a still life made in his studio in 1837, still exists in France. Over the protestations of Isidore Niépce (Joseph's son and successor), Daguerre named the process he had discovered the daguerreotype.

In 1838 Daguerre sought, without success, to raise funds through a public subscription before revealing the secret of his process. Later in the year, he contacted a number of prominent French scientists, to interest them in the promotion of his process. François Arago, one of those contacted, championed Daguerre's cause and announced his discoveries to the French Academy of Sciences, making no mention of Niépce.

While generally each followed his own path, Niépce and Daguerre did communicate with one another and there was some exchange of ideas between them. William Henry Fox Talbot, on the other hand, was unaware of the two Frenchmen's work—though he had probably heard of the Diorama—when he undertook his early experiments in photography. Frustrated with his mediocre drawing skills, Fox Talbot began to make use of the camera lucida and camera obscura. In 1835 he was successful at sensitizing paper with silver chloride. At first he made only contact prints of lace and leaves on paper, but then he moved on to using small cameras (his wife referred to them as "mouse traps") with which he succeeded in producing a number of negatives of his home, Lacock Abbey.

Fox Talbot was typical of well-educated, wealthy Britons in the early nineteenth century. He had a brilliant intellect and the financial resources to pursue whatever subject intrigued him. One of his interests was mathematics, and he contributed many papers in the field to scholarly journals. He was also an authority on classical languages. After his brief period of photographic discovery, Fox Talbot returned to his other varied pursuits and never published any reports of his work.

It was only when he learned of Daguerre's discovery that Fox Talbot resumed his involvement with photography, immediately appealing to Arago for recognition as the true originator of the process. Within weeks after filing his claim, Fox Talbot exhibited some of his "photogenic drawings," first at the Royal Institution and less than a week later at the Royal Society. In the months between his learning of Daguerre's work and the revelation of Daguerre's process, Fox Talbot returned to his experiments. As it turned out, of course, the two men had independently discovered two different photographic processes.

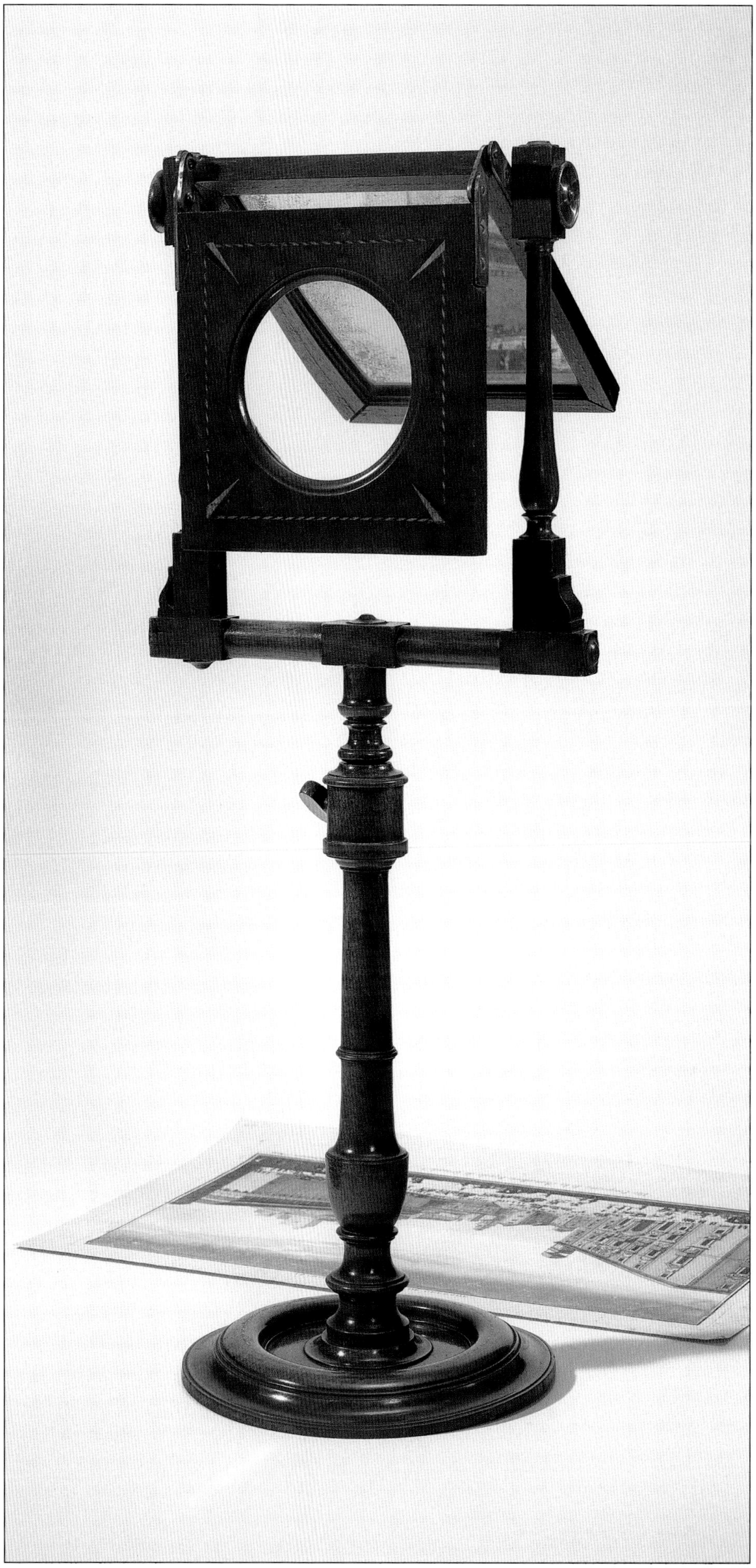

Zograscope, ca. 1830s, prob. American, a tabletop viewer with a special arrangement of mirror and lens producing a pseudo-stereo or enhanced perspective image when viewing prints specifically made for this equipment.

CHAPTER TWO:

PHOTOGRAPHY'S EARLY YEARS

Anonymous, Portrait of a man with a chamfered-box daguerreotype camera, ca. 1856, ambrotype, 4¼" x 5 ½", In thermoplastic case.

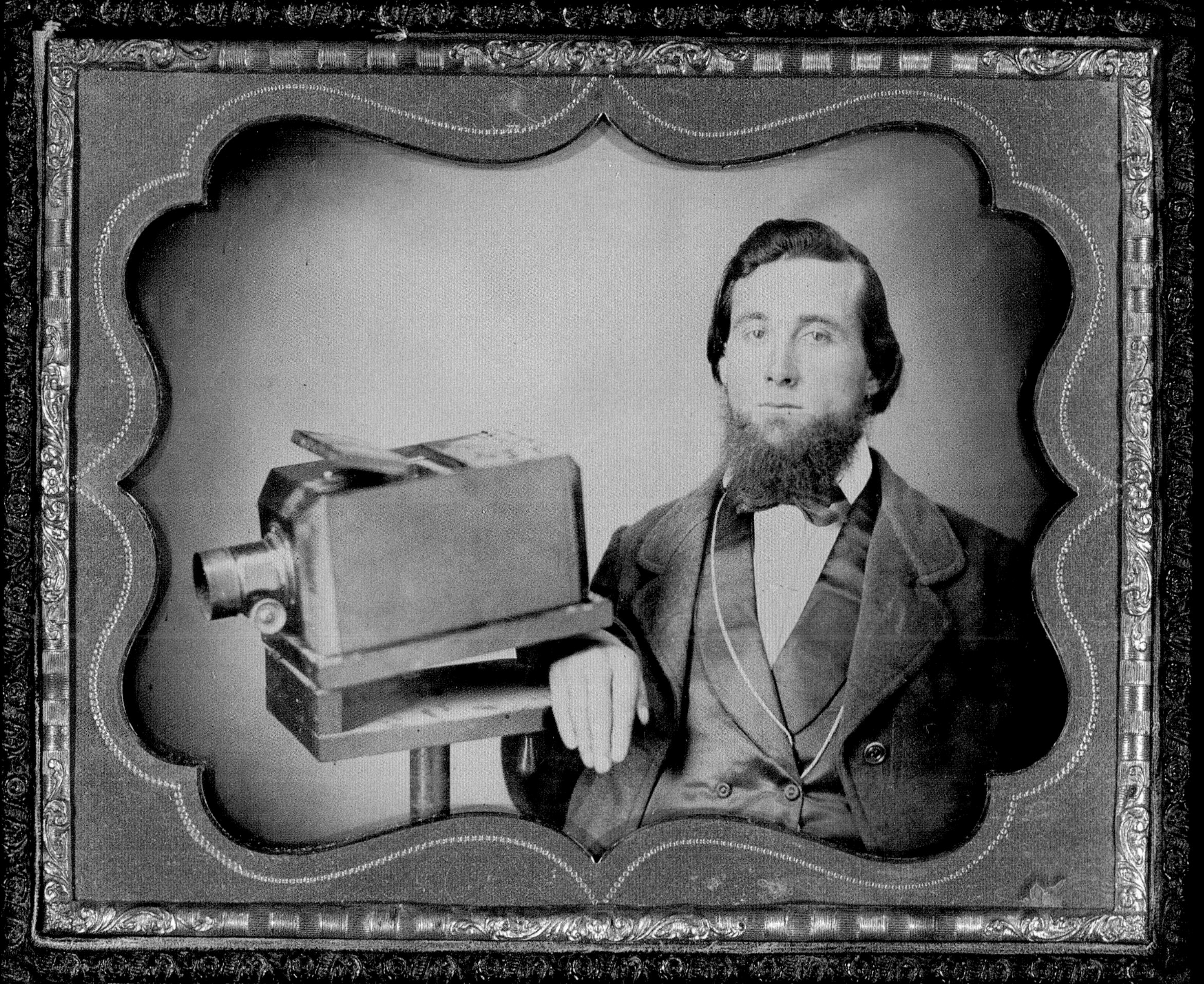

The Daguerreotype

In 1839, a process discovered by Louis Jacques Mandé Daguerre changed forever the way in which man's world was depicted. Whereas previously, drawings, paintings, silhouettes, etchings, and lithographs—all the means of graphic representation ever employed—relied on the human hand to bring them about, now the image produced was the result of a combination of light, optics, and chemistry, with the guidance of man.

On January 7, 1839, the French scientist François Arago, having previously made arrangements with Daguerre, announced Daguerre's discovery to the French Academy of Sciences. Although, the day before, the Paris newspaper *Gazette de France* had announced "an important discovery made by M. Daguerre . . . who discovered a method to fix the images which are represented at the back of a camera obscura," neither that paper nor Arago's presentation revealed the details of the process.

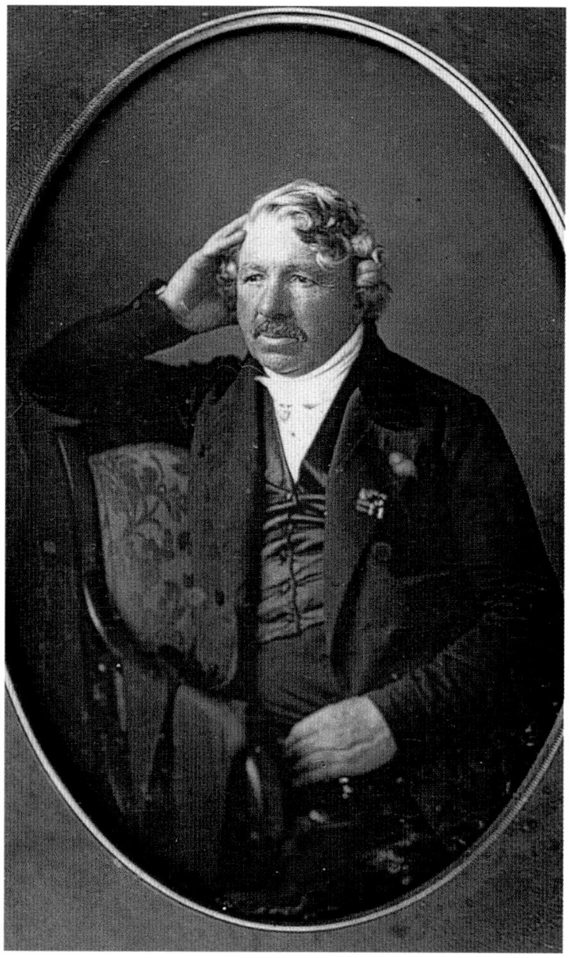

John Mayall, *Louis Jacques Mandé Daguerre*, 1846, Woodburytype, from *Yearbook of Photography*, 1881.

Arago quickly became a staunch supporter of Daguerre and decided that the French government should compensate Daguerre for the rights to his discovery, and that Daguerre should reveal the specifics of his discovery to the world. Accordingly, Arago contacted various officials of the French government, and in June a committee was formed to consider whether or not Daguerre's process was important enough to warrant the compensation. The sum of six thousand francs was proposed as an annual payment, to continue throughout Daguerre's lifetime. In exchange, Daguerre agreed to the announcement and publication of his process, and to the revelation of the technical details of his Diorama.

The bill codifying the arrangements was passed and signed into law in early August. On August 19, 1839, before a joint meeting of the Academy of Sciences and the Academy of Beaux-Arts, Arago presented the process in detail. Not above capitalizing on his process in any way not prohibited by his agreement with the government, Daguerre entered into a contract with Alphonse Giroux, a relative by marriage. Daguerre authorized Giroux to produce equipment related to the process, which would include a statement that it was manufactured under Daguerre's direction, and the publication of brochures providing instructions on the process.

Below: Samuel Bemis, Country road, Crawford Notch, New Hampshire, 1840, daguerreotype, 6½" x 8½".

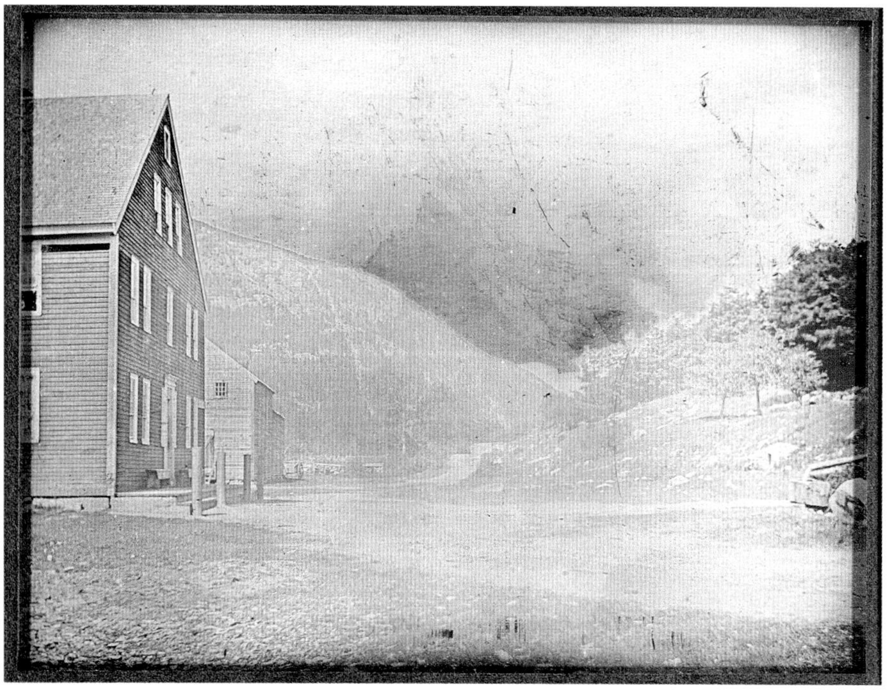

PROFILE: *The Daguerreotype Process*

Proper preparation of the daguerreotype plate was essential to making a beautiful image.

First, the plate was polished or buffed, using a flat, paddle-like "buff stick," covered with buckskin to rub rottenstone or pumice evenly on the plate's surface. Next, a finer abrasive, often jeweler's rouge or lamp black, was applied with a flannel-covered buff stick.

The polished plate was then sensitized. It was placed, silver surface down, over the top of an open, glass-lined fuming or sensitizing box that contained compounds of iodine, which became photosensitive after interacting with the silver of the plate.

A light-tight holder was used to protect the plate until the moment of exposure. Rays of light, upon striking the daguerreotype plate, converted the silver iodide to metallic silver, forming a latent image which became visible after the plate was mercurialized, or placed face down over heated mercury. The image was fixed (rendered permanent) in a wash of hyposulfite of soda, which removed the silver iodide.

An optional last step was gilding—washing the plate with a solution of gold chloride—which increased the image's brilliance. Daguerre did not gild his plates.

Daguerreotypes in most cases came in standard plate sizes: whole plate (6 ½-by-8 ½ inches), half plate (4 ¼-by-5 ½ inches), quarter plate (3 ¼-by-4 ¼ inches), sixth plate (2 ¾-by-3 ¼ inches), ninth plate (2-by-2 ½ inches), and sixteenth plate (1 3/8-by-1 5/8 inches). These plates could be cut down to fit circular and oval cases, lockets, brooches, and other odd-sized pieces of jewelry. Oversized plates were also made, such as the "double-whole" or "mammoth" (9-by-13 inches) or Southworth & Hawes' 13 ½-by-16 ½ inch plate.

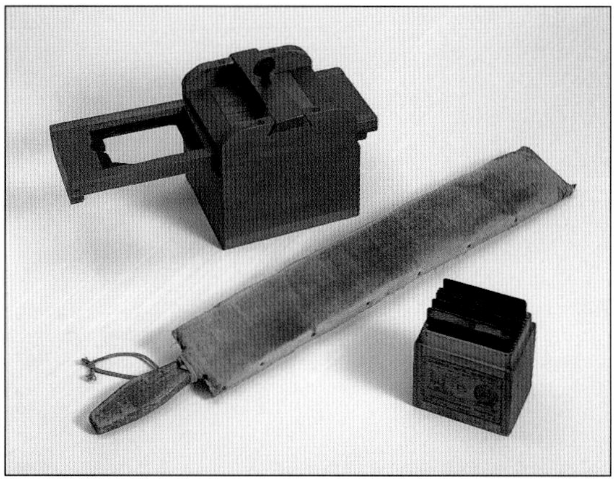

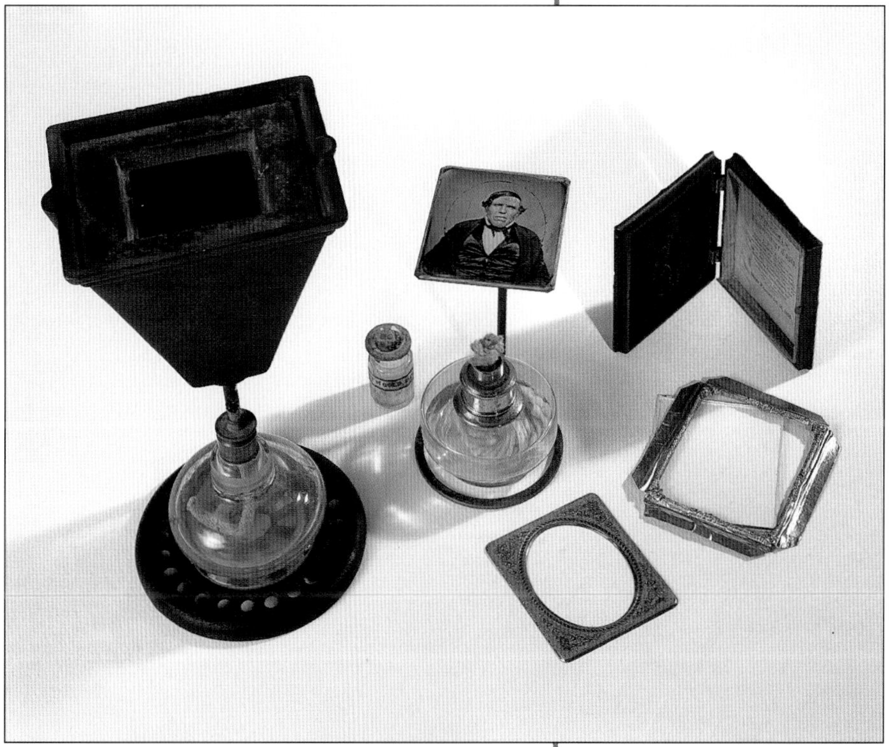

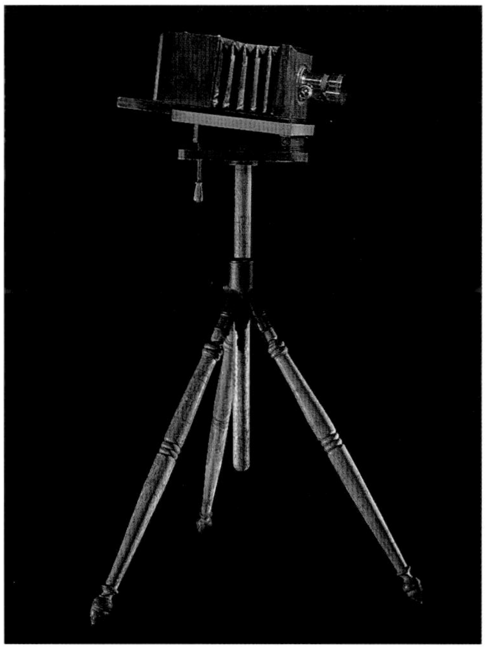

Clockwise from top left:
Daguerreian accessories, ca. 1852. Iodine sensitizing box, buff stick, and Scovill Manufacturing Co. plate box, with unused 3 ¼" x 4 ¼" daguerreotype plates.

Daguerreian accessories, ca. 1853. Left to right: mercurizing stand, gilding stand, daguerreotype case, mat, and preserver.

Lewis-pattern American daguerreotype camera, ca. 1852, for 3 ¼" x 4 ¼" plates. With Holmes Booth and Haydens lens, on classic daguerreian tripod.

FOCUS: *The Daguerreotype Camera*

The principal instrument of photography derives both its name and its form from the camera obscura. The first photographic cameras consisted of two boxes, one tightly fitted into the other to prevent the entry of light, but with enough clearance for the inner one to slide back and forth for focusing. A lens was mounted at the front end with some means of covering the lens to exclude light. The rear section of the camera had a framed sheet of frosted or "ground" glass on which the image was focused. The frame and glass were removable to permit the substitution of the holder for the daguerreotype plate. Daguerre's instruments, as made and sold by Giroux, were additionally fitted with a mirror, mounted so that it tipped back at an angle of 45 degrees. This enabled viewing and focusing the image from above.

The popularity of daguerreotyping in America led to considerable variety in the forms of cameras produced there. After an initial period of some six or eight years,

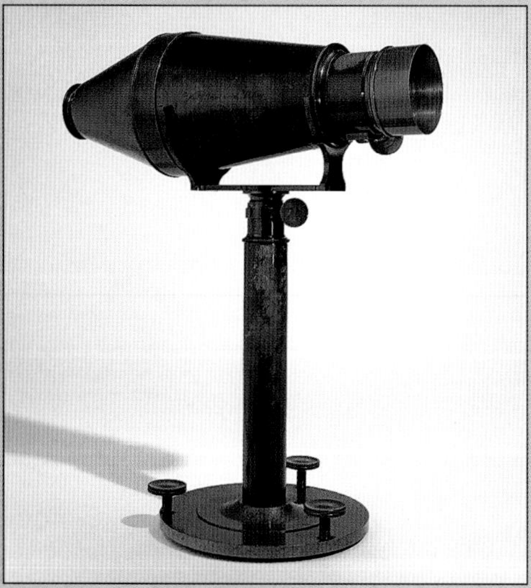

All-metal daguerreotype camera, replica, Voigtländer & Son A.G., 1938. The original was introduced in 1841 by Peter Friedrich Wilhelm Voigtländer.

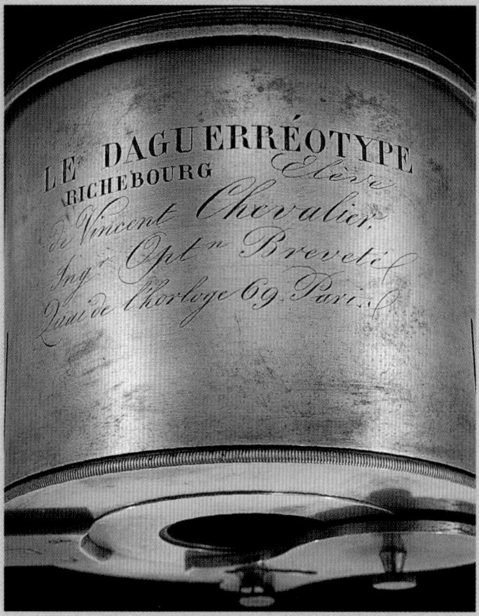

Daguerreian lens, Ambroise Richebourg, ca. 1842. Richebourg was apprentice to Vincent Chevalier until Chevalier's death in 1841, at which point Richebourg took over the business.

three general patterns of cameras emerged on the American scene. One was the so-called chamfered- or American-box camera. In this style the front and rear edges of the camera were beveled. At the rear was an opening through which the ground glass could be viewed. On the top there was usually a pair of hinged doors, through which the plate holder could be slid into one of two slots. The forwardmost slot was used to make photographs of distant objects. The rear one, in conjunction with the lens's sliding or rack-and-pinion focusing, was used for close-ups and copying.

The second type of camera, most often called a Robert's-type—for its association with Bostonian John Roberts—or Boston box ("box" referred to the camera body, frequently sold separately from the lens), was distinctly rectangular, with no chamfering. These cameras operated on the sliding box-in-box manner of Giroux's instruments and had a pair of hinged doors in the top. These served the same function as in the chamfered-box cameras. A characteristic feature of these cameras was the presence of a knob-fronted worm gear which was mounted on the face of the camera and which moved the back portion for focusing. In many instances the lens mount also had focusing capabilities.

The third major type of American daguerreotype cameras employed a bellows. While the use of a bellows in a camera was first proposed in 1839 by Baron Séguier, this design was not employed by European camera manufacturers in the early years. The American bellows-type camera was introduced in 1851 by William and William H. Lewis, of New York City. From the

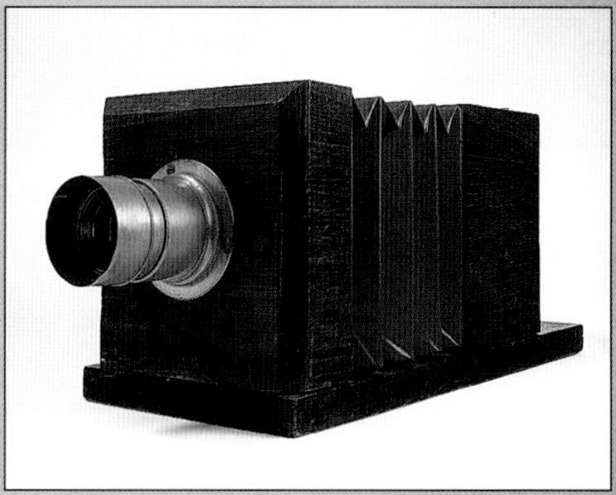

Bellows-style daguerreotype camera, Palmer & Longking, ca. 1854, for 4 1/4" x 5 1/2" plates. Palmer & Longking were the ultimate successors to W. & W. H. Lewis, originators of this style of camera.

front the camera looked a bit like a chamfered-box camera, but it differed in three major respects. First, the body was split into front and rear portions with a bellows positioned between them. Second, the body's parts were mounted on a bed or

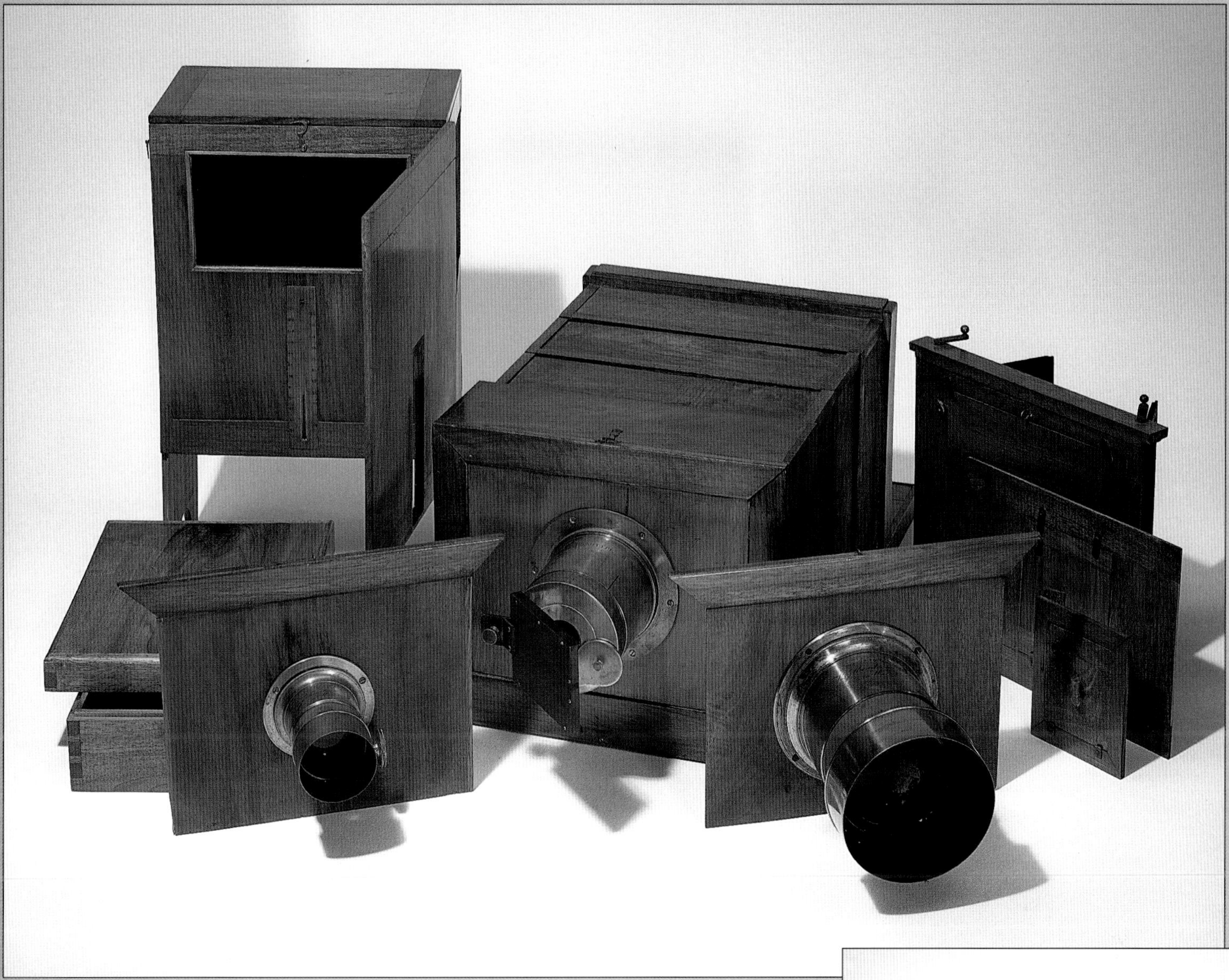

base to which the front section was fastened. The rear portion of the bed was slotted, which permitted the rear body section to be moved backward and forward on it for focusing. A setscrew held that portion in place and could be tightened to maintain a selected position. Finally, in the early models the plate holders were loaded from the side, though top loading was used in later models. This type of camera is most often referred to as a "Lewis-type" camera, as a result of the changing fortunes of the manufacturers. W. & W. H. Lewis were briefly succeeded by Gardner, Harrison & Co., who, after about six months in business, were succeeded by Palmer & Longking. Henry J. Lewis, brother of W. H., continued making this bellows-style camera well into the wet-plate period.

Daguerreian outfit, Ambroise Richebourg, ca. 1842, for 6 1/2" x 8 1/2" plates. In addition to the extra front lens boards and lenses, a mercurizing box, left rear; an iodizing box, left center; and a plate vise, right rear, are present.

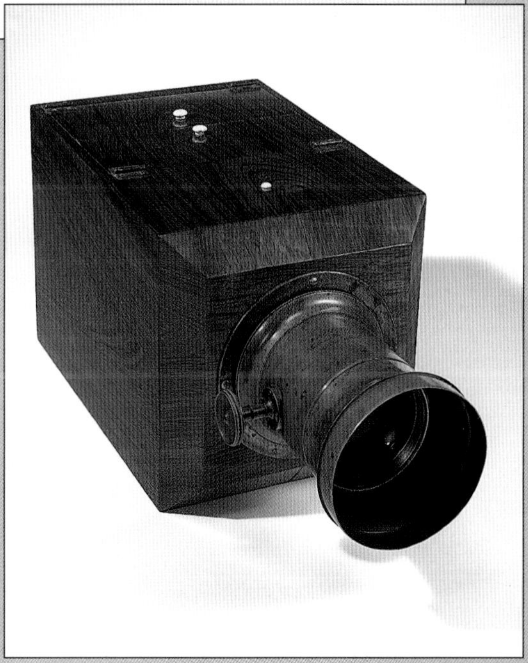

Right: Chamfered American daguerreotype camera, manufacturer unknown, ca. 1850, for 4 1/4" x 5 1/2" plates. The hinged doors on the top allowed the user to position the plate for close-ups and copying.

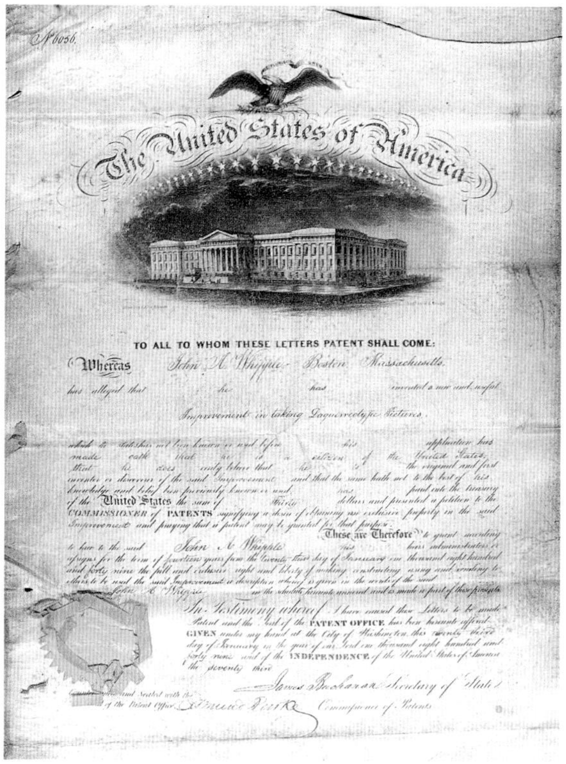

The United States of America

TO ALL TO WHOM THESE LETTERS PATENT SHALL COME:

Whereas John A. Whipple Boston Massachusetts

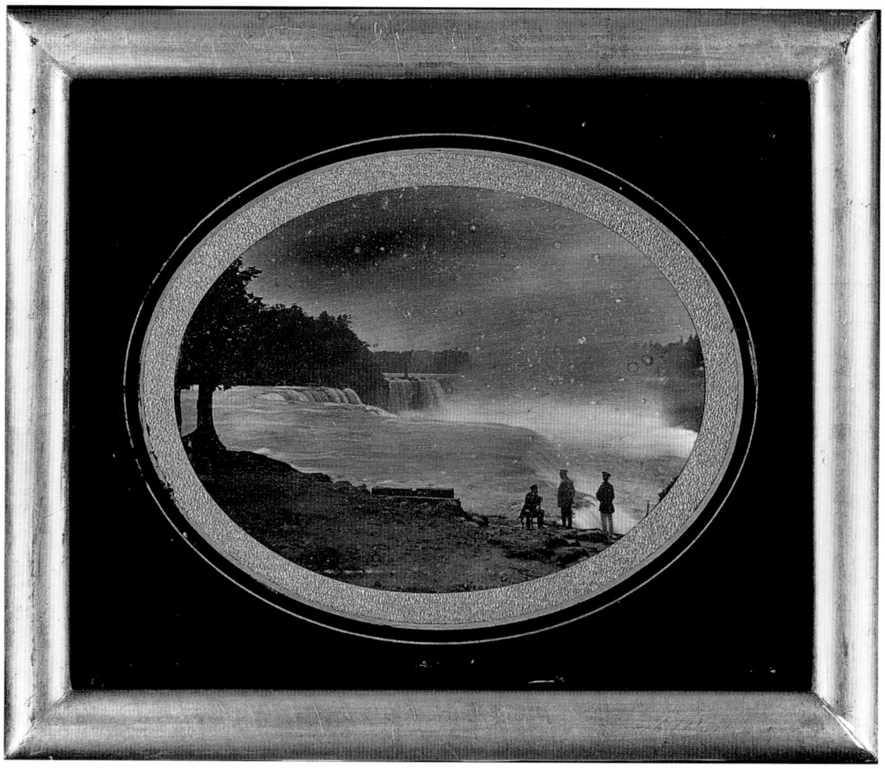

France—Following the revelation of the particulars of Daguerre's process, many people in France tried their hand at making daguerreotypes. N. P. Lerebours, a manufacturer of optical instruments, commissioned daguerreotypes of various historical sites throughout Europe, the Mediterranean, and the Middle East. He then used the results of their efforts to produce engraved plates, and published them in his 1840–1843 work, *Excursions Daguerriennes*. Some Frenchmen even traveled as far afield as Mexico to make daguerreotypes.

With the explosion of interest in viewing and making daguerreotypes came an increase in demand for daguerreotype cameras. While Giroux's Daguerre-endorsed devices had a head start on competitors, many felt that they were too heavy and expensive. It wasn't long before others, including some noted opticians, began to make and market the equipment themselves. Lerebours outfitted the photographers he enlisted with cameras of his own manufacture. Charles Chevalier, who had previously supplied lenses to both Niépce and Daguerre, also marketed his own equipment. This included a collapsible camera, circa 1840, which economized on bulk—though not on weight. Chevalier's camera represented one of the first departures from the camera obscura-based design of Giroux's apparatus.

Marc Antoine Gaudin also designed a daguerreotype camera, the Nouvel Appareil Gaudin (Gaudin's New Camera), around 1841. Made for Gaudin by Lerebours, this camera departed from the standard model in several respects. It had a circular disc with three different-sized holes mounted in front of the lens. These holes made it possible to vary the amount of light passing through the lens, in effect providing variable f-stops. The camera box was significantly larger than the lens and the plateholder sections contained within. This provided enough space for the storage of plates, plate holders, the coating box, and the mercury-fuming box, thus combining the functions of camera body and carrying case. Also, a piece of cloth, attached at the top front edge of the camera, could be used for uncovering and covering the lens to control the duration of exposures. Most other cameras had either a solid, pivoting plate mounted at the front of the lens or relied on the removal and replacement of a lens cap. Another camera, made for a very specialized form of daguerreotyping, was invented by a German-born resident of Paris, Friedrich von Martens. His camera produced panoramic daguerreotypes and relied on

Left: U.S. Patent No. 6056, granted to John A. Whipple for improvements in taking daguerreotypes, January 23, 1849. Original patent for "crayon," i.e. vignetted, daguerreotypes.

Right: Attributed to Platt D. Babbitt, Niagara Falls, ca. 1855, daguerreotype, 6 1/2" x 8 1/2".

Interior of Meade Brothers Daguerreotype Gallery, Broadway, New York, woodcut, from *Gleason's Pictorial Drawing-Room Companion*, 1856.

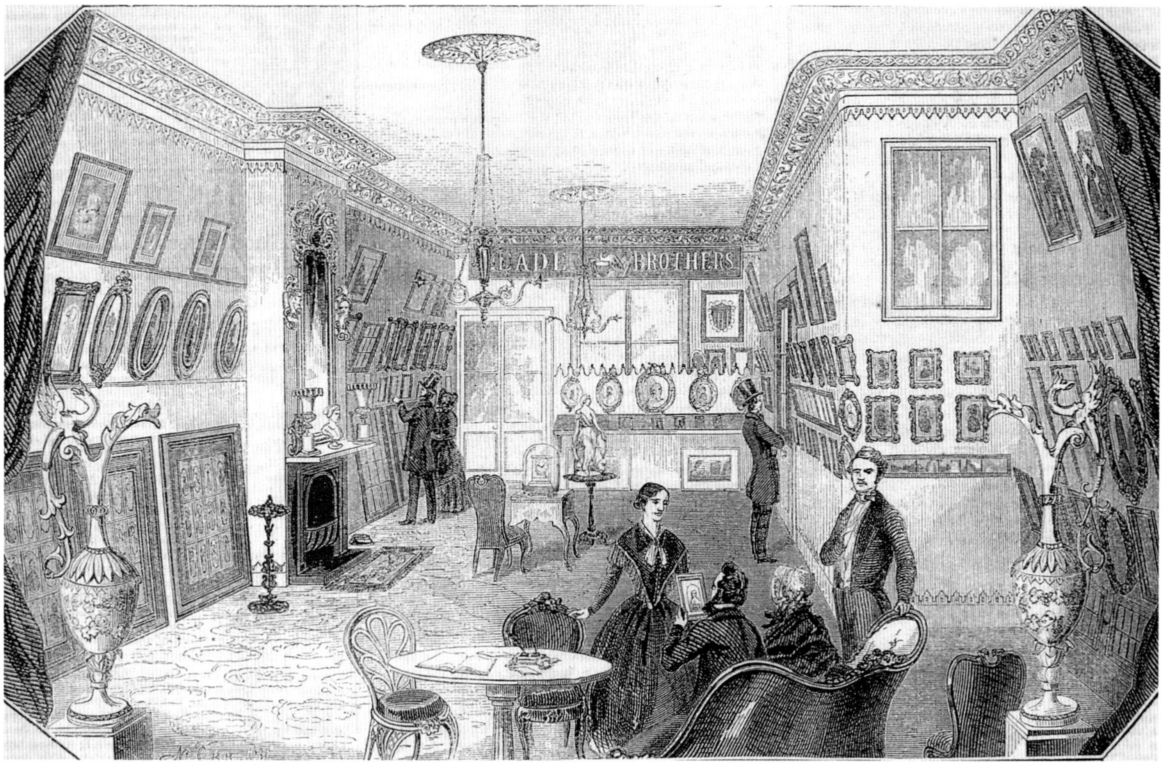

Below: Anonymous, Portrait of a man in uniform, ca. 1850, daguerreotype, 3" x 4", probably German. In black velvet frame.

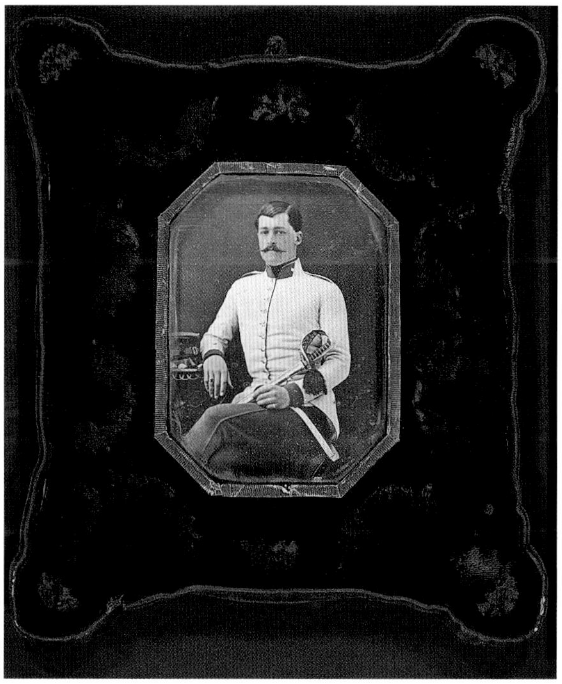

the lens being moved past a curved daguerreotype plate to make the exposure.

The daguerreotype process became so popular in France that in 1847 more than a half-million plates and two thousand cameras were sold in Paris alone. Most early daguerreotypes required relatively long exposures, and as a result were limited to the depiction of outdoor scenes. The first known photograph of a person was accidentally obtained when a man paused on a Paris street corner long enough to get his shoes shined, thus registering on the daguerreotype being made of the street scene at that moment. As the sensitivity of plates and the light-gathering ability of lenses improved, portraits became not only practical but commonplace. By the early 1850s, daguerreotypes that included moving people, animals, and even steamships were being made.

Germany—The first person in Germany to receive a camera for making daguerreotypes was Louis Sachse of Berlin. While in Paris in April 1839, he had arranged for the delivery of six outfits and instructional brochures as soon as they were available. Sachse was not the first in Germany to make a daguerreotype, as his outfits were damaged during shipping and needed repair. Later, though, he had the distinction of making the first daguerreotype portraits in Germany, in April 1840.

Using instructions available in the literature of the day, Theodor Dorffel, also of Berlin, was able to construct his own camera, and by September 15, 1839, was exhibiting it and the daguerreotypes made with it. A few days later, Eduard Petitpierre, a Swiss citizen living in Berlin, received a Giroux outfit and set about making copies of it. Carl

August von Steinheil made daguerreotypes in Munich, in early September, and also constructed a miniature daguerreotype camera that used 8-by-11-mm plates.

In Vienna, Professor Josef Max Petzval designed an f/3.6 lens for daguerreotype cameras. This design was used in the all-metal daguerreotype cameras manufactured by the firm of Voigtländer & Son.

By 1841 a number of daguerreotypists were active in Germany and Austria. Among the most noted were Herman Biow and Carl Ferdinand Stelzner. Biow opened his studio in Hamburg, one of the earliest in Germany, on September 15, 1841. Stelzner, who was originally a painter of miniatures, entered into a partnership with Biow and was credited with great artistry in his daguerreotypes.

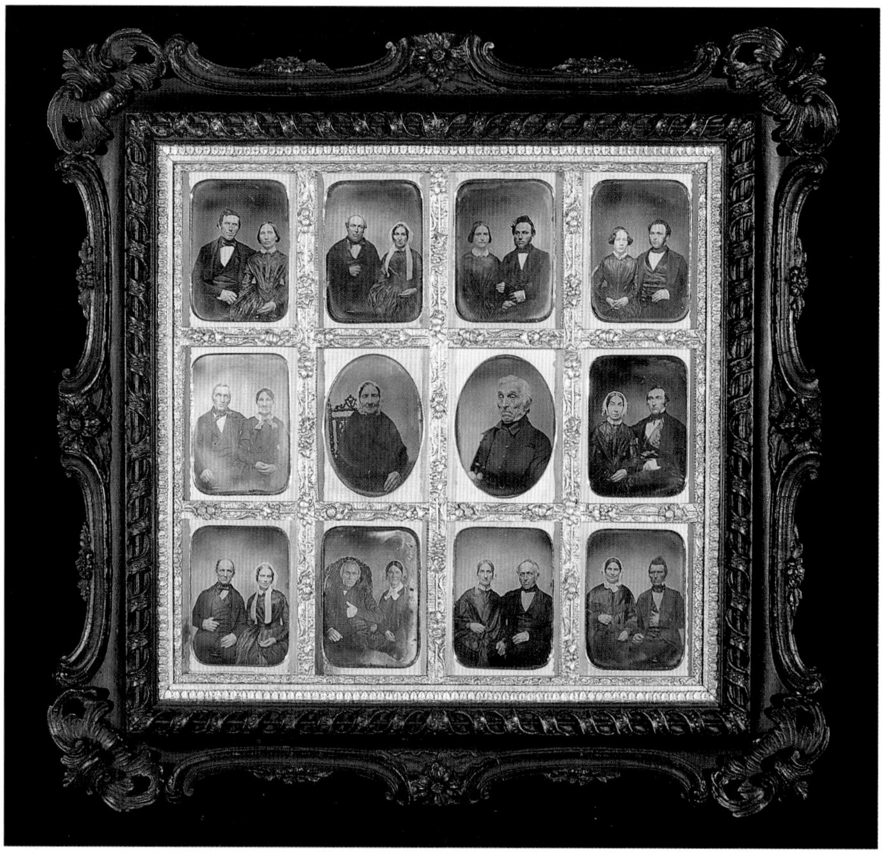

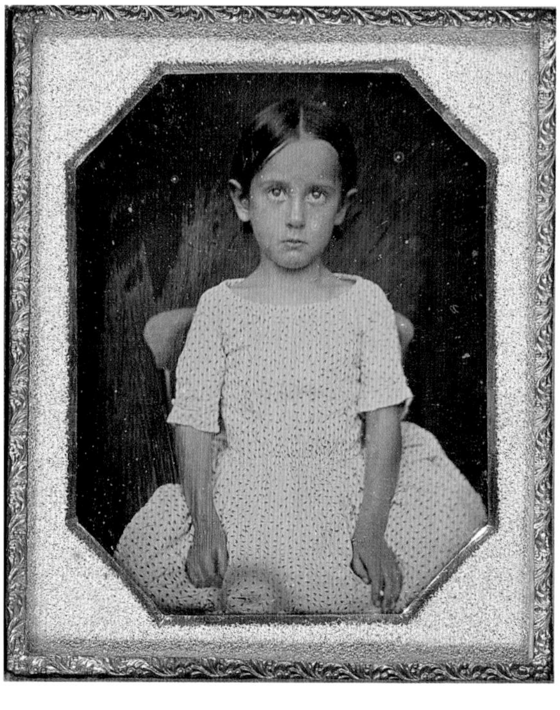

Anonymous, Framed group of family daguerreotypes, ca. 1855, each 4 1/4" x 5 1/2".

Left: Plumbe's Gallery, Boston, Portrait of a young girl, ca. 1845, daguerreotype, 2 3/4" x 3 1/4".

Britain—A few days before the details of Daguerre's process were revealed to the world, in mid-August of 1839, his representative in England obtained a British patent for the process in all of England and Wales. So although Daguerre's discovery was ostensibly for the whole world, not everyone benefited from it. For once, at least, Victorian Britons were second-class citizens. To use Daguerre's process one had to pay a fee and get a license. Because of this restriction, daguerreotypy was slow to develop in Britain, and it was only after portraiture became possible that interest began to grow. Even then, however, the process was not widely used. For most photographers, William Henry Fox Talbot's calotype process remained the preferred method.

Antoine François Jean Claudet, a Frenchman residing in London, bought the first license to use Daguerre's process. He also began importing equipment and images from France. But the first person to open a professional portrait studio in London was Richard Beard. In the early years of his business, Beard was the first in England to use Alexander Wolcott's daguerreotype camera, an American invention that never attained much popularity in its country of origin. The camera used a concave mirror to gather light and focus it on the plate, which was positioned in front of the mirror. A distinct advantage of this type of camera was that the image produced was not reversed, unlike the images obtained from most daguerreotype cameras. A disadvantage of Wolcott's camera was that the use of the concave mirror required longer exposures. Beard's studio was extremely successful and his daguerreotypes were better than the ones produced

PROFILE: *Color on and in Daguerreotypes*

The daguerreotype began to replace the painted, miniature portrait among well-to-do families in the early nineteenth century. While daguerreotypes produced a more faithful rendition of the subject, they lacked the painted portrait's capacity for color.

Thus, from the very early years of daguerreotypes, photographers strove to give color to their product. The simplest approach was to gently apply dry pigments to the daguerreotype. This was done with mixed success, depending on the skill of the colorist. With the aid of a fine camel's-hair brush, such as were sold in tinting sets, the photographer could apply the pigment directly to the fragile surface of the finished plate. The most common applications of color were a slight touch of pink to the cheeks and gold to the jewelry. Less frequently, color was added to backgrounds and clothing, particularly women's dresses and military uniforms.

Some ambitious photographers attempted to produce daguerreotypes in full color. The Reverend Levi Hill, of New York, claimed, in 1850, to have produced blue, red, violet, and orange on the same daguerreotype plate (yellow eluded him). Hill nonetheless was quite reticent about exhibiting his results—he refused to show his "heliochromes" to a committee of daguerreotypists charged with assessing the validity of his claims, showing them instead to Samuel F. B. Morse, who publicly affirmed and praised Hill's color daguerreotypes. In the final analysis, Hill had perhaps accidentally happened upon a method of fixing the results of a photochloride process, known in those days, but was never able to recreate the same conditions.

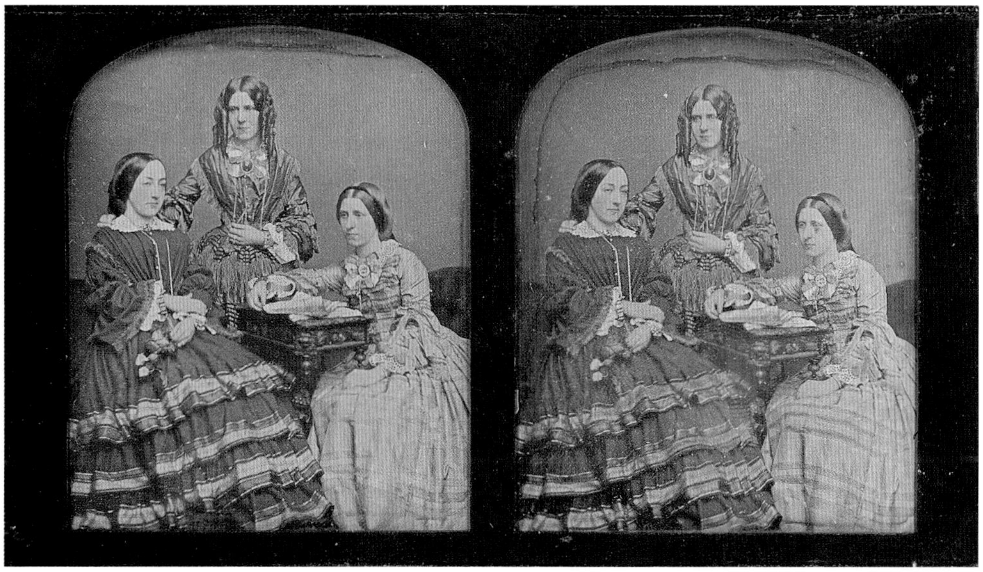

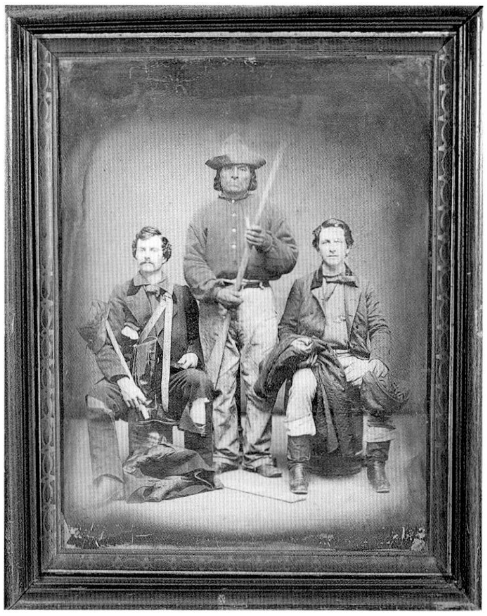

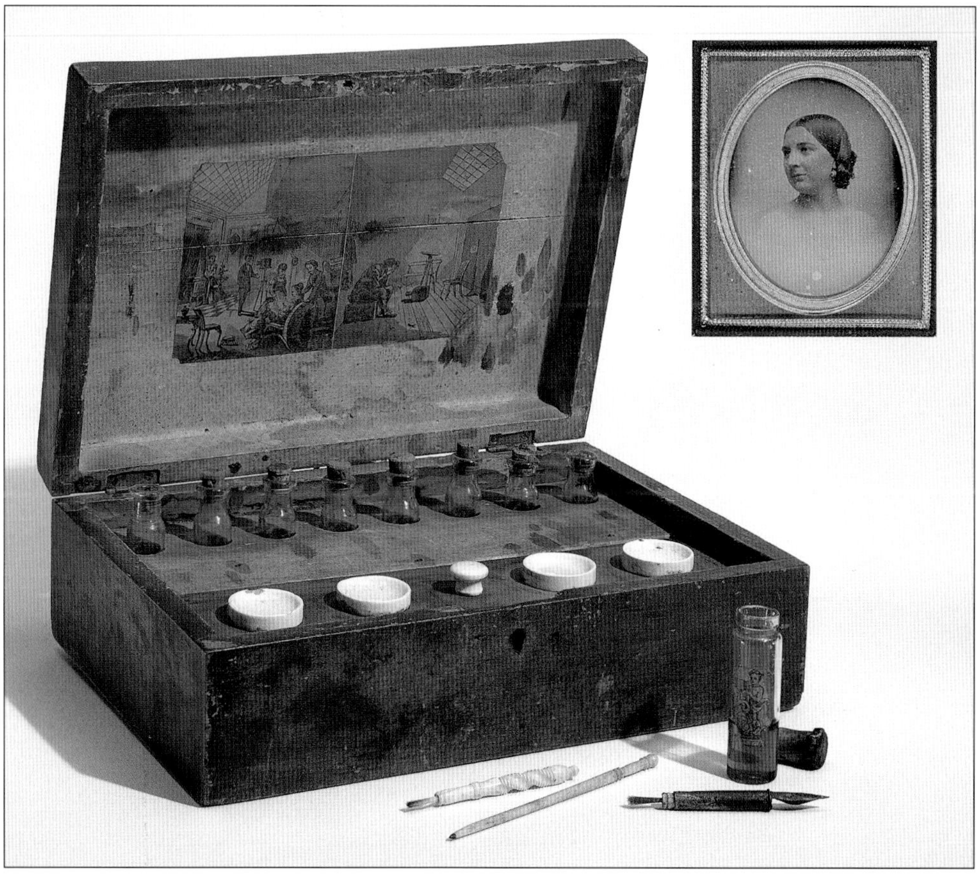

Clockwise from left: T. R. Williams, Tinted stereo pair of three young women, ca. 1850, daguerreotypes, each 2 1/4 x 2 3/4"; Anonymous, Portrait of three men, one with tinted shirt, ca. 1850, daguerreotype. Inset: Anonymous, Vignetted portrait of a woman, ca. 1853, daguerreotype, 2 3/4" x 3 1/4". Note slight tint to woman's cheeks. American daguerreian coloring box, ca. 1848.

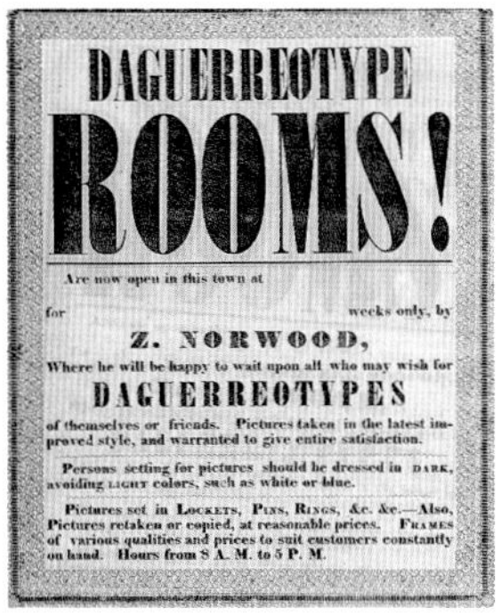

DAGUERREOTYPE

ROOMS!

Are now open in this town at

for weeks only, by

Z. NORWOOD,

Where he will be happy to wait upon all who may wish for

DAGUERREOTYPES

of themselves or friends. Pictures taken in the latest improved style, and warranted to give entire satisfaction.

Persons setting for pictures should be dressed in DARK, avoiding LIGHT colors, such as white or blue.

Pictures set in LOCKETS, PINS, RINGS, &c. &c.—Also, Pictures retaken or copied, at reasonable prices. FRAMES of various qualities and prices to suit customers constantly on hand. Hours from 8 A. M. to 5 P. M.

Broadside for Z. Norwood's daguerreotype rooms, ca. 1855, 9 1/2" x 12". The blank spaces are for filling in the location and duration of the itinerant photographer's visit.

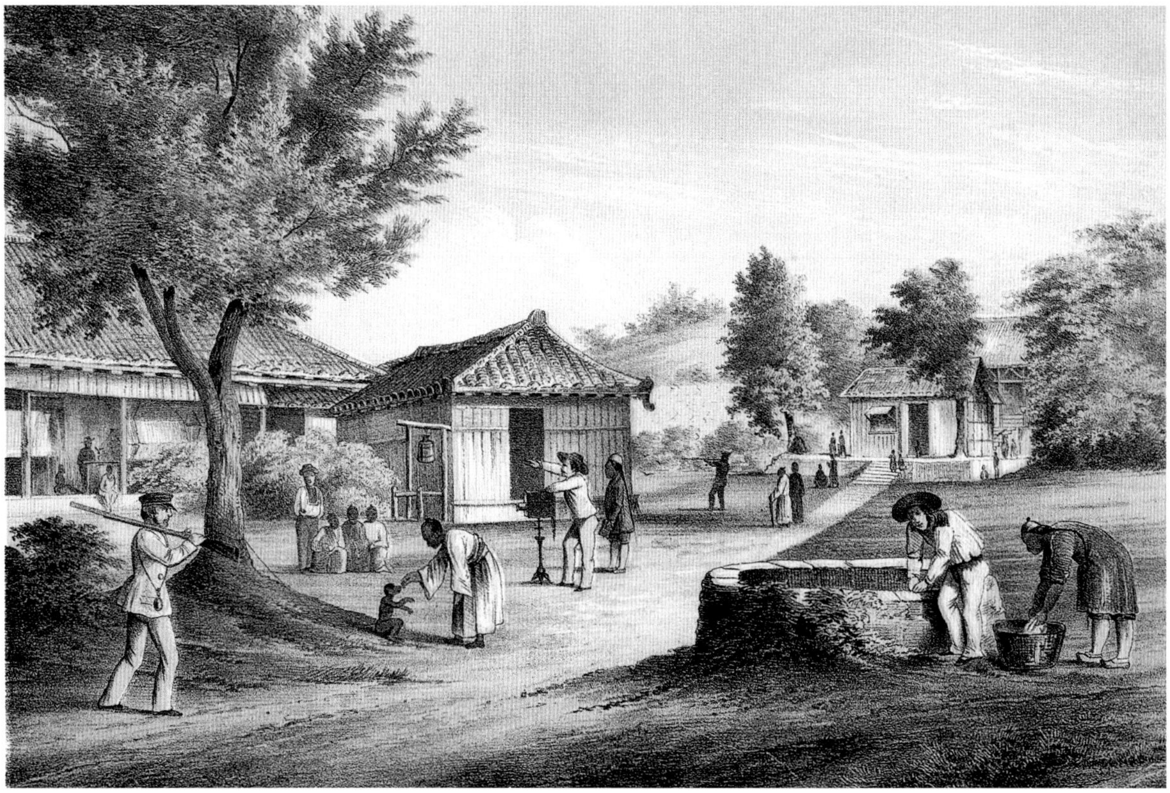

Right: Eliphalet Brown photographing residents of Lew Chew, lithograph, from *Narrative of the Expedition of an American Squadron to the China Seas and Japan, Performed in the Years 1852, 1853, and 1854 Under the Command of Commodore M. C. Perry, United States Navy,* Francis L. Hawks, 1856.

in the studio operated by Claudet. Within a year, however, Claudet's product was acknowledged as superior, both artistically and technically, and his fortunes rose accordingly. By 1843 Beard had shifted from Wolcott's camera to the conventional sliding-box type. This was shown in an engraving copied from a daguerreotype made by Hogg and Johnson in Beard's studio. This engraving, which accompanied a poem, "Lines Written on Seeing a Daguerreotype Portrait of a Lady," appeared in the *Illustrated London News* of August 19, 1843. Claudet gained further prominence in 1853 by photographing Britain's royal family.

Another important daguerreotypist working in Britain was the American John Jabez Edwin Mayall. Having earlier been a competitor of the Langenheim brothers, in 1846 Mayall moved to London, where his business flourished. In fact he was a noted producer of carte-de-visite photographs in the 1860s.

While London was the center of daguerreotypy in Britain, photographers and studios spread throughout the land. Birmingham, Edinburgh, Dublin, Liverpool, Manchester, and York all had active, prominent studios. Even at the height of the daguerreotype's popularity, however, there were still less than a dozen studios in London, a fact that can be attributed to the burdensome cost of a license to use Daguerre's process.

America—Nowhere in the world was the daguerreotype process embraced more enthusiastically than in America. And in no other country were there as many daguerreotypes made. In the early 1850s, more than three million daguerreotypes were made annually in the United States. The superiority of the American product was attested to by the fact that at London's Crystal Palace Exhibition, in 1851, three medals for daguerreotypes—the only ones given—went to Americans: New York's Mathew B. Brady and Martin M. Lawrence, and Boston's John Whipple.

The first American to see an example of Daguerre's work was Samuel F. B. Morse, the inventor of the telegraph and a well-known painter. At the time, Morse was in Paris to promote his recent invention and was invited by Daguerre to his studio to see the results of his photographic work. In return, Morse invited Daguerre to view a demonstration of the telegraph. (Fatefully, during that visit, on March 18, 1839, Daguerre's renowned Diorama was totally destroyed by fire.) Not only was Morse the first American to view a daguerreotype, but he was the first to send word of Daguerre's discovery home to America—in a letter sent in March 1839, shortly before his return. Booklets describing Daguerre's process reached America's shores on September 20, 1839, and Morse, now back in New York City, was the first to purchase a copy. He proceeded to have a camera made by George Prosch, manufacturer of Morse's telegraph instruments, and later an active daguerreotypist in New York and Newark, New Jersey. The camera was finished on September 28, and that same day Morse made his first daguerreotype.

François Gouraud, a Frenchman, arrived in the U.S. on November 23, 1839. He had come as a representative of Alphonse Giroux & Co. to promote Giroux's apparatus and the instructions he published; he was carrying a supply of both with him. While in New York, Gouraud not only exhibited a collection of daguerreotypes but also gave lectures on the process.

At the time the daguerreotype was introduced, America was just entering a sharp economic depression that was to last from the fall of 1839 until the beginning of 1843. It was to be expected that artists would enter this new field, but it was not only artists who did so. Given the potential for unlimited growth, coupled with the unemployment created by the recession, many others looked to this new process as a means of achieving success. Nowhere else in the world was the practice of making daguerreotypes such an egalitarian occupation as in America.

Not long after the introduction of the daguerreotype to America, studios sprang up in all the major cities—first in the East, where the population was concentrated, and then gradually spreading westward. New York City, of course, was an early center of daguerreotype activity. According to Samuel D. Humphrey, editor and publisher of the *Daguerreian Journal*, by 1850 there were more than seventy-five "rooms" (i.e., studios), employing 127 "operators" (daguerreotypists and assistants), eleven women, and forty-six young men. By 1853 the number of studios in New York had grown even higher, with thirty-seven of them located along Broadway, the city's most famous thoroughfare. Many of America's most famous daguerreotypists had galleries on Broadway at one time or another.

The earliest daguerreotype studio in New York was opened in 1840 by Alexander S. Wolcott and John Johnson. In October of the previous year, Johnson had shown Wolcott a description of Daguerre's process and at that time they had made a small camera. The camera used a concave mirror, instead of a lens, to focus the image on the plate. A larger camera was built later that year and Wolcott was granted a patent for his camera in May 1840. This was the first patent related to photography issued by the U.S. Patent Office. Commercially manufactured versions of Wolcott's camera, sold both in America and abroad, were made by the New York firm of W. & W. H. Lewis. William and William H. Lewis later produced their own style of daguerreotype camera, and their family figured prominently in the first fifty years of photography in New York City.

Though their venture was short-lived, in 1840 Samuel F. B. Morse and John W. Draper joined

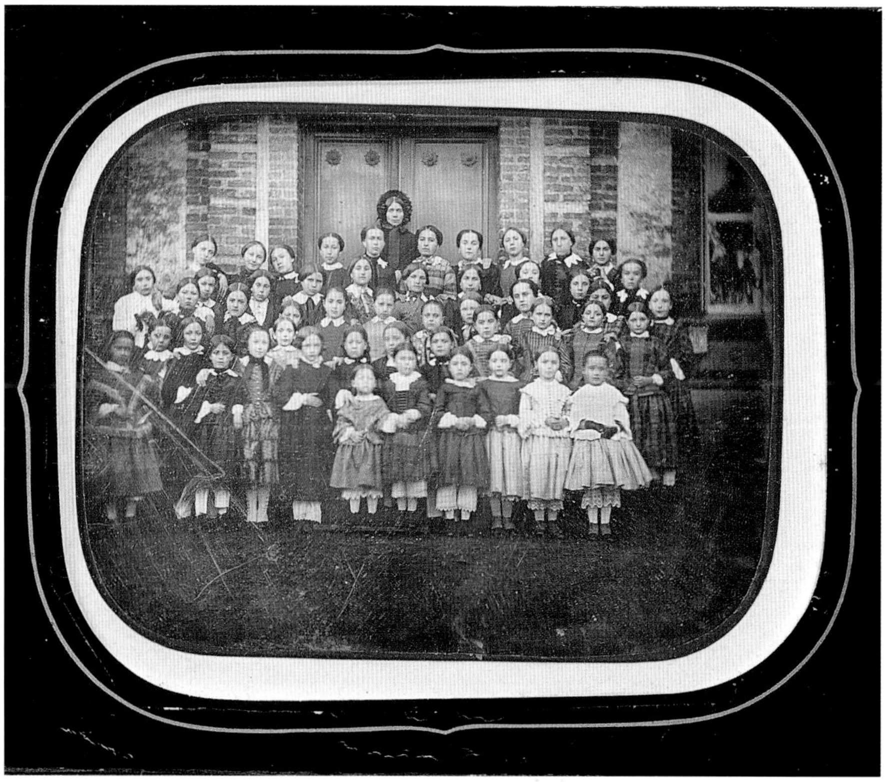

C. H. Perrin, Group portrait, students of a girls' school, Nantes, France, ca. 1855, daguerreotype, 4 3/4" x 6 1/2".

PROFILE: *Stereo*

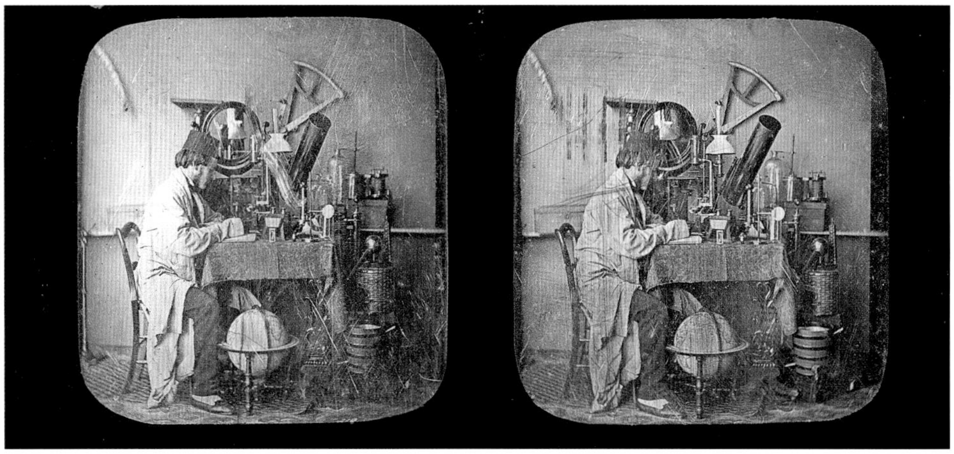

Stereoscopic vision is the process through which the brain combines vision from both eyes into a single, three-dimensional image. This principle has been known for over two millennia. In 1838 Sir Charles Wheatstone, an English physicist and inventor, constructed an instrument that gave a stereoscopic effect to two images of the same subject, drawn from slightly different perspectives. These drawings were positioned in front of and to the side of the viewer's eyes. Immediately in front of the eyes was a pair of mirrors, mounted at a 45-degree angle to the images, which reflected them into the viewer's eyes. This type of viewer was known as a Wheatstone viewer or stereoscope.

Photography was ideally suited to the production of images for the stereoscope, and in 1841, at Wheatstone's request, Henry Collen and William Henry Fox Talbot produced the first photographs for viewing in Wheatstone's instrument. The production of stereoscopic photographs could be accomplished in one of three ways: by shifting a single camera laterally between exposures; by using two cameras with identical lenses; or by using a camera with two lenses and an internal partition.

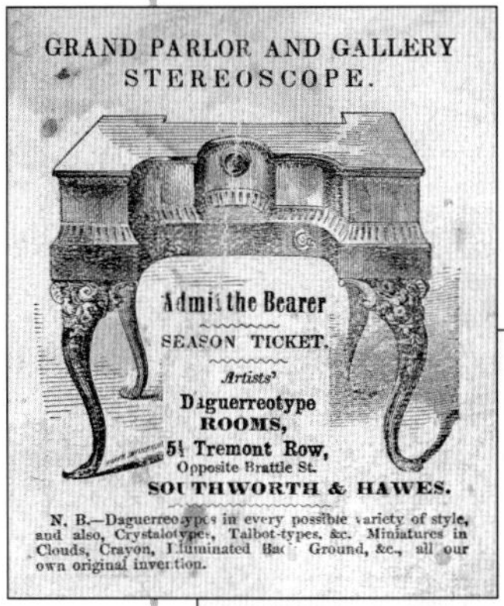

As Wheatstone viewers were somewhat cumbersome, their use was not too widespread. The Boston firm of Southworth & Hawes constructed a large Wheatstone-type viewer in 1855 that they called the Grand Parlor and Gallery Stereoscope. This instrument contained a dozen whole-plate daguerreotype pairs that could be changed mechanically by means of a crank. Admission for viewing was twenty-five cents, fifty cents for a season ticket.

In 1849 Sir David Brewster produced a new kind of viewer. It had the shape of a tapering box, with the daguerreotype housed in one end, and a pair of magnifying lenses (separated by the normal interocular distance) mounted in the other. A hinged panel on the viewer's top was used to admit light. Brewster viewers were made in Paris by the firm of Duboscq and Soleil and were first shown at London's Crystal Palace at the 1851 exhibition.

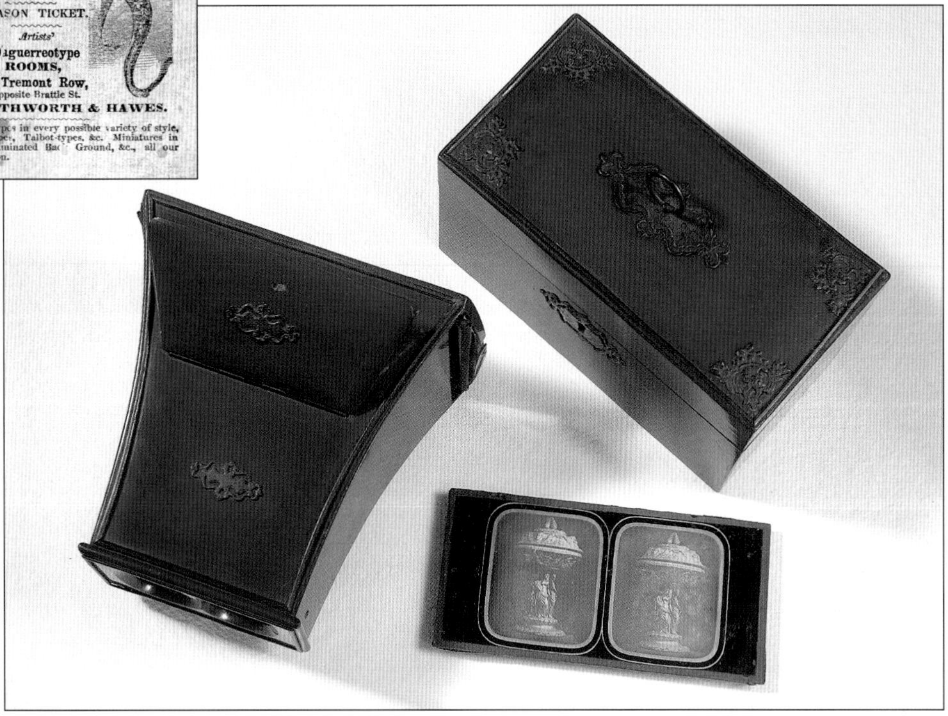

Subsequently, two improvements were made to the Brewster viewer. At the front end, the lenses were remounted into an opera-glass-like extension, some of these providing variable focus. Also, a frosted, or ground glass, screen was installed at the rear, allowing for the viewing of positive transparencies.

While Brewster's stereoscope was the principal type used for viewing stereo daguerreotypes, other folding or collapsible viewers were built into daguerreotype cases. John F. Mascher and John Stull, both of Philadelphia, each invented combined cases/viewers for stereoscopic daguerreotypes, and later ambrotypes.

See opposite for captions.

Opposite, clockwise from top: Attributed to John Benjamin Dancer, Stereo view of man with scientific apparatus, ca. 1853, daguerreotype; Brewster-type stereoscope, matching box for storing views, and stereo daguerreotype, all by C. W. Dixey, ca. 1853; Inset: Season admission ticket for Southworth & Hawes Grand Parlor and Gallery Stereoscope, ca. 1854.

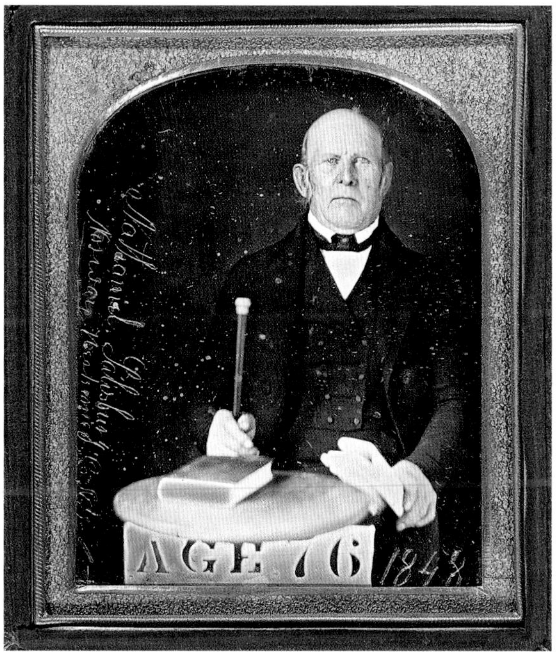

Left: Anonymous, Nathaniel Salisbury, age 76, Norway, Herkimer Co., New York, 1848, daguerreotype, 2 3/4" x 3 1/4". The subject's name and place of residence are scratched on the front of the plate.

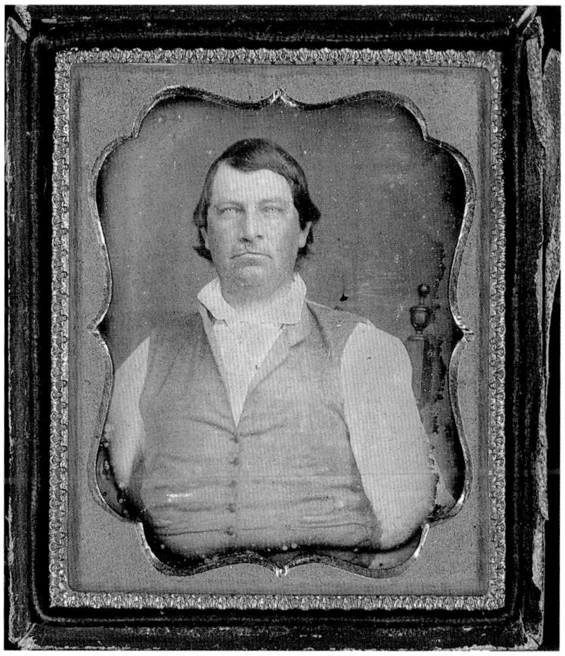

Right: Anonymous, Portrait of a man with a cleft palate, ca. 1855, daguerreotype, 2 3/4" x 3 1/4".

forces to open a New York studio. Another of the city's early daguerreian enterprises was the studio of Jeremiah Gurney. Gurney was certainly the most noted daguerreotypist to fall prey to the dangers of the new process. Due to inhalation of mercury vapors, he was confined to his bed for a protracted period with extreme pain and swelling in his arms and legs. The Meade brothers, Charles R. and Henry, opened their first daguerreotype gallery in Albany, New York, in 1842. Ten years later, they opened another gallery in New York City. Like other noted photographers, they made daguerreotypes of Niagara Falls in the 1840s. Charles R. Meade, who sometimes traveled to Europe, scored one of the greatest coups of the daguerreian era when, in 1848, in France, he made five or six daguerreotypes of Louis Jacques Mandé Daguerre himself, who normally shunned having his portrait taken. Meade's portraits of Daguerre account for more than half of the daguerreotypes ever made of the illustrious father of photography.

Of course the best-known American name from the early years of daguerreotypes in New York was that of Mathew B. Brady. Famous for organizing the effort to photograph the Civil War, Brady was originally a jewel-case manufacturer who turned to making daguerreotype cases. He soon became interested in the Daguerre process and received some instruction from Samuel F. B. Morse. Brady opened his New York studio in 1844 and may have taken daguerreotypes himself in his early years, but due to his failing eyesight and the pressures of managing a popular gallery, he increasingly delegated the actual daguerreotyping to his operators. Quite a few of these operators went on to attain prominence in other cities. In 1851 and 1852, Brady spent eighteen months in Europe, during which time he won the prize medal at the Crystal Palace.

Brady's studio at 359 Broadway was noted for its luxury. The *Illustrated News* for June 11, 1853, reported: "The facilities for first-class pictures appear unrivalled; an additional building has been erected by which, the reception room, ladies dressing-room, and operating rooms are on the same floor, being a desirable arrangement. The ladies dressing-room is fitted up with great taste, and its beauty and convenience will doubtless be appreciated by its fair visitors. The reception saloon is furnished with richness and artistic taste. A large collection of daguerreotypes, of eminent characters, adorn its walls, which are excellently executed, and well worth a visit from all who desire to witness American and European celebrities."

Boston also had early daguerreian activity. François Gouraud, who had first come to New

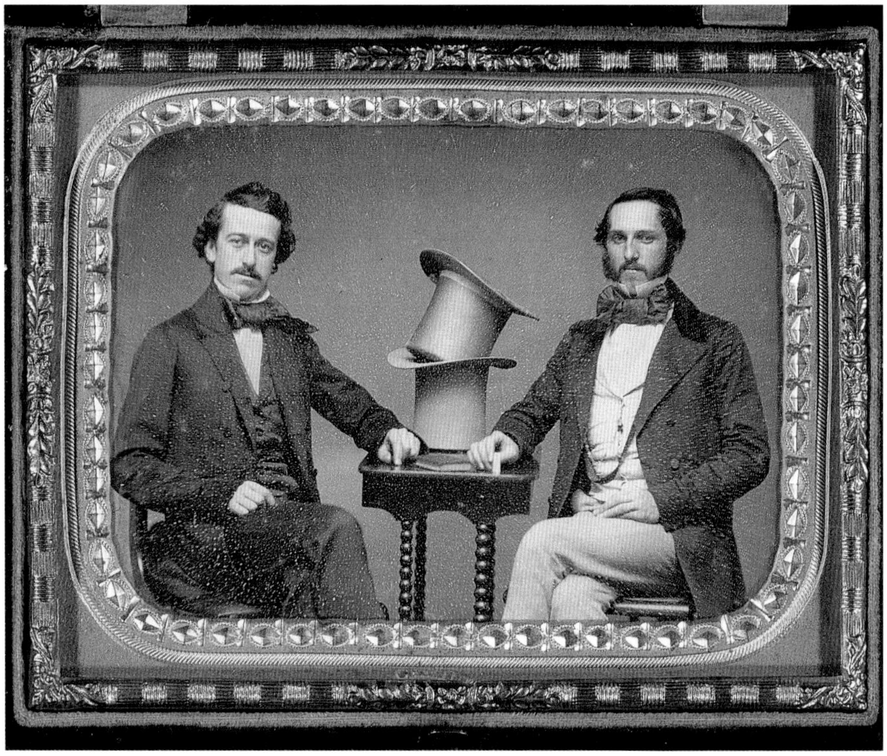

Michael Cahill, Portrait of two men with hats, ca. 1852, daguerreotype, 4" x 4 7/8". In S. Peck thermoplastic case.

York, took a trip to Boston as well. A dentist named Samuel Bemis, who was one of Gouraud's pupils in Boston, purchased an apparatus from Gouraud on April 15, 1840. He then used it to make a daguerreotype of King's Chapel, Boston, and that summer took his equipment to the vicinity of Crawford Notch, New Hampshire, where he made a number of scenic views. Both Albert S. Southworth and John Plumbe, Jr. established businesses in Boston in 1841. Southworth, who had also been present when Gouraud was in Boston making his demonstrations, formed a partnership with Joseph Pennell, a fellow New Englander who had learned the process from Samuel F. B. Morse. Although they launched their business outside of Boston, in 1841 they relocated to the city and began operating as A. S. Southworth & Company. After Pennell left the partnership in 1844, Josiah J. Hawes joined Southworth and the firm became known as Southworth & Hawes. Their portraiture was praised in its day and today they are acclaimed as among the best practitioners of the daguerreian art.

John Plumbe, Jr.'s Boston studio was the first in a chain of galleries he established that extended from the East Coast to the Mississippi, reaching fourteen in number by 1845. Although Plumbe is noted as an early maker of daguerreotypes, history remembers him best as the first person (prior to his involvement in photography) to actively promote a transcontinental railroad. Both Southworth and Plumbe not only made daguerreotypes, but also sold the supplies necessary for making them. Another noted Boston daguerreotypist was John A. Whipple, an enterprising Yankee who used steam to power many of his gallery's operations. Steam supplied the power to clean and polish the plates, to heat the mercury for developing them, and, in summer, to run the fan that cooled the people being photographed. Whipple is also noted for his 1849 daguerreotype of the moon. Also that year he obtained a patent for "crayon" daguerreotypes, which involved the use of a circular mask placed between the sitter and the camera, to give a vignetting effect, and another patent for "crystallotypes," a form of albumen dry plates. James W. Black, another Boston daguerreotypist, became Whipple's partner in 1856. Black is noted primarily for having made the first photograph in the U.S. taken from a balloon, which he did over Boston in 1860.

The news of Daguerre's discovery and process spread from the American Northeast, moving westward and southward to cities such as Washington, D.C.; Utica, Troy, and Rochester, New York; Cincinnati and Cleveland, Ohio; Mobile, Alabama; New Orleans, Louisiana; St. Louis, Missouri; and also to smaller cities and communities. With the discovery of gold in California, daguerreotypists went west, seeking to make their fortunes by exchanging their silver-coated sheets of copper for a more precious metal. Among those making the move were William Shew, Robert H. Vance, and William H. Rulofson. Even Albert S. Southworth made the trip, though he stayed for only two years. Daguerreotypes from California's gold fields have provided us with a vivid record of the mining areas and of those who toiled in them.

One favorite spot of East Coast daguerreotypists who ventured out of their studios was Niagara Falls. Boston's Southworth & Hawes made whole-plate daguerreotypes there in winter. In 1845 William and Frederick Langenheim made

Left: Anonymous, Portrait of a father and son, ca. 1855, daguerreotype, 2 ¾" x 3 ¼". In thermoplastic case.

Right: Anonymous, Portrait of an African American man, ca. 1856, 2 ¾" x 3 ¼".

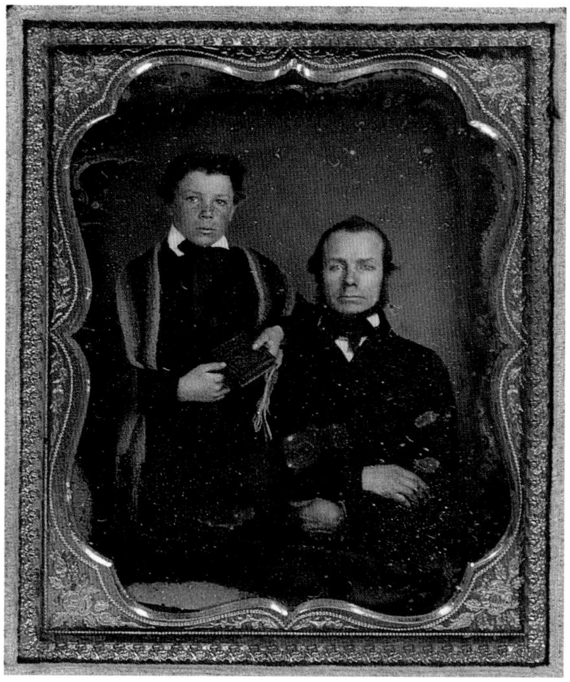

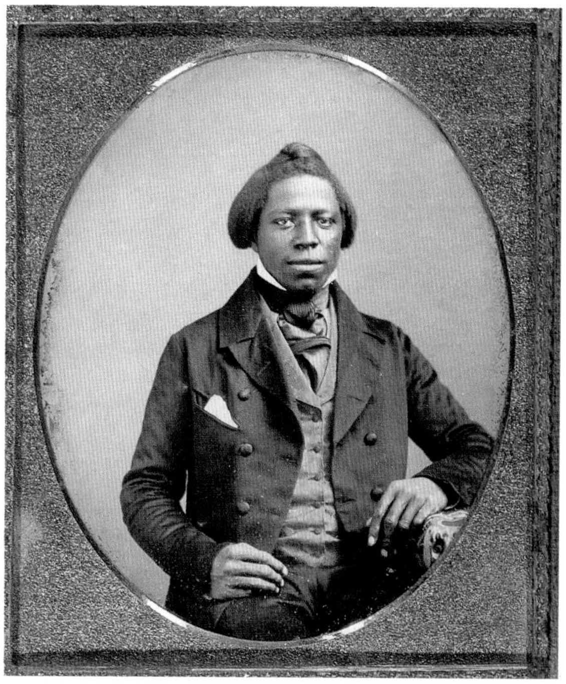

eight sets of five daguerreotype-plate panoramas of the falls, and around 1850–1851 Jesse H. Whitehurst made double-whole-plate daguerreotypes (about 9-by-13 inches) of the falls that he exhibited at London's Crystal Palace in 1852. A permanent fixture at the falls was Platt D. Babbitt, who set up shop there around 1853. Having been granted a monopoly by the government to operate there, Babbitt daguerreotyped groups visiting the falls, and reportedly chased away any potential competitors.

Not all trips were as straightforward as the one to Niagara Falls, though. In 1853 daguerreotypist Solomon N. Carvalho was selected to accompany Colonel John C. Fremont on Fremont's fifth journey to the Rocky Mountains. Carvalho, who had been working out of Charleston, South Carolina, was able to visit a Cheyenne village and make some daguerreotypes, but it was an arduous journey, requiring work in subzero temperatures. At one point, traveling through the snow became so difficult that Carvalho had to abandon his daguerreotype camera and provisions got so low that the group had to slaughter their horses for food.

Other Americans traveled even farther afield. E. Brown sailed to Japan with Commodore Perry and made daguerreotypes there. Augustus Morand went to Brazil, and Charles D. Fredericks, who had a New York studio, journeyed to Venezuela, Brazil, and Argentina. There also was a class of daguerreotypists who had no permanent studios. These were the traveling, or itinerant, photographers, who worked in communities too small to support a permanent studio. Some used their own or rented buggies and wagons to get around, or hired someone to transport them from one place to another. When they came to a town, they set up shop in rented quarters. Others brought their studios with them in the form of daguerreian wagons or "saloons," often parking on the village green. These saloons were horse-drawn and had a skylight in the roof to provide illumination. Inside they had, at minimum: a darkroom area, a camera and tripod, a posing chair, and a head clamp. Additional furnishings depended on the state of the photographer's finances.

Some of these photographers simply went wherever there was a prospect of doing business, and then moved on when the flow of customers tapered off. Others, usually the ones with daguerreian saloons, had a regular circuit they followed each year. In winter, when the sunlight was too dim and infrequent, and the temperatures too low for the chemical reactions to proceed quickly enough, they would close up shop and store their wagons somewhere. Enterprising itinerants even took to the waterways in boats or on barges.

During the era of the daguerreotype in America, virtually nothing was left untouched by the practitioners of the process. The subjects ranged from steamboats to locomotives, from horses and prize bulls to seventeen-year locusts, from buildings and city streets to fires, from statuary to cemetery monuments, from prominent personalities to Native Americans and slaves.

Daguerreotypy also had a number of specialized applications. Edward Anthony's earliest efforts involved documenting the government's survey of the U.S.–Canadian border. John Whipple made astronomical daguerreotypes of the moon and the stars. Daguerreotypes were made to document medical conditions and abnormalities. They were placed on tombstones to commemorate the deceased. They were incorporated into "business cards" and used as marketing aids, to illustrate the products being offered. A very common practice of the day was the daguerreotyping of the deceased. As portraits were relatively expensive, most people didn't have one made in their lifetime. But often families, in remembrance, would commission a daguerreotypist to make a "postmortem" portrait. Southworth's records show that he was hired several times for this task.

For all of the beauty of a good daguerreotype, the process had one distinct drawback—the near impossibility of producing duplicate copies. Only two methods could provide duplicates and both involved extra effort. The photographer could make a second daguerreotype from the original, but the copy was never quite as good, and unless a mirror or prism was used, the image would be reversed. The second method required the use of two cameras, thus adding the expense of a second instrument. (A second exposure on a single camera rarely produced the same result.) In at least one instance, two cameras were used simultaneously. On cards placed in the backs of their daguerreotype cases, James & Company of Boston advertised "Two Likenesses at Once by the DOUBLE CAMERA. Your Choice for 25 Cents." The cards also featured an illustration of the camera. James & Co. was one of the then-infamous cheap daguerreotype parlors, and their 25-cent ninth-plate images (2-by-2½ inches) were generally of mediocre quality. It remained for other photographic processes to provide reproducibility. The first of these in common use was the calotype.

The Calotype

While the news of Daguerre's discovery was received by most with great interest, William Henry Fox Talbot received it with concern. He had been experimenting with photographic processes for some four years already, and to Talbot there was a question of priority of invention, a matter of considerable principle to Victorians involved in science. Thwarted in his attempts to record the scenery on a trip to Italy in October 1833 because he was unskilled at drawing, Talbot turned to the camera lucida and the camera obscura to aid in his endeavors. While he had more success with the former, it was the beauty of the image formed by the camera obscura that captivated him.

By 1835 Talbot had succeeded in using silver chloride to sensitize paper by bathing "salted" paper with silver nitrate. Negatives were then obtained by exposing the paper for several hours in a small camera. But Talbot had never pursued his experiments all the way to a finished positive. When he learned of Daguerre's work, he feared

"Appareil Universel No. 1" sliding-box camera, Maison Charles Chevalier, ca. 1860. A transitional camera that could be used for making 4 ¾" x 6 ½" calotypes, daguerreotypes, or wet-collodion negatives.

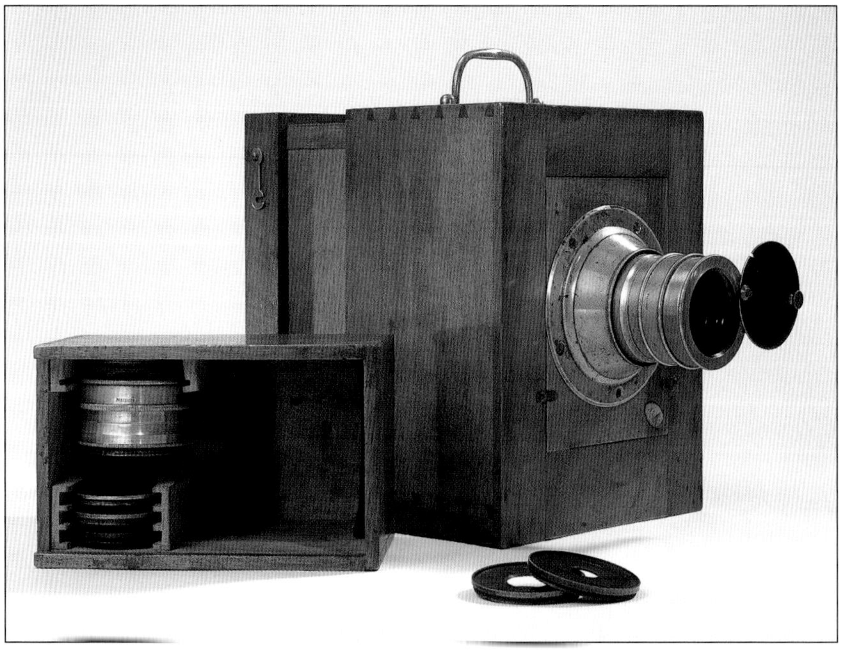

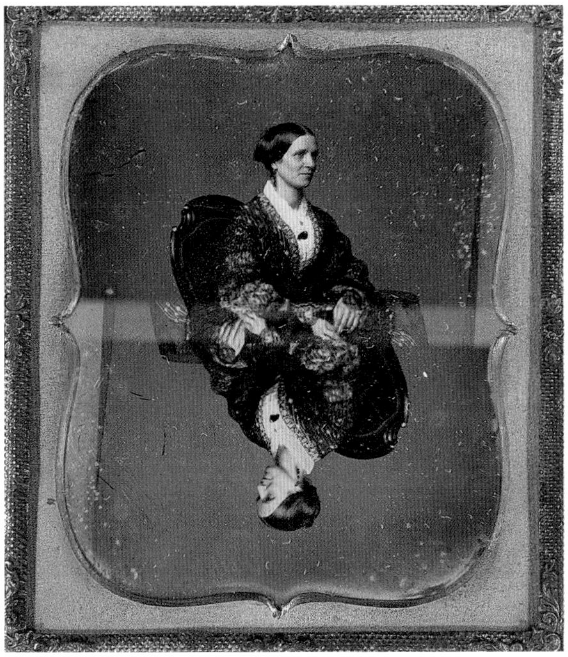

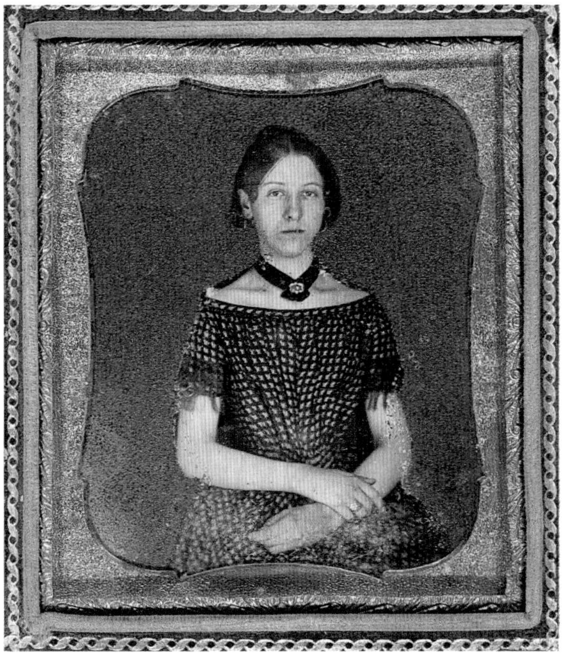

Left: Anonymous, Portraits of a woman, ca. 1852, daguerreotype, 2 3/4" x 3 1/4". Two separate exposures on a single plate. The plate was inverted for the second exposure.

Right: Anonymous, Portrait of a young woman, ca. 1855, 2 3/4" x 3 1/4". The background has been removed by a chemical wash.

that the process was the same as his and set about informing the scientific community of his prior activity. While the effects of light on silver nitrate—it turns it black—were previously known, Talbot had discovered a means of fixing the image, which he called the "preserving process." Talbot reported his work to the Royal Society at a meeting in early 1839, but did not reveal the technical details. The meeting was reported in the *Literary Gazette* of February 2, 1839, thus staking Talbot's claim. That same month, he made his first positive prints by placing a negative print in contact with sensitized paper and exposing it to light.

Upon learning of Talbot's work, two Germans, Carl August von Steinheil and Franz von Kobell, began experiments based on the incomplete reports of the process. They succeeded in dissolving the unexposed silver compounds by using ammonium hydroxide or potassium thiosulfate. Sir John Herschel, a noted astronomer, discovered that hyposulphite of soda—later called "hypo"—worked well in dissolving unexposed silver salts, thus "fixing" (making permanent) the image. Herschel is also credited with introducing the terms "negative" and "positive" to the vocabulary of photography.

Talbot's earlier attempts at producing negatives had relied on using an exposure long enough to produce a visible image. In 1840 he discovered that with shorter exposures—too short to produce a visible image—and with subsequent development, he could get satisfactory negatives. The paper was soaked in silver nitrate and then potassium iodide. Next it was made highly sensitive by washing in a silver nitrate-gallic acid mixture. When the paper was soaked in the same solution, following exposure in the camera, an image slowly appeared. While at first Talbot used potassium bromide for fixing, he subsequently turned to heated hypo. He called this type of print a "calotype," though later the name "talbotype" came into use. Talbot also proposed the additional step of waxing the paper negative, as this improved its transmission of light. Talbot published a lavish book, *The Pencil of Nature*, illustrated with his talbotypes, in six installments between the years 1844 and 1846.

Following the same course as Daguerre, in 1841 he had patented his invention in England, which tended to restrict its use. In 1852, however, bowing to public pressure, Talbot finally relinquished control of the process, except for its use in professional portraiture.

Britain's most noted calotypists were David O. Hill and Robert Adamson. Hill, an artist, hired Adamson, who had studied calotyping under Sir David Brewster. Together they embarked on the mammoth project of calotyping 450 delegates to an 1843 convention that led to the founding of the Free Church of Scotland. This was done to provide Hill

FOCUS: *Daguerreotype Presentation and Display*

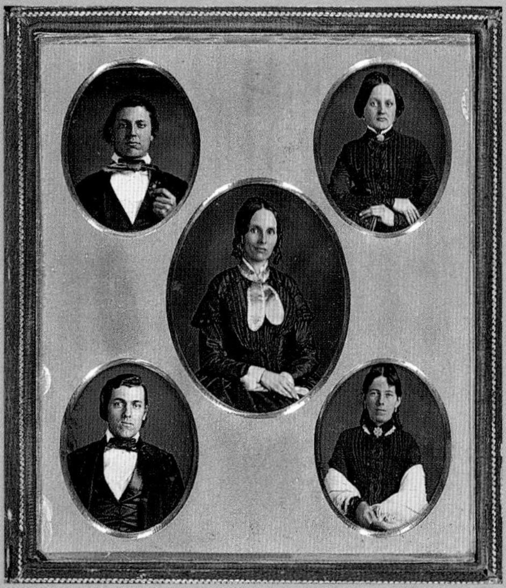

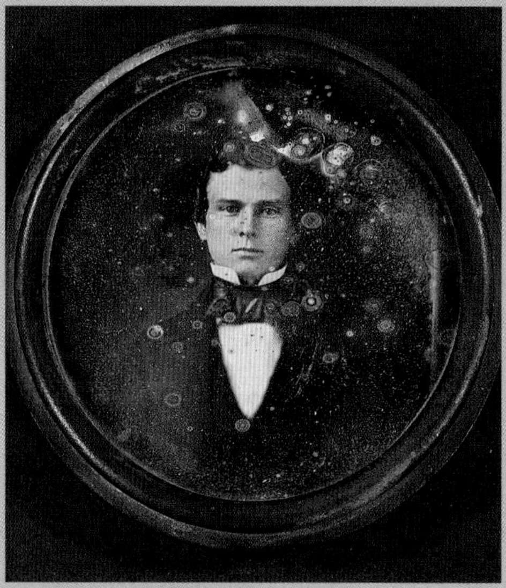

Clockwise from left: Anonymous, Five family portraits, ca. 1850, matte size 4 ¾" x 5 ½". This method was sometimes used to unite several separate but related photographs; Anonymous, Portrait of a man, ca. 1855, daguerreotype, 2 ½" diameter. An example of a monumental daguerreotype, mounted on a tombstone to memorialize the subject; Anonymous, Members of the Houghton family, 1848–1850, framed daguerreotypes, each 2 ½" x 3", stained walnut frame. Name, birthdate, and sometimes age noted above or below each portrait.

Opposite: Anonymous, Clock salesman's sample illustrations, ca. 1858, daguerreotypes. N. L. Bradley, a clock salesman, carried sixteen daguerreotypes of clocks around in a slotted case. The clock type and price were given on the back of each daguerreotype.

The daguerreotype, called the "mirror with a memory" by Oliver Wendell Holmes, is a beautiful object requiring special care and treatment. While the mat, glass, and preserver that often accompanied daguerreotypes at the time of purchase provided sufficient protection, many wished to display them in a grander fashion.

Larger daguerreotypes (and display groupings of small daguerreotypes) were usually placed in frames ranging from the simple to the very ornate. Some were made of finished, veneered, or black- or gold-painted wood. Others were made of gesso, a form of plaster of Paris, which could be cast into a variety of shapes. Thermoplastic frames were made by molding a heated mixture of woody and other fibers mixed with gum shellac. Other types included ornate cases made of wood and papier-mâché, and metal-framed cases covered in leather. The former were covered with black lacquer and inlaid with mother of pearl in floral or other decorative patterns. Many of the frames imported into America had a tortoise-shell pattern in the mat.

The smaller daguerreotypes commonly produced were housed in cases sold by the studios. It was even the practice sometimes for the subject to be photographed holding the case into which the daguerreotype would soon be placed. The earliest cases were hinged at one side, and usually made of leather-covered wood, with a pattern embossed on the leather. Most had a lining of cloth, usually velvet or silk, inside the cover. The photographer's name and address were sometimes stamped into the velvet and, less frequently, onto the exterior.

Practically every manner conceivable was used to house and display daguerreotypes: brooches, lockets—some with multiple compartments—rings, even cuff links, were used for the smaller ones. Some were mounted on top of small boxes and cases. They were even sealed in printed cardboard and used as business cards. In 1855 the Mausoleum Daguerreotype Company even issued a catalog of weatherproof cases, designed to be used to affix daguerreotypes to tombstones.

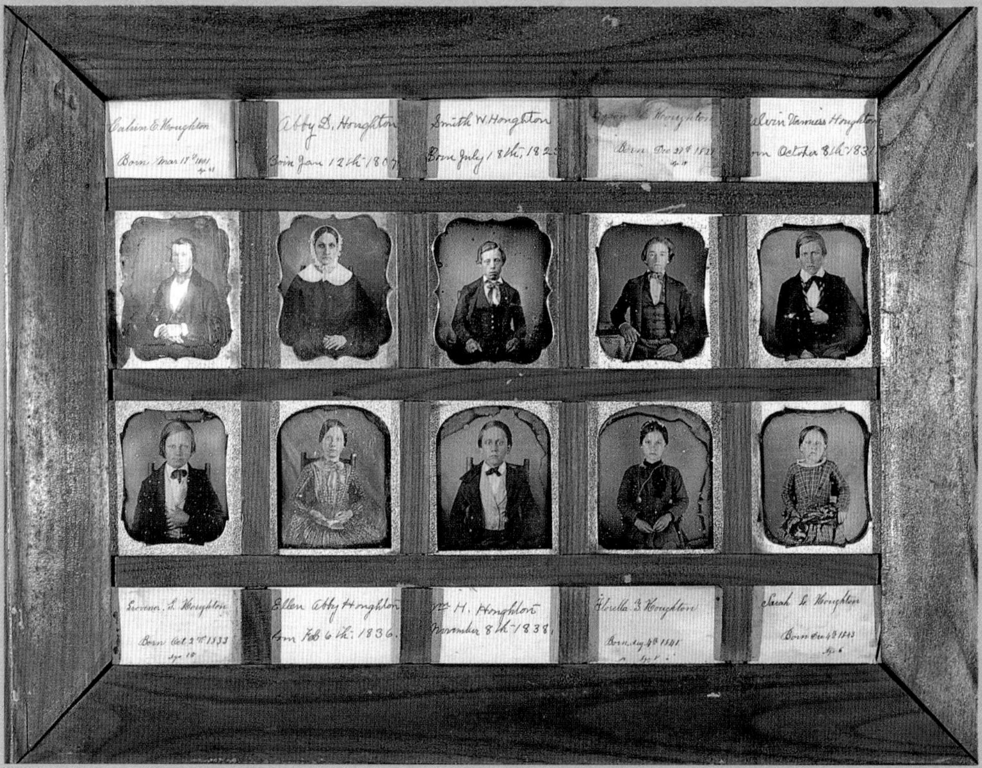

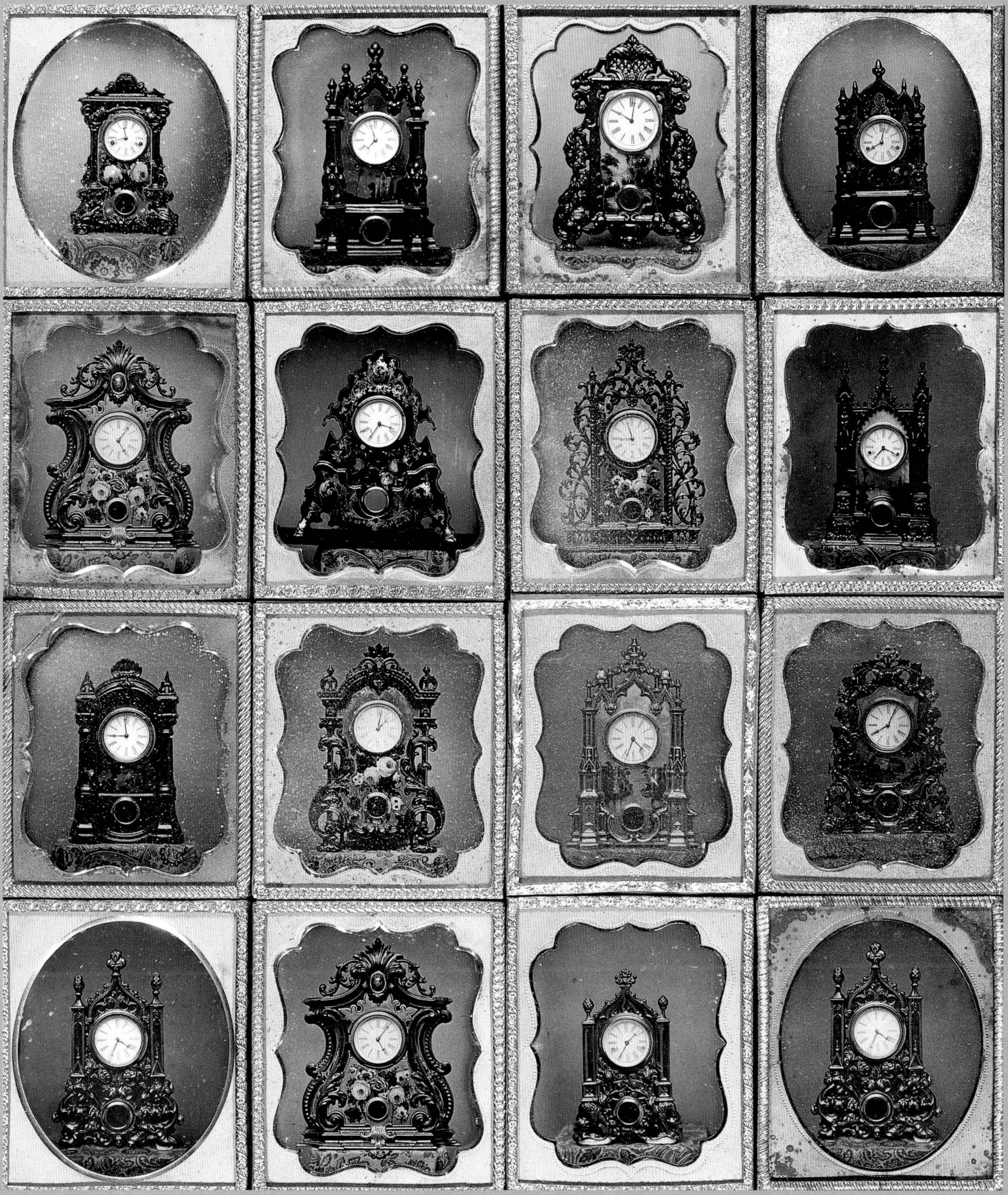

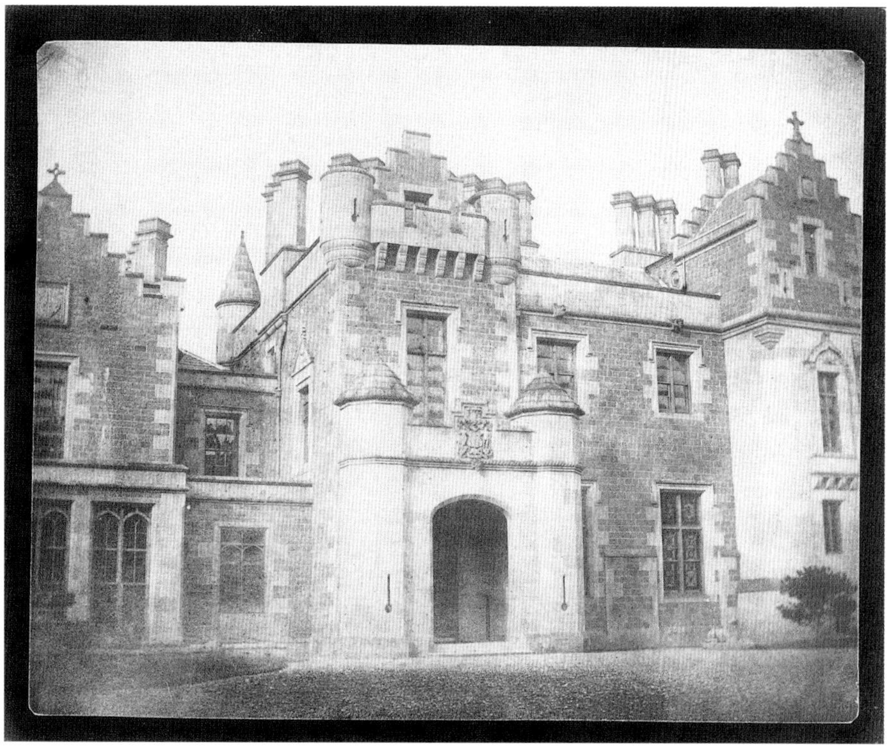

William Henry Fox Talbot, *Hall Door at Abbotsford*, 1845, calotype, 7 3/8" x 9". Plate 5 from *Sun Pictures of Scotland.*

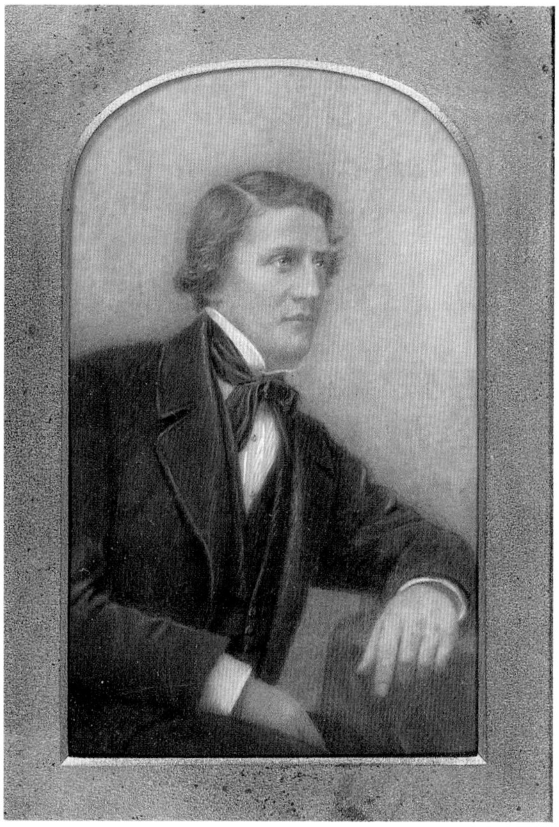

Right: John Mayall, Portrait of a young man, ca. 1855, salt print, 2 3/4" x 4".

with images from which he made a large painting of all the participants in the convention. Hill and Adamson were also noted for their outdoor calotypes of people. These portraits were the exception, however, as the calotype process was used mainly to photograph landscapes and buildings.

In America, the Langenheim brothers secured the rights to Talbot's patent. But they were not successful in their attempts to promote greater use of the calotype. One of the calotype's main advantages was that it allowed any number of positives to be contact-printed from a single negative. Also, it was cheaper to produce a calotype negative than a daguerreotype. On the other hand, the exposures took longer, and many preferred the sharpness of the daguerreotype; its images held up amazingly well even when viewed under a microscope.

In 1850 a significant improvement was made in the sensitive paper used to print negatives: Louis Désiré Blanquart-Evrard dissolved potassium bromide and potassium iodide in egg white and coated the paper with this mixture, which when dry yielded a smooth surface. Then, when the paper was floated face down on a solution of silver nitrate and acetic acid, it became light-sensitive. Following exposure, the paper was toned with the same material as a daguerreotype, then fixed, washed, and dried.

Direct Positives

On May 20, 1839, Hippolyte Bayard met with François Arago and showed him some direct-positive prints on paper that he had produced using a camera obscura. The prints, which he had been making since March 1839, were produced by taking a sheet of paper, prepared in the same way as Talbot's, and soaking it in potassium iodide. The paper was then placed on a piece of slate, loaded in the back of a camera obscura, and exposed. The action of the light on the paper made silver iodide, which appeared white on the darkened paper. The paper was then washed with sodium hyposulfite to stabilize the image. But Bayard's process required lengthy exposures of twenty to thirty minutes, and the announcement of his process was overshadowed by the enthusiasm with which the public and the French government received Daguerre's process. As a result, it never received a large degree of acceptance, and within a few years he abandoned it.

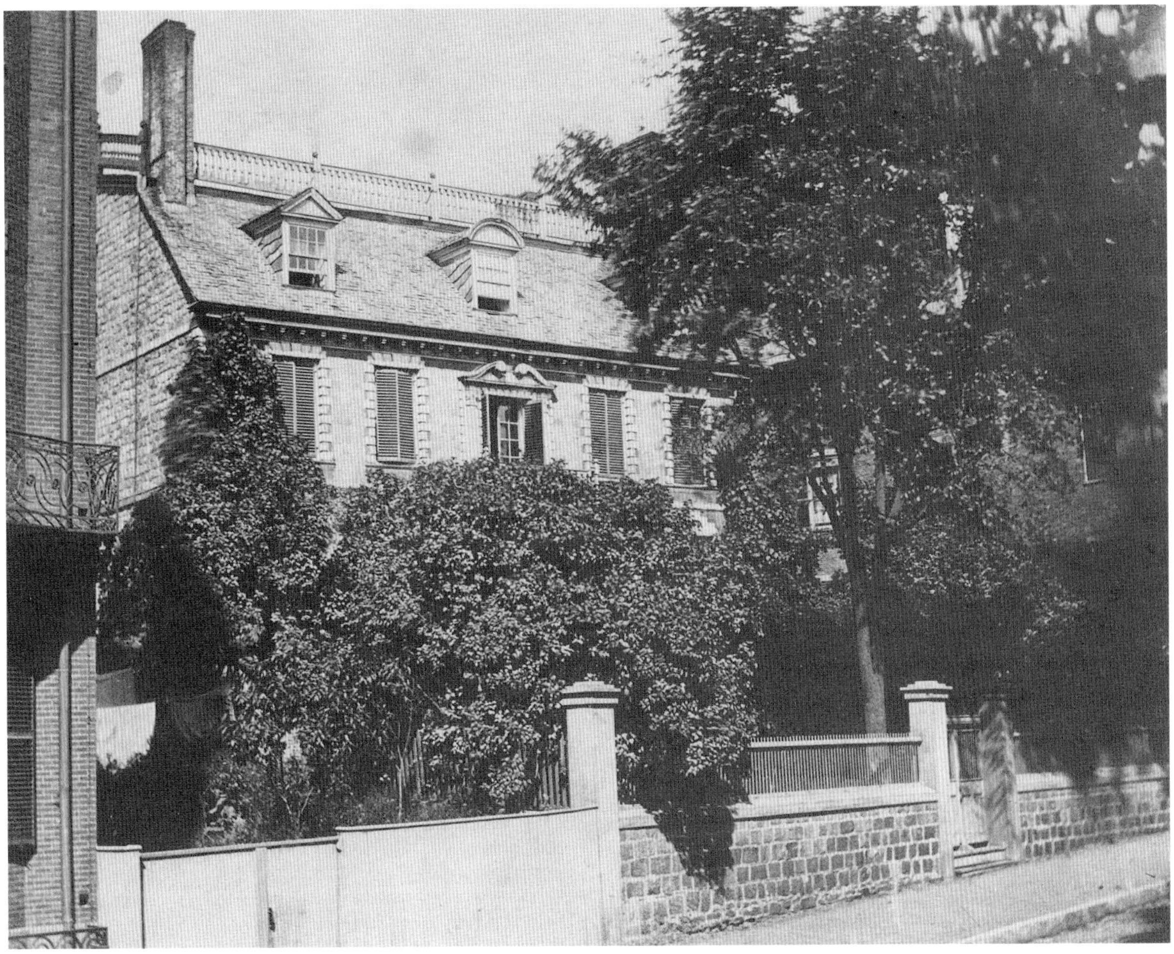

John Whipple, Hancock House, Boston, 1854, crystallotype, from *Homes of American Statesmen.* The house in which John Hancock, a signer of the Declaration of Independence, lived.

Negatives on Glass

In 1847 Claude Abel Niépce de Saint-Victor, the nephew of Nicéphore Niépce, brought full transparency to the negative. Previously, negatives had been made on paper or waxed paper, and as such relied on the transmission of light through paper to make positive prints. This passed onto the positive any features of or irregularities in the paper of the original negative. What Niépce de Saint-Victor did was use a coating of egg white and potassium iodide on a glass plate. Once the plate had dried, it was dipped in silver nitrate and, with the resultant formation of silver iodide, became light-sensitive. Following exposure, gallic acid was used to reveal the image. The negative produced could then be printed on paper, as was done with calotypes.

John A. Whipple began experimenting with glass negatives around 1844, in order to avoid copying the texture of the paper in his photographs. In 1850 Whipple and William B. Jones were granted a patent for the use of albumen on glass, the same technique employed by Niépce de Saint-Victor. The name they gave the results of their process was the "crystallotype." William and Frederick Langenheim also began to use the albumen glass-negative process in 1849—"hyalotypes," as they referred to them. In 1850 the Langenheims were granted a patent for an improvement in this process. One innovation of theirs was the printing of positives from albumen negatives not only on paper, but on glass. These glass-based positives were used in stereoscopes and also in "magic lanterns," by means of which they could be projected.

While albumen paper, as Blanquart-Evrard termed his invention, was used through the end of the nineteenth century, the daguerreotype and its rival, the calotype/talbotype, were not. Their slow but inevitable demise was signaled by the introduction of the wet-collodion process, announced in 1851 by the Englishman Frederick Scott Archer.

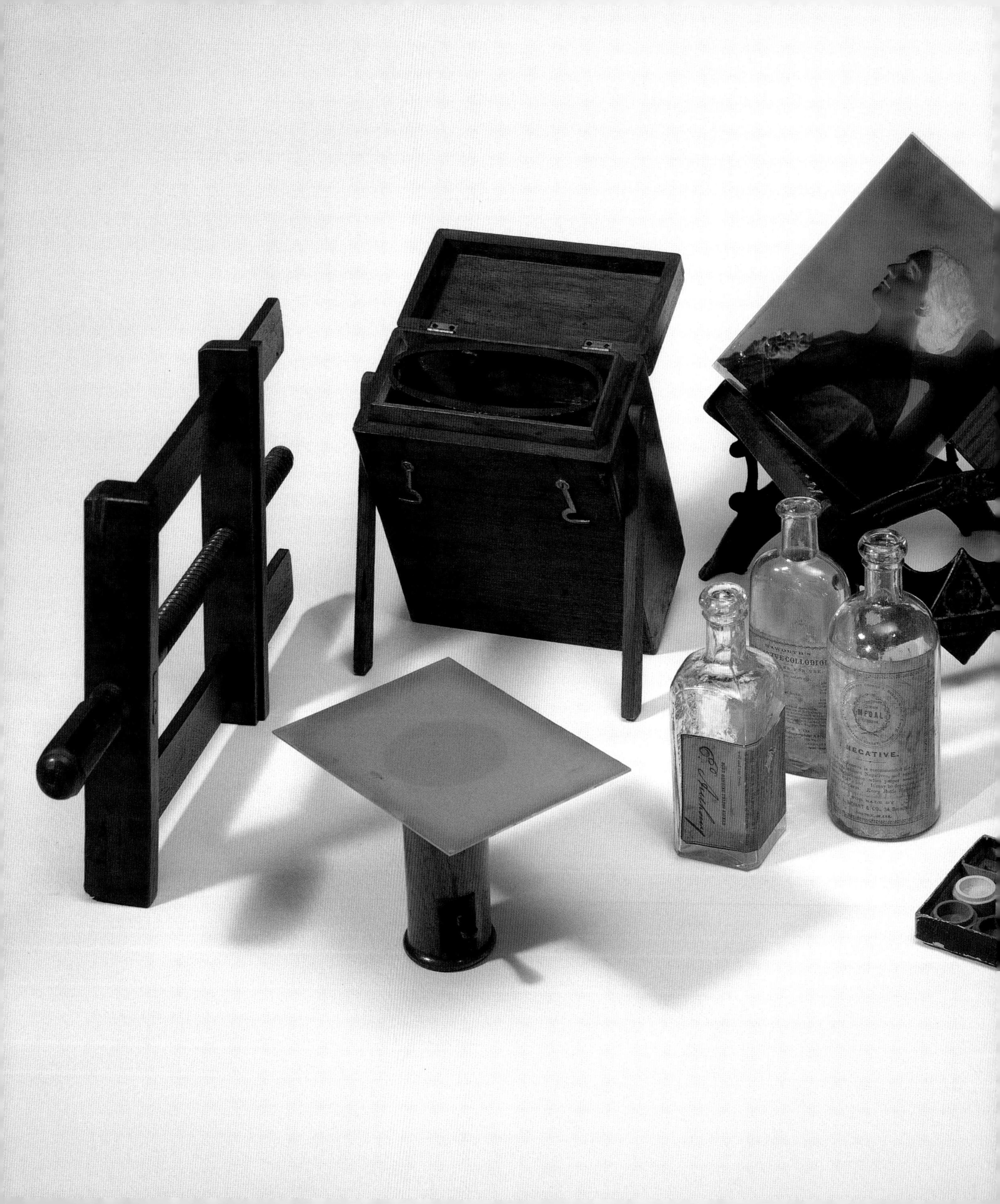
NEGATIVE.

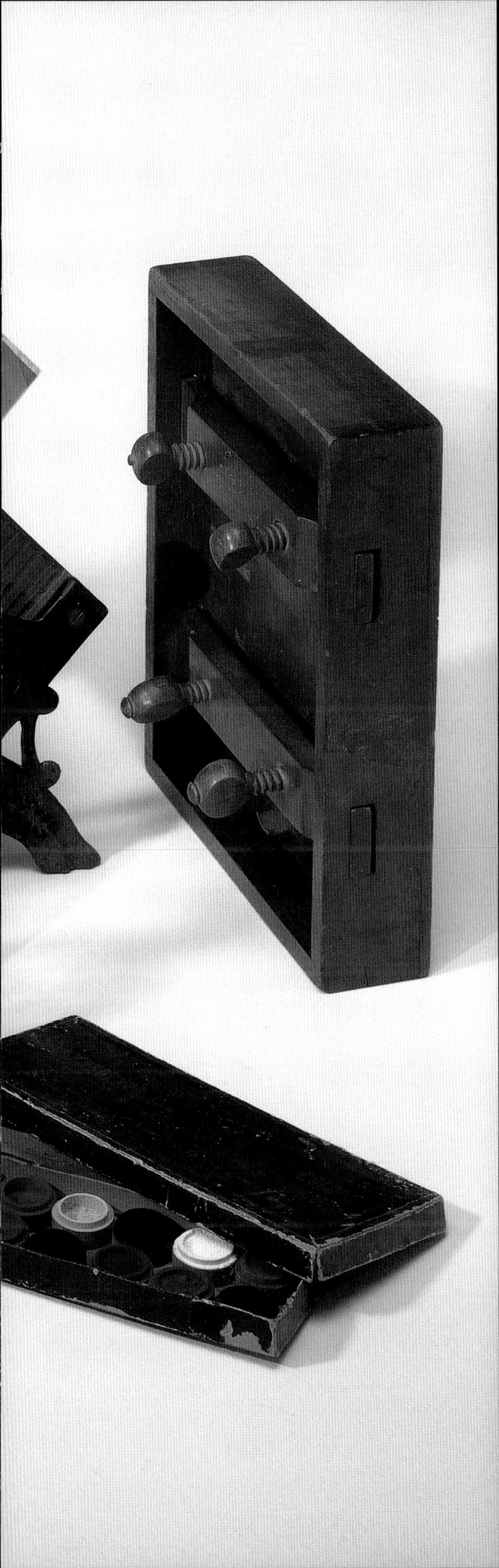

CHAPTER THREE:

THE RISE OF WET COLLODION

Equipment for wet-collodion photography. Clockwise from top left: plate vise; plate bath; plate-drying rack with negatives; printing frame; coloring box; chemical bottles; coated plate on a suction-cup device for holding plates

The Wet-Plate Processes

The introduction of the daguerreotype process to the world led to considerable interest in photography on the part of the more affluent and more informed members of American and European society. It also led to the establishment of studios in most major cities in Europe and in the cities and smaller communities of America. The introduction of the wet-collodion process, however, had a rather different impact. As photographers were already established in business, the number of studios did not markedly increase. The public's interest, though, did gradually grow. This was due to two factors. First, the necessary materials for producing wet-collodion plates were sold to the public at a lower cost. The silver-coated sheets of copper used in making daguerreotypes were far more expensive than sheets of glass and pieces of paper. The second factor was the reproducibility of the photograph. With the new process, a single negative could be used to produce any number of high-quality identical prints at a reasonable price and with a level of detail far surpassing that of the calotype.

In June 1849, Frederick Scott Archer, an Englishman, began experimenting with the use of collodion as a substitute for paper in making photographs. Collodion is a transparent, viscous liquid made by dissolving nitrocellulose ("gun cotton") in ether and alcohol. When the volatile solvents evaporate, what remains is a film that is tough and skinlike. Others before him had used dry collodion as a base for the silver salts, but Archer chose to work with wet collodion. In the March 1851 issue of *The Chemist*, he published his wet-collodion process for photography.

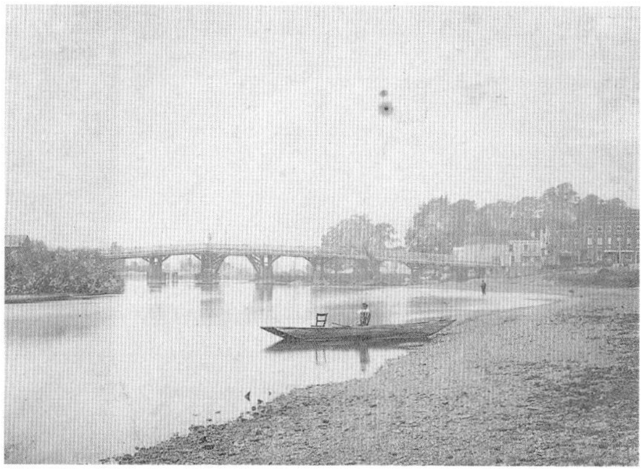

Frederick Scott Archer, *View of the Thames River*, ca. 1857, albumen print from wet-collodion negative, 6" x 8 1/2".

In this process, collodion was used as the vehicle for attaching the light-sensitive chemicals to the glass plate. Because the plate's coating needed to remain moist during the exposure and up to the point of developing in order to preserve its sensitivity, the procedure was referred to as the wet-collodion or wet-plate process. Generally, the plate would remain wet for between ten and twenty minutes at the most, depending on the temperature and humidity of the day. The plate was prepared by dissolving potassium iodide in liquid collodion and then pouring the solution evenly over a sheet of glass. The plate was then dipped, while still sticky, in a solution of silver nitrate. By this process, silver iodide, which was sensitive to light, was produced. The plate, while still moist, was placed in a plate holder, positioned in the camera, exposed, and promptly developed by pouring a solution of pyrogallic acid and silver iodide over it. Hyposulfite of soda was used for fixing, and after washing, the plate was dried. Prints were then made by exposing either calotype or albumen paper while in contact with the now-dry plate.

While daguerreotype plates could be nearly as sensitive as wet-collodion plates, they could not be used to make positive prints in almost unlimited quantities. In addition, collodion plates were more sensitive, more transparent, and more

Below: Folding sliding-box camera, attributed to Thomas Ottewill, ca. 1855, for 9 1/4" x 11 1/4" wet-collodion plates. When collapsed (inset), the camera's outer box had space inside for storing the folded inner box.

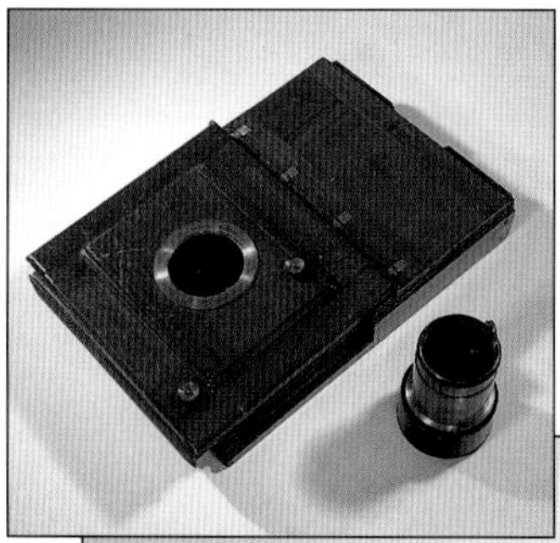

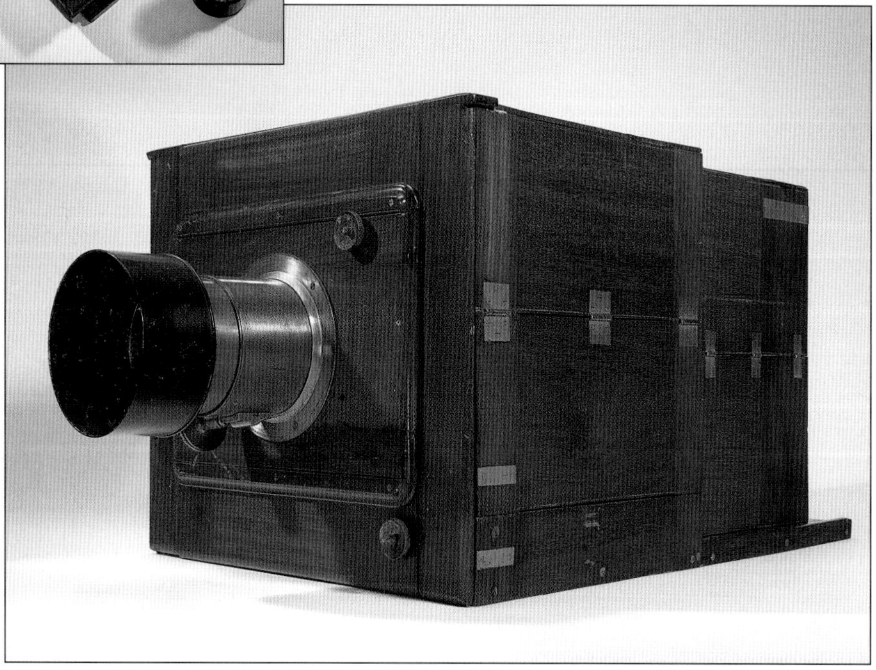

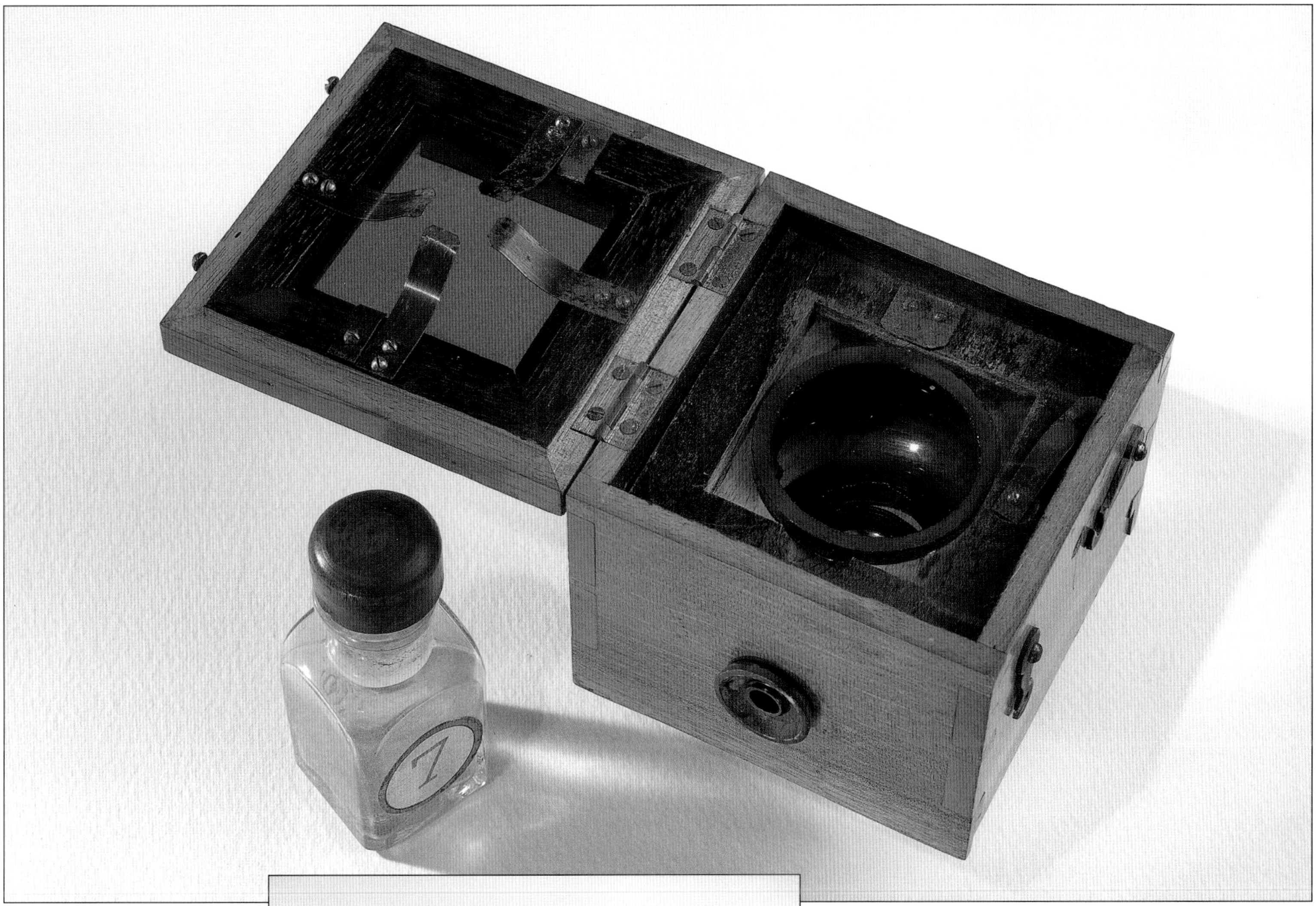

Dubroni Camera No. 1, Maison Dubroni, ca. 1865, for 1 ¾" diameter exposures on 2" x 2" wet-collodion plates. Back open, showing sensitizing/developing chamber.

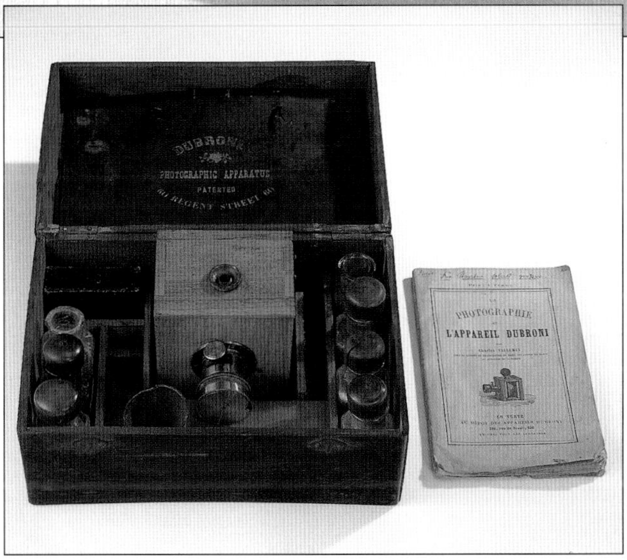

Right: Dubroni Outfit No. 1, Maison Dubroni, ca. 1865. Case containing holding camera and chemicals, and instructions.

uniform if the coating of the collodion was done properly. As good glass—glass with a flat surface—was an expensive material in the mid-1800s, unsatisfactory negatives and those no longer needed were stripped of their collodion emulsions and the glass recycled.

The cameras used for wet-collodion photography were no different from those used to make daguerreotypes. Sometimes a camera that has been employed in wet-plate photography can be identified by the silver nitrate stains at the rear of the camera or on the plate holder. Unless the photographer was careful, the chemicals used in the process ultimately contributed to the deterioration of the camera's and the plate holder's wood. One type of plate holder employed patented glass corners within, for holding the still-damp plates.

In the early 1850s, most cameras were of the sliding, box-in-box type, but gradually there was a changeover to the bellows-style camera. This was especially true of cameras used in the field. To work outdoors in the 1850s, a photographer needed to bring along equipment and chemicals weighing as much as seventy-five pounds. And this was using conventional smaller-sized plates, not the large and heavy glass plates used by photographers of the American West, such as William H. Jackson.

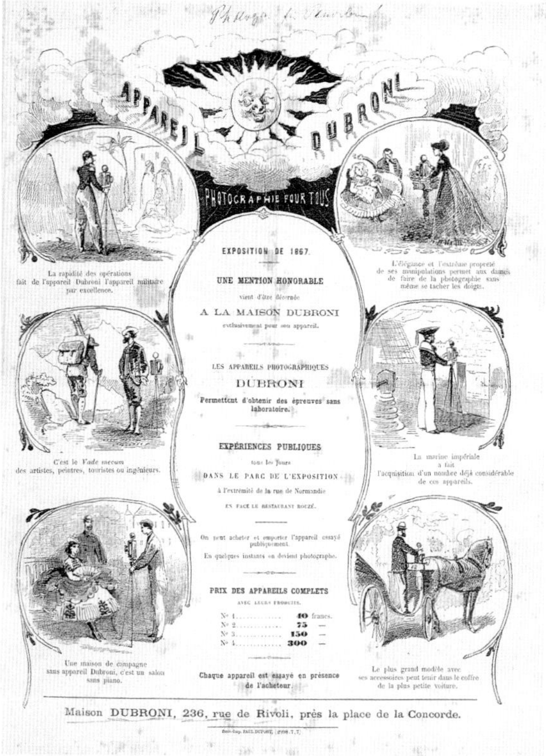

Advertisement for Dubroni Camera, Maison Dubroni, ca. 1868, 9" x 12 ¼".

One unusual camera of the wet-plate period dispensed with the necessity of sensitizing the plate before placing it in the camera and developing it after removal, doing away with the need for a darkroom or dark tent. Called the Dubroni (an anagram of the name of its French inventor, Bourdin), the camera's main element was a central bottle-shaped container of glass or ceramic, mounted between two wooden panels or enclosed within a wooden body. The container's front and rear ends were cut away and ground flat. The lens was positioned at the front, while at the back was an opening with a door, through which a sheet of ground glass could be inserted for focusing. The ground glass could then be replaced with a glass plate that had been coated with bromiodized collodion. On top of the camera was an opening, normally stoppered, through which an India-rubber pipette with a squeeze bulb was inserted. This pipette was used to introduce the chemicals required to sensitize the plate prior to exposure; it was also used to develop and fix the plate once exposed. The open-sided, amber-glass models permitted the user to view the developing process through the sides. In the ceramic and wooden-

PROFILE: *In the Field*

The era of wet-collodion photography was similar to that of the daguerreotype in that studio photographers sometimes ventured into the field, either to make commissioned photographs or to shoot on speculation, in hopes that they would later be able to sell copies of their photographs. Additionally, serious amateurs would occasionally journey into the countryside for a photographic outing.

This was no easy matter. When the photographer left for a day of work, he had to bring with him a camera, tripod, glass plates, chemicals, even the darkened chamber in which he would sensitize and develop the plates. Assuming there were roads, he could use a horse and buggy to transport the equipment. Some professionals had darkrooms built into a cart or buggy. When working on a stream or lake, some used a boat, with a tent set up on board. Often, though, the photographer needed to carry all of his materials himself.

Any lightproof tent could serve as a darkroom, but eventually manufacturers began to offer portable photographic dark tents. These were usually perched on legs, so the photographer had his materials at waist level, and apart from darkness they provided compartments or shelves for chemical bottles and a surface on which to work, and had a tinted panel or window to shield against the harmful rays of light. Water was usually brought into the tent through a tube connected to a container set on top of the tent.

By the late 1860s, such dark tents had become fairly standard. Although dry-plate photography came into general use in the early 1880s, these tents were so well suited to photographers' needs that their production and use persisted through the early 1900s. Many photographers still wanted to develop their negatives in the field, in order to check the results, though by that time they no longer had to sensitize the plates.

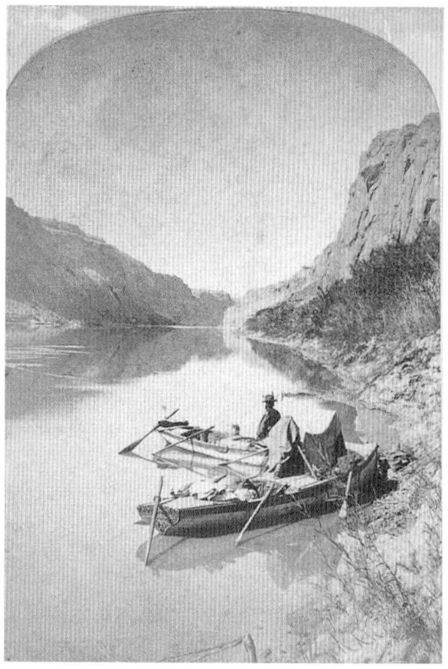

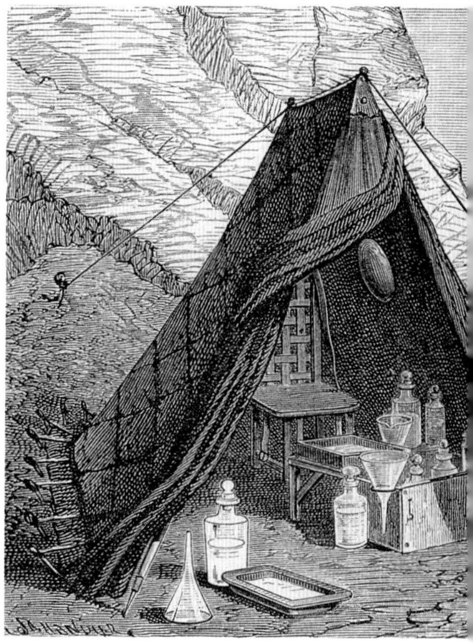

Clockwise from top left: Attributed to John K. Hiller, Photographer's dark tent set up in rear of boat, Glen Canyon, ca. 1875, albumen print, half of stereo pair. Taken during J. S. Powell's Topographical and Geological Survey of the Colorado River.

S. R. Stoddard with Photographer's Dark Tent and Wet-Collodion Photographic Accessories, ca. 1875, albumen print, half of stereo pair. From Stoddard's stereo series *The Walled Banks of the Ausable*.

Wet-plate era photographer in operation in the field, woodcut, from *Les merveilles de la photographie*, Gaston Tissandier, 1874.

Wet-plate photographer in the field with his equipment, woodcut, from *Les merveilles de la photographie*, Gaston Tissandier, 1874. Note the chair in his backpack.

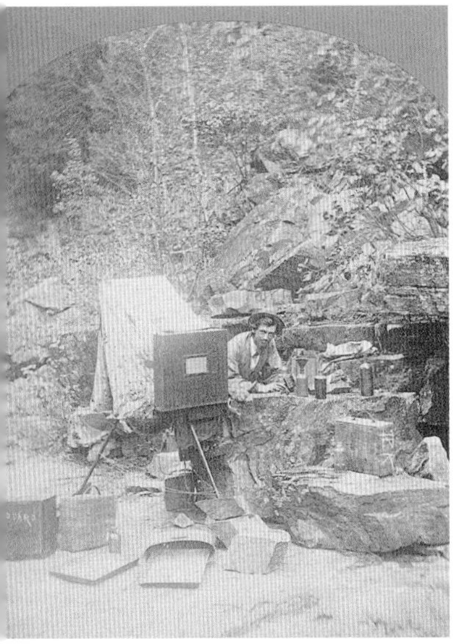

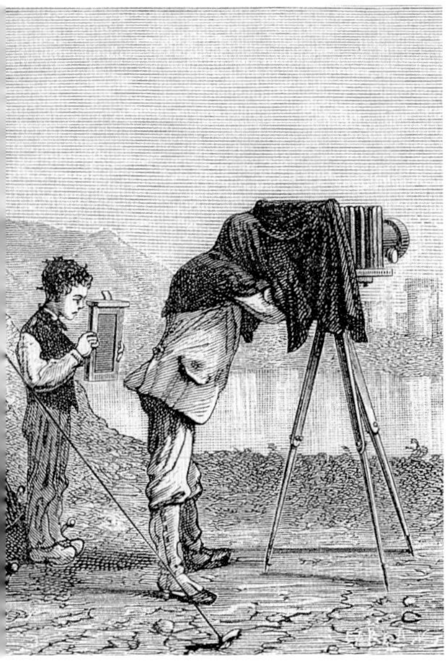

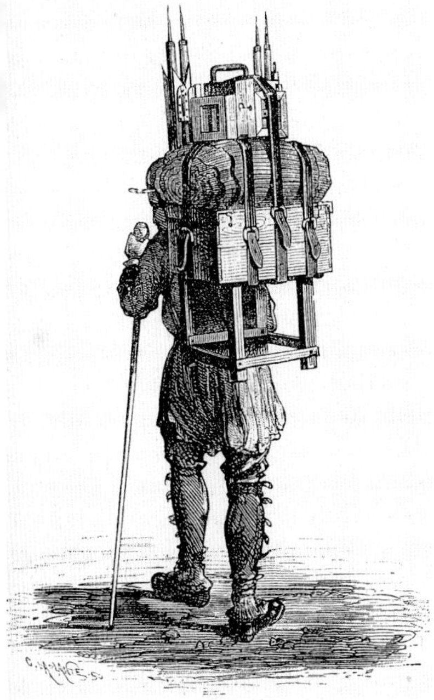

sided models, developing was viewed through a ruby-colored glass window mounted in the rear door. Dubroni cameras were produced in a variety of sizes and were relatively small compared to other cameras of their time. They came in sets, with a compartmented wooden box to hold the camera and chemicals. The small Dubronis could also be mounted on a tripod, and coupled with the fact that they eliminated the need for many of the accessories of wet-plate photography, this made them very popular for use in the field.

The Ambrotype—In July 1854, James A. Cutting of Boston was granted three U.S. patents for variations on the wet-collodion process. The principle behind the ambrotype, as the images produced in this way eventually came to be called, is that when a thin collodion negative is viewed with a black background, it appears as a positive—a principle that had been known since 1840. Cutting's patents were related to modifications of the collodion used, and to the sealing of the image. A variety of materials were used for the black backing, including black cardboard, black cloth, or blackened metal. In some cases, the back of the glass itself was coated with black paint or another opaque substance. Another means of achieving the desired effect involved making the negative on a dark red piece of glass, thus obviating the need for any sort of backing.

Ambrotypes were originally promoted by Isaac Rehn of Philadelphia, Cutting's first partner, as "daguerreotypes on glass." It was only after Rehn showed some of them to Marcus A. Root that Root proposed the name "ambrotype," from *ambrotos*, the Greek word for "imperishable." In the first two or three years after their introduction, ambrotypes gained considerable acceptance and began to supplant daguerreotypes. One reason for their popularity was that while the original image was laterally reversed, the glass plate, being transparent, could be turned over before mounting, making the subject appear laterally correct. Also, ambrotypes lacked the glare produced by daguerreotypes when light struck them from the wrong angle.

Since ambrotypes were produced using the same type of camera as daguerreotypes, they also

Left: Anonymous, Portrait of a young woman, ca. 1856, ambrotype, 3 1/4" x 4 1/4". In reversible case, with velvet backing.

Right: Anonymous, Portrait of a young woman, ca. 1856, ambrotype, 3 1/4" x 4 1/4". Same as previous image but without the black backing, showing the underexposed negative.

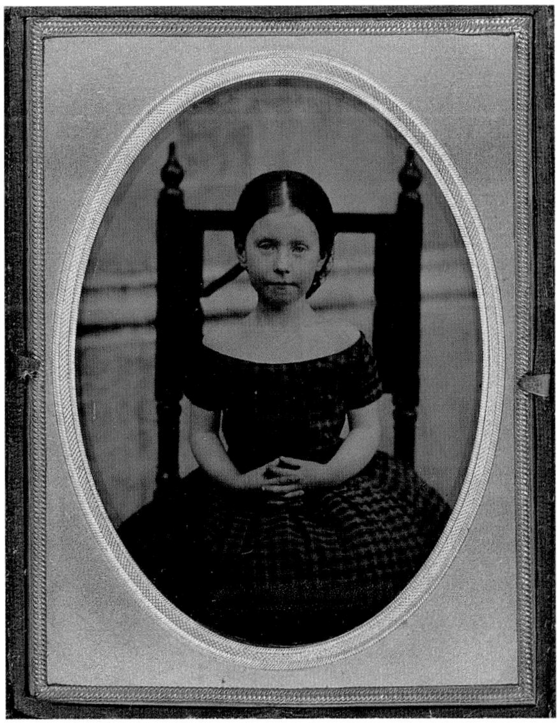

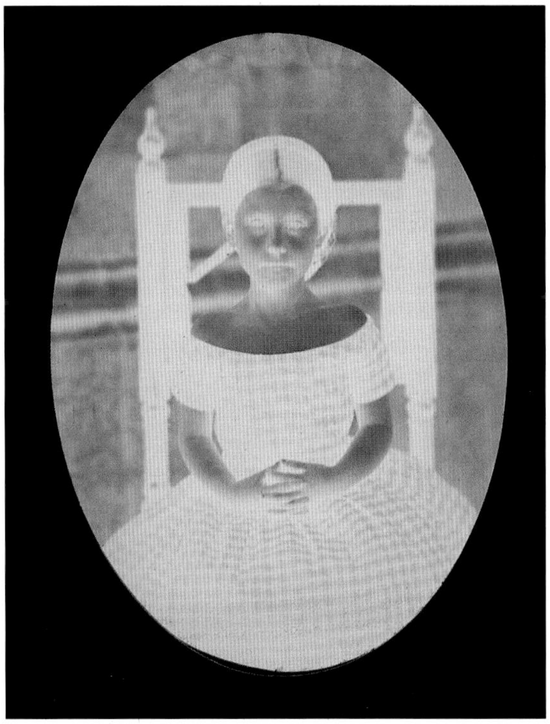

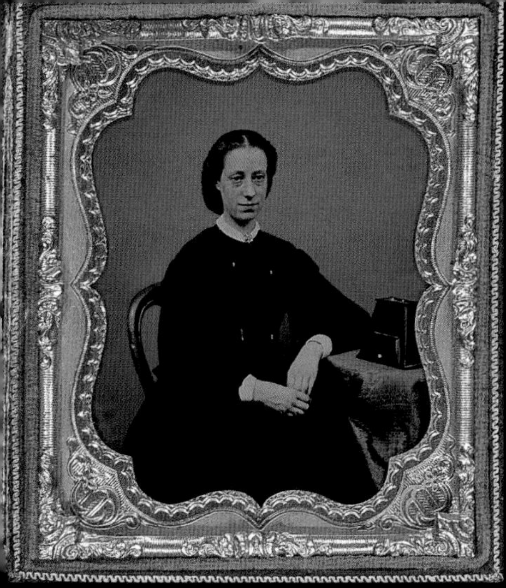

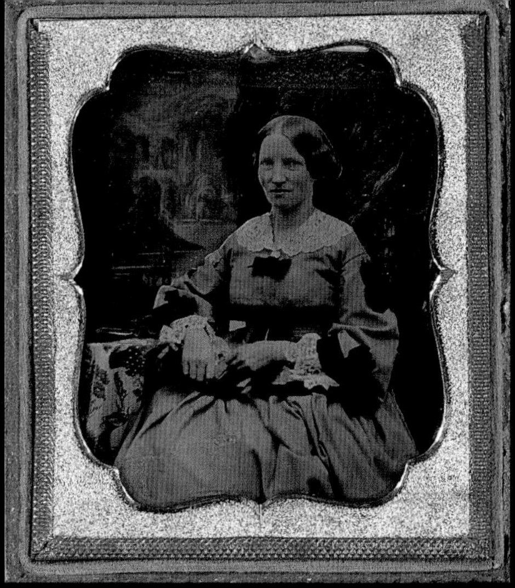

Clockwise from left: Anonymous, Portrait of a woman, with Brewster-type stereoscope, ca. 1856, ambrotype, 2 3/4" x 3 1/4"; Anonymous, Portrait of a woman, with photographically produced background, ca. 1855, ambrotype, 2 3/4" x 3 1/4". The ambrotype of the woman has been superimposed on a separate, photographically reproduced background; "Family Case" with six portraits, photographer unknown, ca. 1860, ambrotypes, each 2" x 2 1/2". Scovill Mfg. Co. hinged accordion-style case, supplied with matching storage box; Anonymous, Portrait of two young women with parrot, English, ca. 1858, tinted ambrotype, 2 3/4" x 3 1/4". The parrot is perched on a headrest/clamp, and a Brewster-type stereoscope is on the table in the background. Gilt wooden frame; Anonymous, Portrait of a woman, ca. 1856, tinted ambrotype, 2" x 2 1/2". With braid of hair attached to velvet lid-liner.

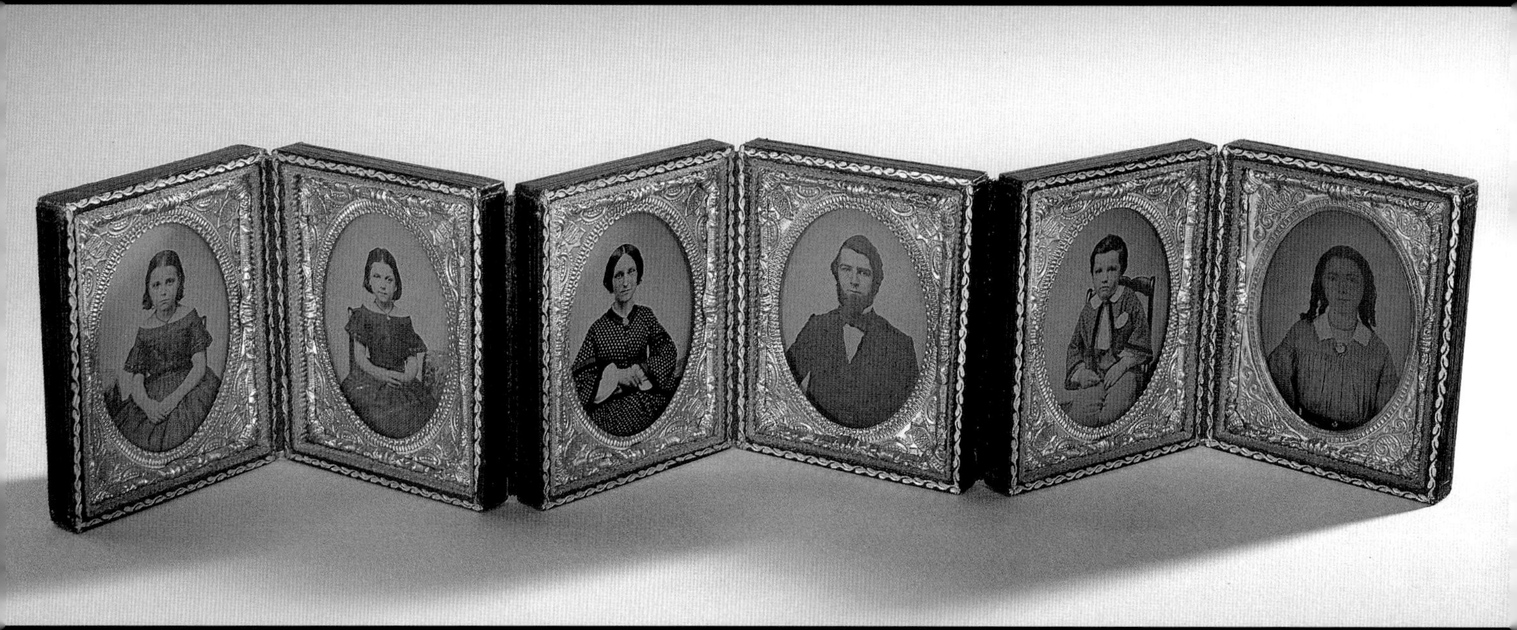

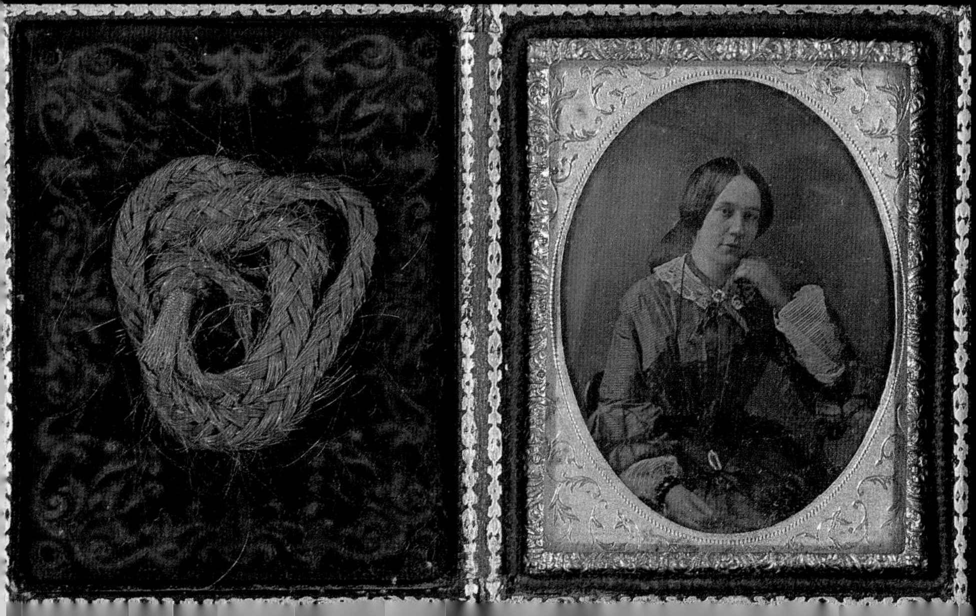

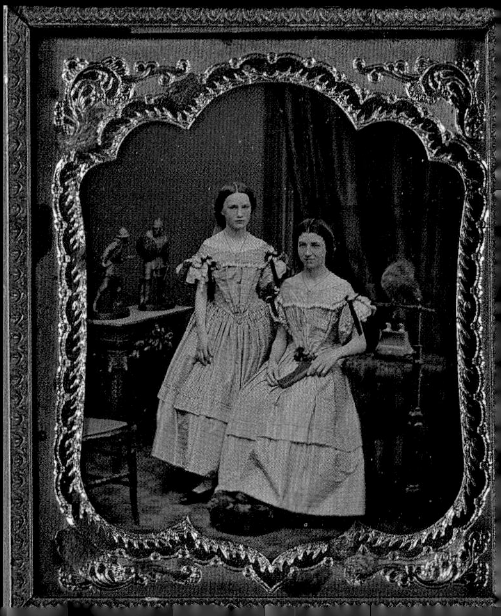

came in the same sizes and could be placed in the same types of cases, mounts, and frames. Some stereo ambrotypes were made and mounted in viewer cases like Mascher's. The exposure times necessary for ambrotypes were on a par with those for wet-collodion negatives. Ambrotypes were used particularly for portraiture, but also, to a lesser extent, in making scenic views. While a good ambrotype can display a very beautiful image, many that were cheaply produced—and there were a lot of them—were of inferior quality, and were thus placed in cheap, paper-covered cases.

Although ambrotypes were quite popular in America, and to some degree in Great Britain, they gained relatively little acceptance in other parts of the world. The year 1856 probably marked the zenith of the ambrotype, as their competition—in the form of paper prints, mostly made from wet-plate negatives—began to rise in popularity. Moreover, another wet-collodion-based form of unique, nonreproducible photograph was winning converts—the ferrotype.

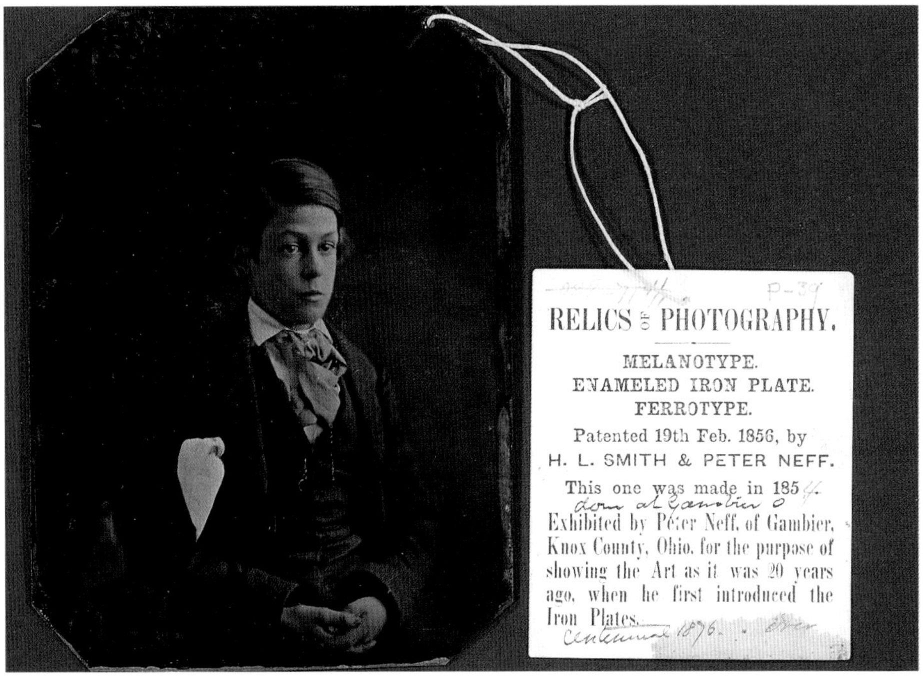

Hamilton Smith and Peter Neff, Portrait of a young man, 1854, melanotype, 4" x 5 1/2". Made two years prior to the patenting of the ferrotype (tintype).

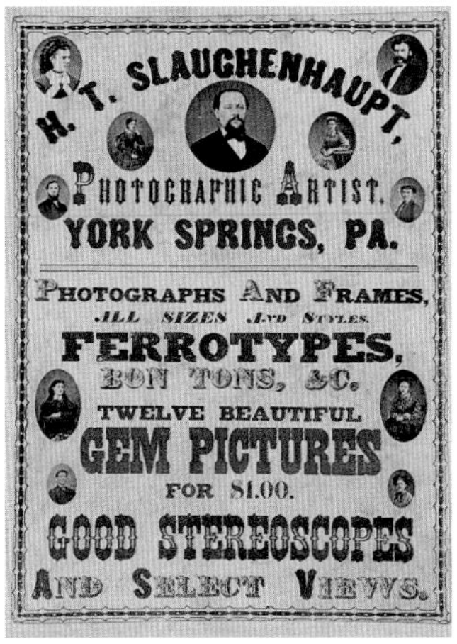

Harry T. Slaughenhaupt, Sign for H. T. Slaughenhaupt's studio, ca. 1875, albumen-print carte de visite, 2 1/8" x 3 1/2" photograph on 2 1/2" x 4" card. Ferrotypes and gems were featured more often than conventional albumen-print photographs.

The Tintype

The Tintype—Like the ambrotype, the ferrotype (or tintype, as it was later called), was another form of positive photograph produced by placing a thin collodion negative emulsion against a black background. Though the idea of producing direct positives on tinned iron originated with Adolphe Martin, a Frenchman, credit for the tintype is usually given to Hamilton Smith of Gambier, Ohio. In 1856 he was issued a patent for "photographic pictures on japanned surfaces." The basic process involved employing a sheet of black-lacquered ("japanned") iron as the base for the same sort of wet-collodion emulsion used in the ambrotype. Almost immediately Smith sold his patent rights to William and Peter Neff, father and son. The Neffs called the new product a melanotype, from the Greek word for dark.

The Neffs began to advertise the process, charging a licensing fee for its use and manufacturing the thin iron plates needed for tintypes. Soon a rival manufacturer, Victor M. Griswold, began to produce plates as well; he referred to his product as ferrotype plates (from the Latin for iron). Although no tin was actually used in the plates, ultimately the term *tintype* entered common usage. With the coming of the Civil War, popular interest in the tintype rose significantly. Many photographers traveled with military encampments and made tintypes of the soldiers. As the plates were durable, much more so than ambrotypes or paper photographs, they were preferred by the troops, who could send them home through the mail more easily.

Initially, tintypes were made in the same sizes as ambrotypes and daguerreotypes and were placed in the same types of cases. The sizes of tintypes changed, though, with the introduction of multilens cameras. These cameras helped to solve the problem of the tintype's nonreproducibility. The use of multilens cameras coupled with camera backs that could vary the position of the plate holder allowed the photographer to take several pictures with fewer exposures—sometimes only one.

Like their predecessors, tintype photos ran the gamut of subject matter—from studio portraits to postmortem pictures, outdoor gatherings to "house portraits" (photos of a house with all of the occupants gathered in front or looking out the windows), as well as animals and still lifes of

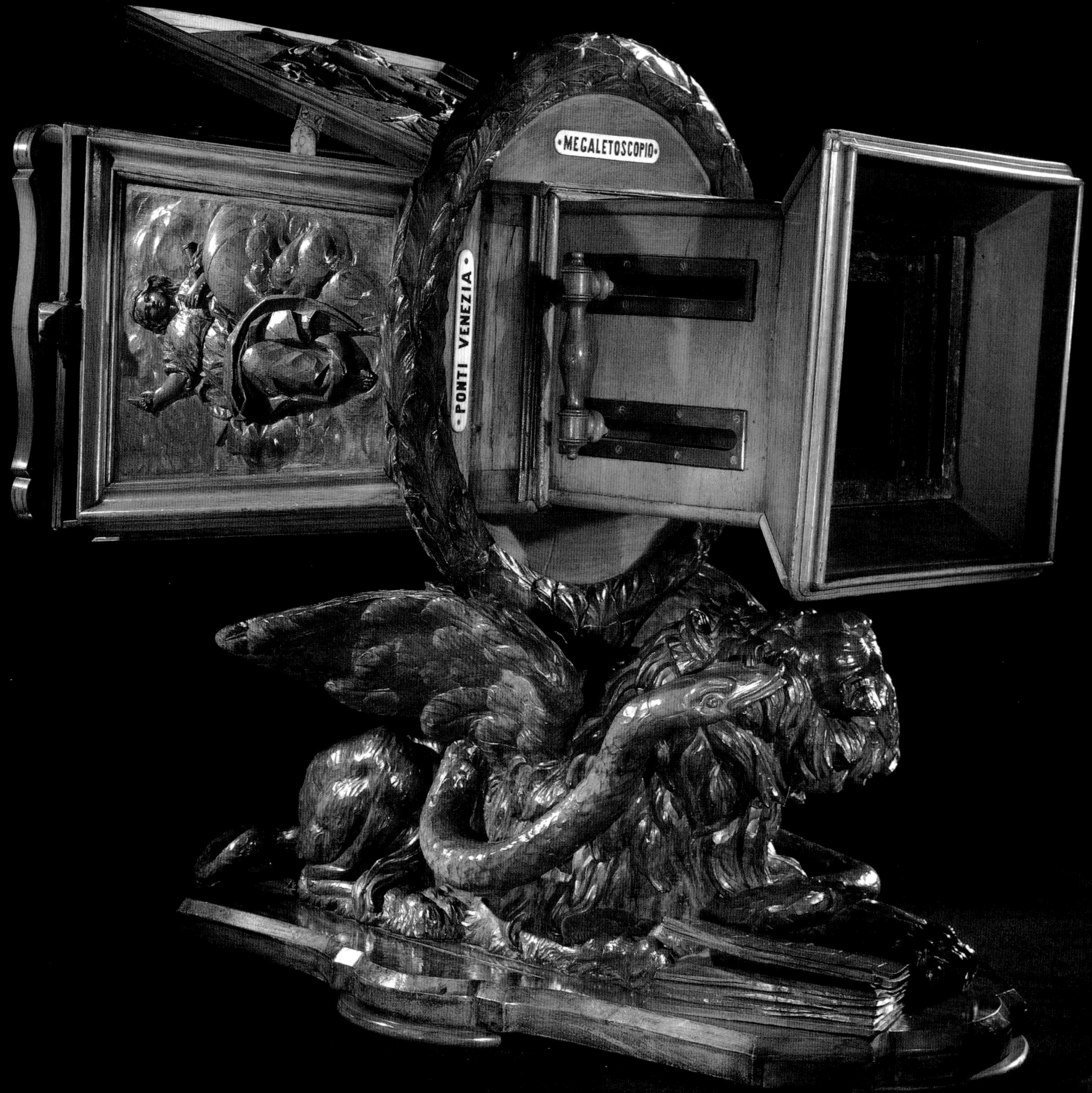
MEGALETOSCOPIO
PONTI VENEZIA

FOCUS: *Ponti's Megalethoscope*

In the 1860s and 1870s most major European cities had at least a few photographic establishments in operation. Often, these studios produced and published views of their cities and surrounding areas. In Venice, the two most active studios were those of Carlo Naya and Carlo Ponti. Both were noted for their architectural views of Venice and published scenic portfolios.

Carlo Ponti invented and patented a unique viewer for the display of his photographs. The Alethoscope, introduced in the early 1860s, was a large table-model instrument for viewing large photographs. In the viewer's front section was a large magnifying lens, shielded from extraneous light by a hood. Levers on either side of the viewer's front section were used for focusing. The forward section of the Alethoscope's body was square, and the section behind that had the shape of a truncated rectangular pyramid, tapering forward. At the rear was a holder into which photographs, each mounted in its own wooden frame, were inserted. A pair of large circular rings surrounded the Alethoscope's body, one toward the front and one at the rear, which allowed for the viewing of both horizontal and vertical scenes. Hinged panels at the rear and on the sides of the Alethoscope directed light into the viewer, illuminating the image.

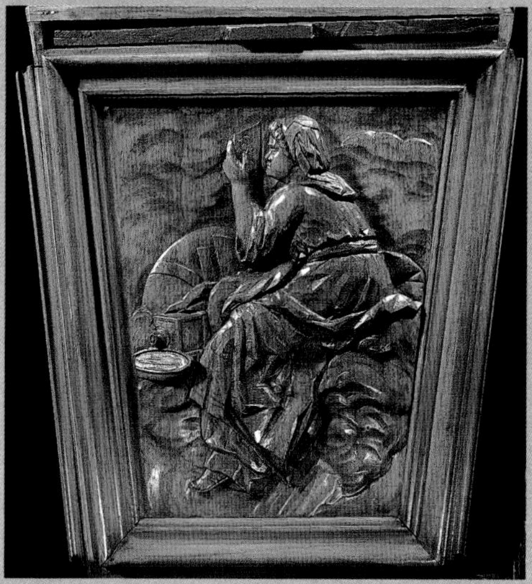

Detail of side panel, Short Model Megalethoscope, Carlo Ponti, ca. 1873, 15 1/4" x 15 1/4". The panel represents photography, with the woman examining negative, camera by her knee.

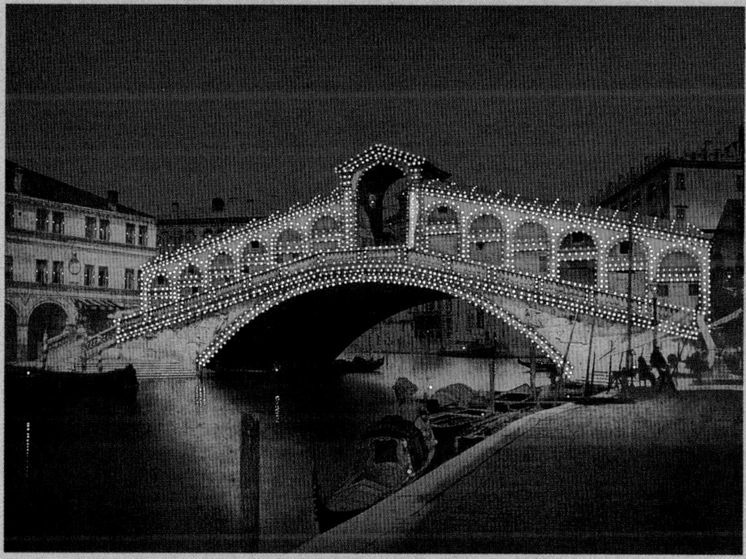

Carlo Ponti, Rialto Bridge, Venice, by night, ca. 1872, albumen print, 10" x 13 1/2", mounted in frame for viewing in Megalethoscope.

By the 1870s, Ponti had redesigned his viewer and had named the new version the Megalethoscope. Among the improvements made were: a two-lens magnifying system that could be interchanged with more powerful lenses; a pair of handles, one on each side, that were connected to rods that adjusted the focus; and a two-blade easel inside the rear that made it possible to accommodate views of various sizes.

The Megalethoscope was manufactured by the Venetian cabinet maker Demetrio Puppolin. Following Ponti's loss of his patent rights to the instrument, around the mid-1870s, Puppolin made copies of the Megalethoscope for the other prominent Venetian photographer, Carlo Naya.

Most models of the Megalethoscope were unadorned. However, a very limited number of ornate Megalethoscopes were produced. One of these viewers had the busts of four different Venetian noblemen carved in high relief on each of the four side panels. On its back panel was carved the figure of a Roman soldier, with sword, vanquishing an enemy. With minor adjustments the instrument could be used as either a stereoscope or a graphoscope. The viewer and its base rested on a matching, marble-topped, carved walnut cabinet with rosewood inlay, in which views for the Megalethoscope were stored. Another viewer was also made of walnut. It had a single carved wooden circular ring for horizontal-vertical shifting, instead of the two rings found in most models. In addition to carved panels on the four sides, the whole viewer rested on a carved base that had the form of a crouching lion, entwined with a serpent.

With the Megalethoscope, Carlo Ponti was obviously attempting to imitate some of the day-night effects created by Daguerre in his Diorama. Beyond being placed in a wooden frame, the photographic views prepared for use in the Megalethoscope were given further treatment. Colors were added to the backs of the albumen prints and pinholes were placed in appropriate places to produce, when the print was illuminated from the rear, the effect of night scenes. In some instances, features, such as figures in a courtyard and a moon in a "night" sky, were added to the print's back.

Opposite: Short Model Megalethoscope, Carlo Ponti, ca. 1873, 15 1/4" x 15 1/4".

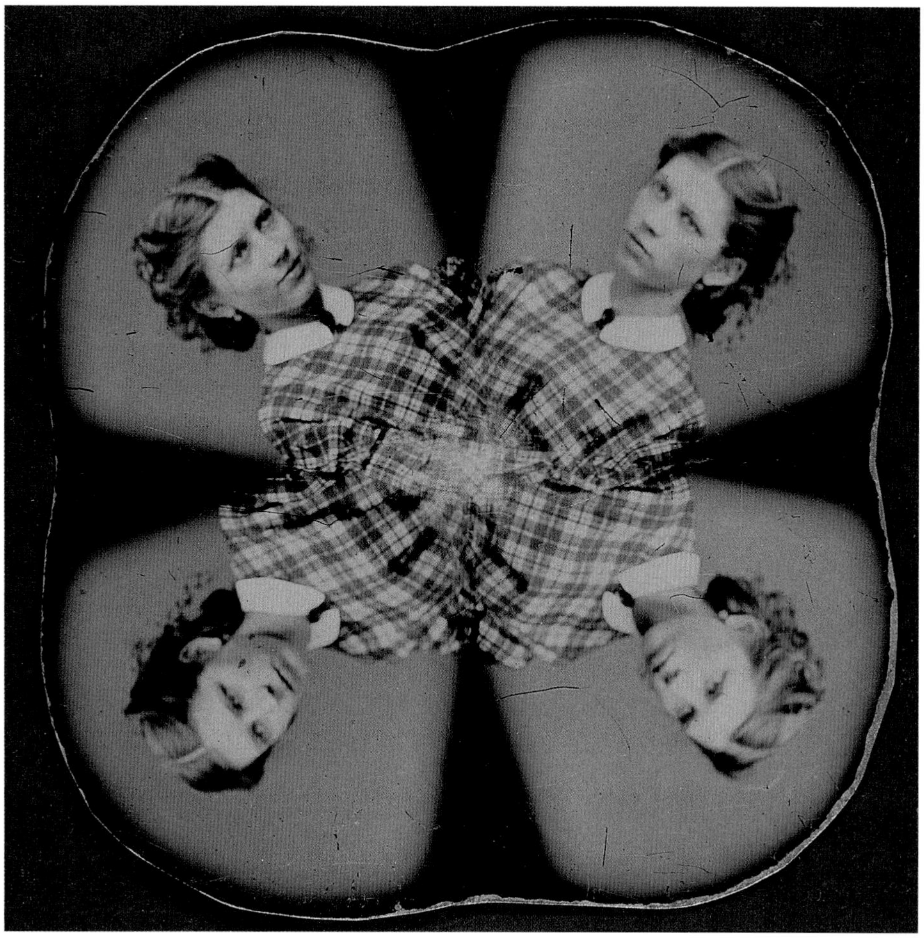

Anonymous, Portrait rosette of a young woman, ca. 1875, ferrotype, 3 1/4" x 3 1/4". Made by rotating the plate and its holder. A V-shaped vignetter possibly used.

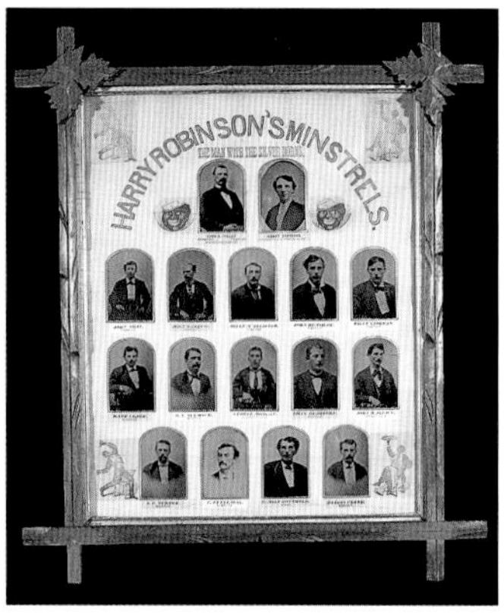

Anonymous, Framed display of Harry Robinson's Minstrels, ca. 1876, sixteen 2 1/2" x 3 1/2" ferrotypes in a 15 1/2" x 19 1/2" mat. With labels indicating positions of members of the group.

everything from flowers to trains. Larger tintypes were generally framed, and in many larger portraits, colored overpainting was used on clothing and the background. Carte de visite-size (2 ½-by-4 inches) tintypes were placed in standard albums. Slightly smaller ones were placed in paper card-mounts of the same size as cartes de visites. The very smallest tintypes, called gems, were mounted in similar-sized card mounts, in small—or tiny—albums, and even in calling cards.

The basic principle of the tintype—a layer of collodion on a black surface—could be applied to a variety of materials. Cardboard, leather, black oilcloth, and enameled paper were all used at one time or another. In fact, in its last days the tintype process was used mostly on coated sheets of stiff paper. While the ambrotype process died out in the 1860s, the tintype process succeeded in making the transition from wet plate to dry plate. With the advent of dry-plate photography in the 1880s, dry ferrotype plates came into use, as did dry glass plates. The tintype was very popular with the photographers who frequented country fairs, parks, and tourist spots, as well as with the street photographers who plied their trade at beaches, boardwalks, and in the city streets. One of the tintype's biggest advantages was the fact that the immediate product was a positive photo. This eliminated the need for a darkroom setup to print from negatives.

The in-camera processing of wet plates following exposure—the production of a finished, fixed negative without having to remove it from the camera—had been around since the early days of the wet-collodion process. (In 1853 Frederick Scott Archer produced a camera with a light-tight area behind the plate-holder section, accessed through black velvet sleeves attached to the camera.) In the early 1900s two Chicagoans, the brothers Louis and Mandel Mandel, pioneered the practical use of a developing fluid, now known as a monobath, which combined developer and fixer. In the period 1910–1930, a variety of cameras designed for street photography used this process. Many were unusual, even garish, in appearance, with the aim of attracting potential clientele. One very popular feature of many of these cameras was their ability to produce "button" photographs. These were made on circular tintype plates, usually one inch in diameter, with a metal rim around them, suitable for mounting in brooches and pins. The tintype positive process survived until after World War II, when it was supplanted by Polaroid photography.

In an attempt to capitalize on the relative speed with which tintypes could be produced, a number of companies in the late 1800s introduced automatic photo machines. The subject only had to insert coins in a slot, sit in a fixed seat, wait for the exposure to be made, and receive his finished photograph shortly thereafter. The National Photograph Machine Company advertised in the October 13, 1894 *Scientific American*, "A nickel dropped in the slot produces a photograph . . . in 35 seconds." At first the photographs were typically printed on "ferrotype cardboard," but beginning in the early 1900s there was a gradual transition to machines that made strips of images on regular photographic paper. Among the early automats were E. Enjalbert's (1889), Giuseppe Sacca's (1890), and the Bosco (1895).

While the tintype was by no means restricted exclusively to America, its popularity there far outstripped its acceptance elsewhere. Generally regarded as unattractive in England and on the Continent, it wasn't until the late 1870s that photographers in Europe began to employ the process. Even then, it was shunned by the better photographers; the most fertile ground for making tintypes was at fairs and by the seaside. But some tintypes were produced out of studios, typically card-mounted and many of them gem-size. A number of English studios advertised themselves as "American Gem" studios or companies, and two French studios placed on their card-mounted tintypes the inscriptions *Portraits-Bijou . . . par La Photographie Americaine* (Gem Portraits by American Photography) and *Photographie Cie. Americaine* (American Photography Company).

The dark tones of the tintype were clearly inferior to the great tonal range of most cartes de visite and, later, cabinet cards. But the immediacy of the process, coupled with its low cost, made it the preferred choice of photographic form for portraits among average and poorer Americans in the late nineteenth century. As a result, tintypes are *the* form of photograph to offer the broadest view of the common man in America at that time.

Cartes de Visite and Cabinet Cards—

The carte de visite, or card photograph, as it was sometimes called, was a 2 ¼-by-3 ½-inch albumen print mounted on a 2 ½-by-4-inch card. Produced in multiples on wet-plate glass negatives, it offered the advantage of almost limitless reprints, with a choice from among the various poses captured on a single plate. The carte de visite was introduced in Paris by André Disdéri in the mid-1850s. As a photographic form, it was not very widely accepted until May 1859, when Napoleon III stopped at Disdéri's studio to have a portrait taken. From then on, the carte de visite quickly gained in popularity, and by 1861, at which time a number of

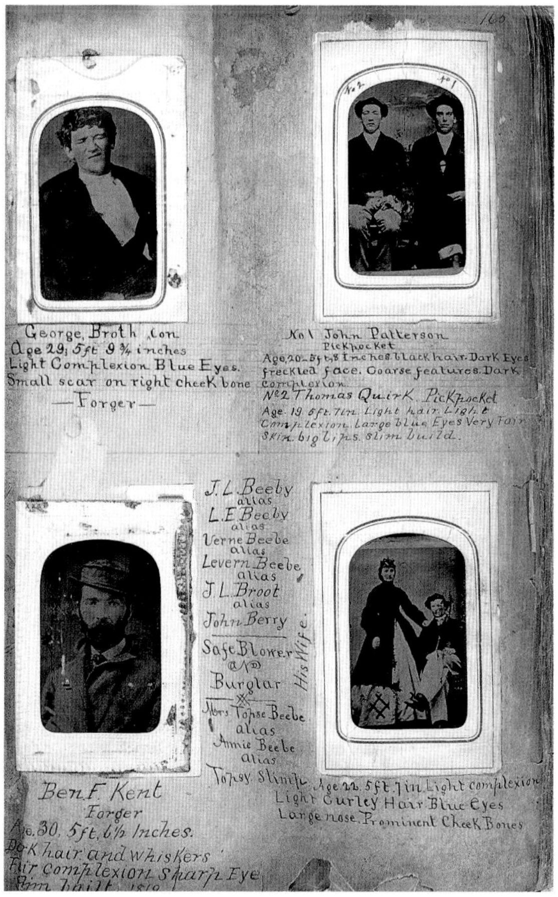

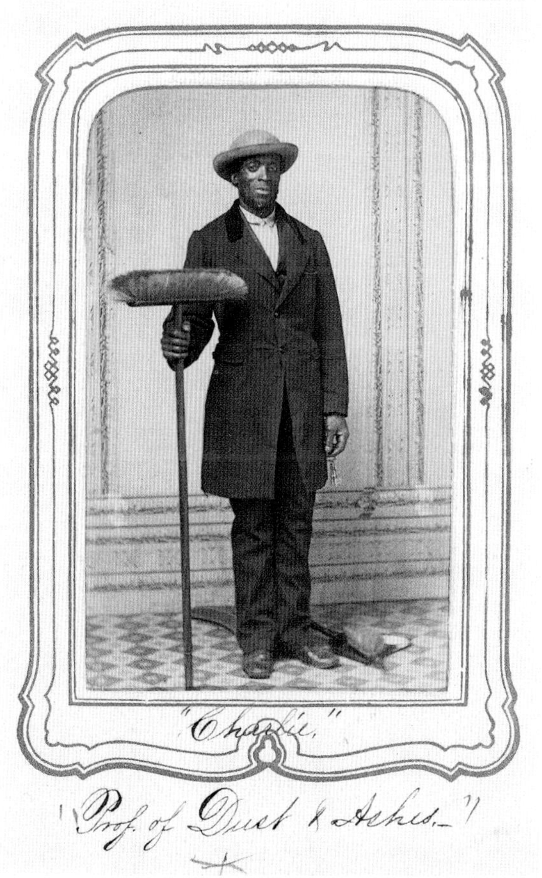

Left: Anonymous, Photographs of wanted American criminals, 1869–1876, ferrotypes, each 2¼" x 3 ½". The ferrotypes are contained in envelope mounts pasted onto a page on which the criminals' names, aliases, and crimes have been written.

Right: Samuel Bowles & Co., Portrait of "Charlie, Professor of Dust & Ashes," 1862, albumen-print carte de visite, 2 ⅛" x 3 ½" on 2 ½" x 4" card. Included with sixty-three student portraits in the Amherst College Class of 1862 Album.

FOCUS: *The Multiplied Image*

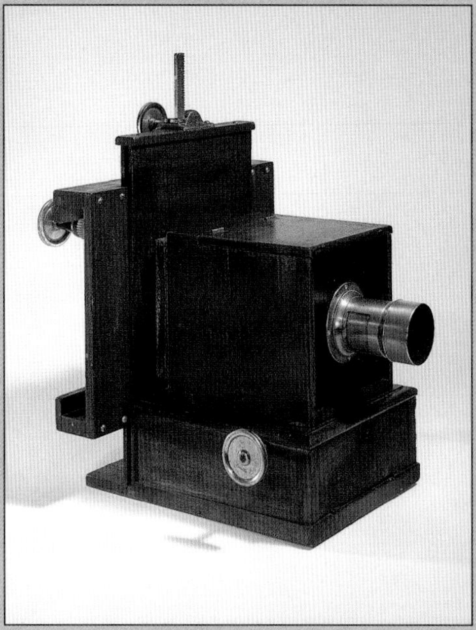

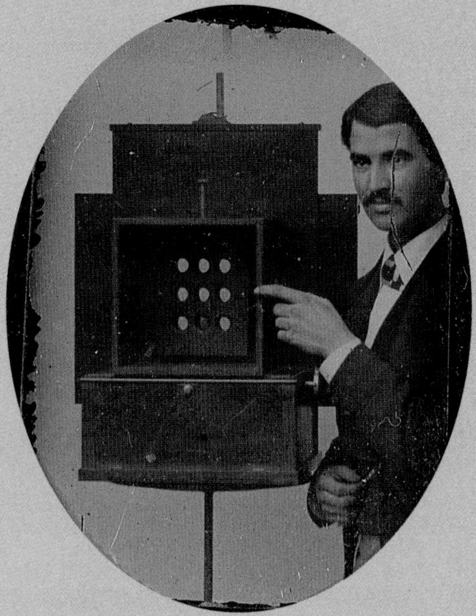

Between the years 1840 and 1860, when the daguerreotype and later, in America at least, the ambrotype were the dominant photographic processes, the only ways to duplicate a photograph were to make more than one exposure, use more than one lens (as in stereo pairs, which could be separated), or rephotograph the original.

The introduction of wet-collodion negatives and the tintype eventually led, however, to the production of multiple images. One way in which multiple images were made was through the use of multiple lenses to produce a number of images on a glass plate or tintype. The albumen prints from the negatives could then be cut apart with scissors or a paper cutter, or in the case of the tintype, the iron sheet could be cut apart with tin snips. In America, John Roberts of Boston pioneered the use of multiple lenses, mounting as many as thirty-two small lenses in the camera's lens board; all thirty-two exposures then were made instantaneously. His cameras were used primarily for making tintypes, and the individual pictures produced, which measured approximately three-fourths of an inch by one inch, were called gems. They were usually placed in carte-de-visite-sized mounts or in small albums.

Another method of obtaining multiple exposures was to use a plate longer than the standard format, mounted in an elongated plate holder, and move the plate holder laterally behind a single lens as successive exposures were made. This method may have been pioneered by Antoine Claudet of London, who used it to make several daguerreotype portraits in succession; the plate was cut after development. On April 10, 1855, Albert S. Southworth of Boston, Massachusetts, was issued a patent for a plate holder that could be moved to bring different portions of the plate into the field of the camera's lens.

An improvement on this principle, in which a larger plate was moved past multiple lenses, was patented on December 4, 1860, by Simon Wing of Boston. Wing pioneered the use of and promoted the sale of multiple-lens, moveable-back cameras in America. He also attempted to

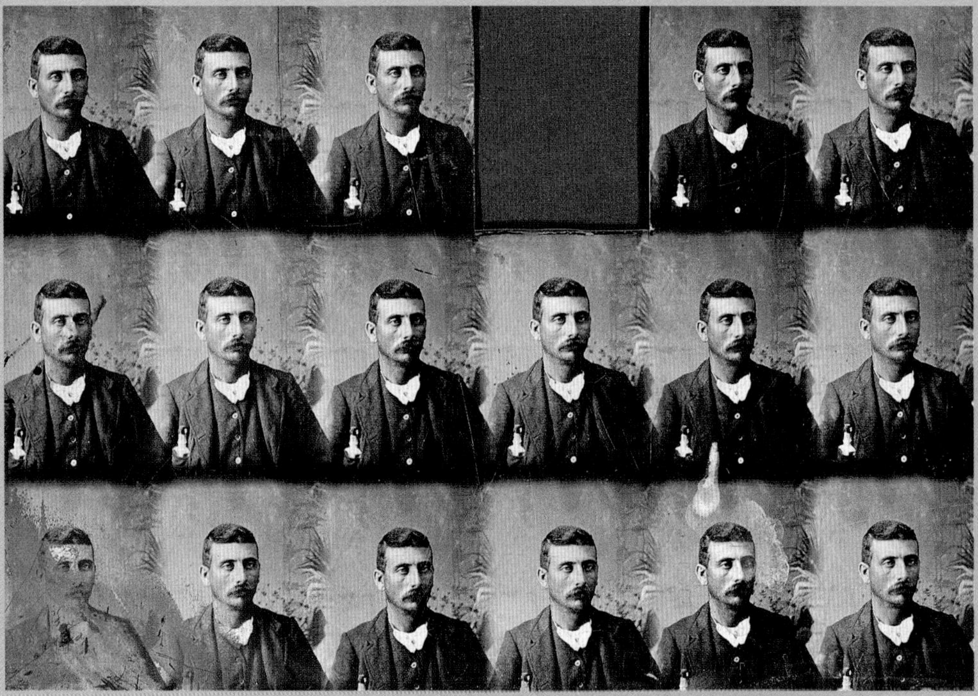

Clockwise from top left: S. Wing Patent multiplying camera, ca. 1865, for 4" x 5" wet-collodion plates, or for single or multiple exposures with a moveable back and/or multiple-lens lens board.

Anonymous, Portrait of man with S. Wing Patent multiplying camera, ca. 1865, ferrotype, 2" x 2 1/2".

Anonymous, Multiple gem portraits of a man, ca. 1865, ferrotype, 1" x 1 1/2" on 4 1/2" x 6 1/4" plate. One of the gems has been removed.

enforce strict licensing for the use of cameras operating under his and Southworth's patents, suing those who didn't pay. A key lawsuit over the matter was finally settled in the U.S. Supreme Court, where the patents were ruled invalid because others had already used the idea prior to the issue of the patents.

The carte de visite is a form of albumen print measuring 2$\frac{1}{4}$-by-3$\frac{1}{2}$ inches and mounted on a 2$\frac{1}{2}$-by-4-inch card. A number of these photos were made on a single wet-collodion plate, contact printed, and cut apart. André Disdéri of Paris applied for a patent for carte-de-visite photographs on November 27, 1854. While Disdéri used a camera with a single lens and a shifting back around 1860, four-lens cameras came into use. These cameras were utilized not only for cartes de visite but also for tintypes.

Yet another form of multilens camera popular in the early 1900s was called the stamp camera. These cameras were not intended to take original photographs, but to copy other photos. A photograph was placed in front of the camera behind a mask, and the camera produced a stamp-sized copy photo. The number of lenses on this type of camera varied, but generally they had nine to fifteen of them. Nowadays passport and identification photographs are made with multilens cameras, typically using Polaroid film.

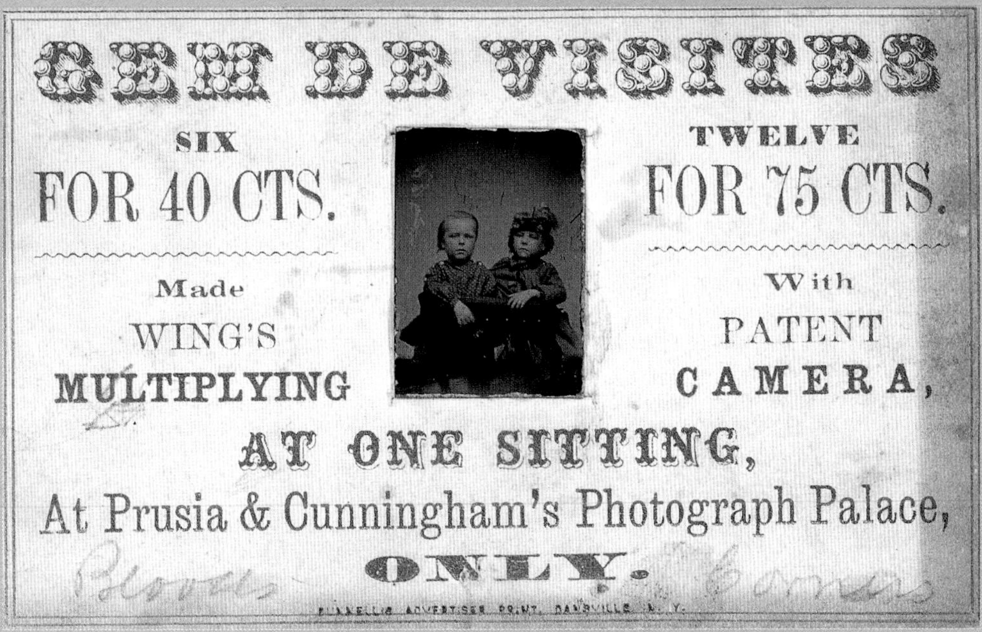

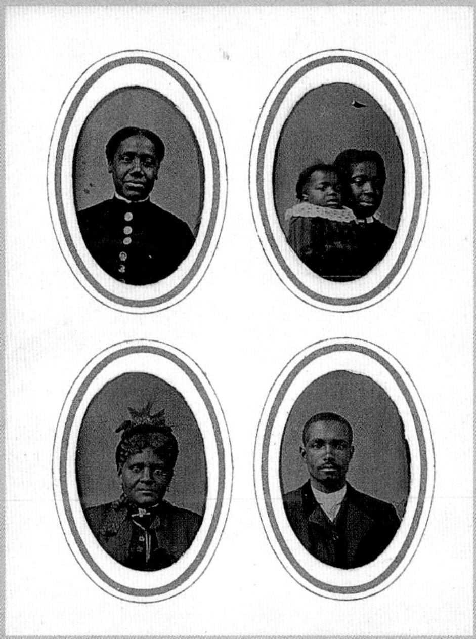

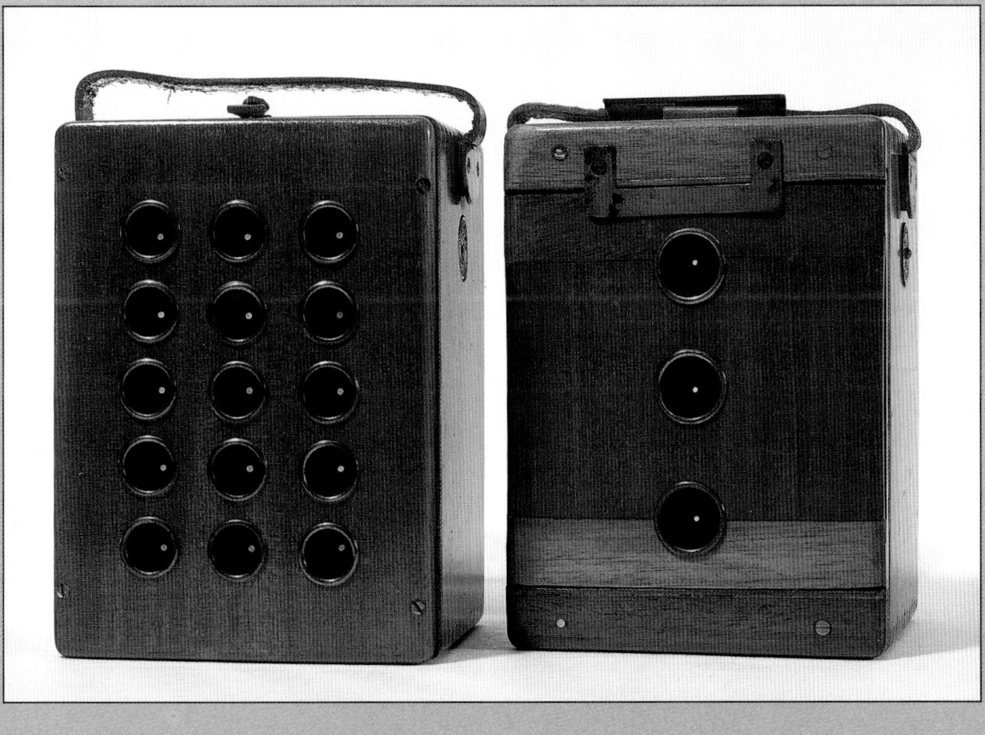

Clockwise from top left: Advertising card for Prusia & Cunningham's Photograph Palace, with portrait of boy and girl, ca. 1863, 2 $\frac{1}{2}$" x 4", with $\frac{3}{4}$" x 1" ferrotype. Uncommon use of the term "Gem de Visite." 1 $\frac{1}{3}$" x 2" albumen print of Civil War soldier mounted on reverse.

Anonymous, Gem tintype portraits of African Americans, ca. 1870, ferrotypes, 1" x 1 $\frac{1}{2}$" in 3 $\frac{1}{2}$" x 4 $\frac{3}{4}$" album. All but three of the album's forty-eight gems are of African Americans.

Multiple-lens cameras by W. Butcher & Sons.
Left: Royal Mail Stamp Camera, ca. 1910, for fifteen exposures, $\frac{3}{4}$" x $\frac{7}{8}$" on 3 $\frac{1}{4}$" x 4 $\frac{1}{4}$" dry plates or film.
Right: Royal Mail Panel Camera, ca. 1911, for three exposures, 1 $\frac{3}{8}$" x 3" on 3 $\frac{1}{4}$" x 4 $\frac{1}{4}$" dry plates or film.

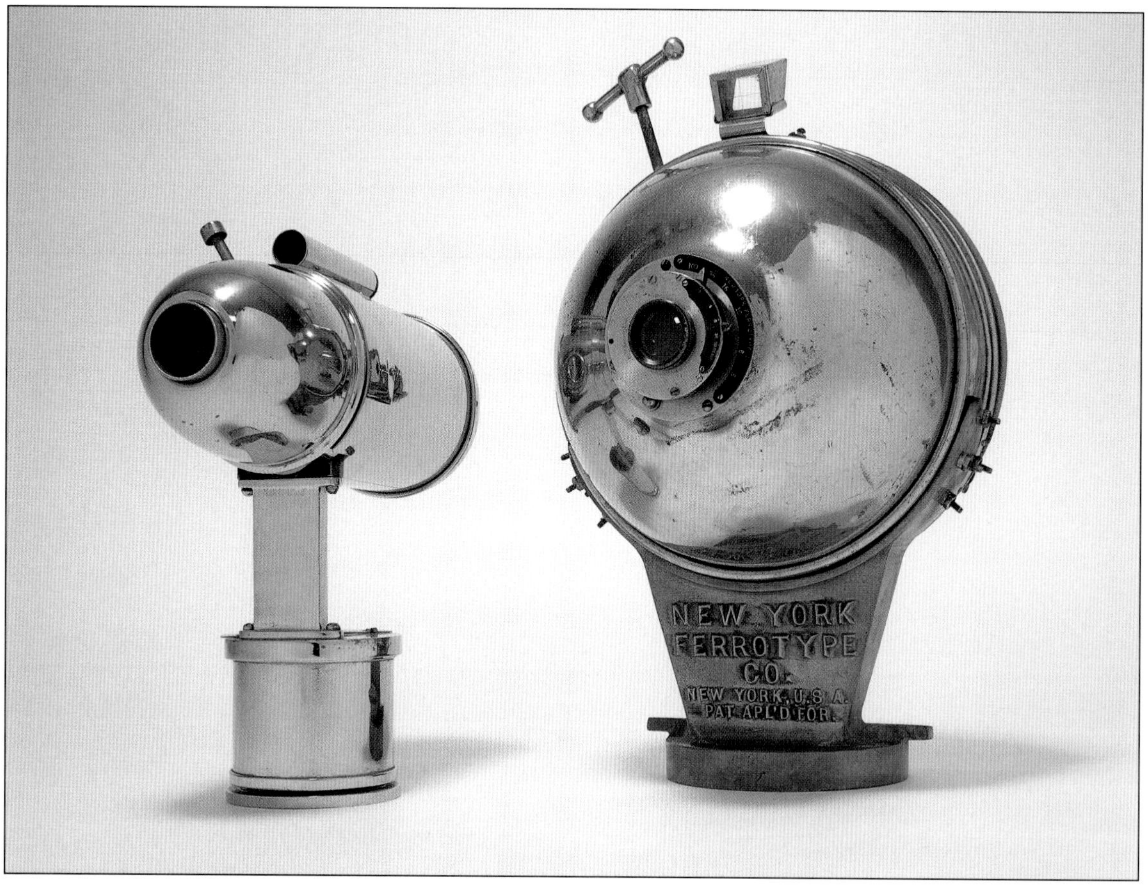

Cameras for making "button" ferrotypes. Left: Automatic button camera, manufacturer unknown, ca. 1930. Sold by a variety of companies under a number of names. Right: Novelty Photo Camera, New York Ferrotype Co., ca. 1918. These cameras were used by street photographers to produce 1" diameter "button" photographs, often placed in pin-backed brooches.

Opposite: Anonymous, Portraits of William C. Canse and Jane Elizabeth Tappen, mounted in their marriage certificate, 1889, albumen-print cartes de visite, 2 1/8" x 3 1/2" on 2 1/2" x 4" cards. Cartes de visite and carte-size ferrotypes were commonly combined with marriage certificates in the years 1865–1890.

other photographers were also offering cartes, Disdéri's studio had a staff of ninety.

A. Marion & Co. introduced the carte de visite in London in 1857, but it wasn't until John Mayall published his *Royal Album of British Nobility* that cartes became popular there. The British eagerly bought thousands of photographs of the royal family. A means for holding these and other images of British notables was realized with the creation of the photograph album. In Austria and Germany, the craze for cartes de visite began around 1859, and "cartomania," as some called it, rapidly spread throughout the rest of Europe.

In America, the first report of card photographs was published in 1859, and in 1860 the Broadway studios began to offer them. By 1861 the card photograph album was being praised as "especially adapted to the cards." While albums had been used before, to hold autographs, etc., the new style of album had recessed pockets on each page. Slots in the faces or at the margins of the pages allowed the cards to be inserted into the recesses. The early card mounts had square corners and thus had a tendency to tear the edges of the album's pockets. Around 1870, cards with rounded edges were introduced, which greatly reduced the potential for damage while placing photographs in the albums.

The outbreak of the Civil War added exponentially to the sales of carte photographs in the United States. Families wanted photos of their loved ones who were going off to war, and soldiers wanted pictures of their families to carry with them. Officers and politicians from both the North and the South were popular subjects for the camera's lens. Cartes de visite of Major Robert Anderson, the hero of the bombardment of Fort Sumter, were produced by E. & H. T. Anthony & Co. in 1861 at the rate of one thousand copies per day for almost two months. Anthony's catalog, issued in November 1862, listed three hundred scenes of the war by Mathew Brady, in addition to a listing of two thousand portraits.

Throughout Europe and North America, little that remained stationary long enough to be photographed escaped portrayal in a carte de visite. In addition to royalty, the military, politicians, and other notables were photographed. Scenes,

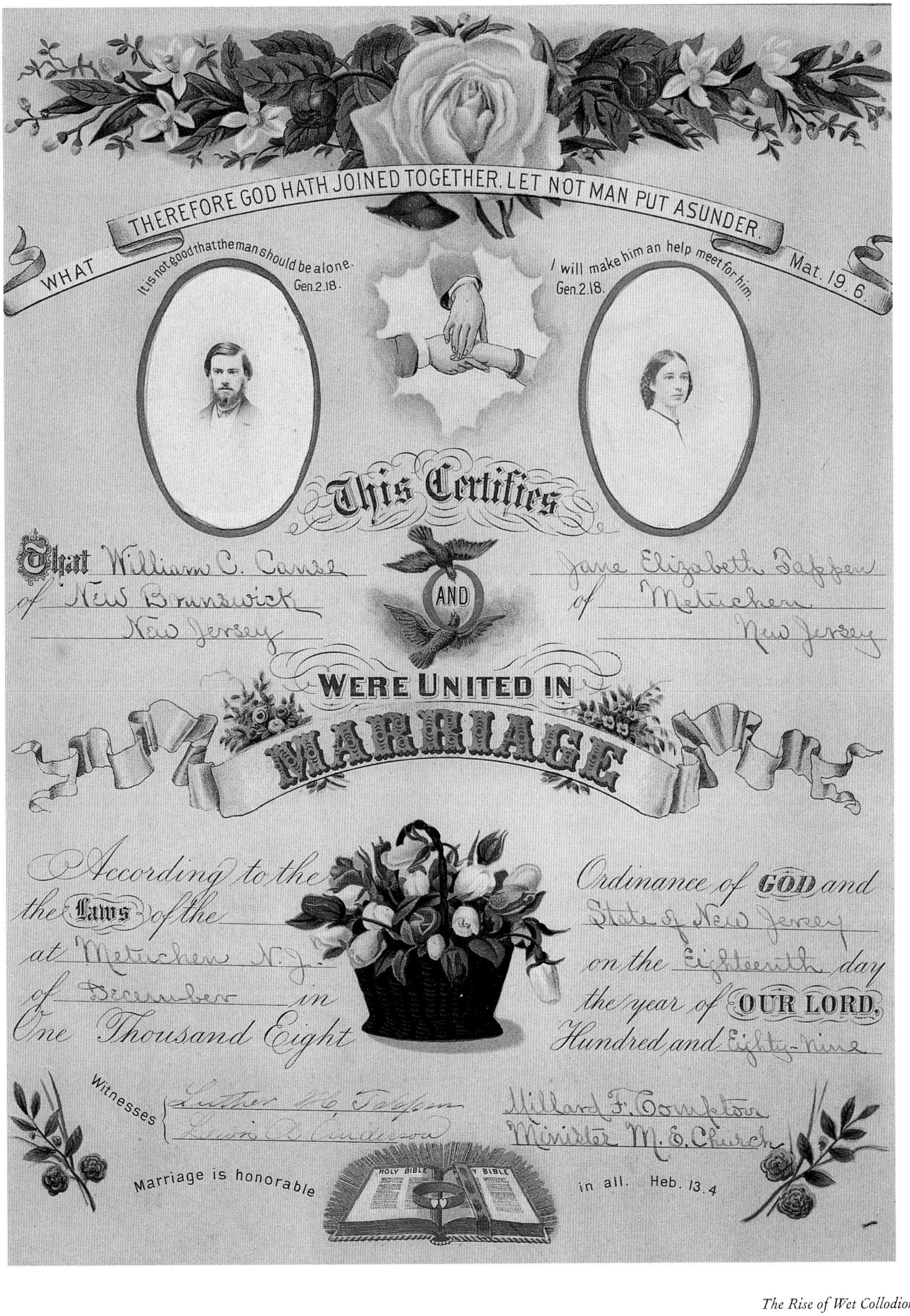
WHAT THEREFORE GOD HATH JOINED TOGETHER, LET NOT MAN PUT ASUNDER. Mat. 19. 6.
It is not good that the man should be alone. Gen.2.18.
I will make him an help meet for him. Gen.2.18.
This Certifies
That William C. Cause
of New Brunswick
New Jersey
AND
Jane Elizabeth Tappen
of Metuchen
New Jersey
WERE UNITED IN
MARRIAGE
According to the Ordinance of GOD and
the Laws of the State of New Jersey
at Metuchen N.J. on the Eighteenth day
of December in the year of OUR LORD,
One Thousand Eight Hundred and Eighty-Nine
Witnesses
Millard F. Compton
Minister M. E. Church
Marriage is honorable in all. Heb. 13.4
HOLY BIBLE
HOLY BIBLE

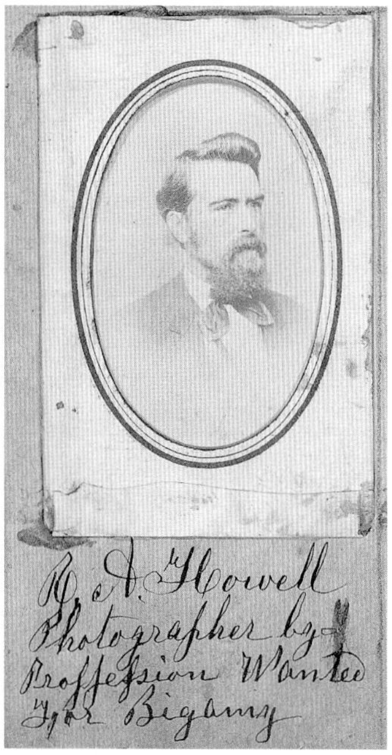

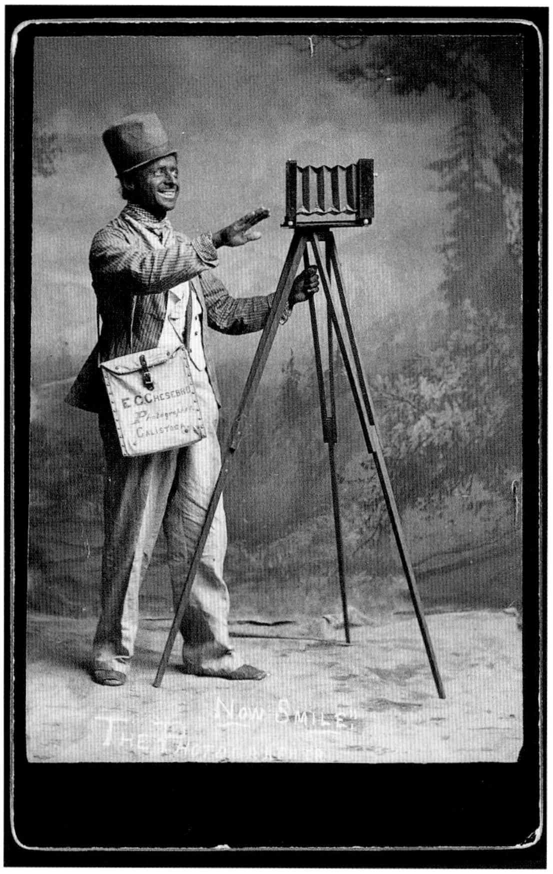

Clockwise from top: Anonymous, R. A. Howell, photographer, wanted for bigamy, ca. 1874, albumen-print carte de visite, 2 1/8" x 3 1/2" on 2 1/2" x 4" card. "R. A. Howell Floating Art Gallery" on back. One of the photographs in an album of known criminals.

Anonymous, E. C. Chesebro, photographer, Calistoga, ca. 1885, albumen-print cabinet photo, 4" x 5 1/2" on 4 1/4" x 6 1/2" card.

John P. Doremus, Doremus's Floating Photograph Gallery, ca. 1875, albumen print, half of stereo pair, on 4 1/2" x 7" card mount. Doremus traveled the Mississippi River on a barge holding his 18' x 76' studio/residence.

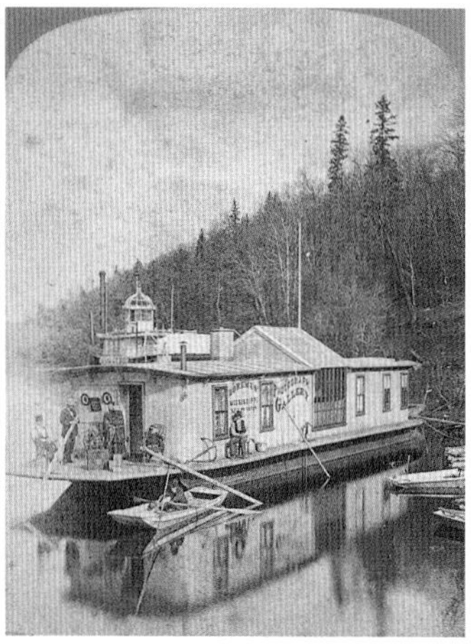

statuaries, buildings, paintings and engravings, authors and poets, actors and ministers, images of all of these became available to everyone through cartes de visite. Cartes were also used to document historic events, medical abnormalities, victims of war crimes, funerals, and the deceased. While the production of cartes de visite lasted into the early twentieth century, it declined in tempo with their waning popularity from about 1880 onward.

Though initially slow emulsion speeds precluded portraits larger than those of the cartes de visite, as time passed and emulsions improved, larger photographs became feasible and popular. By the late 1860s, a new size of photograph, the "cabinet portrait," was ascending in popularity. Introduced in 1862 by George W. Wilson, it was pioneered by the London firm of Window and Bridge. In 1866 the *Philadelphia Photographer* commented on the new cabinet pictures: "It is something like a carte de visite enlarged. The mounting card measures 4 1/4 -by-6 1/2 inches, the print 4-by-5 1/2 inches, and opening in the album 3 7/8-by-5 1/4 inches. Messrs. E. and H. T. Anthony & Company inform us they are manufacturing albums for the new size."

The new size offered the portrait photographer an incentive to improve the lighting, background, accessories, and poses. Since the pictures were larger, any flaws were also enlarged, and so more care in the photo's production was needed. On the other hand, it was now easier for photographers to retouch negatives; imperfections, such as blemishes and wrinkles on the subject's face, could be erased. Within a few years, retouching had become an art in itself and was assigned to special assistants in the larger studios. Not only was it used to remove unwanted features, but also to introduce desired ones. To photographs of people in winter coats posing in front of painted snowy backdrops, falling snow was added by judiciously spattering dark paint or varnish on the negative.

Cabinet cards were originally printed from wet-plate glass negatives, but around 1880 a transition to gelatino-bromide dry plates began. The cabinet's popularity as a form of photograph continued until the end of the nineteenth century, though from the middle 1880s on, the quantities produced declined. A significant factor in this decline, and in the ultimate demise of cabinet photos, was the advent of roll film and the marked increase in amateur photography in the 1890s.

Photographs of Other Sizes—While the carte de visite and the cabinet photo were the most popular sizes of albumen prints in the nineteenth century, they were by no means the only ones. Larger plates were used for a variety of subjects. House "portraits" were quite commonplace, but perhaps the greatest use of larger plates was for exterior scenes. Numerous photos were made of the great cities, cathedrals, harbors, tourist attractions, and even rustic scenes of Europe. Similar photographs were being made in South America, and European photographers traveled far afield, to Egypt,

India, China, and Japan. Tourists could purchase views of practically every location and city they visited.

Subjects other than touristic ones were also recorded, and some of these photographs could be seen as a form of reportage. In the mid-1850s, for instance, Roger Fenton and James Robertson documented the Crimean War. Fenton commonly used 12-by-16-inch and 14-by-18-inch plates, which were so large that the collodion sometimes dried in one spot before the remainder of the plate could be coated. Although Fenton made no photographs of actual battle, he shot many images of troops before and between battles, and of the field afterward. After the Crimean War, Robertson and Felice Beato traveled to India to photograph locations where the Indian Mutiny of 1857 had taken place. Three years later, Beato went on to photograph scenes of the Second Opium War in China.

The U.S. Civil War was exceedingly well documented in cartes de visite, stereographs, and larger-format photographs. The horrors of war were presented to the public via numerous photographs of the dead, found in fields after battle. Following the war, Americans turned their attention to the country's westward expansion, and some photographers took to traveling with surveys and expeditions. One of them was William H. Jackson, who began taking photographs of the West in the late 1860s, and was using 20-by-24-inch plates in the 1870s. Carlton Watkins, whose photographs of California's Yosemite Valley are well known, and Frank J. Haynes, who operated in Yellowstone, were also in that group. That the U.S. Congress designated Yellowstone as America's first National Park was partly due to the fact that legislators had viewed photographs of the area taken by Jackson in 1871.

Additional sizes of portrait photographs introduced around the late 1870s were the Promenade, a 3-by-6-inch photo on a 4-by-7-inch card; the 5-by-8 1/4-inch Boudoir; the 7-by-10-inch Imperial; and the 8-by-13-inch Panel. None of these sizes ever attained great popularity.

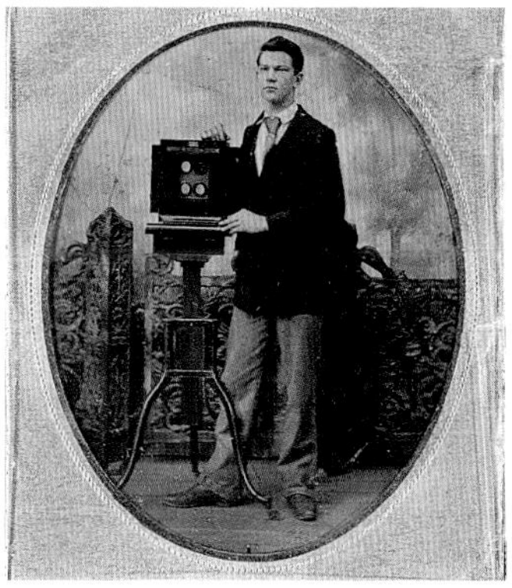

Anonymous, Portrait of man with four-lens studio camera, ca. 1870, ferrotype, 2 3/4" x 3 1/4". Camera is mounted on American Optical Co.'s Acme Stand.

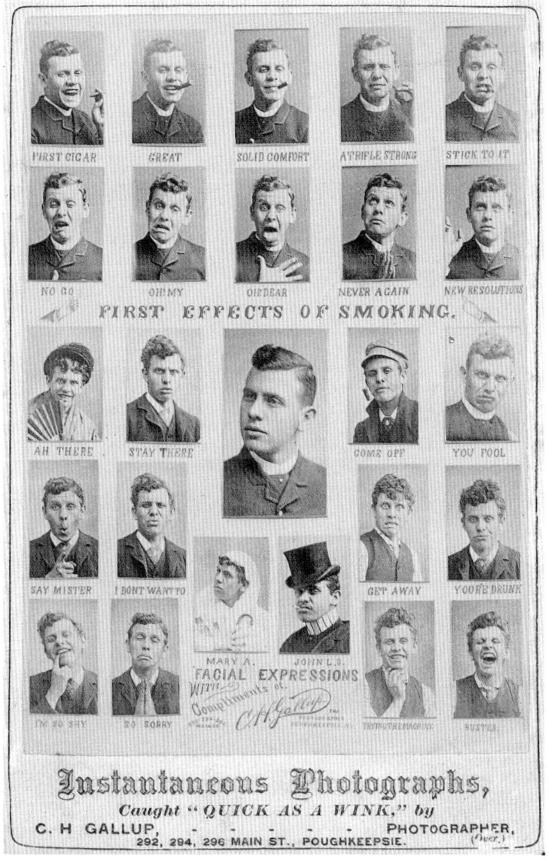

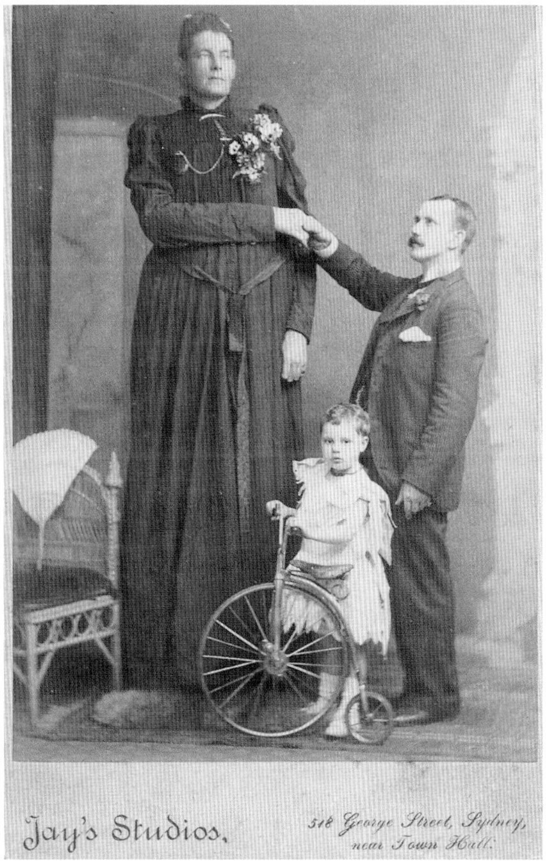

Left: C. H. Gallup, Facial expressions showing the first effects of smoking, ca. 1890, albumen-print cabinet photo, 4" x 5 1/2" on 4 1/4" x 6 1/2" card. Composite of twenty-five photographs and accompanying lettering.

Right: Jay's Studio, Photograph of a female giant, ca. 1885, albumen-print cabinet photo, 4" x 5 1/2" on 4 1/4" x 6 1/2" card. From a collection of 207 photographs and 289 negatives related to giants, assembled by Dr. Charles Dean Humberd.

PROFILE: *Viewing and Displaying Cartes and Cabinets*

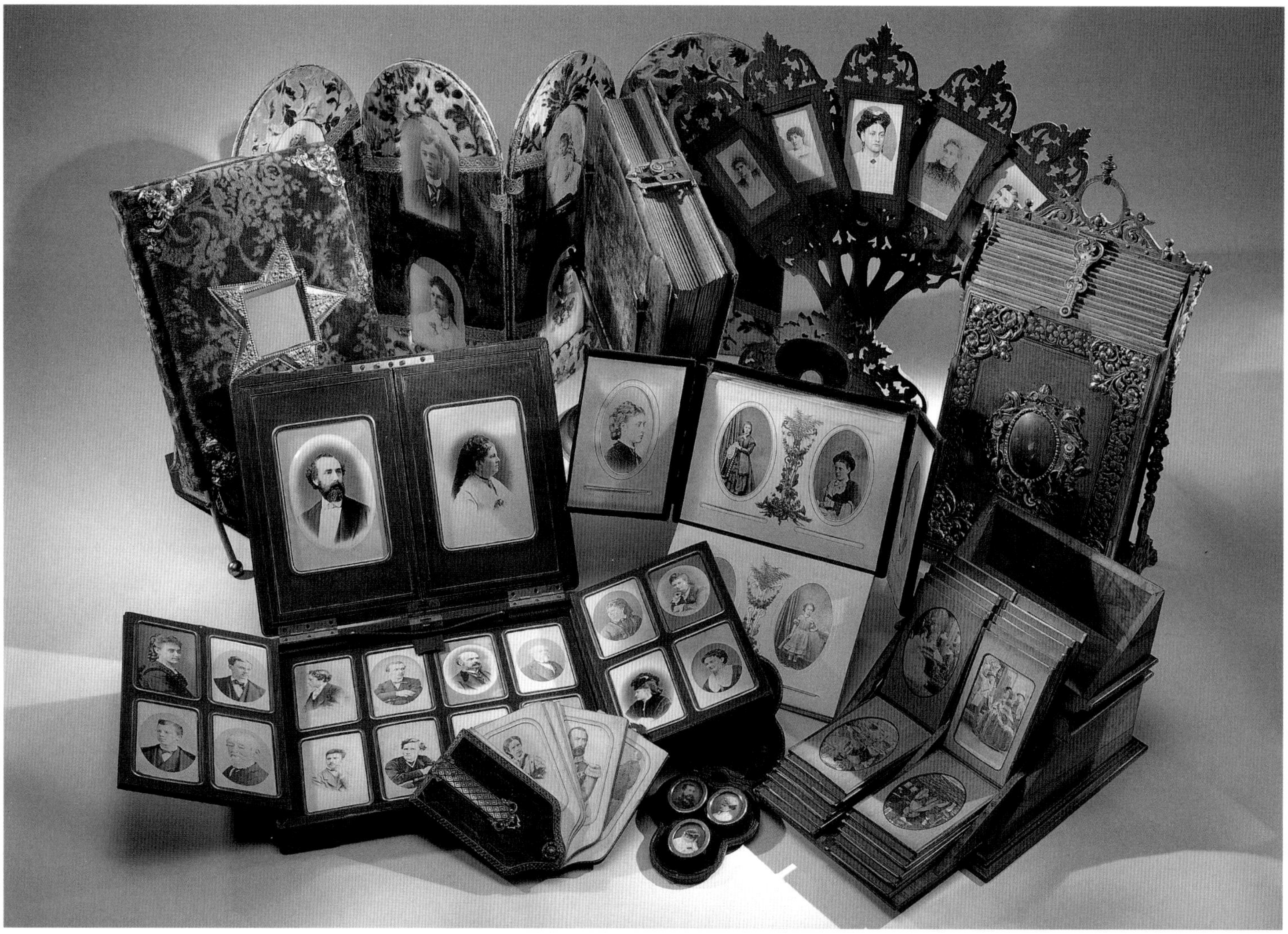

Various means for holding and displaying cartes de visite and cabinet photos, 1870–1900.

The carte de visite's potential for multiple copies prompted a sharp increase in the number of photographic portraits made. Technological innovations allowing up to sixteen small portraits to be exposed simultaneously on a single glass plate lowered the cost of cartes de visite substantially, which made them available to a new segment of society. This significantly changed the cultural role of the portrait; no longer was it necessarily an expensive, unique object. The production of cartes de visite in England alone was estimated to be three to four hundred million per year during the time of their greatest popularity, the 1870s. By comparison, the total population of England a century later, in the early 1970s, was less than forty-six million. As their production increased, so did the display methods designed for them.

Some carte de visite albums held only a dozen cards or fewer, one card to each side of a page. Other albums held between two and four cards on each page. Most albums were covered with leather or velvet and had fasteners that varied from simple brass construction to those ornamented with filigree. Some albums were very exotic, with wood, lacquered, painted, or inlaid covers. Some of the fancier albums surpassed simple book design and opened upward and to the sides.

More sophisticated means of displaying cartes de visite included fan-shaped holders and box-like holders, in which hinged covers opened to reveal pivoting frames. Some mechanical viewers were little more than simple wooden boxes within which the cartes were attached to a band of fabric. The cartes were viewed, two at a time, through a pair of openings in the top. Turning a knob which was connected to internal rollers moved fresh cartes into place. At the other end of the mechanical spectrum were the clock-work-driven viewers. The most elaborate of these devices also played music.

The graphoscope is a magnifying device, usually mounted on a stand, used to view photographs. Pocket-sized graphoscopes were later designed for the viewing of cartes de visite.

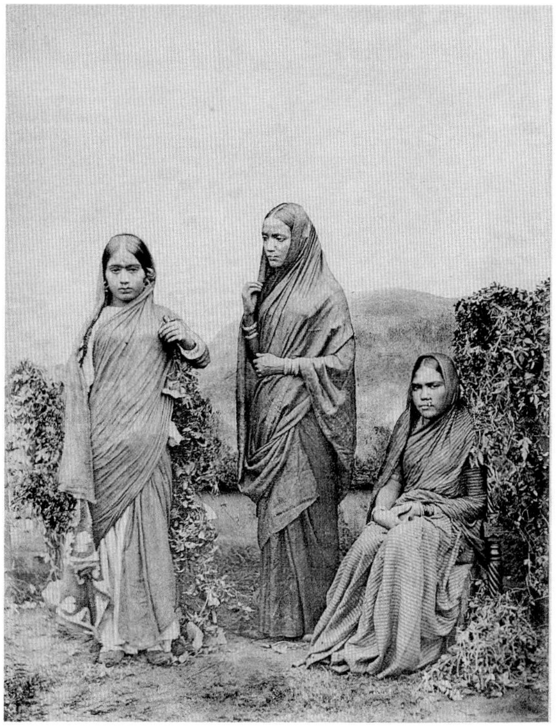

Clockwise from left: William R. Johnson, Muhammadan women of the Konkan, Plate 20 from *Oriental Races and Tribes*, 1866, tipped-in albumen print, 6 3/4" x 8 7/8".

Anonymous, Senior class and faculty, Hampton Normal and Agricultural Institute, Hampton, Virginia, 1876, albumen print, 9" x 12 1/4".

British Ordnance Survey Department, Stonehenge, view from the southwest, from *Plans and Photographs of Stonehenge and of Turusachan in the Island of Lewis*, 1867, tipped-in albumen print, 10 1/4" x 7 7/8".

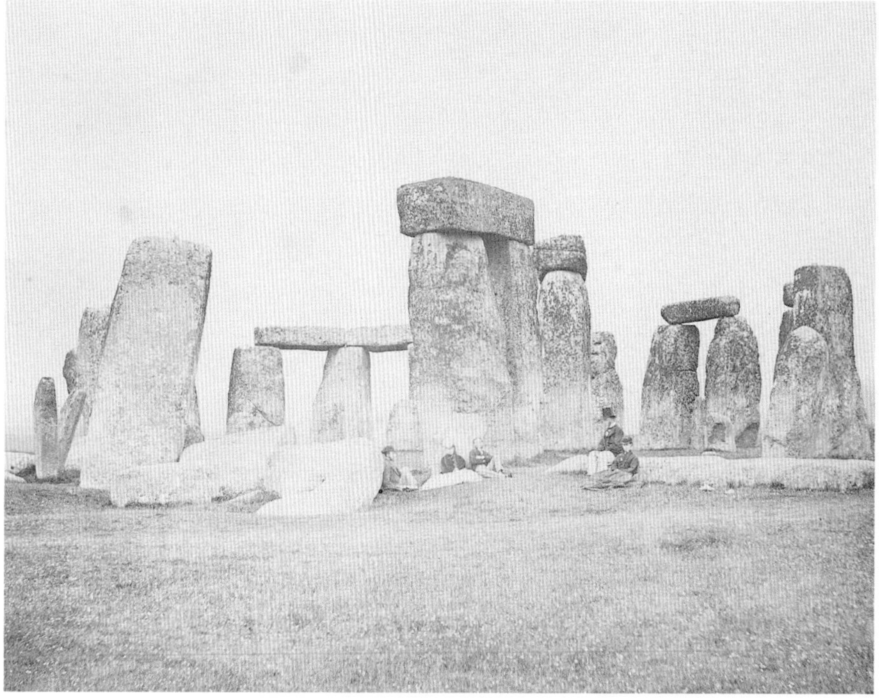

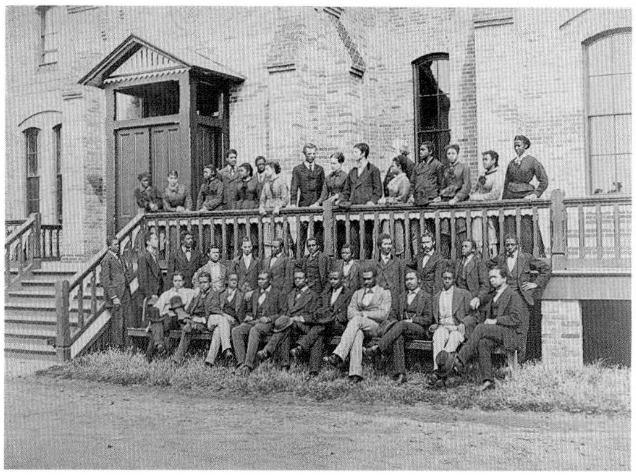

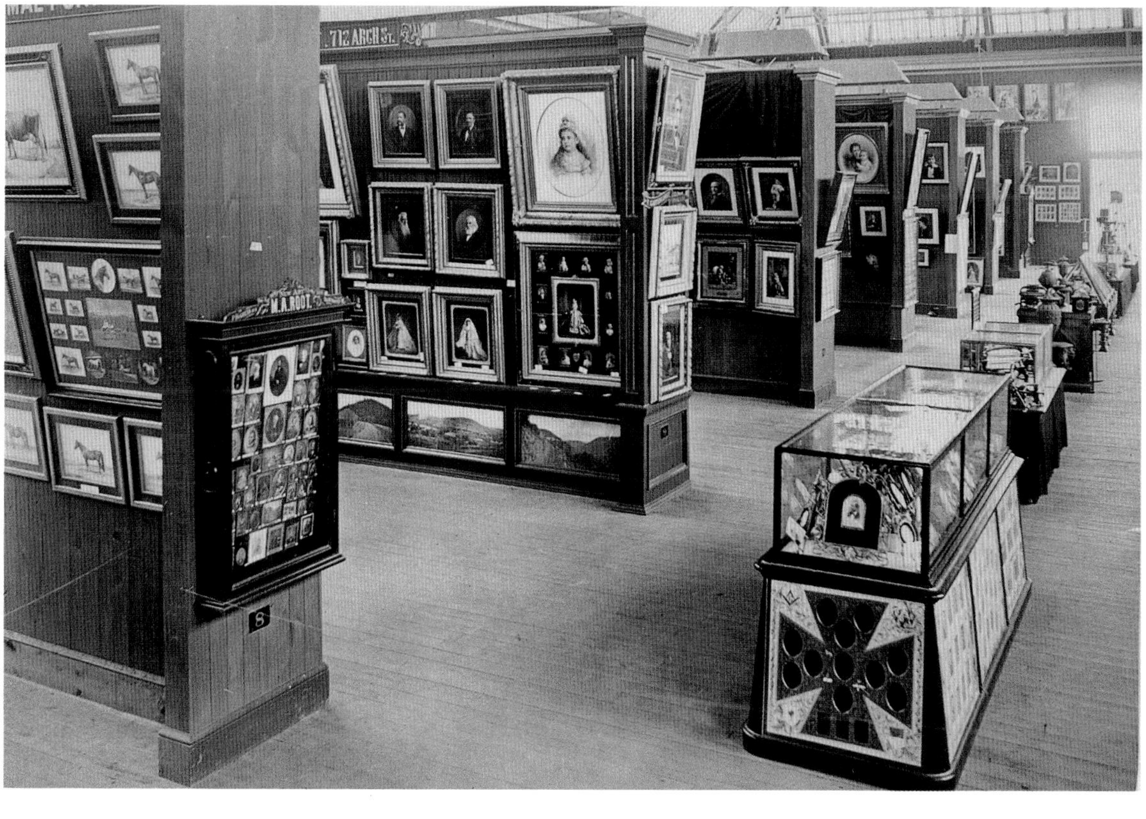

Centennial Photo Company, Photo Hall, international exhibition, 1876, albumen print, 4 3/4" x 7 1/4". Taken at the Centennial Exhibition in Philadelphia.

FOCUS: *The Studio*

Studios in the nineteenth century could be separated into two categories: those that were stationary, and those that were movable. Stationary studios ranged from very simple, one-room establishments that were open only seasonally at beaches and other tourist sites to the great galleries that were popular in the daguerreian era.

Movable studios in some cases consisted of tents, which could be set up at seaside or lakeside resorts or at fairs. In the last three decades of the nineteenth century, a number of the larger photographic dealers carried these tents, which were frequently used by photographers who made tintypes. Some movable studios were too large to be packed up and carried. These varied from large, horse-drawn vans—"saloons," as they were often called—to studios mounted in railroad cars. As in the daguerreian era, boats and barges were also used as platforms for studios, by photographers who plied their trade on rivers and lakes.

With the exception of the galleries belonging to the best-known photographers, the studios of late daguerreian and early wet-plate photographers were fairly simple in their layouts. Backdrops were plain and exhibited little variety. Props were limited to tables on which a few objects were placed and on which the subject would sometimes rest an arm (if sitting) or lean (if standing). Until the advent of faster dry plates, a posing chair and stand were used to keep the sitter motionless.

Many studios of the late nineteenth century had other furnishings, too—more elaborate, painted backdrops, often changeable, and posing chairs ranging from simple wooden affairs to ornate, velvet-upholstered or brocaded pieces, with frills and tassels. In addition, a wide variety of props was available to the sitter. These included

F. D'Alessandri, Studio equipment and products, ca. 1880, tipped-in albumen print, 19" x 12". Cameras, headrest/clamp, posing chairs, and various sizes of photographs.

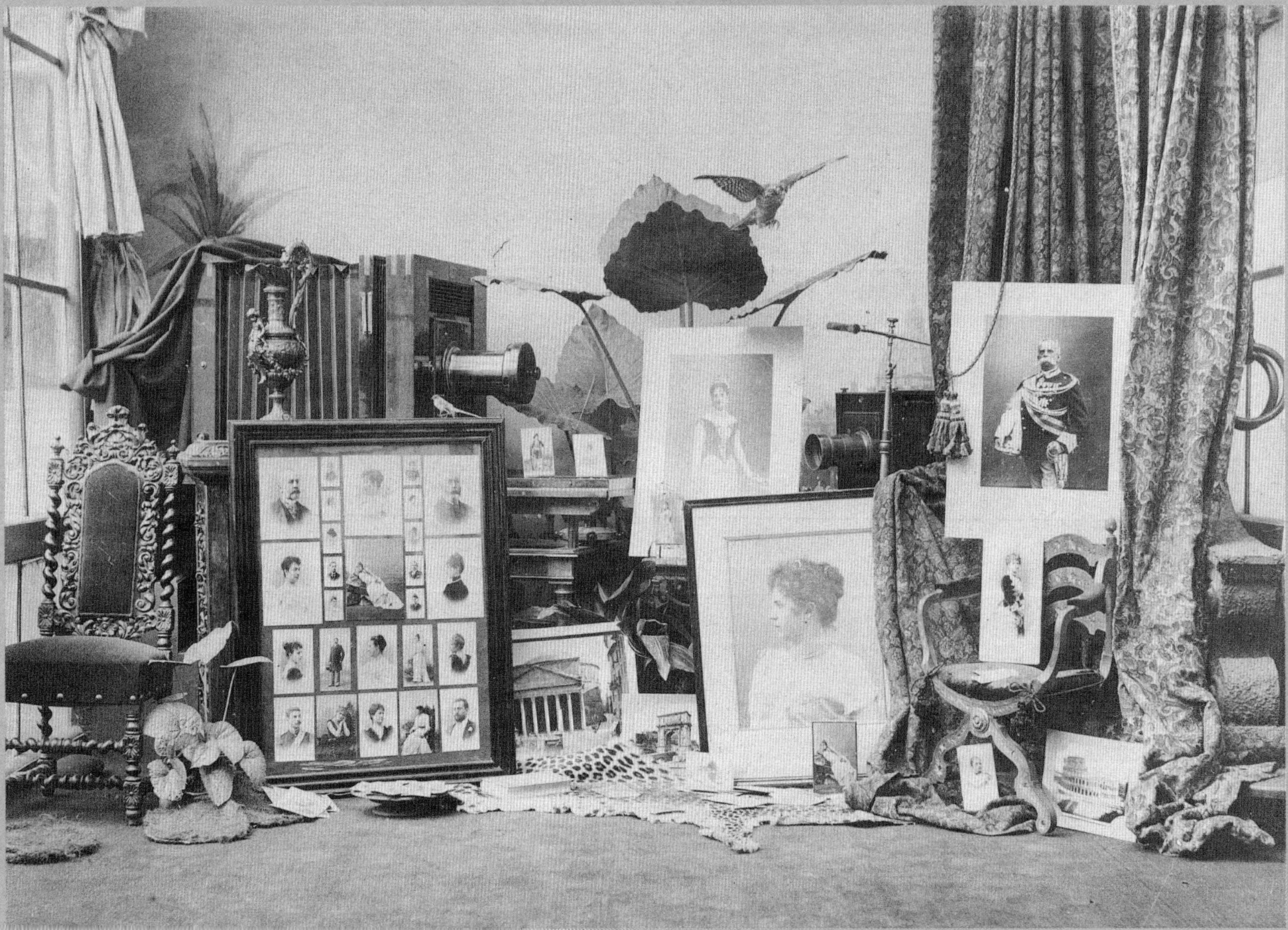

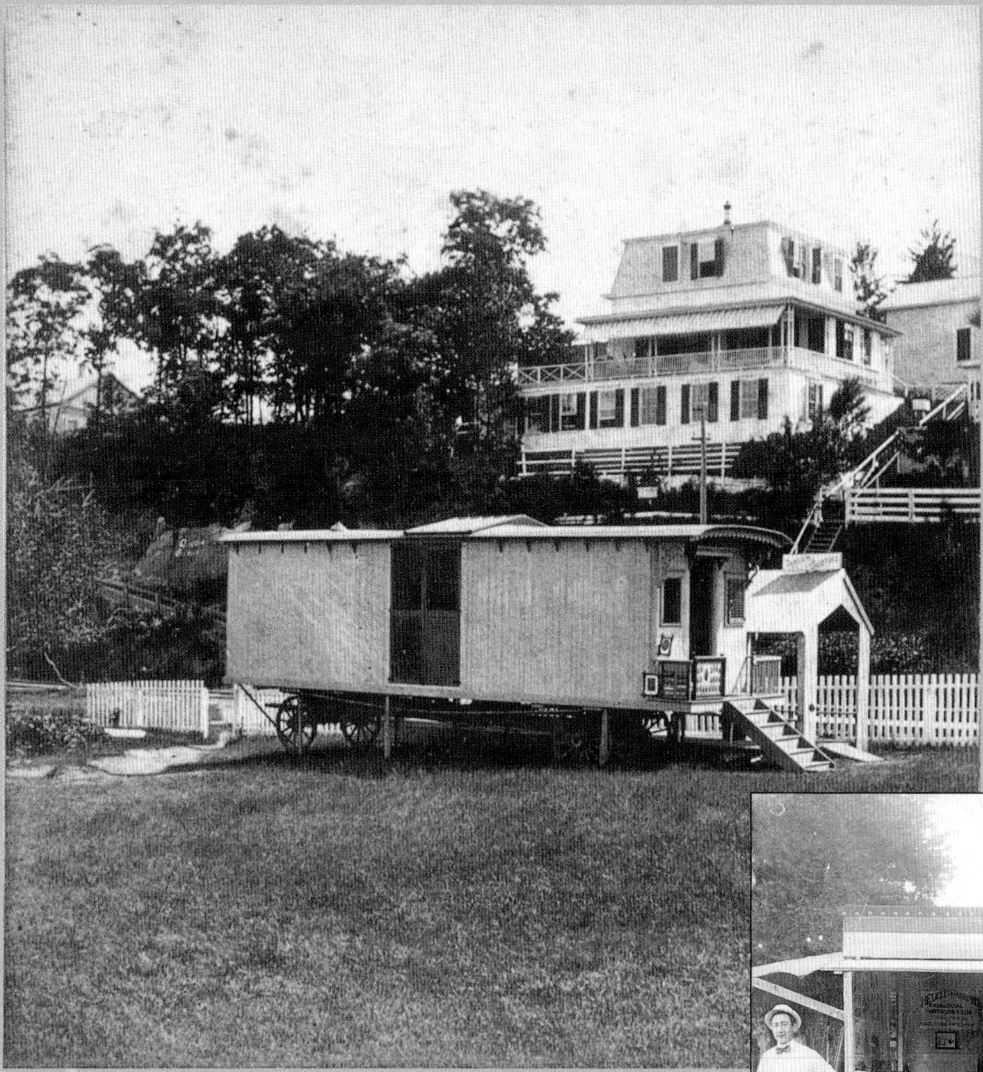

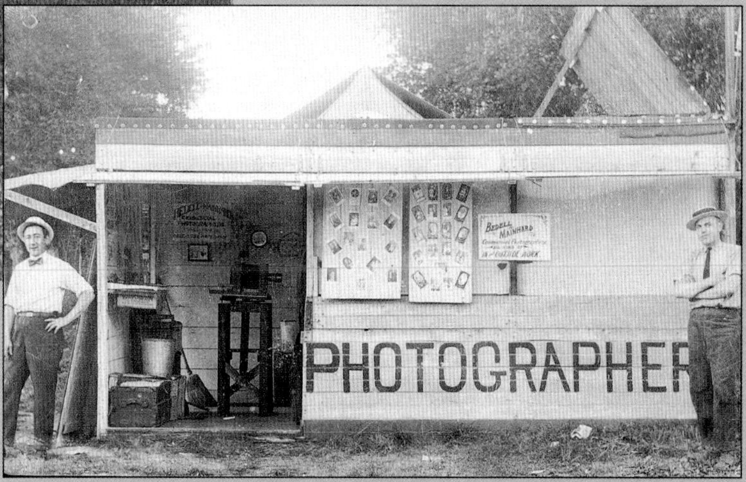

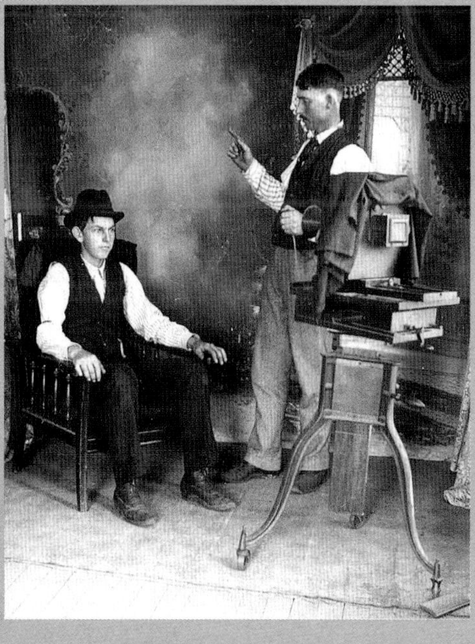

Clockwise from left: Anonymous, Itinerant photographer's traveling studio, ca. 1880, albumen print, half of stereo pair, on 3 1/2" x 7" card mount. Sample photographs displayed beside steps.

Anonymous, Seasonal photographic studio, ca. 1910, gelatino-bromide print. Camera and stand seen through open doorway. Studio intended for summer use.

Anonymous, Photographer in the studio, ca. 1885, albumen print, half of stereo pair, on 4 1/2" x 7" card mount. Multiplying back in use on camera. Acme studio stand.

such items as rustic wooden fences and papier-mâché tree stumps, wood-framed garden walls, papier-mâché balustrades and vases, and even swings, a fairly popular prop for a time.

Of course each studio needed a darkroom. In the days of wet plates, this was the place where both sensitizing and developing occurred. Printing was done out of doors, using daylight as a light source. The earliest enlargers were called solar enlargers, as they too relied on light from the sun. In the dry-plate period, artificial light sources came into use for enlarging in the darkroom. To begin with, enlargers were horizontally oriented; it was only with the invention of electric light that they came to be mounted vertically.

The cameras used in photography studios were for the most part quite large, mounted on a sturdy tripod or a four-legged studio stand, and took plates of 8-by-10 inches and up. The way a camera was equipped was to a large degree determined by the kind of photographs it was used to make. Those for tintypes—except for the larger sizes—and cartes de visite were generally outfitted with multiple lenses and/or sliding backs. Those used to make larger pictures—most often portraits or group portraits—were fitted with single lenses. Of course lenses mounted on lens boards that were interchangeable offered options for a variety of formats.

CHAPTER FOUR:

THE ADVENT OF DRY PLATES

Una hand and stand camera, tropical model, James A. Sinclair & Co., ca. 1915, mahogany construction, for 2 1/4" x 3 1/2" dry plates. While the size and construction (no leather, to avoid tropical mildew) were uncommon, the Una was representative of the British hand-and-stand style of folding plate camera of the period 1895–1930.

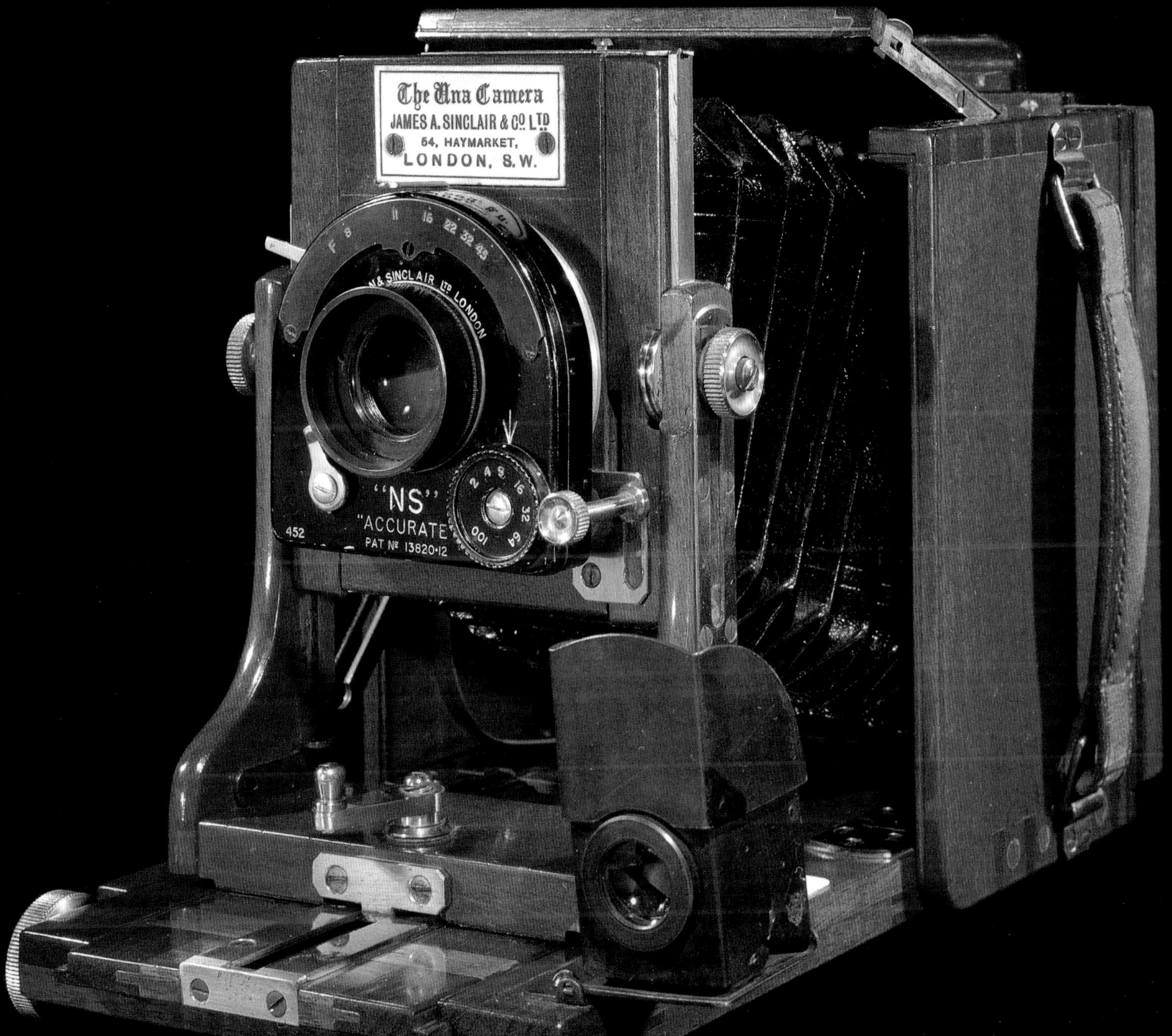
The Una Camera
JAMES A. SINCLAIR & Co. LTD
54, HAYMARKET,
LONDON, S.W.
"NS"
"ACCURATE"
PAT No 13820-12
452

The wet-collodion process offered distinct advantages over daguerreotypes and calotypes. First, a photographer could make an infinite number of prints from a glass-plate negative. Moreover, glass plates eliminated the risk of flaws in the negative paper being transferred to the print. But wet-plate photography had disadvantages as well. To work in the field usually required toting not only the camera and tripod, but also the chemicals for sensitizing and developing plates, and the darkroom in which these procedures were carried out. Also, whether in the field or in the studio, the photographer was working with a silver-nitrate solution that stained hands, clothes—everything it touched. Little wonder, then, that photographers sought a method that would free them of the need to carry their darkroom and chemicals with them, and also make less of a mess. That method was dry-plate photography.

The first attempts at dry-plate photography in fact predated wet plates. In 1847 Claude Abel Niépce de Saint-Victor used egg whites (albumen) as a coating agent for dry plates. Then, in 1850, John A. Whipple and William B. Jones introduced the crystallotype, another form of albumen dry plate. But although the plates could be prepared in advance, they were not very light-sensitive and as a result were not widely used. (Felice Beato, noted for his images of India and China, was one of the few well-known photographers who used albumen dry plates.)

By the mid-1850s, photographers had devised various means of preserving the sensitivity of dry plates for as long as several weeks. Marc Antoine Gaudin, F. Maxwell Lyte, and George Shadbolt were early experimenters with collodion dry plates, but the most popular process was one published by Jean-Marie Taupenot, a French chemist, in 1855. His collodion plates were made with a coating of iodized albumen, then dipped again in a silver-nitrate bath. Once dry, the plate was usable for a few weeks. Still, it could not compete with the sensitivity of wet collodion, which required only one-sixth the exposure time of dry plates.

Tannin plates, a variant form of collodion dry plates, were invented by Major Charles Russell. In his process, published in 1861, tannin was poured over the coated collodion plate. The tannin acted as a sensitizer, but the exposure times required were still six to eight times longer than those with wet collodion, which meant the plates could only be used for nonmoving subjects.

In the early days of photography, the production of plates was the domain of every photographer, amateur or professional. But dry plates, which could be prepared well in advance of exposure, were optimal candidates for industrial prefabrication. Dr. Richard H. Norris, an Englishman, devised a method of coating wet-collodion emul-

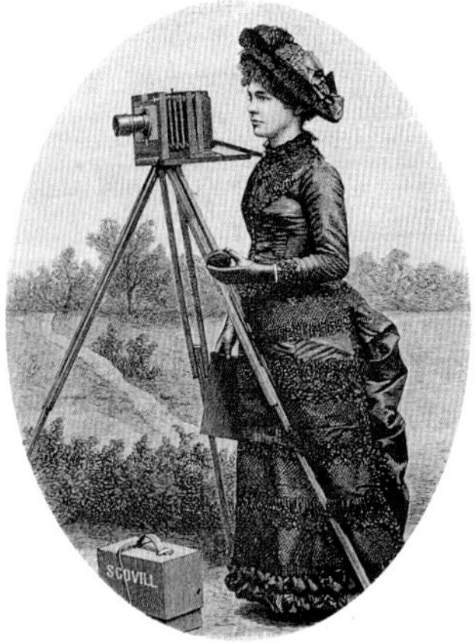

Woman photographer with a Scovill Mfg. Co. view camera, 1882, woodcut, 6" x 9 1/2", from *How to Make Pictures: Easy Lessons for the Amateur Photographer.* In the 1880s, women were often targeted by promotions for photography and photographic materials.

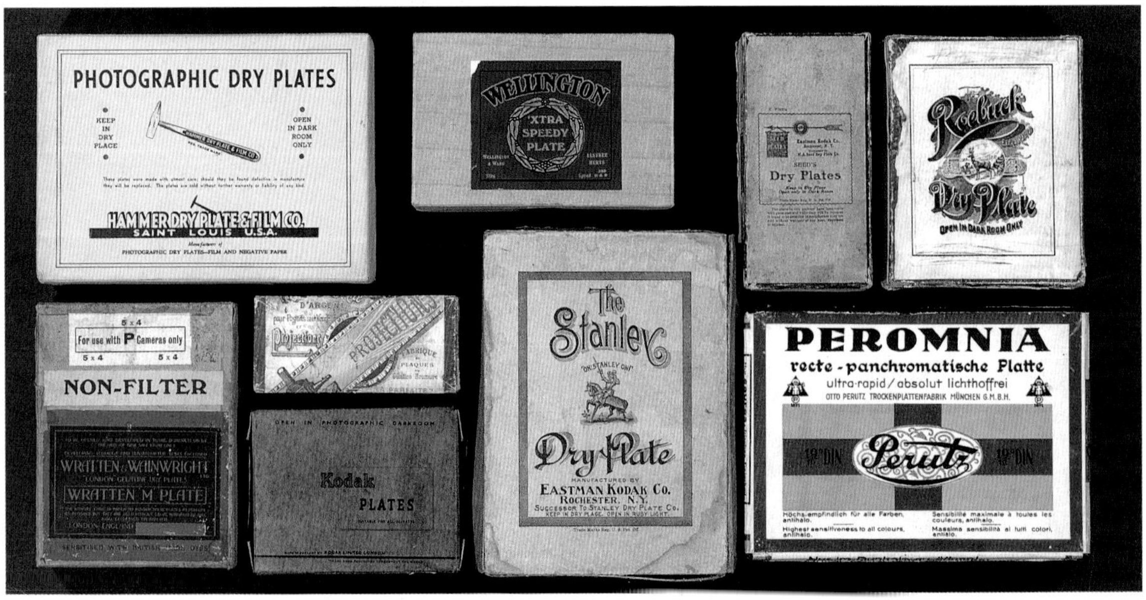

Right: Boxes for gelatino-bromide dry plates. Among the major dry-plate producers represented here are Hammer, Kodak, Stanley, Wellington, and Perutz. Sears, Roebuck was supplied by other manufacturers.

sions with gelatin, resulting in a collodio-gelatin plate. Once dry, these plates could be stored for up to six months. Norris began to market his plates around 1856, and they were in use for about a decade. In 1860, Norris introduced a faster plate that not only matched the wet collodion in sensitivity but lasted as long as a year. Thomas Fothergill, another Englishman, in the late 1850s and early 1860s, marketed plates prepared in a manner similar to Taupenot's, though simplified.

In 1864 the Englishmen William Boulton and J. B. Sayce introduced a collodion emulsion containing silver bromide in place of the long-used silver iodide. This reduced the preparation process to simply pouring the preprepared collodio-bromide solution over the plate and letting it dry.

While Dr. Richard L. Maddox is generally credited with having invented gelatin (gelatino-bromide) dry plates, others had also experimented with the use of gelatin as a substitute for collodion. Although Maddox released information about his process in a paper of September 1871, health problems prevented him from ever perfecting the details. In July 1873, John Burgess of London began selling a gelatin emulsion to be used in making photographic dry plates. His advertisements claimed that plates made with his emulsion were "equal in sensitiveness to the best wet plates." Burgess's emulsion, though, did not sell well, perhaps because the process was impractical: to achieve sensitivity, the emulsion required fermentation at temperatures above 70 degrees Fahrenheit. Burgess instead resolved to make quality preprepared dry plates, and began promoting them in August 1873.

After developing improvements to Burgess's emulsion, Richard Kennett, another British amateur photographer, started to manufacture dry plates in 1876. While his plates were relatively sensitive, they failed commercially. Later that same year, the Liverpool Dry Plate Company and Mawson & Swan, of Newcastle, launched production of gelatino-bromide plates that were as sensitive as wet plates. Less than two years later, a total of fourteen British companies were engaged in dry-plate production.

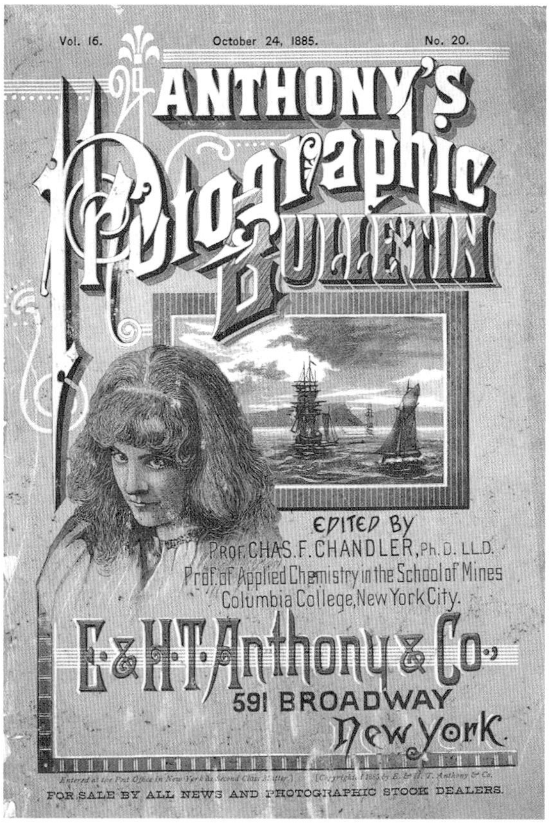

Anthony's Photographic Bulletin, edited by Prof. Charles F. Chandler, E. & H. T. Anthony & Co., October 24, 1885. Both Anthony and its principal competitor, the Scovill Manufacturing Co., published popular photographic journals, aimed at amateurs and professionals, and promoting their own products.

Below: "Le Touriste" magazine camera, E. Enjalbert, ca. 1882, for eight 5" x 7" dry plates. An early form of magazine camera, with plate-changing mechanism at rear.

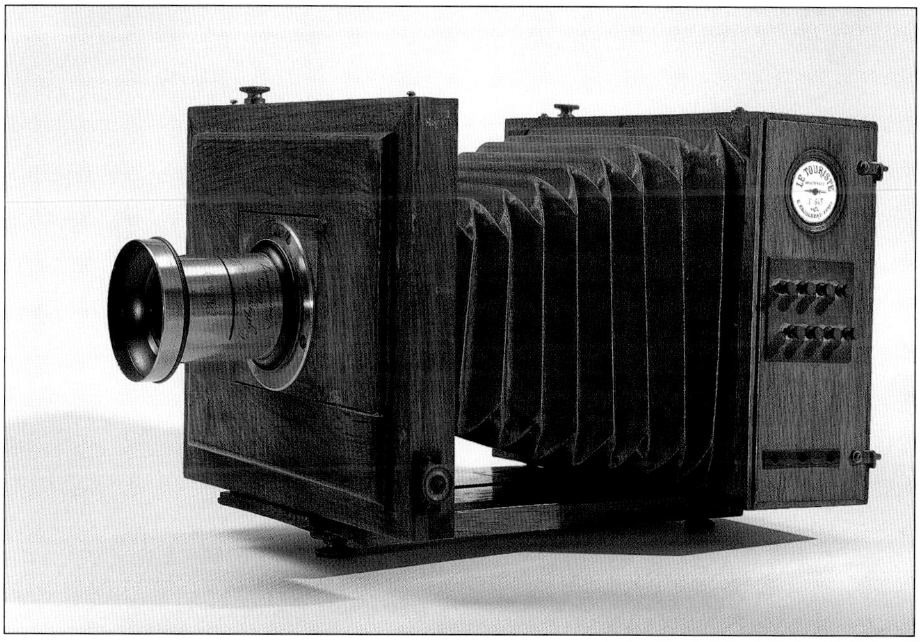

This sudden increase in the number of companies making gelatino-bromide dry plates was due to an innovation in manufacturing—the cooking, or "ripening," process, a new step that yielded a higher-quality plate, at the same time making it easier to produce. Credit for its publication, in 1878, goes to Charles Bennett, who found that greater sensitivity could be obtained by heating the emulsion. While he advocated a temperature of 90 degrees Fahrenheit for a period of two

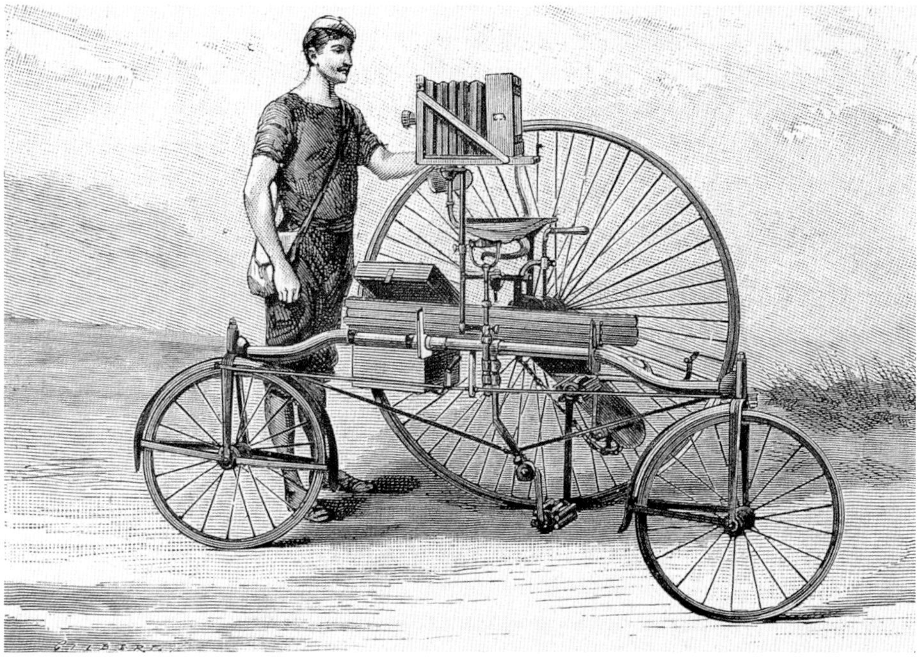

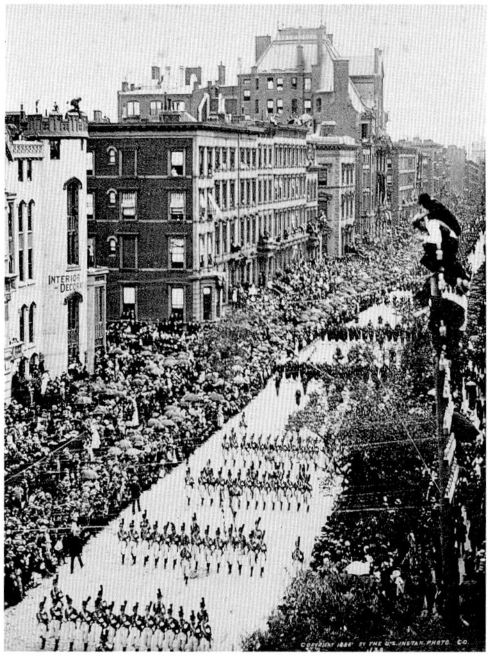

Left: Rudge & Co.'s "Coventry Rotary" photographic tricycle, ca. 1885, woodcut, from *La fotografia moderna*, Alberto Londe, 1889. Special camera mount for the photographer/"wheelman."

Right: Anonymous, General Grant's funeral procession, Fifth Avenue and Fortieth Street, New York City, 1885, tipped-in albumen print, 11" x 14 $\frac{1}{2}$", from *Seven Mile Funeral Cortege of Gen'l Grant*. View down Fifth Avenue from the forty-foot wall of the reservoir.

to seven days, depending on the sensitivity desired, others found that raising the temperature to the boiling point for ten minutes worked just as well and saved considerable time and effort.

Dry plates superseded wet plates more quickly in Britain than on the Continent. In America, they were even slower to gain acceptance. For some photographers, the reluctance to make the switch was a matter of cost and individual preference. Professional wet-plate photographers, to save on expenses, coated their own plates and recycled the glass from unsuccessful exposures. Being accustomed to their own methods, moreover, they did not necessarily welcome the introduction of commercially-produced, less flexible materials. Amateurs were quicker to change to dry plates, and in the 1880s, as camera clubs grew and photography journals multiplied, they also communicated more among themselves than did professionals regarding those changes.

Until the late 1870s, most of the experimentation with dry plates had been done by amateur British photographers. The commercial production of gelatino-bromide plates was based in Britain as well. But in 1877, an American amateur wet-plate photographer had an accident that was to play a pivotal role in the future of photography.

While traveling with his photographic materials, George Eastman of Rochester, New York, who would become the founder of Eastman Kodak, had most of the clothes in his trunk ruined by spilled silver nitrate. Eastman, a shrewd entrepreneur, used this personal frustration as an impetus to make his own dry plates. Though employed as a bank clerk, Eastman began to experiment with the production of dry plates, seeking to eliminate the cumbersome and impractical aspects of the existing processes. After reading up on dry plates in English photography journals, in 1878 he began to make his own, and a year later paid a visit to England to learn more.

On April 13, 1880, Eastman was granted a patent for a plate-coating machine, modeled after a similar machine made by the English company Mawson & Swan, and by September 1880 his plates were being sold commercially by the prominent New York photographic stock dealers E. & H. T. Anthony. In the early 1880s, Eastman's plates had a tendency to lose sensitivity. This was due to the lack of a sulfur-bearing compound—a material necessary to the ripening process—in the gelatin. As a result, Eastman closed down his factory and went to England, where he purchased a formula for a top-quality dry-plate emulsion and the machinery to make the plates. On returning to Rochester, he reopened his factory and resumed dry-plate production. While Eastman's entry into the field of photography was significant, his dry plates were not the first on the U.S. market. John Carbutt's Keystone Dry Plates were introduced in 1879, and E. & H. T. Anthony & Company brought out their Defiance plates in May 1880.

All of the early dry plates were essentially "color-blind"—that is, not very sensitive to color differences, especially in the range of the spectrum between yellow and red. Thanks to discoveries in the period 1873 to 1890, though, the color sensitivity of dry plates increased. These plates were referred to as orthochromatic, as they were still relatively insensitive to red. Panchromatic plates, sensitive to all colors, were first marketed by the British firm of Wratten & Wainwright in 1906.

During the period when amateur photographers were producing their own emulsions and coating their own dry plates, there was, of course, no standard for making exposures. Correct exposure was arrived at by trial-and-error. With the introduction of commercially produced plates, however, sensitivity became reasonably uniform, and a standard exposure system was possible for the first time.

In 1876 Ferdinand Hurter and Vero C. Driffield began investigations into photographic sensitometry—a method of accurately measuring the intensity of light and its effects on dry plates. These measurements could then be used to determine the optimal developing times for all plates and films, given certain brightness ratios, developers, and temperatures. Using their data, published in 1890, it was possible to develop negatives in total darkness with satisfactory results. (The measurement of the sensitivity of photographic emulsions has evolved into standardized rating systems, put forth by such bodies as the International Standards Organization—ISO—and the American Standards Association—ASA.)

The shift to dry plates and the gradual increase in their sensitivity led to marked changes in the use and design of cameras. Before, exposures had been made simply by removing and replacing a lens cap manually; the length of the exposures made any minor irregularity in exposure time unimportant. With the advent of more sensitive plates, exposure times were shorter and so needed to be more accurate.

By the early 1880s, exposures of 1/25 second were common, requiring a reasonably accurate means for controlling exposure duration. In response, a variety of new shutter types was introduced, and as plate and, later, film sensitivity increased further, shutter mechanisms became more sophisticated and precise. By the 1920s, sales

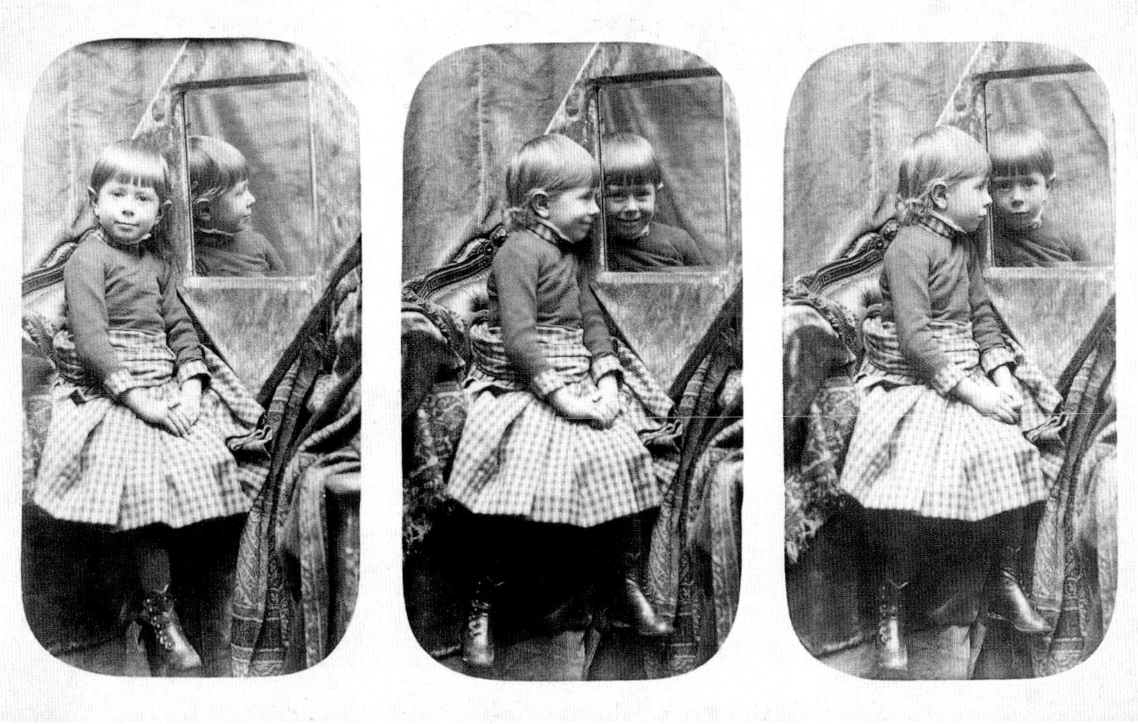

George R. Rockwood, Rockwood's Instantaneous Triplex Portrait, ca. 1880, albumen-print cabinet card. Three portraits combined in a single print.

PROFILE: *Motion Arrested*

A distinct challenge in the early years of photography was how to arrest motion. Landscapes and still lifes presented no problem, but lengthy exposure times meant it was difficult to do portraits of living-and-breathing subjects in the studio. Photographers had to use head rests and other armatures to prevent the sitter from moving. In many outdoor photographs of the wet-plate period, exposures were so long that streets appeared empty or populated solely by phantomlike people who appeared as indistinct blurs.

Only as the sensitivity of plates increased was it possible to stop motion with any degree of success. By the late 1850s, "instantaneous" exposures, on the order of 1/5 second, were being used, but this was the exception, rather than the rule. Some photographers began to specialize in stop-motion work, using humans and animals as subjects. In the 1870s, Eadweard Muybridge, in America, photographed the motion of horses. In the 1880s he produced his famous work *Animal Locomotion*. In the same period, the American artist Thomas Eakins was engaged in motion studies, and Jules Marey, a Frenchman, took photographs of people in motion. All of these photographers employed special equipment developed in the course of their experiments. While multiple cameras were used at first, Marey ultimately invented a camera with a rotating circular plate allowing multiple exposures.

Also in the 1880s, Ottomar Anschütz of Prussia captured the motion of animals on dry plates. While focal-plane shutters—located immediately in front of the camera's plane of focus—had been experimented with by earlier photographers, none had attained any great success. But in 1883, Anschütz developed a camera that used a focal-plane shutter with a slitlike opening between two cloth curtains that swept past the plate. Varying the size of the slit and the tension of the spring that moved the shutter curtains provided a range of speeds up to an unprecedented 1/1000 second. While Anschütz cameras were manufactured by the German firm C. P. Goerz, their basic shutter design was employed in virtually every camera with a high-speed focal-plane shutter made through World War II.

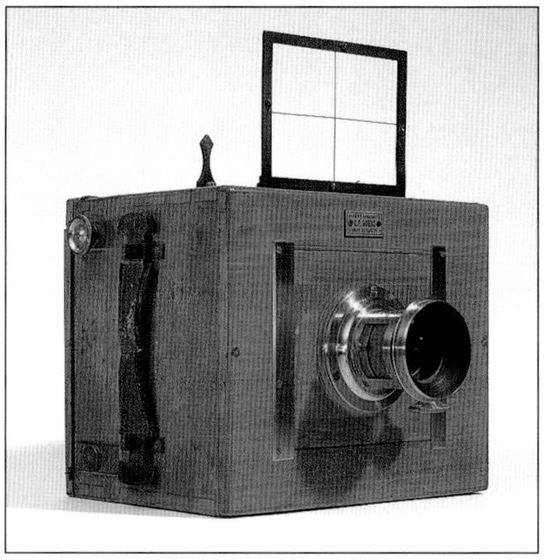

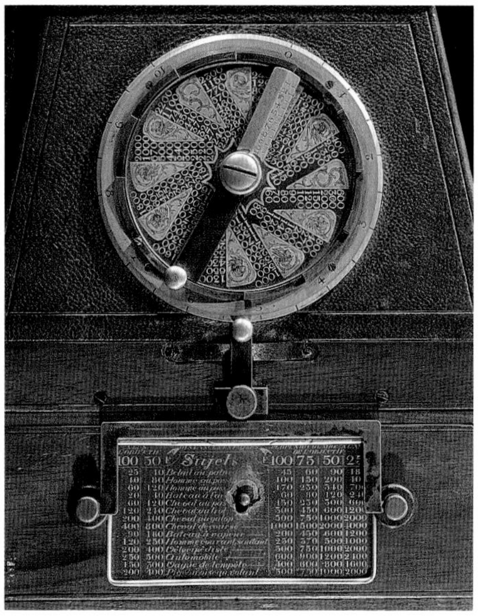

One drawback of the early Anschütz shutters was that they were not self-capping; that is, the slit stayed open while the shutter was being wound. This meant that a plate (or later, the film) could be exposed inadvertently. In 1892, though, Anschütz developed an improved model, and in the early 1900s the Folmer & Schwing Manufacturing Company of New York introduced on its cameras a self-capping shutter, sold separately.

See opposite for captions.

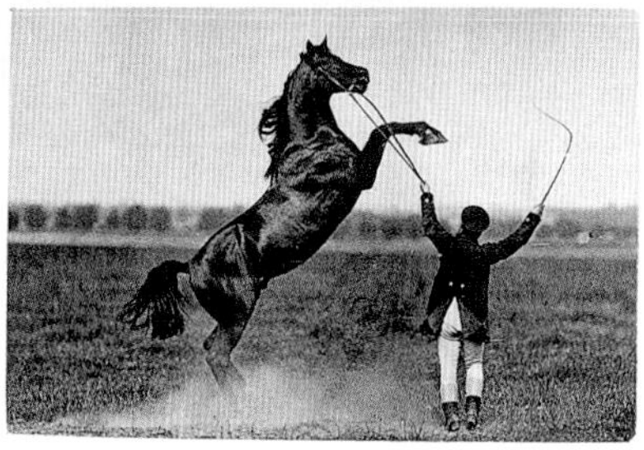

1.

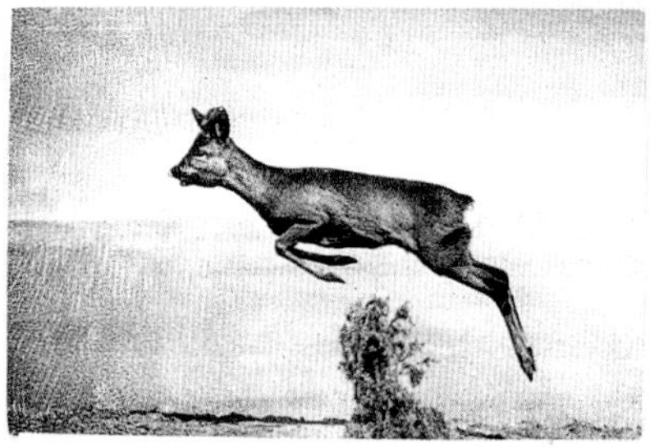

2.

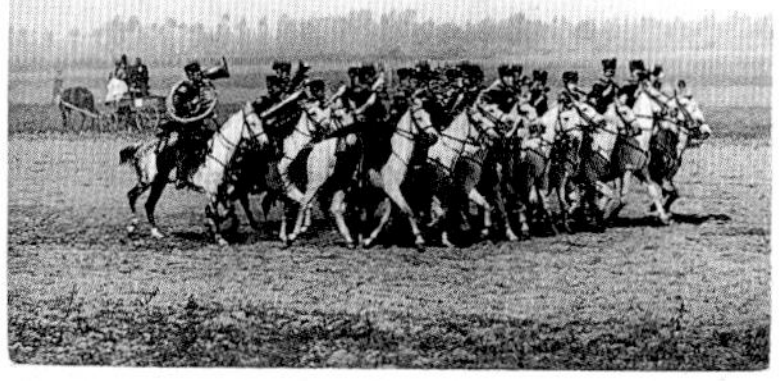

3.

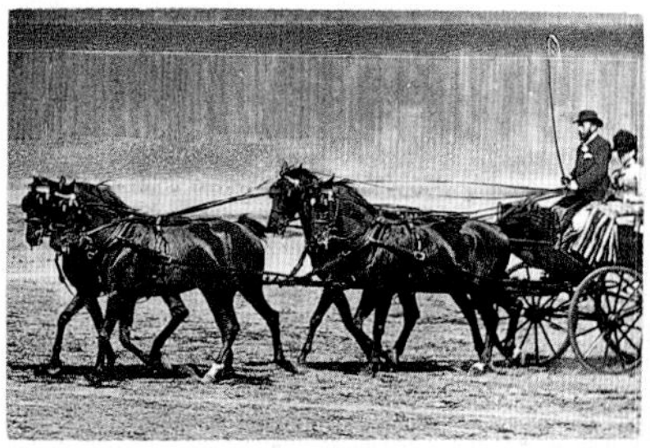

4.

Opposite, clockwise from top: Anschütz camera, improved model, C. P. Goerz, ca. 1892, walnut construction, for 9 x 12 cm dry plates. Cloth focal-plane shutter made rapid shutter speeds possible and facilitated motion-stopping exposures; Shutter of the Sigriste camera, ca. 1900, Guido Sigriste. By means of a focal-plane shutter with variable slit widths and tensions, shutter speeds from 1/40 to 1/5000 second could be attained; Ottomar Anschütz, *Instantaneous Photographs of Animals in Motion*, ca. 1886, collotypes, from *Die Moment-Photographie in ihrer Anwendung auf Kunst und Wissenshcaft*, Dr. Josef Maria Eder, 1888.

of dry plates were distinctly in decline and cameras had become available with shutter speeds as fast as 1/2800 second.

With reduced exposure times, cameras no longer had to be mounted on a tripod or other surface for support. Obviously, there were still limitations in size and weight, but this new freedom led to the creation of a whole new category of camera: the "hand" or "instantaneous" camera.

Thomas Bolas, a British amateur, was one of the first photographers to design a handheld model. He referred to his invention as a "detective" camera—not because it was disguised, but its small size and boxlike shape made it decidedly unobtrusive compared to previous cameras. The first commercially produced hand camera was designed by William Schmid of Brooklyn, New York. Manufactured by E. & H. T. Anthony & Co., Schmid's Patent Detective Camera came on the market in 1883.

Of box-in-box construction, the Schmid's inner box could be moved to permit focusing. Predetermined distances were marked on a brass focusing scale mounted on top of the camera. A rotary shutter was mounted between the camera's front panel and the lens. The tension of the shutter's spring could be adjusted to allow for several shutter speeds. The camera had a small reflecting viewfinder mounted in an upper corner of the body, which meant the photographer could hold the camera at waist level and still be sure that the camera was aimed properly. All of these features, especially this last one, facilitated the inconspicuous use that led to the description "detective."

Schmid's camera was only the first of many boxlike detective cameras manufactured in the U.S. and Europe. In fact, while the "detective" appellation had practically disappeared in America and

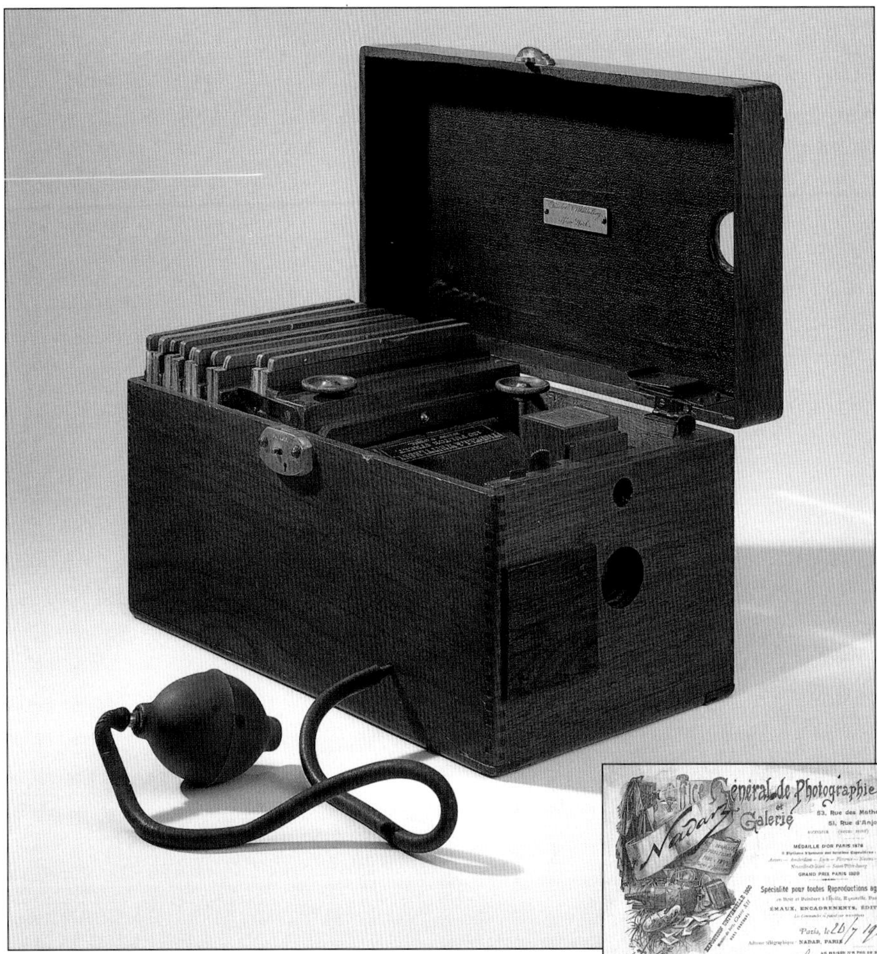

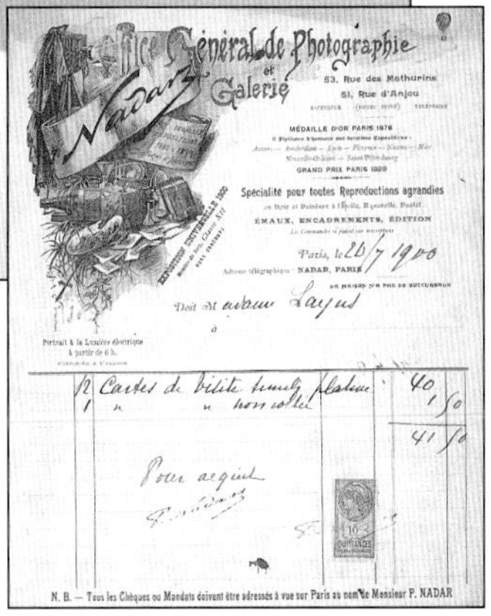
Office Général de Photographie et Galerie
Nadar
53, Rue des Mathurins
51, Rue d'Anjou
MÉDAILLE D'OR PARIS 1878
GRAND PRIX PARIS 1889
Spécialité pour toutes Reproductions agrandies
ÉMAUX, ENCADREMENTS, ÉDITION
Paris, le 20/7 1900
Adresse télégraphique : NADAR, PARIS
Doit Madame Layus
Portrait à la Lumière électrique à partir de 6 h.

12	Cartes de visite timbrés platine	40,
1	" " non collée	1 50
		41 50

Pour acquit

N. B. — Tous les Chèques ou Mandats doivent être adressés à vue sur Paris au nom de Monsieur P. NADAR

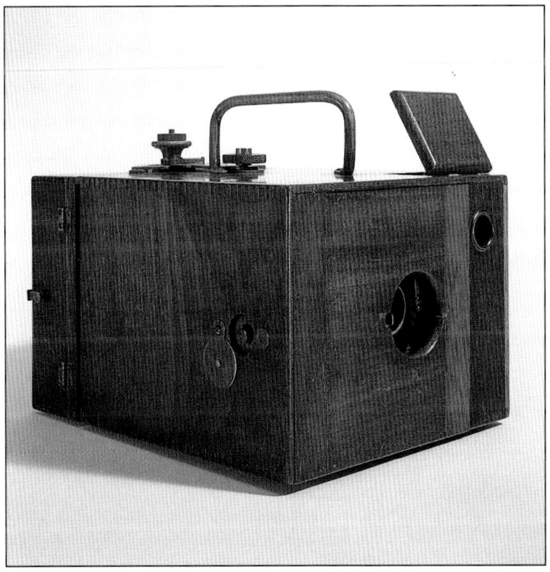

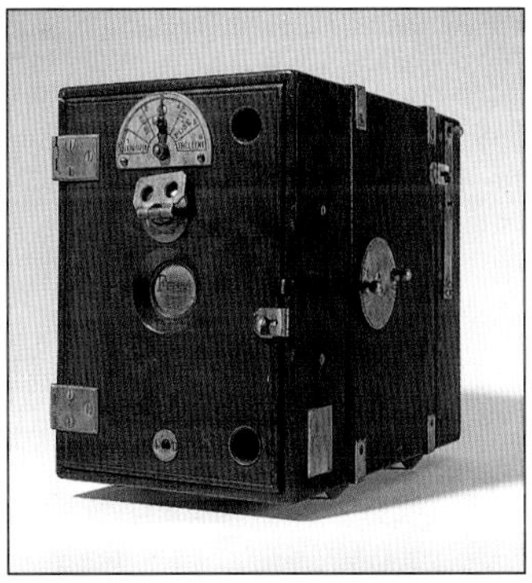

Clockwise from top: T & W detective camera, Tisdell & Whittelsey, ca. 1887, for 4" x 5" dry plates. A popular detective camera in its time; Receipt for the purchase of cartes de visite, Nadar, Office General de Photographie et Galerie, July 20, 1900. Issued for the purchase of twelve mounted cartes de visite, and one unmounted; "Express Détective Nadar" magazine camera, second model, Paul Nadar, ca. 1889, for 9 x 12 cm dry plates. Paul Nadar was the son of Gaspard Felix Tournachon, the famed photographer known as Nadar; Schmid's Patent Detective Camera, E. & H. T. Anthony & Co., ca. 1885, for 4" x 5" dry plates. Schmid's was the first commercially produced "detective," or instantaneous, hand camera. It was also the first to use a viewfinder recessed in the camera body.

FOCUS: *Concealed and "Secret" Cameras*

Spy, disguised, concealed, secret, detective, novelty—all of these terms have at one time or another been applied to cameras whose appearance conceals their function, and thus the intent of their users. At first these cameras were nothing but novelty items, the toys of affluent amateurs, but they evolved into instruments of serious espionage (though the most ominous ones were never advertised to the public).

Cameras have been disguised in a number of ways, often concealed in or on items of clothing such as hats, ties, vests, belts, or shoes. Larger objects have also served to hide cameras, including canes, binoculars, attaché cases, radios, and books—book cameras, especially, came in a rather wide variety. Smaller objects, carried in a pocket or purse, have been used to hide cameras as well—watches, cigarette packs, lighters, women's compacts.

To many, however, the epitome of the concealed camera is the vest camera, invented by an American, R. D. Gray, and introduced in the U.S. in 1886. Soon after, the rights to Gray's invention were acquired by Carl P. Stirn whose brother, Rudolf, began to manufacture them in Berlin. The vest camera was flat and circular, with a lens designed to peep out through the buttonhole of a vest. Most models produced circular exposures on a circular dry plate; six in the smaller model, four in the larger. Stirn Vest Cameras were produced until 1892, and a December 1890 advertisement claimed the company had made more than eighteen thousand of them. This made Stirn's the most common detective camera until the introduction of the Expo Watch Camera in 1905.

One type of detective camera actually looked like a camera. Its deception lay in the fact that it took pictures at right angles to the direction in which it appeared to be aiming, a deceit supplemented by false lenses mounted on the side of the camera. Some regular cameras had a "sneaky" side as well, in that they were equipped with right-angle viewfinders, allowing the user to shoot surreptitiously.

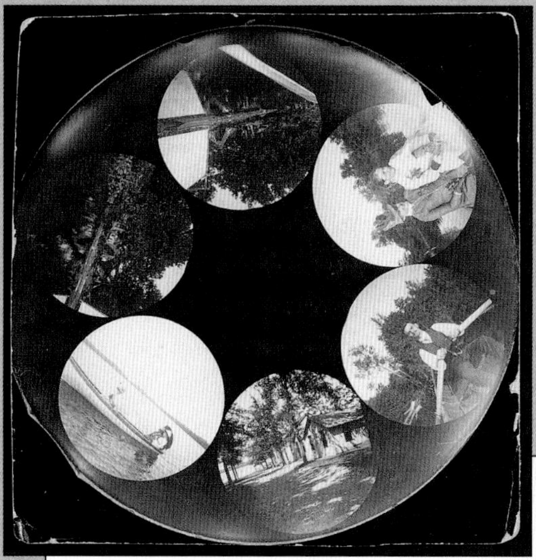

Anonymous, Contact print of negatives made with a No. 1 Stirn Vest Camera, ca. 1892, albumen print, 5 1/2" x 5 3/4".

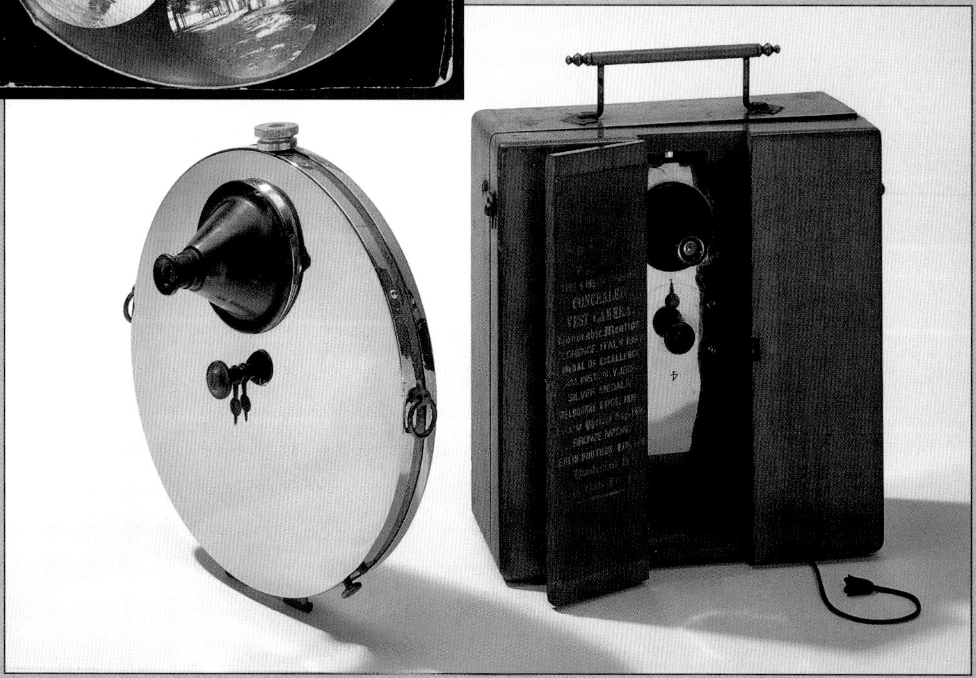

Below: C. P. Stirn's Concealed Vest Cameras. Left: No. 2 Vest Camera, Rudolf Stirn, ca. 1889, for four exposures, 2 3/8" diameter, on 6 3/4" diameter dry plates. Right: No. 1 Vest Camera, Rudolf Stirn, ca. 1891, for six exposures, 1 5/8" diameter, on 5 1/2" diameter dry plates, in walnut carrying case.

Opposite: top row, left to right: Photo-Revolver de Poche, E. Enjalbert, ca. 1883, for ten exposures on 1.8 x 1.8 cm dry plates. The plates were held in a "cylinder" in the top chamber. After exposure—made by pulling the trigger—the cylinder rotated one half-turn, shifting the plate to the lower chamber and recocking the shutter; Krügener's Taschenbuch-Camera, Haake & Albers, ca. 1890, for twenty-four exposures on 4 x 4 cm dry plates, leather-covered wood body. A metal rod moved exposed plates from supply compartment to storage compartment; The Ben-Akiba (photographic cane or walking stick camera), A. Lehmann, ca. 1903, for twenty 1.3 x 2.5 cm exposures on 1.8 cm-wide roll film. The cane's handle not only housed the camera but held three extra rolls of film; John Player Special Cigarettes Camera, left, and Camera-Lite, right. The cigarette camera uses a Russian Kiev Vega mechanism to make 10 x 14 mm exposures on 16 mm film. The cigarette lighter camera made by Suzuki Optical Co., ca. 1950, makes 5 x 8 mm exposures on 8 mm-wide roll film; Steineck A-B-C (Arm-Band-Camera), Steineck-Camera-Werk, ca. 1953, for eight exposures, 5.5 mm diameter, on 24 mm diameter film discs.

Middle row: Pompadour-Kamera (Damen Camera), A. Hesekiel & Co./Certo, ca. 1908, conventional folding camera for 6.5 x 9 cm dry plates, housed in a stylish alligator ladies' handbag.

Bottom row: Goerz Photo-Stereo-Binocle, C. P. Goerz Akt-Ges., ca. 1902, for single or paired exposures on one or two 4.5 x 5 cm dry plates. The camera could function as an opera glass, a field glass, a monocular viewer and single-exposure camera, or a camera for stereo pairs; Deceptive Angle Graphic, Folmer & Schwing Mfg. Co., ca. 1902, for 3 1/4" x 4 1/4" dry plates. One of the few "concealed" cameras made to look like a camera; The Focal Plane "Ticka," Houghton's Ltd., ca. 1909, for 5/8" x 7/8" exposures on 17.5 mm-wide roll film. The Ticka was also made in a non-focal-plane-shutter model and a model with a simulated watch face. Its American counterpart was the Expo Watch Camera.

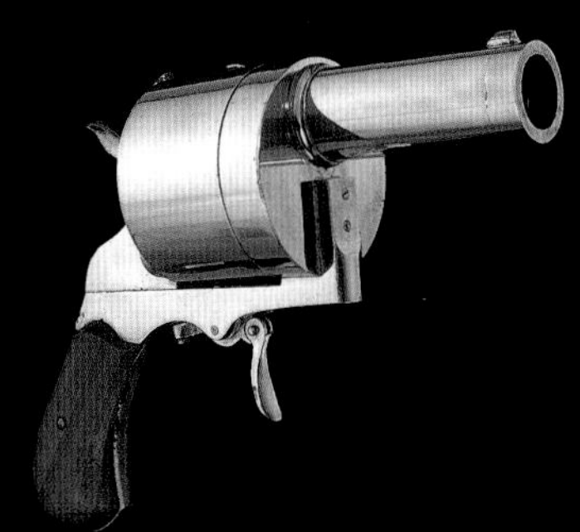
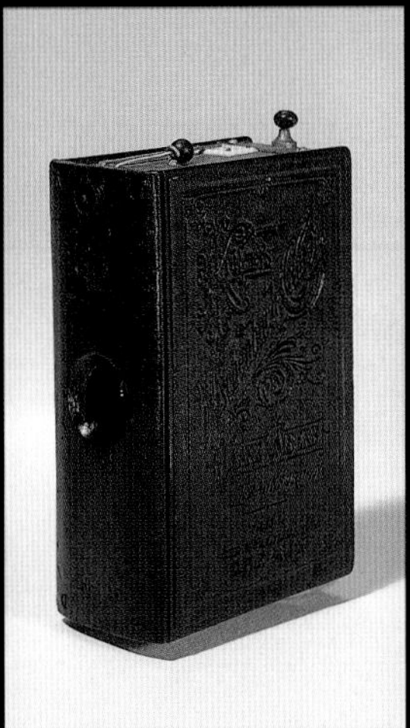
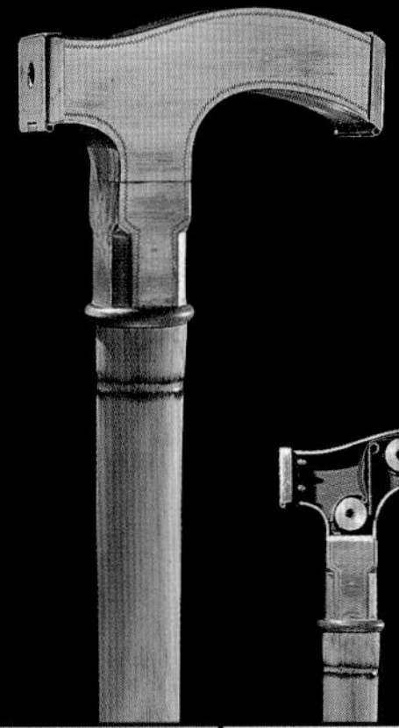
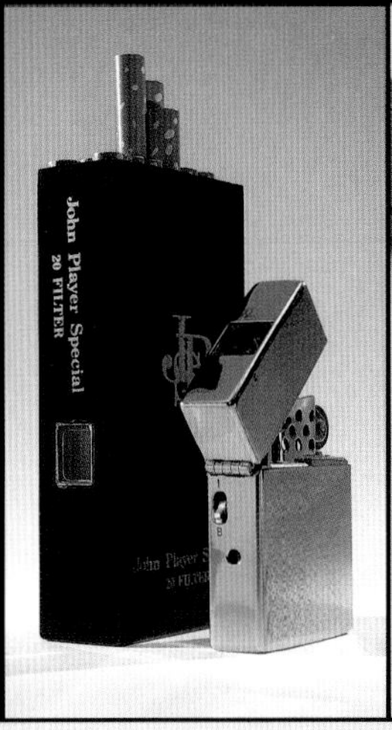
John Player Special
20 FILTER
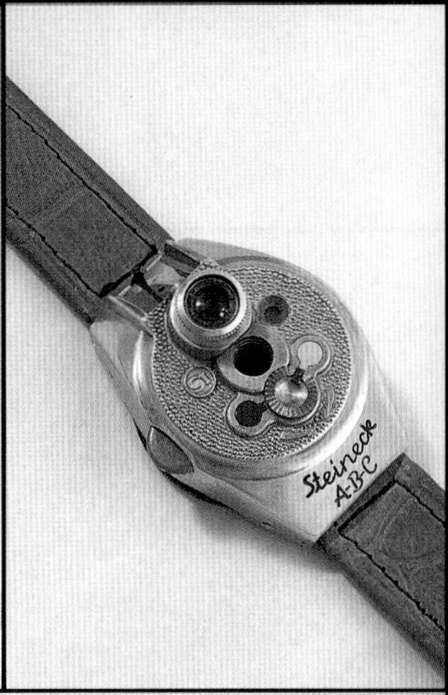
Steineck
A-B-C
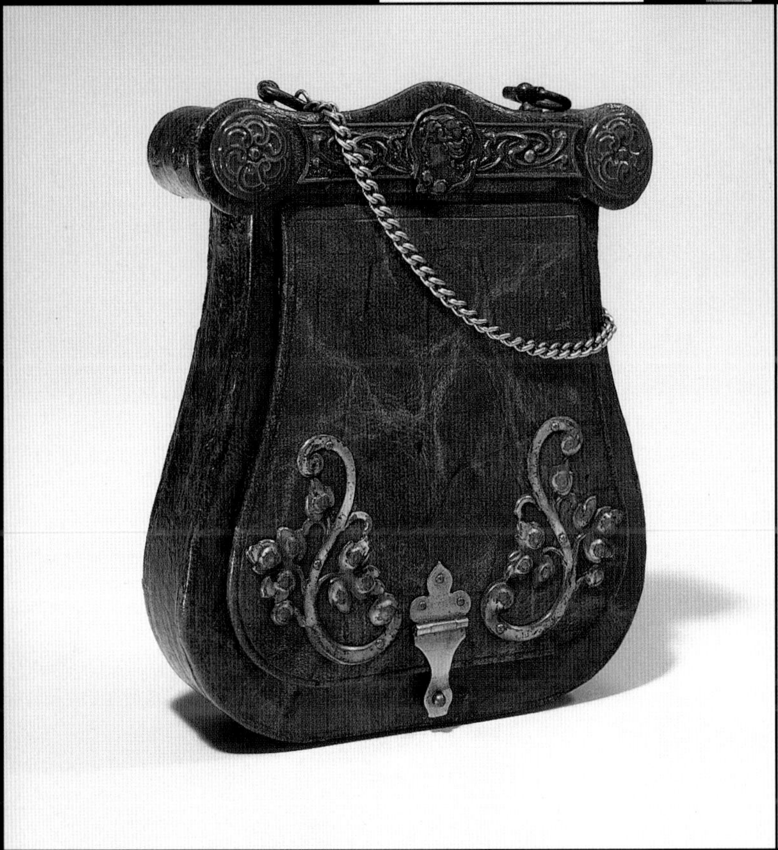
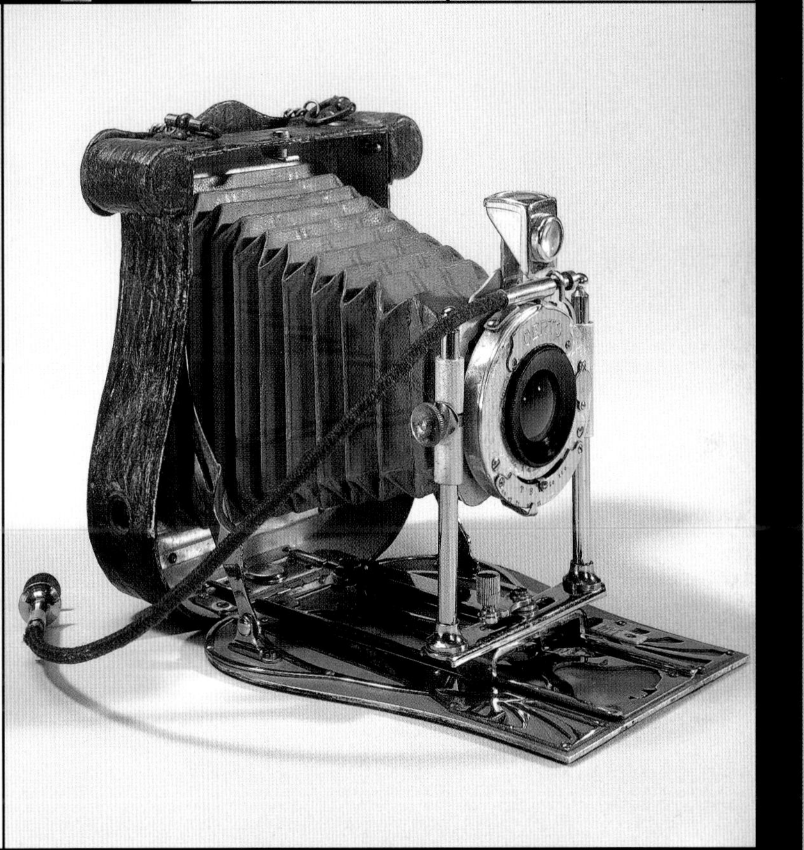
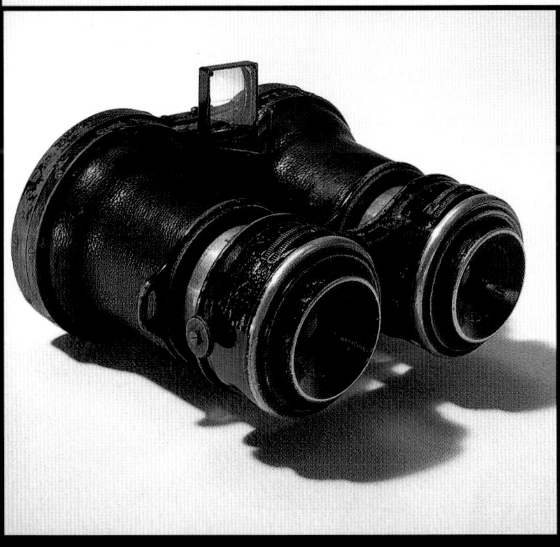
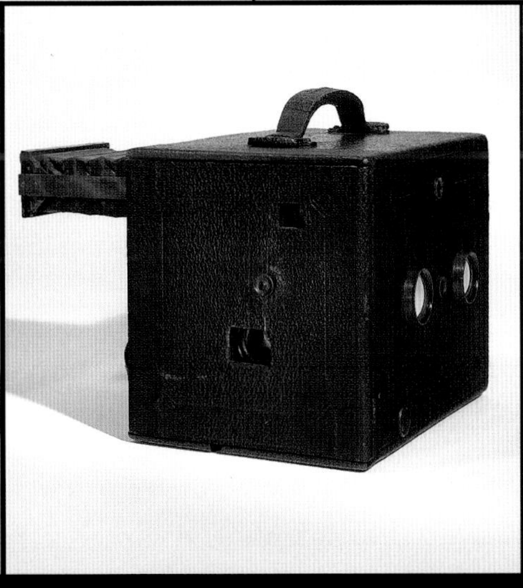
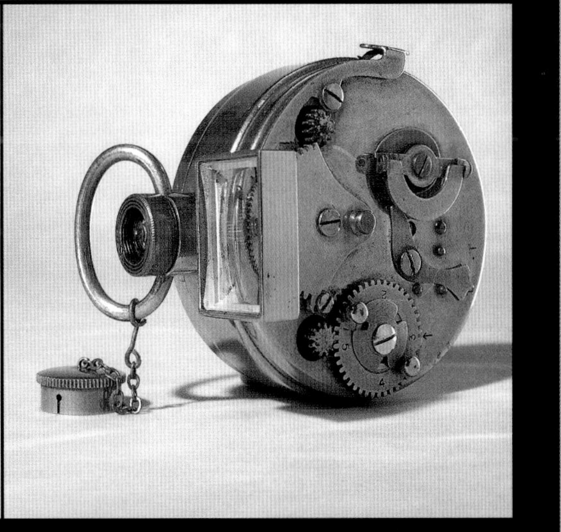

Left: Compass Camera with tripod, made by LeCoultre & Cie. for Compass Cameras, England, ca. 1937, for 24 x 36 mm dry plates or sheet film. Accommodates roll-film back for six exposures on 1 ½"-wide film. No other camera boasted so many features for its size: coupled range finder, spirit level, top and side tripod bushes, extinction meter, built-in lens hood, built-in filters, right-angle viewfinder, and stereoscopic and panoramic heads.

Right: Press permit for using a hand camera at the World's Columbian Exposition, 1893. Amateur photographers were required to have a permit to photograph the exposition. The intent was to discourage professional photographers from competing with the concessions.

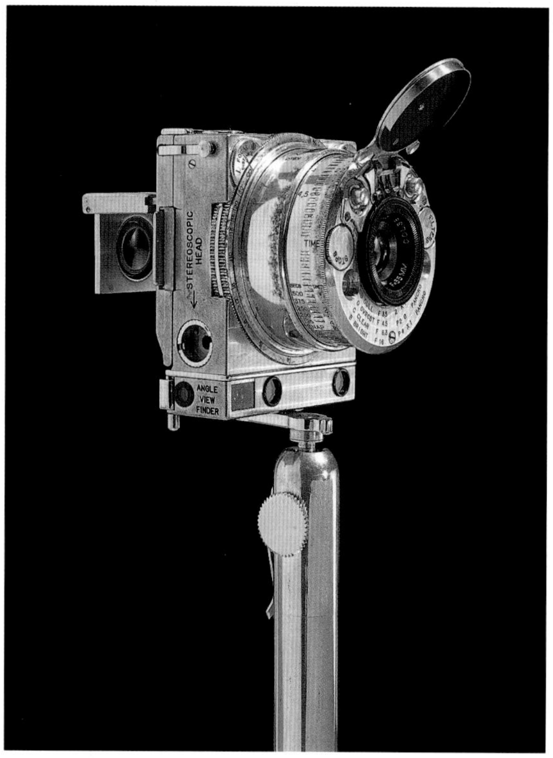

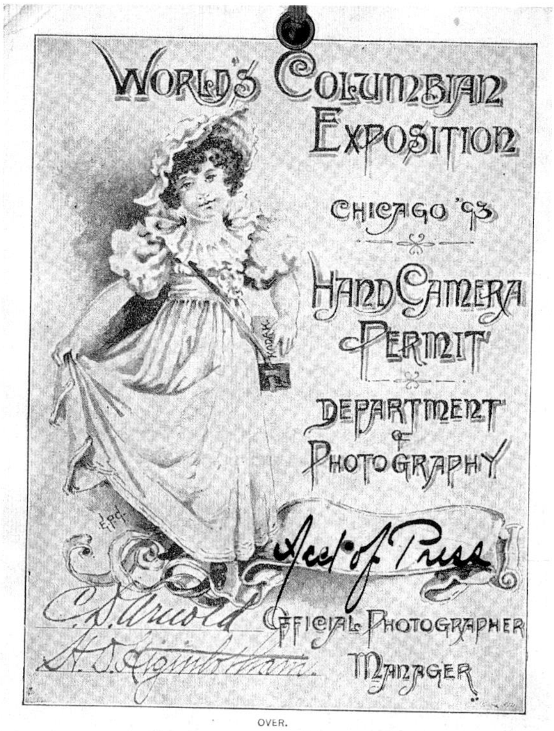

Britain by the early 1890s, giving way to the term "hand cameras," it persisted for some years in France. In that country, from the 1890s up to the 1920s, the term "détective" was used generically to refer to a type of boxlike magazine camera that held a series of plates which were changed mechanically.

While most of the cameras used in the wet-plate/calotype period were of the sliding-box or box-in-box type, from the early 1850s on, cameras equipped with bellows became increasingly common. The bellows made cameras lighter and more compact for carrying, and by the early 1880s the use of bellows cameras, whether handheld or tripod-mounted, was growing in both Europe and the U.S. Handheld varieties fell into one of two groups. The first was cameras whose fronts were hinged at the bottom, the so-called drop-bed cameras. When the front panel folded down, the front standard, which held the lens and shutter, slid forward onto the panel along a track. To focus, most of these cameras used a rack-and-pinion mechanism. The second group of handheld bellows cameras was the "strut" cameras, whose fronts pulled straight outward and were held rigidly in place, attached to the camera body by struts mounted either at the four corners of the front panel, or along the top and bottom, operating in scissors fashion.

The use of dry plates began to decline with the growing popularity of sheet and roll film. Sheet, or "cut," film became available in virtually all of the same sizes as dry plates, and while early versions could not compete with the dry plate's unfailing flatness, in time the advantages of sheet film—its lesser weight and lesser fragility—brought photographers to shift their preference.

At the same time that amateurs were switching to roll film, the production of folding cameras for plates or sheet film that were made in Europe in the 1930s and sold there and in America came to a halt with the outbreak of World War II. And while production of bellows cameras did not resume after the war, dry plates became available once again to meet the demand from owners of prewar cameras. This state of affairs lasted until the number of bellows cameras diminished to the point that it was no longer financially feasible for plate-makers to stay in business. Though dry plates are no longer made for the amateur and professional photography markets, they are still produced for some facets of scientific and technical photographic markets, where the flatness of the surface on which the emulsion is coated is of paramount importance.

PROFILE: *Magnesium Flash*

Magnesium is a silver-white metal—light in weight—that burns with a dazzling, strongly actinic light, discovered in 1808 by Humphrey Davy. After improvements in the refining process in the 1860s, magnesium became affordable. The first successful use of magnesium for photographic illumination was made in 1864 by Alfred Brothers. Later that same year, C. Piazzi Smyth used magnesium wire to illuminate a photograph of the interior of Egypt's Great Pyramid.

Adolf Miethe and Johannes Gaedicke significantly improved magnesium flash powders around 1887 by mixing magnesium, potassium chlorate, and antimony sulfide for a more stable compound. Highly volatile, magnesium was very dangerous. In a two-year period during the 1880s, a total of five people in Philadelphia died from explosions that occurred during the manufacture of magnesium flash powder.

Magnesium flash devices fall roughly into two categories: those that used ribbon or wire and those that used powders. Magnesium ribbon was relatively slow-burning, and could be held flat within flash devices, with one end sticking out through a small opening. The Kodak Magnesium Ribbon Holders, Boots Flasher, and the Pistol Flashmeter were examples of these ribbon-type devices.

Devices that used magnesium flash powder usually had some form of triggering mechanism, such as a cord-activated flint and striker. The Agfa Flash Lamp of 1909 had a covered pan and a key-wound flint wheel. When triggered, the pan opened and the revolving wheel produced sparks. Another type of device was the flash pistol, which used a trigger mechanism to ignite the powder. A few magazine flash devices were made, such as Dr. Ranque's Revolver Photogénique of 1889. This flash stored magnesium powder in a reservoir adjacent to a discharge tube, which was forced in increments past an alcohol lamp, where it ignited.

Only after the invention of flash bulbs, in 1925, and their commercial introduction, in 1930, did the use of magnesium-based flash devices begin to decline.

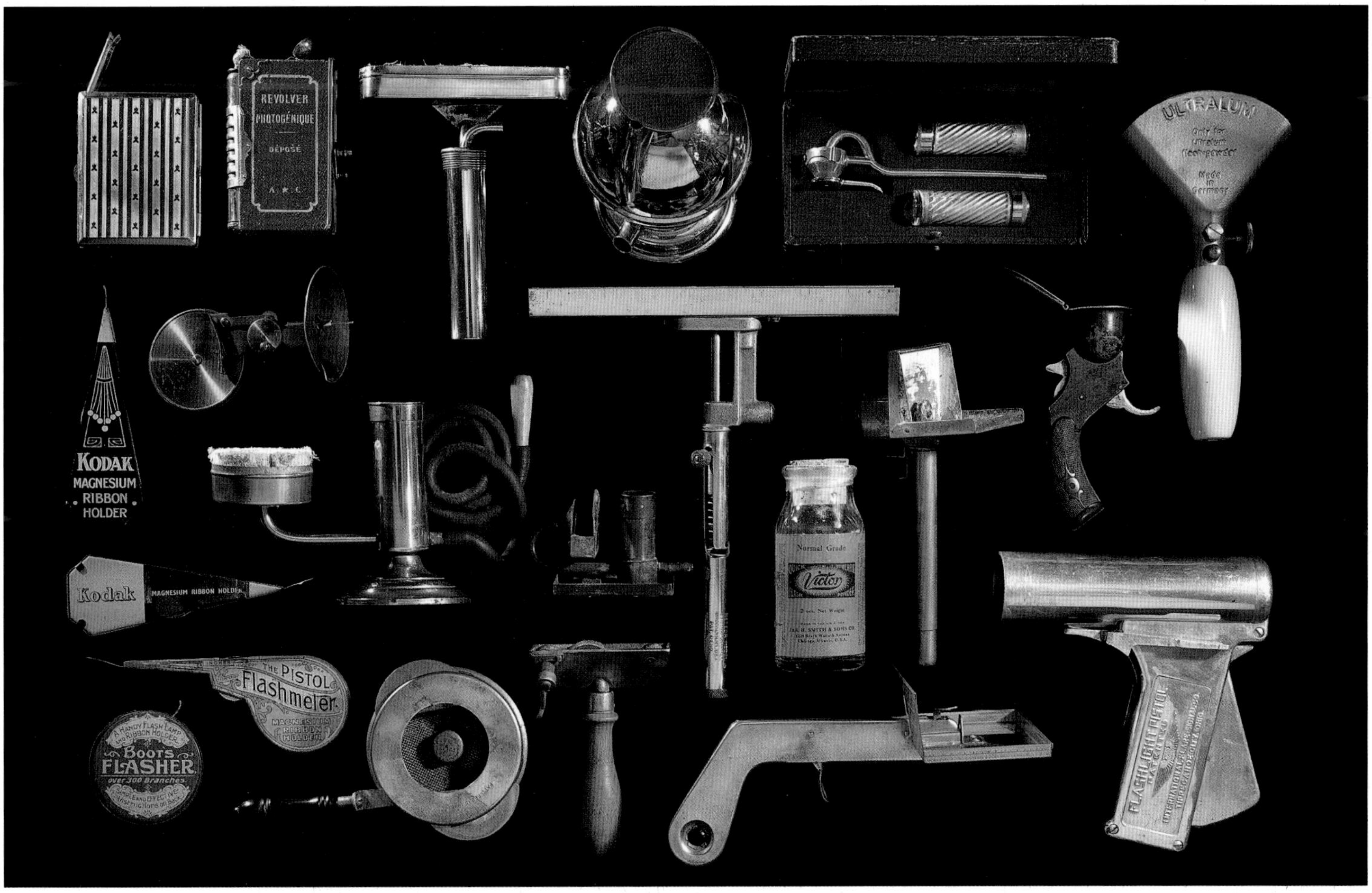

Magnesium flash devices. Including holders for magnesium ribbon, lower left corner (Kodak Magnesium Flash Holder, ca. 1923, left side, second down); flash pistols, lower right corner (Chelsea Flash Light Pistol, center row, second from right); and magazine flash devices, upper left corner (Revolver Photogénique, ca. 1889, top row, second from left).

FOCUS: *Jumelles*

One type of camera developed in the dry-plate era was called the *jumelle* (French for "opera glass"). The first camera to bear this name was the Jumelle de Nicour, invented by Octave Nicour and introduced in 1867. Though it looked more like an opera glass than any of its French successors, Nicour's camera did not become the archetype for future jumelles.

That honor belonged to Jules Carpentier's Photo-Jumelle, introduced in 1892. It should be noted, however, that while Carpentier's prototype did somewhat resemble an angular opera glass, in its ultimate form it bore little resemblance to one. The Photo-Jumelle, for 4.5-by-6 cm plates, had a rectangular-shaped body, with the forward section tapering toward the front. While the camera was equipped with two lenses, only one was used in exposing the plate; the other was for viewing the subject. The rear section of the camera held a series of dry plates in sheaths. A rod at one side was used to change the plate after each exposure.

Not long after the introduction of the Photo-Jumelle, other cameras of the same general type, also called jumelles but from other manufacturers, appeared on the market. Although stereo jumelles were produced, most subsequent cameras had a single lens in front, with viewfinders mounted on the camera's exterior. The jumelle was an almost exclusively French camera; less than a half-dozen models were produced in other countries. Cameras of the jumelle style were made in France until around 1930.

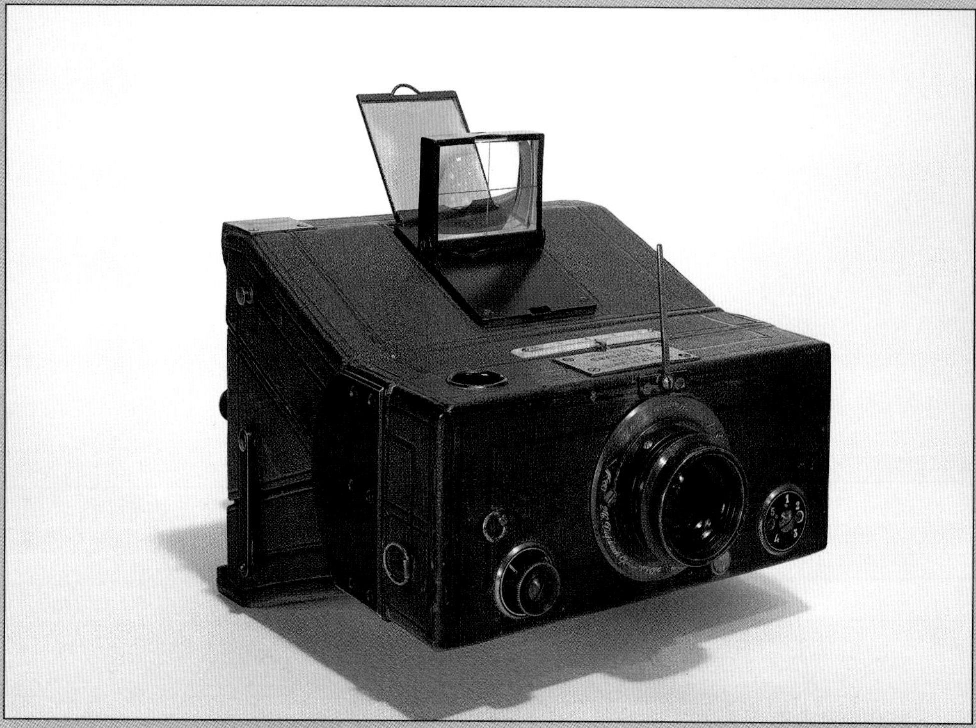

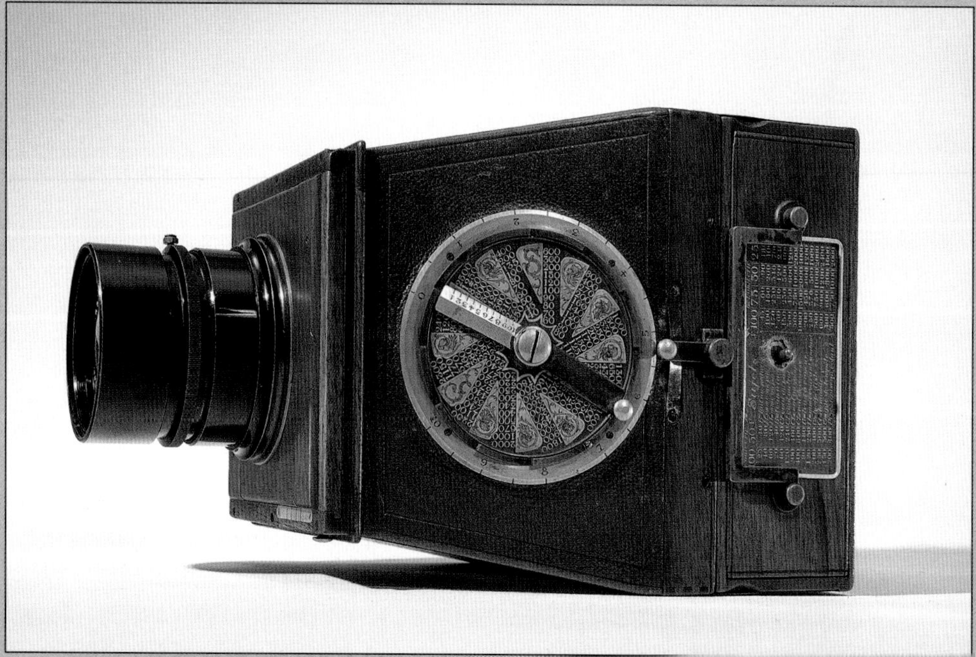

Liévrard Jumelle Pliant, A. Duploich, ca. 1903, for 9 x 12 cm dry plates. Unusual in its collapsible construction. When open it assumes the characteristic jumelle shape.

Left: Sigriste Camera, Guido Sigriste, ca. 1900, for twelve 9 x 12 cm exposures on dry plates. Among jumelle cameras, the Sigriste was noted for its unique shutter offering a great range of speeds.

Opposite: Photo-Binocular of Octave Nicour (Jumelle de Nicour), Geymet & Alker, ca. 1867, for 4 x 4 cm collodion dry plates. One side was for viewing, the other for exposures. Loaded from a fifty-plate drumlike magazine, the camera was designed to be used on a walking-stick tripod, as exposures were long.

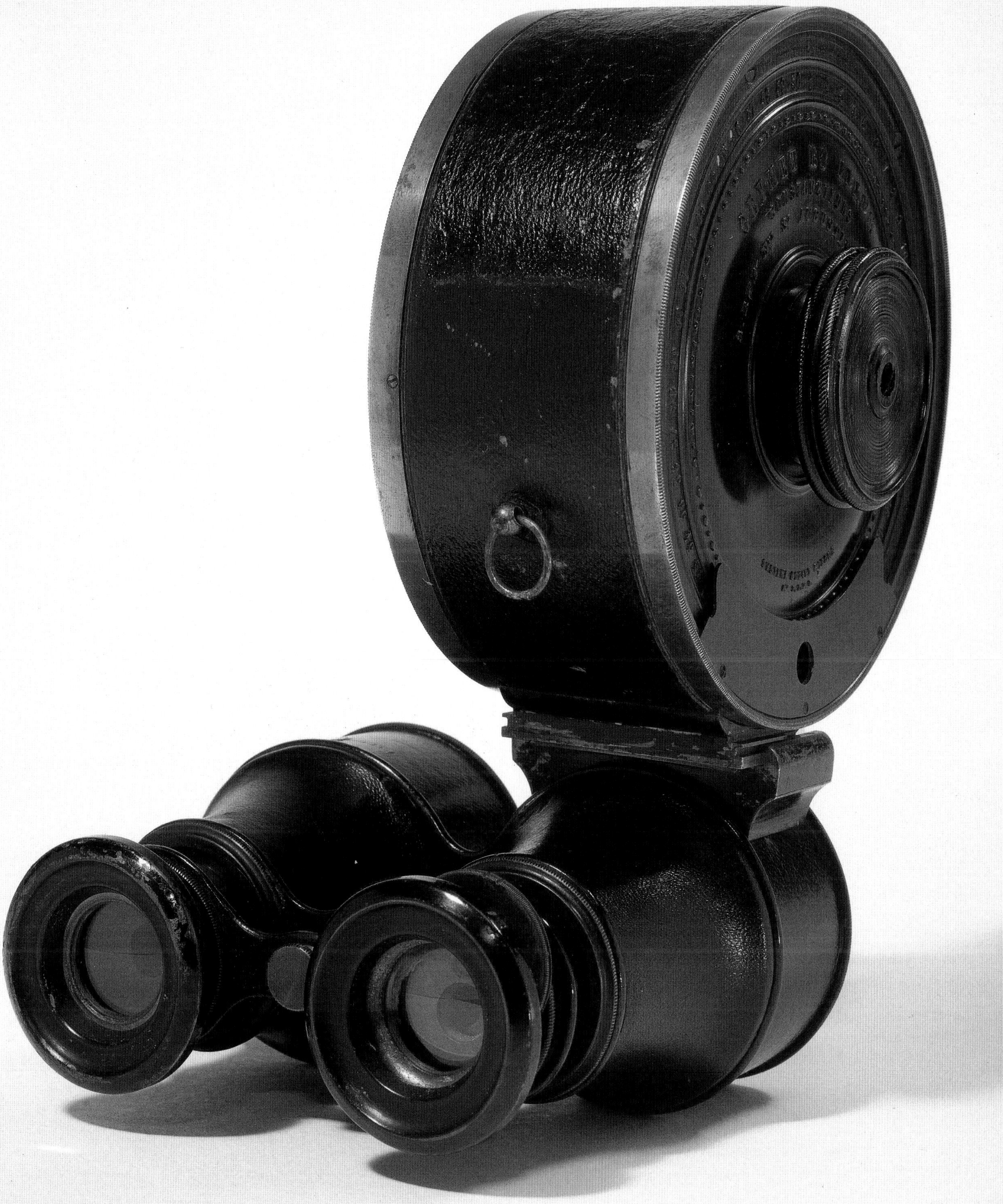

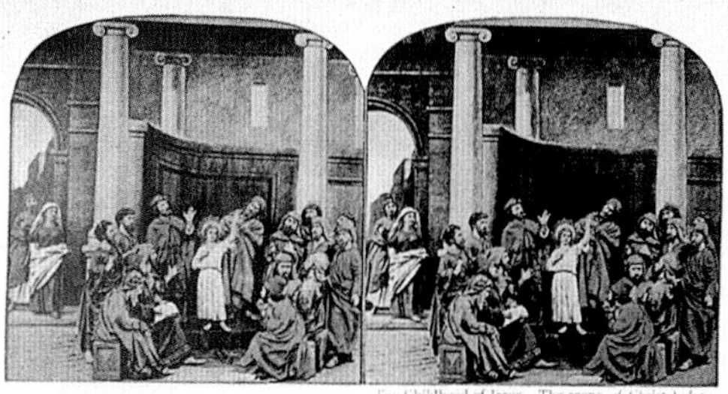

The Childhood of Jesus. The scene of Christ before the doctors in the Temple.

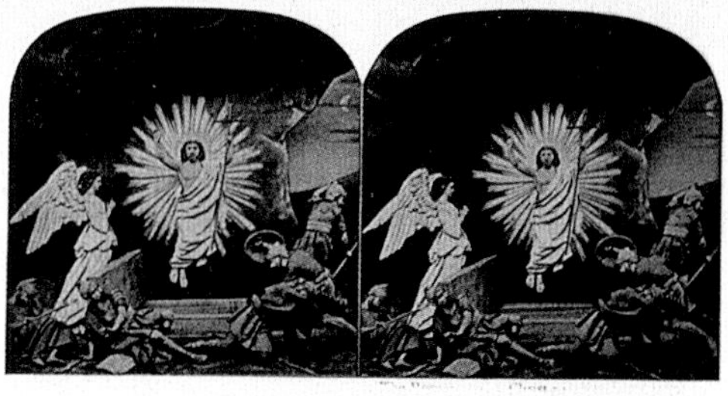

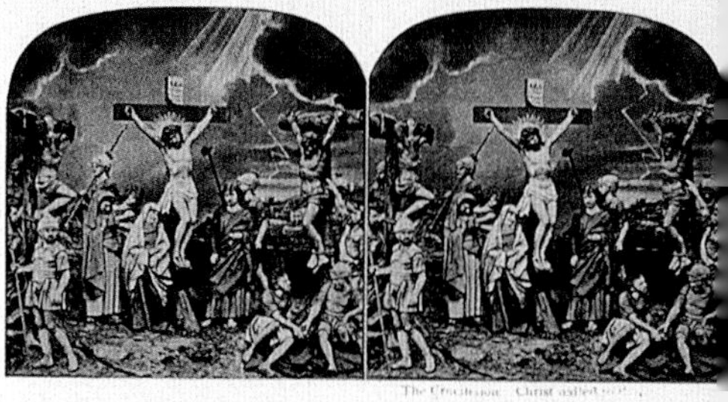

The Crucifixion. Christ nailed to the

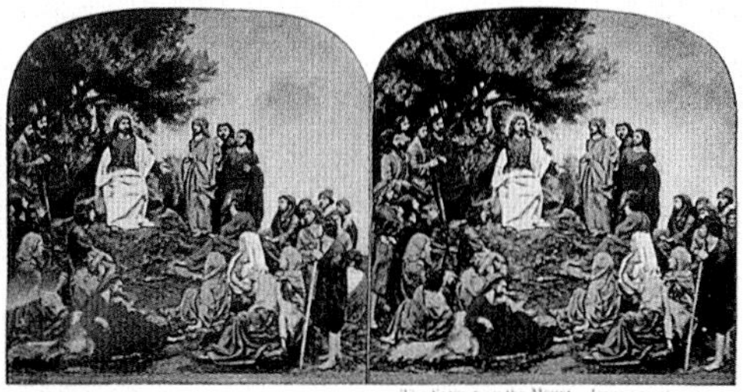

The Sermon on the Mount. Jesus preaching to the multitude.

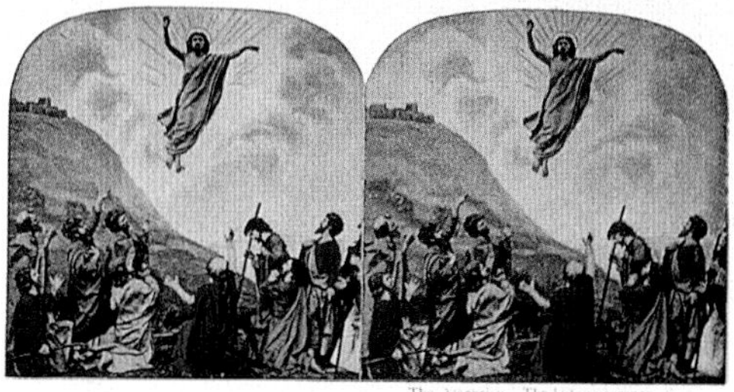

The Ascension. The last appearance of

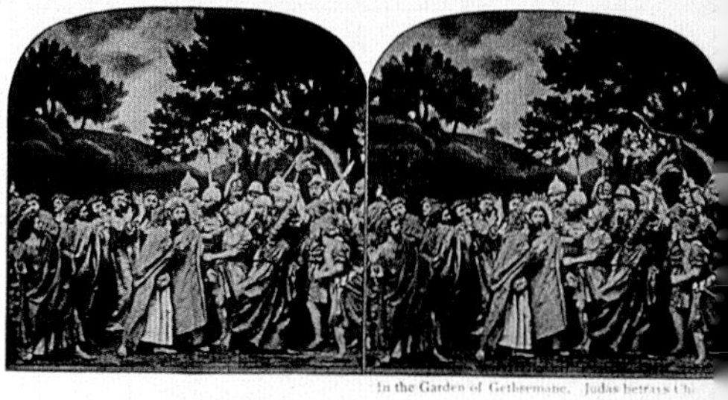

In the Garden of Gethsemane. Judas betrays Ch

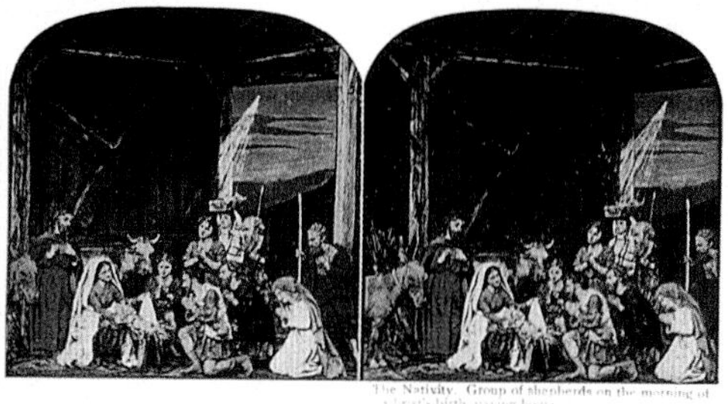

The Nativity. Group of shepherds on the morning of Christ's birth, paying hom

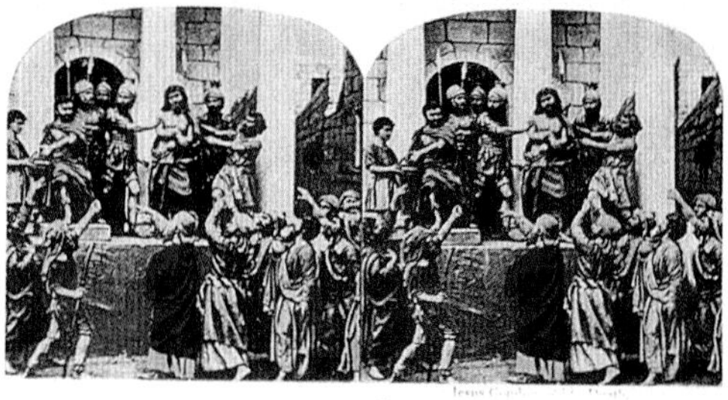

Jesus Co

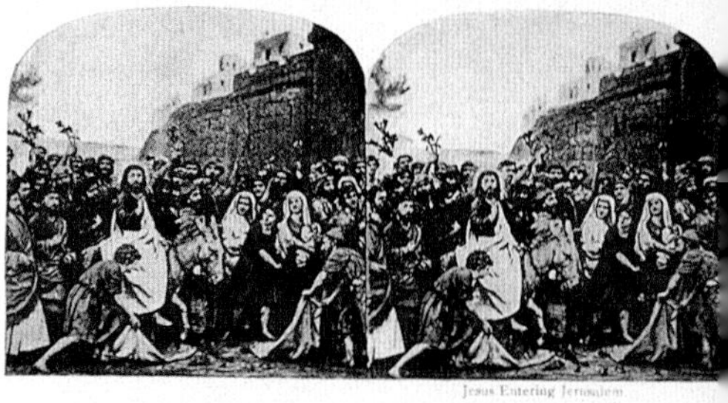

Jesus Entering Jerusalem

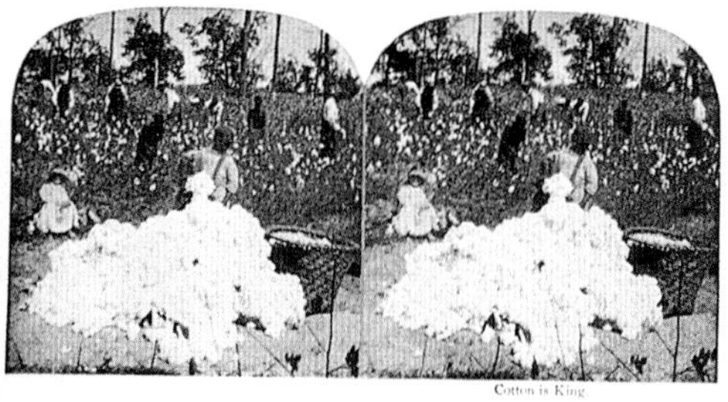

Cotton is King

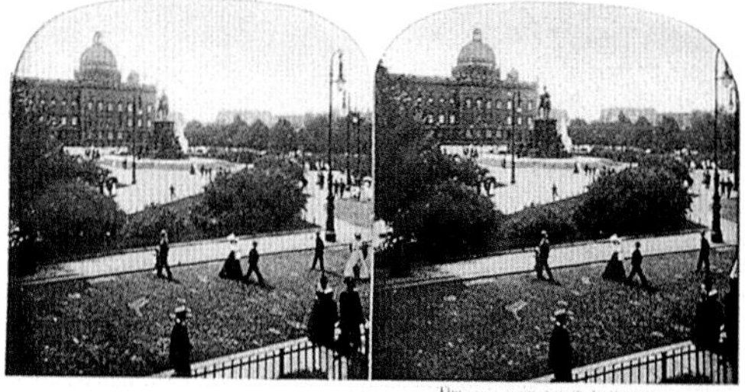

The … Berlin, Germany

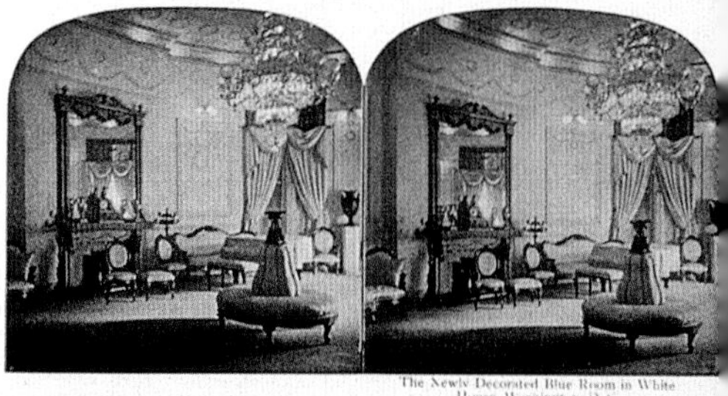

The Newly Decorated Blue Room in White House, Washington, D.C.

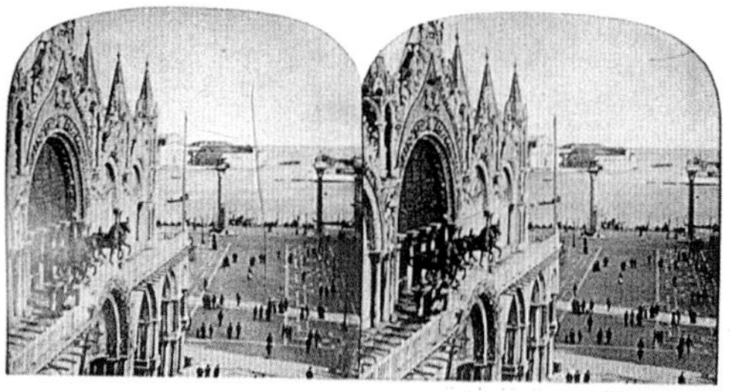

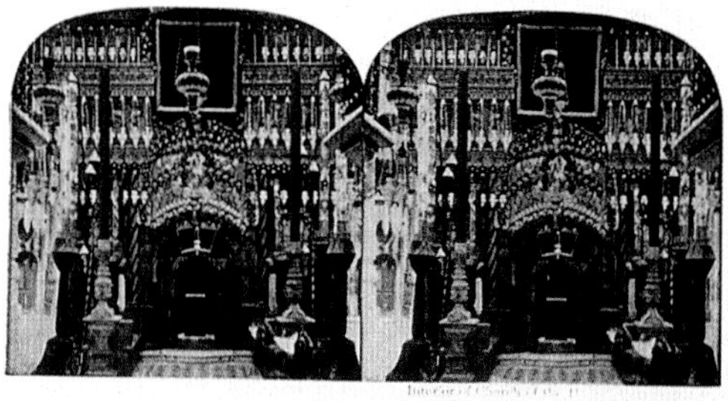

Interior of Church of the …

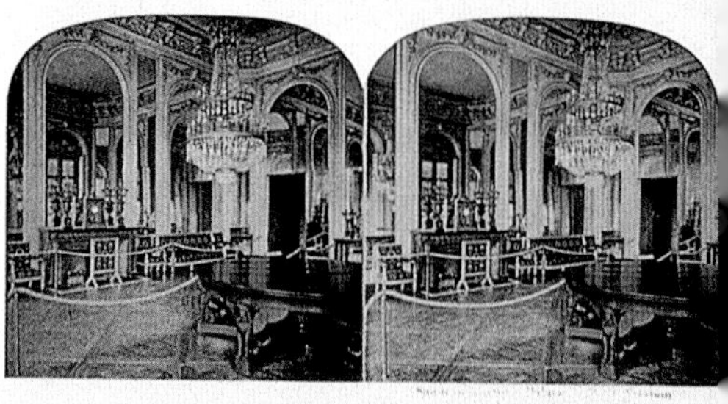

Stock… Palace …

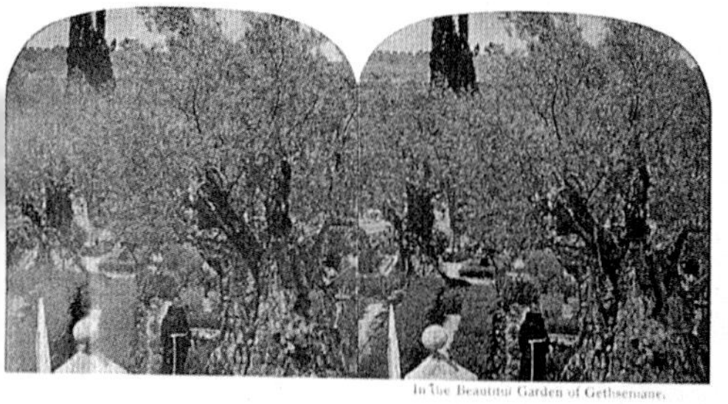

In the Beautiful Garden of Gethsemane.

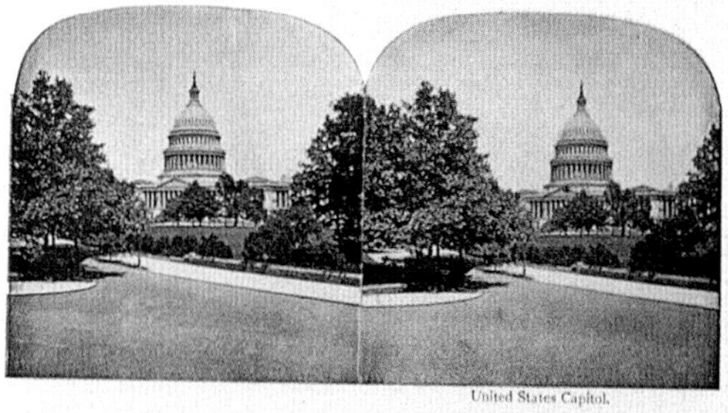

United States Capitol.

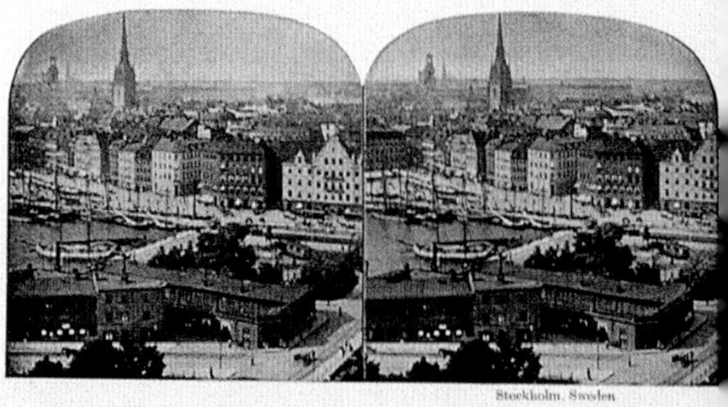

Stockholm, Sweden

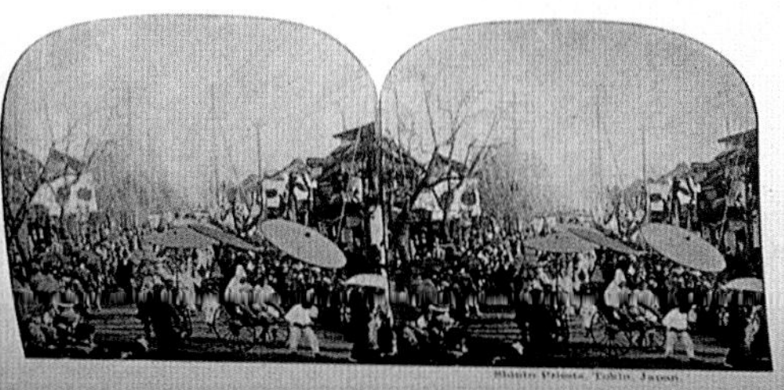

Shinto Priests, Tokio, Japan.

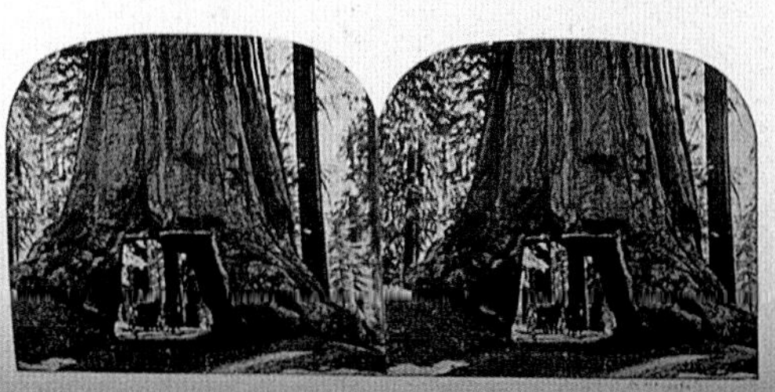

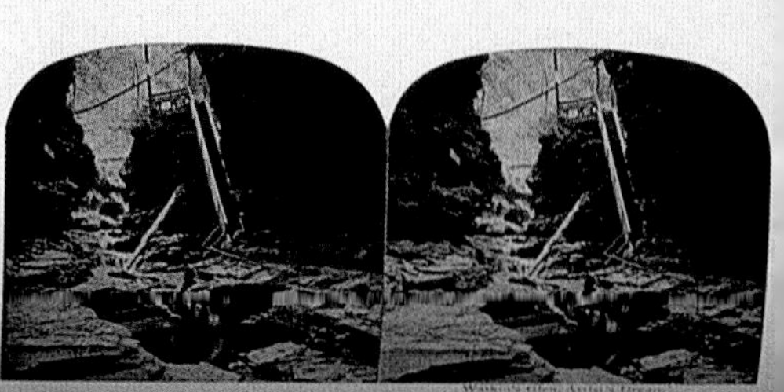

Watkin's Glen, …

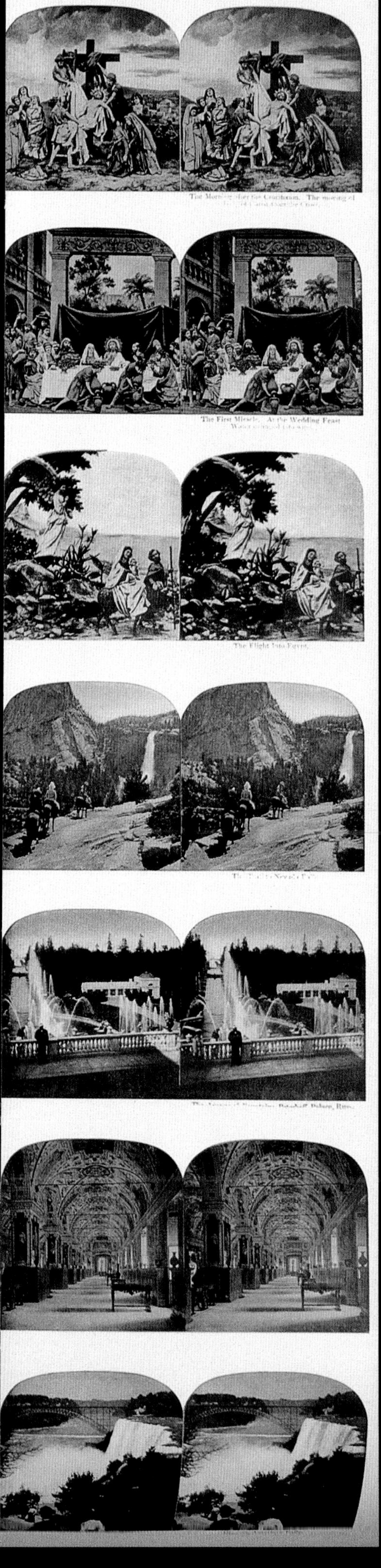

CHAPTER FIVE:

THE ACCESSIBLE IM

Uncut sheet of forty-eight Griffith & Griffith stereo views (twenty-eight shown), ca. 1910, color halftone reproductions, uncut and unmounted.

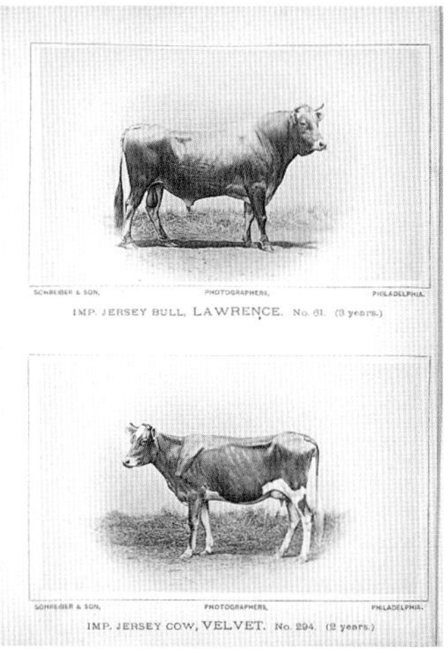

Schreiber & Son, Lawrence, no. 61, and Velvet, No. 294, purebred Jersey bull and cow, 1871, tipped-in albumen prints, from *Herd Register of the American Jersey Cattle Club*, George E. Waring, editor.

When the daguerreotype was introduced to society in 1839, it created quite a stir in scientific and artistic circles, as well as among the upper classes of society. For all the interest, though, the images produced were one-of-a-kind and, even when placed on exhibition, could be seen only by a limited audience. While calotypes offered the potential of multiple images from each paper negative, production of them was controlled by licensing, which also limited the public's access to an image.

How then could the images captured by these processes be seen by greater numbers of people? The answer laid in various forms of mechanical reproduction. Alfred Donné, a Frenchman, used the then-recently discovered electrotype process to make daguerreotype plates into printing plates; N. P. Lerebours's *Excursions Daguerriennes* (1840–1844) contained illustrations printed from copper plate engravings based on careful tracings of daguerreotypes. To the unpeopled originals—remember that exposures then were very slow—the engraver often added people and traffic, to give a greater sense of realism. Throughout the daguerreian era and into the time of wet collodion, many of the illustrations in mass-market publications were printed from engravings or woodcuts based on daguerreotypes and, later, ambrotypes. Among the American journals that carried illustrations of this sort were *Illustrated News* and Frank Leslie's *Illustrated Newspaper*.

Still, these illustrations, even those of the highest quality and accuracy, could not approach the realism and detail of actual photographs. Beginning in the 1850s, a hierarchical relationship developed between mechanically reproduced photographic images and actual photographs. While makers of limited-run publications could afford the luxury of using actual photographic prints "tipped in" (i.e. pasted) to their pages, mass-market publications continued to employ the older, mechanical methods of reproduction. In any case, even the smaller-run publications that used photographic prints generally used very few of them, sometimes only for the frontispiece. The photographically illustrated book, with actual, tipped-in photographs, comprised the high end of Victorian publishing, particularly in the period 1860–1890.

The first publication to utilize tipped-in photographs was William Henry Fox Talbot's six-part illustrated book, *The Pencil of Nature*. Each volume contained from three to seven calotypes. While Part I of *The Pencil of Nature* was issued in June 1844, the final volume did not appear until April 1846. At that time, a British publication called

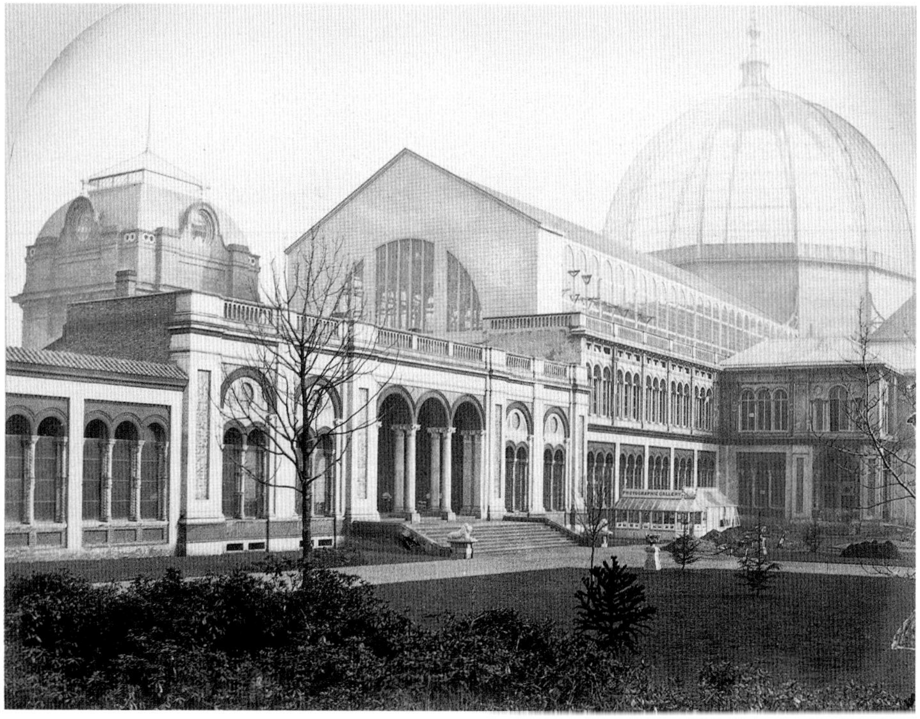

Left: Anonymous, Royal Horticultural Society's exhibition hall, ca. 1862, tipped-in albumen print, from *The Book of the Royal Horticultural Hall*, Bradbury & Evans, 1862.

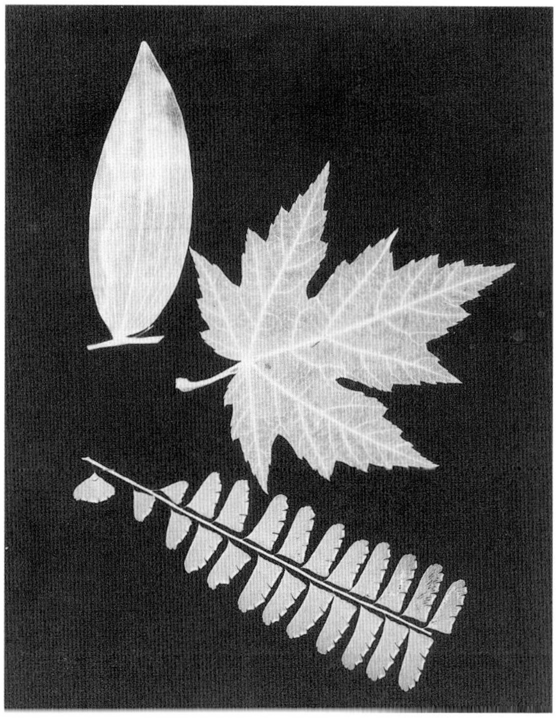

Right: Charles F. Himes, leaf print, ca. 1868, tipped-in albumen print, from *Leaf Prints: or, Glimpses at Photography*, Charles F. Himes, 1868.

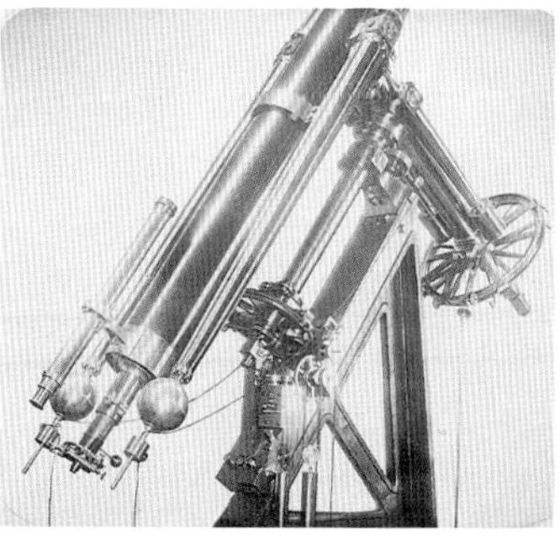

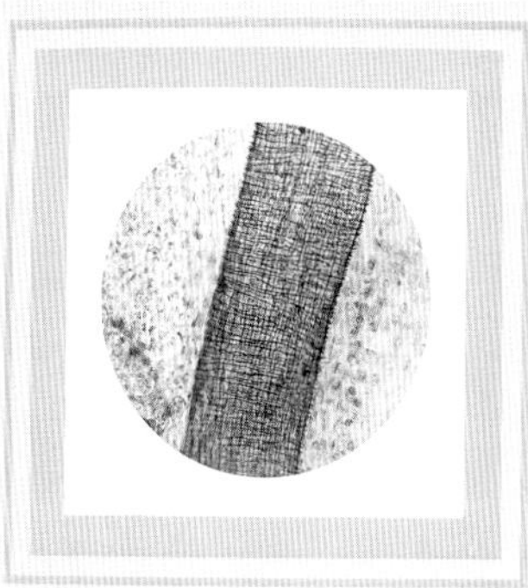

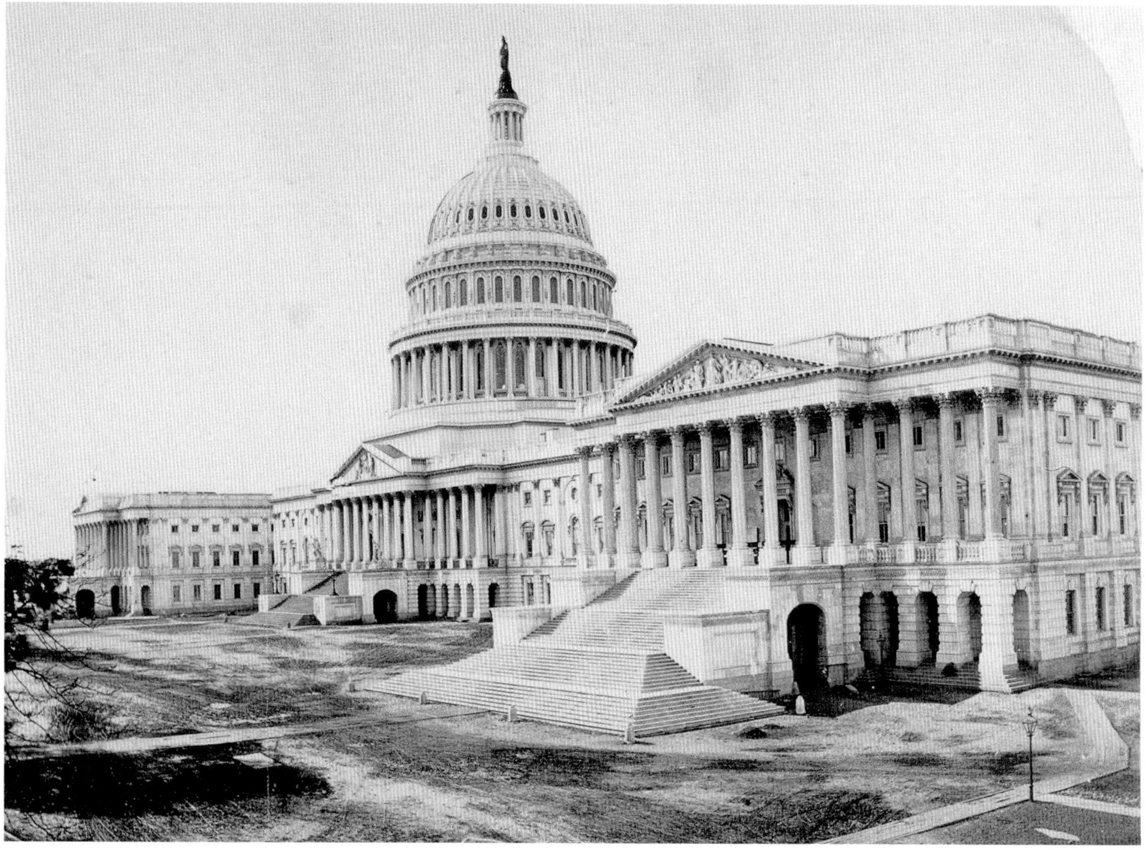

Clockwise from top: Anonymous, Telescope of the Moscow Observatory, ca. 1875, tipped-in albumen print, from *Annales de l'Observatoire de Moscou*, Dr. Th. Bredichin, 1875.

G. W. Wakely, United States Capitol Building, 1870, tipped-in albumen print, from *The Rotunda and Dome of the U.S. Capitol*, S. D. Wyeth, 1870.

Anonymous, Microphotograph of epithelium and muscle cells of a small artery from the mesentery of a frog, ca. 1871, tipped-in albumen print, 6 ¼" x 6 ¼", from *Photographing Histological Specimens by Sunlight; Report of the Surgeon General of the United States Army*, Assistant Surgeon J. J. Woodward, 1871.

The Athenaeum commented, "The labor consequent on the production of photographs is too great to render them generally useful for the purposes of illustration." In 1845, before the second part of *The Pencil of Nature* was completed, Fox Talbot published *Sun Pictures in Scotland*. This was a series of twenty-three prints, without text, based on the works of the popular Victorian writer Sir Walter Scott. *Sun Pictures in Scotland* was published by subscription, with Queen Victoria heading up the list of subscribers. Almost a decade elapsed before the first photographically illustrated book was published in America. That book was *Homes of American Statesmen*, which contained contributions from various writers. It was published by G. P. Putnam & Company, nominally in 1854, though it was already available commercially in December 1853, in time for the Christmas season. The book's frontispiece was a Whipple crystallotype of Hancock House in Boston.

Just as the content of nonfiction books of the mid-1800s varied considerably, so did the kinds of photographs included therein. A cattle register would depict various breeds of cattle, while the report of a fire department might show off a new piece of equipment. Scientific treatises covered a wide variety of areas. Illustrations related to microscopy and microphotography ranged from a man using a microscope to microphotographs of histological specimens, while books on astronomy showed telescopes and views of the moon (or at least photographs of drawings of the moon). Chemistry books might have shown arrangements of laboratory equipment. Medical books, of course, offered a broad range of illustrations commensurate with the many subdivisions of medicine. Photographic illustrations varied from hand-colored images of lepers and amputees—before and after their operations—to forensic illustrations related to murder cases. The first photographic illustration in a medical book depicted two developmentally-disabled individuals. Nature books with tipped-in photographs covered everything from birds of prey to contact prints of leaves.

Tipped-in photographs of buildings and architecture were found in books on subjects as diverse as horticultural societies and the court system, and in straightforward single-topic books, such as *The Rotunda and Dome of the U.S. Capitol*. Anthropological, ethnological, and archeological books bore

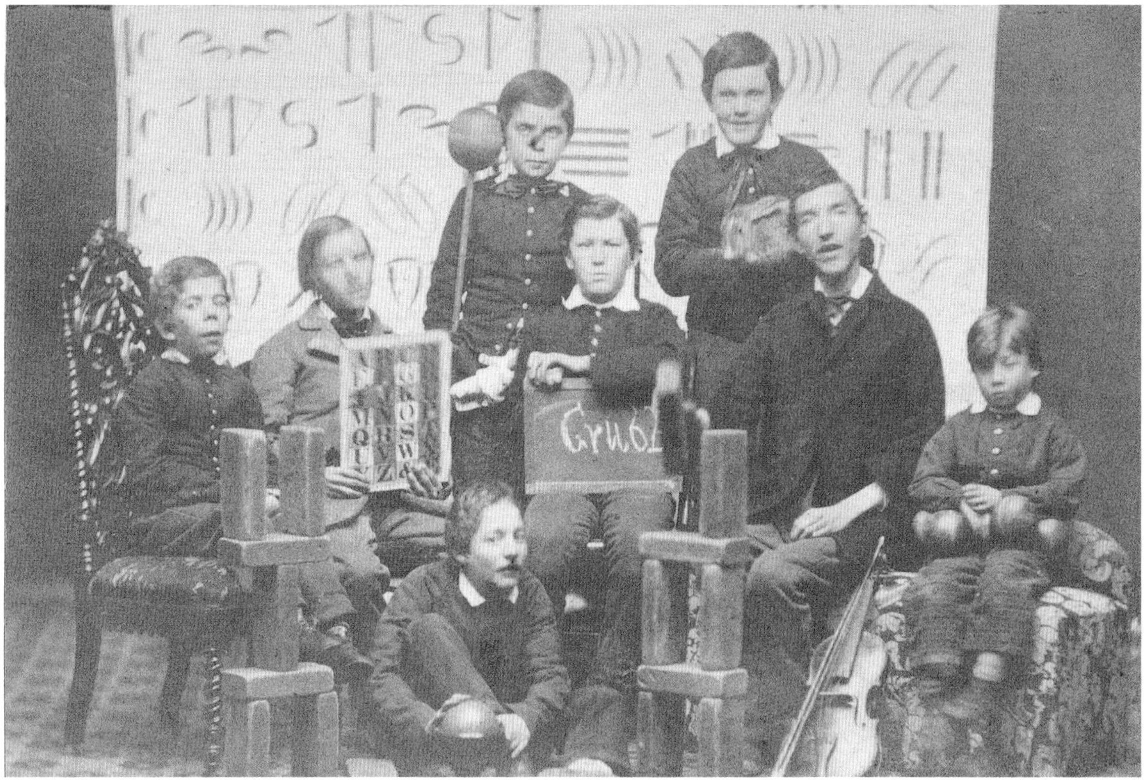

Anonymous, Eight developmentally-disabled male children, ca. 1858, tipped-in salt print, from *The Mind Unveiled; or, A Brief History of Twenty-Two Imbecile Children*, Isaac Newton Kerlin, M.D., 1858. The first American work on psychiatry and the first photographically illustrated medical book in America.

Below: Anonymous, Eleanor Bishop at the casket of her son, Sir Washington Irving Bishop, composite photo, ca. 1889, tipped-in albumen print, from *Human Vivisection of Sir Washington Irving Bishop*, Eleanor Fletcher Bishop, 1889. Presumed to be dead after falling into a trance, Bishop revived during the autopsy, only to perish as a result of the procedure.

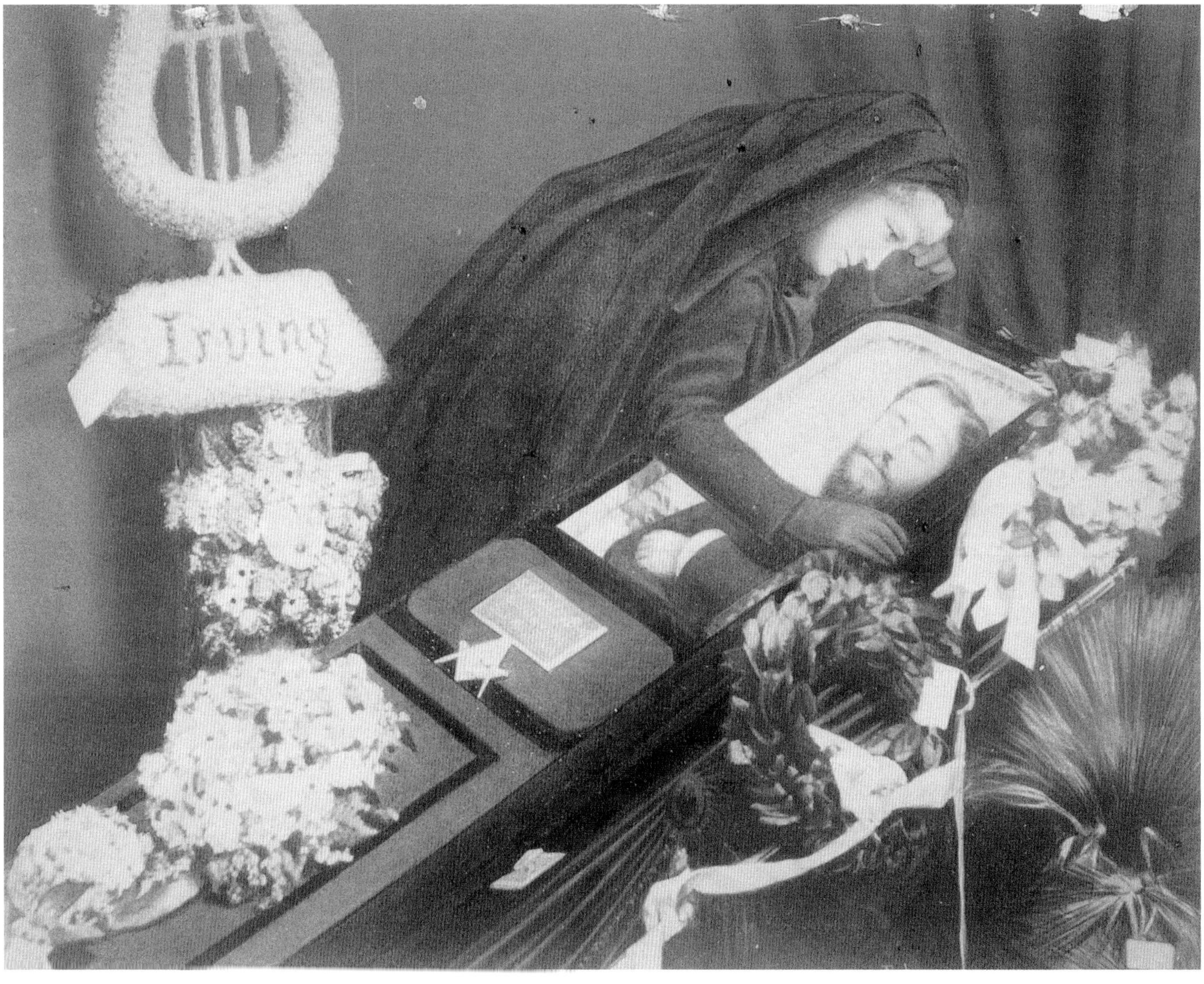

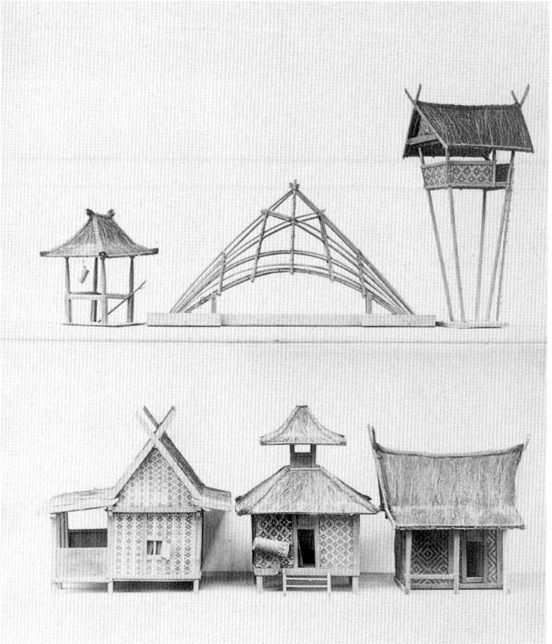

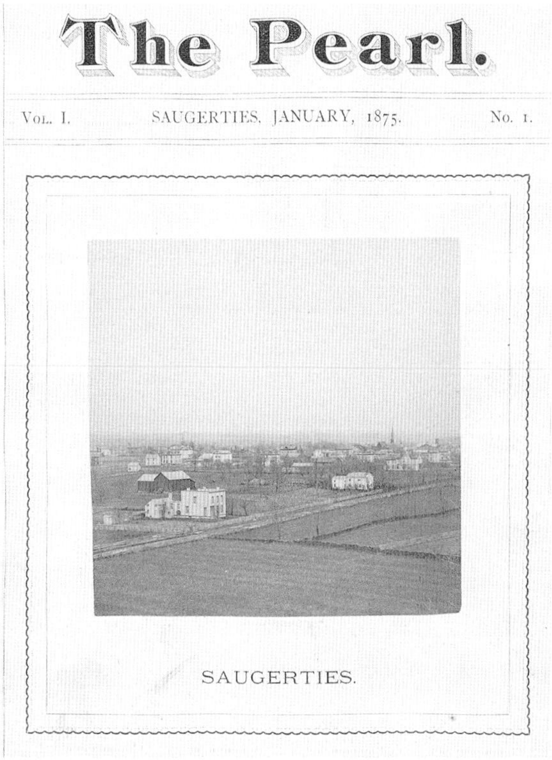

The Pearl.

Vol. I. SAUGERTIES, JANUARY, 1875. No. 1.

SAUGERTIES.

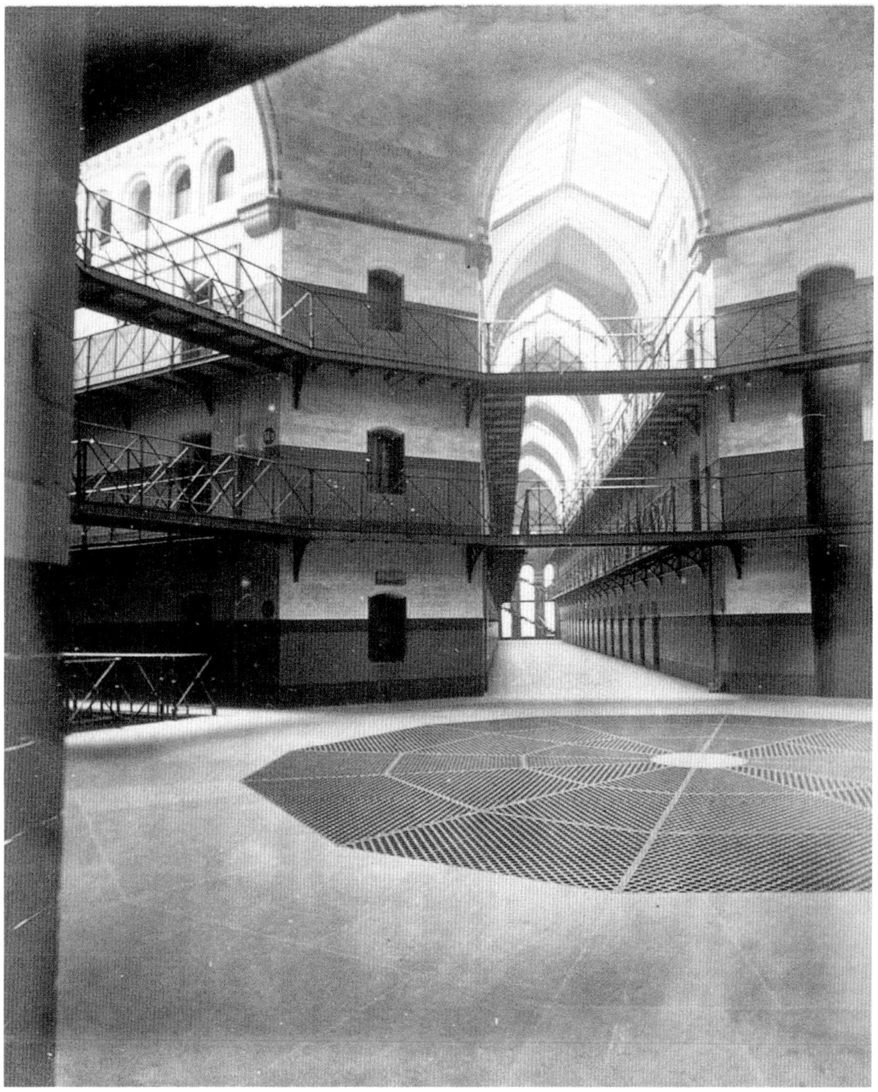

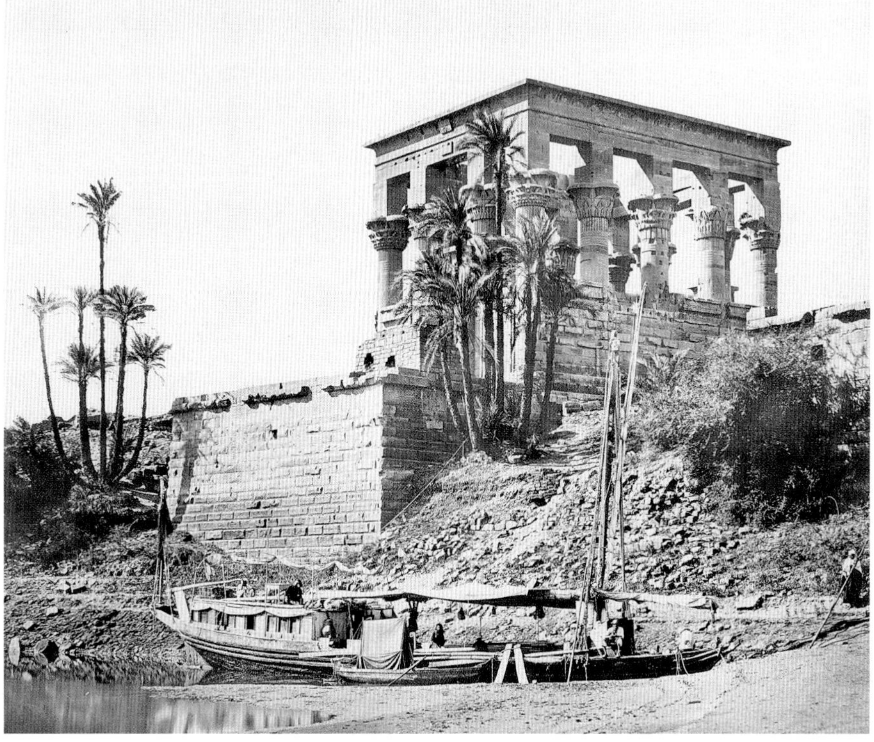

Clockwise from top left: Anonymous, Artifacts from Java, ca. 1866, tipped-in albumen print, from *Reise der Österreichischen Fregatte Novara um die Erde*, Anthropologischer Theil, Dr. A. Weisbach, 1867.

Anonymous, Central Hall, showing corridors, Lancaster County Gaol, ca. 1870, tipped-in albumen print, 3" x 4", from *A Description of the Hundred of Salford Assize Courts of the County of Lancaster*, E. Chadwick, 1870.

Francis Frith, Egyptian temple, ca. 1858, tipped-in albumen print, 19" x 14 3/4", from *Egypt: Sinai and Jerusalem*, with descriptions by Mrs. Poole and Reginald Stuart Poole, 1860.

Anonymous, View of Saugerties, New York, 1875, tipped-in albumen print, from *The Pearl*, vol. 1, no. 1, January 1875, Leon Barritt and Edward Jernegan.

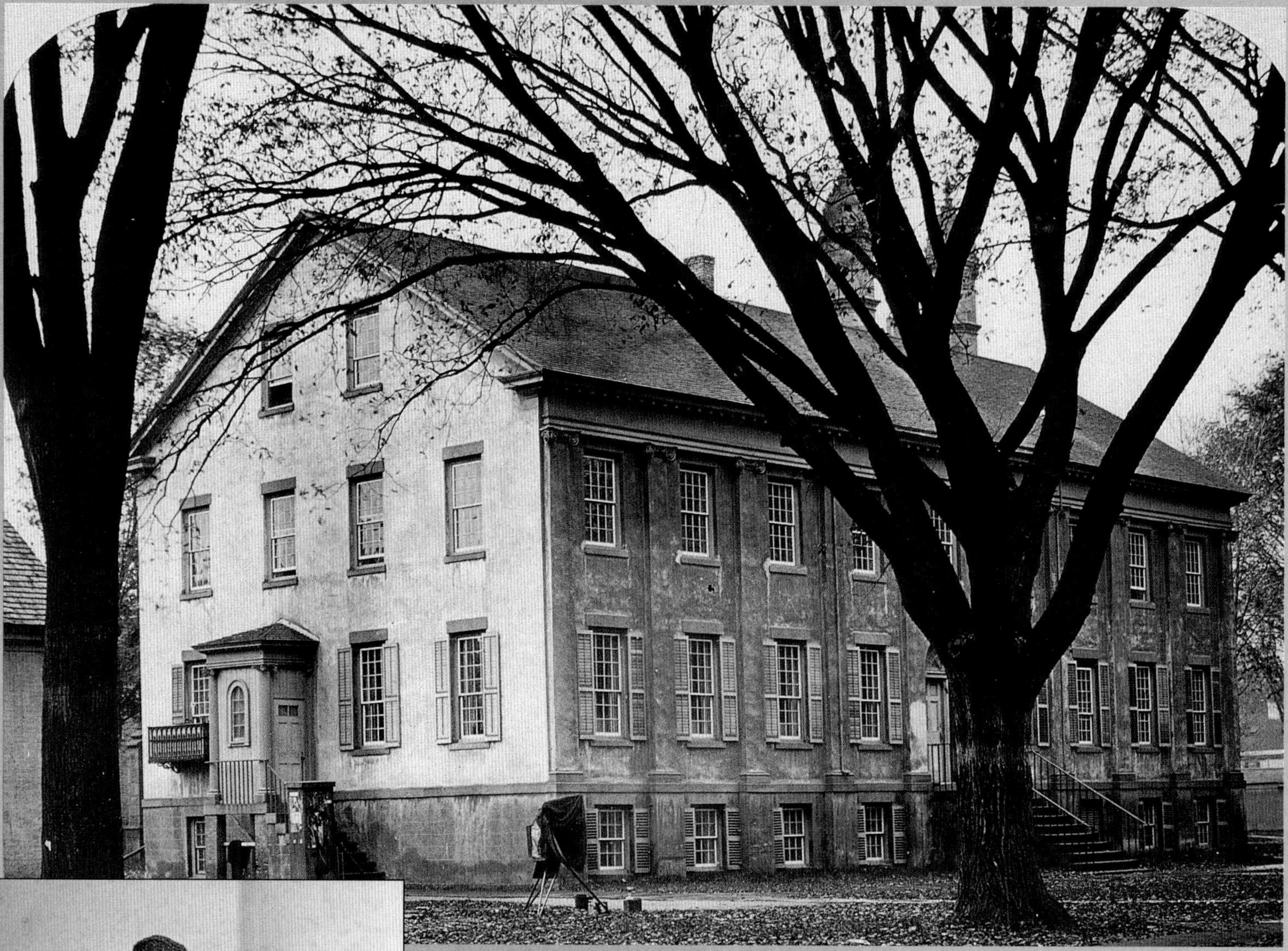

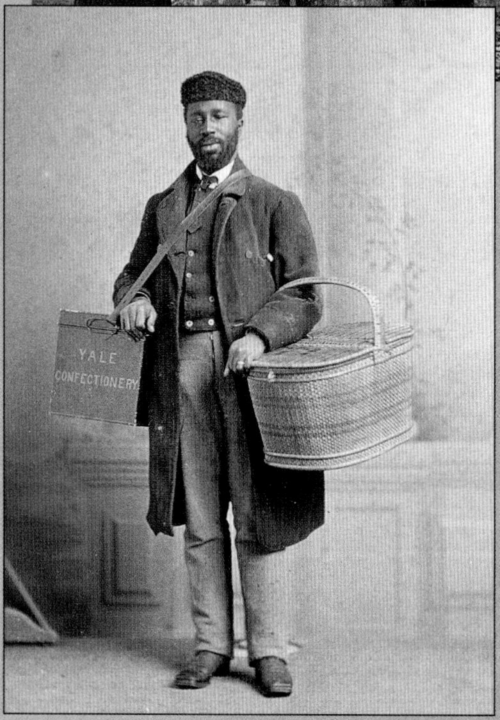

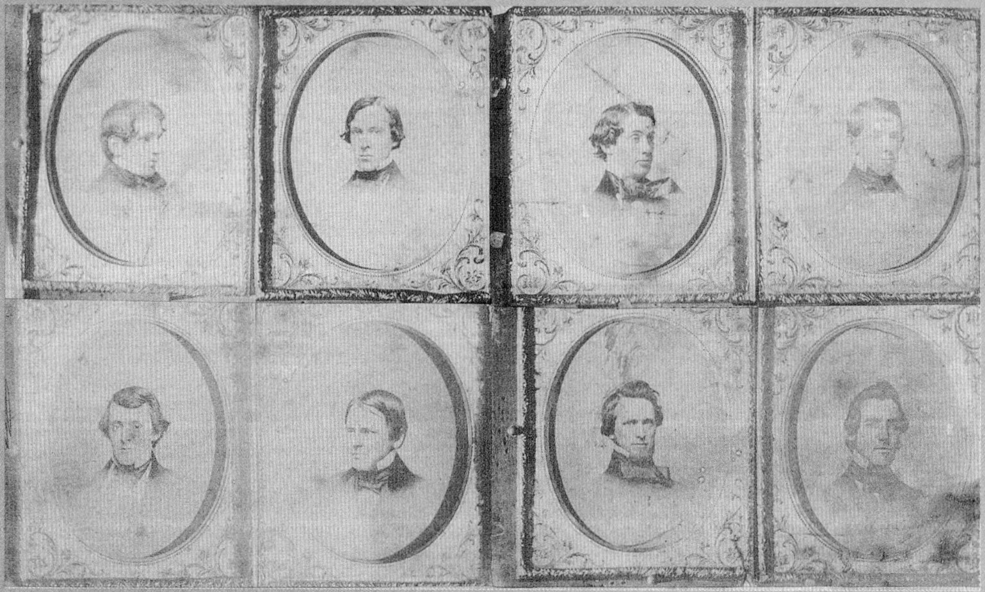

Clockwise from top: Anonymous, Campus building, Yale College, 1869, tipped-in albumen print, in Yale College class of 1869 album. Photographer's dark tent visible in center; Anonymous, Daguerreotypes of students of Harvard College's class of 1852, 1852, tipped-in albumenized salt prints, each daguerreotype copy 2" x 2". The 9 3/4" x 11 1/2" album contains eighty-six copies of daguerreotypes, mounted on eleven pages; Anonymous, African American vendor of "Yale Confectionery," 1869, tipped-in albumen print, 3 3/4" x 5 1/2", in Yale College class of 1869 album.

FOCUS: *The College Album*

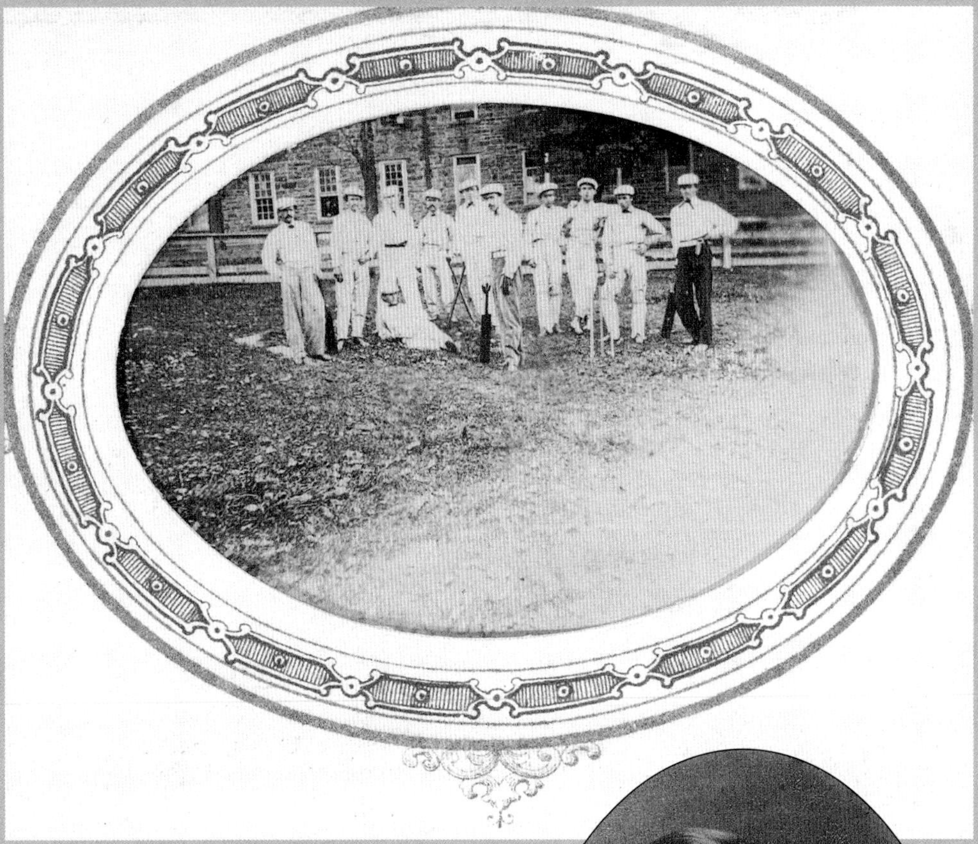

What twentieth-century American high school or college graduate isn't accustomed to seeing, if not owning, an album commemorating their graduating class? Portraits of classmates, sometimes autographed, are the highlight of these albums, though sports teams, school activities, and sometimes campus or school scenes are frequently pictured as well.

College graduating classes were first pictured photographically by means of daguerreotypes. In most cases, there was only one set of them, so they were not distributed to members of the graduating class. Sometimes, however, copy daguerreotypes were made of the individual daguerreotypes grouped together. By 1852 daguerreotypes of seniors at Harvard were being copied to albumenized salt prints, producing a class album. With the introduction of the wet-collodion process, copying daguerreotypes was no longer necessary. Albumen prints could be made directly from the glass plates, which yielded better prints than calotypes. This also meant it was possible to produce class albums in greater, though still relatively limited, quantities. In any case, classes in colleges and universities were not particularly large in those days, so the number of prints required was not too great. Sometimes students would even assemble their own albums, with individual photographs of their classmates and some of their written comments.

Given the ease of use and capabilities of the new wet-plate photography process, the producers of college class albums began to include photos of subjects beyond the standard portraits of the graduating class. In addition to faculty portraits, they presented photographs of sports teams, campus buildings, students' rooms, and campus employees, a trend that has continued to the present day.

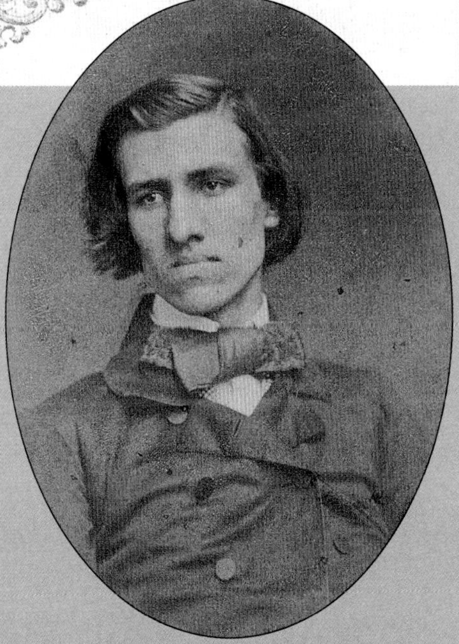

Top: Anonymous, Cricket group, the College of New Jersey, Princeton, 1866, tipped-in albumen print, class of 1866 album. The College of New Jersey later became Princeton University. **Bottom:** Anonymous, Portrait of T. Gilchrist, ca. 1854, tipped-in albumenized salt print, 3 ½" oval, in scrapbook of Princeton College classes of 1853–1856, assembled by Edward Spencer, '55.

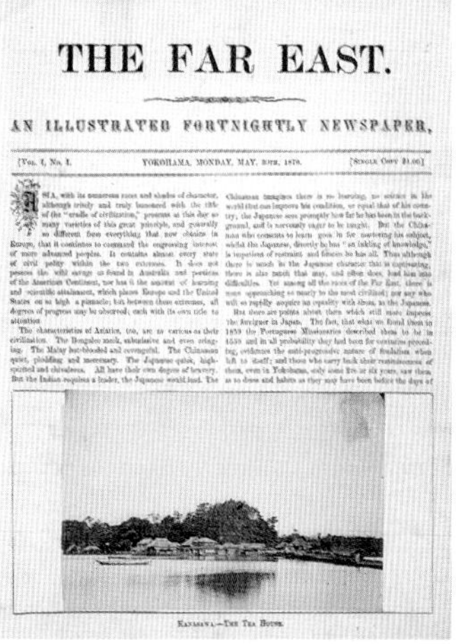

THE FAR EAST.

AN ILLUSTRATED FORTNIGHTLY NEWSPAPER.

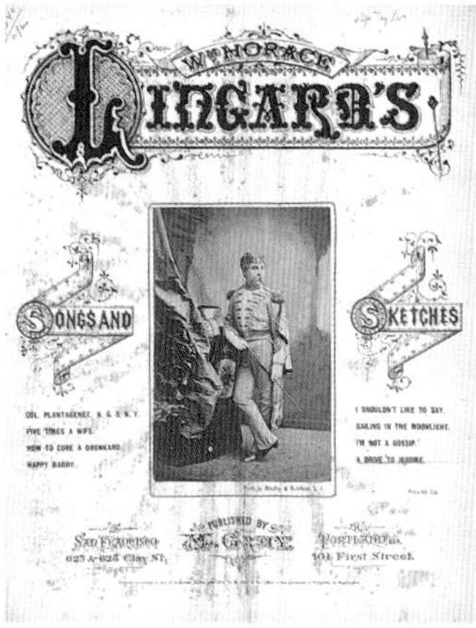

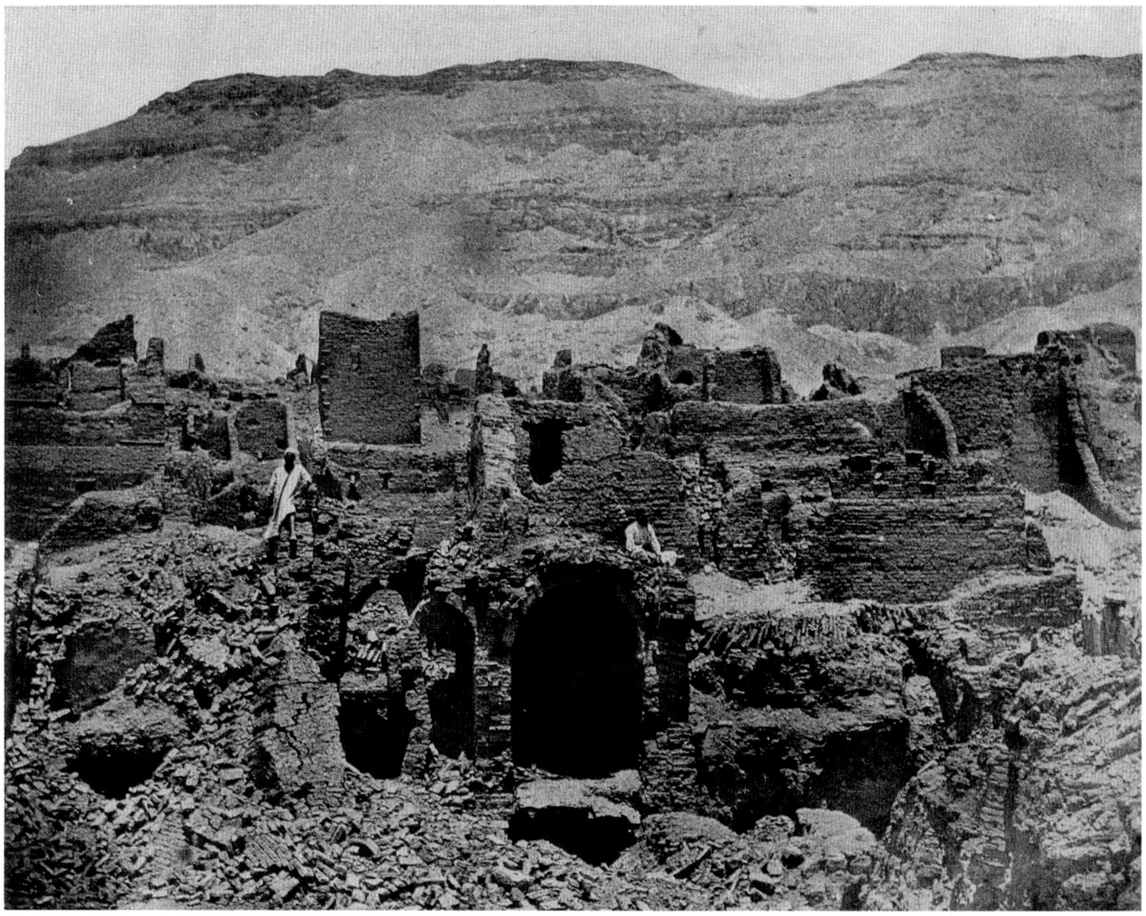

Clockwise from top: Anonymous, The Tea House at Kanasawa, 1870, tipped-in albumen print, from *The Far East,* vol. 1, no. 1, May 1870, J. R. Black, editor.

Maxime Du Camp, *Ruines de la Ville de Papa*, Médinet-Habou, Thèbes, ca. 1852, tipped-in salt print, 6 1/2" x 8 1/2", from *Egypte, Nubie, Palestineet Syrie,* Maxime Du Camp, 1852.

Bradley & Rulofson, Portrait of William Horace Lingard, 1874, tipped-in albumen print, on cover of *A Drive to Jerome*, sheet music by W. H. Lingard.

images of artifacts from various societies, of peoples from distant parts of the world, and of the ruins of ancient civilizations. Travel volumes covered all parts of the world, from the American West to Africa, and from South America to Asia. Many of the matted and framed albumen prints of foreign locations found individually in current photographic collections and exhibitions were formerly bound in large books. One of the more unusual—and bizarre—photo-illustrated books was the *Human Vivisection of Sir Washington Irving Bishop*. That book, written by Bishop's mother, described how her son fell into a trance and, being presumed dead, had an autopsy performed on him while he was—at least for a few moments—alive. One of the book's three tipped-in photographs was a composite showing the mother leaning over her son's open casket.

The purpose of a dealer's or manufacturer's catalog is to sell products, and photographic illustrations are perfect for this use. Prior to the advent of the halftone, tipped-in photographic prints were the best available option. As this manner of illustration was expensive, the use of these prints was usually reserved for relatively deluxe items. A number of catalogs for large—and high-priced—items were illustrated in this manner. The products touted ranged from lathes to locomotives.

Some small-circulation periodicals also bore albumen prints. An early example of these was *The Far East*, an illustrated fortnightly newspaper published in Yokohama, Japan. The cover of its premiere issue, dated May 30, 1870, had an albumen print of a tea house in Kanasawa. *The Pearl*, first published in January 1875 in Saugerties, New York, had mounted on its front page an albumen print of Saugerties. Other printed media that sometimes bore albumen prints were sheet music and compilations of songs. W. H. Lingard's *Songs and Sketches*, published in San Francisco in 1874, had a Bradley & Rulofson albumen portrait of William Lingard on its cover; Edith Louise Wagner's *Dimple Waltz*, written in the 1880s when she was seven years old, had on its front page an oval albumen print of the composer.

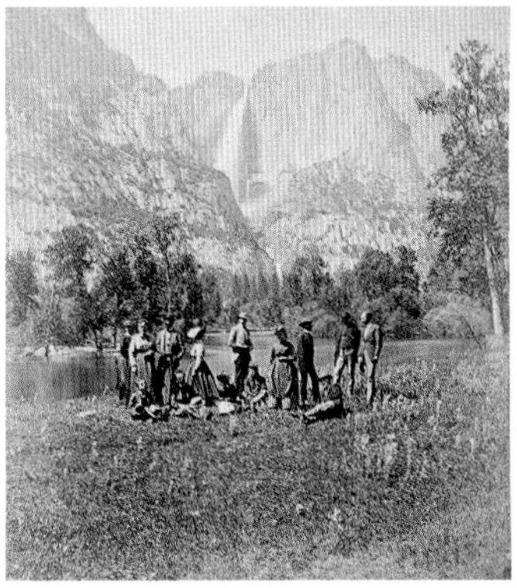

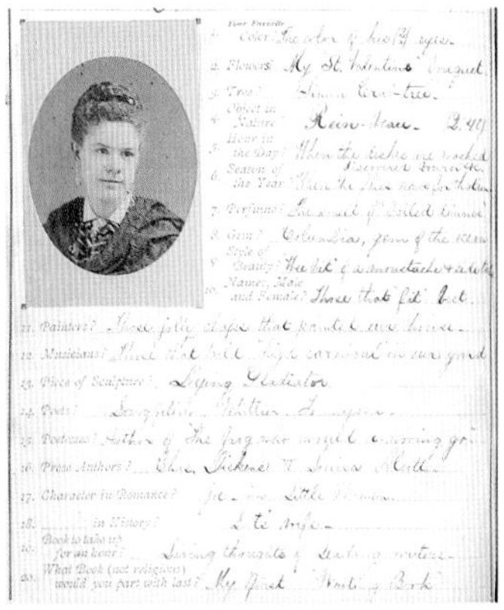

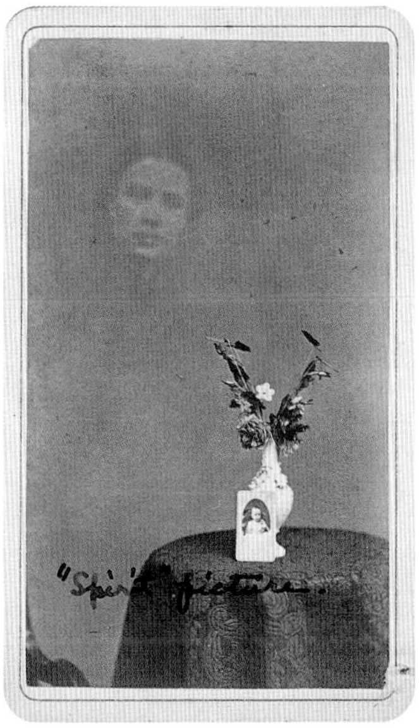

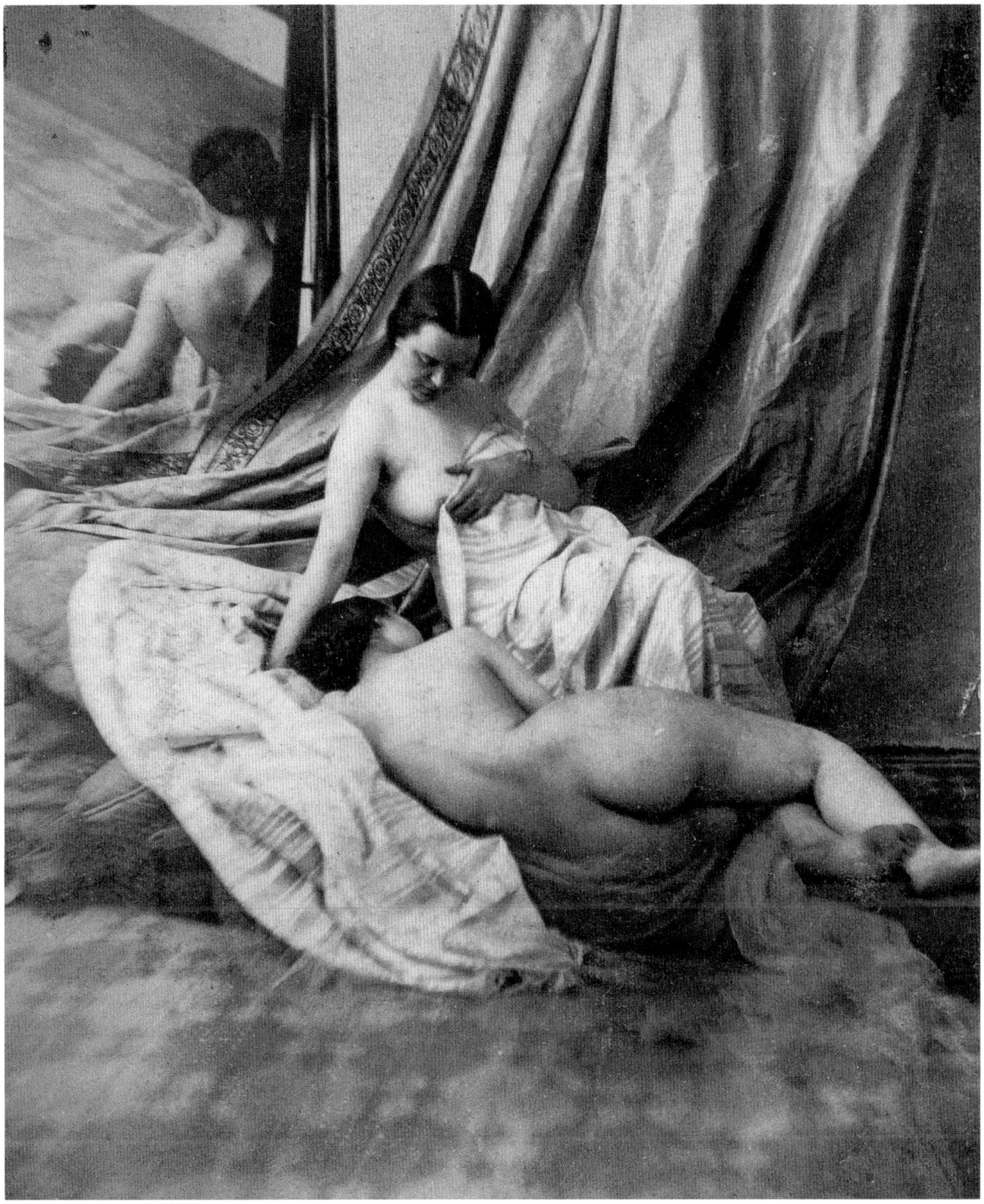

Clockwise from top left: John P. Soule, Yosemite Valley, ca. 1870, tipped-in albumen print, from *The Wonders of Yosemite Valley and of California*, Samuel Kneeland, M.D., 1871; Anonymous, Portrait of two nude women, ca. 1855, salt print, 7" x 8 1/2"; Anonymous, Spirit photograph, ca. 1880, albumen-print carte de visite, 2 1/8" x 3 1/2" on 2 1/2" x 4" card; Anonymous, Portrait of Miss Annie Suzette Trescott, 1873, tipped-in albumen print, 2 1/8" x 3 1/4", from *Mental Photographs, an Album for Confession of Tastes, Habits and Convictions*, Robert Saxton, editor, 1869.

In some instances, printed matter was designed to hold photographs but was sold without them. Examples of this are marriage certificates and family trees, onto which the buyer pasted photographs. Another do-it-yourself publication was *Mental Photographs, an Album for Confession of Tastes, Habits and Convictions.* This booklet from the late 1860s used a two-page-per-person format. It was designed to hold the photographs of friends, adjacent to which were spaces for recording the friends' characteristics and tastes.

Books with tipped-in photographs were beyond the financial reach of most of the population, but of course photographs were also sold individually. As previously pointed out, cartes de visite were very popular in the 1860s. They showed people what heroes, villains (John Wilkes Booth cartes sold well after Lincoln's assassination), and eminent figures, whether political, theatrical, or literary, looked like. Likewise, landscape images and photographs of works of art were exceedingly popular and were frequently included in family albums.

PROFILE:

Photo-Illustrated Passes and Tickets

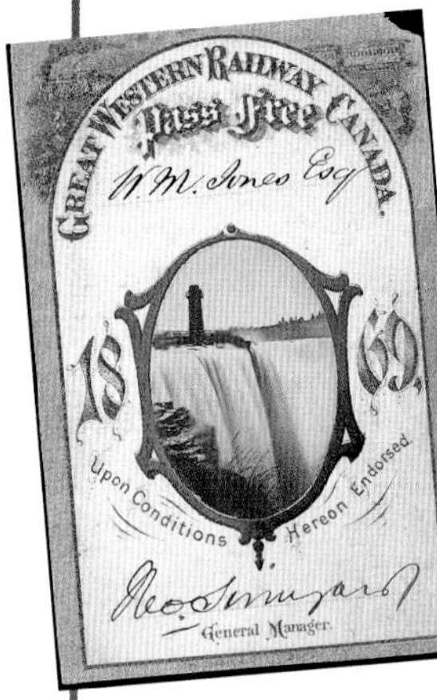

In today's society, photo IDs are commonplace. Driver's licenses, passports, some credit cards, and even senior citizens' transit cards, in some cities, are all familiar examples. But the photo ID is not a twentieth-century invention. Licenses and passes with photographs attached have existed for over 130 years. Prior to the discovery of photography, identification papers relied on verbal descriptions to associate the user with the document. With the advent of photography, though, the process of identification became much simpler.

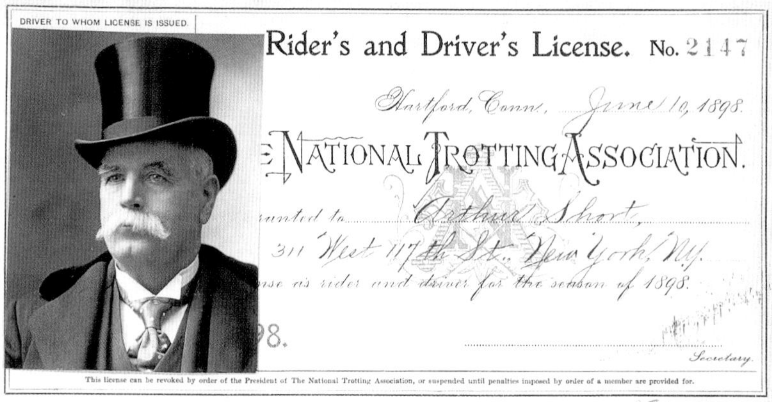

Free pass for the Great Western Railway Canada, issued to W. M. Jones, Esq., 1869, albumen print, 1 1/2" oval, on 2 3/8" x 3 5/8" printed card. **Above:** Rider's and driver's license of Arthur Short, 1898, gelatino-bromide print on printed card.

As early as 1869, the Great Western Railway of Canada issued free passes with photographs on them. In addition to the user's name and a number, the passes bore albumen prints of Niagara Falls and the suspension bridge. While single-admission tickets to an event rarely included a photograph, multiple admission tickets and season passes often did. The twenty-admission ticket to the 1939–1940 New York World's Fair, for instance, had a photograph of the bearer attached. Nowadays, in place of photographic prints, most identification cards employ digital technology, which greatly simplifies reprinting.

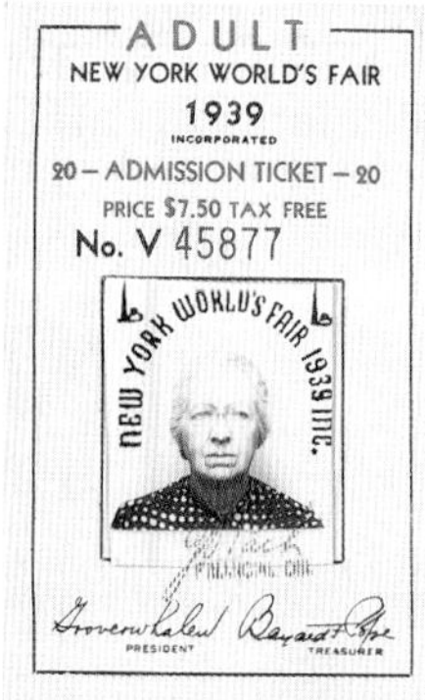

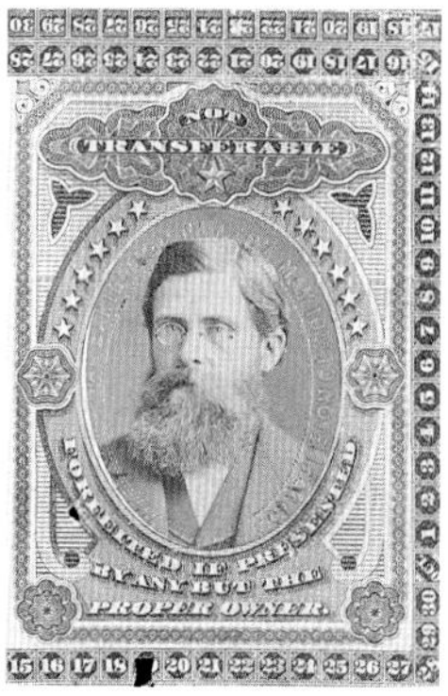

Left: Adult 20-admission ticket to New York World's Fair, 1939, gelatino-bromide print, on printed card. With coupons, one to be torn off by gateman each time Nellie B. Sergent entered the fair.

Right: Press ticket of Simon Mardner for the United States International Exhibition, 1876, albumen print on card. Mardner was the representative of Philadelphia's German-language newspaper, *Sonntags Zeitung* (Sunday Times).

Other photographic subject matter was also widely available, though much of it appealed only to smaller audiences. One example of this was the "spirit" photograph, produced by means of double exposure, with an ethereal image adjacent to the people in the photograph. Some of these, with rather clumsy props or double exposures, purported to show various ectoplasmic emanations. As far as the unclothed human figure is concerned, the dividing line between "art" photography and erotic photography has to some extent always been in the eye of the beholder. Studies of the human form—more often female than male—were available through various sales agencies, some of which

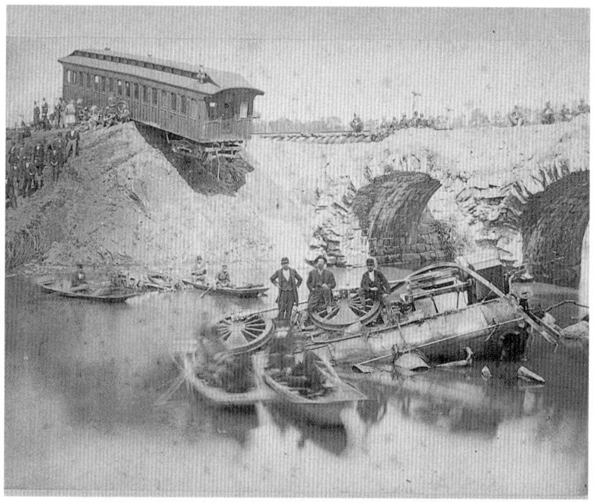

advertised "art studies" in popular publications. While distinctly pornographic photographs were also available, they were usually attainable only through clandestine channels.

Photographs were also used to document news events, though these were not necessarily widely distributed. An example of documentary photographs of limited distribution were those of prisoners of the Crimean War, 1854–1856. On the other hand, more sensational images, such as of train wrecks, had greater commercial potential. Sometimes photographs were intended for circulation among a local public. Often this was for product promotion, with the photograph of the product attached to a printed flyer or a card. In other instances, local authorities would use a photo-illustrated circular to attempt to locate a missing person or to apprehend criminals.

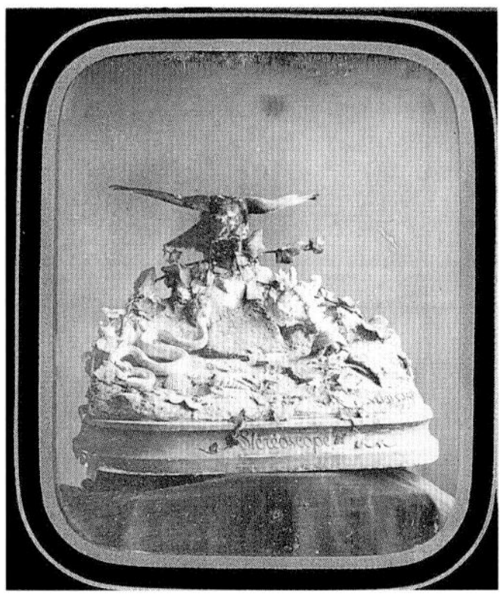

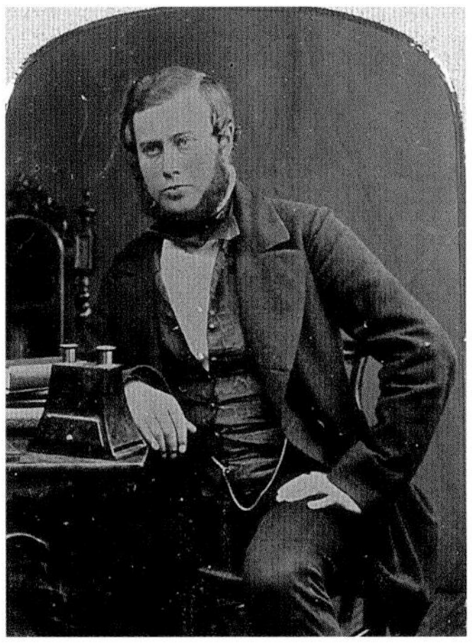

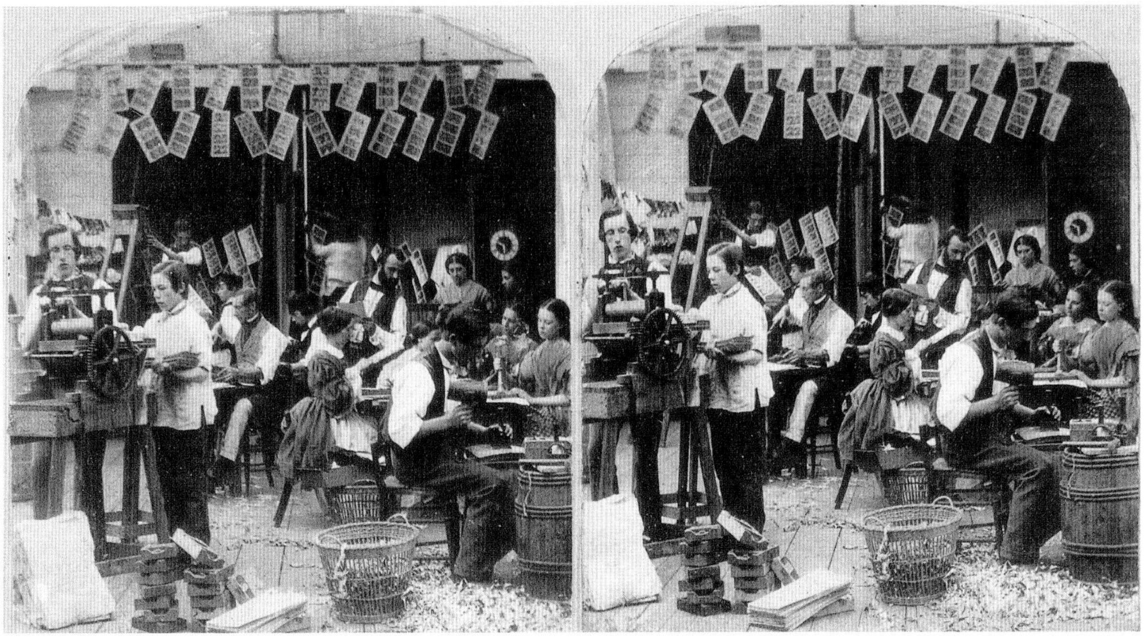

Opposite: Anonymous, Train wreck, ca. 1875, albumen print, 6 1/4" x 8 1/4". The exposure was long enough to show the motion of the boats in the foreground.

Clockwise from top left: C. W. Dixey, Picture of the statue stereoscope, signed "Malsieux," ca. 1852, one half of stereo pair of daguerreotypes, each 2 1/4" x 2 3/4"; Anonymous, Interior of stereoscopic manufactory, ca. 1860, stereo pair of tinted albumen prints, on 3 1/2" x 7" card mount; Anonymous, Tor Mountain, from Dinis Island, the lakes of Killarney, English, ca. 1865, one half of stereo pair of tinted albumen prints, on 3 1/2" x 7" card mount; Brennen's Daguerreotype Portrait Gallery, Portrait of a man with Brewster-type stereoscope, one half of stereo pair of ambrotypes, each 1 1/2" x 2".

One of the most popular and pervasive uses of photographs in the 1800s was the production of stereo images. The introduction of the wet-plate process and the ability to produce salted and albumen prints from negatives led to an increase in the popularity of the stereo image. Not only could many prints now be produced from a single negative, but the cost of the prints decreased significantly. The age of mass-produced stereo images had arrived. Early paper-print stereograms, however, did not possess the uniformity of quality that became standard by the 1880s. It was not uncommon to encounter misaligned stereo pairs or pairs in which one of the prints was noticeably lighter than the other. Only two common photographic forms of the mid-1800s, tintypes and ambrotypes, were not widely employed in the production of stereograms. This was because both were unique positive images, and therefore had to be rephotographed in order to be duplicated.

By the early 1860s, it was common for albumen stereo prints to be tinted. Although in many cases the tinting was done very skillfully, the practice was discontinued, by and large, within a decade. Another form of stereo photograph available at the time was the "tissue," so named because of the very thin paper on which it was printed. Rather than being mounted on a card, like a regular stereogram, tissues were mounted in

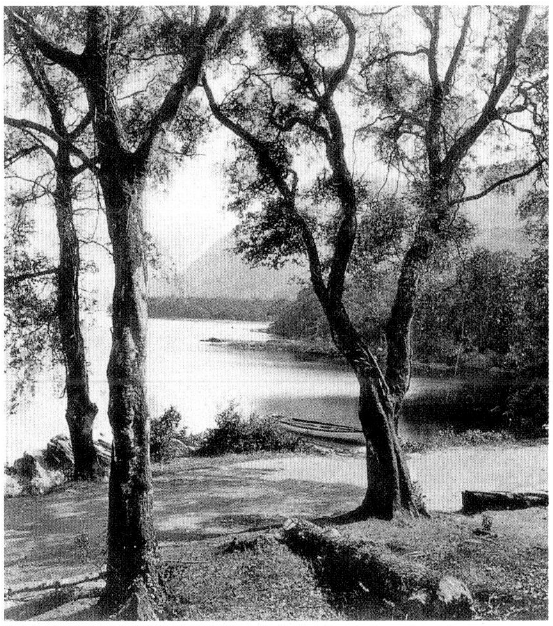

cardboard frames. Usually the back of the tissue was tinted, so that the colors were invisible in ordinary reflected light and only appeared when the light source was positioned behind the tissue. Thus front-lit "day" scenes could be converted into "night" or "sunset" scenes. Sometimes, too, the tissue was pricked with tiny pinholes, which, when illuminated from behind, made objects in the picture, such as streetlamps, appear to glow.

The most common handheld stereo viewers were of the Brewster type, despite the fact that they were felt to cause a strain on the eyes. Very ornate viewers were also available to those who could afford them. But when the more comfortable

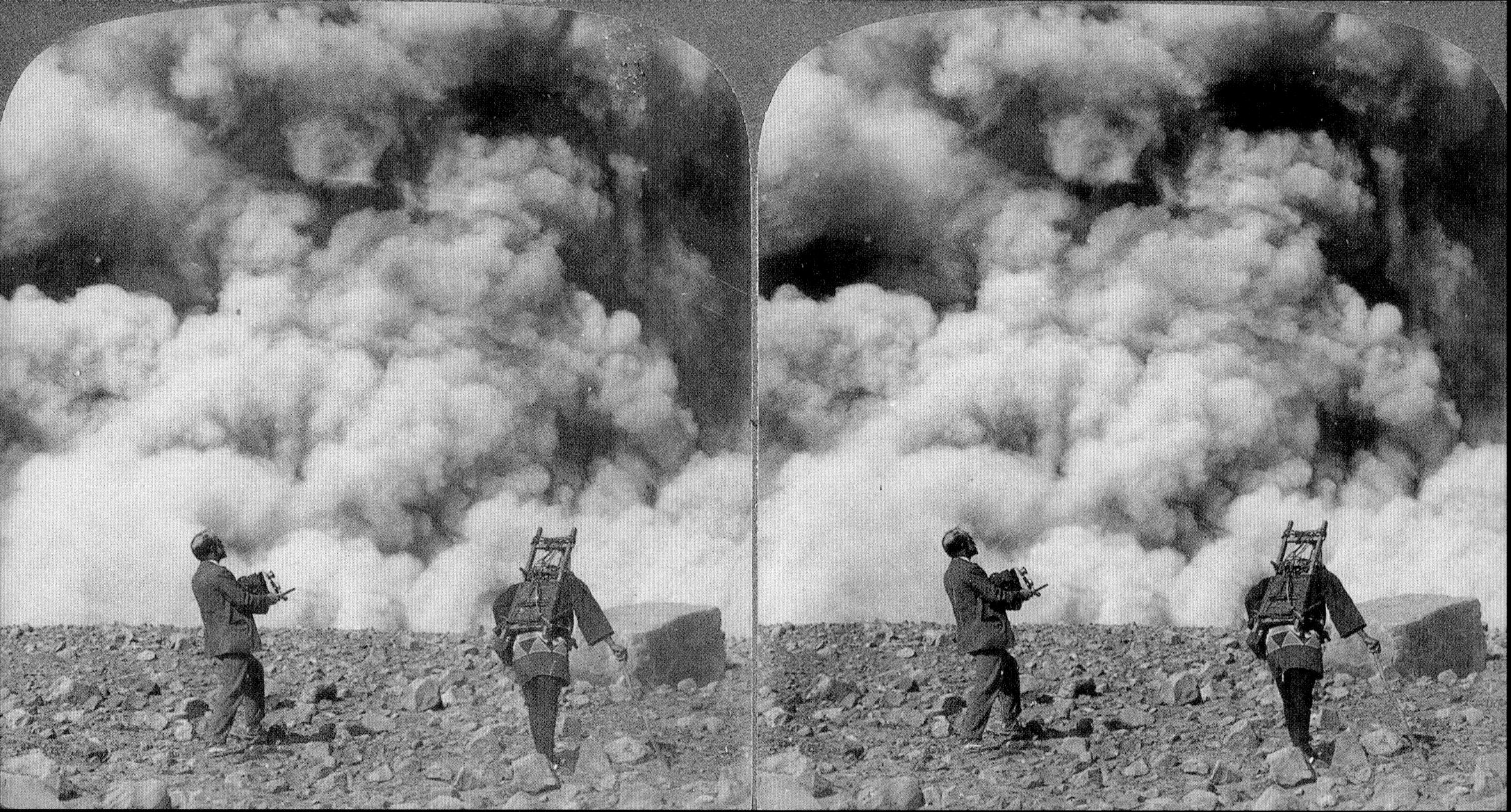

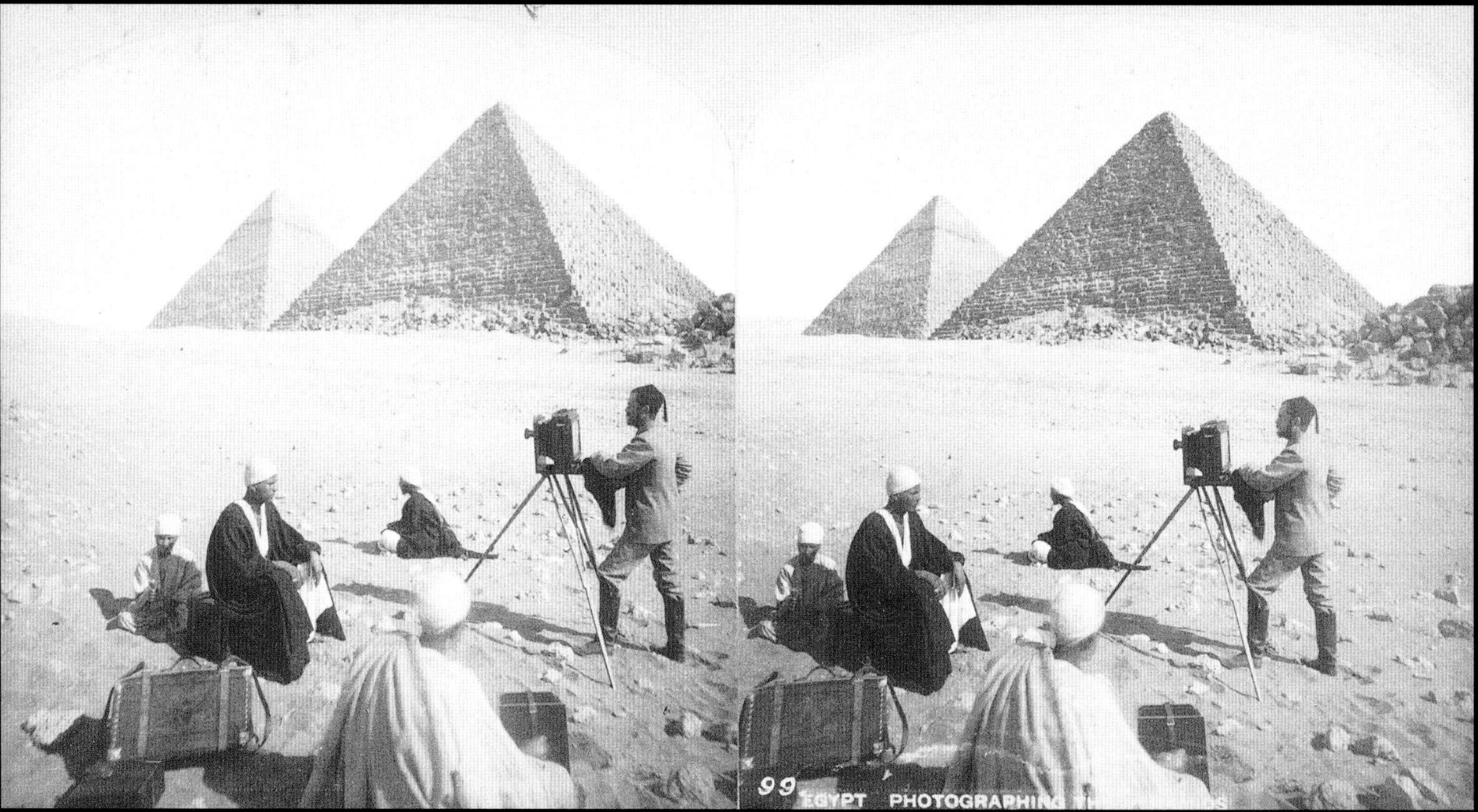

Top: Anonymous, A Sudden Explosion of Asama-yama Volcano, Japan, Underwood & Underwood, 1904, stereo pair of gelatino-bromide prints, on 3 1/2" x 7" card mount. Sudden enough to startle a nearby photographer. **Bottom:** Anonymous, Photographing the pyramids, ca. 1895, stereo pair of gelatino-bromide prints, on 3 1/2" x 7" card mount. The photographer is using a European tailboard camera.

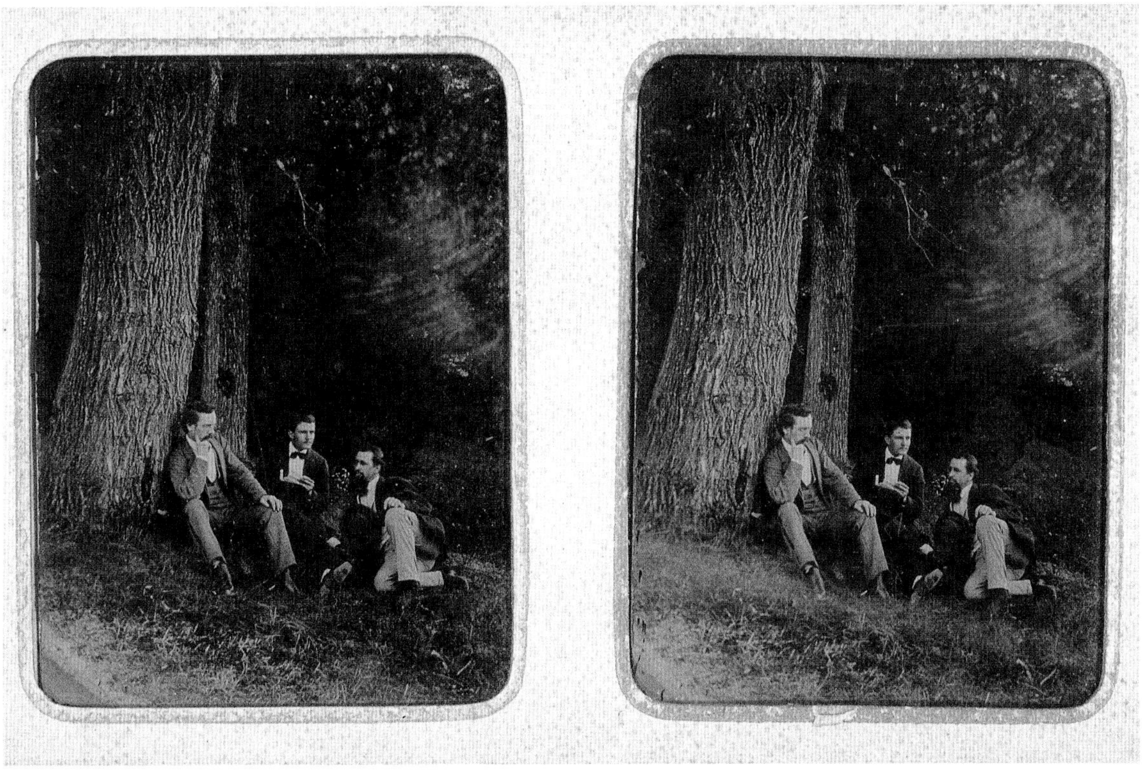

Anonymous, Portrait of three men in a forest, ca. 1870, stereo pair of ferrotypes, each 2 3/8" x 3", in 3 1/2" x 7" card mount.

Holmes-Bates stereo viewer appeared on the market in the late 1860s, it paved the way for wider acceptance of stereo imagery.

By the 1880s, most middle- and upper-class homes in the U.S. and Europe owned several stereo cards, sometimes even a whole library, and at least one stereoscope to view them with. By this point, stereo cards, given the sense of three-dimensionality they offered, considerably outnumbered cartes de visite. With perhaps the exception of personalities and non-three-dimensional art—paintings, engravings, etc.—stereo cards covered all the same subjects as had the cartes de visite. Civil War scenes and events, foreign locales, architecture, pictures staged for humor, and more—stereo cards of all of these subjects afforded viewers a three-dimensional look at the world. While they were generally sold individually, many were also issued in series. "A Visit to the 'Central Park' in the Summer of 1863" was just one of the sets of New York City scenery published by E. & H. T. Anthony & Company. In other instances, stereo cards were issued in boxed sets on topics as varied as views of the Holy Land and interior views of Sears, Roebuck & Company.

While the heyday of stereo cards was in the 1800s, they enjoyed periodic revivals in the twentieth century. This was due to a variety of factors, the most significant being the advent of roll film and the arrival of World War I. The public appetite for images of the war was enormous. Not only were series of stereo cards of the war issued, including deluxe boxed sets, but also smaller, less expensive stereo transparencies were produced in a 45-by-107 mm format. In the years 1920–1932, a number of small stereo cameras appeared on the amateur market in Europe, some of which accommodated roll films. Following World War II, the availability of 35 mm Kodachrome, for transparencies, helped to spur the stereo boom of the 1950s. In the early 1980s, an attempt made to revive stereo with the four-lens Nimslo camera never really caught on. The negatives were printed into 3-D photos with lenticular (double-convex) screens, which didn't require a separate viewer. And while the three-lens, one-time-use Image Tech cameras, which also produce lenticular prints, are still on the market, prints are only available from a limited number of sources.

FOCUS: *Stereo Viewers*

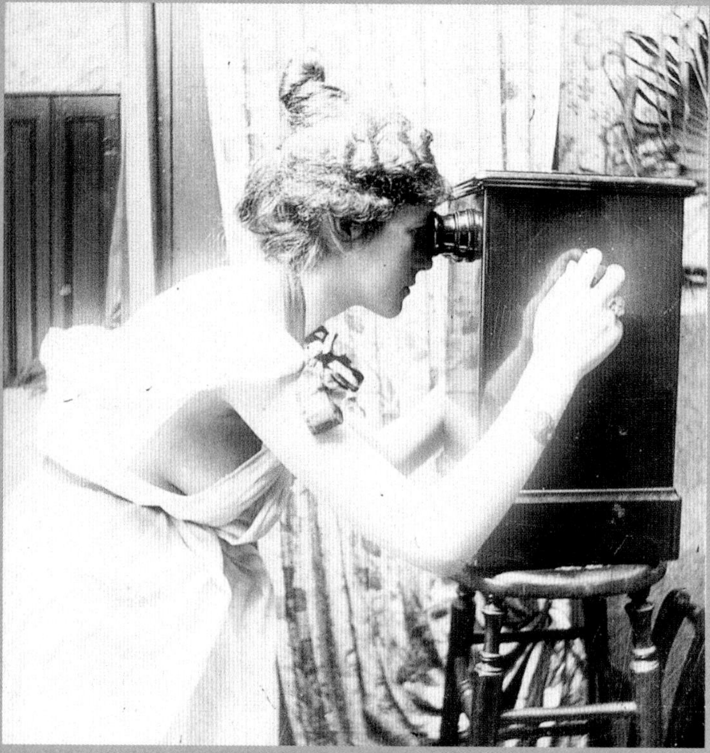

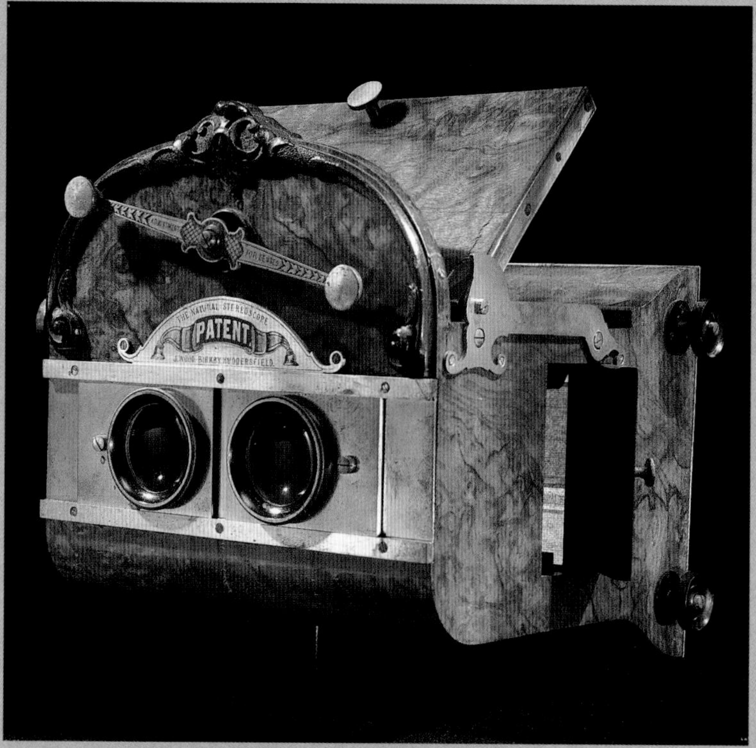

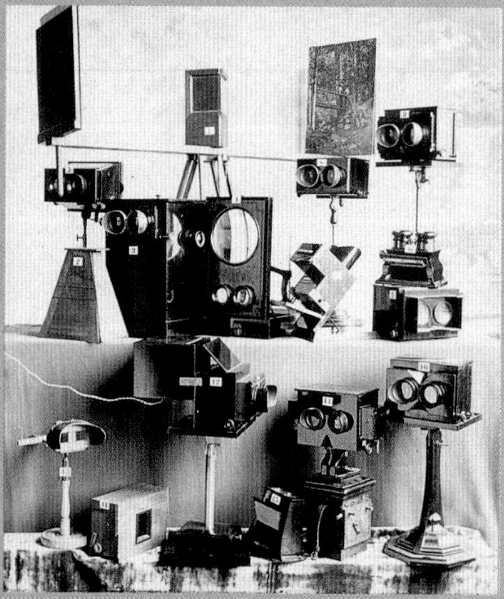

Clockwise from top left: Anonymous, Woman with table model Beckers-type stereoscope, ca. 1875, half of stereo pair of albumen prints, on 3 ½" x 7" card mount; The Natural Stereoscope, John Hirst Jr., & Joseph Wood, England, ca. 1863, walnut veneer. Interocular adjustment, rack-and-pinion focusing, translucent tinted filters to alter the light cast on the card or transparency; Anonymous, Exhibition of stereoscopes, probably French, ca. 1905, gelatino-bromide print, half of stereo pair. A great variety of stereoscopes, including Wheatstone-type, top; Beckers-type, top shelf, second from left; stereoscope-graphoscope, top shelf, center; Ives Kromskop, top shelf, second from right; Brewster-type, top shelf, right; and Holmes-Bates-type, bottom row, left.

Prior to 1860, most stereoscopes were manufactured in England or Continental Europe, especially France. As discussed in Chapter Two, the first stereoscopes were patterned after Sir Charles Wheatstone's design, which was first announced in 1838. This model was in use until around 1850, when Sir David Brewster introduced his popular stereoscope. His design featured a pair of lenses located at one end and a sheet of glass at the other, for illuminating transparencies. In addition, it had a hinged top panel which, when open, admitted light for viewing daguerreotypes and card-mounted photographs. The characteristic Brewster stereoscope tapered toward the lenses. A considerable variety of Brewster-type viewers were produced in both rigid (often mounted on stands) and collapsible forms.

As time passed, the designs of stereoscopes became even more varied. Stereoscopes that folded into containers resembling books and notebooks were produced. In addition, a type of stereoscope for viewing stereo pairs that were tipped into books was made. One example of this type was the Mirror Stereoscope of Smith, Beck & Beck, of London.

The next major advance in the design of stereo viewers was the introduction of the multiple-view stereoscope. The popularization of that type of viewer was in considerable part due to the design patented in 1857 by Alexander Beckers, a German-born American. In Beckers's device a number of stereo photographs were contained within the cabinet of the viewer. These stereographs were usually transparencies but could also be card-mounted prints. Beckers's design, which used belts to move the images at right angles, established a standard in America and Europe through the nineteenth century. Variations on Beckers stereoscopes ranged from simple wooden models to elaborate enameled and decorated ones. While other multiple-view stereoscopes were patented and produced in the nineteenth century, their numbers never approached the total number of Beckers-type viewers made.

In 1894 Jules Richard, of Paris, introduced a camera that would bring stereo photography into a new age. The Verascope used 45-by-107 mm glass plates to produce a pair of 42-by-47 mm exposures. While there were slight changes in that camera's features over the years, it never appreciably deviated from its original form in the thirty-plus years in which it was produced. Not long after the 45-by-107 mm format was introduced 6-by-13 cm format stereo cameras also began to appear on the market, and stereo transparencies in both of these formats became popular.

In 1900 Richard introduced a viewer that, like the Beckers model, accommodated multiple stereographs. Richard's stereoscope differed, though, in that it used a tray form of storage and was more compact. It became known as the Taxiphote, and was quite popular in France.

Thirty-five millimeter stereo photography, which became popular after World War II, will be considered in Chapter Nine.

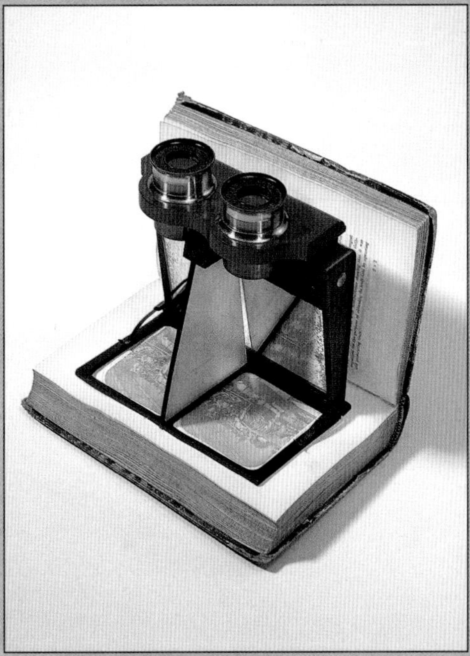

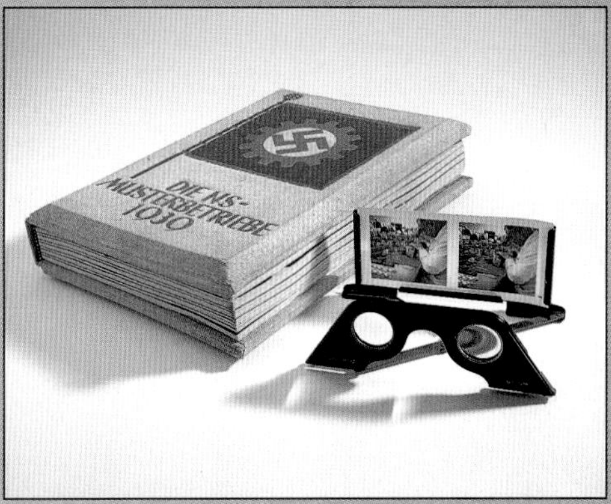

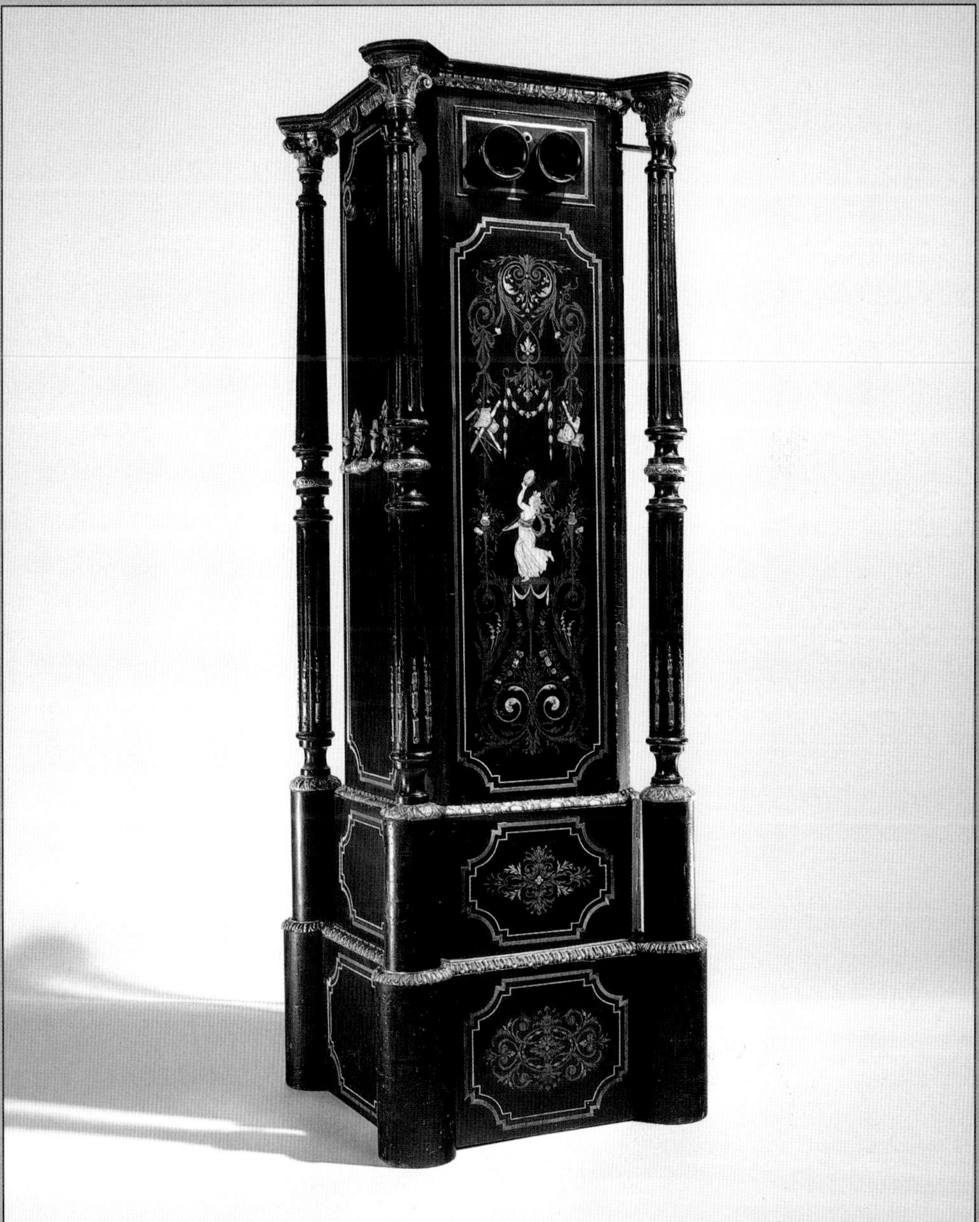

Clockwise from top left: Smith, Beck & Beck Book Stereoscope, England, ca. 1862, for viewing stereo pairs of photographs tipped into books; Raumbild Stereoscope and *Die NS—Musterbetriebe 1939*, Raumbild-Verlag, 1939. Viewer, with $2\frac{1}{4}$" x 5" stereo silver print, can also be laid against views in book. Book contains twenty-four tipped-in silver print stereographs of exemplary German industries; Ornate Floor Model Parlor Stereoscope, probably French, ca. 1875, for up to two hundred stereographs. Inlaid, ebonized finish. Pedestal case inlaid with ivory and cut-brass panels of classical figures; $50\frac{1}{2}$" high.

CHAPTER SIX:

THE ROLL-FILM REVOLUTION

L'Escopette (Pistolet), Boissanas, ca. 1889, walnut and brass construction, for 110 68 x 72 mm exposures on 2 3/4" roll film for the Kodak. Probably the first non-Eastman camera to use Kodak film. Folding legs facilitate time exposures. Name translates as "blunderbuss."

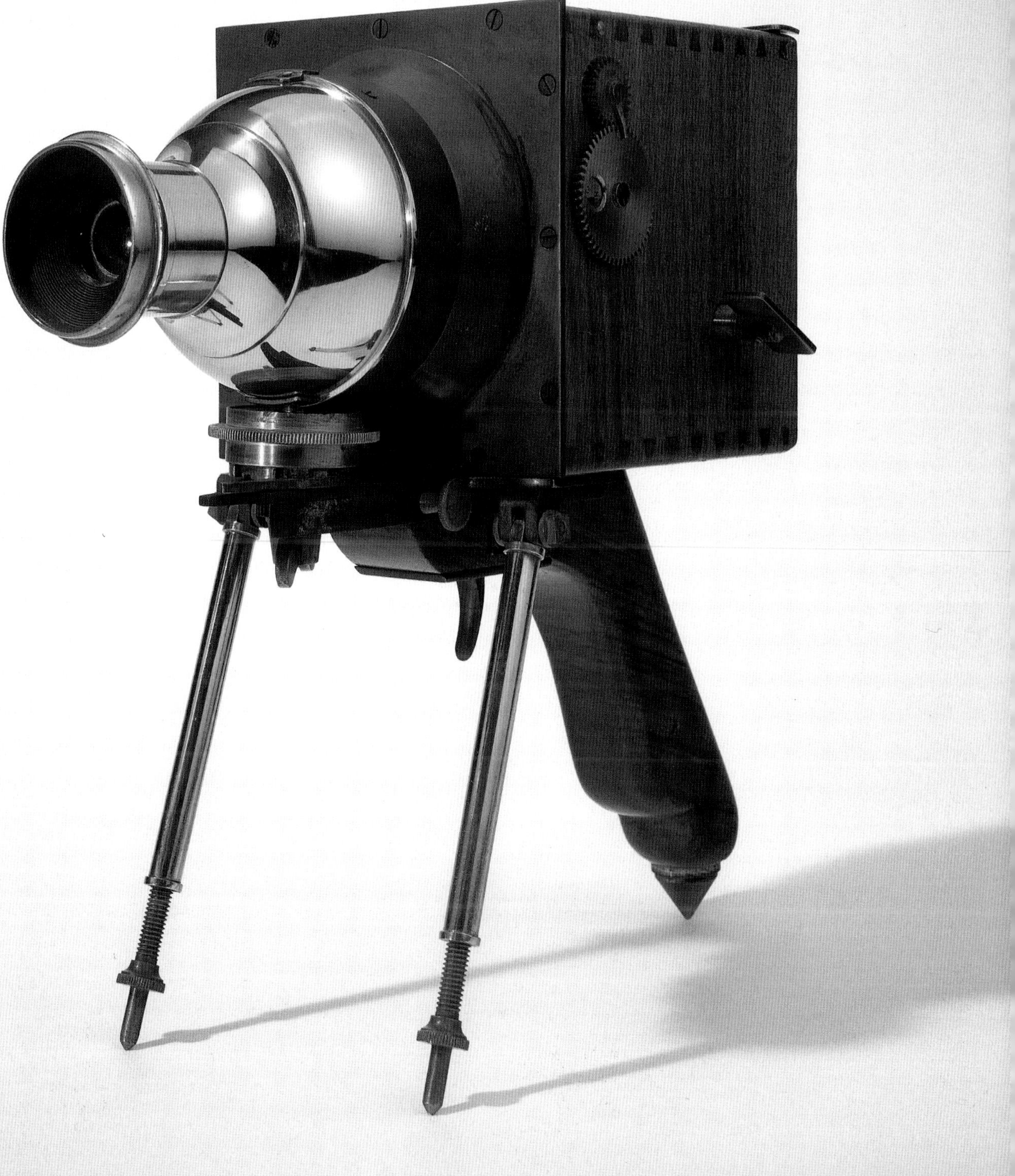

Almost as soon as glass-plate photography became feasible, innovators sought to streamline and, ultimately, to supplant the bulky plate negatives and their surrounding apparatuses. On March 22, 1854, the British Patent Office issued a provisional specification for a roll holder for flexible film to Arthur J. Melhuish and J. B. Spencer. The roll holder, a special back that could be attached to a camera, wound a length of sensitized waxed paper, prepared using Talbot's formula, from one roll, past the plane of focus, to another. For purposes of development, the roll had to be cut up. The holder used a glass pressure plate to keep the film flat. Although offered commercially, the Melhuish-Spencer roll holder was never widely used.

Several other photographers produced their own variations of flexible, rolled film. In each case, the design needed to address functional problems specific to roll film while matching the consistency of plates. A particular problem was how to ensure reliable advancement of the film—in other words, how to avoid the overlap of frames without wasting valuable film. Photographers' mistrust of early roll films was augmented by some prominent mishaps.

In 1875 Leon Warnerke, a Russian living in England, described his new roll film and holder to a meeting of a photographic society. His film differed significantly from preceding ones in that it was a "stripping" film, in which transparent gelatin or collodion was coated on an opaque roll of paper. Once the exposures had been developed and fixed, the transparent layer was separated, or "stripped," from the paper base by soaking the film. Then the negative was mounted on a sheet of glass and was printed. Warnerke's first holder used hundred-exposure lengths of film, though he later reduced it to forty. The film was etched with lines to indicate the space required by individual negatives. Although Warnerke's roll holder was mechanically sound, it wasn't feasible for use with simple amateur cameras. In 1877 William H. Jackson, the noted photographer of the American West, used a Warnerke roll holder and a considerable amount of "English tissue" on one of his trips west. To his alarm, however, upon developing the film Jackson discovered that none of the four hundred negatives he had shot had been exposed.

Another roll-film system was developed, along with a compatible camera, by Professor E. Stebbing, a Parisian. His roll film, like other designs, was flawed: it tended to distort during the development process. Not until George Eastman, ever aware of emerging photographic trends, turned his attention to the problem was a reliable roll film produced.

Eastman filed for a patent for a stripping film in March 1884, and hired William H. Walker, a fellow resident of Rochester, New York, to design a suitable holder for it. Walker had managed a com-

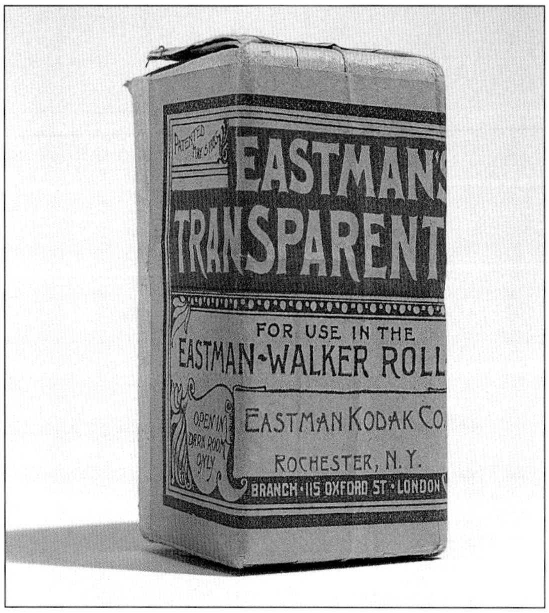

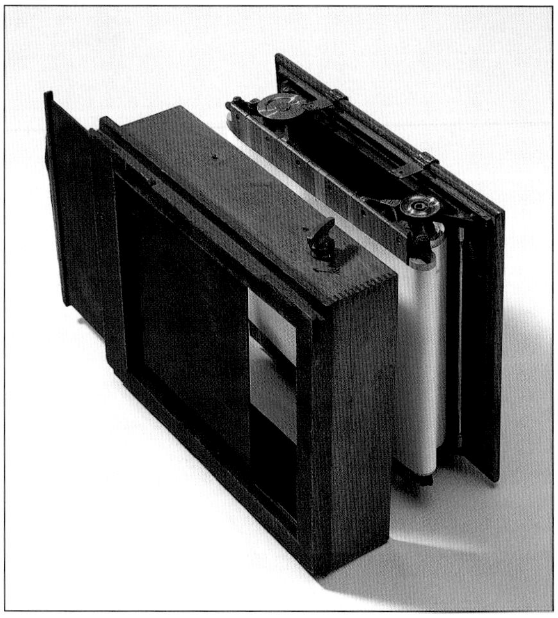

Left: Box of Eastman's transparent film for use in the Eastman-Walker roll holder, Eastman Dry Plate & Film Co., ca. 1893.

Right: Eastman-Walker roll holder, Eastman Dry Plate & Film Co., ca. 1887. Open to show mechanism.

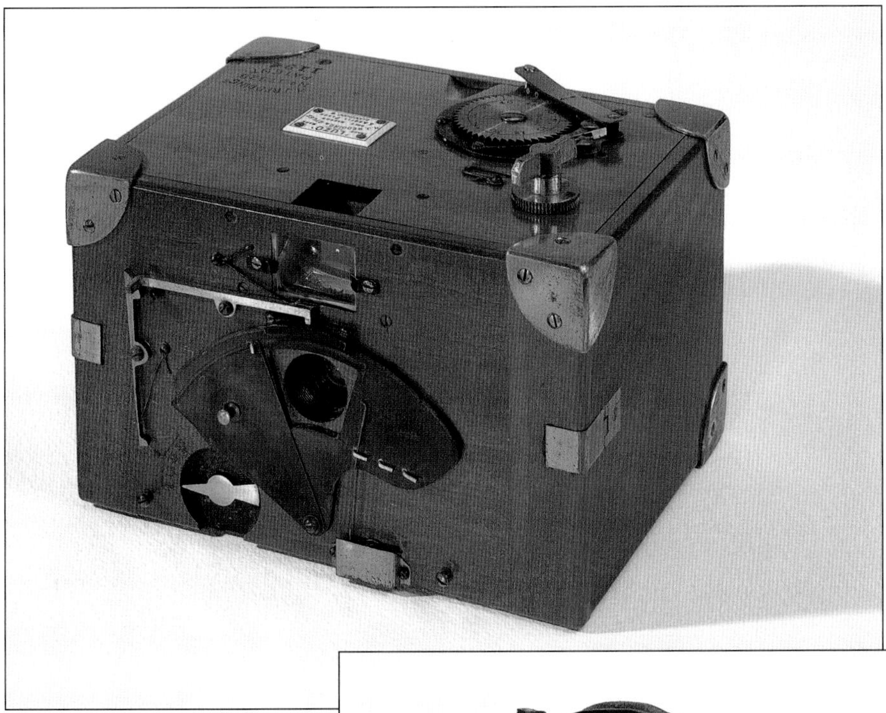

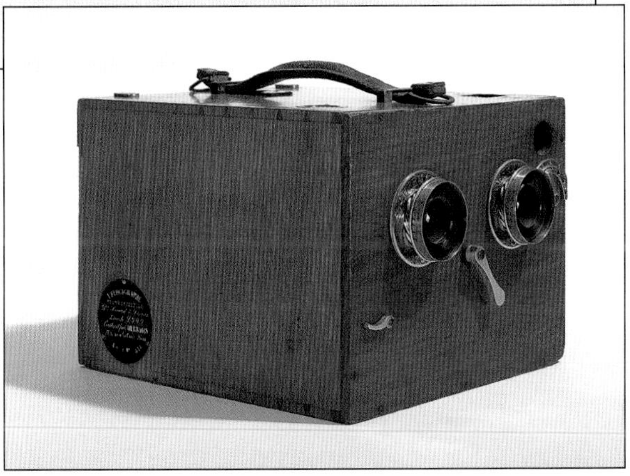

No. 3a Luzo, Redding & Gyles, ca. 1896, Spanish mahogany construction, for forty-eight exposures, 3 ¼" x 4 ¼", on roll film. When introduced in 1889, the Luzo was called the New Detective Camera.

Right: Stereo Vélocigraphe, J. Fleury Hermagis, ca. 1895, mahogany construction, for twelve stereo pairs on 9 x 18 cm dry plates. A falling-plate form of magazine camera.

pany that manufactured a product called Walker's Pocket Camera. The design of this device was so precise that all of its parts were fully interchangeable from one camera to the next, a noteworthy feat for the time.

Together, Eastman and Walker labored to create a roll holder that was functionally sound, aesthetically pleasing, and could fit easily onto the back of existing dry-plate cameras. In addition, their roll holder employed a mechanical film counter, the first of its kind. In August 1884, they filed for a patent, and in anticipation of great success Eastman changed the name of his company from the Eastman Dry Plate Company to the Eastman Dry Plate & Film Company.

When introduced on the market in 1885, Eastman and Walker's roll holders and films met with some skepticism. This changed in mid-1885, when, at the International Inventions Exhibition in England, three British groups awarded Eastman and Walker their highest medals. Subsequent reviews in the *London Times* and the *British Journal of Photography* were generous in their praise. Even William H. Jackson, having been furnished with an Eastman-Walker roll holder, wrote glowingly of it.

A crucial facet of Eastman's business was the aggressive pursuit and control of all patents related to photography. When he discovered that David Houston of North Dakota had been granted a patent for a roll holder with an improved exposure counter, he bought out the patent, along with one other, for five thousand dollars. He made improvements to the stripping film and renamed it American Film. Moreover, in 1886 the Eastman Dry Plate & Film Co. introduced a photofinishing service for professional photographers. Negatives sent in could be enlarged to prints as large as 25-by-30 inches.

But it remained for the introduction of one Eastman product in July 1888 to revolutionize photography: the Kodak. A simple, fixed-focus camera, the Kodak reduced picture-taking to a total of three steps: 1) pull the string (to cock the shutter); 2) turn the key (to wind the film); 3) press the button (to make the exposure). True to the advertising slogan "You press the button, we do the rest," the Kodak was sold already loaded with film. After finishing the roll, the user then sent the camera to the Eastman Dry Plate & Film Co. For a charge of ten dollars, the company developed the negative images, stripped the film from its paper backing, transferred it to a sheet of glass, and printed and mounted the prints. These were then returned to the customer, along with the reloaded camera. For the first time, the process of taking pictures, from exposure through printing, was so simple that even those with no special knowledge could participate.

Roll film was an essential element in the explosion of amateur photography. While many roll films had previously appeared on the market, they generally attached (with a roll holder) to the back of a folding-bellows camera. These cameras required a fair degree of competence to make successful images. After the Kodak, roll film, along with the service of photofinishing, would be inextricably tied to amateur photography. Although the Eastman Dry Plate & Film Co. had introduced photofinishing for users of its American Film in 1886, the service was not restricted to users of any particular camera system, and one could correctly say that photofinishing as an industry began with the Kodak. Not long after it came on the market, the company began to provide instructions for those venturesome photographers who wanted to do the developing themselves. Soon a number of companies were offering photofinishing for Kodak and other types of films. As it happened, photofinishing became such a major and time-consuming activity at Eastman's company that eventually it was discontinued.

In 1889 the Eastman Dry Plate & Film Co. announced two new products. One was a new model of camera, the No. 1 Kodak, introduced late in the year. It differed little from its predecessor except that it was equipped with an improved shutter that was simpler and less expensive to produce. The second product, transparent roll film, eased the process of photofinishing and printing, and thus helped to further the boom in amateur photography.

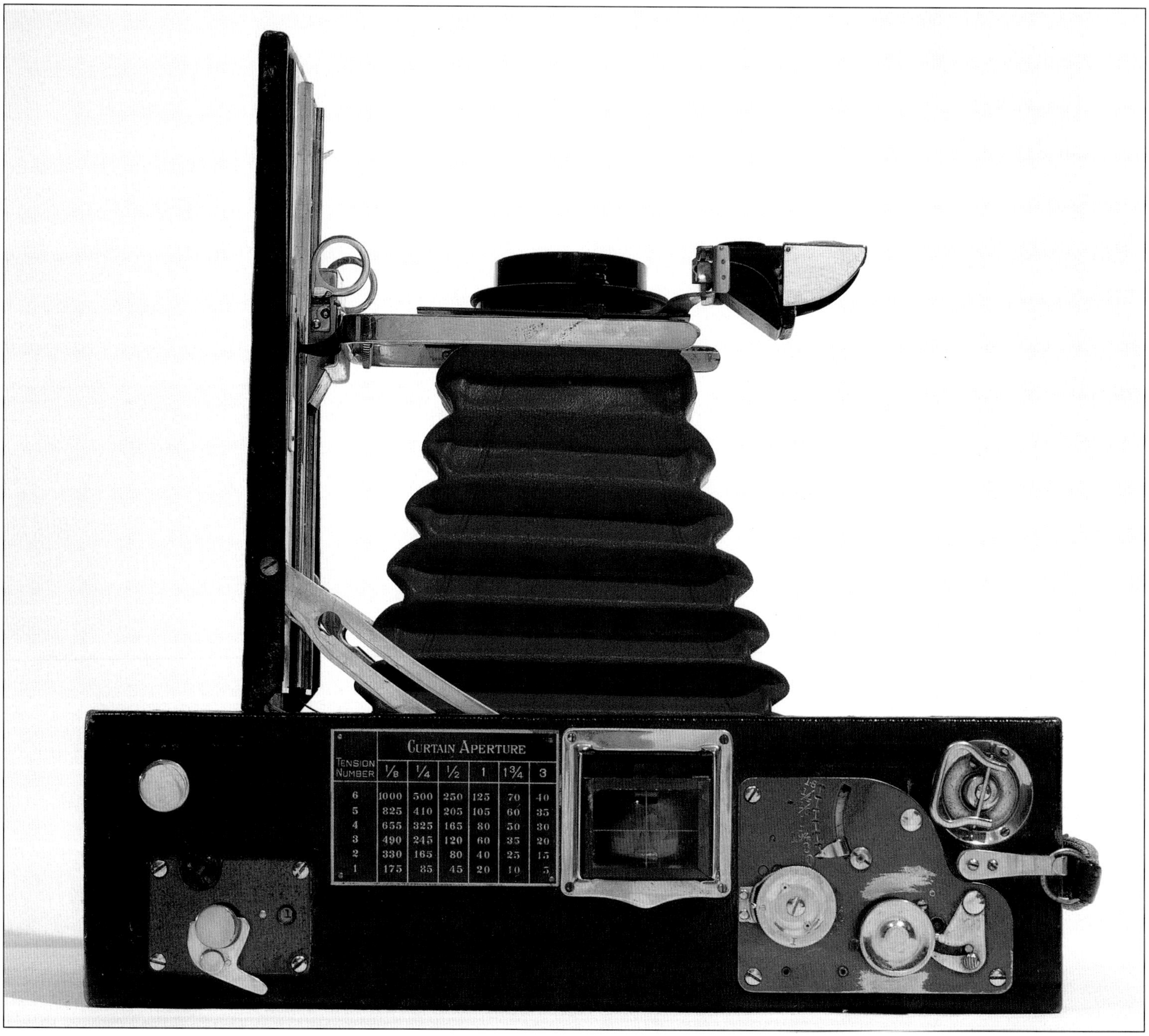

No. 4A Speed Kodak (shown on its back), Eastman Kodak Co., ca. 1910, for six exposures, 4 1/4" x 6 1/2", on No. 126 roll film. The reason for the word "speed" in the camera's name came from the fact that it was equipped with the Kodak Focal Plane Shutter, which offered shutter speeds of up to 1/1000 second.

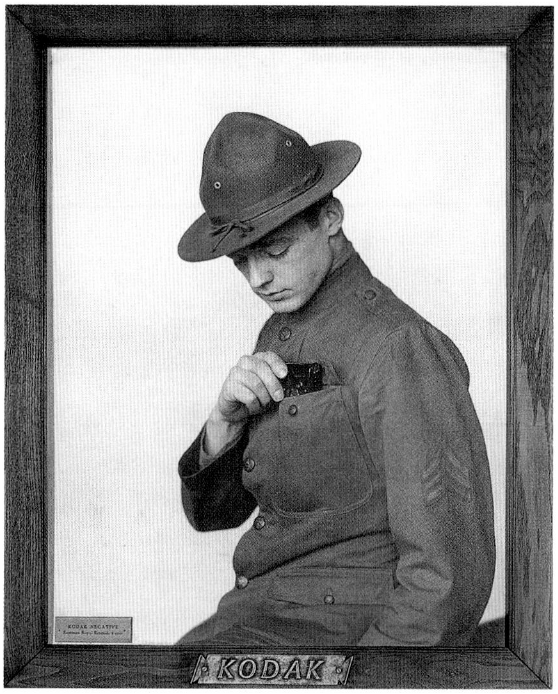

Anonymous, Portrait of a soldier, framed bromide print. Illustrates the Vest Pocket Kodak's convenient size and the fact that Kodak film and paper were used.

PROFILE: *The Kodak*

The Kodak, a relatively simple box camera, was arguably the most influential camera produced since the announcement of Daguerre's discovery. It was introduced by the Eastman Dry Plate & Film Co. in July 1888. The camera measured 3 ¼-by-3 ½-by-6 ¾ inches and was made of wood covered in morocco leather. Inside, behind the plane of focus, was a roll-holder mechanism which accommodated a length of 2 ¼-inch stripping film sufficient to produce one hundred 2 ½-inch-diameter exposures. Behind the camera's front panel was a 57 mm, f/9 periscopic lens and a rotating, horizontal-cylinder shutter with a single, fixed speed and a provision for making time exposures. To make prints, the user sent the camera back to Eastman's company, which would develop, mount, and print the film, and reload the camera all for ten dollars.

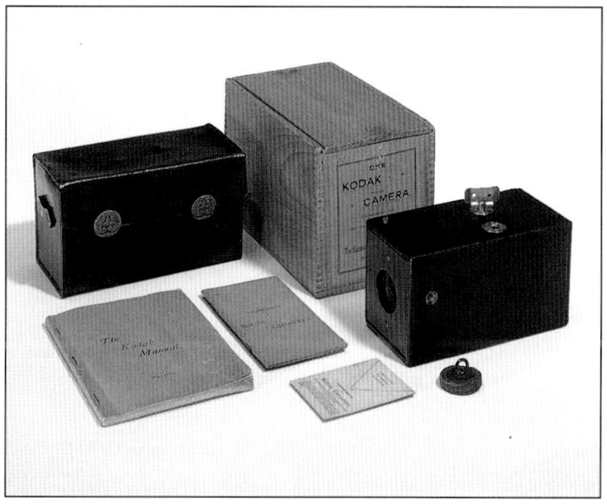

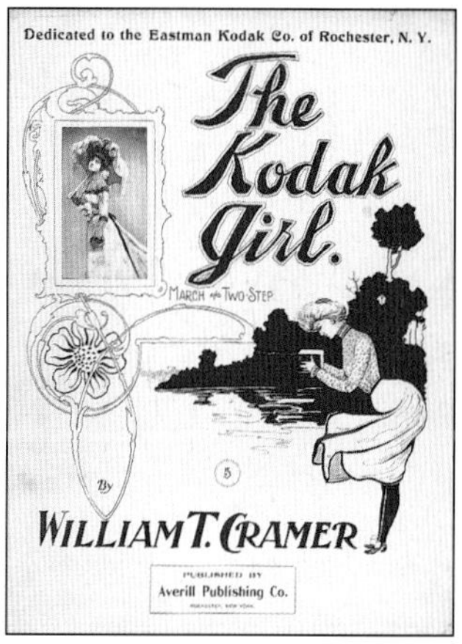

Left: The Kodak, made by Frank Brownell for the Eastman Dry Plate & Film Co., 1888, for 100 exposures, 2½" diameter, on 2 ¾" roll film. With case, shipping box, *Kodak Manual, Memorandum of Kodak Exposures*, "Angle of View" memorandum, and felt plug for time exposures. **Right:** William T. Cramer, *The Kodak Girl*, sheet music dedicated to the Eastman Kodak Co., Averill Publishing Co., 1902. Halftone of the familiar Kodak Girl at upper left.

Sold for twenty-five dollars, the Kodak and its felt plug came in a wooden box, with a carrying case, a copy of the *Kodak Manual*, the *Memorandum of Kodak Exposures*, and a small card that showed the angle of view of the lens, as the camera had no viewfinder. The *Memorandum of Kodak Exposures* enabled the user to record, for all hundred exposures, the date, time, subject, distance, light conditions, exposure length, and whether or not the felt cap was used. Kodak cameras were often used for trips abroad, where a great number of exposures would be desirable.

By the mid-1890s Kodak had become a household word. The Kodak Girl became the company's symbol of a "modern" photographer. In fact, the word Kodak became almost synonymous with photography. When George Eastman created the word Kodak, purportedly because it was a strong name—he thought the initial letter *K* was "firm and unyielding"—he undoubtedly never anticipated the meaning that would accrue to that name in the time since its introduction.

In August 1886, George Eastman had hired chemist Henry M. Reichenbach to assist in certain aspects of the improvement of roll film. Late in 1888, Reichenbach succeeded in producing a transparent film from a solution of nitrocellulose in wood alcohol that was flowed onto a smooth glass plate. The problem was that as it dried, the film's surface became irregular and wavy. Reichenbach continued his experiments, and early in 1889, by using a camphor solution to which he added a solution of amyl acetate and fusel oil, he was able to produce a satisfactorily flexible, transparent film. Later that year, Eastman's Transparent Film came to market, freeing photographers from the daunting task of stripping the emulsion off a paper backing and transporting it to a glass support for printing. This new product was so widely preferred to stripping film that production of the company's American Film was discontinued in 1891.

In 1890 Eastman introduced seven new sizes and styles of cameras and no less than five new film sizes. Among the cameras, only the No. 2 Kodak, which produced exposures three-and-a-half inches in diameter, used the round format of the original Kodak. All of the others produced rectangular images. Now that cameras comprised a significant element in the company's product line, the company once again revised its name, becoming the Eastman Kodak Company.

The cover of the company's 1902 catalog bore an illustration of a flourishing green oak tree. The word *Kodak* was spread across its leafy branches. To one side of its trunk was the phrase "The Growth and Triumph of an Idea." At the tree's base, intertwined with its roots, were acorns partially cut away to reveal rolls of film. Although Eastman's company repeatedly brought out new designs and models of cameras, it was the sales of the films used in these cameras that was now at the heart, or root, of its business.

The success of the Kodak was not lost on other photographic manufacturers. In 1890 Thomas H. Blair's camera company bought the rights to manufacture the Hawkeye, a "detective" camera for 4-by-5-inch dry plates, from the Boston Camera Company. These cameras could be equipped with holders for Eastman's roll film. In 1891, not long after the introduction of the No. 4 Kodak Camera, the Blair Camera Company, also of Boston, introduced the Kamaret. This too was a roll-film camera, but its construction differed from the Kodak in one significant respect: its film rollers were located at the plane of focus, but its supply and take-up spools were positioned forward of the focal plane. This made for a significant reduction in the camera's length. That feature of the Kamaret had been patented in 1889 by an Englishman, Henry Good. Both the Kodak and the Kamaret had mechanical exposure counters, as the films used were too sensitive to permit viewing the exposures through colored glass.

In December of 1891, the same year that the Kamaret was introduced, Eastman offered a new camera, the Daylight Kodak, in three different sizes. The name indicated its most important feature: the film could now be loaded in subdued light, whereas previously, all film loading had to be done in the darkroom. As the 1892 Kodak catalog described, "This is accomplished by having a section of black paper fastened to each end of the film, which covers the film while loading." The film's spool was housed in a lightproof cardboard carton inserted into the camera's back, and the film was wound onto a spool in a similar carton. In the Daylight Kodak, exposures were counted by a mechanical device that had an

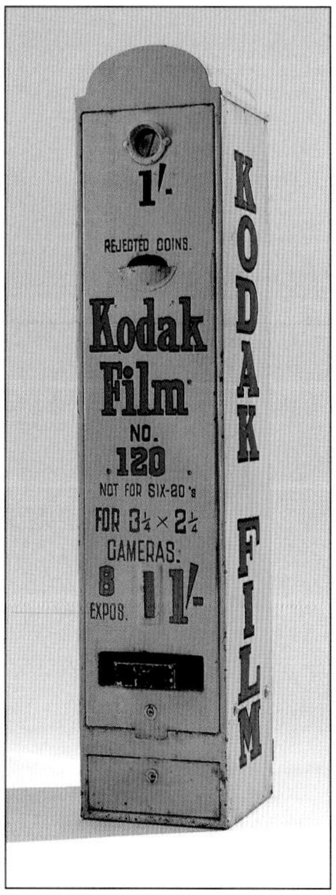

Left: Dispenser for No. 120 Kodak Roll Films, Kodak Ltd., England, ca. 1935. Coin-operated machine for dispensing roll films.

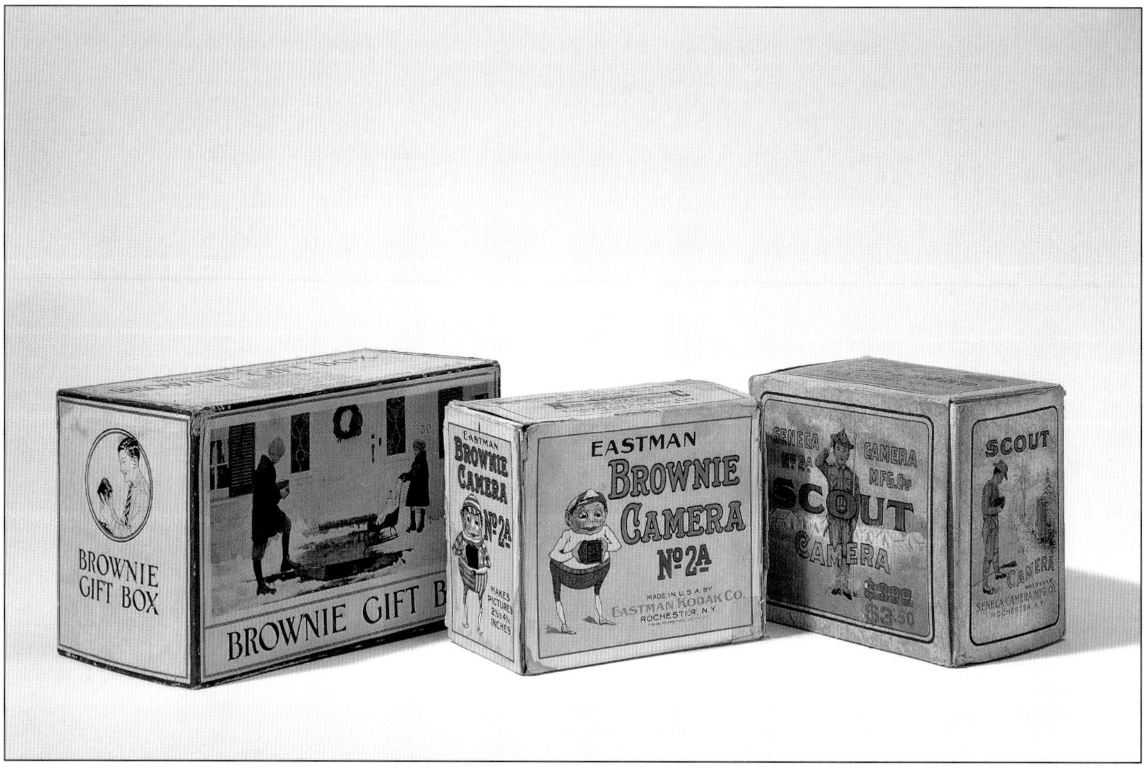

Right: Colorful boxes used to promote box camera sales. Left: Brownie Gift Box, ca. 1924. Center: No. 2A Brownie Box, ca. 1908, with Brownie Imp illustrated. Right: No. 2A Seneca Scout Box, ca. 1915. The Brownie Gift Box contained a camera and accessories.

"automatic" lock to stop the advancing film at the proper point.

In 1892, the Boston Camera Company introduced a camera that completed the advances in roll-film technology that spurred the incredible growth of amateur photography in the 1890s. The paper backing of stripping film had disappeared with the advent of transparent film. Now only the single band of nitrate film was needed. The company's Bulls-Eye Camera reincorporated paper backing into the design of roll film. But in this case the film, rather than being attached to the backing, was simply wound on the spool together with it. While some early roll-film systems, prior to Eastman's, had yellow or orange windows to let the user view the film and ensure proper positioning of exposures, increases in emulsion sensitivity necessitated abandoning them. The Bulls-Eye Camera had a new system for accurately positioning exposures. The black paper that backed the film had numbers printed on it, spaced at negative-length intervals. In the center of the camera body's back was a small, D-shaped window (later changed to round) with a piece of red celluloid in it. This was used to view the exposure numbers on the backing paper. The backing paper blocked light from exposing the film and allowed for daylight loading as well. The four most important features of roll-film cameras were now in place: transparent film, film spools positioned forward of the plane of focus, numbered backing paper visible through a red window, and easy daylight loading.

George Eastman attempted to consolidate his control of the industry by systematically gaining control of the patents for all of these elements. Although he believed he owned the rights to the production of transparent film, even that patent did not come easily. After an application process fraught with difficulty, the U.S. Patent Office had recognized the Rev. Hannibal Goodwin as "the first inventor of the successful photographic film pellicle," or transparent film, in September 1898. Goodwin died early in 1900, shortly after the Goodwin Film and Camera Company had been established, but before film production had begun. In 1901 Anthony & Scovill, the successors to E. & H. T. Anthony & Co., purchased a majority holding in the Goodwin Film and Camera Co. from Goodwin's widow, and by late 1902 the film was being produced. Anthony & Scovill brought suit against Eastman Kodak for infringing upon the patent that they now owned. In 1914 Goodwin's priority was

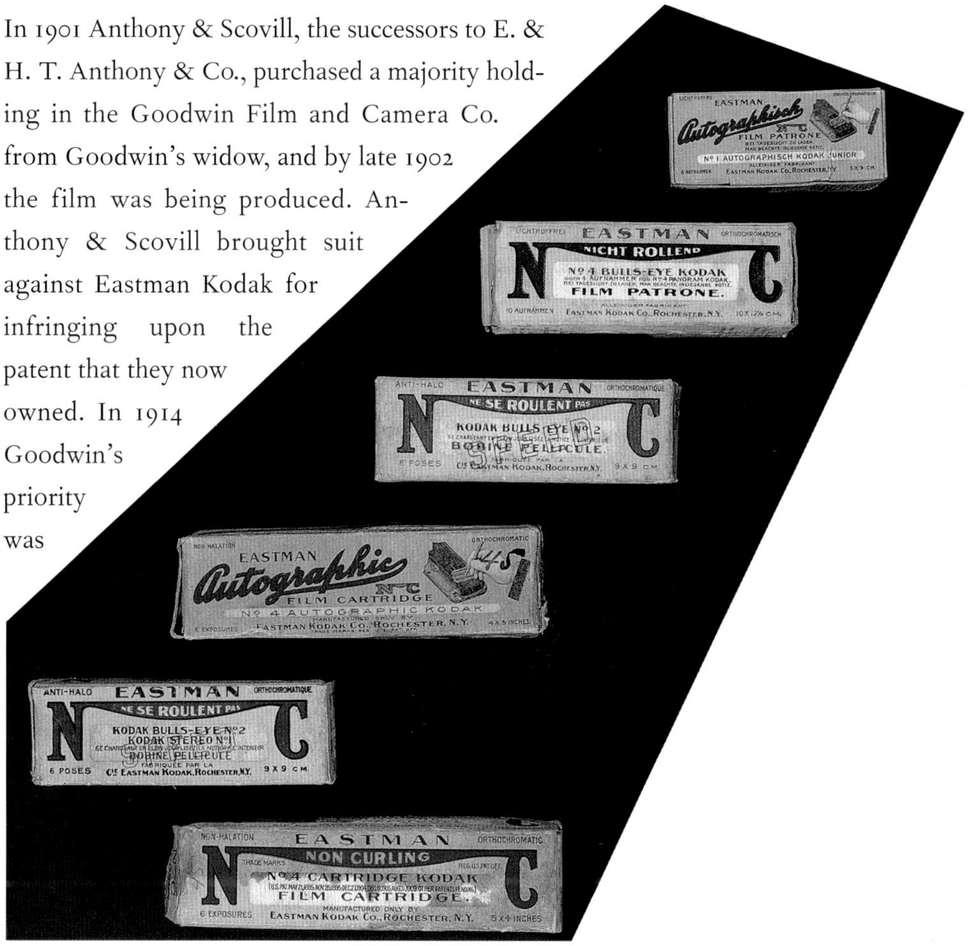

Kodak boxes for roll film, ca. 1905–1935. Types shown include NC (non-curling) and Autographic films.

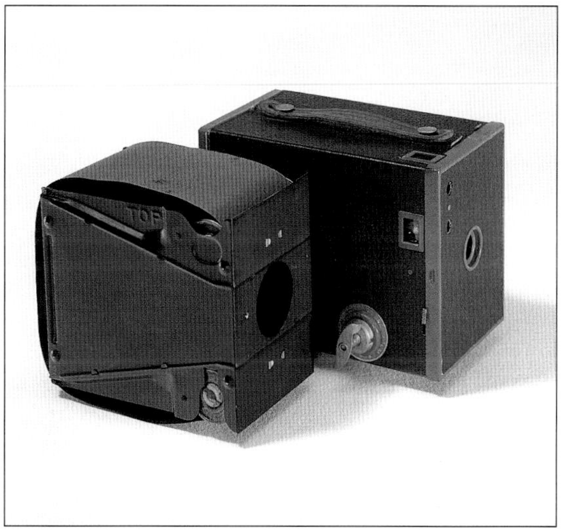

Left: Blue No. 2 Brownie, Model F, Eastman Kodak Co., ca. 1930, for eight exposures, 2 ¼" x 3 ¼", on No. 120 roll film. Brownies of this type were also available in black, brown, gray, red, and green. Shown with film carrier.

reaffirmed, the infringement was upheld, and George Eastman paid Ansco, successor to Anthony & Scovill, five million dollars in cash.

While Eastman had sought an injunction against the American Camera Manufacturing Company in 1894 over roll-film and film-roller patents, his move was denied. Eastman had begun to realize the competitive advantage of the Bulls-Eye, based on patents for the daylight-loading system invented by Samuel Turner and the front-roll

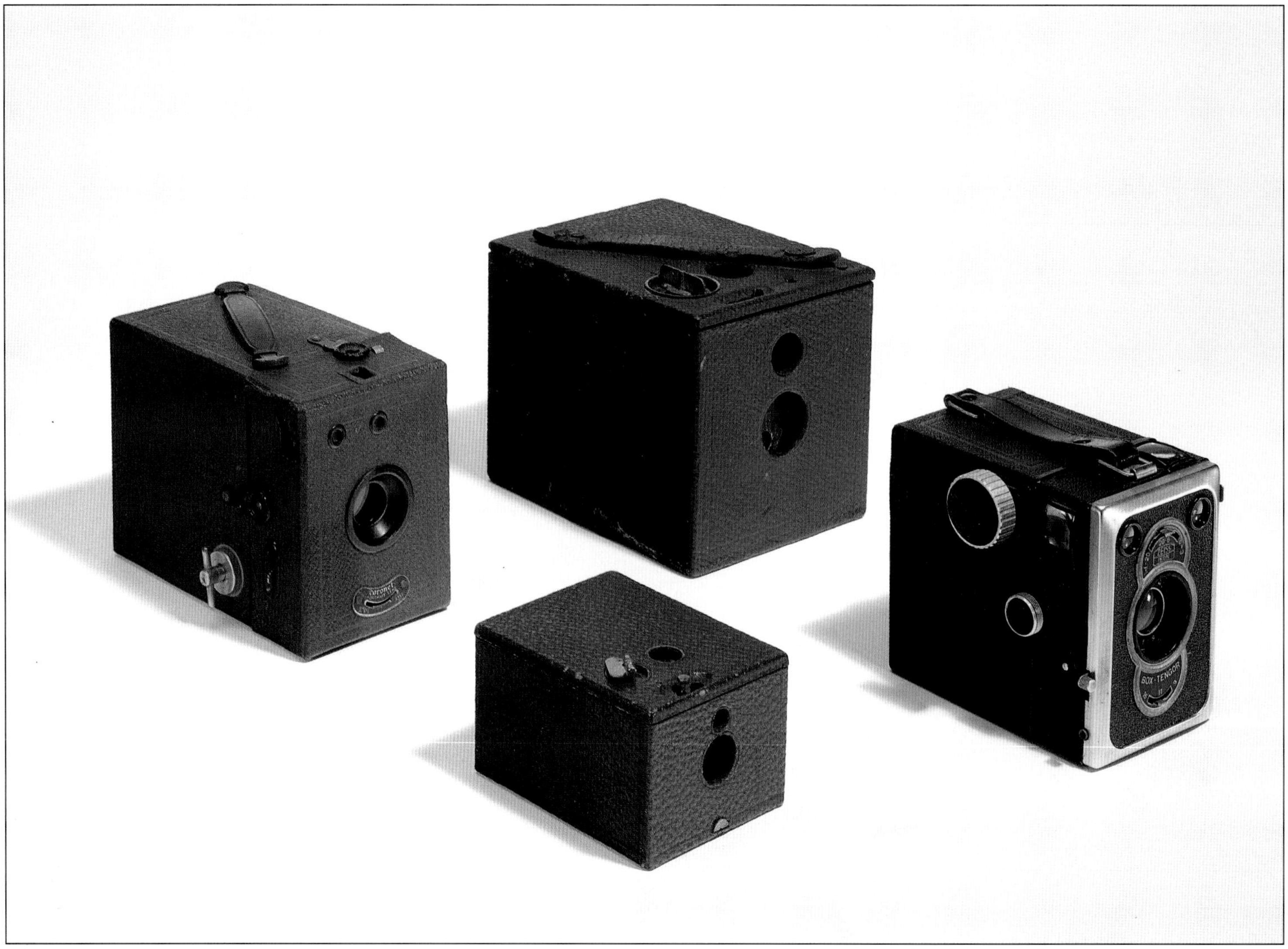

Box cameras for roll film. Clockwise from left: Coronet Box with portrait lens, green model, Coronet Camera Co., ca. 1935, for 2 1/4" x 3 1/4" exposures on 120 roll film; No. 2 Bulls-Eye, Eastman Kodak Co., ca. 1898, for 3 1/2" x 3 1/2" exposures on No. 101 roll film; Box Tengor, Zeiss Ikon, ca. 1951, for 6 x 9 cm exposures on No. 102 roll film; Pocket Kodak, Eastman Kodak Co., 1895, for 1 1/2" x 2" exposures on No. 102 roll film.

design invented by David Houston. In July 1895 the Pocket Kodak, a small but extremely well-made camera, was introduced. It used Turner's daylight-loading system, for which Eastman had obtained a nonexclusive license. The Pocket Kodak quickly became wildly popular. Between July and December, one hundred thousand were made. In contrast, the total production of the original Kodak had reached only 5,200. In order to gain full control of the Turner patent, then, Eastman bought the Boston Camera Co. and all its assets in August 1895 and immediately began marketing the Bulls-Eye Camera. Unfortunately for him, that purchase did not give Eastman the rights to Houston's front-roll system, which were owned by Thomas H. Blair. So, in 1898, Eastman bought Blair's American Camera Manufacturing Co.

Now that George Eastman had succeeded in gaining control of most patents for roll film, other camera companies had to avoid using this type of film. Most accomplished this with magazine cameras—cameras that employed some mechanical means for changing the dry plates (or, later, sheet films) they used. Many used falling-plate mechanisms, in which a series of plates were stacked vertically at the camera's back. After making the exposure, the photographer pushed a lever to move the plate forward and down, into a reservoir in the bottom. A spring inside the back pushed the remaining plates forward toward the plane of focus. Some plate-changing mechanisms were quite complicated—even to the point of absurdity. One magazine camera used an arrangement most resembling a locomotive turntable and roundhouse. In America alone, from 1885 to 1905, dozens of magazine cameras were made and marketed. In Europe, where Eastman's patent control was no less vigorous, the magazine camera was the dominant form

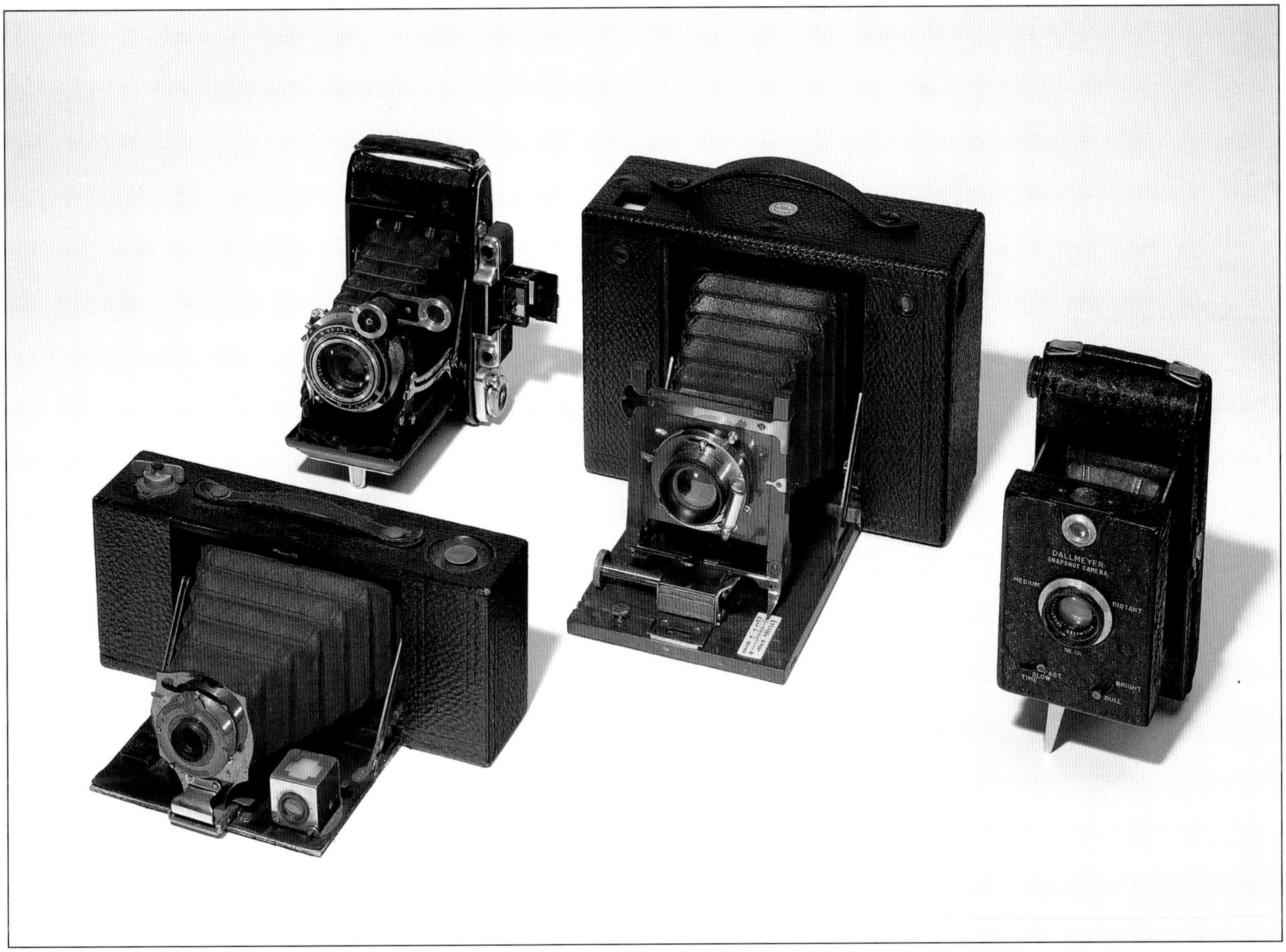

Folding cameras for roll film. Clockwise from top left: Super Ikonta C, Zeiss Ikon, ca. 1950, for 6 x 9 cm exposures on No. 120 roll film; No. 4 Cartridge Kodak, Eastman Kodak Co., ca. 1898, for 5" x 4" exposures on No. 104 roll film; Snapshot Camera, made by Houghton-Butcher for J. H. Dallmeyer, Ltd., ca. 1935, for 2 1/4" x 3 1/4" exposures on No. 120 roll film; 2A Folding Pocket Brownie, Eastman Kodak Co., ca. 1910, for 2 1/2" x 4 1/4" exposures on No. 116 roll film.

of amateur hand camera and retained a significant presence on the market until World War I.

In the early 1900s, folding and box-form cameras for roll film began to proliferate. Ever mindful of the need to create new markets, Eastman Kodak's advertising for the Brownie Camera, introduced early in 1900, was aimed specifically at children. The camera, well-made and simply constructed, cost one dollar. A six-exposure transparent film cartridge cost an additional fifteen cents. A Brownie developing and printing outfit cost seventy-five cents. In one issue of Kodak's Trade Circular in 1900, dealers were exhorted to "Plant the Brownie acorn and the Kodak oak will grow." In May, Kodak announced the formation of the Brownie Camera Club of America, open to "any boy or girl under 16 years of age," living in America, its possessions, or Canada, and, of course, owning a Brownie Camera. Competitions were held, offering prizes for photographs made with a Brownie Camera.

After the success of the Brownie, Kodak decided to court female photographers with the Vanity Kodak, introduced in April 1928. Manufactured in several colors, these cameras, a variation on the Vest Pocket Kodak, Model B, came with matching cases. Also available was the Vanity Ensemble: a Vanity Kodak in a colored case that also contained a lipstick, compact, mirror, and change purse. In 1929, the year in which Essex automobiles became the first to be manufactured in colors other than black, the less fancy—but still colored—Kodak Petites were introduced. Also that year, Kodak brought out colored Brownies, and in 1930 the Art-Deco Beau Brownie Cameras arrived on store shelves.

Another novel camera offered by Eastman Kodak was the Autographic, which used a special

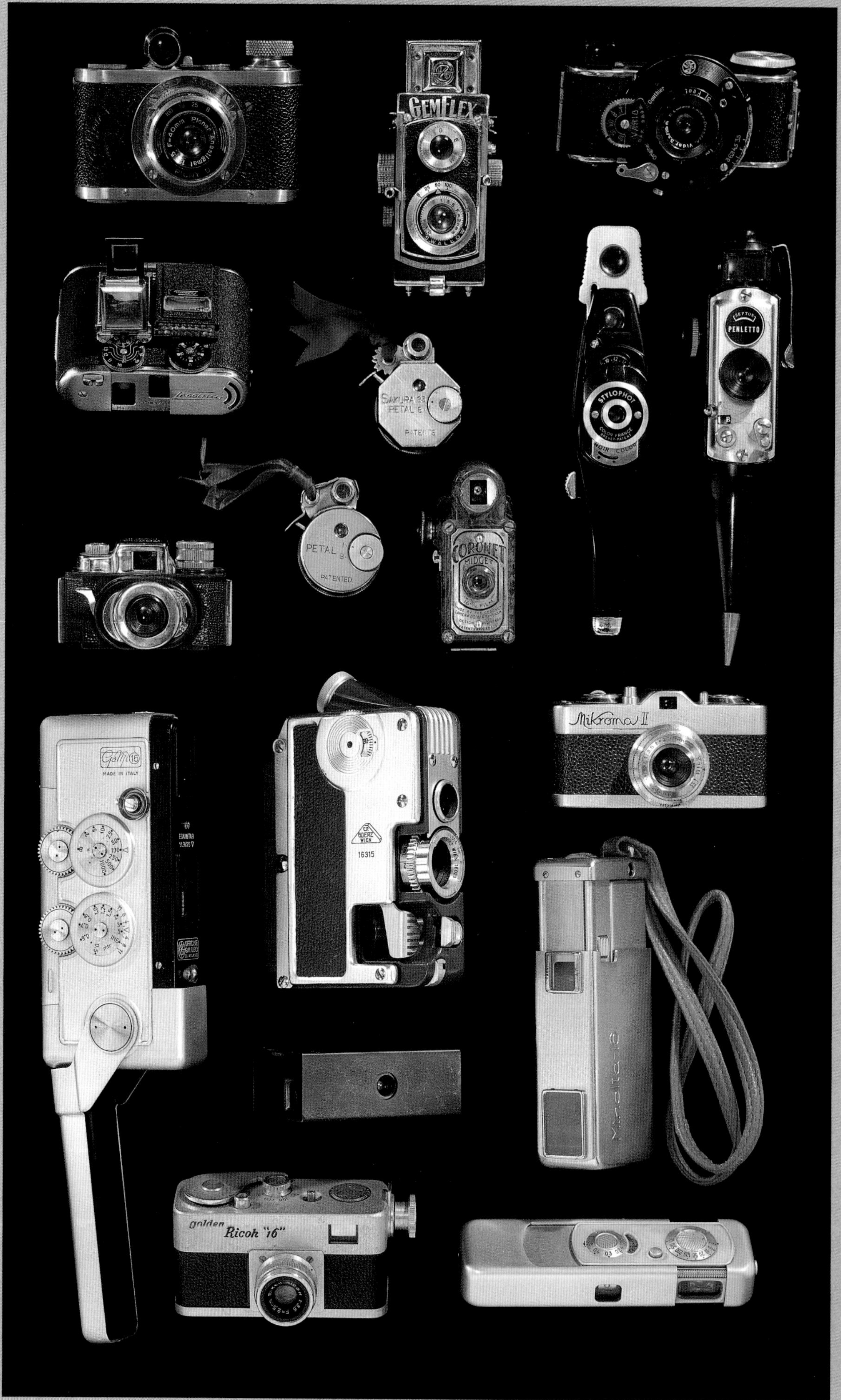

Subminiature Cameras, 1932–1980. Representative examples include: **Top row, center:** GemFlex, Showa Kogaku, ca. 1949, for 14 x 14 mm exposures on 17.5 mm paper-backed roll film. **Right side, second from top:** Septon Penletto, Harukawara, ca. 1953, for exposures on 17.5 mm paper-backed roll film. **Top row, right:** Mini-Fex, Fotofex-Kameras, ca. 1933, for thirty-six 13 x 18 mm exposures on 16 mm paper-backed cine film; probably the first precision subminiature. **Second row, second from left:** Petal, Sakura Seiki Co., ca. 1948, for six exposures, 5 mm diameter, on 25 mm diameter film; slightly postdates the St. Peter Optical Co.'s round Petal (third row, second from left). **Third row, center:** Coronet Midget, Coronet Camera Co., ca. 1935, for six exposures, 13 x 18 mm, on special 16 mm film, bakelite construction, in five colors: black, red, brown, green, and blue. **Second row from bottom, center:** Camera-X or Matchbox Camera, Eastman Kodak Co., ca. 1944, for ½" x ½" exposures on 16 mm film; a true "spy" camera, made for the war by the U.S. Office of Strategic Services.

FOCUS: *Miniature and Subminiature Cameras*

Miniature, subminiature, ultra-miniature—these terms are all used to refer to cameras that are small and produce small-format pictures. Being relative judgments, the terms have been applied to cameras of varying sizes at different times. In 1914, cameras using vest-pocket-size, 127 mm film were referred to as "miniature" cameras. An article, "Modern Miniature Cameras," in the *British Journal Photographic Almanac* for 1933, mentioned the small Rolleiflex and the Pilot Reflex, both of which used 127 mm film. To many in the 1930s, though, miniature cameras were the 35 mm cameras that were appearing on the market—Leicas, Contaxes, etc.—in ever increasing numbers.

William White, in his book *Subminiature Photography* (1990), defined subminiature cameras as "all cameras smaller in size than those regularly used in 35 mm photography." Joseph D. Cooper never specifically delineated what a miniature camera was in his book *ULTRA-Miniature Photography* (1958). He did, however, cover the Compass camera, which produced 1-by-1 ½-inch exposures, and he included cameras using 16 mm, Minox (9.5 mm), and 8 mm film. William Henry Fox Talbot built small experimental cameras in the 1830s that made 1-by-1 inch (25 mm square) negatives.

In 1858 William Skaife, an Englishman, introduced his perfected Pistolgraph. This small camera produced 1 1/8-by-1 1/2-inch exposures on wet-collodion plates. A camera that was by no means miniature but which produced exposures on small, 2-by-2 cm dry plates, was Enjalbert's Photo-Revolver de Poche. Marion's Metal Miniature Camera came in various sizes, the smallest of which, available in 1886, used 1 1/4-by-1 1/4-inch dry plates. Many other very small cameras of the 1880s and 1890s that took small pictures were designed to be concealed. These included Lancaster's Patent Watch Camera of 1889 and the Photoret, a watch camera, of 1894. The Expo and "Ticka" Watch Cameras, introduced in the early 1900s, were among the first subminiature cameras to make use of roll film.

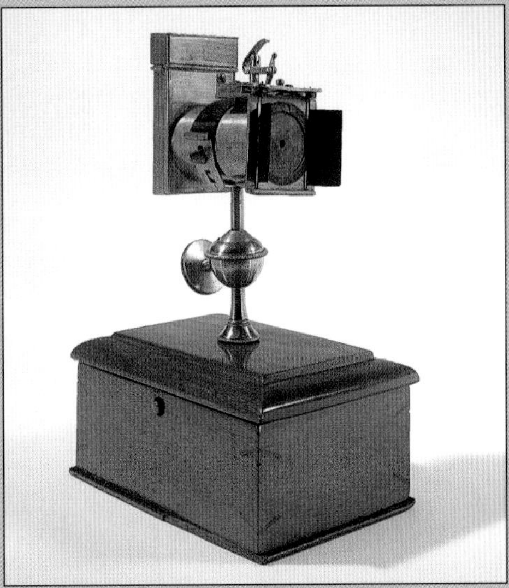

Pistolgraph, Thomas Skaife, ca. 1859, all-brass construction, for 1 1/8" x 1 1/2" exposures on wet-collodion plates. By removing the back lenses it could be used as an enlarger. Reportedly, Skaife was arrested for aiming his Pistolgraph at Queen Victoria while attempting to "shoot" her picture.

Until 1923 most subminiature cameras had to use special plates or films made specifically for them. In June 1923, however, the Eastman Kodak Co. introduced the Cine-Kodak movie camera, accompanied by 16 mm cine film. Kodak did not produce a subminiature camera until World War II, when it made the OSS "Camera-X" or Matchbox Camera. Kodak's 16 mm cine film became the standard size for virtually all subminiature cameras. Perhaps the cheapest—and in most cases the flimsiest—subminiature cameras were the "Hit-type" cameras. These little cameras produced 14-by-14 mm exposures on 17 mm paper-backed roll film. They were produced in Japan by the hundreds of thousands in the quarter century following World War II.

Metal Miniature Camera, Marion & Co., ca. 1888, nickel-plated brass construction, for 2" x 2" exposures on dry plates. With slip-on guillotine drop shutter. Considered a "miniature" camera in its time.

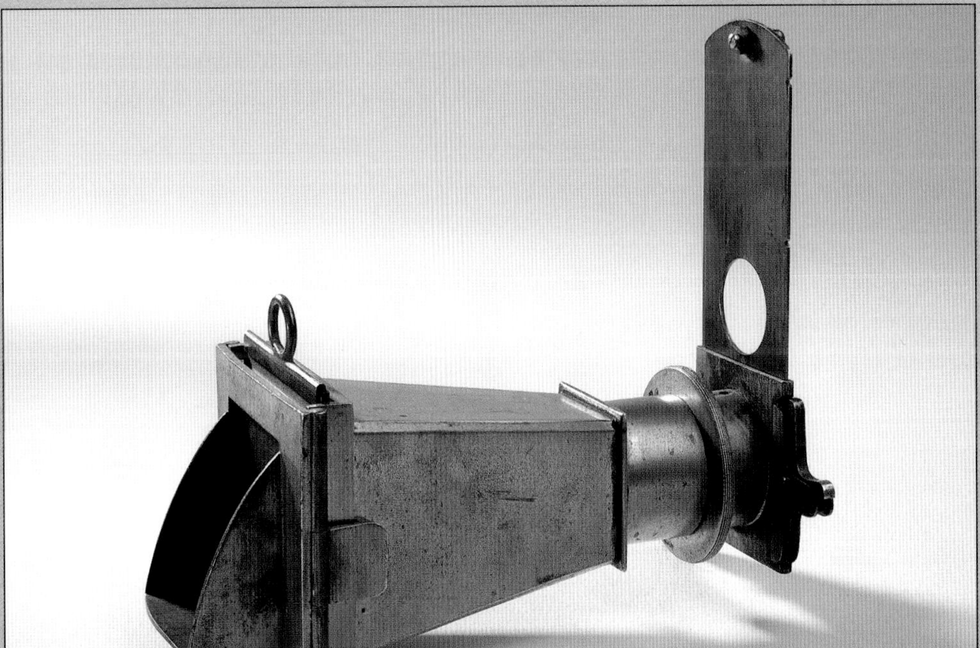

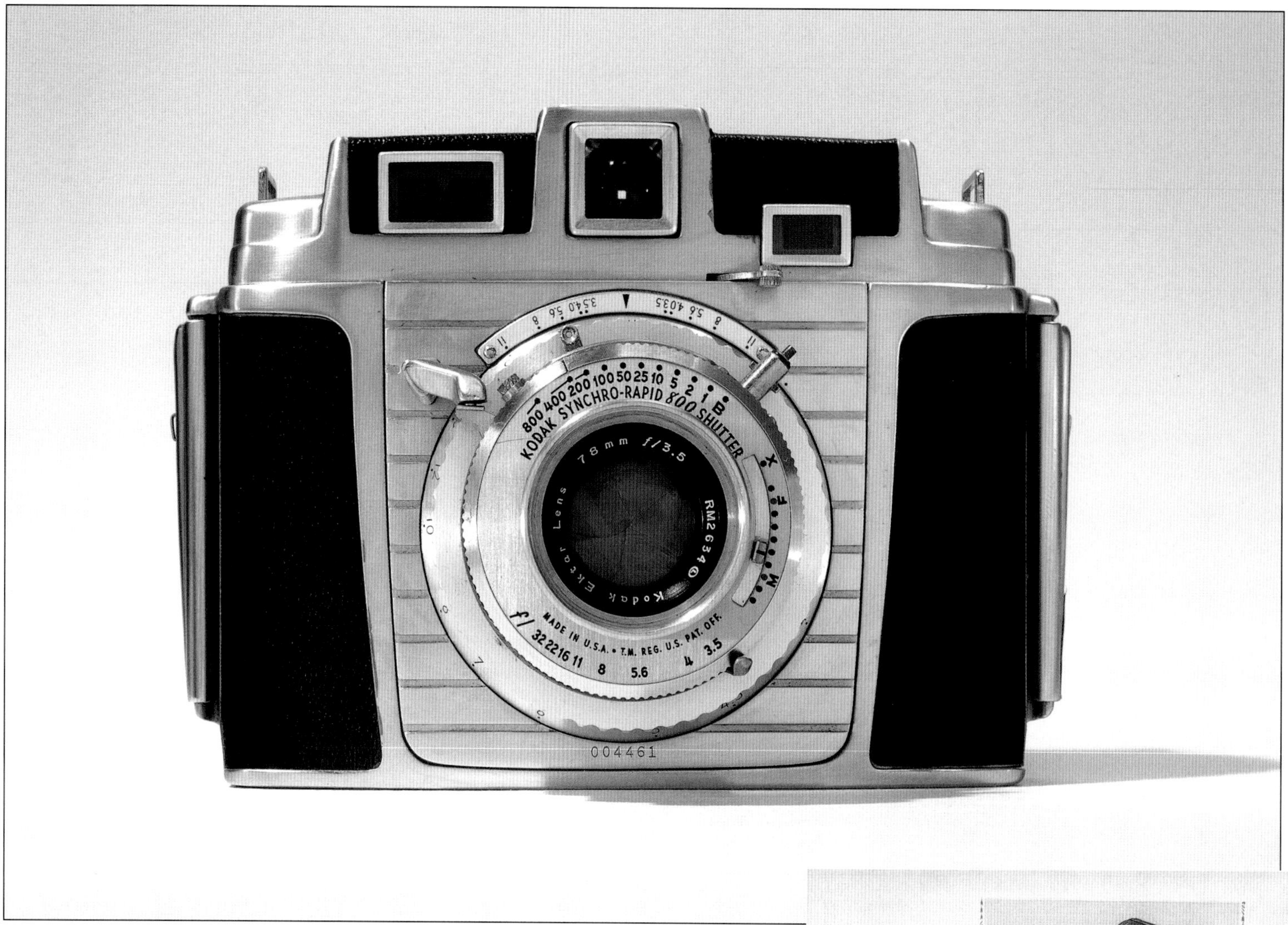

Kodak Chevron, Eastman Kodak Co., ca. 1954, for twelve exposures, 2 ¼" x 3 ¼", on No. 620 roll film. Built-in flash synchronization, coupled rangefinder, parallax correction, and lever-operated film advance.

Right: Advertisement for Vanity Kodaks, Eastman Kodak Co., 1928. Colorful ads for the colored Vanity Kodak cameras appeared in many popular journals in mid-1928.

roll film and had a modified back. The film had a red paper backing that, when written on with a stylus, permitted the passage of light through the back of the film to the emulsion. The user could write notations on each frame through a trapdoor in the camera's back. When the negatives were developed, the notation appeared on one of the margins, and in printing was transferred to the photographic print. Thus a notation such as "Aunt Nellie's Birthday" could be affixed to the photo at the time of its exposure.

The influence of roll film on professional and particularly amateur photography can hardly be overstated. Roll film is more compact, less expensive, and far more user-friendly than plate film, and as a result, vastly more accessible to the amateur. The interest in amateur photography that began in the 1890s blossomed in the twentieth century. This rapid growth can be discerned by examining the production numbers for Kodak cameras.

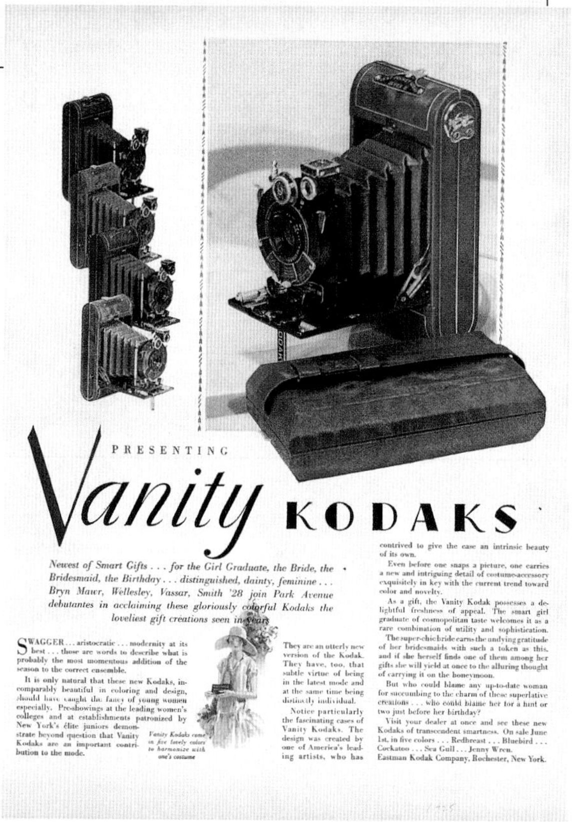

Certainly the number of cameras sold reflects to an extent the number of photographers using new cameras, which in turn suggests the number of photographs made—with new cameras alone. (It should be noted that the focus here is the rate of increase, rather than the specific numbers.)

The original Kodak and the No. 1 Kodak had a total production, from 1888 to 1895, of about fifteen thousand. For the Pocket Kodak, from 1895 to 1900 (the period in which it was produced) the number was 147,000. Production of the Brownie in the nine months of its existence was 245,000 cameras. Between October 1901 and 1921, production of the larger No. 2 Brownie Camera totaled more than two and a half million. These figures demonstrate the rapid growth in the production of cameras from only one manufacturer—granted, the most significant one—in only one country. They have also been chosen selectively from only the first three decades or so of viable roll film. A later figure, from the period 1963 to 1982, shows that more than 140 million Kodak cartridge-loading (Instamatic) cameras were sold.

In addition to the standardization and simplification afforded by roll film, the mass production of cameras utilizing it made them much more affordable. At the time the twenty-five-dollar Kodak was introduced, the average annual earnings of a nonfarm employee were $466. That meant it took nearly three weeks' wages to purchase a Kodak. In 1895, the Pocket Kodak was priced at five dollars, or less than a week's wages. At two dollars, the No. 2 Brownie, introduced in 1901, could be bought for two days' earnings of a worker in manufacturing. And the one-dollar price tag of the Brownie, in 1900, put it within the reach of young people with pocket change earned doing odd chores.

In the years since the introduction of paper-backed roll film, there have been many improvements. The original roll films had a tendency to curl after developing, fixing, and drying, in some cases curling as tight as a pencil. Kodak solved that problem by introducing its NC (non-curling) film in 1903. The sensitivity of film has increased tremendously since then, to the point that films with an ISO rating of 3200 are now available. Likewise, the ability of black-and-white film to register different colors of the spectrum—both visible and invisible—has gradually improved. Film has evolved from orthochromatic to panchromatic and infrared. Emulsions have become increasingly fine-grained, yielding crisper enlargements, even from smaller negatives.

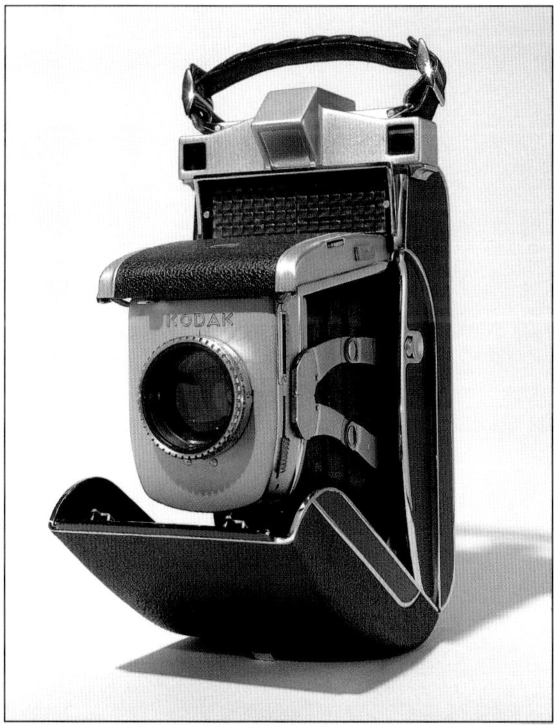

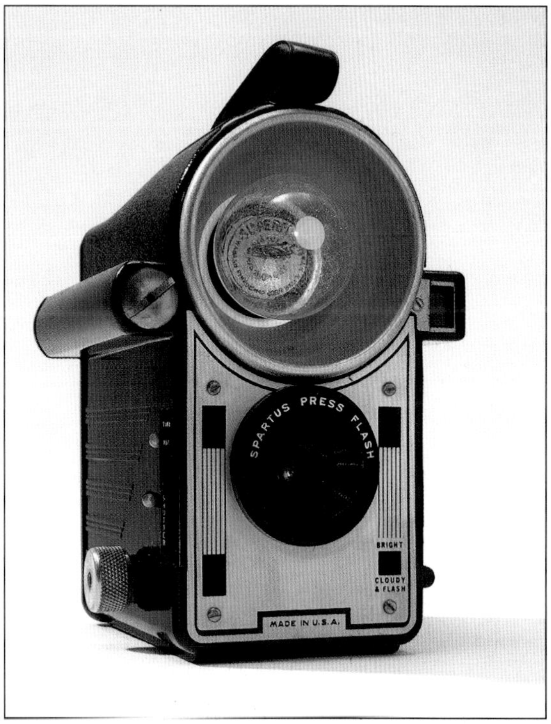

Left: Super Kodak Six-20, Eastman Kodak Co., ca. 1939, for eight exposures, 2 1/4" x 3 1/4", on No. 620 roll film. The first camera with automatic exposure control. A light-metering cell controlled the diaphragm aperture.

Right: Spartus Press Flash, Spartus Corp., ca. 1954, for eight exposures, 2 1/4" x 3 1/4", on No. 120 roll film. Introduced in 1939, this was the first camera to have a built-in unit for flash bulbs. Also appeared under the names Falcon Press Flash, Galter Press Flash, and Regal Flash Master.

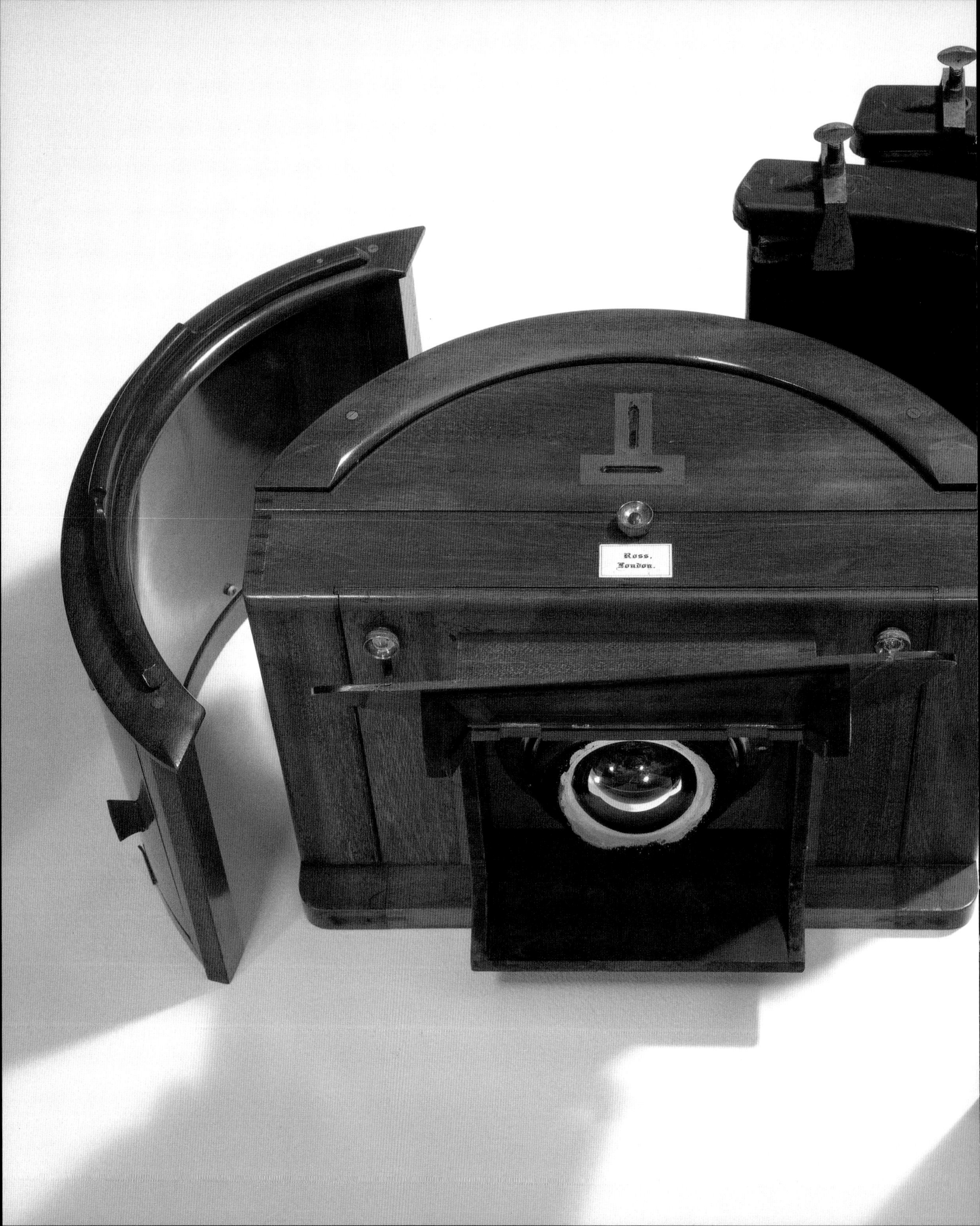
Ross,
London.

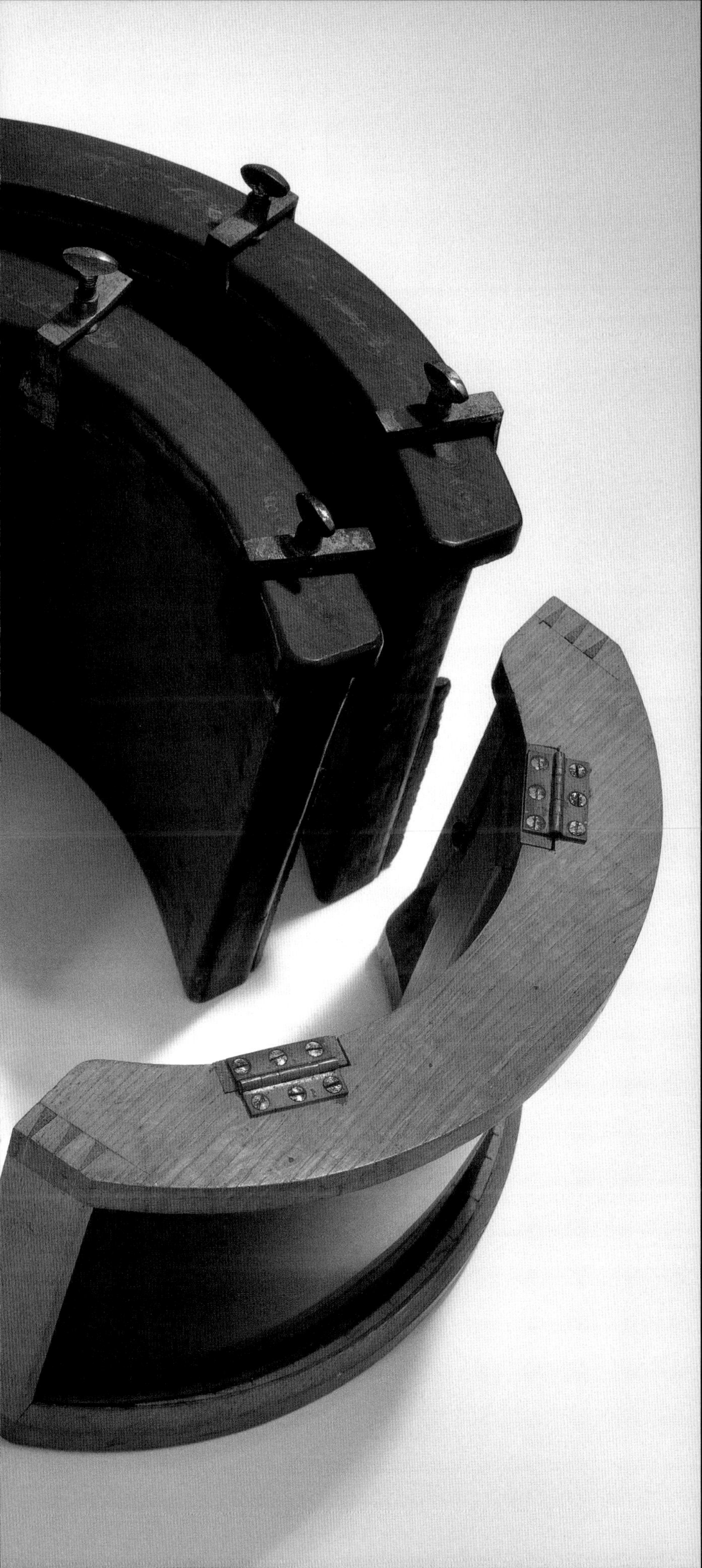

CHAPTER SEVEN:

THE ALL-SEEING EYE: DIVERSITY IN THE CAMERA

Sutton's Panoramic Camera, Thomas Ross, ca. 1861, mahogany construction. Shown with mahogany plate holder, left; two hard rubber tanks, rear; and printing frame, right.

The applications of photography since its inception have been numerous and diverse. Often, advances in technology and the evolution of cameras themselves have made different types of photography possible. In other cases, cameras have been modified with a particular use in mind, resulting in highly specialized equipment. This consideration of the camera, in its various forms, will be organized into two sections. The first section will group cameras by their defining features, such as twin-reflex and single-reflex cameras, while the second will survey several categories of cameras designed for special use, such as medical and underwater cameras.

Stereo Cameras

Stereo photography has been around since 1841, when William Henry Fox Talbot and Henry Collen produced pairs of photographs for viewing in Sir Charles Wheatstone's stereoscope. As the type of stereoscope invented by Sir David Brewster in 1851 (which mimicked human vision by presenting two perspectives of an image) became popular and the demand for images to be viewed in his instruments increased, the need to assure the proper positioning and amount of shift of the camera became more important. This was particularly true in photographing human subjects, which required a quick shift in camera position.

One obvious way to adapt a camera's structure for stereographic production would have been to incorporate two lenses into the design. However, in the 1850s lenses were very expensive, so alternative solutions were devised. Many stereo cameras, such as those produced in London by Latimer Clark and Negretti & Zambra, were mounted on a base that allowed the camera to slide on tracks between two fixed positions. Among cameras of this design, Powell's Portable Stereoscopic, made in the late 1850s by Horne & Thornthwaite, was especially popular.

In 1856 John Benjamin Dancer introduced a two-lens stereo camera to the photographic society in Manchester, England. Although it could accommodate single wet-collodion plate holders, it was intended for use with a plate-changing magazine for dry-collodion plates (3 ¼-by-6 ¾ inches), which could be attached below the body. Mounted in front of the camera's lenses was a metal-plate shutter; by pivoting the plate, the lenses could be uncovered and re-covered to provide simultaneous exposure. Joseph John Pyne's Tourists' Stereoscopic Companion camera had a similar shutter design.

Left: Stereoscopic camera, Latimer Clark, ca. 1855, mahogany construction, for sequential paired exposures, 2 3/4" x 3 1/4", on 3 1/4" x 6 3/4" wet-collodion plates.

Right: Stereoscopic camera, J. B. Dancer, ca. 1856, mahogany construction, for twelve paired exposures on 3 1/4" x 6 3/4" dry-collodion plates housed in lower changing box. Could also be used for single wet-collodion plates. Pivoting brass shutter.

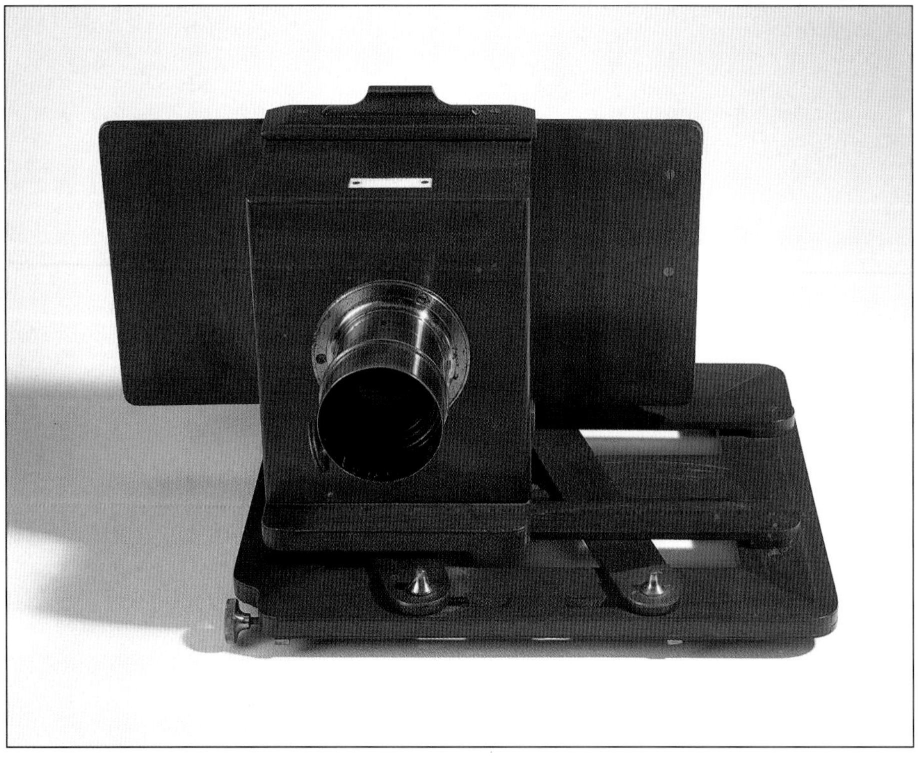

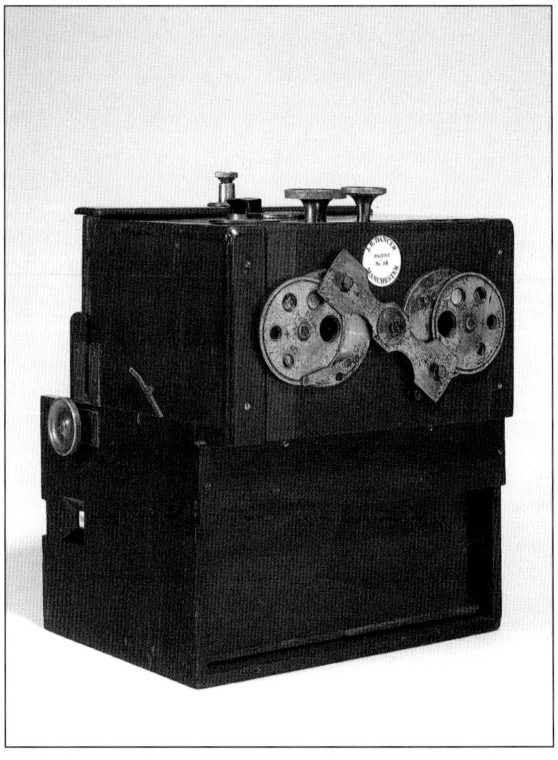

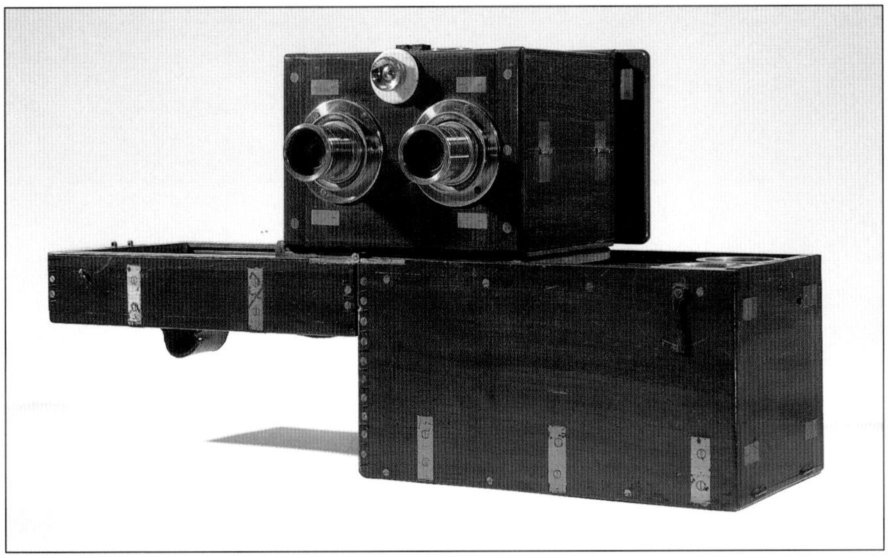

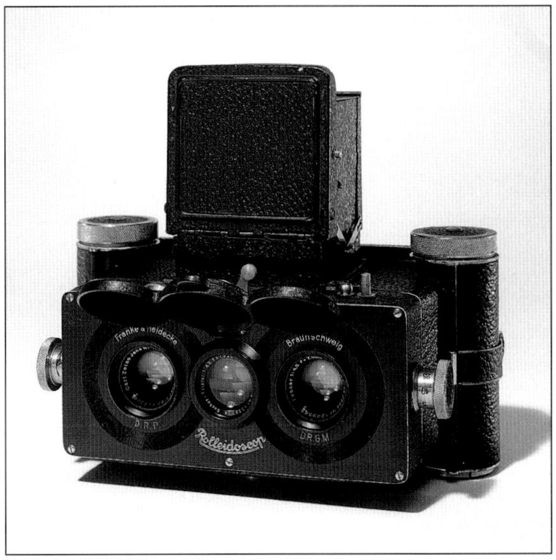

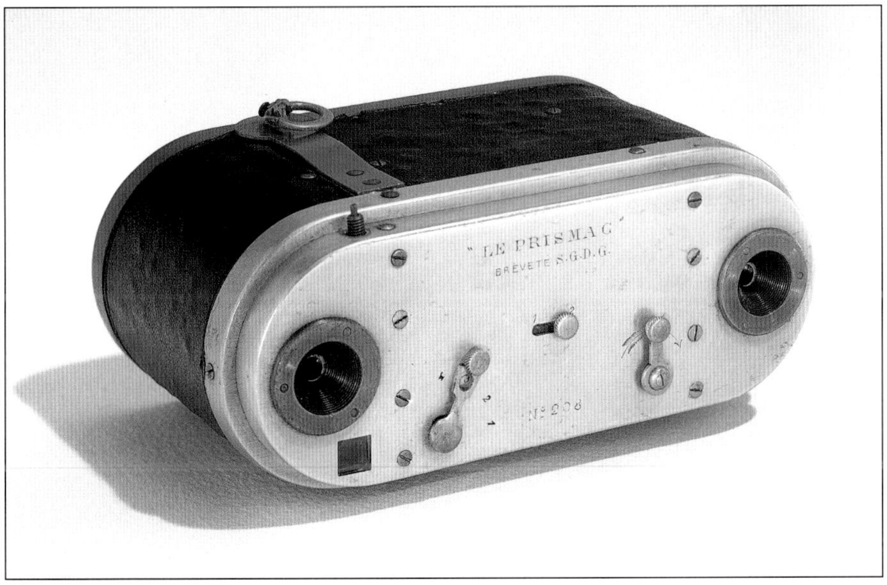

Clockwise from top left:
Collapsible stereoscopic camera, Horne & Thornthwaite, ca. 1864, mahogany construction, for paired 2 3/4" x 3" exposures on dry-collodion plates. Top of case acts as track for lateral shifts.

Rolleidoscop, Franke & Heidecke, ca. 1931, for paired exposures, 6 cm x 6 cm, on No. 120 roll film. The Rolleidoscop and the Heidoscop (for dry plates) led to Rolleiflex's line.

Le Prismac, A. Devaux, ca. 1905, for 4.5 x 4.5 cm paired exposures on No. 102 roll film.

As bellows-view and studio cameras came into greater use in the late 1860s and 1870s, stereo cameras incorporating these features became more common. While rigid-bodied two-lens stereo cameras had a rigid septum (an internal partition that prevented the two images from overlapping on the plate), bellows cameras had cloth ones to allow for closure. As the interest in stereo photography decreased, bellows cameras often doubled as regular view/field cameras. This dual function was effected in one of two ways. The more common was to have the lenses mounted on an interchangeable lens board. Once a single lens was mounted and the septum removed, nonstereo images could be made. Stereo cameras could also be converted to panoramic cameras in a similar manner. Another, less expensive way to take stereo photographs was to use a single lens mounted on a lens board that had a greater-than-normal shift.

Around 1900, stereo photography underwent a revival as a trio of stereo formats developed. Along with the 45-by-107 mm format of Jules Richard's Verascope, the 6-by-13 cm format of a number of French jumelles and German stereo cameras also flourished. In America the standard format used in the Holmes-Bates stereoscopes persisted.

One unusual stereo camera of the early 1900s was Le Prismac, designed by Deloyé. This apparatus, whose name derived from the prisms it used, made paired 4.5-by-4.5-cm exposures on 102 mm roll film. The film traveled in a forward path within the body, perpendicular to the camera's front. The pair of 90-degree prisms, mounted behind the lenses, directed the images onto the film. This design eliminated the need for the customary switching of left and right exposures to ensure proper viewing.

In the 1920s and 1930s, stereoscopes were more popular in Germany and France than in the U.S. The French and German markets offered simple box cameras for roll film and plates, in addition to a number of quite sophisticated models. One stereo camera that used roll film was the Rolleidoscop, manufactured by Franke & Heidecke in two sizes. The smaller model took 4-by-4-cm pairs on 127 mm film; the larger, 6-by-6-cm

PROFILE:

Johnson-Harrison Pantascopic

In 1862, Johnson and Harrison introduced their Pantascopic Camera, which came equipped with traditional optics. The whole camera was rotated by a built-in clockwork mechanism, while the sensitized wet-collodion plate (of conventional shape and not curved) moved laterally in a direction opposite to that of the camera. A slit-cloth cover on the front of the plate holder moved along the plate, producing a continuous, uniform exposure with an arc of 110 degrees. Johnson and Harrison's first Pantascopic model produced 7 ½-by-12-inch negatives; a later model, marketed by the Pantascopic Company, produced 4 ½-by-7-inch negatives.

The first photographic panorama book illustrations, made from negatives taken with Johnson and Harrison's second-model Pantascopic Camera, appeared in the sixth-annual edition of *The Royal Album: Court Directory and General Guide* (Spottiswoode & Co., London, 1866). Though otherwise unremarkable, this edition, in the third and final part, the "Illustrated Guide to London," contained eight 3¾-by-7-inch panoramic albumen photographs made with Johnson's camera, earning it the honor of being the only nineteenth-century book illustrated with single-plate panoramic photographs.

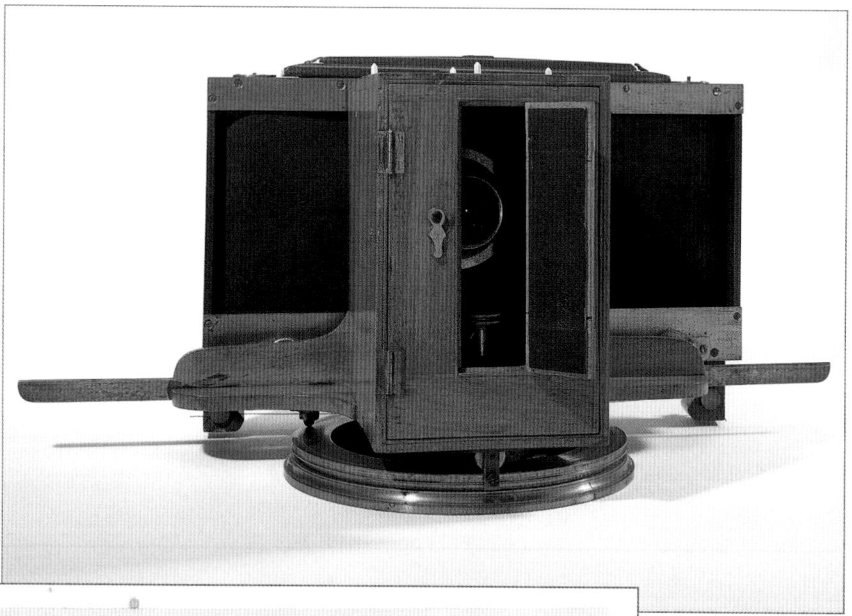

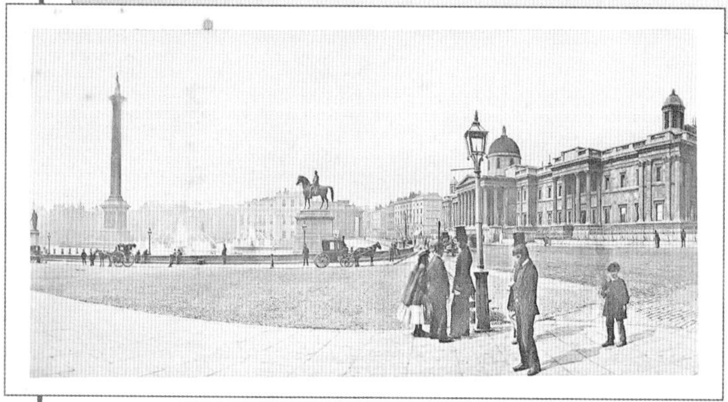

Johnson-Harrison Pantascopic Camera, ca. 1864.

Left: Anonymous, Panoramic view of Trafalgar Square, ca. 1866, tipped-in albumen print from *The Royal Album: Court Directory and General Guide.*

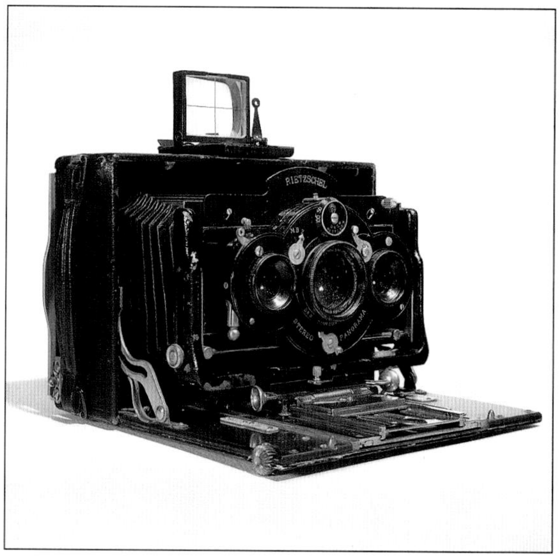

pairs on 120 mm film. These cameras had a large viewfinder that projected an image of each exposure onto its ample viewing screen. In its day, the Rolleidoscop was considered by many to be the finest stereographic camera in the world.

In the years following World War II, stereo photography became popular yet again, this time in the 35 mm format. Some of these cameras will be considered in a later chapter.

Panoramic and Wide-Angle Cameras

The angle of clear vision for the human eye is roughly 60 degrees. The angle of view for a "normal" camera lens is 45 to 50 degrees. Wide-angle photographs are those that cover a field of view appreciably greater than that of a normal camera, i.e., 65 degrees or more. A panoramic picture is a wide-angle photograph whose width-to-height ratio is larger than usual.

Cameras that produce wide-angle and panoramic photographs can be separated into two basic types. The first is similar to a traditional camera in that neither the lens nor the camera moves, and all of the film or plate is exposed at once. A lens with a wider-than-normal field of view generates a panoramic result. The second type consists of those cameras in which there is motion of the lens in relation to the film or plate, or of the film or plate in relation to the lens. Only a thin vertical section of the film or plate is exposed at any one time.

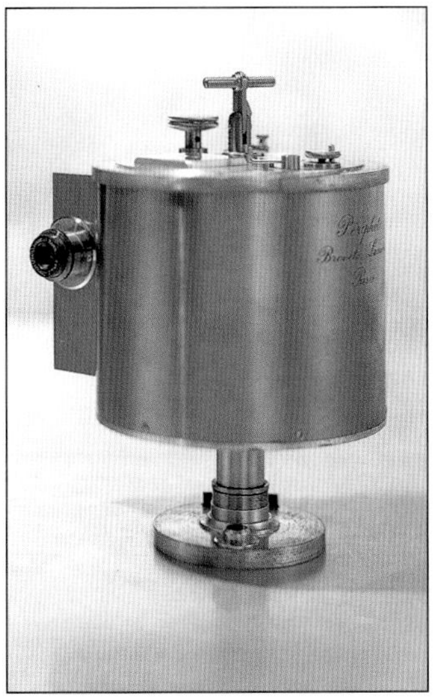

Opposite: Universal Heli-Clack, Type III, Hch. Rietzschel, ca. 1912, for paired 7 x 9 cm exposures on dry plates. Could also be used with center lens only for single exposures.

Above: Périphote, Lumière Bros., ca. 1901, aluminum construction, for six 2 3/4" x 15" exposures on roll film, up to 360-degree angle covered. Image projected onto film by means of prism.

Right: Al-Vista Panoramic camera, Model 5F, Multiscope & Film Co., ca. 1905. Shown with conversion front, right, for conventional exposures on 4" x 5" dry plates.

The first camera designed specifically to take panoramic photographs was a daguerreotype camera produced in 1844 by Friedrich von Martens. This was a pivoting-lens camera that moved in an arc of 150 degrees to expose a curved daguerreotype plate. Von Martens used his camera to make tableaux of Paris. In 1854, following the introduction of the wet-collodion process, he switched to flat glass plates.

The next significant development in wide-angle/panoramic cameras came in 1860, with Englishman Thomas Sutton's invention of a camera that used curved glass plates for the wet-collodion process. Its fixed-position lens was a spherical shell of flint glass filled with water which covered an angle of 120 degrees. Sutton's camera and lens were produced in multiple sizes by Frederick Cox and, later, by Thomas Ross.

The Pantascopic Camera of John R. Johnson and John A. Harrison, patented in England in 1862, was a panoramic camera in which the lens remained stationary but the camera body pivoted on a central axis. A flat glass plate, coated with wet collodion, was moved past a narrow vertical slit at the plane of focus. The camera's motion covered an angle of approximately 120 degrees.

Other notable pivoting panoramic cameras manufactured in the late nineteenth century include Stirn's Wonder Panoramic Camera (1890), designed by Canadian J. R. Connon and made in Berlin by Rudolf Stirn, and the Cyclographe (1890) by J. Damoiseau. Both devices were capable of making full 360-degree panoramas but could also expose lesser segments of film.

The early 1900s brought additional models with 360-degree capabilities: the Lumière Périphote (1901), the Cirkut Camera (1904), and the Ernemann Rundblick-Kamera (1907). Of these, the Cirkut Camera was the most widely known, and it is also the only one still in use today.

Until to the 1890s, panoramic cameras were considered too expensive for middle-income amateur photographers. In 1896, however, Peter N. Angsten and Charles H. Gesbeck of Chicago were granted a patent for the Al-Vista Panoramic camera. Made by the Multiscope & Film Company, their camera worked on the pivoting-lens principle, using roll film set in a curved interior. The

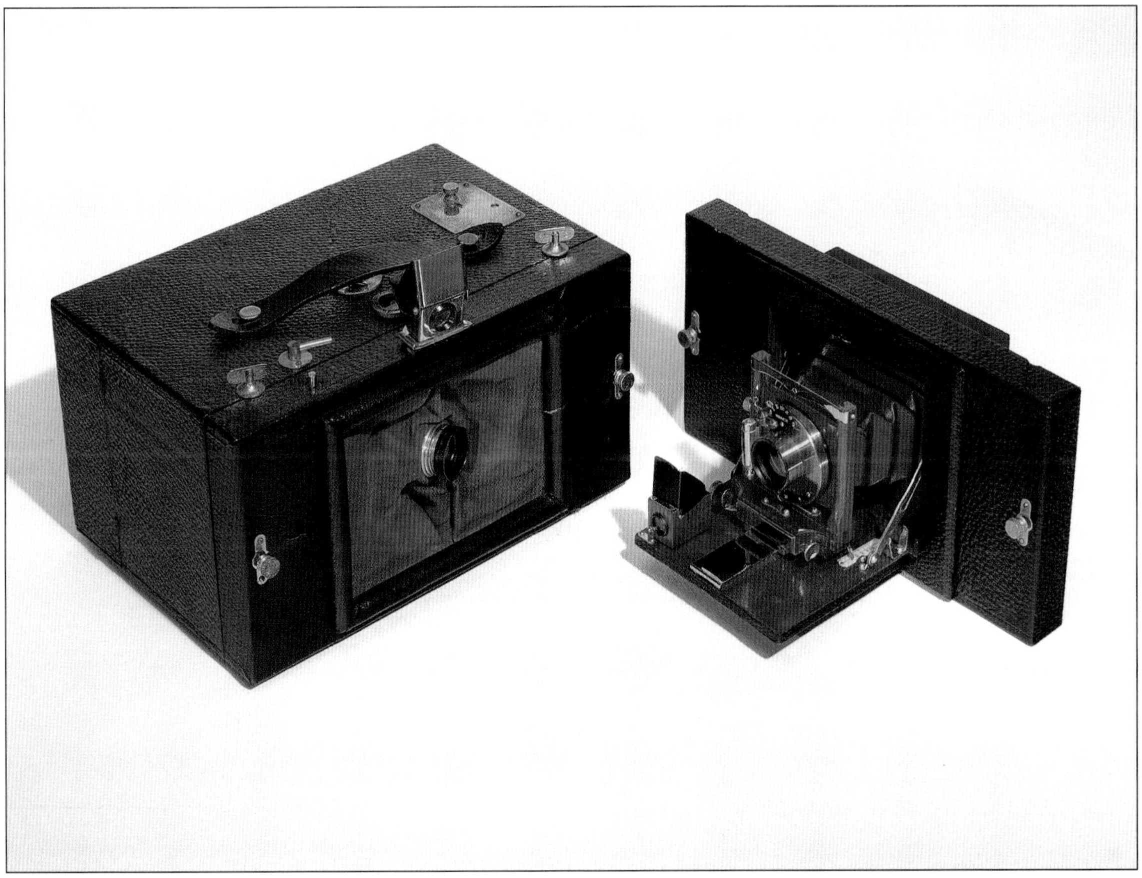

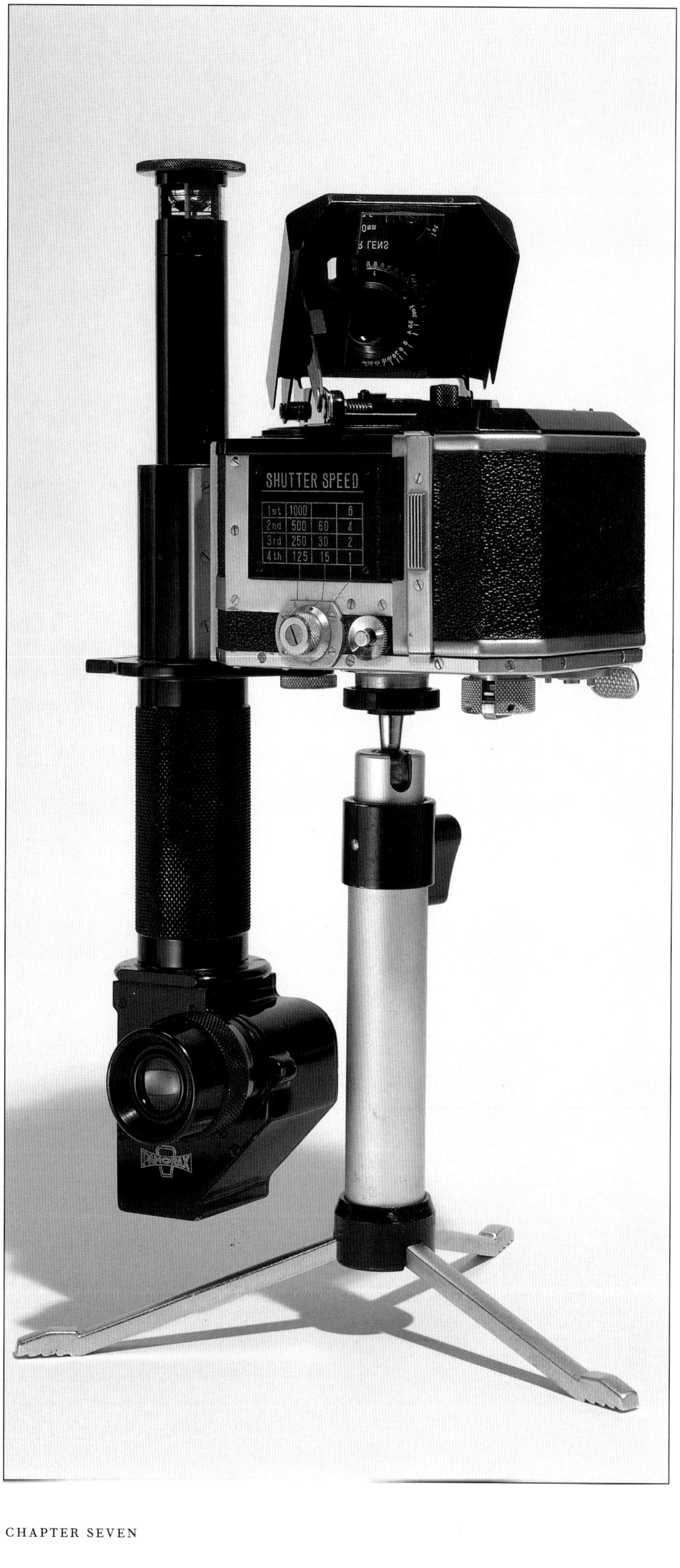

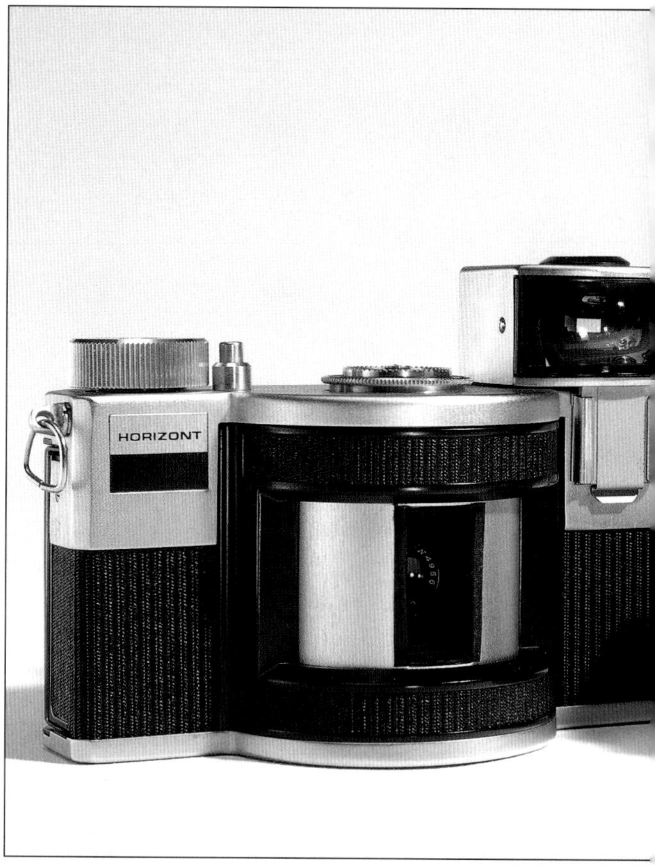

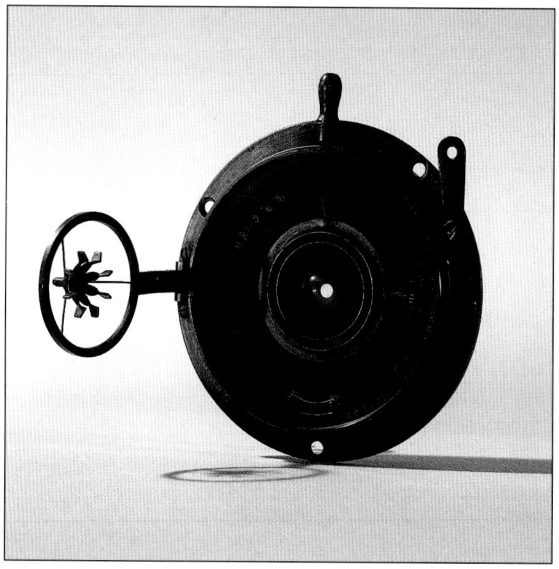

Clockwise from left: Panorax-ZI 360E, Panorax Optical Co., ca. 1958, for exposures from 24 x 42 mm up to 24 x 230 mm on No. 135 roll film, up to 360-degree angle covered. Unusual in its use of mirror and prism to direct image onto film wound on drum.

Above left: Horizont, K. M. Z., Russia, ca. 1968, for twenty-one exposures, 24 x 58 mm, on No. 135 roll film, 120-degree angle covered. Above right: Viscawide-16 ST-D, Taiyokoki Co., Ltd., ca. 1961, for ten exposures, 10 x 46 mm, on specially loaded 16 mm film, 120-degree angle covered.

Hypergon lens, C. P. Goerz, ca. 1906.

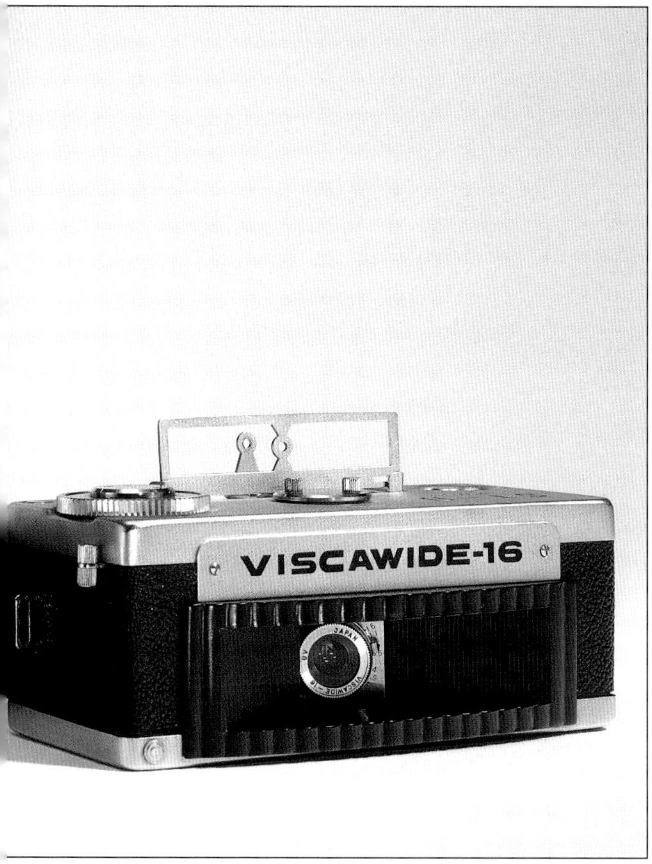

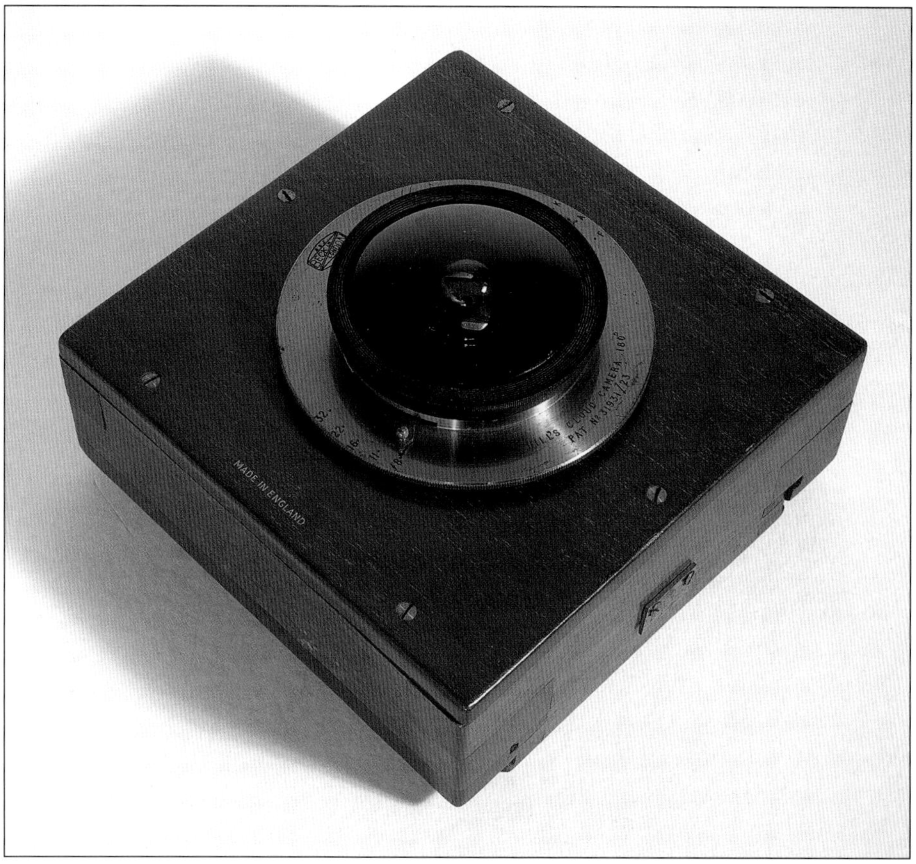

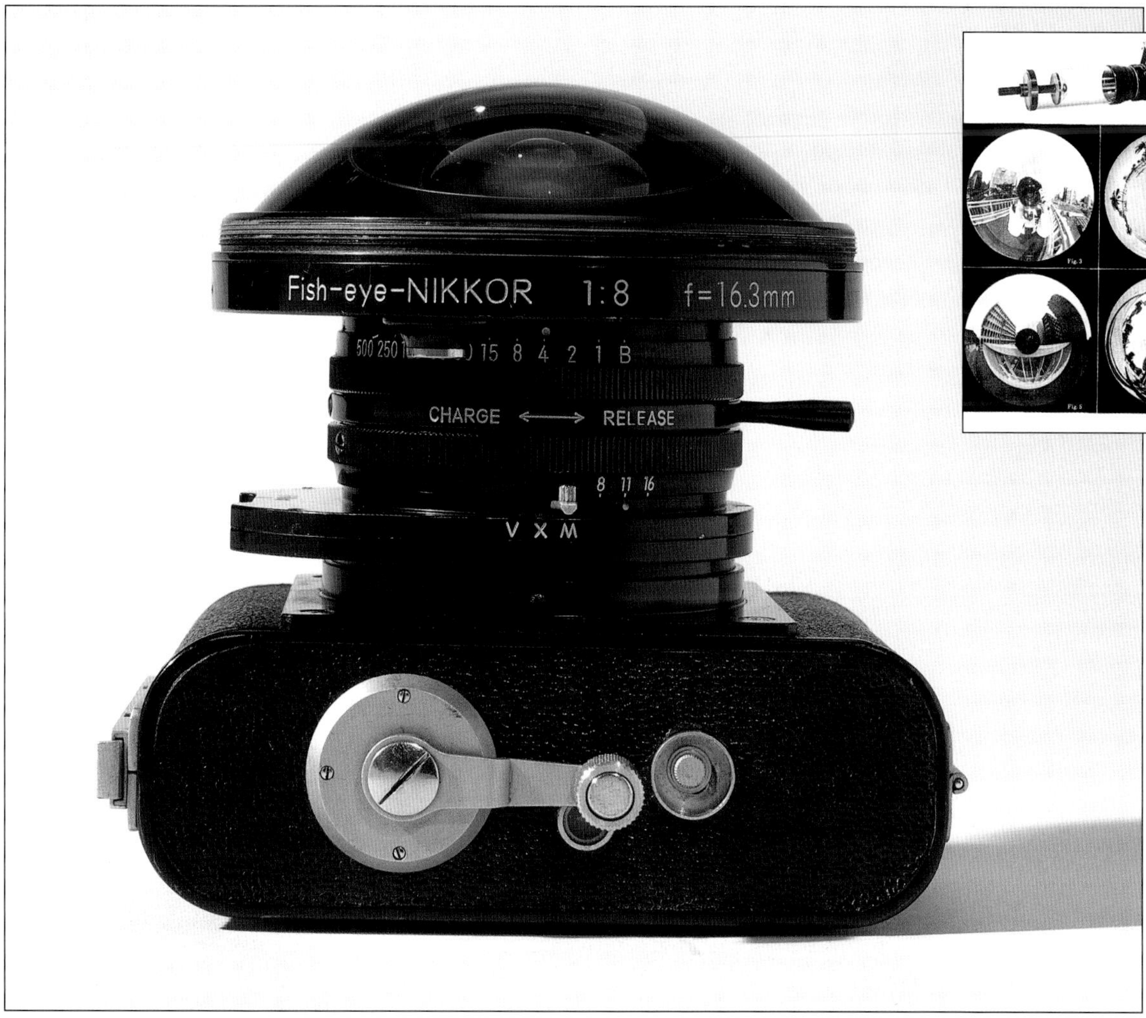

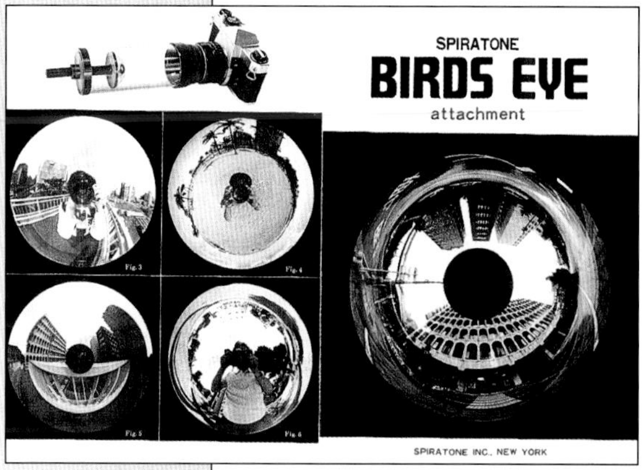

Clockwise from top right: Hill Cloud Camera, R.& J. Beck, ca. 1924, for circular exposures (2 1/2" diameter) on 3 1/4" x 4 1/4" dry plates or sheet film, mahogany body construction.

Pamphlet for Spiratone Birds Eye attachment, Spiratone, ca. 1976.

Nikon Whole-Sky Camera with Fish-eye Nikkor lens, Nippon Kogaku, K. K., ca. 1961, for 2 1/4" x 2 1/4" exposures on No. 120 roll film.

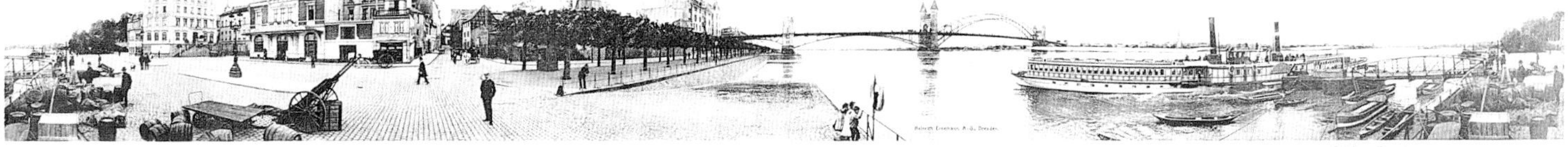

Anonymous, View of Rhine River at Bonn, 360-degree view, ca. 1910, collotype, 4" x 37", taken with Ernemann-Rundblick-Camera.

swing of the lens on some models could be adjusted to cover various lengths of film. Al-Vistas were affordable, too—costing thirty dollars in 1901. (A worker in manufacturing made an average of $511 per year.) The most versatile model was one in which the camera's front, with its pivoting lens, could be removed and replaced by a conventional bellows-equipped front section, complete with lens and shutter. The camera's back could be fitted to hold 4-by-5-inch dry plates. The Al-Vista inspired a similar pivoting-lens panoramic camera, produced by Eastman Kodak in 1899.

The Hypergon lens, designed in 1900 by E. von Hoegh and manufactured by C. P. Goerz, was a wide-angle anastigmat lens offering a flat field and freedom from distortion over an arc of 135 to 140 degrees. Because illumination fell off markedly at the field's outer edge, mounted in front of the lens was a long-toothed cogwheel. To prevent the image of the wheel from appearing on the film, the wheel was spun during exposure with puffs of air produced by squeezing an air bulb.

Fish-eye and *sky* are terms applied to lenses that project the image of a full hemisphere (180 degrees) onto a finite circle in the focal plane. The earliest example of such a lens was the Hill Sky lens, introduced in 1924. Designed by Robin Hill and made by R. & J. Beck, of London, the lens was mounted on a flat, boxlike body. Because it was used for meteorological observation, the apparatus was called the Hill Cloud Camera. In 1960 Nikon introduced a 180-degree fish-eye lens, mounted on a special camera body that used 120 mm film. This outfit was called the Nikon Whole-Sky Camera. Some of the approximately thirty of these cameras that were manufactured were used by the Japanese Bureau of Meteorology. More affordable to the average photographer was the Spiratone 12 mm, f/5.6 prime lens, which came "complete with lens cap [and] deluxe zipper case with strap." An unusual ultra-wide-field accessory was the Birds Eye attachment, also sold by Spiratone. This accessory produced pictures of the camera and the field surrounding it through the use of a hemispherical reflector mounted directly in front of, and facing, the lens.

Single-Lens Reflex Cameras

The 35 mm single-lens reflex camera, or SLR, was the dominant form of camera used by serious American amateur photographers from the 1970s to 1990 or so, owing mainly to two factors. First, unlike cameras with a ground-glass or focusing screen, SLRs allowed for viewing of the subject right up to the moment of exposure. Second, SLRs eliminated parallax, or the discrepancy between what is seen in the viewfinder and what is projected onto the film.

Although SLRs did not catch on with amateurs extensively until around 1975, their design principle dates back more than a century to the reflex camera obscura. That instrument had a mirror in the rear, positioned at a 45-degree angle to the lens so the image reflected upward onto a screen at the top of the camera. The first single-lens reflex camera was patented in August 1861 by Thomas Sutton, an Englishman. As Sutton described his instrument, "The ground glass lies horizontally beneath your eye, and you look down upon it and see the picture erect thus obtaining a very perfect idea of the composition."

Over twenty years passed before the production of the next SLR. In July 1884, Calvin Rae Smith of New York City was granted a patent for a camera that had "a mirror arranged on the shutter to reflect the image in the focus of the lens on the focusing-glass." The mirror was located at a 45-degree angle on the upper portion of the shutter assembly. By late 1884, Smith's invention was being advertised as the Patent Monocular Duplex camera. While the original model took 3 ¼-by-4 ¼-inch dry plates, in later years the Monocular Duplex was offered with the option of an Eastman-Walker holder for roll film.

The single-lens reflex became increasingly popular in the 1890s. High-selling models included Loman's Reflex, made in Holland; the Vanneck reflex, from W. Watson & Sons of London; and, from France, Tourtain's Orthoscope. In Germany the firms of Krügener, Wünsche, and Hüttig all made SLRs, and Dr. Adolph Hesekiel's company made a particularly attractive model. While a number of these cameras used the mirror-on-shutter mechanism, Dr. Hesekiel's employed a roller-blind shutter and an independently-mounted mirror .

In the fall of 1902, the Folmer & Schwing Manufacturing Company introduced the single-lens reflex camera that was to dominate the American market: the Graflex. While at least a half-dozen other makes of the SLR were produced in the U.S. between 1900 and 1915, none could match the performance of the Graflex's focal-plane shutter, attached at the back of the camera's body. This shutter provided a considerable range of speeds through combinations of the variable width of the opening in the shutter curtains and the tension of the spring that operated the shutter.

As the single-lens reflex camera made inroads with a variety of photographers, specialized versions began to appear on the market. In the 1930s came smaller-format SLRs such as Bentzin's Primarflex, Schmitz & Thienemann's Patent-Sport Reflex, Mentor's Compur-Reflex, and Ihagee's Exakta Model B. Naturalists and bird watchers could use SLRs equipped with tele-

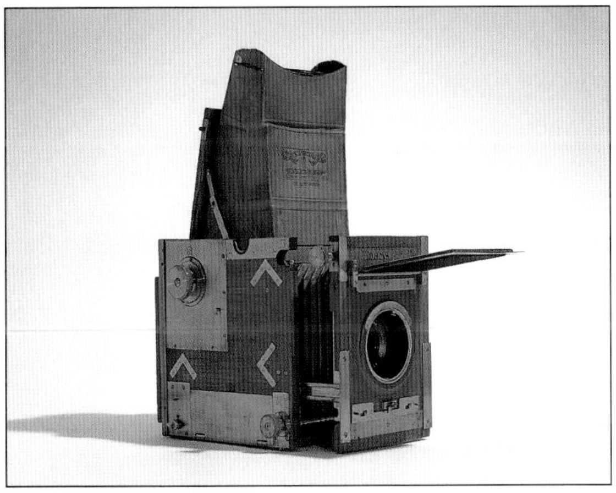

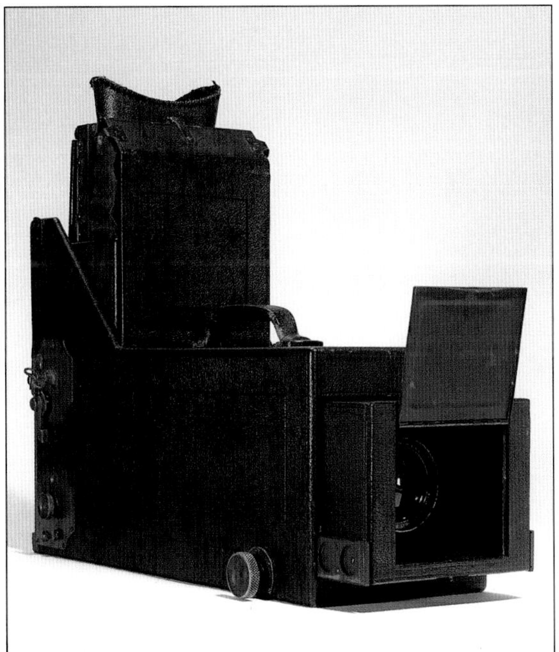

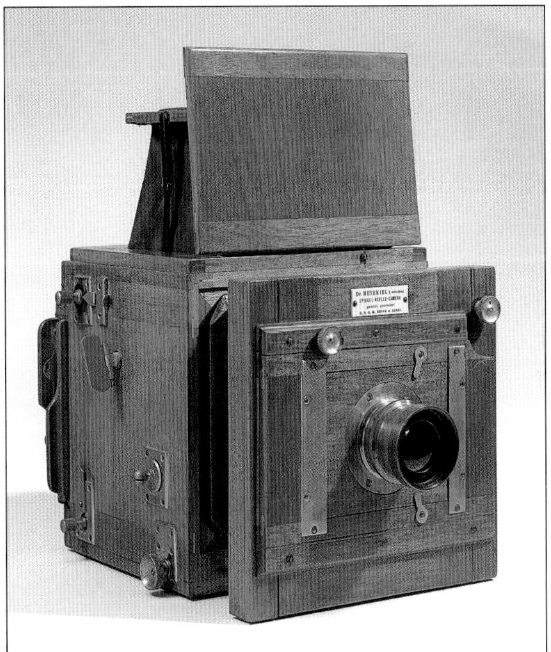

Clockwise from top left: Minex De Luxe Tropical Reflex, Adams & Co., ca. 1925, teak construction, for 3 ¼" x 4 ¼" exposures on dry plates or sheet film, storage in base for two plate holders.

Dr. Hesekiel's Original Spiegel-Reflex-Camera, Dr. A. Hesekiel, ca. 1894, walnut construction, for 9 x 12 cm exposures on dry plates.

Naturalists' Graflex, Folmer & Schwing Division of Eastman Kodak Co., ca. 1910, for 4" x 5" exposures on dry plates or sheet film. Focusing hood shifts from vertical to horizontal viewing by means of built-in mirror.

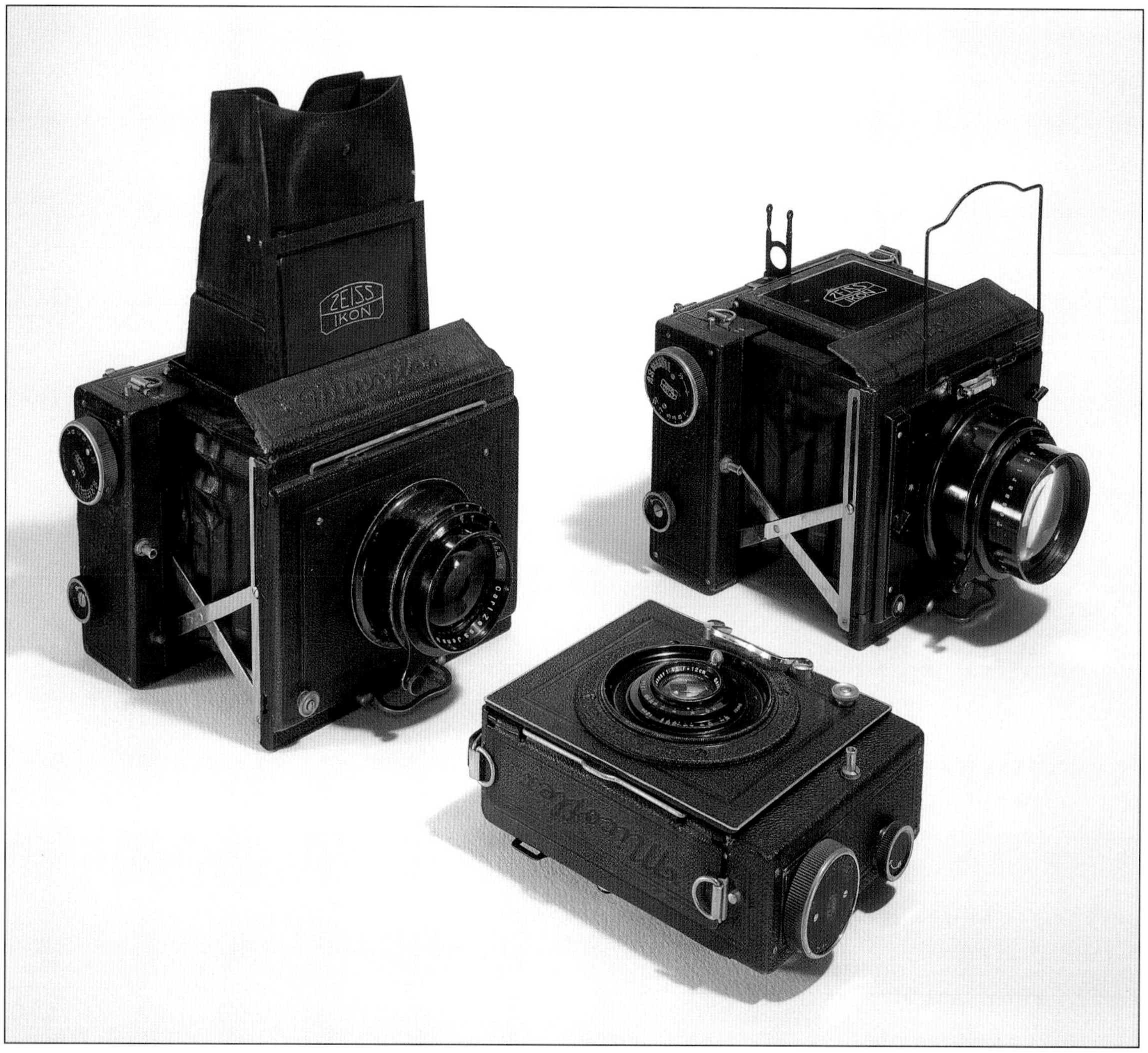

Miroflex cameras, Zeiss Ikon. Rear left: Miroflex B, ca. 1930, for 9 x 12 cm exposures on dry plates or sheet film, 165 mm f/3.5 Tessar lens, hood raised for reflex viewing. Rear right: Miroflex B, ca. 1927, for 9 x 12 cm exposures on dry plates or sheet film, 165 mm f/2.7 Tessar lens, frame-finder extended. Front: Miroflex A, ca. 1928, for 6.5 x 9 cm exposures on dry plates or sheet film, 120 mm f/4.5 Tessar lens, collapsed.

Opposite: Academy cameras, mahogany construction, Marion & Co. Left: ca. 1881, for 1" x 1" exposures. Right: ca. 1885, for 3" x 3" exposures.

Opposite, inset:
Left: Fallowfield's Twin-Lens Camera, Jonathan Fallowfield, ca. 1910, mahogany construction, for 3 1/4" x 4 1/4" exposures on dry plates. Right: New Artist's Hand Camera, London Stereoscopic Co., ca. 1889, mahogany construction, for 3 1/4" x 4 1/4" exposures on dry plates.

photo lenses, such as the Birdland camera (1904), by Sanders & Crowhurst, the Folmer & Schwing Naturalists' Graflex (1907), Dallmeyer's New Naturalist camera (1900), and the Jagd-Ango (1910), by C. P. Goerz.

Developments in the 35 mm single-lens reflex will be considered in a later chapter.

Twin-Lens Cameras

Though both have a pair of lenses, twin-lens cameras make a single exposure whereas stereo cameras produce a pair of photographs. In twin-lens cameras, one lens has a shutter and actually makes the exposure, while the second lens is used for viewing and focusing.

Twin-lens cameras can be separated into two categories. (In both, the image on the viewing screen is approximately the same size as the negative the camera produces.) The first type, the simple (nonreflex) twin-lens camera, has two sections: one is used for viewing and has its ground-glass screen at the back; the other is for making the exposure. The first camera to operate on this principle was not actually a twin-lens camera but a sliding-box stereo camera. Disdéri's stereoscopic camera of 1864 had an upper focusing chamber with a pair of lenses aimed at its rear ground-glass screen. The lower chamber had a similar pair of lenses for making stereo photographs. Regular, nonreflex twin-lens cameras had either a solid body, with a partition between the viewing and exposure chambers, or a pair of bellows. The first production-run solid-bodied model was the Academy, introduced by England's Marion & Company in 1882. The camera, whose viewing screen was held at eye level, had a twelve-plate magazine that supplied the lower exposure compartment.

More common in nonreflex twin-lens cameras was the use of bellows, mounted either one section

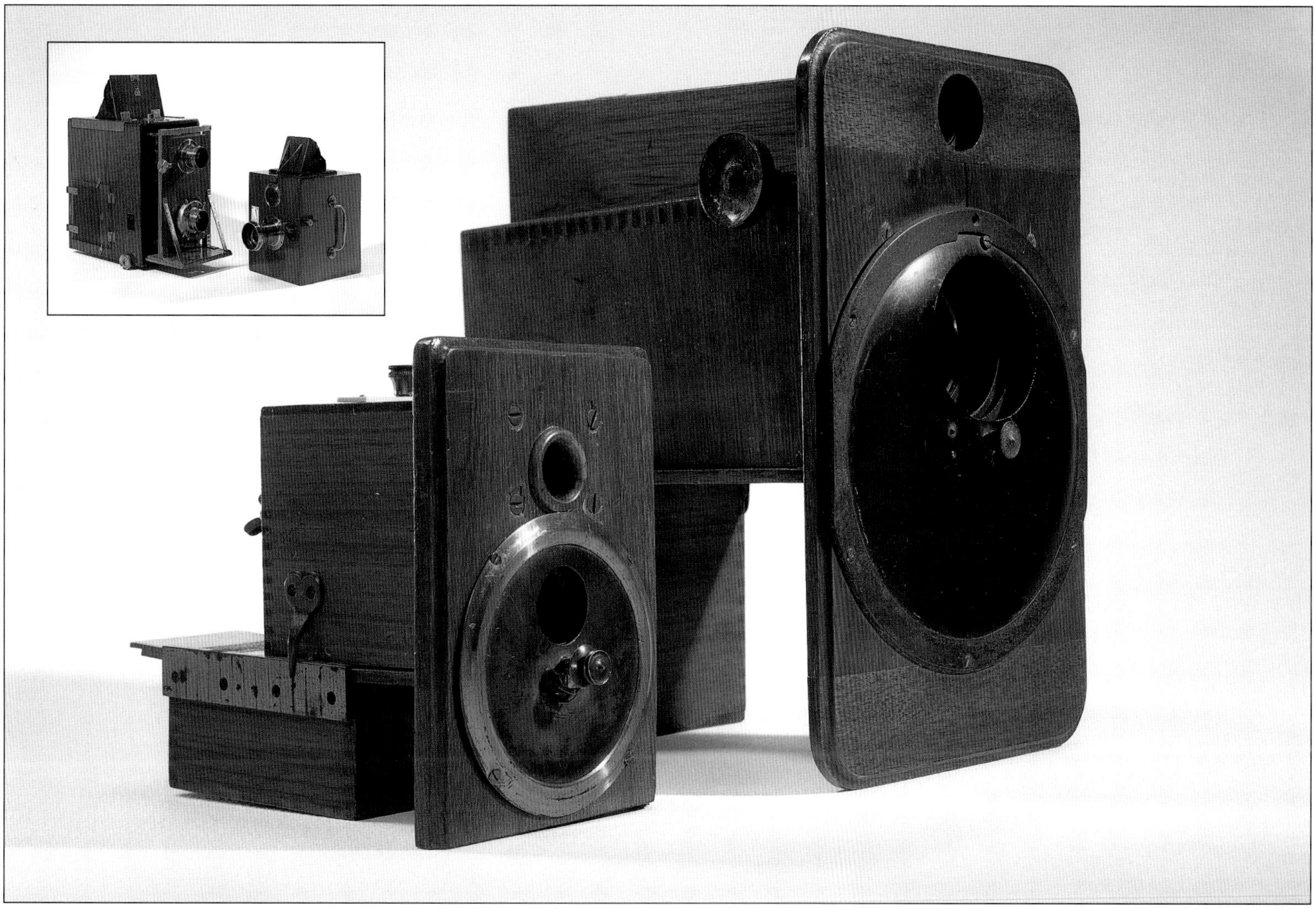

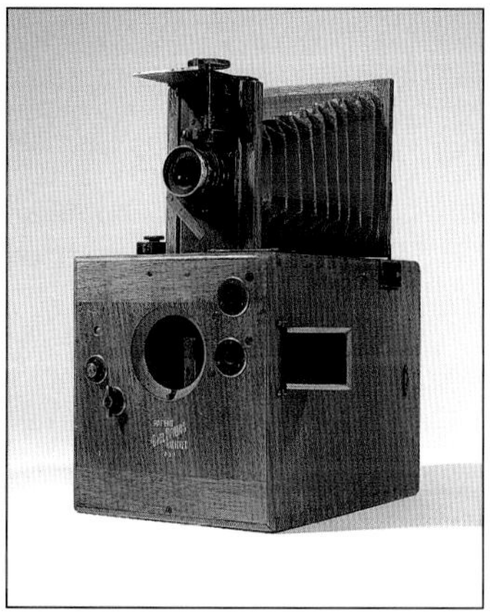

Bruns Detective Camera, Christian Bruns, ca. 1883, for 9 x 12 cm exposures on dry plates.

above the other or side by side. The first over-under bellows model was made circa 1889 in France, by B. Marion. The camera was handheld and, like others of its type, used at eye level. In 1890, Russia's N. N. Apostoli made an apparatus strongly resembling Marion's, and in 1893, Christian Bruns of Munich came out with a magazine camera, an unusual hybrid twin-lens model, which, in addition to a pair of small reflecting viewfinders mounted in its boxlike body, had a bellows eye-level viewing compartment that could be mounted atop the camera. Another notable twin-lens camera of this general type was Folmer & Schwing's Graphic Twin-Lens Special (1904), with over-under bellows that could be retracted into its boxlike body. Two German twin-lens cameras of the 1930s were the Eder Patent (1934), a folding plate camera with a pair of bellows mounted side by side, and the Bentzin Primarette (1937), a collapsible model with an over-under arrangement.

The second type of twin-lens camera is the one familiar to most people, the twin-lens reflex (TLR). This apparatus uses a mirror mounted at a 45-degree angle in the upper viewing compartment to reflect the light onto a viewing screen, or "brilliant" lens, in the top. The first known twin-lens reflex was a one-of-a-kind model made in 1880 by R. & J. Beck, London, at the commission of G. M. Whipple, superintendent of Kew Observatory. Beck's camera, like nonreflex twin-lens cameras, offered users the advantage of being able to view the subject while the exposure was being made.

In the next two decades, a profusion of twin-lens reflexes appeared, both in Europe and in America. Virtually every major British manufacturer, including Ross, Lizars, and Adams, had at least one TLR in its line. The Excell was made by the Belgian firm of Armand le Docte. Perhaps the best known of the German TLRs was Dr. Krügener's Simplex Magazin Camera (1890). In

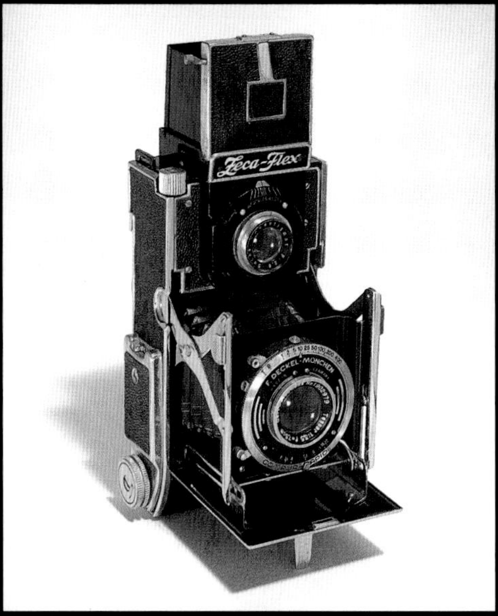

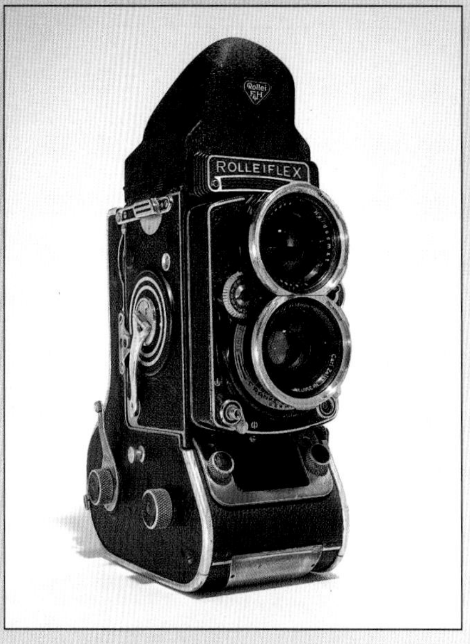

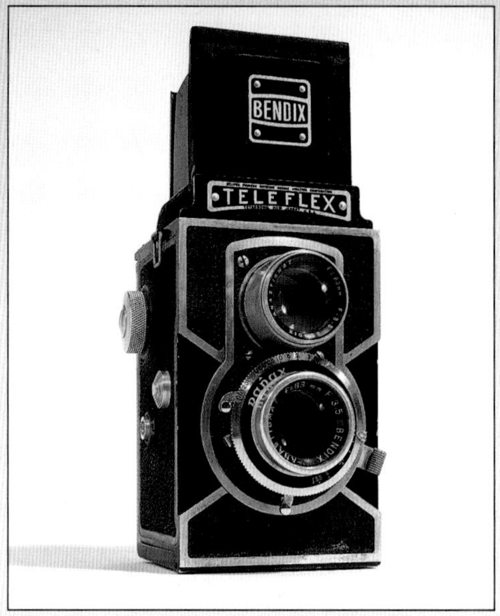

Clockwise from top left: Zeca-Flex, Zeh-Camera-Fabrik, Paul Zeh, ca. 1937, for 6 x 6 cm exposures on No. 120 roll film. One of the few folding twin-lens reflex cameras.

Rollei Wide, Franke & Heidecke, ca. 1962, for 2 ¼" x 2 ¼" exposures on No. 120 roll film. The only Rolleiflex with 55 mm lens.

Teleflex Prototype, Eclipse Pioneer Division, Bendix Aviation Corp., ca. 1946, for 2 ¼" x 2 ¼" exposures on No. 120 roll film.

Twin-lens reflex cameras. Left: Excell Twin-Lens Camera, Armand le Docte, ca. 1890, for 8 x 10.5 cm dry plates. Center: Twin-Lens Ideal, Adams & Co., ca. 1895, for 3 ¼" x 4 ¼" exposures on dry plates. Right: New Model Folding Twin-Lens Camera, Ross & Co., ca. 1906, for 3 ¼" x 4 ¼" exposures on sheet film.

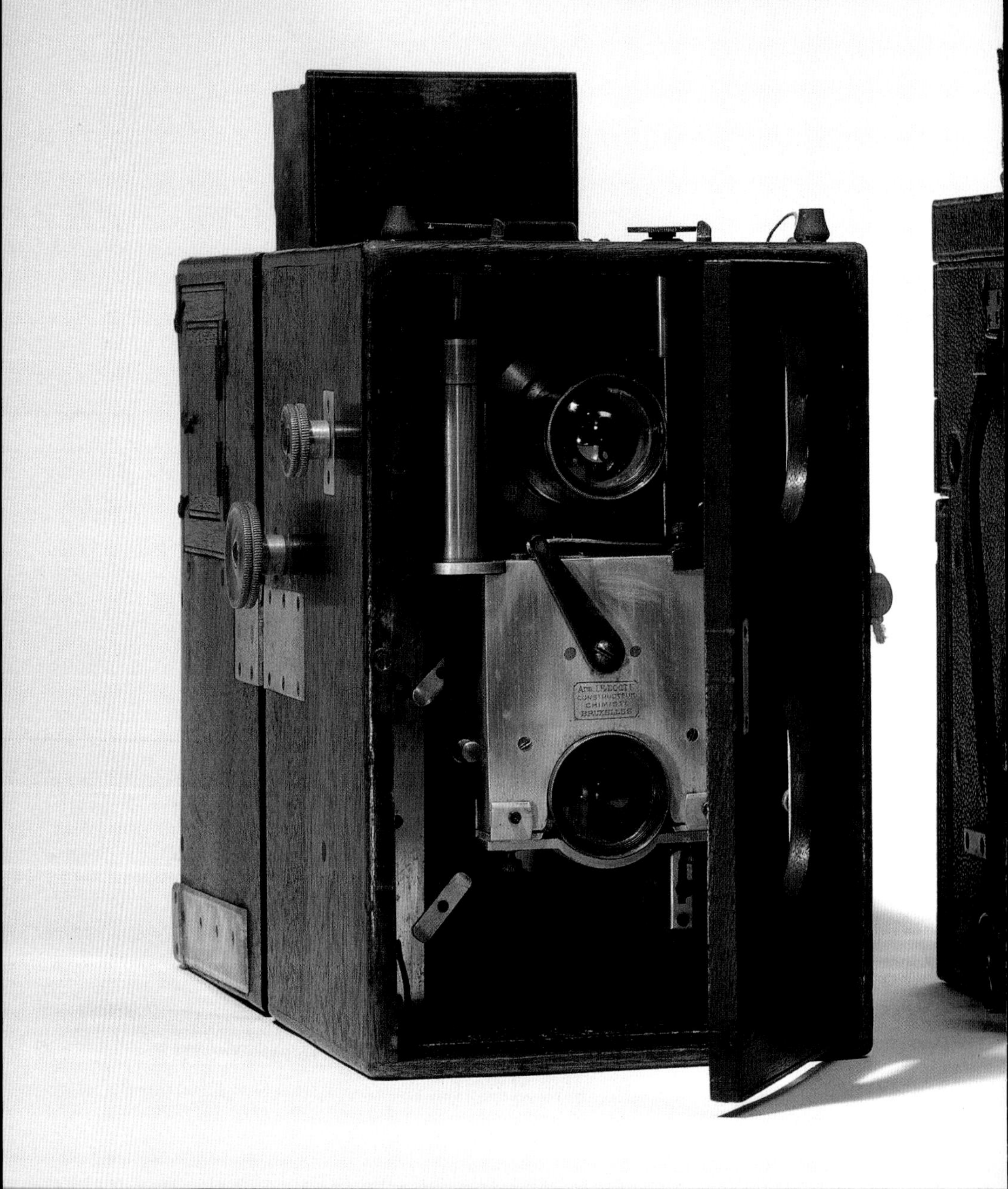

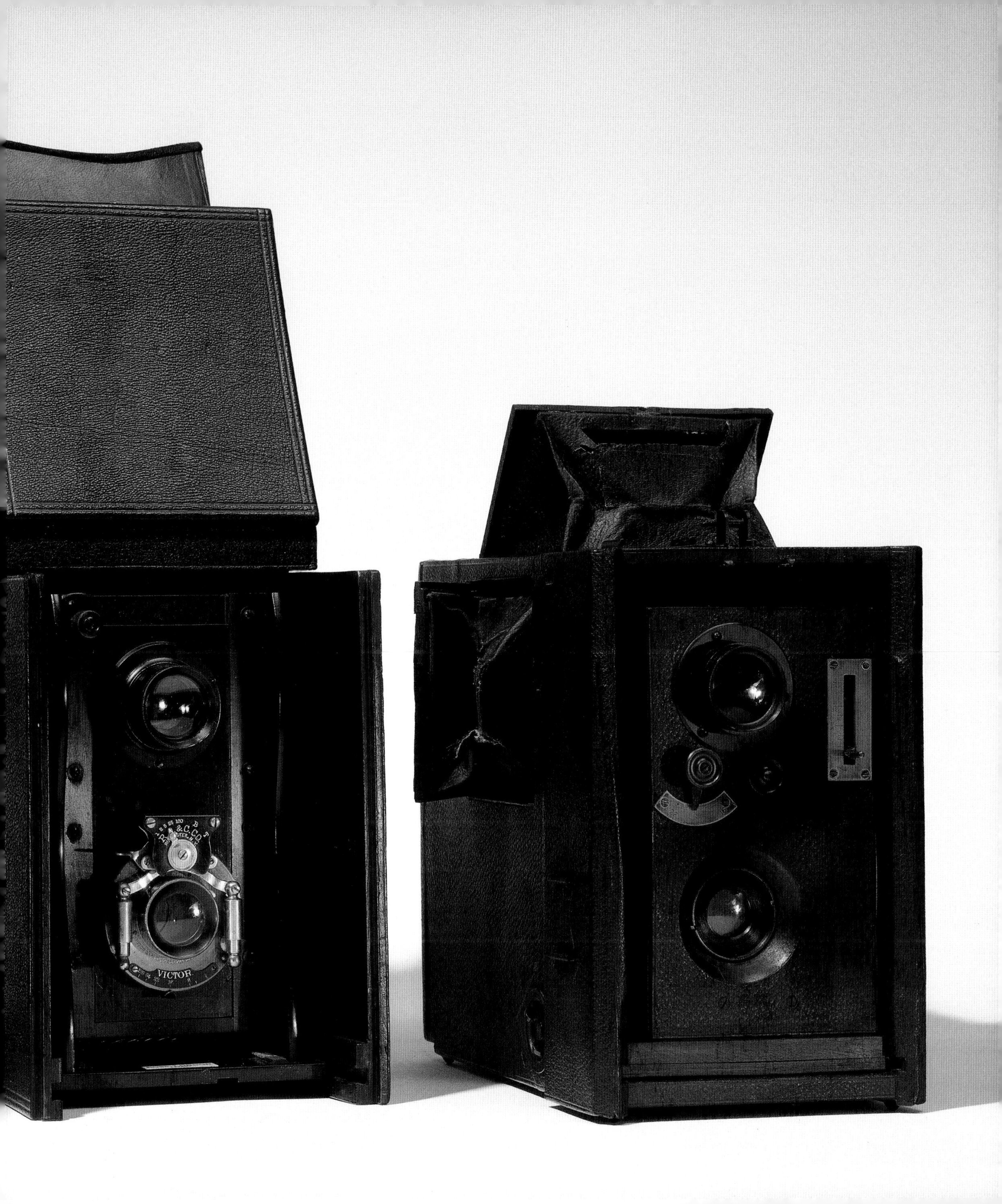
VICTOR

America, three different twin-lens reflex cameras were produced in the late 1890s; the most common was Folmer & Schwing's Twin-Lens Graphic. Production of the twin-lens reflex died during World War I.

For more than a decade, the design lay fallow. Then, in 1928, the German firm of Franke & Heidecke introduced a "miniature" twin-lens reflex, the Rolleiflex, producing 6-by-6-cm (2 ¼-by-2 ¼-inch) negatives on 117 mm roll film. This format remained popular for several decades, and in fact TLRs of this type are still manufactured today, though only in a limited number of models, in China.

The 6-by-6-cm twin-lens reflex enjoyed considerable popularity in the years following World War II. Rolleiflexes and their companions, the Rolleicords, tended to dominate the field, but the 1950s and 1960s saw a wave of Japanese TLRs appear on the market. Special-lensed TLRs from both Japan and Germany included the Tele-Koniflex (1955) and Tele-Rolleiflex (1959), both of which sported telephoto lenses, and the Rollei Wide (1961), which had a wide-angle lens. The various models of the Japanese Mamiyaflex C (1957) offered fully-interchangeable lenses.

The Voigtländer Superb (1933), which bucked the trend by having its film move side to side, horizontally, instead of the conventional, vertical, bottom-to-top orientation, was one of the more unique twin-lens reflex cameras of the 1930s. The speed markings on its Compur shutter were engraved backward so they could be viewed from above through a correcting prism. The Superb's most distinct feature, however, was its viewing lens, which, as one focused on nearer subjects, tilted downward to compensate for the parallax problem of most twin-lens reflexes.

Other Camera Types

Aerial Cameras—Over the years, a variety of means have been used to raise cameras above the earth's surface. Balloons, kites, blimps and dirigibles, airplanes and helicopters, gliders, rockets,

PROFILE:

Dr. Neubronner's Doppelsport

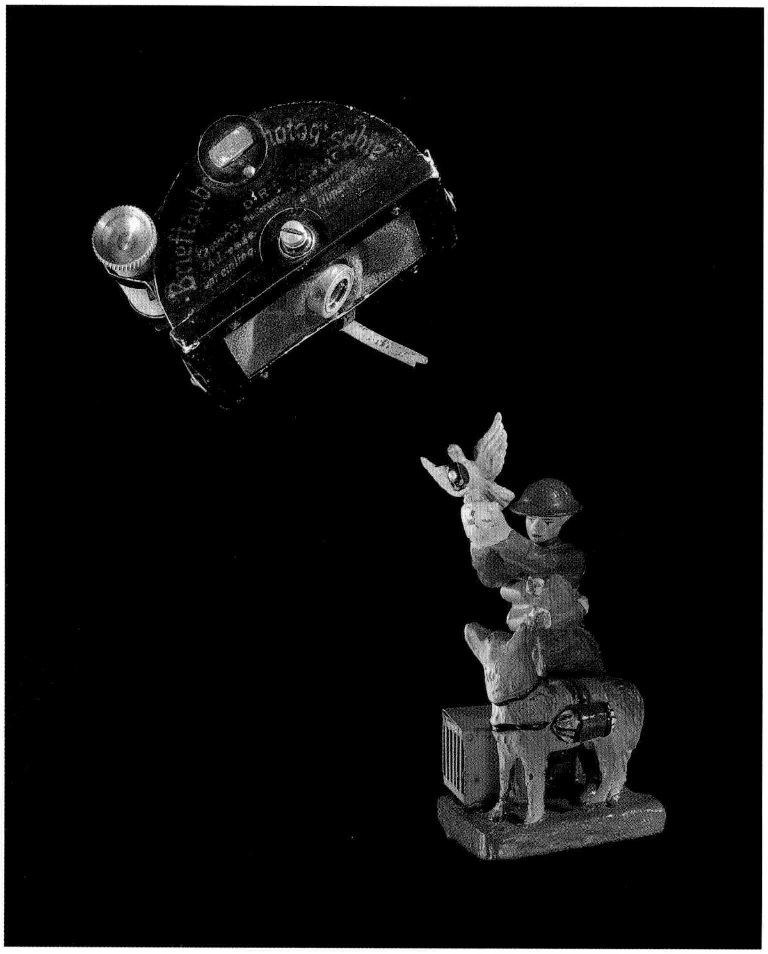

Above: Doppelsport pigeon panoramic camera, Dr. Julius Neubronner, ca. 1913, for 3 x 8 cm single exposures on curved sheet film. Below: Toy soldier holding homing pigeon wearing Doppelsport Camera, Elastolin, ca. 1936, 9 cm high.

Unquestionably, the most unusual aerial camera ever made was Dr. Julius Neubronner's Doppelsport. This little camera, patented in Germany in 1903 by Dr. Julius Neubronner, was designed to be mounted on the breast of a carrier pigeon. Continuing development led, in 1912, to a miniature pivoting-lens panoramic camera, also pigeon borne. All of Neubronner's cameras took only single exposures and had timing devices to delay the moment of exposure until the pigeon —one hoped—was above its target. Homing pigeons were trained to carry these cameras. The German military was interested in the panoramic model prior to World War I. In the 1930s, Elastolin, a German toy maker, made a 9-cm-high toy German soldier who held in his raised hands a pigeon equipped with a Doppelsport. The soldier, who on his chest and back had pouches that held pigeons, also had beside him a dog with similar pigeon-containing pouches. A cage to hold pigeons stood at his feet. A variant version had the soldier outfitted in a British or American uniform, also with the dog and cage.

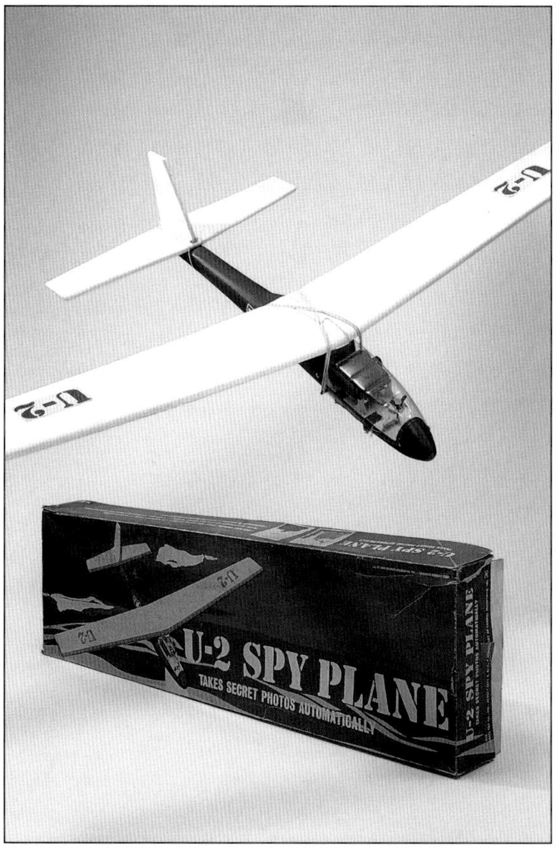

drones, and even birds have all at one time or another been employed to this end.

Until the late 1870s, most aerial photography was accomplished with conventional apparatus by such photographers as James W. Black (U.S.), Henry Negretti (England), James Glaisher (England), and Nadar (France). In 1885 Jacques Ducon made photographs of the Ile St. Louis in Paris from a balloon captained by Gaston Tissandier. Kite photography was introduced in 1887 by the Belgian Arthur Batut, who used a custom-made lightweight camera whose shutter was controlled by a timing device. One of the most effective uses of kites in aerial photography was by George Lawrence, in his photographs of San Francisco after the 1906 earthquake and fire. In making his views, Lawrence used a battery of seventeen kites to hold aloft a pivoting-lens panoramic camera. For one of the prints he was paid eight thousand dollars.

The applications of aerial photography for surveillance led to the use of balloons and kites for military purposes. During the U.S. Civil War, in battles around Richmond, Virginia, General George McClellan used photographs taken from a balloon by the team of Allan and LaMontain to map the terrain in the area. During the Spanish-American War, a kite photographic system devised by William A. Eddy was used in Puerto Rico by the U.S. Army Signal Corps. With the fairly extensive use of aircraft—both airplanes and dirigibles—in World War I, it was only natural that aerial photography would be relied upon for intelligence purposes. In the forefront of aerial camera design in this period were the British firm of Thornton-Pickard and the Folmer & Schwing Division of America's Eastman Kodak. Aerial cameras were heavily used in World War II as well. To the present day, many advances in aerial camera design are developed for the military. After all, the sole purpose of the U-2 airplane of the Cold War era was to carry high-altitude aerial cameras.

In the past few decades, a number of amateur aerial cameras have appeared on the market, from the Dunford Flying Machine (1979), a kite, priced from $20 to $100, depending on size, to the Astro-Cam 110 rocket and camera (1987), priced at $29, to a tethered helium-filled balloon (1990) costing $425, to the Re-Con Spy Plane (1999), for $100.

Photogrammetric/Surveying Cameras—Photogrammetry, the science of obtaining land surveys using photographs, has inspired the design of many specialized cameras. The father of photogrammetry, Colonel A. Laussedat, used the camera lucida for topographic work as early as 1849. Since then, photogrammetric cameras have come to include such elements as a level, compass, and film plates that register compass direction directly on the negative.

In the early 1860s, Auguste Chevalier invented a surveying/photogrammetric camera called the Planchette Photographique. This apparatus was a modified panoramic camera with a viewing field of 180 degrees. Photos taken with the camera were mounted on a card that had an arc of 180 degrees printed on it, around the edge of the area where the photograph was placed. Other surveying cameras include the Photo-Theodolite, made by J. Bridges-Lee of London,

Clockwise from left: U-2 Spy Plane, Gabriel Toy Co., 1965, for 16 exposures on No. 127 roll film, blue plastic and Styrofoam glider containing Empire-Baby camera with catapult launcher. Clockwork self-timer triggers one exposure per flight.

Anonymous, Seine River and Ile Saint-Louis, Paris, from a balloon at an altitude of 600 meters, ca. 1885, tipped-in photoglyptique, from *La Photographie en Ballon*, Gaston Tissandier, 1886.

Aerial camera, Konishiroku Co. Ltd., ca. 1944, for 5" x 7" exposures on 7-inch-wide film. Japanese World War II aerial camera.

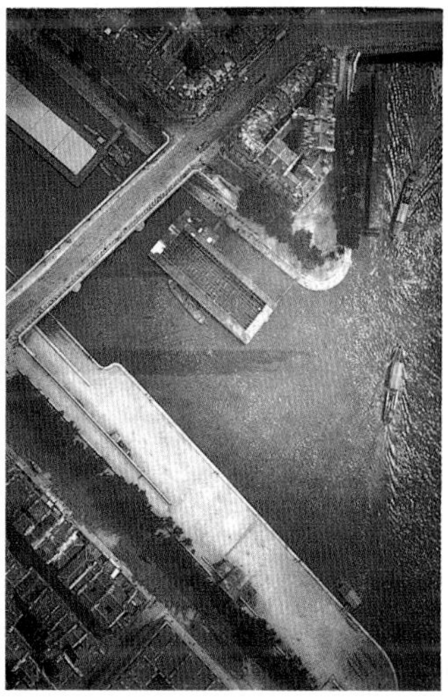

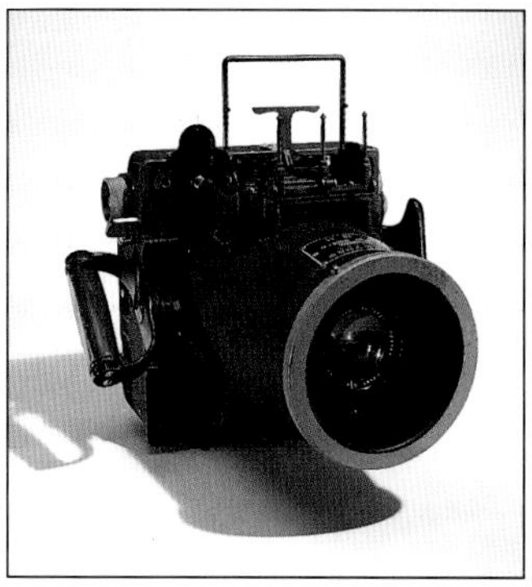

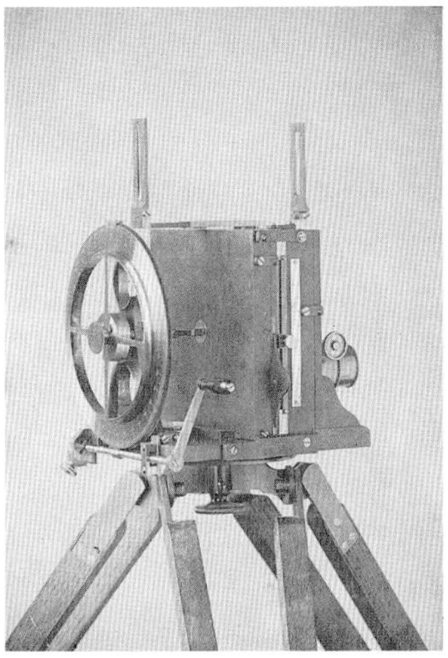

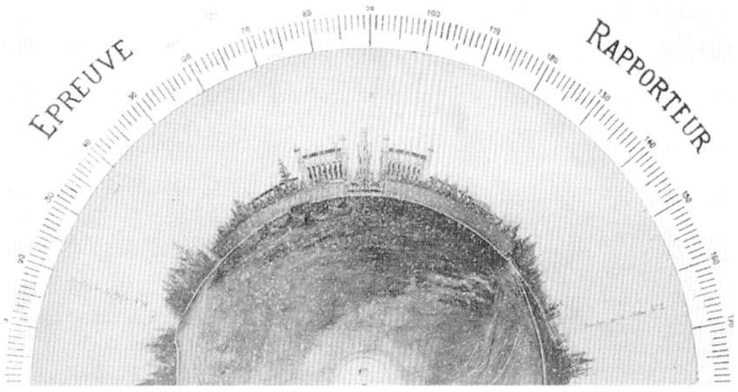

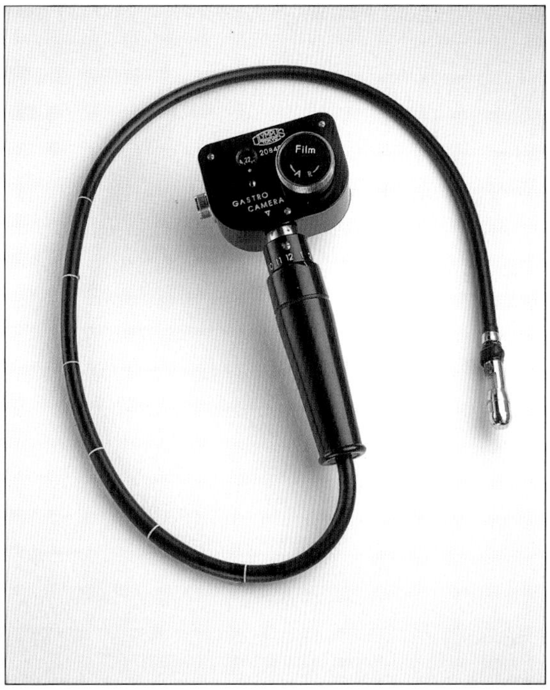

Clockwise from top left: Anonymous, Illustration of Planchette Photographique, invented by M. A. Chevalier, tipped-in albumen print, from *Notice sur la Planchette Photographique*, J. Dumaine, 1862.

Anonymous, "Demi Tour d'Horizon" test made with the Planchette Photographique, 1862, tipped-in albumen print, from *Notice sur la Planchette Photographique*, J. Dumaine, 1862.

Gastro Camera GT-F, Olympus Optical Co., ca. 1964. First gastric camera to use fiber optics.

and the Sanger-Shepherd Photo Survey camera. The latter, introduced in 1910, claimed to map the detail of an area in one-tenth the time it would take a surveyor using a plane table.

Medical Cameras—In the nineteenth century, most of the cameras used in medical photography were conventional models modified to suit the user's particular needs. Often a special mount or stand was used to allow patients or procedures to be photographed from special angles. Until the invention of the flashbulb in the 1930s, if a surgical procedure was to be photographed it had to take place in an operating room well-illuminated by skylights.

Albert Londe, one of the pioneers of medical photography and director of the photographic service laboratory in a Paris hospital, designed a special variable-speed shutter for recording objects or people in motion. His camera was often used to take photographs of postures and of the expressions of disturbed patients.

In the 1930s, specially-made cameras, produced in small quantities, became available for medical applications. For example, the Burton Clinical Camera, invented by A. E. Alderman, used a large flashbulb mounted behind the camera body and a very large reflector placed behind the camera to supply the necessary light. The Burton made single exposures. Other highly-specialized cameras included those for photographing the fundus (the inner surface of the eye, farthest from the pupil), endoscopic cameras, for photographing into body cavities, and cameras for dental photography. One company, Lester A. Dine, Inc., of Long Island, New York, modified the Kodak Starflash, 126 Instamatic, and 110 Pocket Instamatic cameras for dental and medical photography.

While most medical cameras were used for photography of external parts of the body, the endoscopic variety, noted above, were far more invasive. Though the camera body itself remained outside the patient's body, interchangeable tubes enabled photographs to be taken within the opening. Most invasive of all, perhaps, was the Olympus Gastro Camera GT-F. Introduced in 1964, it was the first gastric camera to employ fiber optics. The f/10, 4 mm lens and a flash lamp were located at the end of the tube. The thirty-exposure 6-mm roll film and reflex viewer were located externally. The images it produced measured 4.5 centimeters in diameter.

Underwater Cameras—Initially used only by serious amateurs or members of the scientific community, underwater cameras were often one-of-a-kind or produced in very limited quantities. The first underwater photograph is believed to have been made in 1856 by William Thompson, an Englishman. He placed a 4-by-5-inch camera that took dry-collodion plates in a watertight box and lowered it to a depth of eighteen feet. After a ten-minute exposure, he brought the camera up and developed the plate. Although the water pressure had caused the box to leak, a weak but discernable image was obtained.

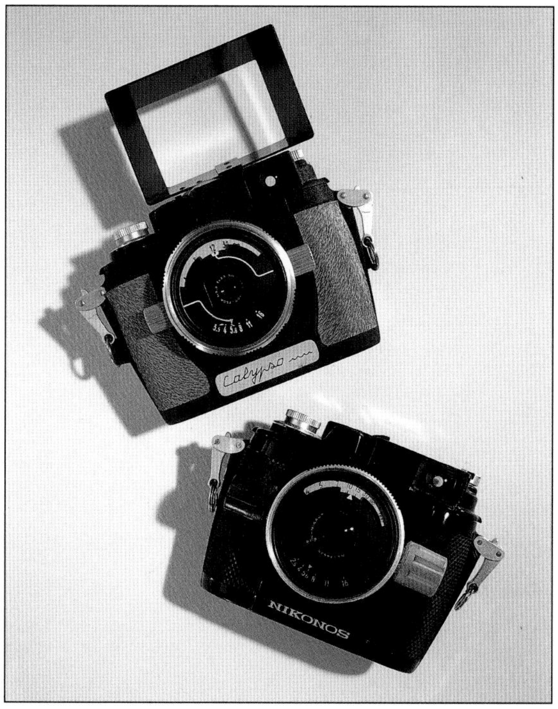

Above: Calypso, Spirotechnique, ca. 1962. Capable of withstanding pressure at depths up to 180 feet. Below: Nikonos (I), Nippon Kogaku K. K., ca. 1964, good to a depth of 160 feet.

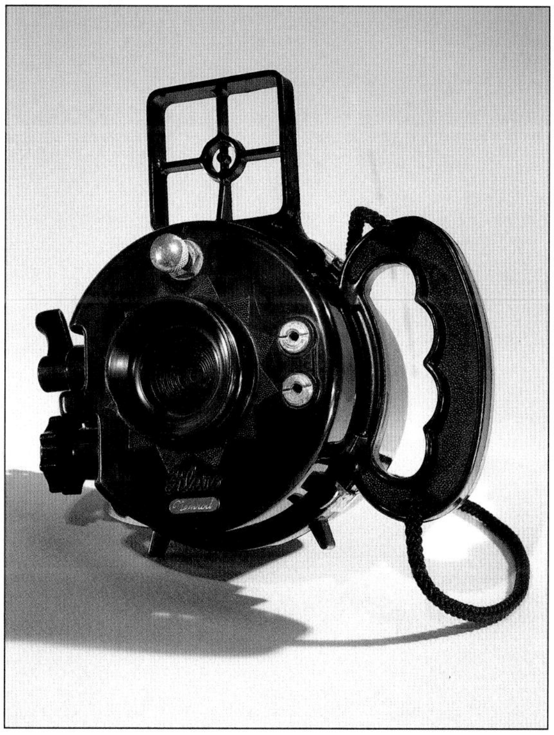

Below: Siluro Underwater camera, Nemrod Metzler, S. A., ca. 1962, Novodur plastic construction, flash synchronization, lead weights inside to counteract buoyancy.

Because of the minimal light available at any appreciable depth in the water, it was not until the development of powerful electronic flash units, by the American scientist Harold Edgerton in 1938, that undersea photography became feasible. Due to the expense of the equipment, however, it remained the province of the scientific community. Amateur photographers were relegated to constructing their own devices for shallow-water photography, as evidenced by the occasional "how to" articles that appeared in *Popular Photography* in the 1940s and 1950s.

In 1957 a company called Healthways introduced the Mako Shark, a cylindrical plastic underwater camera. Available with or without flash, the Mako Shark used 120 mm roll film on the innards of a Brownie Hawkeye and was effective only in relatively shallow water. An underwater camera whose design was apparently based on the Mako Shark was the Siluro, made in Spain and introduced around 1960. It, too, used 120 mm roll film. With a body made of Novodur plastic, the Spanish Siluro worked at depths up to roughly 120 feet. Neither of these cameras, though, was truly suited for anything beyond amateur use.

The needs of serious amateurs and professionals were finally met in 1960 with the introduction of the French-made Calypso, which produced standard-format exposures on 35 mm film and could withstand the pressure in waters as deep as 180 feet. Recognizing its potential, Nippon Kogaku, the makers of Nikon, purchased the rights to the Calypso and by 1963 were manufacturing and marketing it as the Nikonos. An electronic flash unit was sold separately. The Nikonos II, released in the early 1970s, offered interchangeable lenses. Automatic exposure was introduced with the Nikonos IV-A in 1980.

Today, amateur photographers wishing to delve beneath water can purchase a single-use 35 mm camera. Fuji, Konica, Kodak, and Agfa all sell inexpensive models.

Sequence Cameras—Sequence photography essentially began with Eadweard Muybridge and his attempts to "stop" the motion of a running horse. In his experiments, conducted in California from 1872 to 1878, Muybridge found he was unable to obtain successful results using a single camera and so instead employed a battery of cameras. Sequence photography could not exist until plates or film of sufficient sensitivity and shutters of sufficient speed came into use.

Sequence photography remained the province of scientists, or very serious amateurs, for nearly a

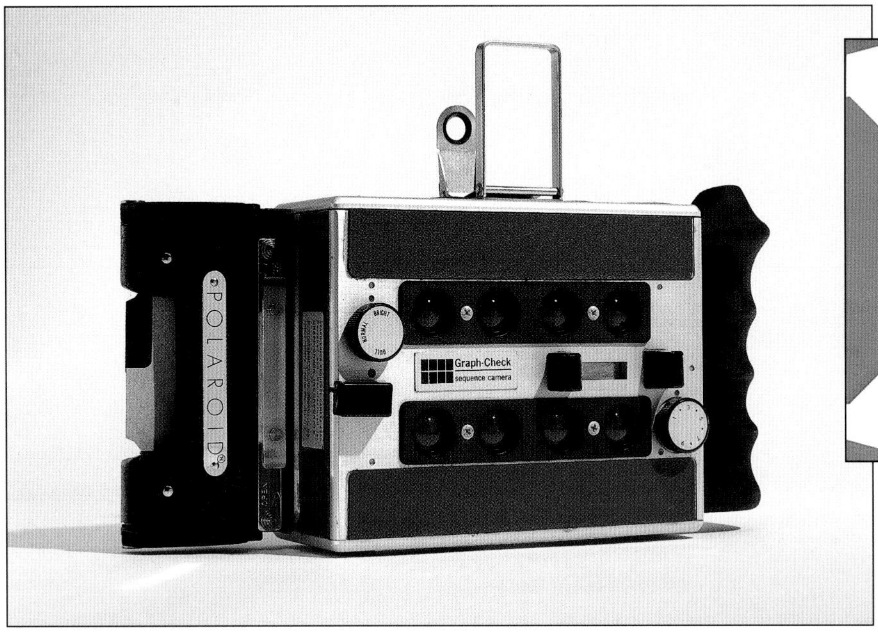

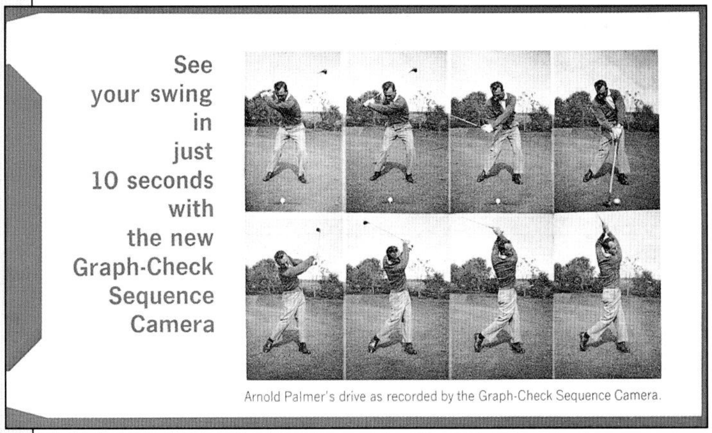

Clockwise from top left:
Graph Check Sequence Camera, Graph Check, Inc., ca. 1965.

Anonymous, Arnold Palmer's golf swing, ca. 1965, promotional item, sample eight-shot sequence photo taken with Graph Check Sequence Camera.

Left: Micromeccanica, Fotomicro, ca. 1932, for fifty 3 x 4 cm exposures on roll film, spring wind for rapid sequence. Right: Le Pascal, Japy Frères & Co., 1899, for twelve 4 x 4.5 cm exposures on 4.5 cm-wide roll film, leather-covered wood construction, spring wind for rapid sequence.

century. Hulcher cameras were among the few commercially available, if expensive, sequence cameras. The Hulcher 70 of the early 1950s used 70 mm film, and with speeds of up to 1/2000 second could record as many as fifty frames per second. Electronic flash, used stroboscopically, proved a helpful tool for sequence photographers. Frequent intense-light emissions of extremely brief duration enabled movement to be recorded on film as a series of "frozen" images. Even motion too fast to be perceived by the human eye could be arrested and analyzed. A bullet passing through a sheet of glass, a falling drop of water—these and innumerable other movements were at last revealed in detail.

Amateurs, too, gained access to this field with the introduction of the Graph Check Sequence Camera in the mid-1960s. The camera, which remained on the market for more than a decade, had eight separate lenses and a shutter that operated in sequence for each of the lenses. The Graph Check made eight separate exposures on a sheet of 4-by-5-inch film and accommodated a holder for Polaroid film, offering near-instant results. Cheap, plastic four-lens sequence cameras began to appear on the market around 1990. Sporting such names as Action Tracker, Sports 35, Mekai, and Catch 4, the single-speed cameras made four exposures on a single frame of 35 mm film, which could be processed in any one-hour photo lab. In the late 1990s, the Fuji Photo Film Company, Ltd., introduced a disposable/recyclable eight-lens 35 mm camera named the Golf; promotions in

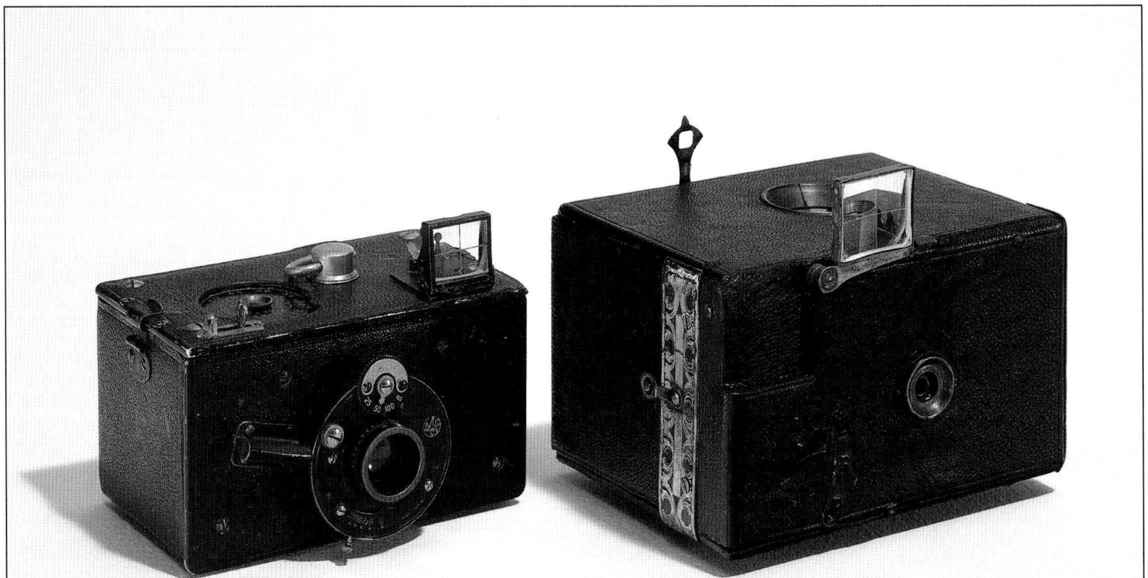

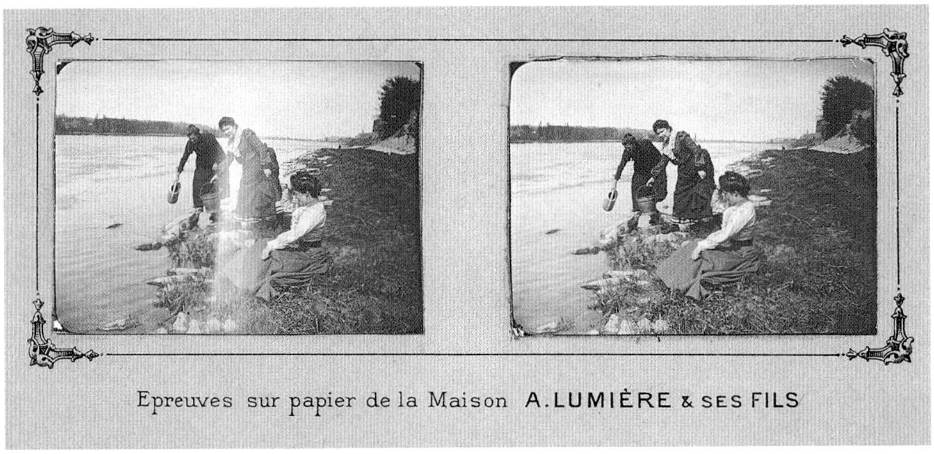

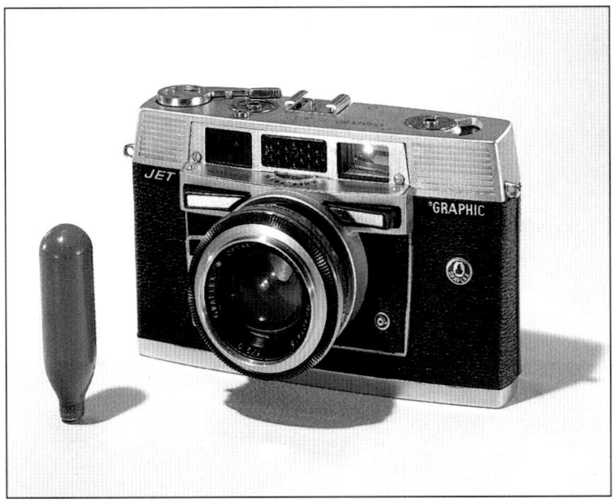

Left: Anonymous, Women at the waterside, ca. 1900, silver print on Lumière paper, 4 x 5.5 cm exposures mounted in 3 ½" x 7" card. Made in succession with Le Pascal.

Right: Graphic Jet, Kowa Co. for Graflex, ca. 1961, for 24 x 36 mm exposures on No. 135 roll film. Rapid advance powered by CO_2 cartridge.

the U.S. offered buyers a professional analysis of their golf swing.

Rapid-Wind Cameras—Today, almost every camera sold offers automatic film advancement as a standard feature, but this was not always the case. Until as recently as a decade ago, cameras required manual advancement or winding. To make this process more efficient, rapid-wind mechanisms were devised.

The rapid-advance concept was first employed in the plate-changing mechanism of magazine cameras, but it was most effective with roll-film cameras. The first roll-film camera to use rapid film advance was Le Pascal, introduced by Japy Frères & Company, of Belfort, France, in 1899. The small, wooden-bodied box camera made 4-by-5.5-cm exposures on special 4.5 cm roll film. In the process of tensioning the spring-wound advance mechanism, the film was wound onto a take-up spool. Then, when the release button was triggered following each exposure, the film was rewound onto the original supply spool.

In 1924 Ansco, an American company, introduced the Semi-Automatic Ansco, a folding roll-film camera with a spring-wound film-advance mechanism. After the exposure was made, the user pressed a lever that activated the mechanism and wound the film to the next exposure. The next year, Ansco introduced the Ansco Automatic No. 1A, which differed from the Semi-Automatic in that the lever on the advance mechanism was coupled to the shutter release so that only a single motion was needed to trip the shutter and advance the film.

In 1934 the first 35 mm rapid-wind camera was introduced: the Robot. Manufactured by Otto Berning & Company of Germany, it made 25-by-25 mm exposures on standard 35 mm film and had a large knob on top for winding the clockwork mechanism. While the Leica of the 1930s was not a rapid-wind camera, it gained rapid film-advance capability with the introduction of the accessory spring-wound Leica-Motor, in 1938. In 1939 Leitz also introduced an electric Leica-Motor. This was used in the 250-exposure Leica Reporter cameras.

Two other rapid-wind cameras that deserve mention are the Graphic Jet and the Bell & Howell Foton. The 35 mm Graphic Jet, manufactured around 1961 by Kowa for Graflex, was notable because in place of a spring- or electric-wind mechanism it used the power supplied by gas escaping from standard CO_2 cartridges, the kind used to carbonate beverages. The Foton, introduced in 1948 by Bell & Howell, was a rapid-wind camera with a spring motor drive. With a capacity of six frames per second, a single winding of the camera's spring would provide up to fifteen frames of advancement. The Foton used interchangeable lenses, one standard and two telephoto.

Instant Cameras—"Pictures while you wait" is a concept that has been around since the early twentieth century, when street photographers used tintype cameras to satisfy the public's wish for souvenirs of outdoor occasions. In November 1948, Edward Land changed "while you wait" to "instant" with the Polaroid Land camera. Polaroid went on to dominate the instant-camera market to

PROFILE: *Stanhopes and the Pigeon Post*

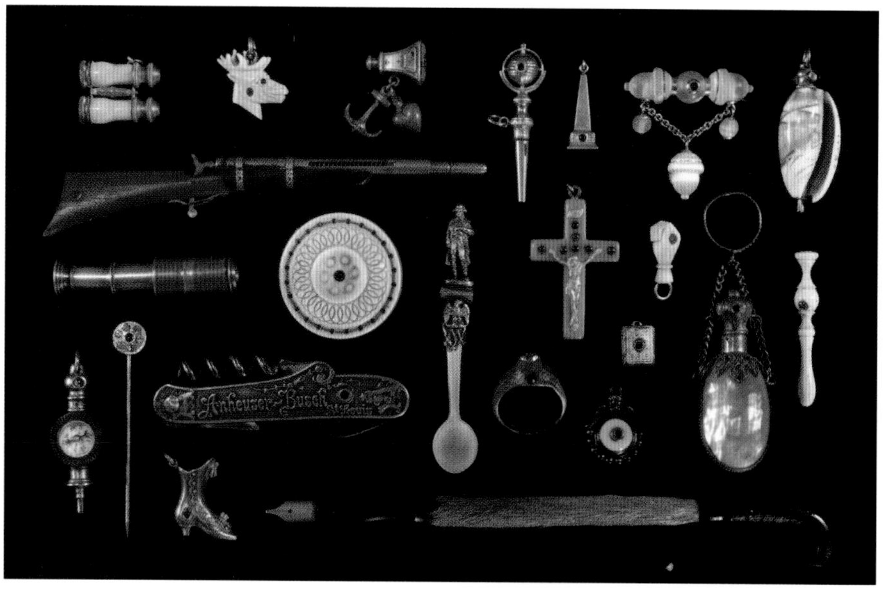

John Benjamin Dancer made the first microscopic images, known as microdots, in 1840. By 1852, Dancer was using the recently-introduced wet-collodion process to make microscopic images of portraits, paintings, and newspaper pages. These tiny photographs were mounted in the manner of conventional microscope slides, complete with cover slip.

In 1856 Dancer showed some of his images to Sir David Brewster, famous for his design of stereoscopic viewers. Brewster thought of several means by which to view microphotographs, including his suggestion to an Italian jeweler that he construct a brooch which would carry a microphotograph, magnified by one of the precious stones.

These tiny images, along with their viewing lenses, came to be called stanhopes, after Lord Stanhope, who designed the lens arrangement used in the viewers. Stanhope photo-lens systems were placed in every type of object imaginable: not only lockets, brooches, and bracelets, but rings (Queen Victoria wore one), pendants, hatpins, tiepins, and earrings. In addition to these conventional articles of adornment, they were also placed in pens, cane handles, buttonhooks, pocket knives, crucifixes, and miniature replicas of binoculars, monoculars, telescopes, and rifles.

In 1860 René Prudent Dagron, a Parisian, introduced a series of small, brass, multilens cameras designed to produce multiple images for stanhopes. Each model used a different size wet-collodion plate, but most measured approximately 4-by-8.5-cm. Between nine and twenty-five lenses could be mounted at the camera's front. A sliding back made it possible to take seventy-two exposures on a nine-lens model and four hundred and fifty exposures on a twenty-five-lens model.

In 1870, during the Franco-Prussian War, Dagron's camera was used to make microphotographs of letters, which were carried by pigeon between generals in Paris and Tours. Microphotography was also used to cut down on the bulk of overseas transports carrying letters to and from U.S. military personnel during WWII, in a process known as airgraph, or, popularly, V-mail.

Stanhopes. Each object contains a microphotograph with a magnifying lens to facilitate viewing.

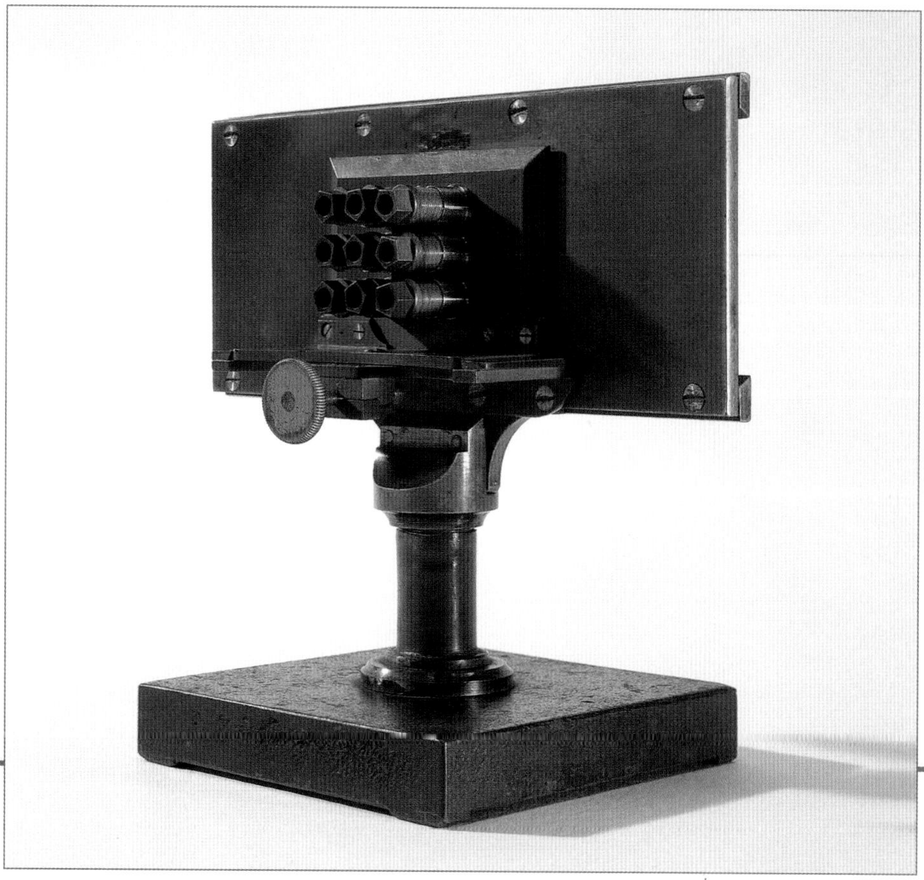

Left: Dagron microphotographic camera, ca. 1860, all brass construction, used in conjunction with "Chambre Noir."

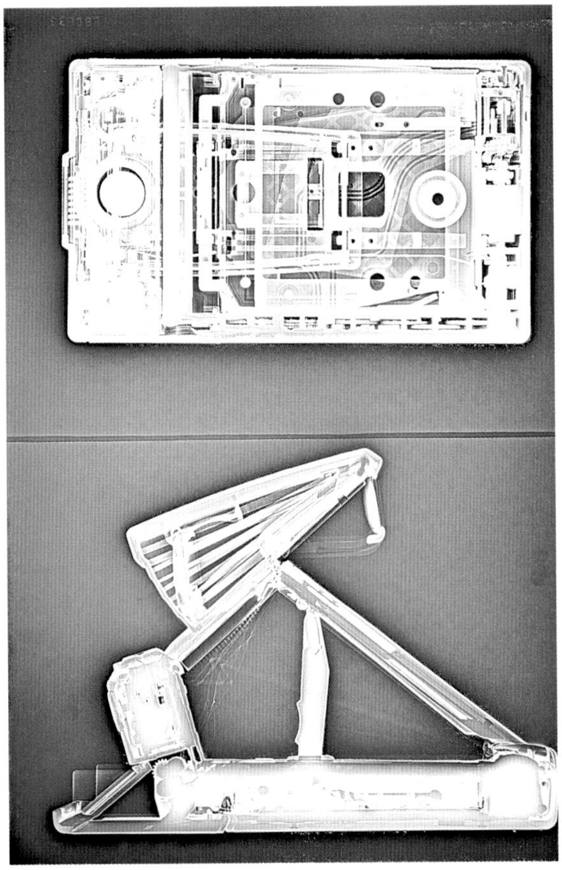

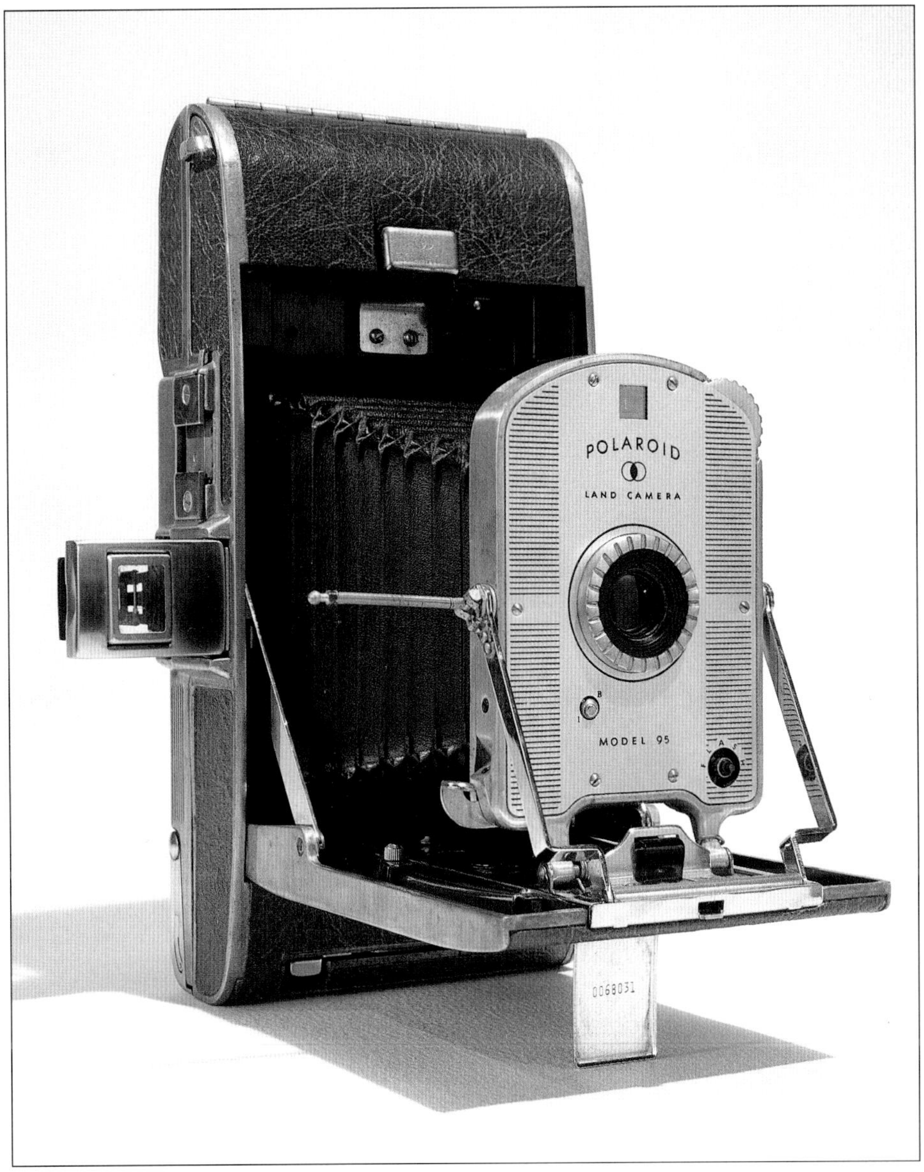

such a degree that its name is now synonymous with the format.

The Polaroid Model 95 Land camera looked very much like a conventional folding camera for roll film. However, the Land camera used a unique, peel-apart film that had, adjacent to each exposure segment, a small pod of developing chemicals. After the film was exposed, and as it was pulled from the camera, the pod burst and a pair of rollers spread the developing chemicals evenly across the film's surface. The developing time was just sixty seconds. The approximately 3¼-by-4¼-inch photographs produced, eight to a roll, were sepia in color.

Early advances in Polaroid products included the introduction of black-and-white roll film (1950) and ASA (ISO) 3000 film (1959). In 1960 developing time was reduced to fifteen seconds. In 1963 the Polaroid 100-Series Land camera was introduced and Polacolor film packs became available. In October 1972, a markedly-different product, the Polaroid SX-70 Land camera, was introduced. This folding single-lens reflex camera used a battery in the film pack to power a motor that spat out the photos, which then developed in minutes before the user's eyes. In 1976 significantly less expensive, rigid-bodied Polaroid Land cameras using SX-70 film came on the market. Sonar-operated auto focusing was introduced in July 1978 with the SX-70 Sonar OneStep Land camera. For professionals a Land camera roll-film back, which used the same film as the Model 95, was introduced back in 1951, and in 1958 the 4-by-5 Land Film Holder #500, which used individual film packets, was added to the company's line.

Polaroid also manufactures film backs that can be attached to a wide range of professional and digital cameras, transforming them into instant cameras. Often these film backs are used to check lighting and exposure prior to shooting standard film.

Left: Anonymous, X-ray of Polaroid SX-70 Land camera, ca. 1972. The camera made ten 3⅛" x 3⅛" exposures on SX-70 Land film. Motorized print ejection powered by battery in film pack.

Right: Polaroid Model 95 Land camera, Polaroid Corp., 1948, for eight 3¼" x 4¼" exposures on Type 40 Land film. Prints developed in sixty seconds.

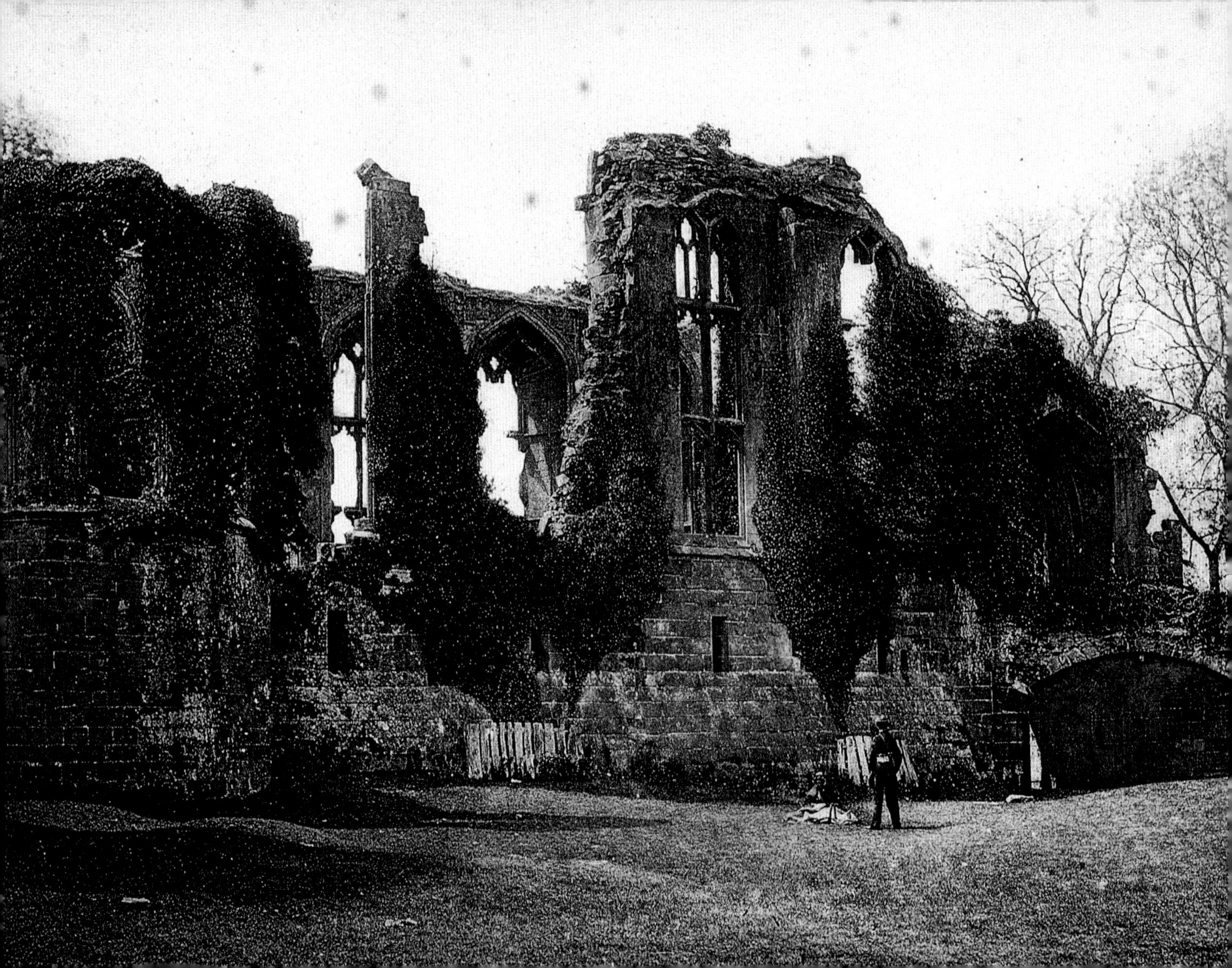

CHAPTER EIGHT:

REPRODUCTION OF PHOTOGRAPHS: PRINTS AND PROCESSES

Francis Bedford, Banquet hall, Kenilworth, 1863, photoelectric engraving (Dallastype), presented to subscribers of the *Photographic News*, January 1, 1864

Photographic Prints

Most photographic prints produced since the introduction of photography are silver prints, meaning that some compound of silver which forms photosensitive salts was used to make them. (Although not technically a photographic print, the daguerreotype is also a silver-based image, but produced on a silver-coated sheet of copper rather than on paper.) The first prints to contain silver were those produced by William Henry Fox Talbot in 1835, before the public introduction of photography. In preparing his paper, Talbot dipped it in a sodium chloride (table salt) solution and then, after drying, in silver nitrate. The silver chloride formed by this action was significantly more sensitive to light than was the silver nitrate. After fixing, the negative produced could then be contact printed onto the same type of paper to produce a positive. This process was called the salted-paper process. Subsequently Talbot prepared paper with potassium iodide and silver nitrate to make silver iodide. This produced a latent image that could be developed and printed in the same manner. The end result was called a Talbotype or calotype.

The wet-collodion process was used to produce negatives—as well as ambrotypes and tintypes—but not for making paper prints. Until the advent of albumen paper, prints from collodion negatives were made using one of Talbot's processes. In 1847 Louis Désiré Blanquart-Evrard invented a modification of the calotype process that yielded a greater tonal range. Blanquart-Evrard's process involved two successive baths of potassium iodide and silver nitrate. Subsequently Blanquart-Evrard proposed using albumen (egg white) as a material to help the silver salts adhere to the negative paper. This led to the use of albumen in making paper for positive prints, thus creating albumen paper. The process of printing on it was called "printing out," because a visible image was produced on the paper by exposure alone; no development was necessary. Unless toned, however, the image was unstable. Albumen paper was most widely used for the printing of wet-collodion negatives.

Peter Mawssley first produced gelatin silver bromide paper in 1873, which printed so rapidly that a few seconds' exposure to gas or other artificial light was enough. Mawssley's was a developing-out paper, which meant that chemical development in darkness was necessary to bring forth the latent image resulting from exposure. Recognizing the potential of developing-out gelatin bromide paper, George Eastman began manufacturing it in the mid-1880s. Eastman's company used this paper in its portrait-enlarging service for professional photographers. By 1900, having replaced albumen paper, bromide developing-out paper was the universal standard.

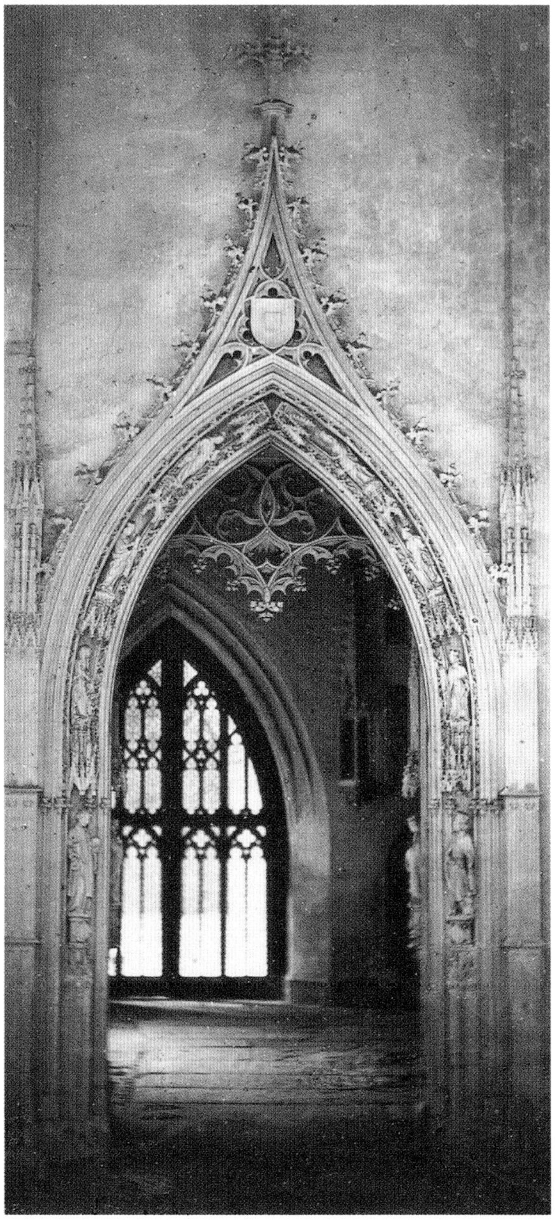

Herm. Emden, Mainz Cathedral, 1858, tipped-in salt print, 2 1/2" x 6 1/2", from *Der Dom zu Mainz*, published by Victor V. Zabern, 1858.

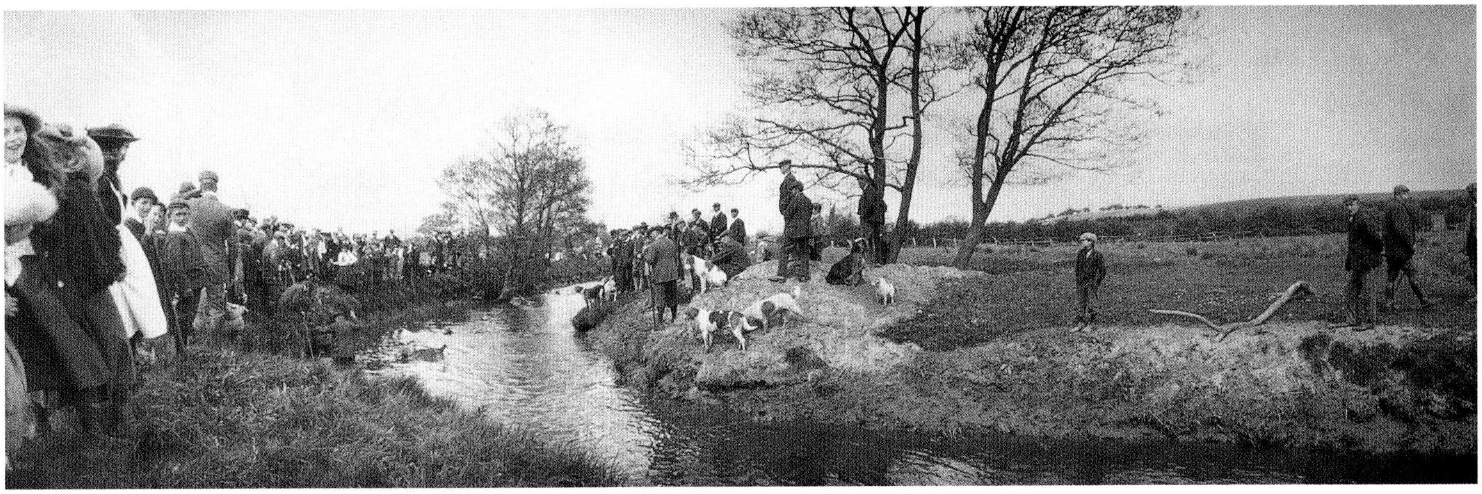

J. R. Crosse, Otter hunting at Stoke and Wollerton, ca. 1905, gelatino-bromide print, 3 1/8" x 11 3/8". Probably made with No. 4 Panorama Kodak.

Right: Mathew B. Brady, Principal officers of the Japanese Embassy, New York, ca. 1860, albumen print, 7" x 8 1/2".

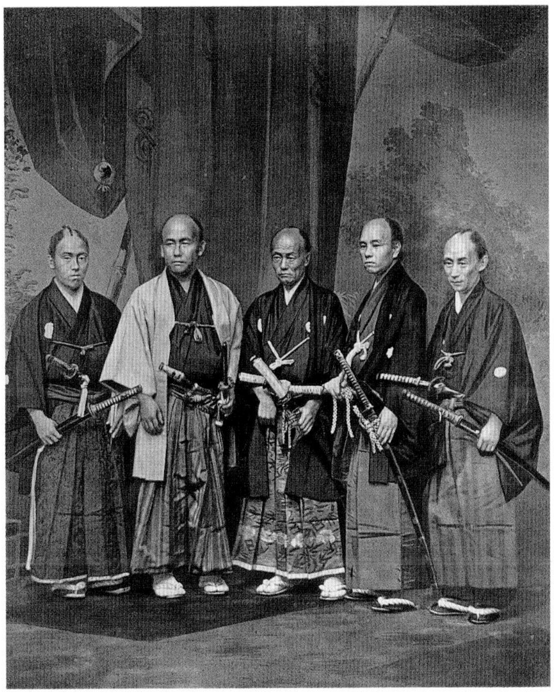

Gelatin silver chloride paper came in two types, developing-out and printing-out. Josef M. Eder and Giuseppe Pizzaghelli are credited with introducing, in 1881, gelatin silver chloride paper that was developed out. Slower than bromide paper, it was more suited to contact printing than to enlargement. Velox was the name of one popular brand of this paper. Printing-out gelatin silver chloride paper was in turn introduced by Captain William de W. Abney in 1882. More than twice as sensitive as albumen paper, it was also said to be more permanent. The most popular of these papers was Eastman Kodak's Solio.

Josef M. Eder is also credited with the invention of chloro-bromide gelatin paper. Announced in 1883, Eder's paper, which gave prints a warm brown tone, was used chiefly for contact printing by artificial light.

Although silver-based technology dominated the production of photographic prints, other printing technologies did exist. One early alternative was the cyanotype. Invented by Sir John Herschel, the cyanotype was distinctive because of its blue color—*kyanos* is the Greek word for dark-blue substance. After discovering that ferric (iron) salts were photosensitive, a finding he announced in 1842, Herschel realized he could sensitize paper for printing by combining potassium ferricyanide with ferric chloride or ferric ammonium nitrate. Exposure to light under a negative produced a blue positive image on the paper. Washing in water made the paper a deeper blue and removed the remaining light-sensitive chemicals. While Herschel's process had its practitioners in the late 1800s and early 1900s, it never entered into general use. Photographic albums with cyanotypes can be found, as can stereo cyanotypes. Some of the earliest cyanotypes are contained in Anna Atkins's 1843 volume, *Photographs of British Algae: Cyanotype Impressions.* The cyanotype process, also known as the blueprint process, has seen its greatest use in the duplication of architectural plans and other diagrams.

Carbon prints rely on the fact that the sensitivity of bichromates (also called dichromates) depends on the presence of organic substances. In 1855 Alphonse Poitevin patented a photographic process that involved the mixing of powdered carbon with bichromated gelatin. This substance was

FOCUS: *Stamps and Photography*

Considering the impact photography has had on culture, science, and our everyday lives, it has often been passed over by the post offices of the world when issuing celebratory or commemorative stamps.

The eminent historians of photography Alison and Helmut Gernsheim have drawn attention to a remarkable episode involving stamps that occurred in South Africa during the Boer War (1899–1902). When the defenders of Mafeking ran short of stamps, the British Lieutenant Colonel

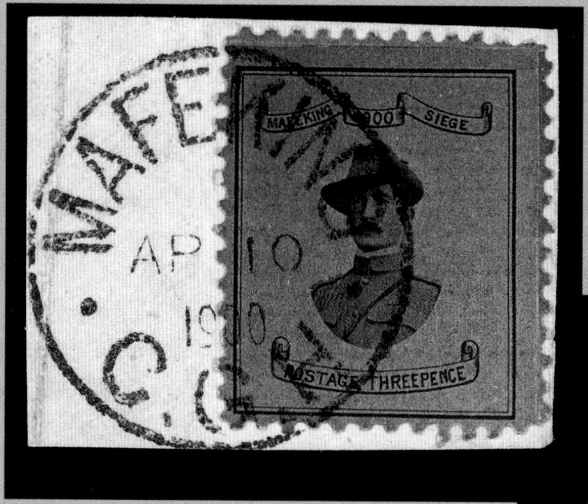

E. J. Ross, Portrait of Lt. Col. Baden Powell on threepence "Mafeking Siege" postage stamp, 1900, cyanotype.

Right: E. J. Ross, Portrait of Sergeant Major Warner Goodyear on one-penny "Siege of Mafeking" postage stamp, 1900, cyanotype.

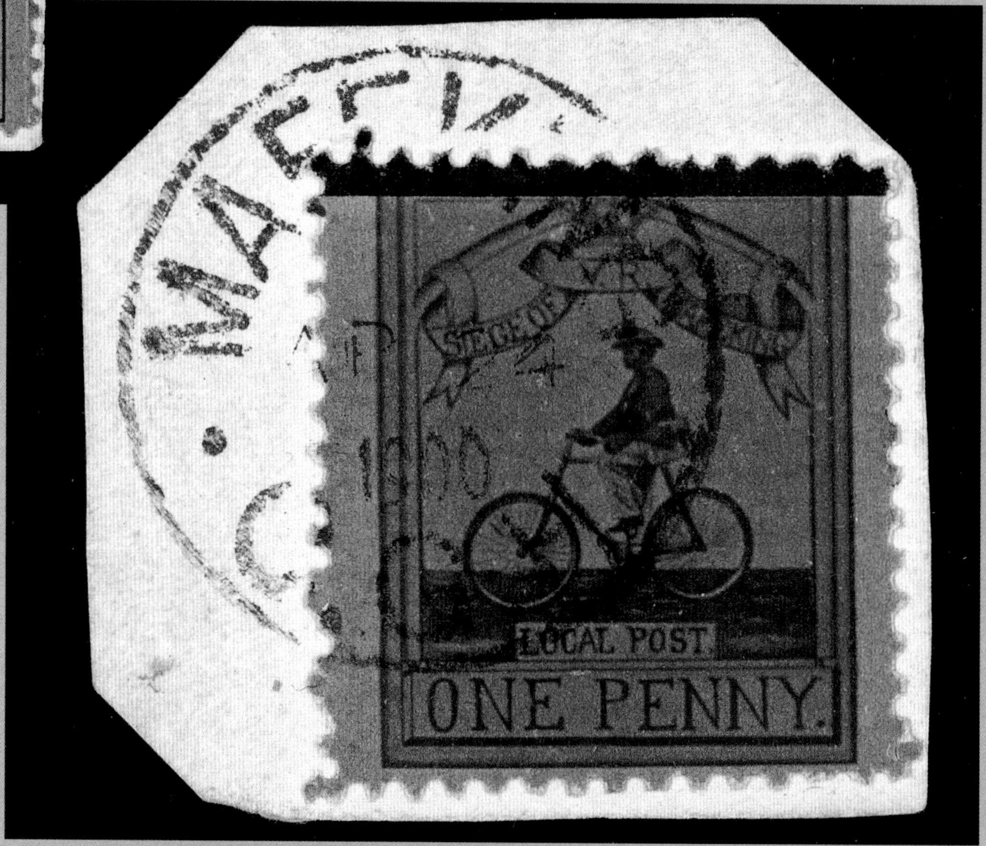

Baden Powell turned for help to amateur photographer E. J. Ross, who suggested they produce new stamps photographically. Due to a shortage of eggs, however, albumen could not be used, so instead the stamps were made using the cyanotype process. Two denominations were printed in that way, one bearing the likeness of Lt. Col. Powell. They were inscribed "Siege of Mafeking" and "Mafeking 1900 Siege."

The only country to issue a substantial number of photography-related stamps was the German Democratic Republic (East Germany), all between 1955 and 1972. Some were part of special sets promoting the *Leipzig Messen*, the vast technology and commerce fairs for which the city is famous. One portrayed Carl Zeiss, founder of the Zeiss works; another, Ernst Abbe, one of the nineteenth century's foremost optical designers and a core member of the Zeiss foundation. There was also a stamp of John Heartfield, the master of photomontage—and the only photographer ever to be honored in this fashion. Other East German stamps illustrated photographic products, as well as movie, TV, and still cameras. Among the latter is a picture of an Exakta with a microscope in the background. Still others depicted slide and overhead projectors.

During the 1960s and early 1970s, many nations—among them Anguilla, Australia, Barbados, Canada, Congo, Czechoslovakia, France, West Germany, India, Iran, Monaco, the Netherlands, Antilles, the U.S.S.R., and Umm al Qaiwain—issued stamps related to motion pictures, or used perforated film as a symbolic frame around the subject. In 1944 the United States celebrated in stamps the fiftieth anniversary of motion pictures and, in 1975, D. W. Griffith's hundredth birthday. Two years later a U.S. stamp commemorated the fiftieth anniversary of talking pic-

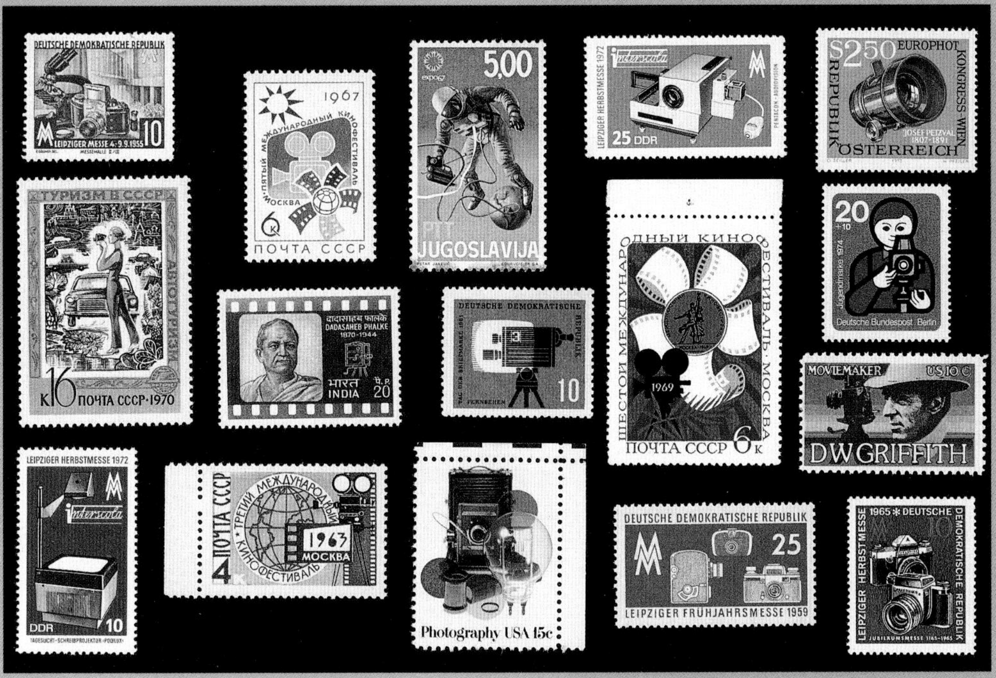

tures (i.e., movies with sound). In what must be considered the historically most significant "photographica" stamp, France in 1939 celebrated the hundredth anniversary of Arago's announcement of "the invention of photography." Superimposed on a meeting of the French Academy of Sciences, headed by Arago, were medallion portraits of Niépce and Daguerre. (That the stamp gives the wrong date for the meeting is a well-known fact.) In 1955 France also honored the Lumière brothers, Auguste and Louis, for their contributions in the field of color photography and motion-picture projection.

A U.S. stamp of 1940 portrayed Samuel F. B. Morse, and a 1947 stamp pictured Thomas Edison. In 1954 the United States issued the only stamp to honor an individual for his contributions to photographic technology: George Eastman. The stamp, available cancelled on its first day of issue, illustrated, on a variety of caches, cameras, Eastman's birthplace, his mother, his first factory, and Eastman himself.

Many giants of photography, Fox Talbot, for example, have yet to be honored with a stamp. Indeed, Great Britain, where so many pioneers of photography lived and worked, has never issued a single photography stamp. In 1873, however, Austria issued a stamp on the occasion of the Europhot photographic congress in Vienna. This stamp paid tribute to early lens designer Joseph Petzval, whose lens graced the famous Voigtländer metal daguerreotype camera. Photography itself was best promoted with the Soviet Union's 1970 stamp picturing a female photographer in action, and by Senegal's 1967 stamp promoting the "International Tourist Year" with an open-mouthed hippopotamus. In 1974 West Germany produced an attractive Jugend-Marke (stamp) with an illustration of a boy using a camera.

Of course, photography has long played an important role in providing imagery for postage stamps, but it was only after World War II that the use of actual photographs on stamps became widespread. Perhaps the most famous stamp based on a photograph is the 1945 U.S. stamp depicting Joe Rosenthal's picture of the raising of the American flag by U.S. Marines on Mount Suribachi, Iwo Jima.

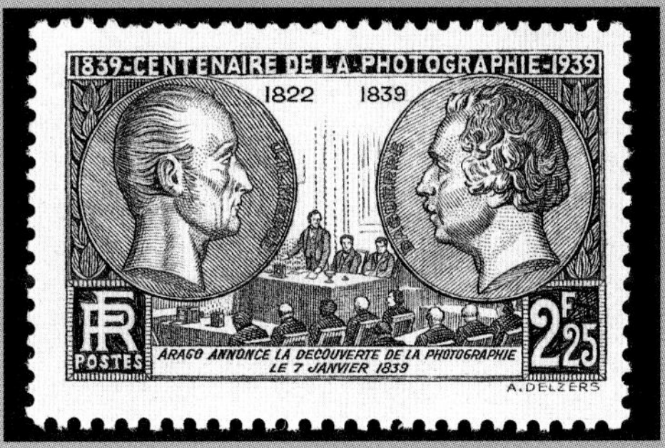

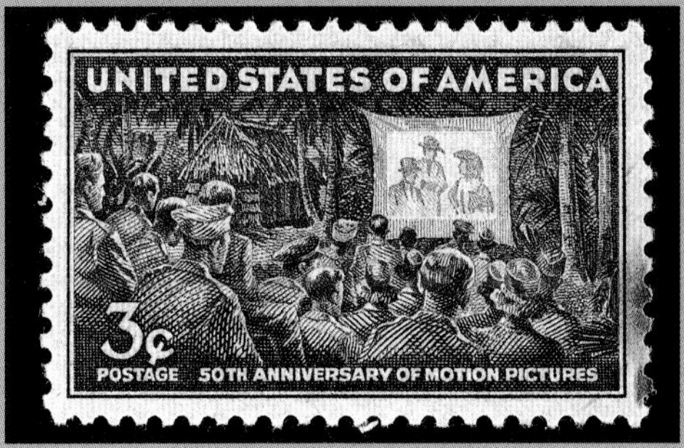

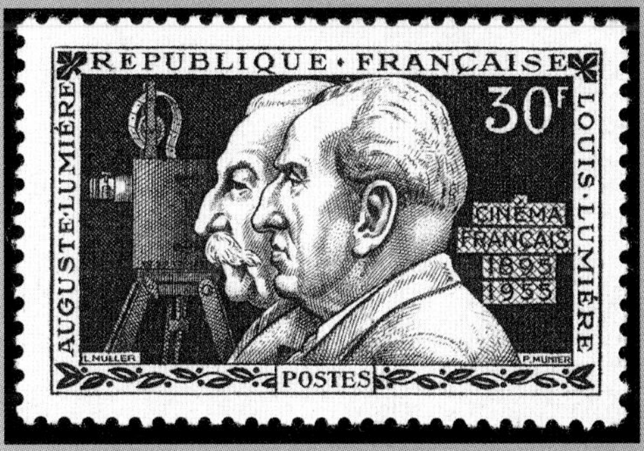

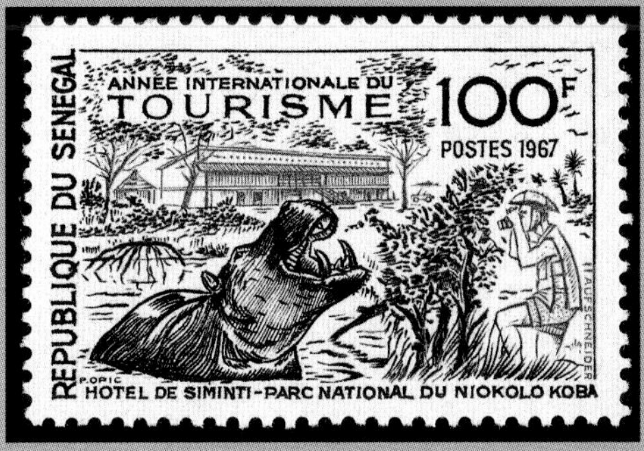

Clockwise from top left:

Photography-related postage stamps.

French "Centenary of Photography, 1839–1939" 2.25-franc postage stamp, 1939.

American "50th Anniversary of Motion Pictures" 3-cent postage stamp, 1944.

Senegalese "International Year of Tourism" 100-franc postage stamp, 1967.

French "Cinéma Français, 1893–1933" 30-franc postage stamp, 1933.

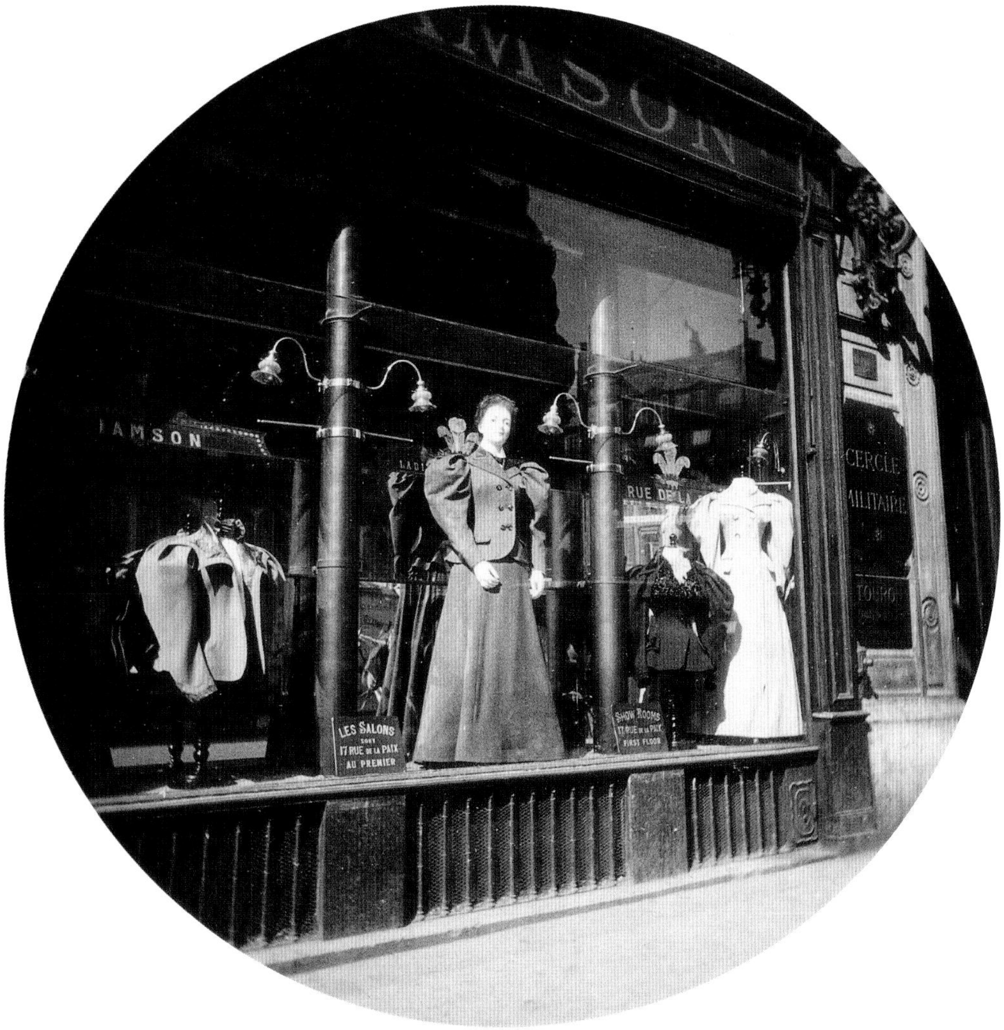

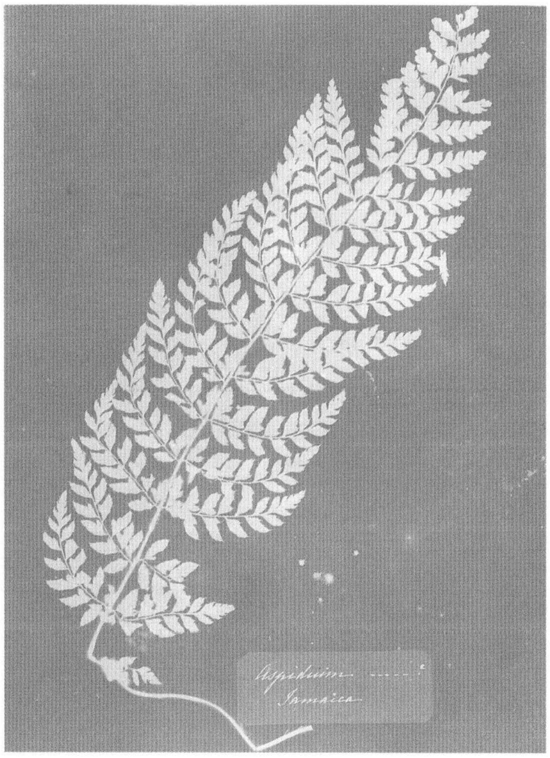

then spread on paper and, with a negative placed above it, exposed. Where light reached the coating, an insoluble gelatin, containing pigment, was formed. Like a pencil drawing, carbon prints were less susceptible to fading than silver-based prints, but they were not suitable for producing halftones, the intermediary shades of gray between white and black. Although a number of photographers sought to improve on the process, it wasn't until 1866 that Joseph W. Swan perfected a ready-made carbon tissue. His tissue consisted of paper coated with a carbon-gelatin mixture and presoaked in a bichromate solution. Next, a negative was placed on the gelatin side of the paper and exposed. The carbon tissue was then attached to a sheet of supporting paper and the original backing paper removed by soaking in hot water. This process dissolved the unexposed gelatin, leaving a carbon print that possessed gradations of pigment. Carbon tissue, originally manufactured by Mawson & Swan, was available in three shades of color and various levels of contrast.

GLOSSARY

Albertype
Invented by Josef Albert, of Germany, in 1879. The first workable collotype process. Sometimes referred to as Albert-type or Albertotype.

Artotype
An early collotype process in which the plate receives two separate coatings of bichromated gelatin.

Collogravure
A form of collotype in which gelatinobromide of silver films are converted into collotype printing surfaces. Invented in 1893 by Georges Balagny, a Frenchman.

Collotype
Based on the use of bichromated gelatin, which turns insoluble following exposure to light. An exposed and washed collotype plate is similar to lithographic stone. Known also as photo-collotype, in Germany as *lichtdruck*, and in France as *phototypie*.

Dallastype
Invented by Campbell D. Dallas. A photograph's halftones are reproduced by inducing reticulation in bichromated gelatin, producing a grain similar to that in a collotype. Also known as Dallastint.

Electro-Phototypy
The making of halftone printing blocks. A halftone is made by photographing onto a gelatin plate through a ruled screen. After development but before drying the plate is heated, swelling the gelatin into relief. Following this the plate is used as a mold for electrotyping. Sometimes referred to as photo-electrotype.

Electrotype
Engraved plates are pressed into beeswax. The resulting mold is covered with a solution of graphite and electroplated with copper. When the copper thickens it is removed and fortified with type metal for use in printing.

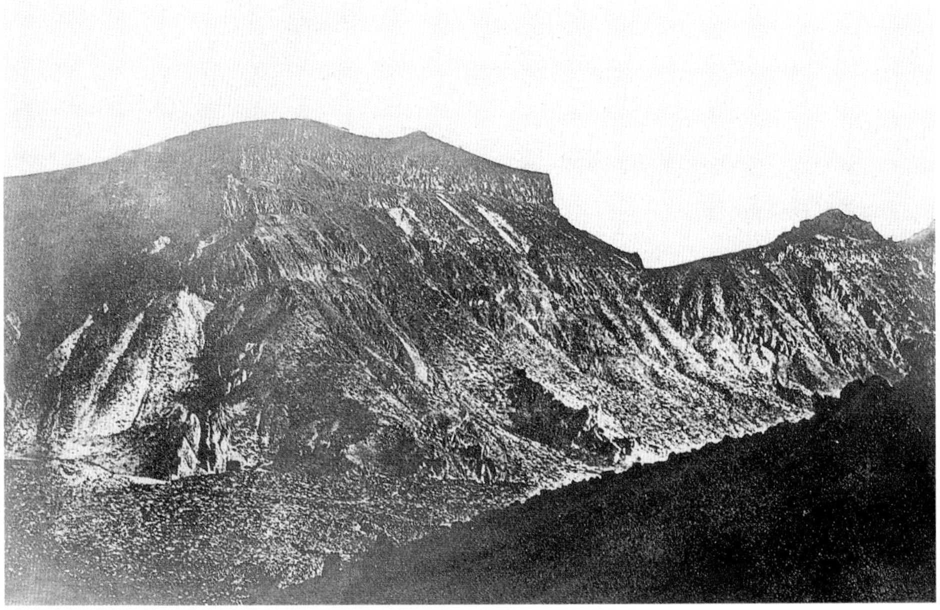

Opposite, top: Anonymous, Shop window, Paris, 1895, gelatino-bromide print, 3 1/2" diameter print on 3 7/8" x 4 3/4" paper. From album of 229 prints made with No. 2 Kodak camera.

Opposite, bottom: Anna Atkins, Aspiduim, Jamaica, ca. 1850, cyanotype, contact print, 8" x 10".

Above: Anonymous, Mount Guigara and the interior of the south wall of the great crater, Tenerife Experiment of 1856, 1856, printed in ink from a photoglyptic steel plate prepared by William Henry Fox Talbot.

Right: Cover of *American Phrenological Journal*, May 1858, bearing a portrait of Mathew B. Brady, photographic woodcut (Price's process) made from an ambrotype.

Two additional nonsilver prints are platinum prints and palladium prints. William Willis, an Englishman, was the first to develop a satisfactory platinum process, which he patented in 1873. In 1880 his company, the Platinotype Company, began to sell platinum paper. In Willis's process, iron oxalate and potassium chloroplatinate were coated on paper. Exposure caused the ferric salts to turn to ferrous salts to a degree determined by the amount of exposure. Developing in potassium oxalate dissolved the ferrous salts, leaving behind metallic platinum. The remaining ferric salts still subject to light's action were dissolved with hydrochloric acid. The platinum gave the print a silver-gray color and delicate halftones. Moreover, platinum is very stable, which made the prints extremely long-lasting.

Palladium is a rare metallic element of the platinum group. Its chemical kinship with platinum allowed it to be used in a similar manner in producing photographic prints. The sensitizing and developing processes for palladium prints were almost the same as those used in platinum printing. Prints resulting from the use of palladium tend to be brown in color.

Photomechanical Reproduction

Photomechanical reproduction involves the use of a photographically-prepared plate to print pictures or copies mechanically, such as with a printing press. Credit for the first photomechanical reproduction belongs to Joseph Nicéphore Niépce. In the early 1820s Niépce found that bitumen of Judea (a form of asphalt) became insoluble if exposed to light. After thinning some bitumen of Judea with oil of lavender, Niépce coated a plate with the solution. Next he placed the plate under an engraving soaked in oil (rendered transparent) and exposed it to the sun. Several hours of exposure made the bitumen insoluble where it had been struck by the light. The unexposed bitumen could then be dissolved, leaving a negative impression of the engraving on the plate. In further experiments, Niépce tried using a base of zinc or pewter rather than glass. In 1826, using a plate of pewter, Niépce copied an engraving of Cardinal d'Amboise. He dissolved the unhardened bitumen and then etched the exposed metal beneath the dissolved bitumen area. After an engraver deepened the lines, prints were made. Thus, photomechanical reproduction was born.

Early photographs were made on plates, suggesting that it would be relatively simple to use them in mechanical printing. In 1839 the Parisian Alfred Donné treated daguerreotypes with nitric acid to create printing plates, but as the etching

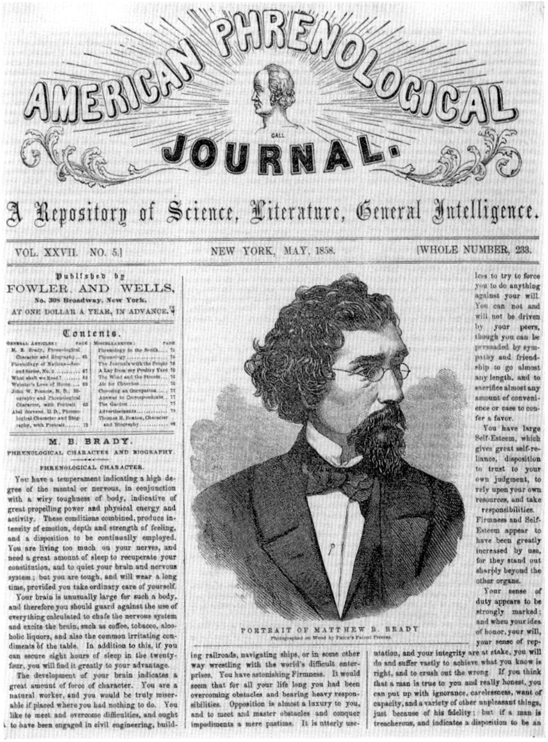

AMERICAN PHRENOLOGICAL JOURNAL.

A Repository of Science, Literature, General Intelligence.

VOL. XXVII. NO. 5.] NEW YORK, MAY, 1858. [WHOLE NUMBER, 233.

Published by FOWLER AND WELLS, No. 308 Broadway, New York. AT ONE DOLLAR A YEAR, IN ADVANCE.

Contents.

M. B. BRADY. PHRENOLOGICAL CHARACTER AND BIOGRAPHY.

PHRENOLOGICAL CHARACTER.

You have a temperament indicating a high degree of the mental or nervous, in conjunction with a wiry toughness of body, indicative of great propelling power and physical energy and activity. These conditions combined, produce intensity of emotion, depth and strength of feeling, and a disposition to be continually employed. You are living too much on your nerves, and need a great amount of sleep to recuperate your constitution, and to quiet your brain and nervous system; but you are tough, and will wear a long time, provided you take ordinary care of yourself.

Your brain is unusually large for such a body, and therefore you should guard against the use of everything calculated to chafe the nervous system and excite the brain, such as coffee, tobacco, alcoholic liquors, and also the common irritating condiments of the table. In addition to this, if you can secure eight hours of sleep in the twenty-four, you will find it greatly to your advantage.

The development of your brain indicates a great amount of force of character. You are a natural worker, and you would be truly miserable if placed where you had nothing to do. You like to meet and overcome difficulties, and ought to have been engaged in civil engineering, building railroads, navigating ships, or in some other way wrestling with the world's difficult enterprises. You have astonishing Firmness. It would seem that for all your life long you had been overcoming obstacles and bearing heavy responsibilities. Opposition is almost a luxury to you, and to meet and master obstacles and conquer impediments a mere pastime. It is utterly useless to try to force you to do anything against your will. You can not and will not be driven by your peers, though you can be persuaded by sympathy and friendship to go almost any length, and to sacrifice almost any amount of convenience or ease to confer a favor.

You have large Self-Esteem, which gives great self-reliance, disposition to trust to your own judgment, to rely upon your own resources, and take responsibilities. Firmness and Self-Esteem appear to have been greatly increased by use, for they stand out sharply beyond the other organs.

Your sense of duty appears to be strongly marked; and when your idea of honor, your will, your sense of reputation, and your integrity are at stake, you will do and suffer vastly to achieve what you know is right, and to crush out the wrong. If you think that a man is true to you and really honest, you can put up with ignorance, carelessness, want of capacity, and a variety of other unpleasant things, just because of his fidelity; but if a man is treacherous, and indicates a disposition to be an

PORTRAIT OF MATTHEW B. BRADY

Halftone
A) A glass plate, ruled with at least two sets of parallel lines crossing to form a grid, is placed in front of an emulsion to break up a photograph into a series of dots, facilitating the reproduction of tones of gray. Known in France as *simila-gravure.*
B) The tonal gradation of a photograph is reproduced using a pattern of dots of a single color, created by interposing a screen between the camera and subject.

Heliotype
A modification of the collotype process, devised by Ernest Edwards. A waxed glass plate is coated with a layer of bichromated gelatin containing a small amount of chrome alum, which hardens the gelatin and makes it insoluble but permeable. The dried gelatin is removed from the glass and the undersurface contact printed with a reversed negative. The film hardens at the back following exposure to light and then is attached to a pewter plate under water. After the bichromated salt is washed away the plate may be used for printing.

Photo-Aquatint
A modification of the photogravure process, developed by Thomas Huson. Differs from regular photogravure in that a single strength of etching solution is used.

Photogalvanography
A glass plate is coated with bichromated gelatin containing a silver salt. After drying it is contact printed with a transparency and washed with cold water to remove the unchanged bichromate. The gelatin swells proportionally in relation to the tones of the picture. After being electroplated the copper is removed, backed with type metal, and printed. Sometimes called Pretsch's process or photographic galvanography.

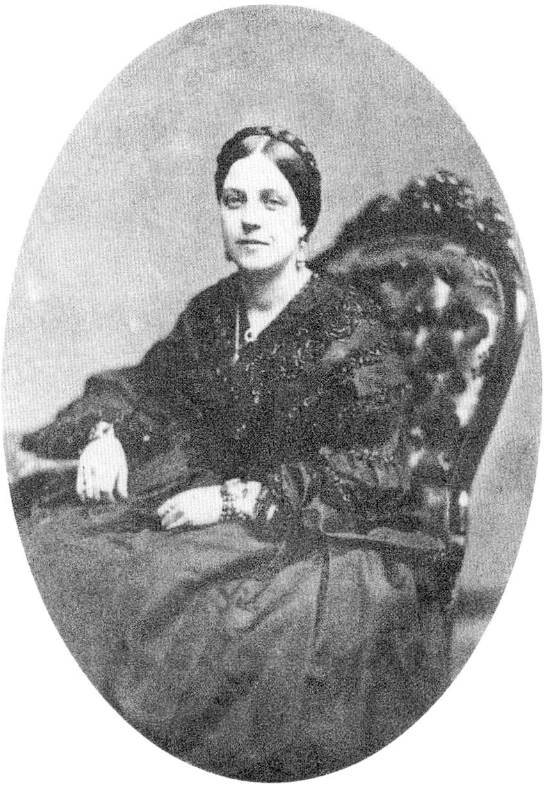

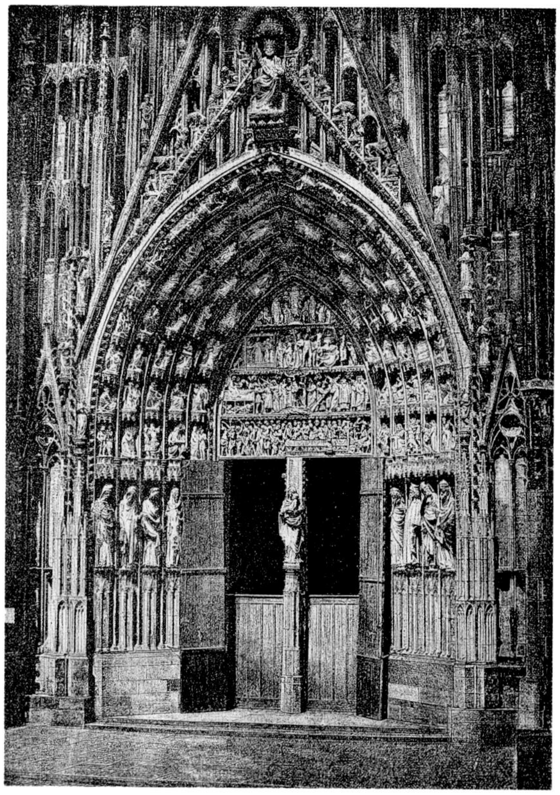

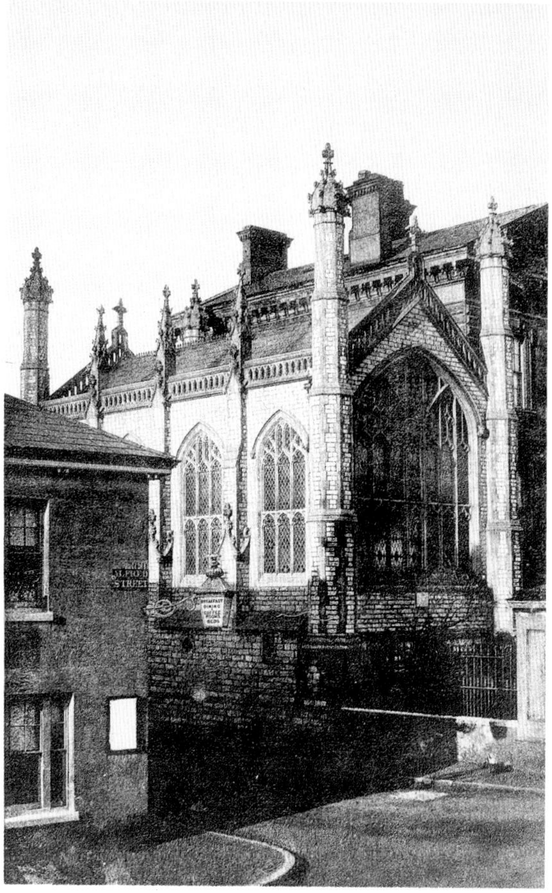

was not very deep the plates did not yield more than about forty faint prints. Josef Berres, an Austrian, obtained better results by using daguerreotypes made on solid silver plates, which could be etched more deeply than Donné's silver-coated copper plates. After experimenting with the process, Berres succeeding in making up to five hundred prints from a single plate. In 1840 he published the pamphlet *Phototyp nach der Erfindung des Prof. Berres in Wien* in an edition of two hundred, with each copy containing five prints from etched daguerreotype plates. Berres's was the first publication with illustrations produced by a photomechanical process.

In the early 1840s, the Frenchman Hippolyte Fizeau had much success with etched daguerreotypes, though his process was considerably more complex than the one practiced by Berres. After boiling the daguerreotype in potassium hydroxide, Fizeau etched the plate in nitric acid, filling the etched parts with linseed oil, and electroplating the plate with gold. Then, after removing the oil, he etched the plate again. A final electroplated coat of copper, which was harder than the silver, made the plate ready for printing. Lerebour's 1841–1843 *Excursions Daguerriennes* contained two prints by Fizeau.

It soon became clear that the method of printing from plates made directly from daguerreotypes lacked commercial potential. First, because

Opposite, clockwise from top left:

Anonymous, Portrait of a woman, ca. 1858, photolithograph (Bradford's process), 5 1/8" x 7 1/8" on 5 3/4" x 7 3/4" sheet, L. H. Bradford & Co.

Anonymous, Porch of Strasbourg Cathedral, ca. 1860, photogalvanograph (Pretsch's process), 6 1/4" x 8 1/2".

R. Murray, Chapel of the Southampton Infirmary, 1862, photo-zincograph, from a calotype negative, from *On Photo-Zincography and Other Photographic Processes Employed at the Ordnance Survey Office, Southampton*, Captain A. De C. Scott, London, 1862.

Right: Anonymous, Girl with scoliosis, ca. 1876, tipped-in Woodburytype, from *Spinal Diseases and Spinal Curvature*, Lewis A. Sayre, M.D., London, 1877.

Below: Rockwood & Co., Old Dutch church, "Sleepy Hollow," ca. 1868, heliographic engraving.

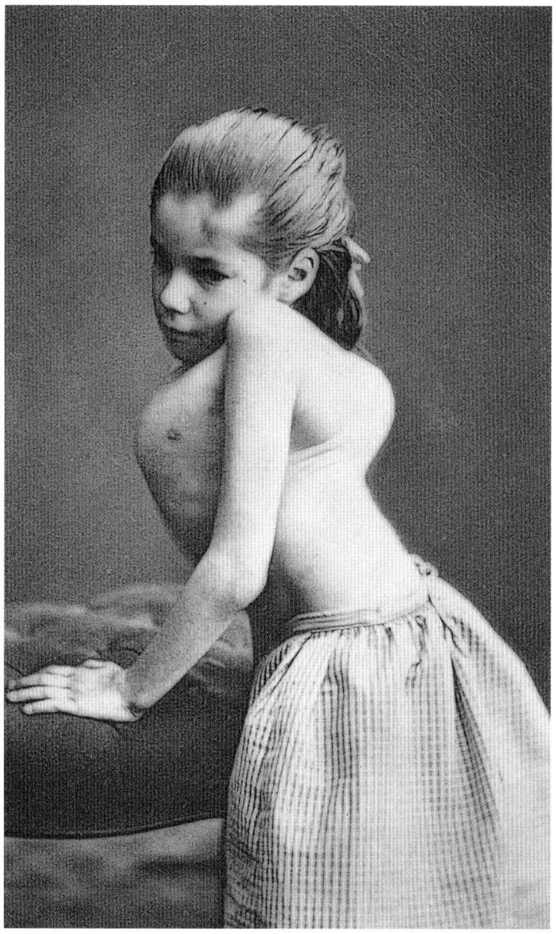

each plate was a unique original, any attempt to print the image meant running the risk of losing the photograph entirely. Moreover, once the plate was exhausted, no means existed for reproducing it. Prints made directly from photographic plates were also not commercially viable because of the highly skilled labor and costly materials required for their production. Thus, printers attempted to devise more sophisticated means of employing photography's illustrative power.

A woodcut is an engraving on wood or a print from such an engraving. Cutting into a wooden plate leaves raised lines, or characters, which then may be pressed, i.e., printed, onto paper to produce illustrations. In the 1840s, engravers began to use photographs as sources for their woodcuts. First the photograph was drawn onto the wood block and the unmarked areas cut away. Since the drawing and engraving had to be laterally reversed in order not to produce a mirror-image print, often the engraver drew the photograph from its reflection in a mirror. The main difference between the

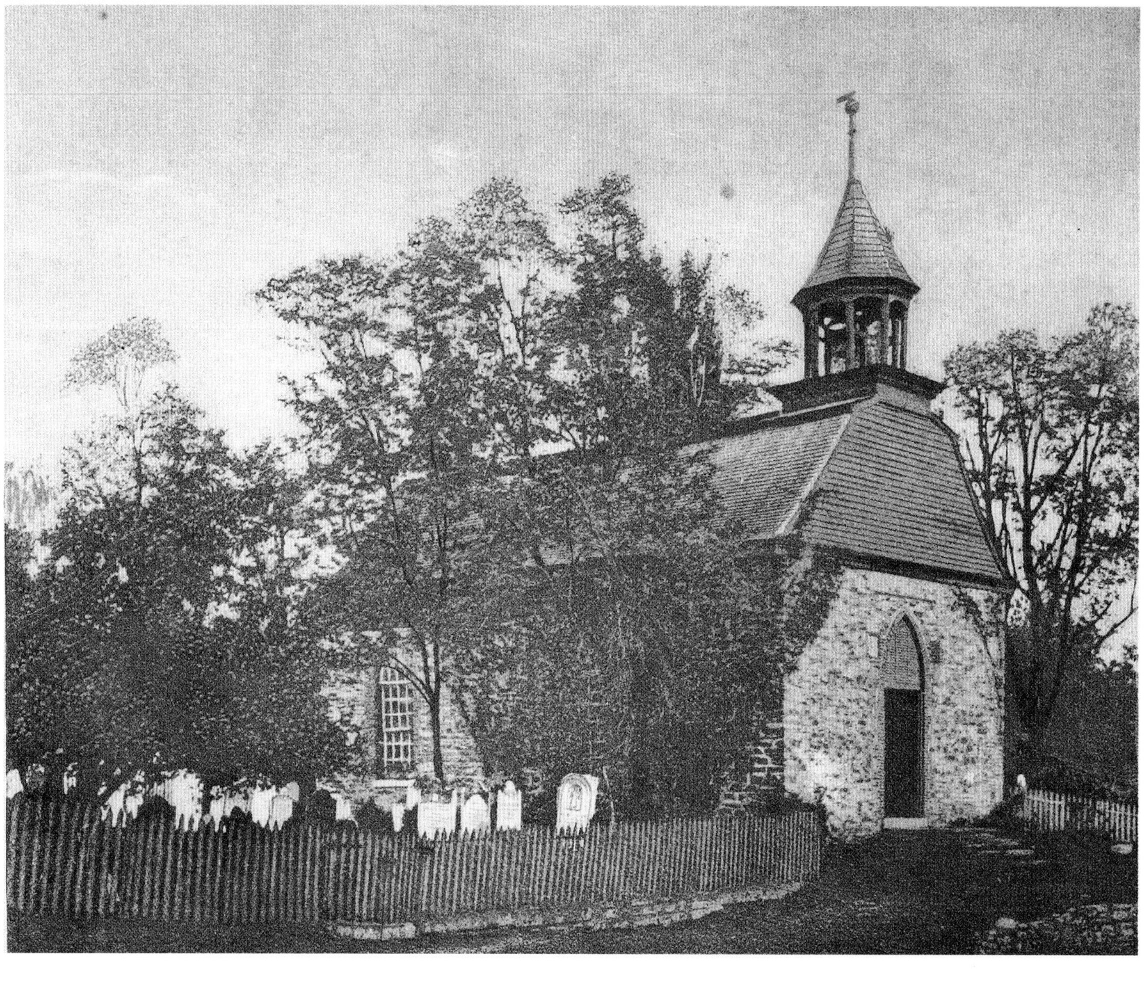

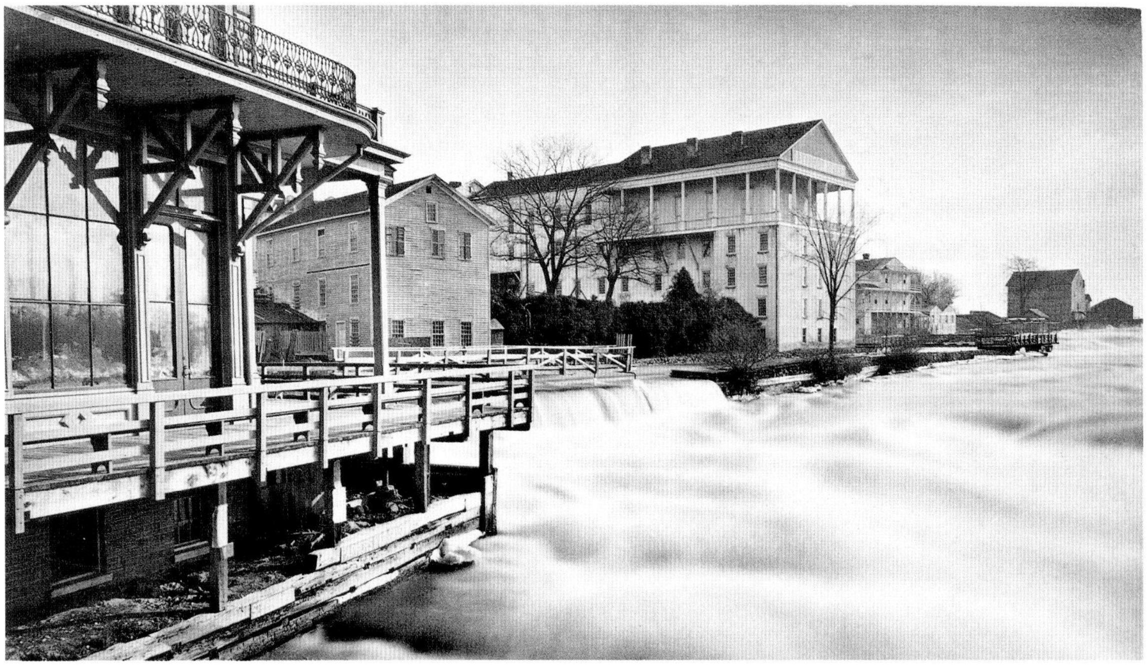

Photoglyphic engraving
A form of photogravure. A metal plate coated with gelatin is sensitized with potassium bichromate. After exposure under a negative the plate is dusted with powdered resin and melted. The cooled plate is etched with a fluid that penetrates in proportion to the varying thickness of the hardened gelatin. Invented by William Henry Fox Talbot. Also known as photoglyphy.

Photogravure
A copper plate is dusted with resin which is solidified by heating. Carbon tissue printed under a transparency is transferred to the plate and then developed. When dry, the plate is etched in a succession of baths so that the depth of etching is proportionate to the picture's tones, with the shadows being the deepest. After inking the image is printed from the plate. Sometimes referred to simply as gravure, or, in Europe, as heliogravure.

Phototint
A) A halftone block process invented by Cocking. The process consists of printing from two negatives, one ordinary and the other prepared by hand. Produces striking effects of light and shade. B) Another name for collotype.

Phototype
Name given to a once-secret process invented by F. Joubert. It has since been applied to the collotype and also to halftone blocks.

Stannotype
Modification of the Woodburytype in which the bichromated gelatin relief is faced with tin foil. Devised by Walter Woodbury in 1881.

original photograph and the print of it from a woodcut was that the prints were lacking halftones. Crosshatching was used to suggest shading. If large numbers of prints were needed, the wood pattern could be pressed into wax or clay and molten type-metal poured into the impression. Then prints could be drawn from the more durable metal plate.

The advent of the wet-collodion process, in 1851, introduced the potential for printing a photograph directly on a wood block. This eliminated one step—drawing on the block—and made the engraver's job easier and the results more accurate. In the 1850s, J. D. Brinckerhoff of New York became the first to print a photograph on wood successfully. *The Photographic and Fine Arts Journal* of February 1855 carried his first published effort. While Brinckerhoff didn't bother to patent his process, Robert Price of Worcester, Massachusetts, and C. B. Boyle of Albany, New York, both obtained patents for reproducing portraits by means of woodcuts. Price was granted a patent in May 1857, and Boyle in February 1859. Use of the various photo-on-wood processes increased in the years leading up to 1865, and soon after, they entered into general use.

Photography on zinc was probably first used by the Parisian Gillot in 1859. In America, however, the process was relatively unexplored until the 1880s. When a zinc plate is coated with a mixture of bichromate and albumen, it becomes sensitive to light. Exposure of a reversed image on a coated zinc plate causes the coating to harden where the light—representing dark areas in the original subject—strikes it. Next, when the zinc plate is lightly inked and washed, the unaffected albumen dissolves. Re-inking the plate and treating it with acid etches the zinc areas not protected by hardened albumen. If the plate is then mounted on a wood block, it can be used for printing. Halftones cannot be reproduced with this process.

The "swelled-gelatin" method was patented in 1875 by Louis Levy and David Bachrack, Jr., both of Baltimore. After photographing the original image in reverse, a heavy glass plate, coated with gelatin and bichromate, was placed under the negative and exposed. The gelatin/bichromate mixture hardened where exposed to light, and when washed in cold water the gelatin not affected by light would swell. By pouring plaster over the plate, Levy and Bachrack obtained a relief that could be used to make a wax impression, which they then electroplated with copper. The final print was produced by inking the copper. Levy and Bachrack's method was also incapable of yielding halftones.

In November 1854, Paul Pretsch, an Austrian living in England, took out a patent for a process he called photogalvanography. In his process a

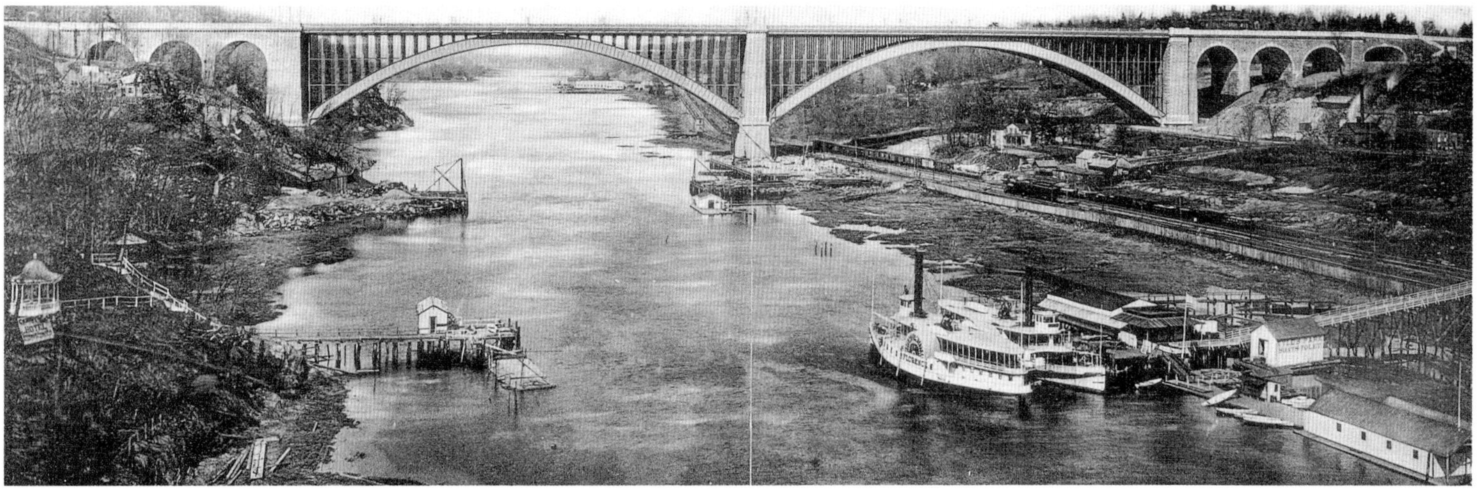

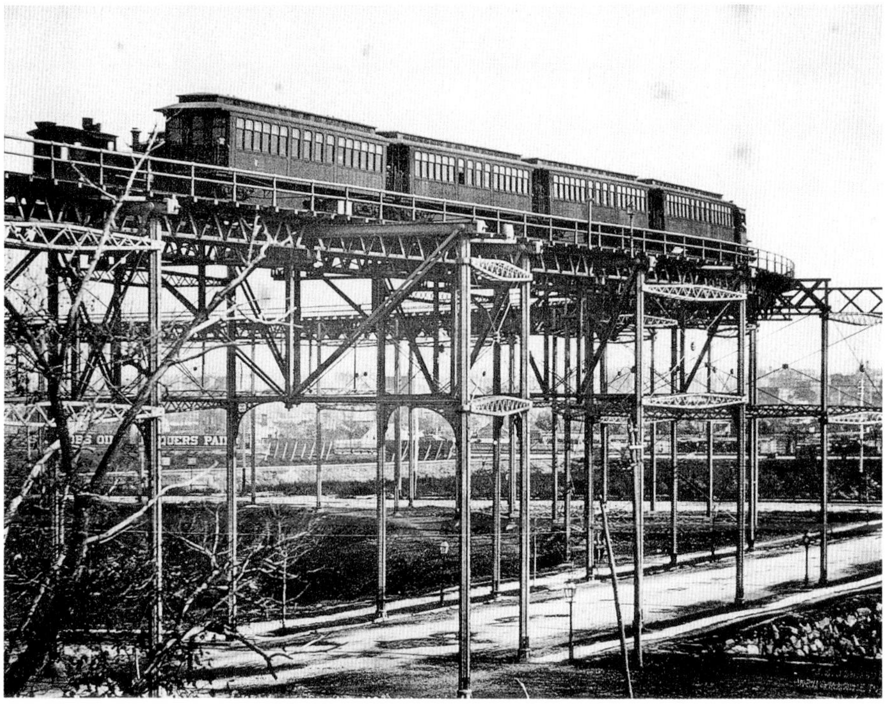

Opposite: George Barker, Disfigured banks, village shore of upper American falls, ca. 1879, tipped-in heliotype print, from *Special Report of New York State Survey on the Preservation of the Scenery of Niagara Falls*, James T. Gardner, Albany, 1880.

Top: Anonymous, The Washington Bridge, general view from the south, ca. 1888, Albertype, from *The Washington Bridge Over the Harlem River at 181st Street, New York City*, William R. Hutton, 1889.

Bottom: J. S. Johnston, Elevated railway, New York City, ca. 1888, collotype, from *Views of New York*, published by Brentano's, 1889.

glass sheet was coated with a gelatin of dichromate, potassium iodide, and silver nitrate. The dried coating was then contact printed from a transparent positive and washed in cool water. Upon washing, the gelatin would swell and reticulate, making a relief corresponding to tones in the negative. Next a mold of gutta-percha (one of the first natural plastics exploited by humans) was made of the surface; after separation, the mold was electroplated with copper, duplicating the surface of the original. Finally a second, thicker, electroplate was made over the first, and the resultant plate was ready for printing, though generally some retouching by an engraver was needed to produce a truly satisfactory surface. The 1856 publication of *Photographic Art Treasures*, using Pretsch's process, created a stir, as it was the first publication of photographs to utilize printer's ink. Not only was this new process faster than engraving, taking weeks as opposed to months or years, it was also less expensive.

In 1863 Campbell D. Dallas, who modified Pretsch's process after the patent lapsed, revealed the Dallastype, an improvement over the previous process in that it did not require retouching by an engraver. However, as the intermediate tones of photographs were too costly and/or difficult to attain with the Dallastype, it was generally used only for the reproduction of line illustrations.

The Woodburytype, invented by Englishman Walter Woodbury in 1866, was the first commercially successful photomechanical process to reproduce intermediate tones. Woodbury's process also used bichromated gelatin film exposed under a negative. When washed in warm water, the film yielded a gelatin relief of the negative, which could then be used to make an impression on a lead plate. Thanks to the hollows in the plate, which held varying amounts of ink, the result was a print displaying continuous shades of dark and light. The Woodburytype was principally used for book illustrations. Of all the prints produced by photomechanical processes, the Woodburytype is the closest to a photograph in appearance.

In 1869 Josef Albert, the court photographer of Bavaria, patented a process of his own invention called the Albertype. Though subsequent modifications of the process bore different names, all of these prints are now collectively referred to as col-

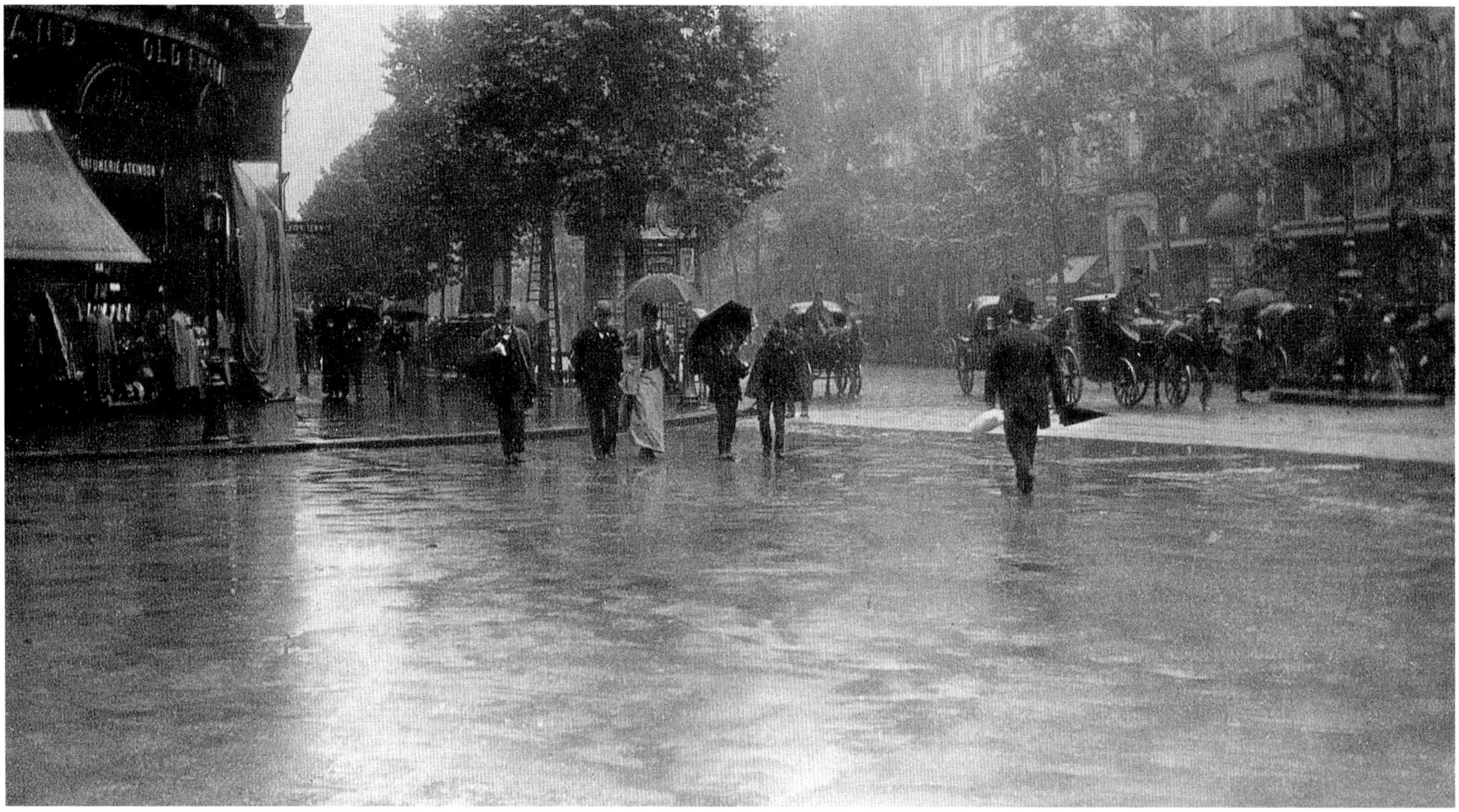

Swelled-gelatin process
A heavy glass plate is coated with a thick layer of bichromated gelatin. The plate, after drying, is contact printed with a line negative. When placed in cool water the unexposed gelatin swells. The exposed sections remain hardened. After swelling, the plate is placed in a hardening bath and coated with plaster. The dried plaster is then used as a matrix for a wax mold for electrotyping.

Woodburytype
A relief image on bichromated gelatin is covered with lead and placed in a press. The mold created in the lead is then inked and printed. The process was patented in 1866 by Walter B. Woodbury. Known in France as *photoglyptie*.

Zincography
A photolithograph transfer is put on a zinc plate for printing. Developed by Colonel Henry James. Also known as photozincography.

lotypes. Like the Woodburytype, the Albertype used bichromated gelatin, but Albert used a hardened base of bichromated gelatin coated on a glass plate in order to help an upper, bichromated gelatin layer adhere to the plate. Then, when the negative was contact printed on the plate, the exposed sections of the upper gelatin coat would harden. The treatment of plates in Albert's process was similar to that of Woodburytypes, with thick inks used for shadows and thinner ones for halftones. Albert was able to obtain more than two thousand prints from the gelatin without it deteriorating, and in view of its greater simplicity and lower cost the Albertype eventually came to supplant the Woodburytype.

In 1879, Austrian Karl Klic invented the photogravure, often referred to simply as gravure. In this process, resin dust is placed on a copper plate and melted. Then a sheet of pigmented paper coated in gelatin is sensitized with bichromate. After contact exposure through a positive, the sheet is soaked in water and placed gelatin-side-down on a copper plate. Once the paper backing is removed, the gelatin is washed in warm water, leaving behind only the insoluble portions, with

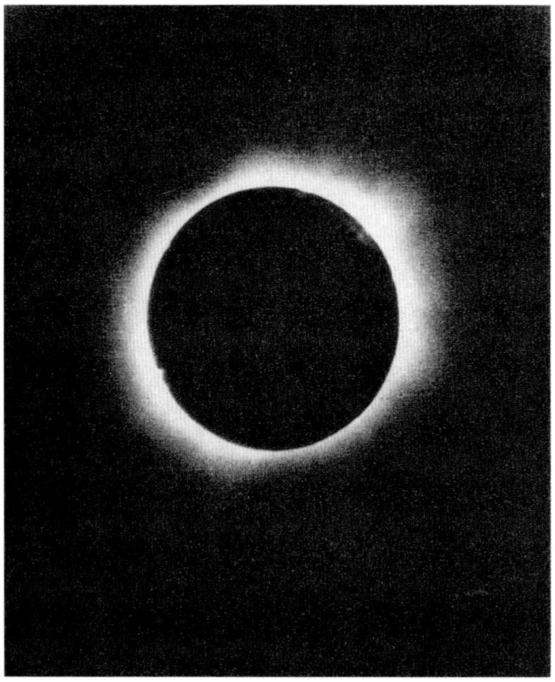

highlights thicker than shadows. In etching, the ferric chloride works deeper where the gelatin is thin, thus producing depth where the shadows are located. The plate is then inked and printed.

For all the success of the various methods devised for mechanically printing photographs by the 1880s, one distinct problem still existed:

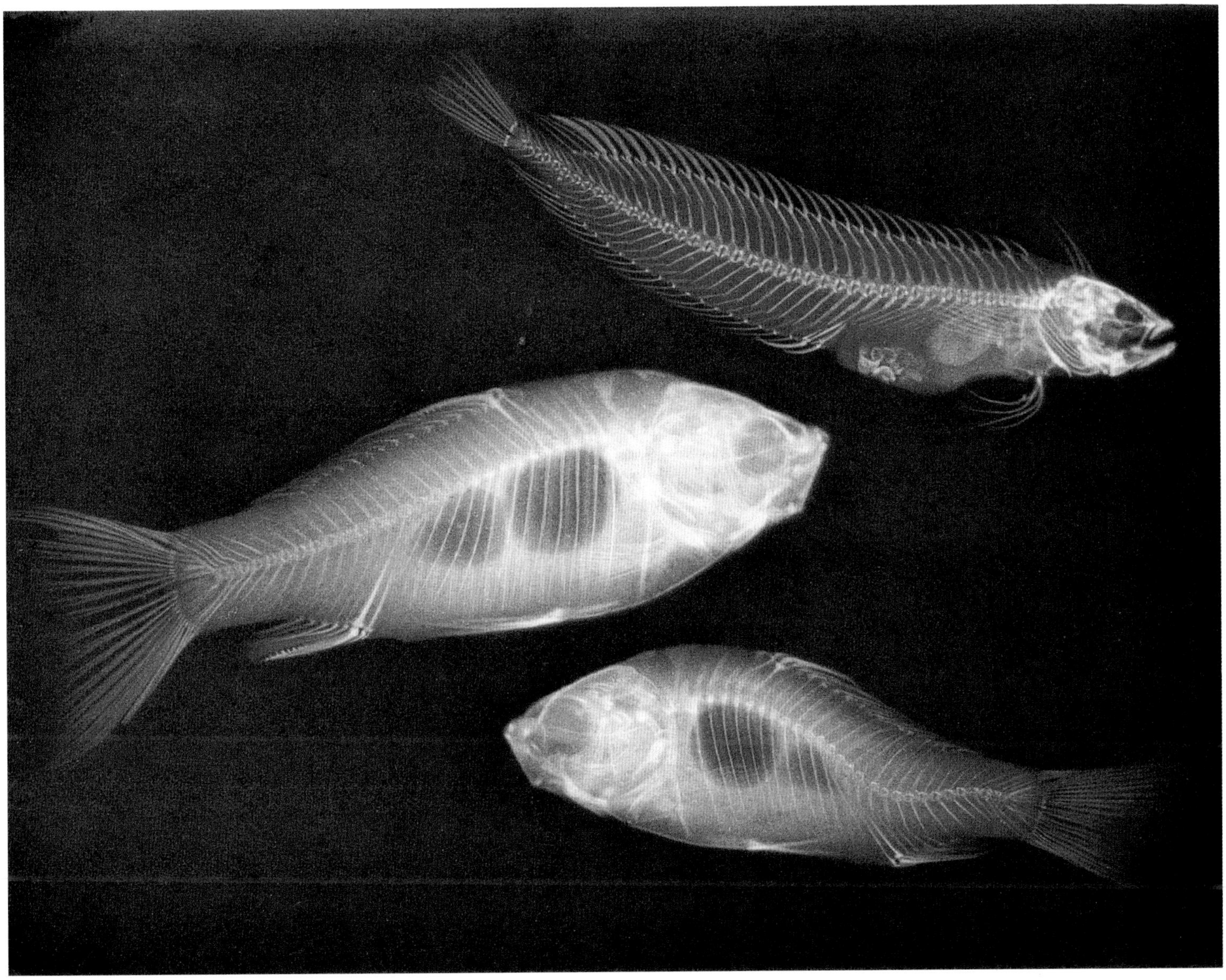

Opposite, top: Alfred Stieglitz, *A Wet Day on the Boulevard*, 1895, photogravure, 6" x 3 1/4", from *Photographic Times*, December 1895.

Opposite, bottom: Dr. Busch, Total eclipse of the sun, July 18, 1851, heliogravure, from a daguerreotype, from *Die Photographie der Gestirne*, Dr. J. Scheiner, 1897.

Above: Eder & Valenta, X-ray of three fish, halftone, from *K. K. Graphische Lehr u. Versuchsanstalt in Wien*, 1888–1913, directed by Josef Maria Eder, 1913.

they could not be printed in conjunction with type on an ordinary printing press. Mechanically-printed photographs had to be bound or tipped into books in the same manner as a photographic print.

Halftone reproduction would eventually allow for the simultaneous printing of text and photographic images. Fox Talbot is considered to have pioneered the halftone screen when, in October 1852, he used folded gauze to evenly divide a photograph into small parts.

In the 1860s and 1870s Joseph Swan proposed using ruled lines as a screen for photographs. Among the others who worked with screens was F. W. Eggloffstein, who in 1865 was granted the first U.S. patent for use of a screen in photoengraving. Frederick Ives, who debuted his process in 1881, is credited with introducing halftones to magazine illustrations. But it was Stephen H. Horgan who developed the use of halftone printing for newspapers. The March 4, 1880 issue of the *New York Graphic* was the first newspaper to publish a halftone. Horgan's halftone plate was made by placing a screen with fine parallel rulings between the negative and a glass plate with a bichromated gelatin surface. After exposure, the procedure was similar to that of other bichromated gelatin processes. The resulting plate produced the kind of dot-based image—though much more coarse in those days—still seen in today's newspaper illustrations.

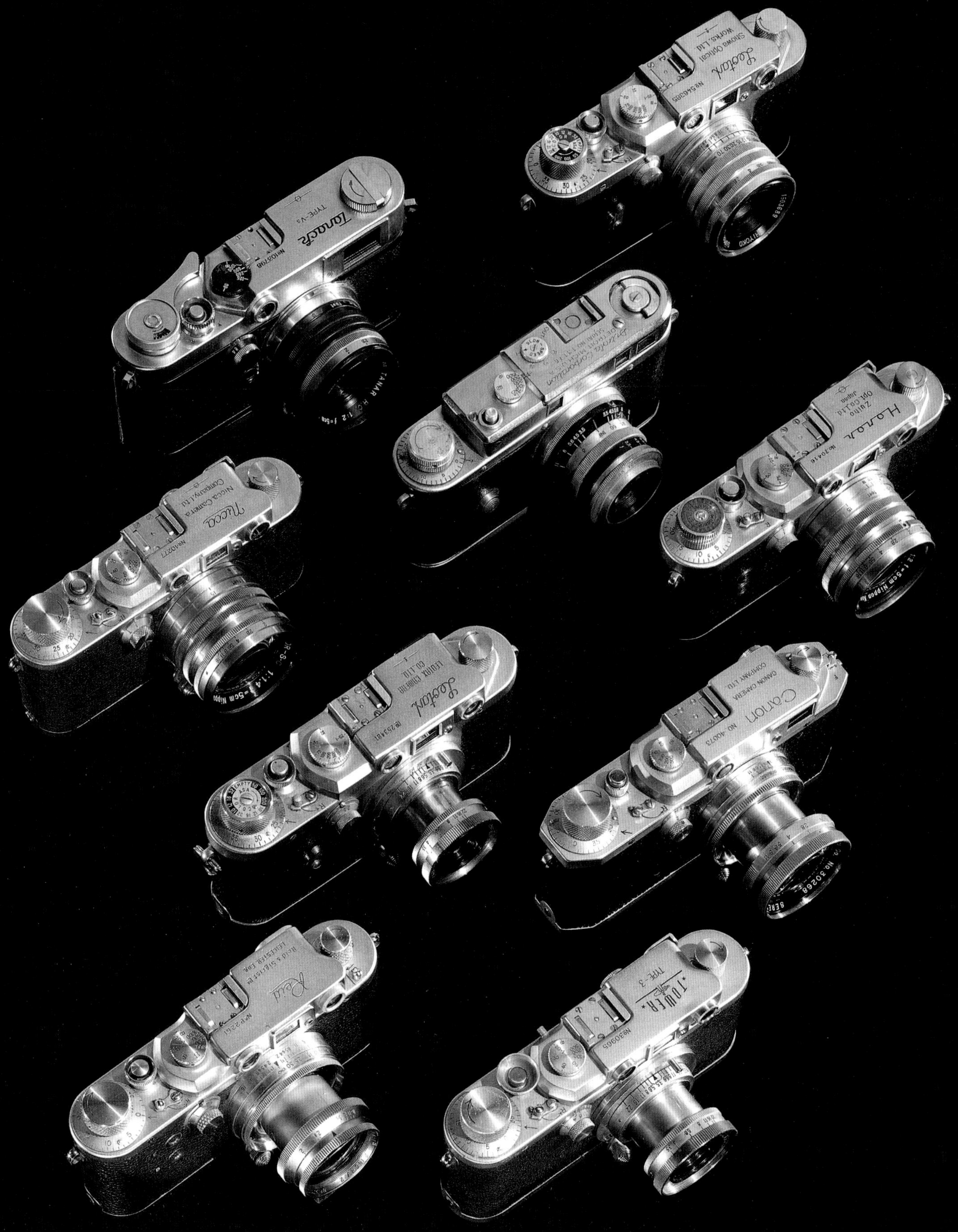
Leotax
Tanack
Nicca
Canon
TOWER

CHAPTER NINE:

THE 35 MM CAMERA

Leica copies. All for 24 x 36 mm exposures on No. 135 roll film. Top row, left to right: Tanack IIIF, Tanaka Kogaku, ca. 1954; Leotax F, Showa Kogaku, ca. 1955. Second row, left to right: Nicca IIIA, Nicca Camera Works, 1951; Detrola 400, Detrola Corp., ca. 1941; Honor S1, Zuiko Optical Co., ca. 1957. Third row, left to right: Leotax T, Kyoei-Sha Co., 1955; Canon IIB, Canon Camera Co., ca. 1950. Bottom row, left to right: Reid, Reid & Sigrist, ca. 1958; Tower Type-3, Nicca Camera Works for Sears, Roebuck & Co., 1952, same as Nicca IIIa.

In the last three decades of the twentieth century, cameras designed to use 35 mm film dominated the amateur and professional photographic scenes. Film of this size was first made in 1889 for use in motion-picture machines. As a film width for production-model still cameras, it was first employed in 1913, and, though a camera using the 24-by-36 mm format on perforated 35 mm-wide film was introduced in 1914, the format did not become standard until the late 1920s. From then on it gradually gained in popularity, until it reached its present position as the standard photographic format.

This discussion of 35 mm cameras is broken into three segments, covering the years 1900–1925, 1926–1945, and 1946 to the present. The end of the first period is marked by the introduction, in 1925, of what would become the gold standard of 35 mm cameras, the Leica. In the years following its introduction, the Leica would inspire many imitations. While modeled after the Leica in many respects, cameras of the second period share with their predecessors a remarkable ingenuity and diversity of design that cannot be found amongst the 35 mm cameras of today.

1900–1925

In 1889, W. Laurie Dickson, chief assistant in Thomas Edison's laboratories, was working on a motion-picture camera that could be used in a new type of viewer. The camera was called the Kinetograph, and the viewer, the Kinetoscope. This viewer used a loop of film that permitted repetition of the movie without rewinding. Edison and Dickson approached George Eastman, whose Transparent Film, available late in 1889, could be contact printed for use in the Kinetoscope. Early samples of the transparent film showed a tendency to tear slightly where the camera's and viewer's toothed rollers engaged the film's perforations. At Eastman's urging, Henry Reichenbach, Eastman's main film chemist, developed a double-coated film that withstood repeated use.

The film supplied to Edison and Dickson was the same hundred-exposure-long film used in the Kodak and No. 1 Kodak. In Edison's laboratories the film was slit lengthwise, with the two resulting pieces attached at the ends to create the length needed for the loop. As the Kodak film was 2 ¾-inches wide—70 mm in metric units—slitting it in

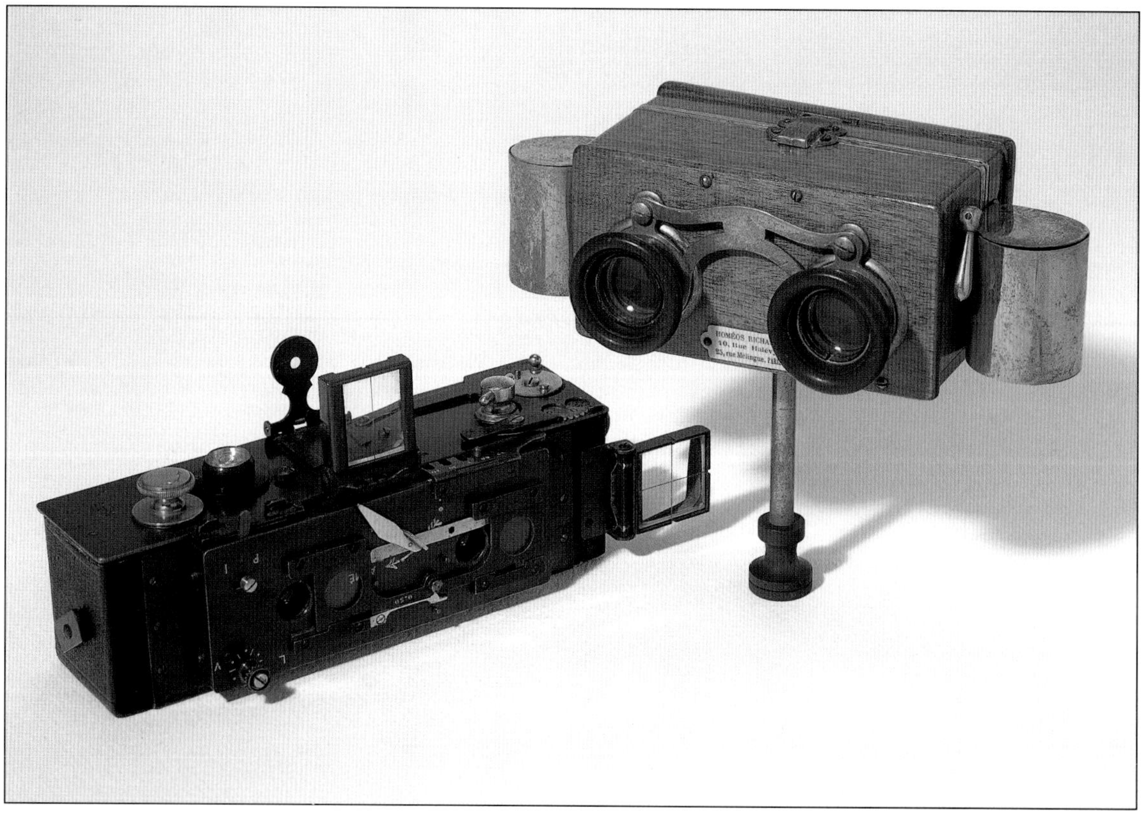

Homéos, Jules Richard, ca. 1914, all-metal construction. Shown with Richard stereoscope for viewing 35 mm filmstrips of positive pairs.

Contax-related cameras. Back row, left to right: KE-4 (1) 70 mm Combat Camera, Signal Corps Model, Graflex, Inc., ca. 1953, for 5.5 x 7 cm exposures on 70 mm roll film; Nikon S, Nippon Kogaku K. K., ca. 1952, for 24 x 36 mm exposures on No. 135 roll film. Front row, left to right: Contax II, Zeiss Ikon, ca. 1938, for 24 x 36 mm exposures on No. 135 roll film; Contax (I), Zeiss Ikon, ca. 1934, for 24 x 36 mm exposures on No. 135 roll film.

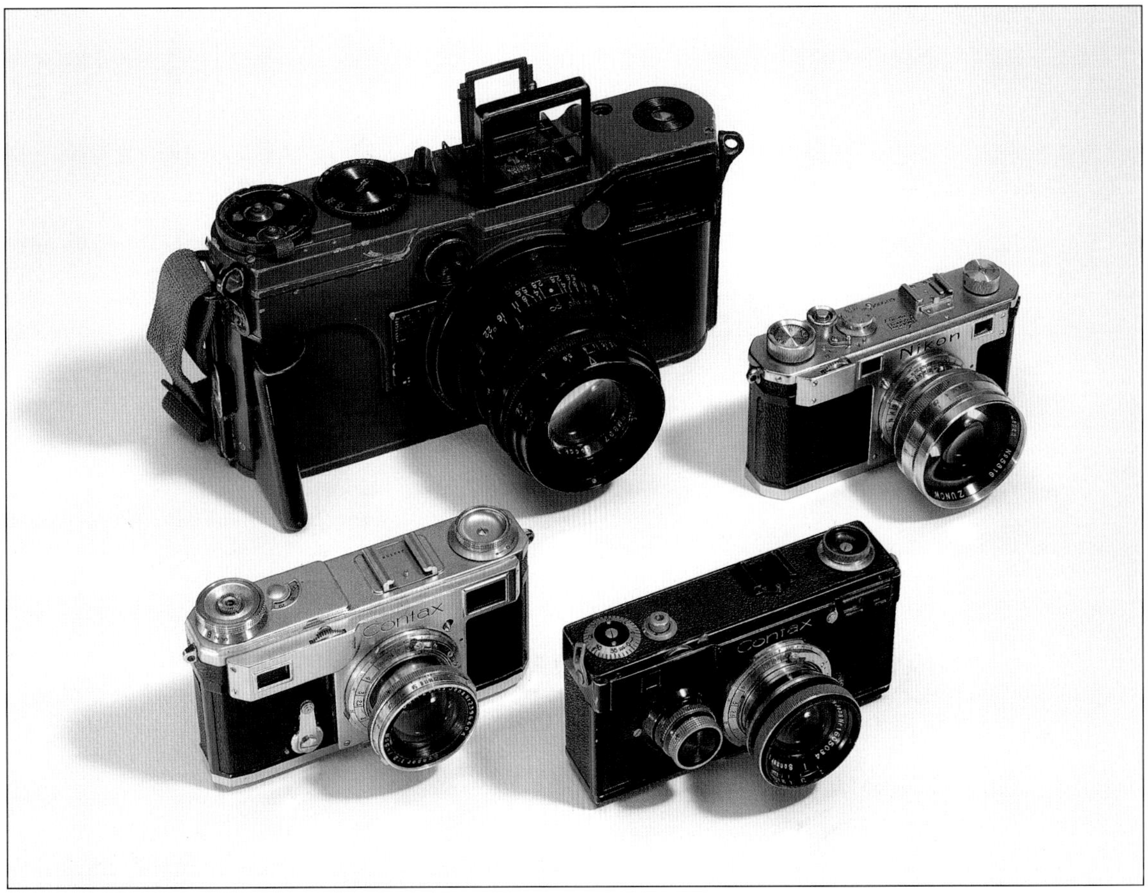

half produced 35 mm-wide film. When the two strips were pieced end-to-end, they yielded an approximate fifty-foot length. Each frame in Kinetoscope film was 18-by-24 mm and had four perforations per frame on each side of the film.

At the turn of the century, a variety of film widths competed with Edison's 35 mm film, made by Kodak. As a result, anyone wanting to show movies was faced with various film dimensions from several companies. In the early 1890s, the Lumière brothers in France introduced the projection—rather than Kinetoscope viewing—of motion pictures, using 35 mm-wide film in the Cinématographe, their combination camera-printer-projector. Their film had one round perforation on each side of each movie frame, but, observing the popularity of Edison's film, they modified their Cinématographe to accommodate it. This made many more pictures available for projection in their machines. In 1907 a number of companies involved in the production and marketing of cameras, projectors, and films entered into a voluntary agreement, called the Motion Picture Patents Agreement, which established 35 mm as the standard for motion-picture film. This width remains in general acceptance today for films shown in theaters around the world.

As 35 mm film became the standard for motion-picture film, it also presented itself as a possible size for still photography. One of the first still cameras to incorporate 35 mm film, the spark-drum camera, was introduced by Dr. Lucien Bull, of Britain. Something of a hybrid between a still and a movie camera, it was used to make stereoscopic pairs of exposures at a rate of up to two thousand per second. Parallel three-foot lengths of 35 mm film were wound around a rotating drum. A very bright, brief electric spark was used to illuminate the film, and the result was fifty-four pairs of exposures. The camera was used to make motion studies of such things as bursting soap bubbles and the movements of dragonflies. As this was a specialized piece of equipment for scientific purposes, very few were made, and many would not consider it to be in the mainstream of 35 mm still-camera development.

In 1905 Rene Millaud, Honorary Secretary-Editor of the French Chamber of Deputies, asked the Gaumont company to make a small, one-of-a-kind camera for him. Disguised as a dictionary, this camera used 35 mm film. In the years 1905–1910 Millaud used the camera to take photographs during sessions of the Chamber. These were regularly published in the French weekly, *L'Illustration*. While the photographs created quite a stir within the Chamber, their source was unknown until Millaud revealed it himself in a 1938 article in *Photo-Revue*.

While 35 mm film was employed in still cameras in several prototypes, one-of-a-kind, or novelty cameras, it was not until 1912 that this format was considered for commercial production. Once again, the cinema played a role.

Henry Herbert, of the New York firm of Herbert & Huesgen, importers of professional movie equipment, discovered that left-over short lengths of 35 mm film, too short to be used in the cameras of movie studios, were readily available for one-third the regular cost of cine film. Herbert asked his chief technician, Paul Dietz, to undertake the design of a still camera to use this low-priced 35 mm film. The camera that resulted from that design was the Tourist Multiple. It was made by the New Ideas Manufacturing Company, of New York, and was patented and introduced in 1913. As such, it qualifies as the first publicly-sold production-model still camera using 35 mm film. The camera used fifty-foot lengths of film, loaded in a magazine, to produce 750 exposures on a single load of film. The negative format, 18-by-24 mm, was the one used in conventional motion-picture cameras. The camera's body could be used as a component of a projection lantern; an enlarging accessory was anticipated, but never produced.

The Tourist Multiple's manufacturers claimed that it "will take the pictures of an entire summer, of a complete European tour, of a voyage around the world, of vacation trips to the tropics or the arctic regions, or extended journeyings in any part of the world." Unfortunately, tourism abroad was sharply curtailed with the outbreak of war in 1914. Production of the Tourist Multiple was suspended

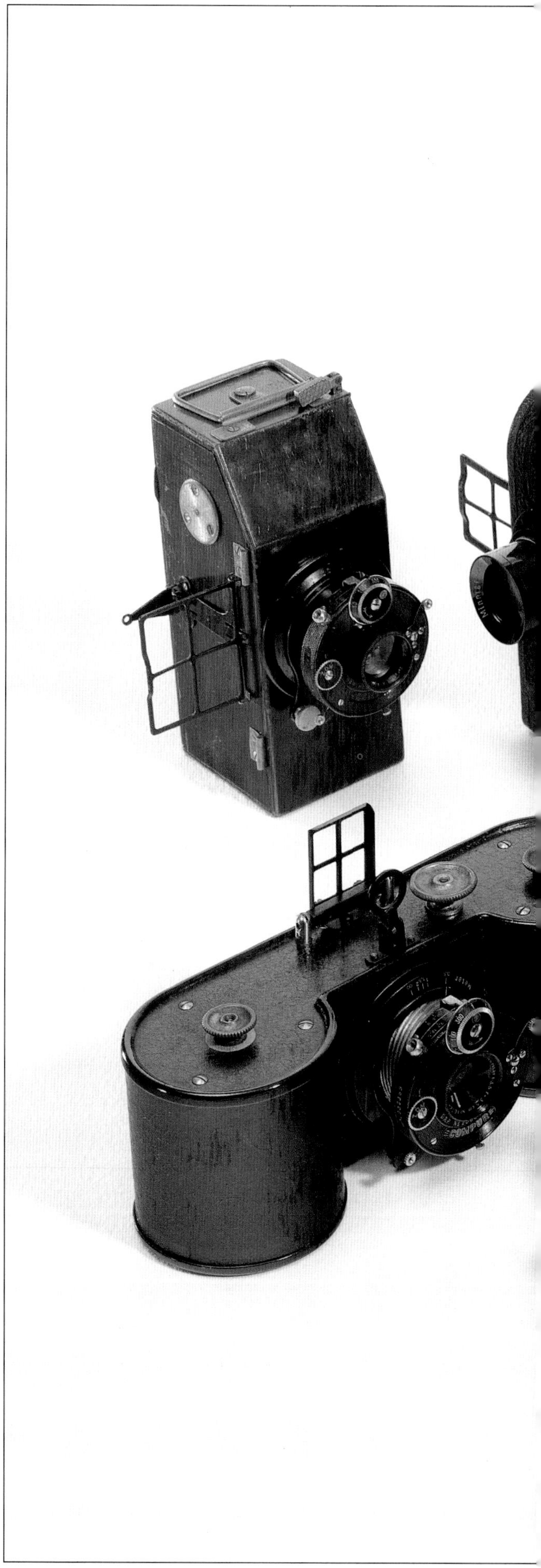

Early 35 mm cameras. Back row, left to right: Sico, Simons & Co., ca. 1921; Minnigraph, Levy Roth, ca. 1915; Le Cent-Vues, Model 1, Établissements Mollier, ca. 1925; Tourist Multiple, New Ideas Mfg. Co., ca. 1914; Photo-Ciné Sept, André Debrie, ca. 1924. Middle row, left to right: Esco, Model I, Seischab & Co., ca. 1922; Amourette, Österreichisches Telephon AG (ÖTAG), ca. 1926; Éka, E. Krauss, ca. 1926. Bottom row, left to right: Photoscopic, La Cinéscopie, ca. 1924; Le Furet, Model I, E. Guérin & Co., ca. 1926.

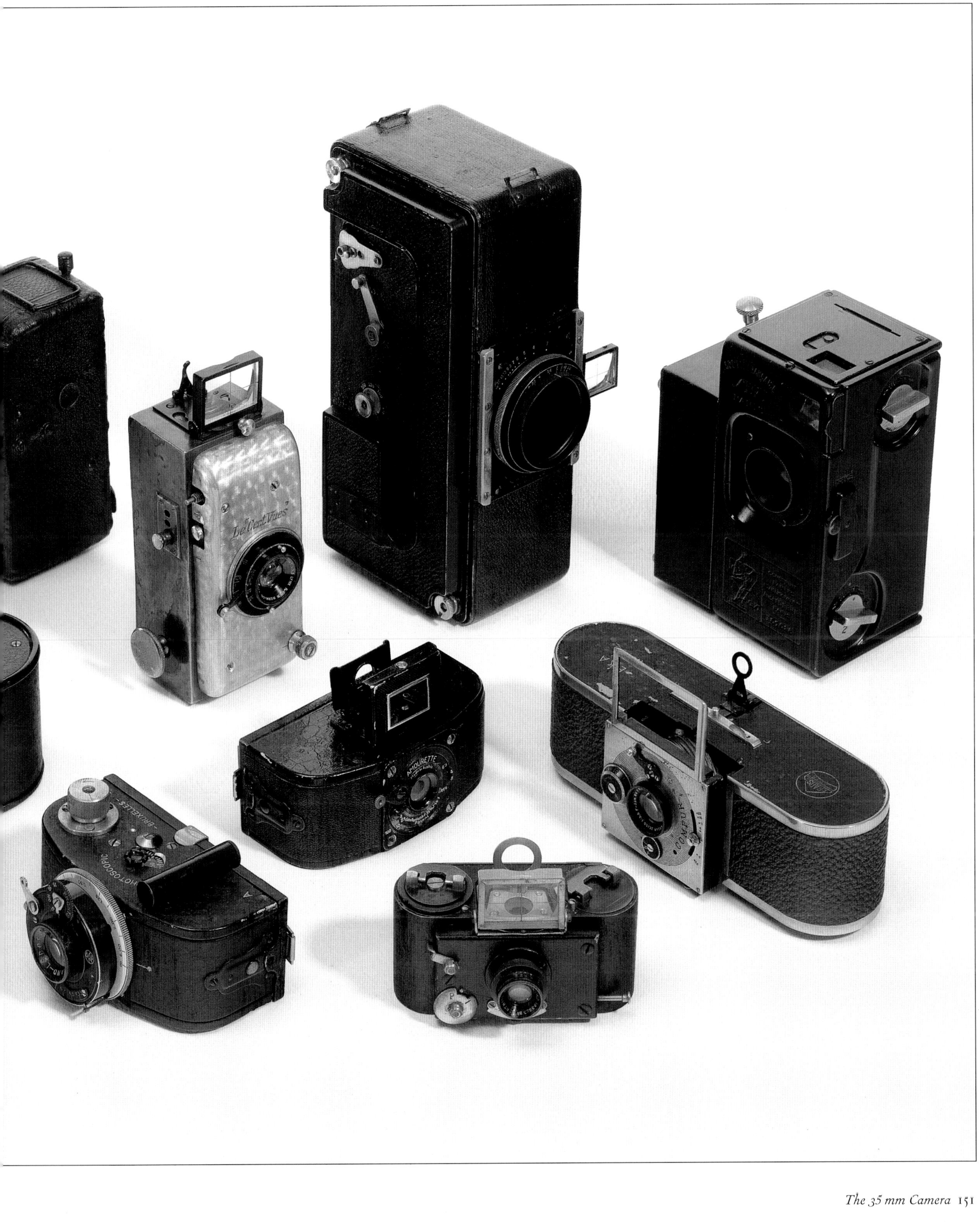
AMOURETTE
COMPUR
BRUXELLES

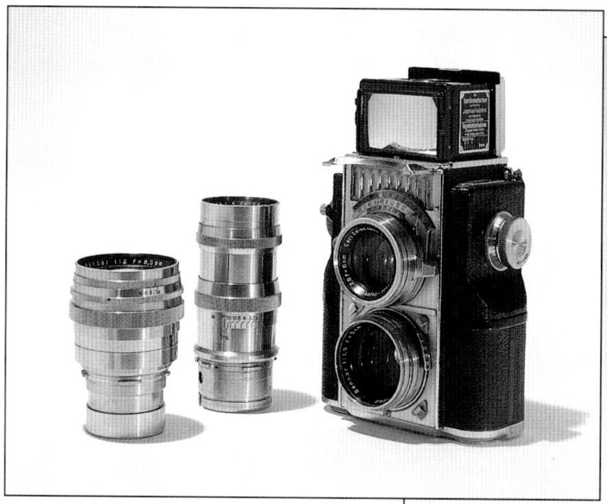

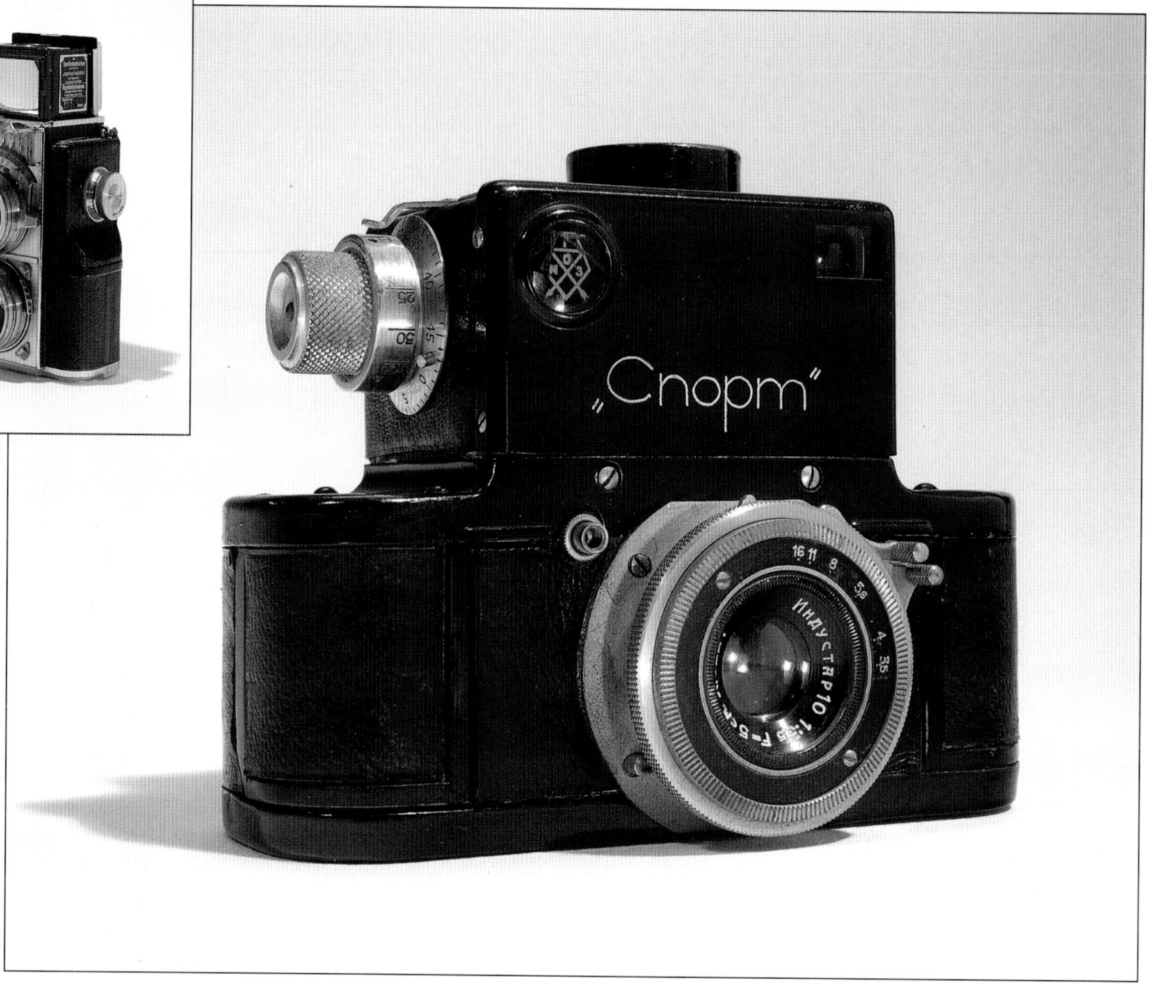

Contaflex, Zeiss Ikon, ca. 1936, for 24 x 36 mm exposures on No. 135 roll film. Built-in noncoupled photoelectric exposure meter. Shown with other interchangeable lenses.

Right: Cnopm (Sport) G101, GOMZ, ca. 1938, for 24 x 36 mm exposures on special cassette loads of standard 35 mm film.

for the duration of the war—the factory where it was made was requisitioned—and the camera's production was never resumed following the end of World War I.

After the Tourist Multiple, several 35 mm cameras were designed in France, Germany, and Britain. Like the Tourist Multiple, these cameras hardly had time to take hold in the market before the outbreak of the war halted their production.

The Homéos camera, manufactured by Jules Richard, of Paris, was patented in 1913 and introduced later that year. It was a stereoscopic camera that produced twenty-seven stereo pairs, 2.5-by-1.9-cm, or, in later models, fifty-four single exposures on standard cine film. Reports suggest that ten cameras were sold in 1913 and a few hundred in 1914. The war then interrupted production, which was slowly resumed thereafter.

The Simplex Multi-Exposure Camera was manufactured by the Multi-Speed Shutter Company, of Long Island, New York. It was introduced early in 1914. The camera, which used standard, perforated 35 mm cine film, offered interchangeable formats. On a single fifty-foot magazine load of film, it could produce four hundred full-frame (24-by-36 mm) or eight hundred half-frame (18-by-24 mm) exposures. A lever was used to change the format. In 1915 the Simplex Multi-Exposure Camera, Model B, was introduced. This version not only possessed a simpler lens and shutter, but also used only the four-hundred-exposure 24-by-36 mm format. Around that time, the earlier model, with the interchangeable formats, was redesigned and designated the Simplex Multi-Exposure Camera "Special." There is no record of any of these models having been produced past 1916.

The Minnigraph camera was probably put on the market in 1914, though 1913 and 1915 have also been suggested as the date. Made in Berlin by the firm of Levy-Roth, the Minnigraph was a simple camera with an all-metal body, a single-speed shutter and an f/3 lens. Although basic, the camera was versatile: it could be used to copy negatives and contact-print positives, as an enlarger, and as a projector. In 1916, three more models of the Minnigraph were introduced, offering different lens options as well as other slight changes. The camera was advertised as late as 1917, but its production does not seem to have survived the war.

In late 1914 the "Centum" Film Camera was reviewed and advertised by Newman & Sinclair, Ltd., of London. It had a box-like shape and used "standard cinematograph film"—perforated 35 mm—in rolls for twelve, twenty-five, or one hundred exposures. The advertisement for the camera stated "Ready early in 1915." While at least one example must have been seen in order to have been reviewed, the actual quantity made is unknown. As Britain was at war at the time, commercial production was probably never initiated.

According to an advertisement in the 1930 *British Journal Photographic Almanac*, the Talbot "Invisible" camera had been on the market for fifteen years, placing its introduction in the year 1915. This unusual camera looked like the front half of a belt and was meant to be worn around the waist. A lens was positioned in the center of the front, tending to belie the camera's belt guise. Located at one end of the camera was a supply cassette and, at the other, a take-up one. A brochure for the camera stated that the film was supplied in one-meter lengths, enough to make thirty pictures, but this had been changed by hand to read ½ meter for fifteen pictures. It is not known how long the camera was produced after 1930.

While virtually all of the cameras introduced before World War I used perforated 35 mm film, one camera that was placed on the market in America in 1916, the No.00 Premo, did not. The simplest of box cameras, the little camera used paper-backed 35 mm film—Kodak's No. 35—to produce 32-by-44-mm exposures. These exposures were wider than the standard because the film had no perforations. The No.00 Premo was produced by Kodak's Rochester Optical Division until 1922.

With one major exception, 35 mm camera design and production lay dormant in the years immediately following World War I. That exception was Tartara's Autocinephot (see Chapter 7). That camera's introduction, in 1919, came less

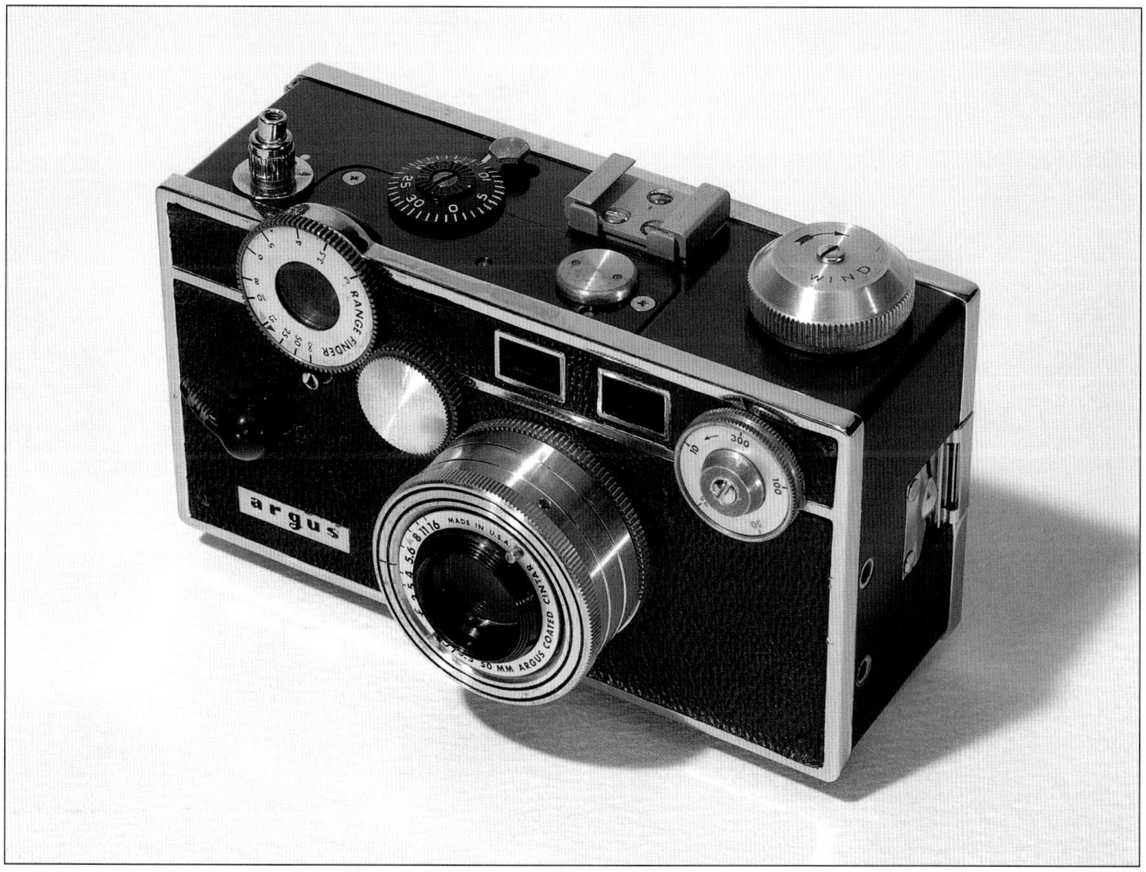

Argus C3, Argus Inc., ca. 1945, for 24 x 36 mm exposures on No. 135 roll film. Often referred to as "the brick."

than a year after the war ended, and it may well have come too soon, before European countries—even the victors—had entirely recovered.

In the period 1920 through 1925, a number of still cameras that used 35 mm film were introduced. As the references for some of these are rather sketchy, approximations are given for some of their dates of introduction. In 1920 Simons & Company, of Berlin-Charlottenberg, introduced the Sico camera. The shape of its all-wood body was very similar to that of the Minnigraph. The camera produced twenty-five exposures, 30-by-40 mm, on unperforated, paper-backed roll film specially spooled for the camera. Also in 1921, the Italian firm of Morsolin introduced the Argus. The horizontally-oriented camera produced 30-by-40-mm exposures on unperforated cine film.

The Esco camera, which was introduced in 1922, was produced by Seischab & Co., of Nuremberg, Germany. In the tradition of some of its predecessors, the camera used a large-load magazine to produce four hundred exposures, 17-by-24-mm in size, on "Normal-Kino-Film" (standard movie film). The camera's body was enlarged at both of its rounded ends, to accommodate the large film magazines. This gave an appearance later echoed by the 250-shot Leica Reporter. A model of the Esco with a better shutter was marketed in 1929. Another notable occurrence of 1922 was the reintroduction of the Italian Tartara's Autocinephot, as the French Photo-Ciné Sept. Another camera reputed to have been introduced in 1922 is the Phototank, manufactured by the French firm of V. Houssin. The metal-bodied camera bore a vague resemblance to a World War I tank, which may well account for its name. It produced 24-by-24-mm exposures on a fifty-exposure length of unperforated 35 mm film. Only a limited number of the cameras were produced.

The year 1924 saw the introduction of several cameras using 35 mm film, whose resemblance to one another is a matter either of imitation or of theft. Those were the Photorette, Photoscopic, Amourette, Lutin, and Cinescopic. Early in 1924 the Vienna firm of Photorette-Gesellschaft exhibited its Photorette camera. It made seventy-five exposures, 18-by-24 mm, on a length of perforated 35 mm film. The metal body had a flat back, with

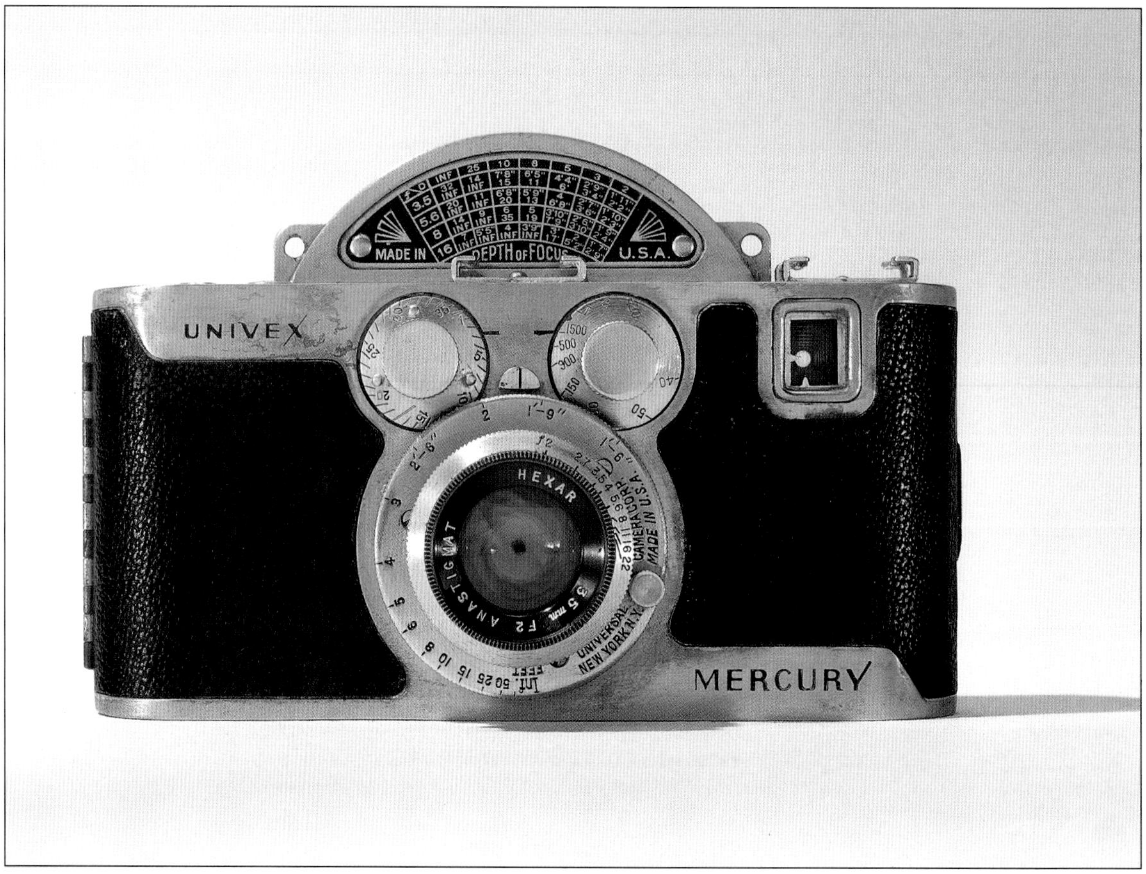

Univex Mercury, Universal Camera Co., ca. 1939, for 18 x 24 mm exposures on specially spooled, standard perforated 35 mm film, rotary focal-plane shutter.

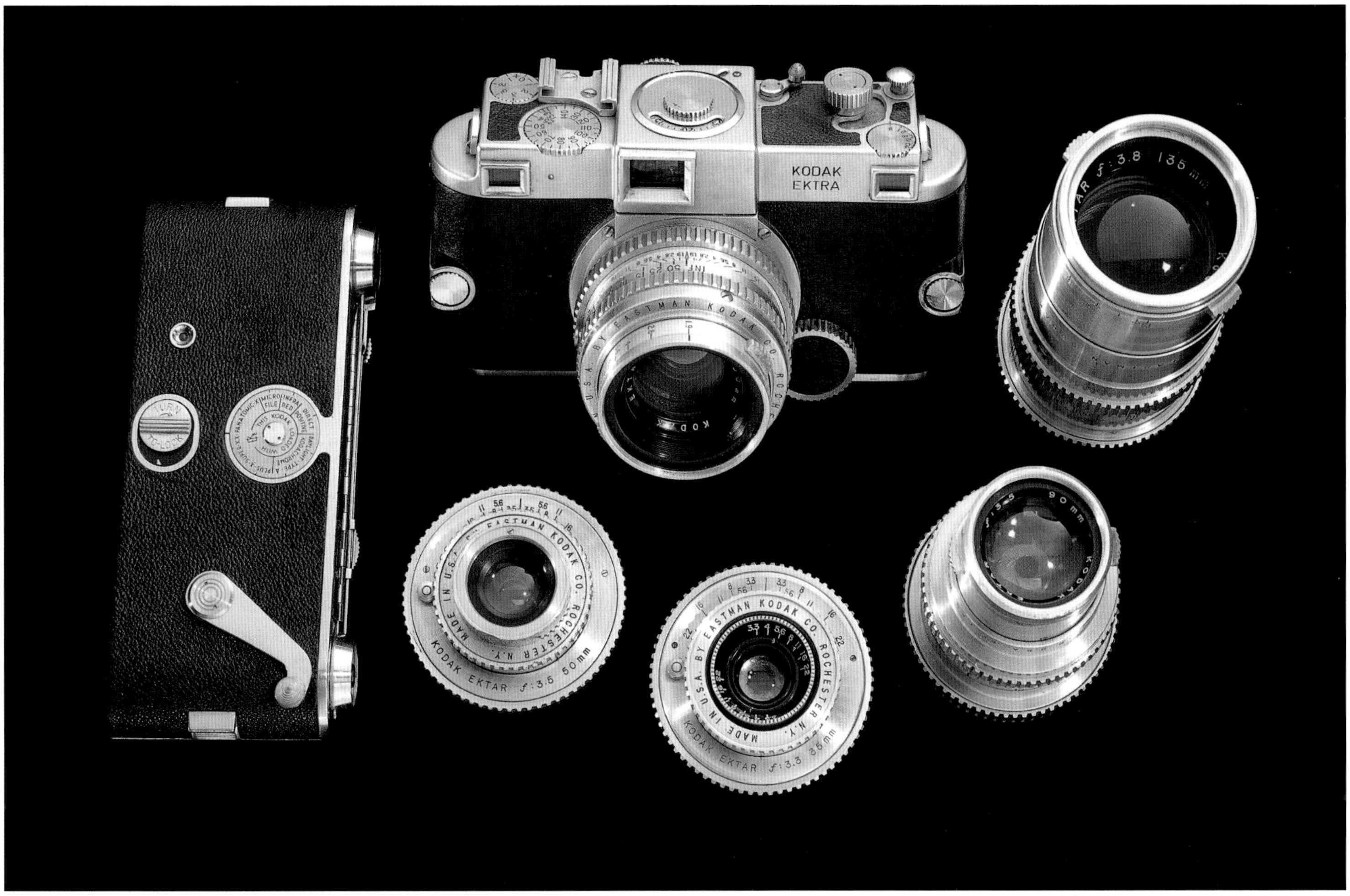

Ektra, Eastman Kodak Co., ca. 1941, for 24 x 36 mm exposures on No. 135 roll film. Shown with magazine back and interchangeable lenses of focal lengths from 35 to 153 mm.

sides curving toward the back, and a folding frame-type viewfinder on top. In 1924 Andre van Remoortel, a Belgian, produced the Photoscopic camera, a flat-backed camera with sides that curved toward the back. The camera used sprocketed 35 mm film to produce 24-by-24-mm exposures. It had a tubular optical viewfinder on top. Apparently some Austrians visited van Remoortel in Brussels, at which time he showed them plans and working sketches for his camera. Thus, the remarkably similar Amourette appeared in 1925, producing fifty exposures, 24-by-24 mm, on perforated and unperforated 35 mm film. The camera was manufactured in Vienna by Österreichisches Telephon AG (ÖTAG), and in Berlin by Robert Glombeck. The camera had a flat back, sides that curved toward the back and a folding-frame-type viewfinder on top. Also in 1925 Le Lutin appeared on the French market. It not only looked like the Amourette, it *was* the Amourette, bearing a different name for sale in France. Beney Frères were the exclusive agents for it. In 1929 van Remoortel split with his Belgian partner and designed and manufactured the Cinescopic 35 mm camera. In size and proportions it resembled the Photoscopic, including its tubular optical viewfinder. However, its sides curved all the way around to the back. It, too, produced 24-by-24-mm exposures. It was manufactured until 1939.

The French Cent-Vues camera was another 35 mm camera introduced in 1924. It was built by Mollier, Paris, and made one hundred exposures—*cent vues*—18-by-24 mm in size on perforated film. The aluminum-bodied, vertically-oriented camera had a simple guillotine shutter. A later model of Le Cent-Vues, introduced around 1929, also produced one hundred exposures on magazine-loaded 35 mm film. It had an interlens shutter. Another small box camera that used paper-backed, unperforated 35 mm film—as did the No.00 Premo—was the Ernemann Unette. The beautifully-made, wooden-bodied camera was introduced in 1925.

PROFILE: *The Leica and Its Imitators*

The Leica A camera was introduced in 1925 by Ernst Leitz of Wetzlar, Germany. It was the culmination of years of development by Oskar Barnack, a Leitz employee. In the years 1911–1913, Barnack designed a small metal camera that used standard perforated cine film. The project was put on hold during the war, but development was resumed in the 1920s. In 1924 a "pilot" run of thirty Leica (LEItz CAmera) cameras was manufactured. While these cameras had many of the features used in the 1925 Model A, the pilot-run cameras had a non-self-capping focal plane shutter. The Model A had a self-capping one, plus a frame counter that prevented accidental double exposure. A later model, the Leica B, featured a Compur shutter, which provided for slow shutter speeds.

The Leica A, which was sold to the public, established the basic body pattern used by most 35 mm cameras for most of the twentieth century. The optics of Leica's lenses raised standards across the industry. Over the years Leicas became fitted with slow-speed provisions for the focal-plane shutters, with range finders (the world's first 35 mm range finder) and, after World War II, with flash synchronization.

Not only was the Leica the single most influential camera, it was also the most imitated. The first imitator, the Fed, was produced in Russia, starting in 1932. The original Fed was an exact copy of the Leica II. The Kwanon X, introduced by Seiki Kogaku Kenku Sho in 1933, looked almost exactly like the Leica II. It was the first of many Japanese-made Leica copies. Over the years Leica copies have been manufactured in America, Australia, Austria, China, the former Czechoslovakia, France, Germany, Hungary, Italy, Japan, Russia, Switzerland and the United Kingdom. But the greatest number by far were made in Japan, mostly in the years following the Second World War.

Leica I (A), Ernst Leitz GmbH, ca. 1926. For other examples, see Leica copies on page 146.

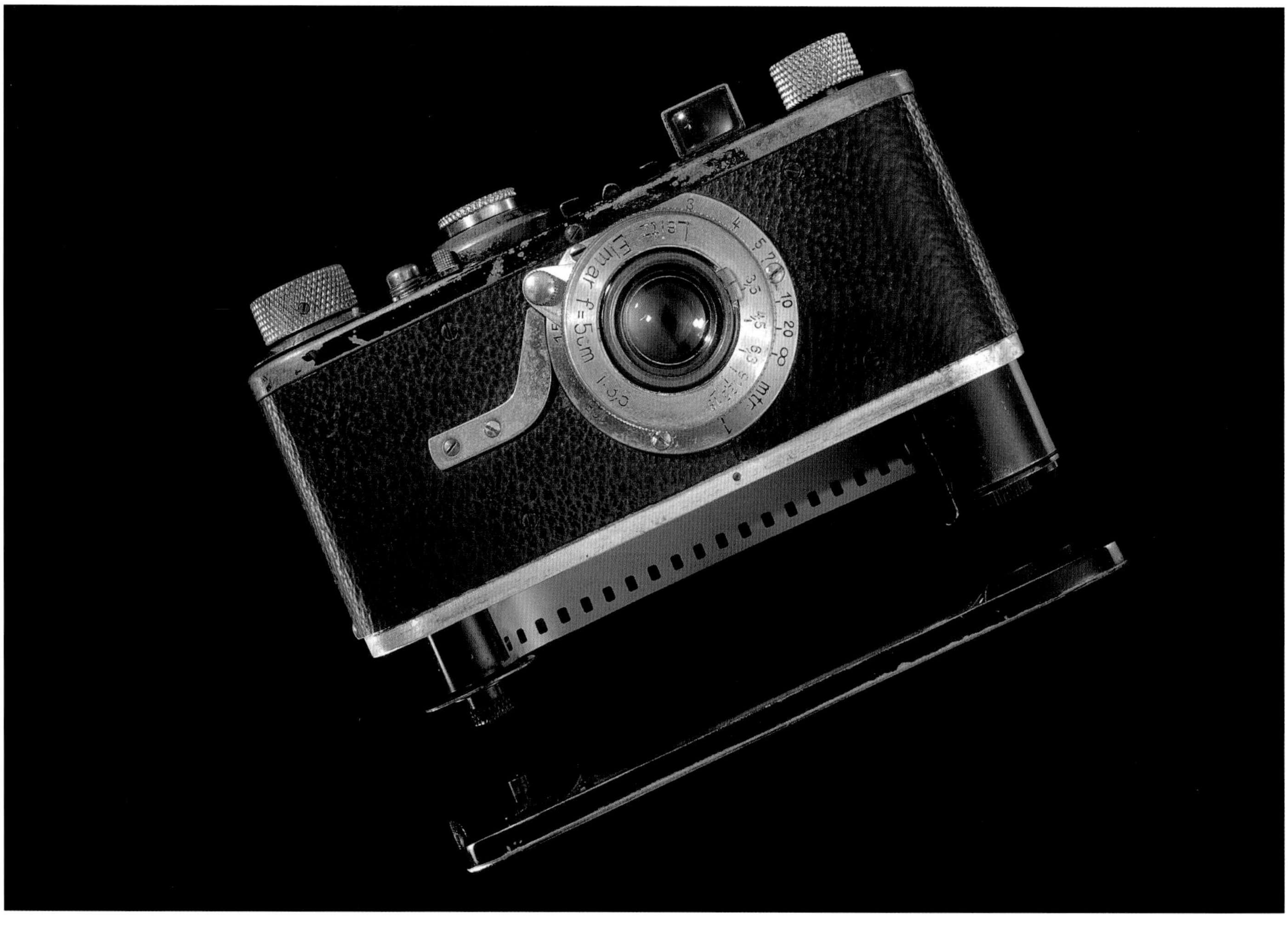

Initially built to produce 18-by-24-mm exposures, it was redesigned in 1926 to give larger, 22-by-33-mm exposures, still on the same size film. Production of the Unette was continued for a few years after Ernemann was absorbed by Zeiss Ikon. The Japanese firm R. Konishi & Co. produced an Unette copy in 1926, named the Record. It made 22-by-32-mm exposures, also on paper-backed 35 mm film.

1926–1945

While the Leica, introduced in 1925, was unquestionably the most influential 35 mm camera ever made, that influence took hold gradually. Photographers both amateur and professional would come to expect the optical precision, anastigmat focal-plane shutter, and interchangeable lenses of the Leica. However, in the time between the Leica's introduction and its proliferation, a few of what would now be considered non-standard 35 mm cameras came onto the market. Le Furet (the ferret) was a tiny (1 ⅞-by-2-by-3 ½ inches) metal camera that produced twenty-five to thirty exposures, 25-by-35 mm on standard perforated cine film. (The camera initially was advertised as taking 37.5 mm-wide exposures, but was modified early on.) The camera was manufactured by E. Guerin & Company, Paris, and introduced in 1926. Le Furet could also be had, on special order, in an 18-by-24-mm format. Le Furet evolved through three models. The first and second (1929) used rotary shutters, the first a single-speed, the second a three-speed. The third model of the camera (1930) had a Compur shutter. At some point the firm of Leroy assumed manufacture of Le Furet.

In December 1926 Ansco Photoproducts, Inc., of Binghamton, New York, announced the Ansco Memo camera. The little, vertically-oriented camera made fifty exposures, 18-by-24 mm, on standard perforated cine film loaded into special cassettes. The very first model had a finished wood exterior, but shortly after the camera's introduction, leather covering became standard. In 1928 Ansco merged with the German firm

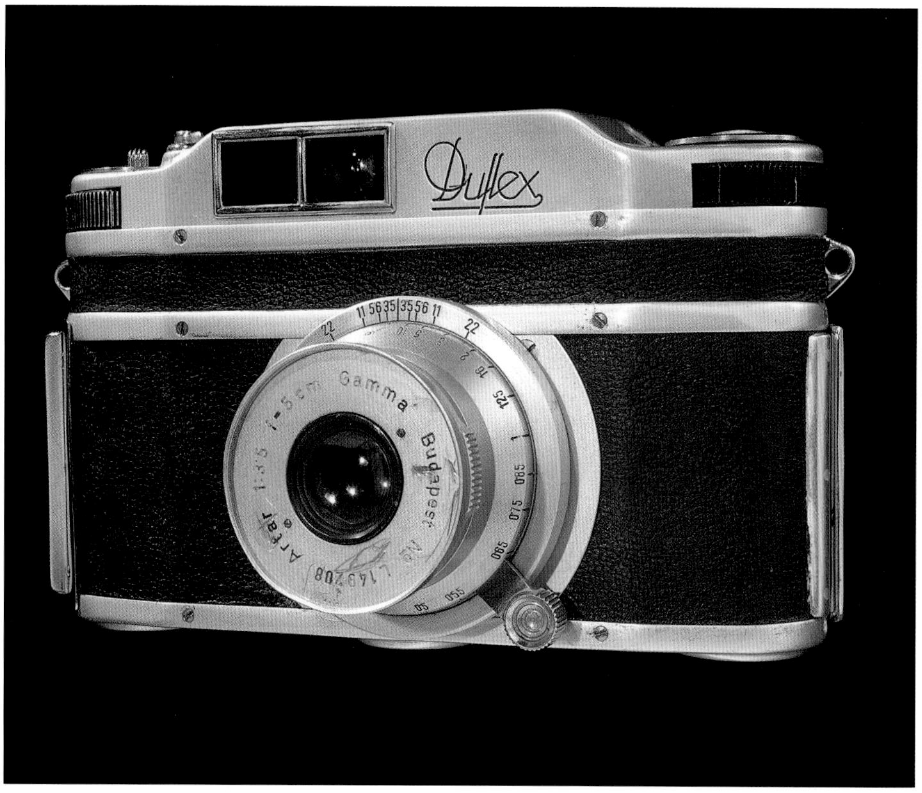

Duflex, Gamma Works, 1948, for 24 x 26 mm exposures on No. 135 roll film, instant return mirror, separate viewing and focusing windows.

Agfa. While the camera was produced for at least another year after that, by 1930 it was being sold at close-out prices. The camera was available with various lens and shutter options; there was a Boy Scout Memo manufactured; and a special copy-camera outfit was produced. Two different versions of projectors were manufactured for use with positives made from Memo exposures.

Around 1928 the horizontally-oriented Ellison "Kamra" was introduced. The camera, whose body was made of black bakelite, produced four hundred exposures, 24-by-36 mm, on a magazine load of standard 35 mm cine film. The lens was mounted behind a front panel that swung down. The Ellison "Kamra" never sold well, and its manufacturers convinced the QRS Company, of Chicago, to acquire the rights to manufacture the Ellison. The redesigned, smaller, brown bakelite camera was reintroduced in January 1929 as the QRS Still Kamra. One of the reasons the QRS was smaller was that it used only enough film to produce forty exposures, 24-by-36 mm in size. Shortly after the QRS was introduced, the QRS Company acquired the DeVry Corporation and renamed the camera the DeVry Still Kamra, as the DeVry name was better known in the photo-

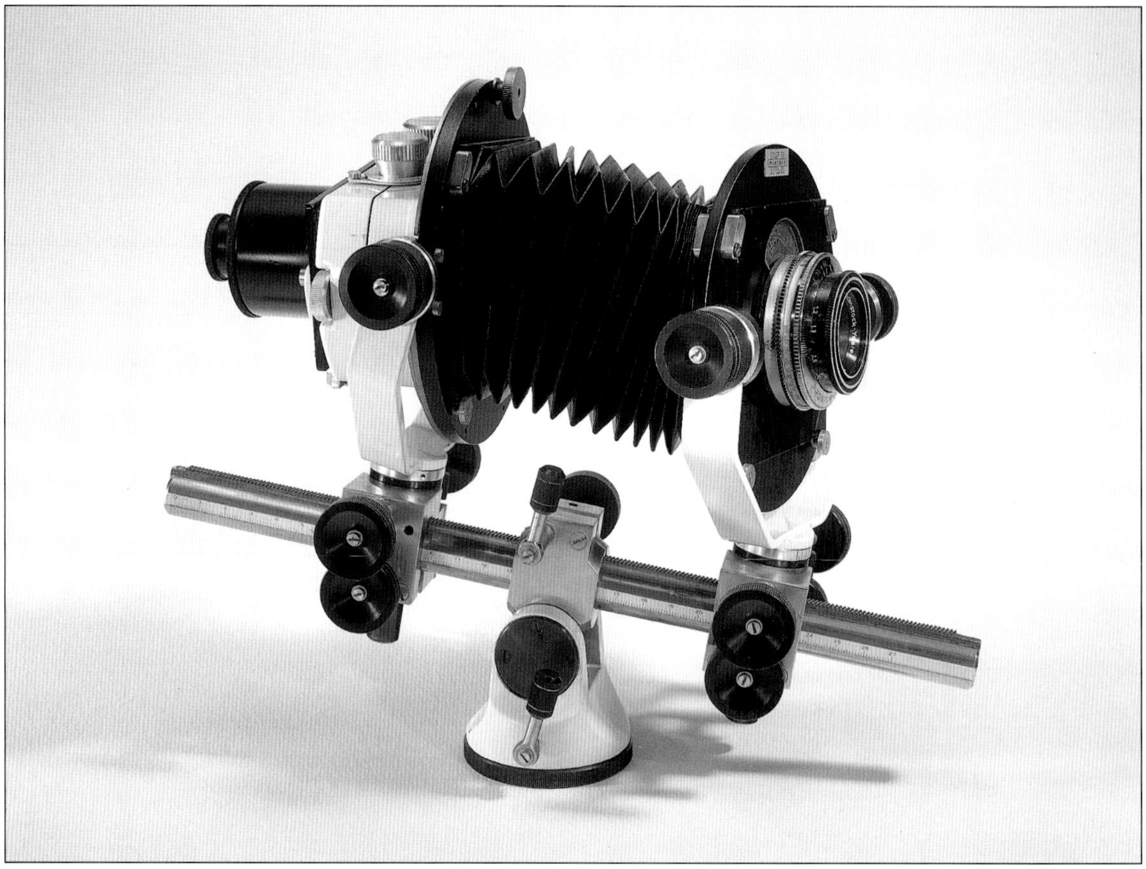

K. I. Monobar, Kennedy Instruments, Ltd., ca. 1951, for 24 x 36 mm exposures on No. 135 roll film, a monorail view camera with full movements.

graphic industry—QRS was known for its production of player-piano rolls. The QRS and DeVry Kamras, with their backs removed and their bodies mounted in front of a lamp unit, could be converted into projectors for positive filmstrips. By early 1932, production of the cameras had been discontinued.

As time passed, the 24-by-36-mm format on "cine" (perforated 35 mm film) became the standard for "miniature" cameras, and the choice of cameras in that format grew more diverse. The first bellows-equipped 35 mm camera was the Peggy camera, introduced in 1931 by G. A. Krauss, Stuttgart, with a strut-supported, collapsible front. It was followed in 1934 by the Peggy II, equipped with a coupled range finder. Another notable 35 mm bellows camera was the Kodak Retina, the first of a long line of Kodak cameras bearing that name. The Retina, introduced in 1934, was manufactured in the German factory acquired with Kodak's purchase of the Dr. August Nagel Camerawerk. The Super Nettel was another 35 mm bellows camera introduced in 1934, by Zeiss Ikon. In contrast to the interlens shutters of the Peggys and Retinas, the Super Nettel had a focal-plane shutter. Some think of the camera as a sort of "folding Contax." The German Welta Kamera-Werke was another prolific producer of folding 35 mm bellows cameras in the 1930s.

Introduced in 1932, the Contax (I) was Zeiss Ikon's answer to the Leica. Unlike the Leica's first model, the Contax, from the start, came equipped with interchangeable lenses and with a long-base rangefinder. It also had a vertically-moving metal focal-plane shutter. Various models of the Contax were produced until 1961.

In the 1930s the first 35 mm single-lens reflex cameras were produced. The Kine Exakta—"kine" because of the cine film it used—was introduced at the Leipzig New Year's Fair by the Ihagee Kamerawerk, Dresden, Germany. With the Leica and Contax on the scene, the production of a 35 mm Exakta was a logical extension of the vest pocket Exaktas already in existence. The camera had a waist-level viewfinder with a collapsible hood, in which was mounted a round magnifier. When the magnifier was lowered into position, the viewfinder front acted as a sports finder. The through-the-lens viewing, 35 mm format, and the multitude of accessories available for the Kine Exakta made it an extremely popular camera with the scientific community for many years. It did, however, have a left-handed film-wind lever and shutter-release button which many found awkward. SLRs bearing the Exakta name were in production through the late 1970s, though in the later years they were manufactured in Japan.

Another 35 mm SLR introduced in 1936 was the Sport, produced by GOMZ, Leningrad, Russia. The Sport was an improved version of the Gelveta, which was designed by A. O. Gelgar and produced from 1934–1935. It had a raised section above the camera's body that housed the focal-plane shutter mechanism, effectively doubling the camera's height. Located in the top of that section was the round lens of a chest-level viewfinder. The Sport used a special 35 mm cassette that held a fifty-exposure film length. The lens used a Contax-type and -size bayonet mount, and was removable, though no other focal-length lenses were available.

In 1938 another 35 mm single-lens reflex, the Praktiflex, was introduced by Kamera-Werkstätten AG, Dresden. The camera had a fixed, waist-level reflex finder with a hinged cover. The central section of the cover could be swung down to provide an eye-level frame finder. Introduced later than the Sport and Kine Exakta, the Praktiflex had more of an influence on mainstream postwar 35 mm SLR development than did the other two cameras. Its body style served as the basis for the body styles of a significant number of postwar single-lens reflexes. The Prakticas and Pentacons have bodies—excluding the pentaprisms—designed along these lines. Some Japanese SLRs' body designs followed in this pattern as well. The Praktica of around 1949 established the 42 mm screw-thread lens mount that became a standard for the industry.

A few other pre-World War II cameras deserve mention here. The twin-lens Contaflex—not to be confused with the postwar Contaflex SLRs—was introduced in 1935 by Zeiss Ikon. An elaborate camera with a number of then novel features, it has been referred to as the "flagship of their fleet." Its features included a built-in exposure meter, an f/2.8 viewing lens—providing a very bright finder image—a built-in Albada finder in addition to the reflex one, and a whole array of interchangeable lenses. It was the most expensive camera of its day. With the f/1.5 Sonnar it cost $435, which was almost equal to the cost of a two-door sedan. Production of the Contaflex was discontinued in 1939 because of Germany's entry into the war.

Three significant American 35 mm cameras of the prewar period, quite different from one another, are the Argus Miniature Camera (1936), the UniveX Mercury (1938), and the Kodak Ektra (1940). Announced in 1935 by the International Research Corporation, Ann Arbor, Michigan, the Argus—later designated "Model A"—appeared on dealers' shelves in the spring of 1936. The camera had a black bakelite body, a 1/25- to 1/200-second shutter, and an f/4.5 anastigmat lens. The camera was very well made and well received, as was its selling price of $12.50. The Argus Model A was but the first of a series of Argus 35 mm cameras, the best-known of which was unquestionably the long-lived "black brick," the Argus C-3 (1939–1966).

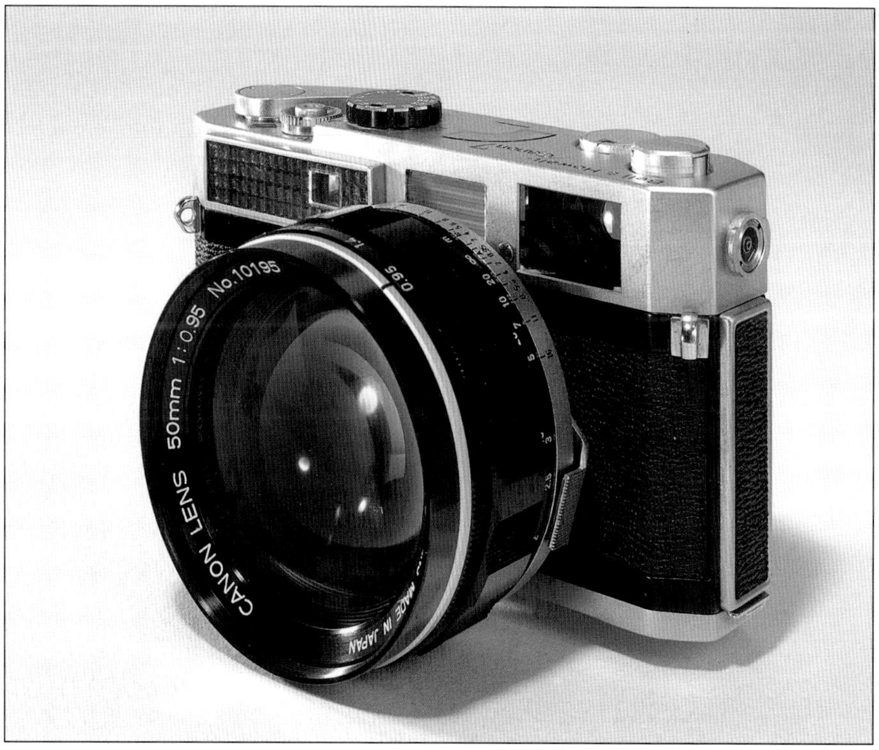

Canon 7, Canon Camera Co., ca. 1962, for 24 x 36 mm exposures on No. 135 roll film, with ultrafast 50 mm f/0.95 Canon lens.

PROFILE: *Exposure Devices*

Not until uniformly-prepared dry plates were introduced did the accurate determination of exposures (based on a combination of shutter speed, aperture, and, later, film speed) became possible. The earliest and least accurate exposure devices were exposure tables, or calculators. Ranging from simple to complex, calculators assigned a speed figure for each type of dry plate and combined it with data for lighting—a function of the time of year, latitude, time of day, and weather—to provide recommendations for various shutter speeds and lens openings. Such calculators were available up until World War II.

More accurate than calculators, extinction meters were introduced in the 1850s. A filter of graduated density indicated proper exposure at the number that was just barely visible (almost extinct) while looking at the subject. Some cameras of the 1930s, such as the Argus A2 and A2F, had extinction meters built in.

Comparison photometers were based on the principle of extinction meters but employed a light-source of standard intensity. Actinometers measured light according to the chemical change it produces—specifically, in a piece of paper that has been sensitized to light. The piece of paper exposed to and darkened by the light is compared to a standard degree of darkness or tint to determine the proper exposure time. (These devices were also called tint meters.)

Electric photometers measure the amount of light falling onto a photoelectric cell, and separate into two main types: reflected-light meters and incident-light meters (measuring the amount of light falling directly on a subject). Early electric photometers used selenium while today's light meters use cadmium sulfide in photoelectric cells.

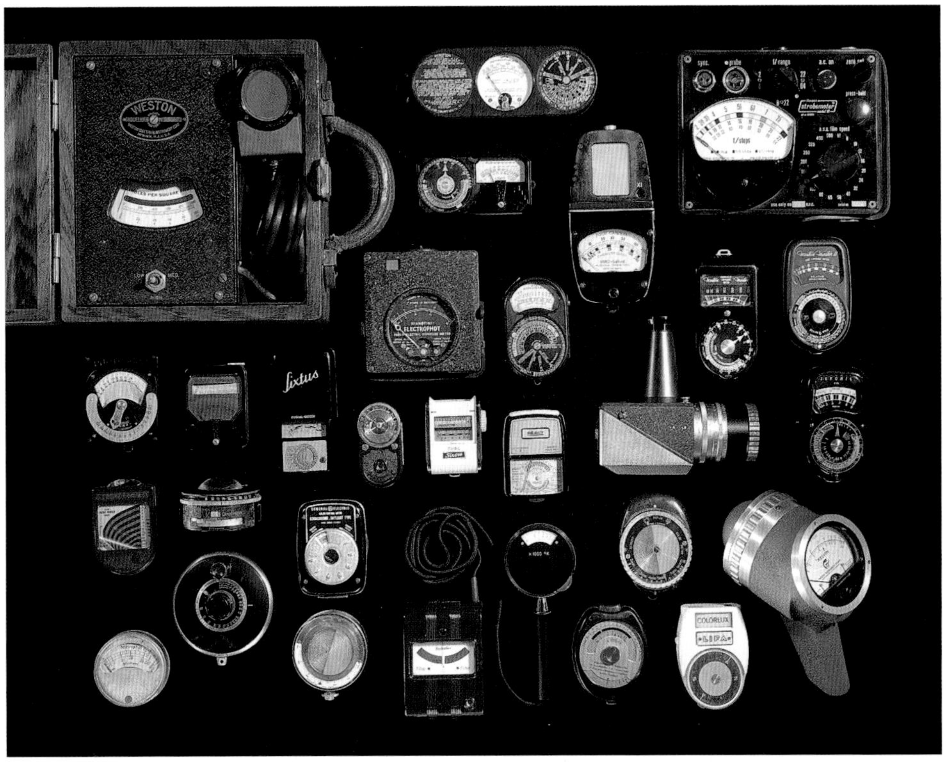

Photoelectric meters. Representative examples include: Second from left, third down: Rahmstein Electrophot, ca. 1931. Lower right corner: Spectra Three-Color Meter, Photo Research Corp., ca. 1958.

Right: Calculators, actinometers and extinction meters. Representative examples include: Calculators: Top left, Le Posographe, A. Kaufmann, ca. 1925. Actinometers: Bottom right, Adams's Stopwatch Meter, Adams & Co., ca. 1914. Extinction Meters: Right, second from top, Photomètre, J. Decoudin, ca. 1894.

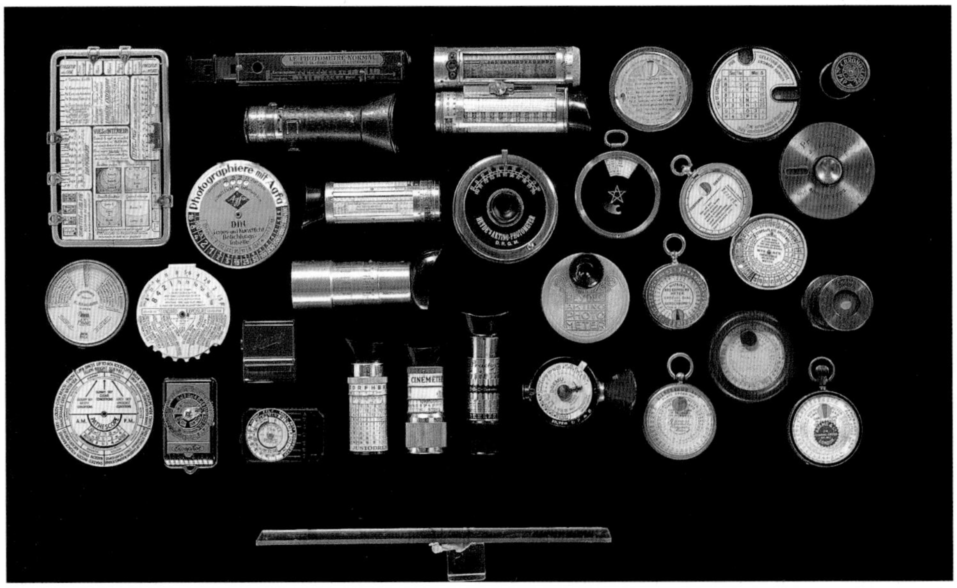

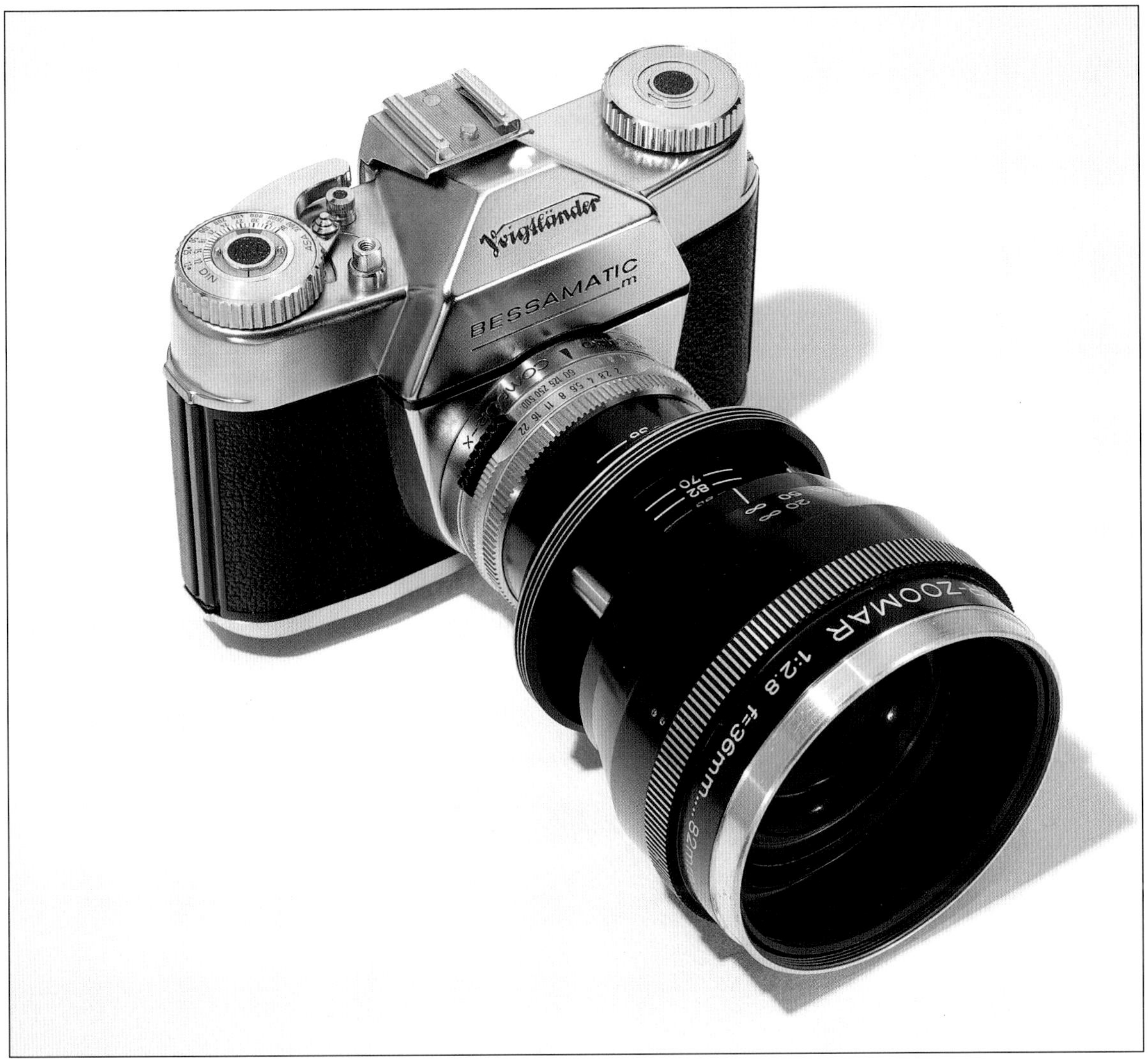

Bessamatic, Voigtländer & Son, ca. 1960, for 24 x 36 mm exposures on No. 135 roll film, with Zoomar 36-82 mm f/2.8 lens—the first zoom lens for an SLR.

The UniveX Mercury, introduced in late 1938 by the Universal Camera Corp., New York, was a rather unusual 35 mm camera in both appearance and construction. All of the Mercury's controls—except the shutter release button—were located on the front of the camera. On top of the camera was a dome-shaped protuberance that housed the upper part of the shutter. While most 35 mm cameras of the day used either interlens shutters or cloth—or metal—curtain focal-plane shutters, the Mercury had a rotating, circular shutter that operated at the plane of focus. Turning a wind knob simultaneously cocked the shutter and wound the film. The film format was half-frame (18-by-24 mm) and the film was packaged in eighteen- or thirty-six-exposure rolls. The film was 35 mm sprocketed film, but it came on special spools—not in the then-standard cartridges—and it had paper backing to protect it while loading and unloading the camera.

The Kodak Ektra was the finest 35 mm camera ever produced by the Eastman Kodak Co. It was introduced in January 1941, when Europe was already embroiled in war, and it was intended to take the place in the market of the increasingly scarce Leicas and Contaxes. Among the Ektra's features were a 1 to 1/1000 second focal-plane shutter, an f/1.9 lens, interchangeable film backs, and five interchangeable lenses. The camera had an automatic finder and parallax adjustment for those lenses. In addition to these features, though, the Ektra also had problems. The rapid-wind and shutter-release controls were located on the left-hand side of the camera's top, the interchangeable backs were awkward to remove, and the shutter was problematic. Production of the camera was halted shortly after America entered the war. The camera was officially discontinued in 1948, but very few of these expensive cameras were made after the war.

1946–PRESENT

Camera production in general was slow to resume in the years immediately following World War II, and 35 mm cameras were no exception. The production of sophisticated 35 mm cameras was particularly slow. Benefiting from America's policies toward conquered nations, however, the German and Japanese camera industries began not only to resume camera production halted during the war, but also to introduce new models and designs. High-end functionality such as internal flash synchronization and coated lenses soon became standard features of German and Japanese cameras.

By the 1950s a considerable number of 35 mm cameras were competing with each other on the consumer market. The battle that was really shaping up was the one between the rangefinder models and the 35 mm SLRs. Quality German-made rangefinder cameras like the Leica, Contax, and Retina were being joined by Japanese products such as the Canon, Minolta, and Nikon (the Nikon S was the first Nikon to be officially imported into America). But the SLRs were beginning to come on strong themselves. The East German Pentacon, West German Edixa Reflex, and Japanese Asahiflex—later joined by the Asahi Pentax—were among the first. The year 1959 saw the introduction of the Nikon F, the first SLR from Nippon Kogaku, which quickly rose to prominence in the industry.

In this competition, SLR 35 mm cameras suffered one pronounced disadvantage: the image seen on the ground-glass focusing/viewing screen was laterally reversed. That is, objects to the right in a person's field of vision appeared in the viewing screen to be to the left. Similarly, a moving object passing from left to right in front of a viewer appeared in the SLR's viewing screen to be coming from the right—a problem for one attempting to follow a moving subject in an SLR's viewfinder.

The solution to this problem lay in the pentaprism—a five-sided prism that corrects an image laterally by means of multiple internal reflections. A trio of single-lens reflex cameras pioneered the pentaprism. The Gamma Duflex, made by Hungary's Gamma Works, introduced in 1947, offered eye-level viewing and focusing, through the use of a porroprism and an instant-return mirror. While the porroprism offered eye-level viewing, the image was still laterally reversed. A prototype model, the Duflex System Reflex S, was also made by Gamma. While it had a roof pentaprism, providing laterally-corrected eye-level viewing, it was never put into regular production.

The East German Contax S, made by VEB Zeiss Ikon, East Germany, appeared in 1949. To its Praktiflex-like body was added a roof pentaprism, which provided a laterally-corrected image. The Contax S and its offspring, the Contax D (1952), appeared on the U.S. market bearing a variety of names, as the U.S. courts frowned upon the use of the Zeiss Ikon and Contax names by East German firms. The Pentacon line of SLRs descended from the Contax S. The Pentacon, along with the Praktica, is credited with introducing the 42 mm screw-type lens mount.

The Italian Rectaflex, made by Rectaflex S.P.A., Rome, was also introduced in 1949, and was equipped with a roof pentaprism and a split-image rangefinder. Although the Rectaflex was an early postwar SLR of high quality, and although it had the advantageous feature of a pentaprism, it

Instamatic 154, Eastman Kodak Co., ca. 1956, for twelve or twenty 28 x 28 mm exposures on No. 126 roll film, spring wind for rapid advance.

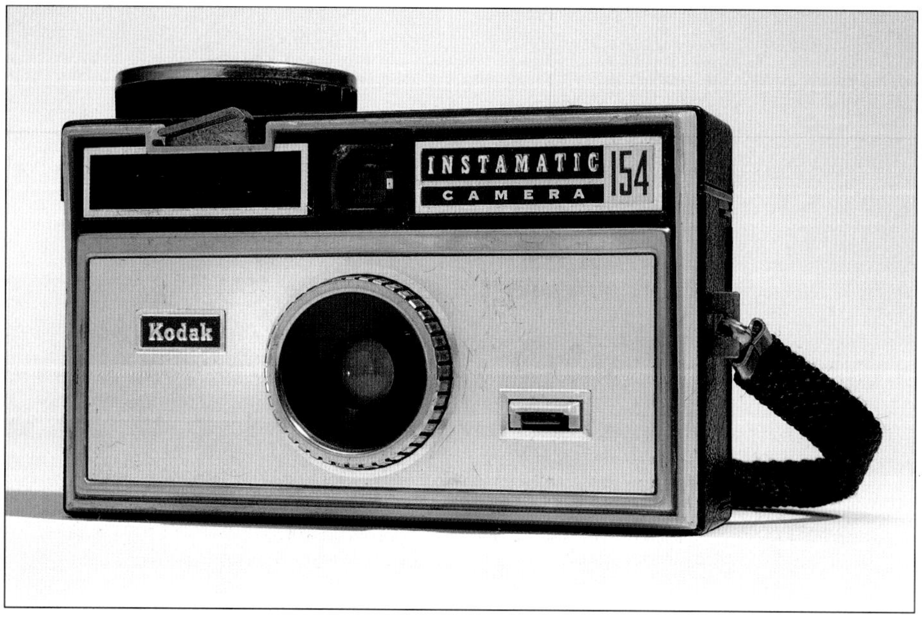

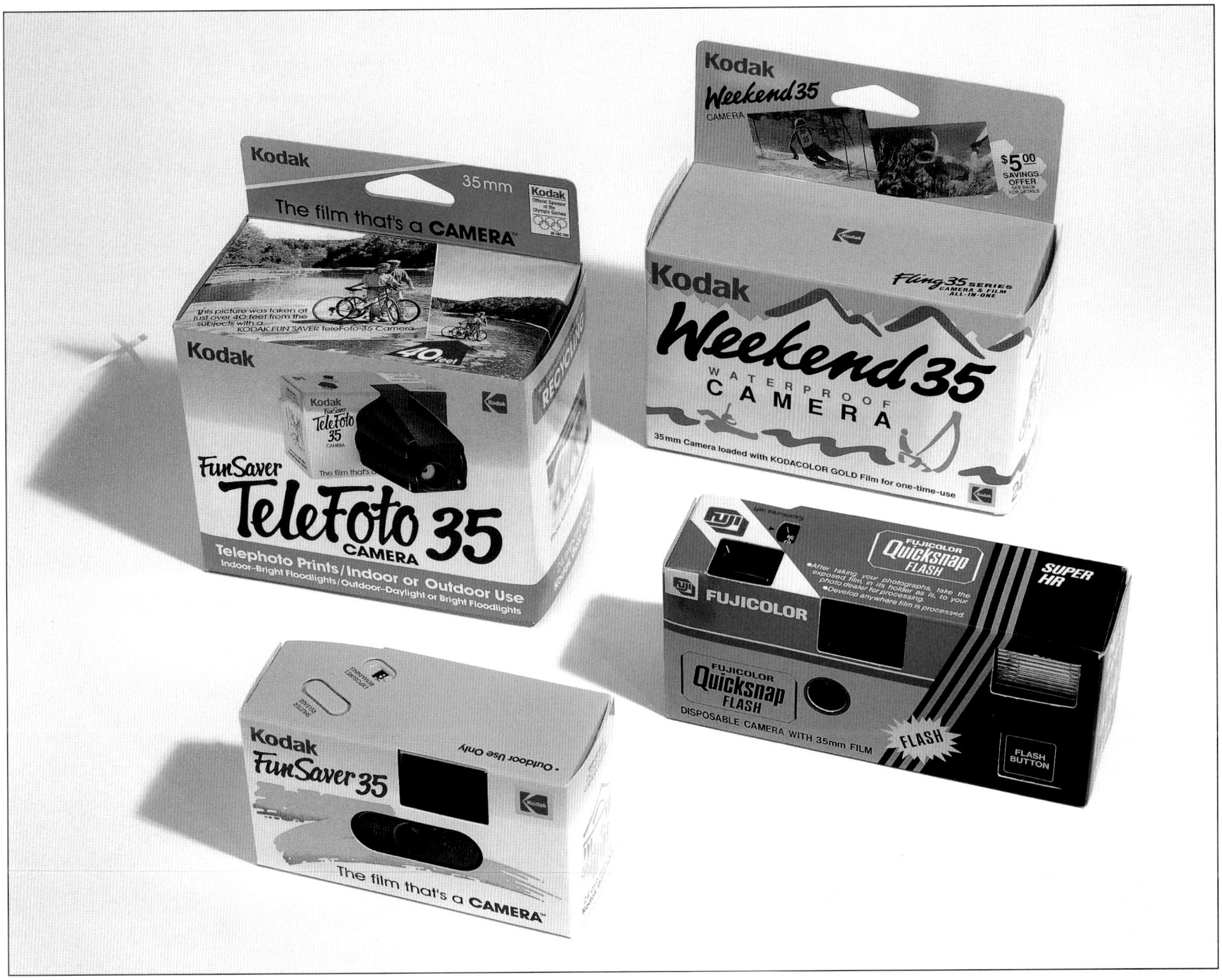

One-time-use cameras. All for 24 x 36 mm exposures on standard No. 135 roll film. Rear, left to right: FunSaver TeleFoto 35, Eastman Kodak Co., ca. 1991; Weekend 35, Eastman Kodak Co., ca. 1989. Front, left to right: FunSaver 35, Eastman Kodak Co., ca. 1991; Fujicolor Quicksnap Flash, Fuji Photo Film Co., Ltd., ca. 1988.

nonetheless did not survive past the mid-1950s. The question of priority among these three pentaprism SLRs—the Duflex System Reflex S, the Contax D, and the Rectaflex—is resolved by the fact that the design of the Contax S camera's pentaprism can be traced back to a 1937 Zeiss Ikon development.

In roughly the first half of the 1950s, there was a boom in the popularity of stereo cameras using 35 mm film. This was due in part to the availability of 35 mm Kodachrome transparency film—a transparency is an attractive way to view three-dimensional images—and also due to a surge in the popularity of amateur photography in general.

In the last half of the twentieth century, various innovations and improvements changed the lenses used on 35 mm cameras. With its f/1.8 Ernostar lens, the 4.5-by-6-cm Ernemann/Zeiss Ikon Ermanox camera of the mid- to late-1920s and 1930s had pioneered fast—wide aperture—lenses on mass-produced cameras. In the 1930s, fast lenses came to 35 mm cameras with the f/1.5 lenses available for the Leica and Contax cameras. It wasn't until 1961, though, that a lens with an aperture much wider than f/1.5 was available for 35 mm cameras. In that year the Canon 7 rangefinder camera was introduced. Also introduced in that year, to go on the Canon, was an f/0.95 Canon lens. Another notable accomplishment in lenses for 35 mm cameras accompanied the 1959 introduction of the Voigtländer Bessamatic. That was the availability of the f/2.8, 36–82 mm Zoomar lens to fit the Bessamatic. It was the first use of a zoom lens on an SLR. Other lenses developed for 35 mm cameras were perspective control lenses. These operated much in the way that rising/falling and lateral-movement fronts worked on view cameras. Because of the critical nature of the results, they were used on single-lens reflexes.

Autoexposure in 35 mm SLRs first appeared in the little-known (and not widely sold) French Savoyflex Automatique, introduced in 1959 by Royer. The camera's exposure was controlled by a selenium cell located above the lens. The first autoexposure 35 mm SLR to appear on the American market was the Konica Auto-Reflex of 1967. Its meter was positioned on the right front, below the shutter controls. An uncommon feature of the Auto-Reflex—reminiscent of the 1914 Simplex—was its interchangeable formats. By moving a switch, one could shift between standard, 24-by-36-mm exposures and half-frame, 18-by-24-mm ones. The Topcon Super D, introduced by Tokyo Kogaku in 1963, was the first 35 mm SLR with through-the-lens metering. Autofocus in a 35 mm camera made its debut with the Konica C35AF in 1977. It used an active-infrared AF rangefinder. The camera also had CdS autoexposure.

The standardization of 35 mm film with perforations, used in 35 mm cameras from the 1930s on, didn't mean that in the following years all 35 mm film had the four perforations per side of each frame. In fact, a number of non-standard-perforation 35 mm-wide films have appeared—and disappeared. Discounting such maverick films as those produced for the Rocamco cameras of the 1930s, there were two major appearances of non-standard 35 mm film. The first of these came from Eastman Kodak in 1935, with the first of the Bantam cameras. The Bantam line ranged from a simple, collapsible-bellows model with an f/6.3 lens to the streamlined, Walter Dorwin Teague-designed Bantam Special, equipped with a rangefinder, an f/2.0 lens and a sophisticated shutter. The feature that the Bantam cameras all had in common was the film they used, designated No. 828. This 35 mm-wide film was paper-backed. Although it had perforations, there were only

PROFILE: *35 mm Stereo Cameras*

The first 35 mm stereo camera produced after World War II was the Verascope F40, introduced in 1946 by Jules Richard, Paris. It produced 24-by-30-mm pairs. In America the camera was marketed as the Busch Verascope F40. The Verascope F40 marked the start of the period in which 35 mm stereo became popular. Certainly the Stereo Realist of 1947 contributed greatly to the interest in America. In the period 1946–1958, no fewer than three dozen different 35 mm stereo cameras were manufactured, most in Germany and America, and most between 1952 and 1955. The formats for the stereo pairs were either 24-by-23 mm or 24-by-30 mm, with 24-by-23 mm predominating.

Two 35 mm stereo cameras deserve special consideration. These are the View-Master and the Nimslo. The View-Master was produced in two models, the View-Master Personal Stereo Camera (1952) and the View-Master Stereo

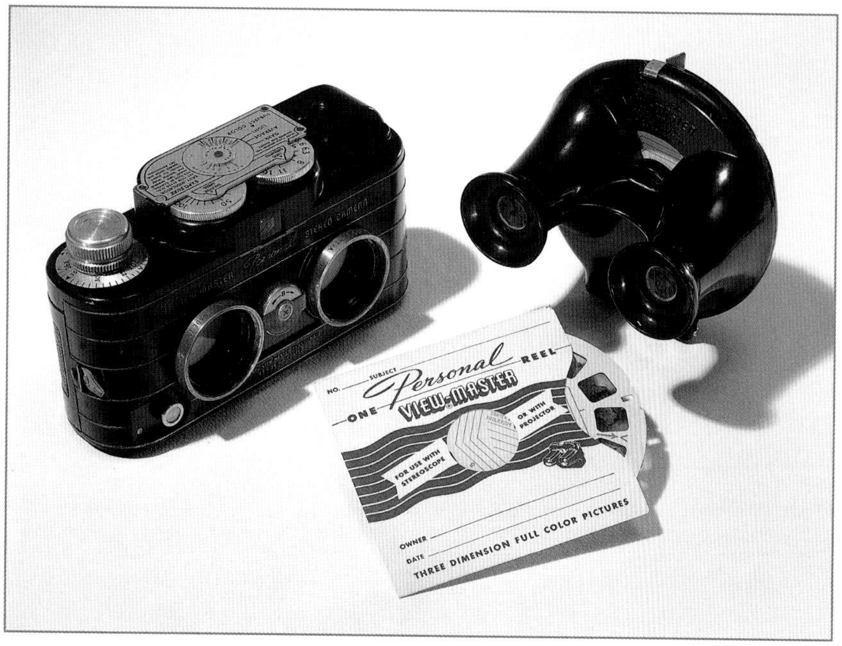

View-Master items. Left: View-Master Personal Stereo Camera, Sawyers Inc., ca. 1952. Center: View-Master reel, in sleeve. Right: viewer for View-Master reels, Sawyers Inc., ca. 1952.

Color Camera (1962), both of which produced 11-by-12-mm stereo pairs. The View-Master is significant because it produced the size of stereo pairs that were mounted in disc-shaped View-Master reels. The stereo pairs could be mounted in the reels by the photographer, but the main significance of the reels is their commercial marketing to generations of children and families. Hundreds of different subjects have been available on View-Master reels over the years. The reels could be viewed in any of the more than one hundred viewers marketed since they were introduced. Projectors for showing single View-Master frames were also made. The Nimslo 3-D Camera, introduced in 1980, was the first amateur 35 mm stereo camera to produce lenticular stereo photographs. Nimslo cameras were at one time or another manufactured in Japan and in Great Britain.

eight perforations per roll, because the perforations were used not to advance the film, but to stop it. As the film was wound, a pawl would engage the perforation and stop the film's advance. Releasing the pawl after the exposure would permit further advancing of the film. The format produced, wider than the standard 35 mm because of the perforation spacing, was 28-by-40 mm. Bantam film was used in a moderate number of other makers' cameras.

The other main use of 35 mm-wide film without the standard perforations was in Kodak's Instamatic cameras. The film used in these cameras, designated No. 126, was once again paper-backed with a single perforation per frame. Again, a pawl engaged the perforation to stop the film's advance. The main—and important—difference from Bantam film was that 126 film was housed in a "drop-in" cartridge. Preparing an Instamatic for use involved opening the camera back, dropping in the cartridge, closing the back, and advancing the film until it was arrested by the pawl's action.

The first Instamatics were introduced in March, 1963. Within the Instamatic family of cameras, there were usually at least four models introduced at a time: a simple model, a model with autoexposure, a model with rapid wind, and a model with autoexposure and rapid wind. All of the Instamatics could use flash bulbs, and as the flash bulb technology changed, new Instamatics were introduced. AG-1 bulbs, Flashcubes, Magicubes, and FlipFlash were steps in the Instamatic evolution. Quite sophisticated models were produced and even an Instamatic Reflex, from Kodak A.G., Stuttgart, was made. Kodak Instamatics were manufactured in America, Argentina, Australia, Brazil, Canada, Columbia, Germany, Spain and the United Kingdom. Hundreds of models of cameras using 126 film were manufactured over the years by other companies. The last year of Instamatic production was 1987, and at the end of 1999, Kodak discontinued 126 film.

The first disposable camera, introduced in America in 1887, had a paper bellows, a pinhole opening, and a single glass plate within. After use the camera was torn open in the darkroom, the plate was developed and the camera discarded. Another such camera was introduced at the 1900 Paris exhibition.

In the late 1940s and 1950s, a series of mail-in, disposable cameras that used 35 mm film were marketed. The cardboard-bodied Picture Box (1940s) and Photo-Pac (ca. 1950) used strips of 35 mm film, pulled through the camera by means of an attached paper strip. The body could be mailed in for film processing. Sometimes the inner, heavy-cardboard bodies were recycled. The Imp (1951), Pro (1953), and Mini-Mate (1971) were plastic-bodied 35 mm cameras that were mailed in, in the same manner as the Picture Box and Photo-Pac. Their plastic bodies were reloaded by the processing labs for reuse.

In 1987, Fuji Photo Film Company Ltd. brought out its 35 mm QuickSnap "film with lens" disposable camera. Kodak responded in 1988 with its disposable Fling. Fuji's QuickSnap Flash disposable was countered with Kodak's Flash version of the Fling. Konica also entered the field, and soon enough, disposable cameras from China began appearing. The "disposable" appellation was dropped around 1990, in response to environmental concerns. Now most one-hour photo labs recycle the components of the cameras.

In the past decade, various special one-time-use cameras have been introduced, including underwater, close-up, telephoto, convertible-format, sequence, and even a 35 mm twin-lens reflex. The public has become very enamored of these convenient cameras; one-time-use cameras now represent a significant segment of the 35 mm camera market.

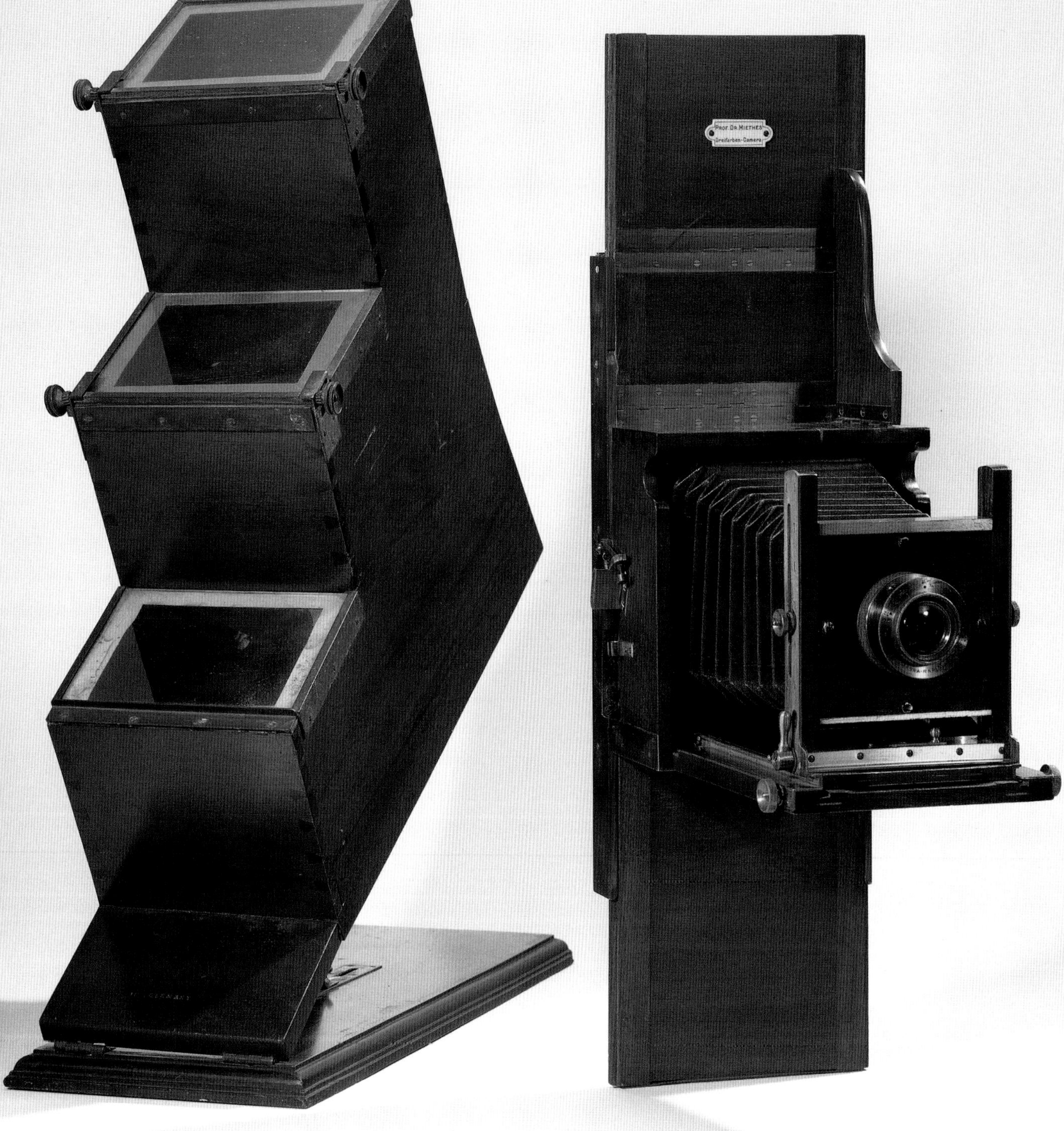
PROF. DR. MIETHES
Dreifarben-Camera

CHAPTER TEN:

THE QUEST FOR COLOR

Left: Viewer for combining images from color separations made from Miethe Three-Color Camera.
Right: Miethe Three-Color Camera, W. Bermpohl, ca. 1903, mahogany construction, for three 9 x 12 cm color separations on 12 x 30 cm dry plates (and later, sheet film).

While daguerreotypes and calotypes captured the public's attention, they were lacking in one regard: they could not reproduce color. Photographers and their assistants tried to get around the problem by manually adding color to pictures. Daguerreotypes, though, were especially tricky to color because of their delicacy. Powdered pigments, often mixed with gum arabic, were applied to the surface of a dry daguerreotype using a fine brush. The excess pigment was then removed with puffs of air from a rubber squeeze bulb. Once the desired coloring had been achieved, the colorist moistened the daguerreotype by breathing on it. Since gum arabic becomes insoluble in water when mixed with the bichromates of the plate, this helped affix the colors permanently.

The coloring of calotypes was much easier, as the colors, either watercolor or transparent oil, adhered readily to the paper's matte surface. An additional advantage to the coloring of calotypes was the fact that each one was printed from a negative and was therefore reproducible. If the coloring was unsatisfactory, a new print could be made and colored. Although undertaking to color a daguerreotype offered greater financial compensation, it was also considerably more risky than coloring a calotype.

The introduction of Blanquart-Evrard's albumen paper in 1850 presented more of a challenge than calotype paper. The surface of albumen paper was smooth and slightly glossy, and therefore difficult to penetrate with paint. This presented a problem for colorists, as albumen paper was the popular choice of print medium for many years. As late as the 1890s, following the advent of silver-based emulsions, the largest manufacturer of photographic paper in Europe used the whites of some eighteen-million eggs per year in the production of albumen paper. Fortunately, colorists were able to utilize oil-based paint with some degree of success.

Gelatin-emulsion photographic papers came into use in the 1880s, simplifying the colorization process: their surface absorbed watercolors quite effectively, particularly if the gelatin was moistened in advance. So simple was this process compared to the coloring of daguerreotypes and prints on albumen that specialized technicians were not the only ones to attempt coloring photographs. Around the turn of the century, do-it-yourself tinting kits were sold to the public.

The images produced by hand-coloring were unique and often beautiful but lacked the attribute that made photographs so special: the unflinch-

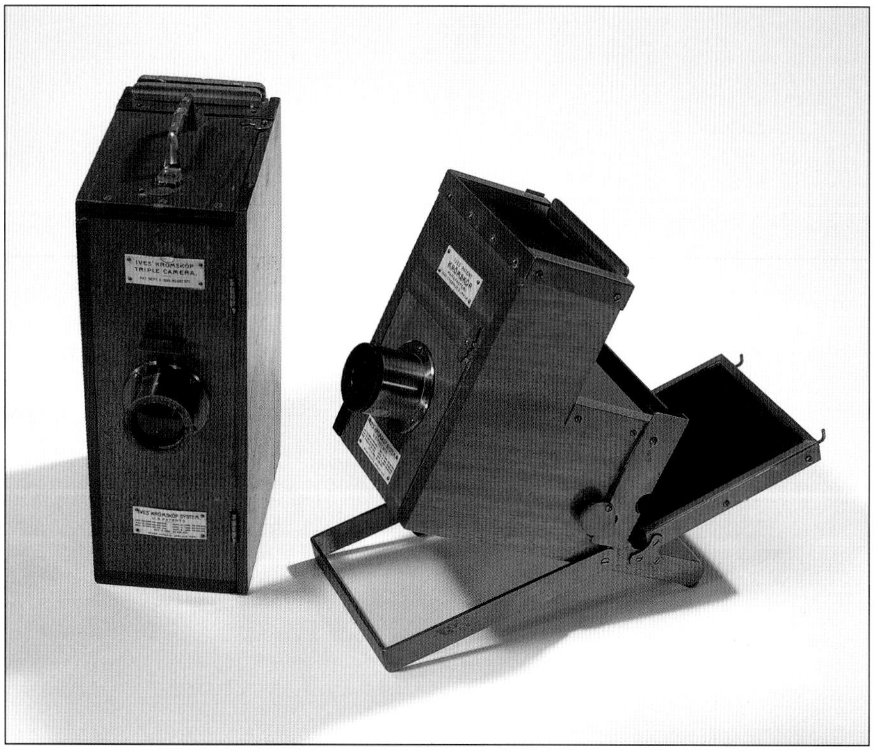

Left: Left: Kromskop camera, F. E. Ives, ca. 1900, mahogany construction, for three simultaneous 2 1/4" x 2 1/2" exposures on 2 1/2" x 8" dry plates. Right: Kromskop viewer, F. E. Ives, ca. 1900, mahogany construction, for combining images from three positive 2 1/4" x 2 1/2" transparencies on a single 2 1/2" x 8" plate into a single additive color image.

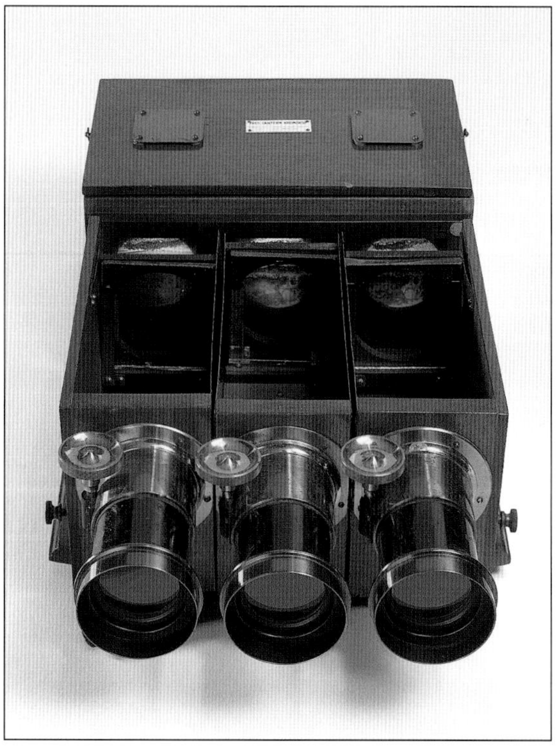

Right: Lantern Kromskop attachment, F. E. Ives, ca. 1900, mahogany construction, to be attached to a light source for projecting three separate 2" x 2" glass positives—with red, green, and blue filters to achieve color image.

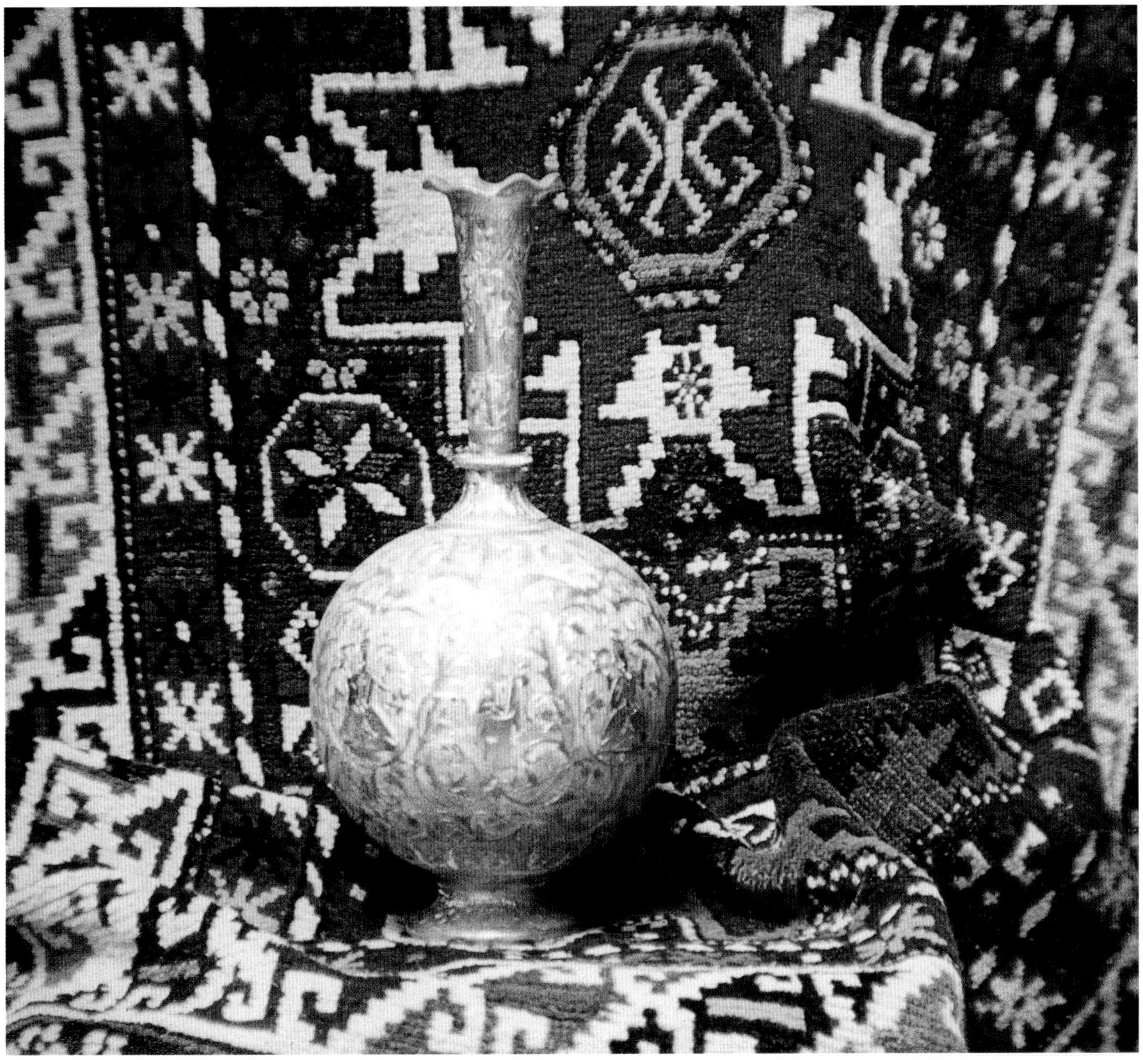

Anonymous, Vase with rug, ca. 1950, 9" x 10" print made from original Ives Kromogram color separation.

ingly precise reproduction of the world as seen through a camera lens. In order to capture color in the same way that values of light and dark were captured in a photograph, a more sophisticated understanding of the nature of color and light was needed.

The human eye is incapable of distinguishing the various wavelengths of visible light that make up the "white" light of the sun. In order to see its constituent colors—red, orange, yellow, green, blue, indigo, violet—sunlight must be passed through a prism, by means of which it is separated into bands of equal wavelength (seen as bands of color). This was discovered by Sir Isaac Newton in 1669 and communicated to the Royal Society of London in 1672. Before Newton, notions of white light had been based on Aristotle's theory that white light was a homogenous entity of a single wavelength, and that color was a modification (rather than a component) of this light.

Color may also be produced through subtractive synthesis. When white light strikes a surface, all of the light that is not the same color as the object is absorbed; the rest is reflected. Thus an object that looks green is reflecting mostly green light while absorbing the other colors of the spectrum.

Another important principle in color theory is additive synthesis, which holds that all colors can be created through the combination of two or three primary colors. One major stumbling block in early attempts to reproduce color in photography was that the primary colors are not the same for pigments and light. Painters had long known that red, yellow, and blue could be mixed to create all colors; however, the primary colors for light are red, *green*, and blue. Only through experimentation did photographers and scientists discover this.

Employing the theory of primary colors put forward by Thomas Young, English physicist

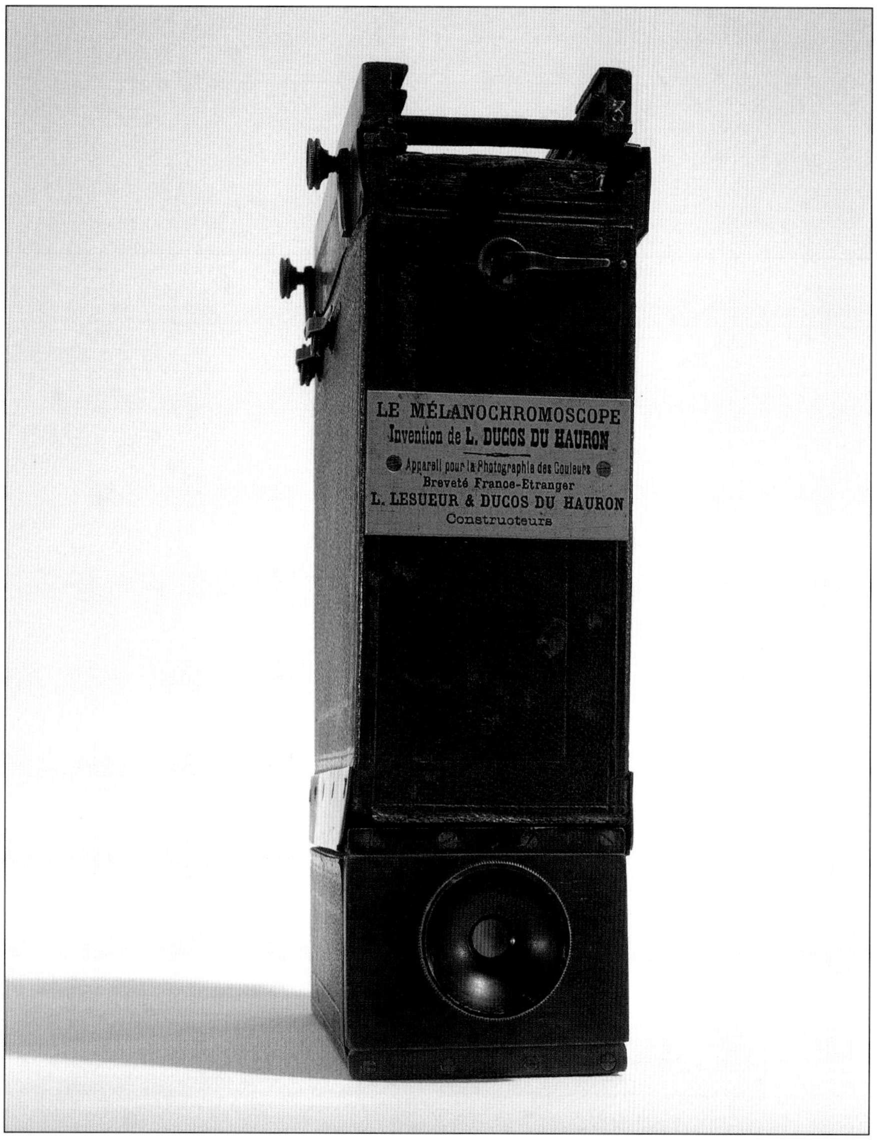

Le Mélanochromoscope, L. Leseur & Ducos du Hauron, ca. 1900, for three simultaneous 35 x 35 mm exposures on 43 x 130 mm dry plates and for viewing positives made from plate. Combined camera and viewer.

James Clerk Maxwell was the first person to incorporate color in a photographic reproduction. For his demonstration of the process to London's Royal Institution in May 1861, Maxwell enlisted the help of photographer Thomas Sutton, who made three separate negatives of a bow formed with multicolored ribbon. For one calotype negative, a container of red liquid was placed between the camera and the bow. According to the principle of subtractive synthesis, this negative recorded every color of the ribbon except red, which was filtered out. Using the same technique, Sutton produced two more negatives, using filters of green and blue solution, and the positives were then projected separately through red, green, and blue filters. The superimposition of the three images on a screen approximated the colors of the ribbon. Maxwell's demonstration was a success, though it was later discovered that it succeeded partly by chance. Black-and-white films at the time were not sensitive to the full range of the spectrum, particularly red, so the negative made through a red filter had actually recorded ultraviolet light reflecting off the red areas of the ribbon.

Despite the success of Maxwell's demonstration, he conducted no further research or experiments in the field of color photography, instead turning to the study of Saturn's rings, which led him to propose his famous kinetic theory of gases in 1857.

In 1862 the Frenchman Louis Ducos du Hauron invented the Chromoscope viewer, which assembled a color image from three filtered black-and-white transparencies. Apart from its mistaken use of filters that were red, yellow, and blue, the design of the Chromoscope was otherwise sound. When du Hauron presented his ideas to the French Photographic Society in 1868, he found that a colleague, Charles Cros, had also been working on three-color photography. The discoveries of du Hauron and Cros would eventually serve as the foundation of color photography, yet for decades they lay dormant. It was not until the invention of dyes that extended the sensitivity of emulsions to colored light that their theories were put into practice.

In 1892 the American inventor Frederic E. Ives achieved what was probably the first practical color projection of three black-and-white diapositives (positive transparencies made from negatives), based on a principle he demonstrated in 1888 with a triple-projection lantern. The Frenchman Léon Vidal gave a similar demonstration using three separate lanterns in 1892. That same year Ives developed and patented the Photochromoscope, a three-color camera that came with a separate viewer. The camera made use of reflectors, filters, and prisms; the viewer used colored filters and light-reflecting mirrors to reunite the three diapositives. A stereo camera and companion viewer, which produced brilliant images (known as Kromskops), were introduced commercially in 1895. The single-lens Photochromoscope also appeared on the market that year, though its name was changed to the Kromskop Triple Camera. The negatives produced by both cameras were called Kromograms.

In 1897, nearly thirty years after his discovery of three-color photography, du Hauron perfected his Chromographoscope, followed in 1899 by the Melanochromoscope. The latter invention, manufactured by L. Leseur and du Hauron, was a combined three-color camera and viewer. Using lenses, mirrors, and green, red, and blue filters, the camera produced negatives that were subsequently converted to diapositives. These could be placed where the camera's plate holder had been and viewed by transmitted light, thus converting the Melanochromoscope into a viewer.

The color photographs discussed up to this point were achieved using transmitted light to unite, by means of a viewer or projector, the separate images produced by three-color photography. Another way was to use color screens placed within the camera between the lens and the film emulsion. After development and reversal, the resulting diapositive was viewed through the same screen, thus recreating the colors of the original subject. Brian Coe's book *Colour Photography* (1978) shows photomicrographs of sixteen different color screen plates and films from the years 1895 to 1935.

Du Hauron was the first to propose the use of a screen for color photography. Although he never made it, the plan for his screen was to contain tiny blue, yellow, and red lines; the colors of the subject would be reconstituted by viewing the diapositive through the same screen used to make the photograph. John Joly of Dublin was the first to actually produce such a screen, using a machine to rule the lines—colored with ink, ten per millimeter—on the glass screen. A diapositive, obtained from a negative made through the glass screen, was then bound in front of a similar, carefully registered screen. When viewed in front of a light source, a good rendition of the subject's original colors was obtained; the one drawback, aside from the amount of labor that the process entailed, was that the vertical lines from the glass screen were evident in the image.

Several other ideas for the use of screens were formulated over the next few years. In 1903 the Lumière brothers announced the development of a color screen for making and viewing color transparencies. Their design used colored grains of

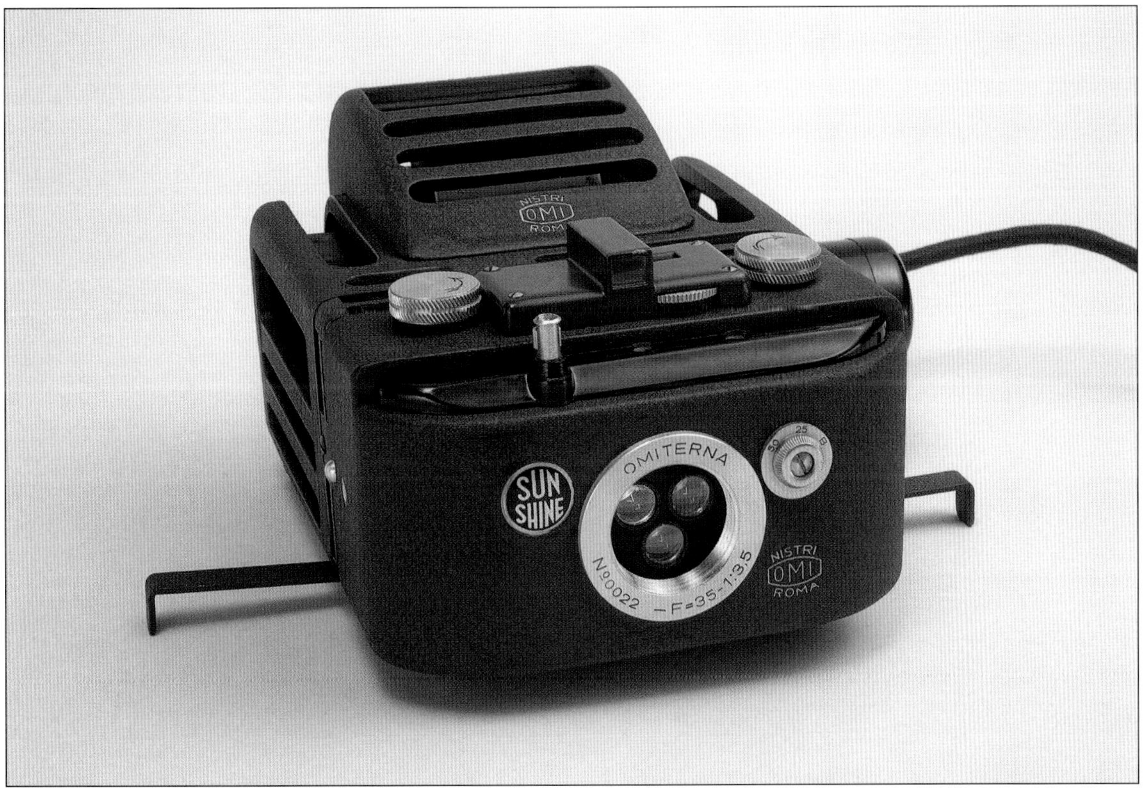

Sunshine Three-Color Camera/Projector, Ottico Meccanica Italiana (OMI), ca. 1947, for three simultaneous 9 x 11 mm exposures on No. 135 color transparency film. Lamp housing fits to camera back for projection.

starch rather than vertical lines. Equal quantities of red-orange, green, and violet grains were mixed and then coated on top of a glass plate, which in turn was covered with a gelatin emulsion. The subject was then photographed with the glass surface of the plate toward the camera's front and, once developed by the reversal process, the plate was ready for viewing. After problems in the production process were worked out, the plates were introduced commercially under the name Autochrome in 1907. To use the Autochrome in a conventional camera, a yellow filter was needed to compensate for the emulsion's extra sensitivity to blue light. Autochromes were the first truly successful color plates, and they remained the dominant format for color transparencies through the first half of the twentieth century. In 1909 the French firm of Jougla & Company introduced Omnicolor plates, invented by du Hauron. These had a red, green, and violet screen printed on them with oil-based pigments. Although more sensitive, the color quality of Omnicolor plates did not equal that of the Autochromes, and as a result they were not particularly successful. In 1911 Jougla was acquired by the Lumière firm.

A number of other color screens for plates appeared in the remaining years prior to World War I. One of these was Louis Dufay's screen plate, in which pairs of lines of complementary colors were laid at right angles on top of lines of noncomplementary colors; this resulted in a screen of green lines alternating with rows of red and green squares. Announced in 1908 as Duplicolor, by the time it came on the market in 1909 Dufay's invention had been renamed Dioptichrome. Revisions of the screen were introduced in 1910 and 1912. Another screen design, published in 1912, was the invention of Geoffrey S. Whitfield of London. Through a complex series of dying and bleaching steps, a screen of red, green, and blue squares was laid down on a plate coated with collodion. In 1913 Whitfield's plates

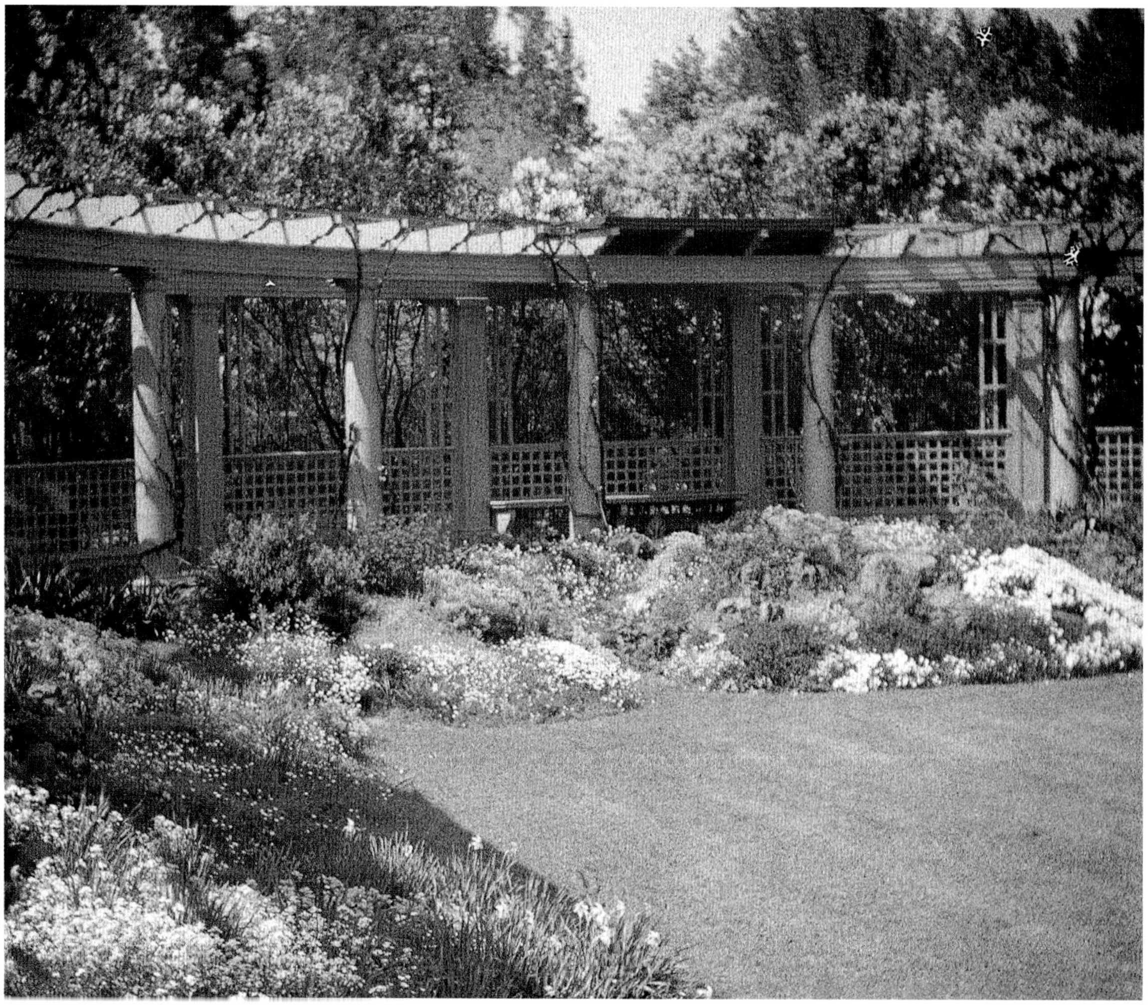

Anonymous, George Eastman's garden, ca. 1907, Lumière Autochrome, 3 1/4" x 4 1/4".

made their commercial debut in Britain under the name Paget Colour Plates. Yet another screen plate, patented by J. H. Christensen in 1908, was acquired by Agfa in Germany and introduced there in 1916 as the Agfa Color process.

After World War I, the change in black-and-white photography from dry plates to sheet films accelerated and a number of manufacturers of screen plates for color began to introduce sheet films—and, subsequently, film packs and roll films—for color. These, like their predecessors, were coated with screening pigments. Lumière introduced Filmcolor in 1931. Agfa brought out Agfacolor in 1932. Dufaycolor also appeared in 1932, but only as movie film. In 1935 it was introduced in roll film, sheet film, and film packs. Dufaycolor remained in production until the 1950s.

Subtractive synthesis in color photography is achieved, in essence, by removing certain colors of the spectrum by means of absorption; the remaining colors are reflected, rendering them visible. In 1862 du Hauron discovered a way of making color prints on paper. His method, patented in 1868, involved making three negatives of a subject, each using a different-color filter: one green, one orange, and one violet. From these, three positive prints were made on semitransparent paper: the print from the green-filtered negative in magenta, from the orange-filtered negative in cyan, and from the violet-filtered negative in yellow. If the three positives were then carefully placed in register atop one another, the result was a color print. The complementary colors of green, orange, and violet—respectively, the blue-red magenta, the blue-green cyan, and the red-green yellow—would subtract, or absorb, the primary colors in relation to the density of the complementary colors.

Du Hauron designed a camera that simultaneously made all three of the exposures required for subtractive color photography by employing three lenses in combination with mirrors or "reflectors." These reflectors permitted the passage of some light onto a lens and sensitive plate while reflecting the remainder to another lens and plate. Many subsequent camera designs employed a single lens at the camera's front, with internal reflectors or prisms to convey the light to the three different plates. Cameras of this type, exposing three different plates at once, came to be called "one-shot" color cameras.

The development of one-shot color cameras proceeded slowly until the introduction of dry plates. The various designs differed in their arrangements of the semitransparent reflectors and the prisms, and sometimes there were slight differences in the colors of the filters. One of the relatively early one-shot color cameras was patented in 1897 by E. T. Butler; eight years later he patented an improved model. The Butler One-Shot Camera was commercially available into the mid-1930s.

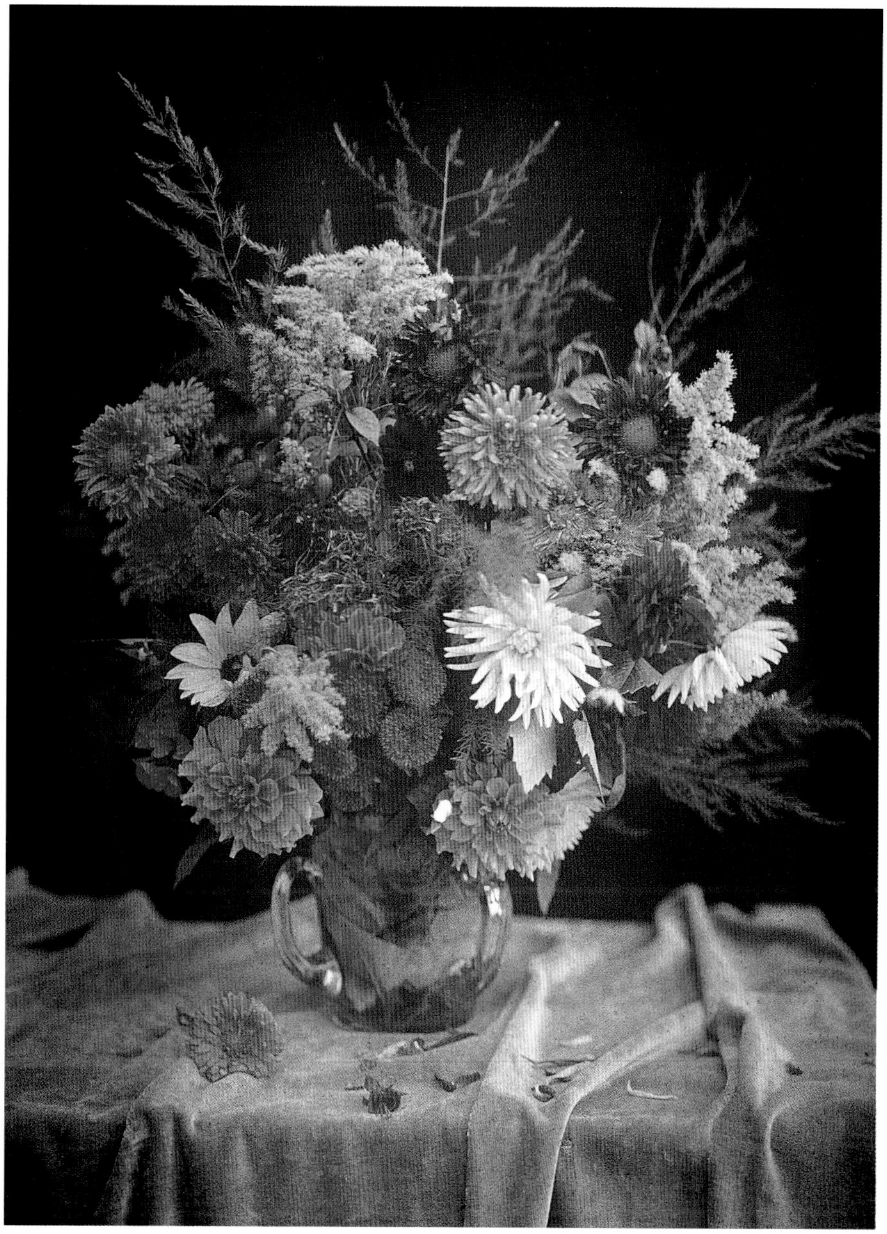

Anonymous, Vase of flowers, ca. 1910, Dufay Dioptichrome screen-plate transparency, 3 1/4" x 4", mounted on 9 1/4" x 11 1/4" black card.

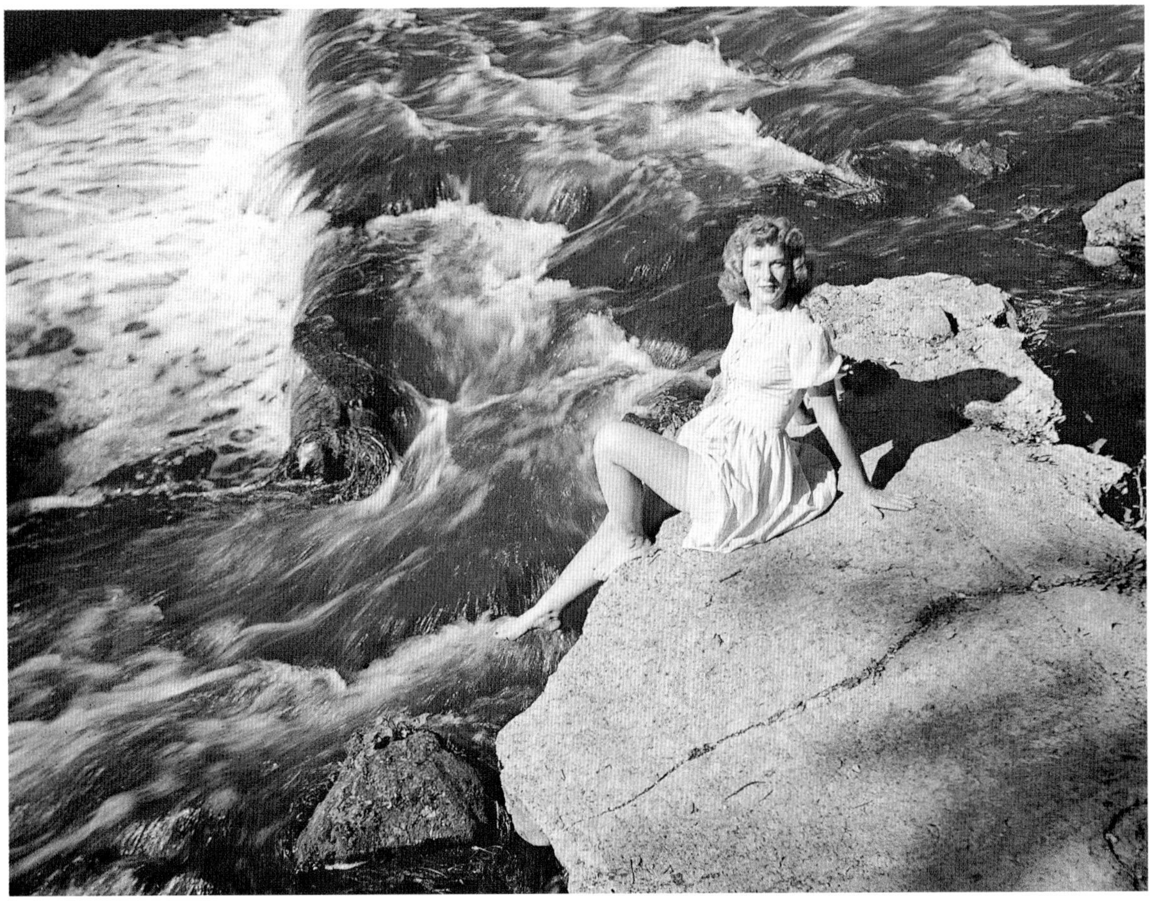

Dr. Walter Clark, Woman at waterside, ca. 1935, Dufaycolor transparency, 2 1/2" x 3 1/4", mounted between 3 1/4" x 4" glass plates.

Below: Butler Three-Color cameras, improved models, manufacturer unknown, ca. 1905, mahogany construction, for three simultaneous exposures on three separate dry plates. Rear: for 4 3/4" x 6 1/2" plates. Front: for 2 1/2" x 3 1/2" plates.

The Sanger-Shepherd Camera, invented by Edward Sanger-Shepherd, was introduced in 1902 and could make either transparencies for subtractive prints or paper prints. Some of the Sanger-Shepherd's features were also employed in later one-shot cameras such as the Bermpohl of the 1920s and 1930s, and the Devin Color Camera of the late 1930s and early 1940s. The Sunshine, made by Italy's Ottico Meccanica Italiana in 1947, could be converted from a one-shot camera to a projector.

In 1924 the Jos-Pe color camera, by Joseph P. Welker, was introduced, with a design patterned on an earlier one-shot camera by Ives. The Jos-Pe came in two sizes, for 9-by-12-cm or 4.5-by-6-cm plates. While one-shot color cameras varied somewhat in shape from one to the next, there were no significant differences in design among the mainstream models. One unusual camera, however, was the Mikut, which appeared in 1936. Measuring 3 3/4-by-4-by-6 inches, the Mikut weighed only three pounds and made three exposures on a 2-by-6-inch plate, using a system of prisms to separate the light for the three separate exposures. The Mikut was a

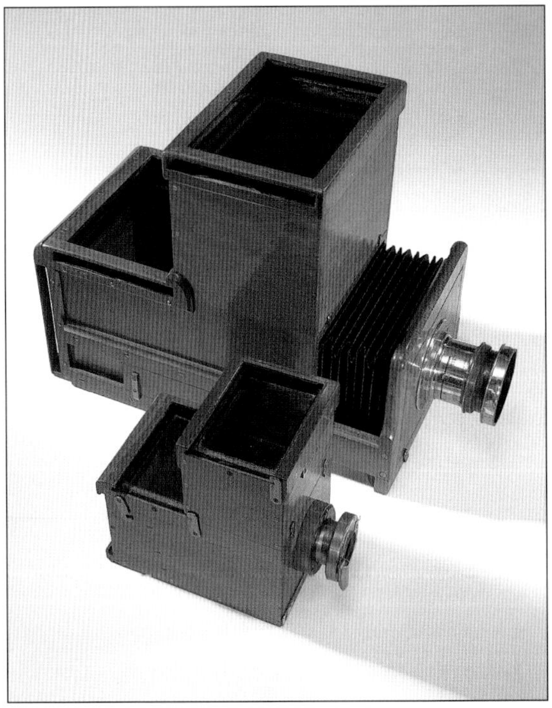

"system" camera, introduced together with the Mikut Projector and Enlarger. The illuminating system had three projection lamps, allowing the Mikut to be used in additive color synthesis (through projection) or subtractive synthesis (by means of prints).

One-shot color cameras were crucial whenever movement—or potential movement—of the subject between exposures was a factor. Color sliding backs, however, could still be used for still lifes or landscape shots. Some cameras were constructed with such backs while in other instances repeating backs were attached at the rear of conventional plate cameras. In the early 1900s, Professor Adolph Miethe designed a color camera with a repeating back, manufactured and sold by W. Bermpohl, Berlin. Although not a one-shot camera, its back was vertically oriented so it could be dropped in rapid succession from the first plate's position to the remaining two. A separate viewer, for those who wanted to see color transparencies, was also made. Professor Miethe's color camera was sold up through the early 1930s. Also in the early 1900s, Sanger-Shepherd & Company produced a repeating back as an accessory for conventional cameras. The German firm Linhof also manufactured and sold a three-color drop back, one form of which was designed to fit the Speed Graphic.

In addition to the additive and the subtractive syntheses of color, there is another method of obtaining color photographically, based on the creation of interference patterns between light waves. This process was perfected in 1891 by Gabriel Lippmann, a physics professor at the Sorbonne. A glass plate was coated with a near-transparent, fine-grained emulsion, placed in contact with a film of mercury, and exposed with the plate's surface facing the camera lens. Once the plate was developed, the colored image appeared as a brilliant positive only when viewed by reflected light at a suitable angle. Although the Lippmann process was able to reproduce color realistically, it required exposures more than ten thousand times longer than those for conventional emulsions. And while the use of faster lenses was proposed to reduce exposure times, all things considered, the process was still impractical.

In 1895, following work by du Hauron and Ives, the Lumière brothers patented a process for printing in subtractive colors from separation negatives. Their process, which had potential for commercial application, made use of bichromated gelatin, with silver bromide added, coated on paper. Following exposure, the three thin sheets were transferred to glass, where they were developed and stained. After the images were removed from the glass, the yellow image was glued to a sheet of paper. Then the thin cyan and magenta sheets were added. Transparencies could be obtained by removing the assembled tissues and placing them on glass. Prints produced by this method were shown at the 1900 Paris Exhibition

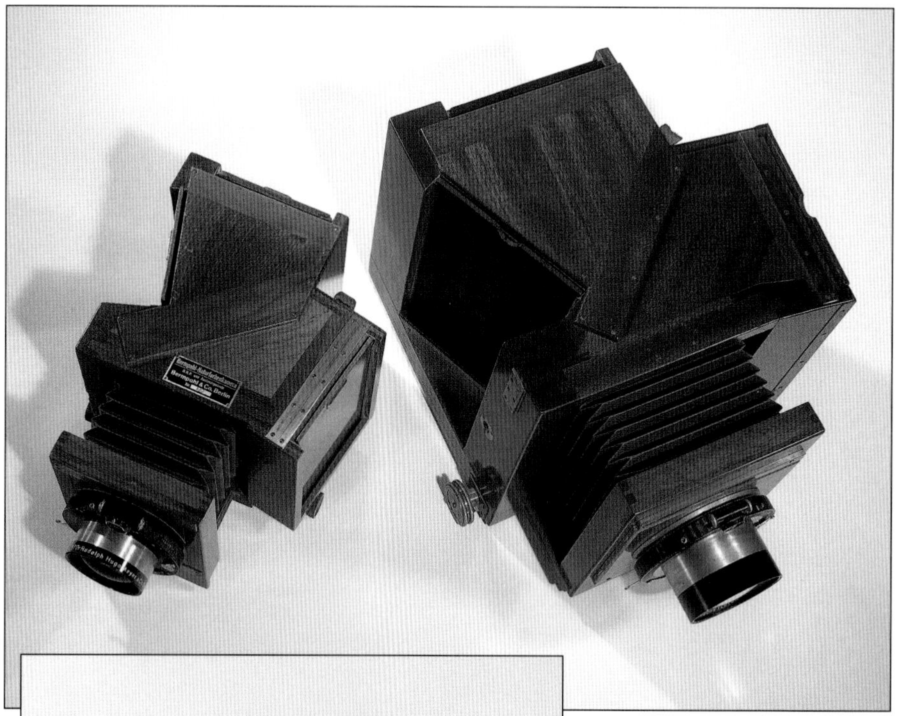

Bermpohl Naturfarbenkameras, Bermpohl & Co., ca. 1930, mahogany construction, for three simultaneous exposures on three separate dry plates or sheet film. Left: for 9 x 12 cm plates or film. Right: for 5" x 7" plates or film.

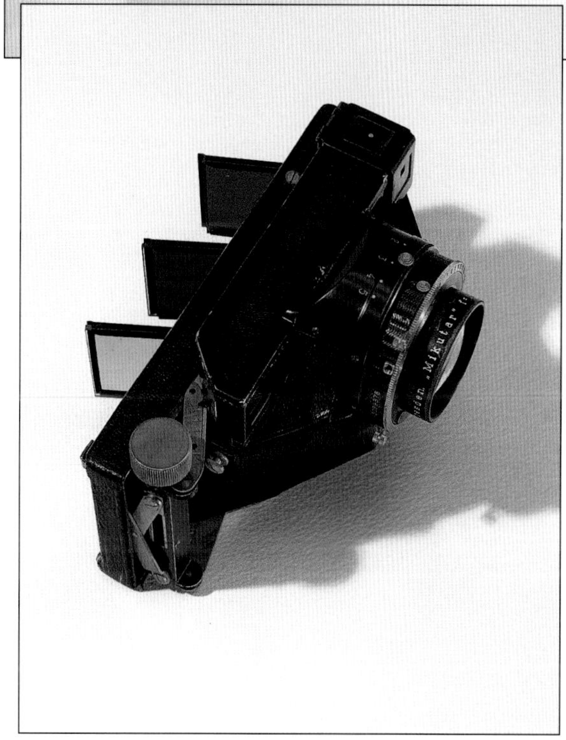

Left: Mikut Color Camera, Oscar Mikut, ca. 1936, for three filtered simultaneous 4.5 x 4.5 cm exposures on 5 x 15 cm glass plates. Subsequent positive transparencies were projected with a separate Mikut projector.

Page 176: Alfred K. Wittauer, Woman with airplane, 1939, Dufaycolor transparency, 2 1/4" x 3 1/4". Taken at Kodak Research Laboratories for comparison with Kodachrome transparency.

Page 177: Alfred K. Wittauer, Woman with airplane, 1939, Kodachrome transparency, 2 1/4" x 3 1/4". Taken at Kodak Research Laboratories for comparison with Dufaycolor transparency.

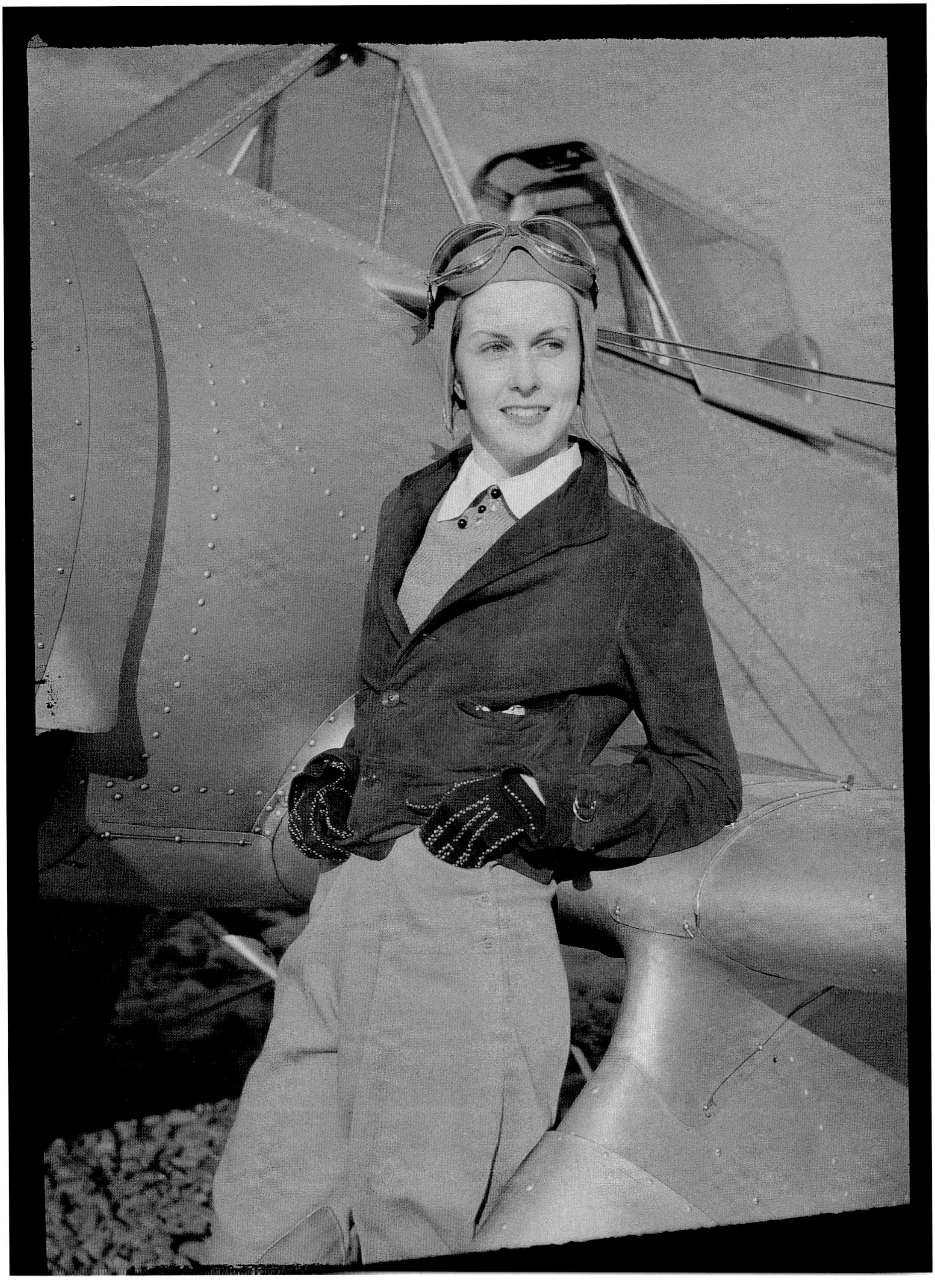

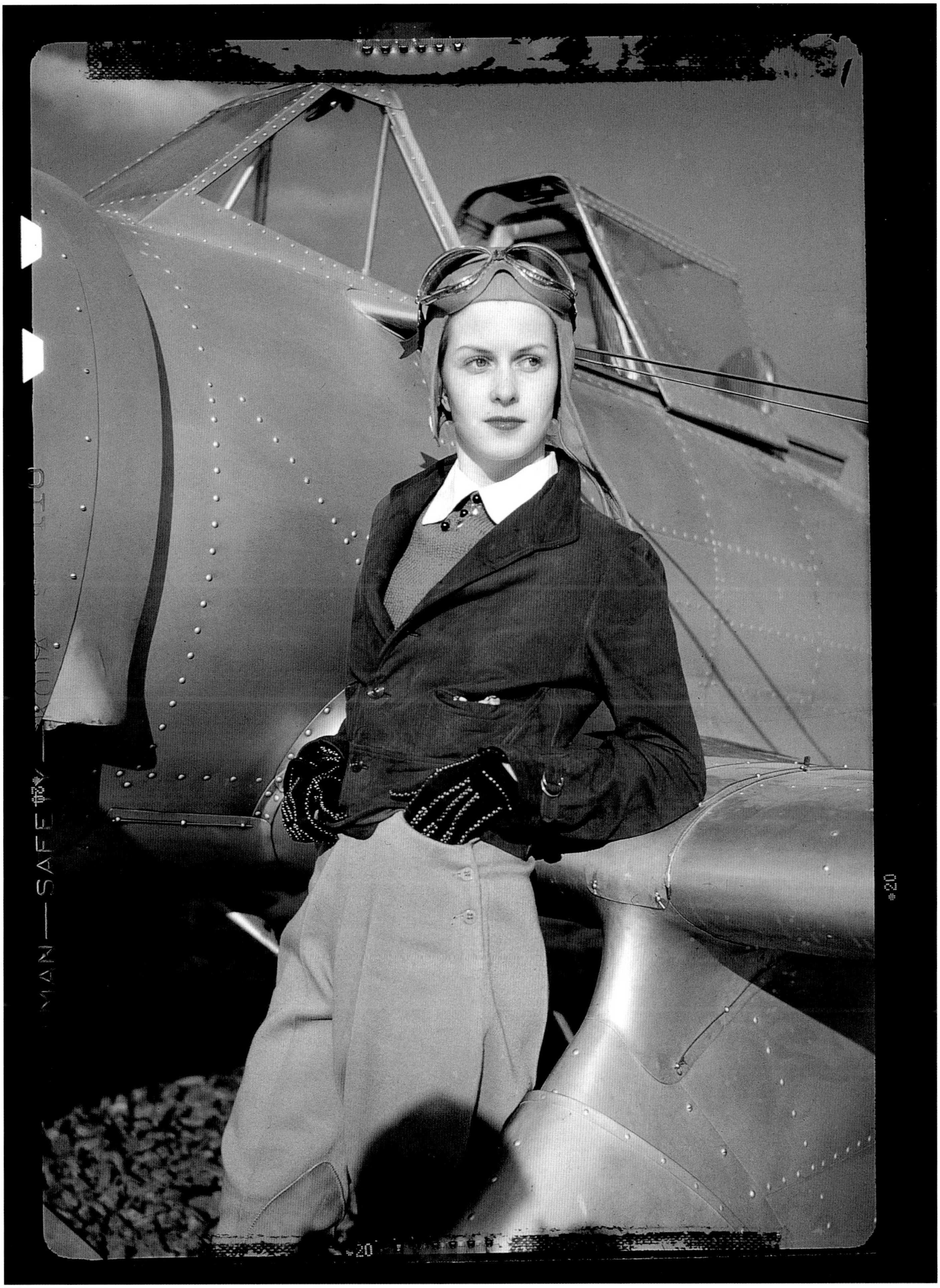
MAN — SAFE

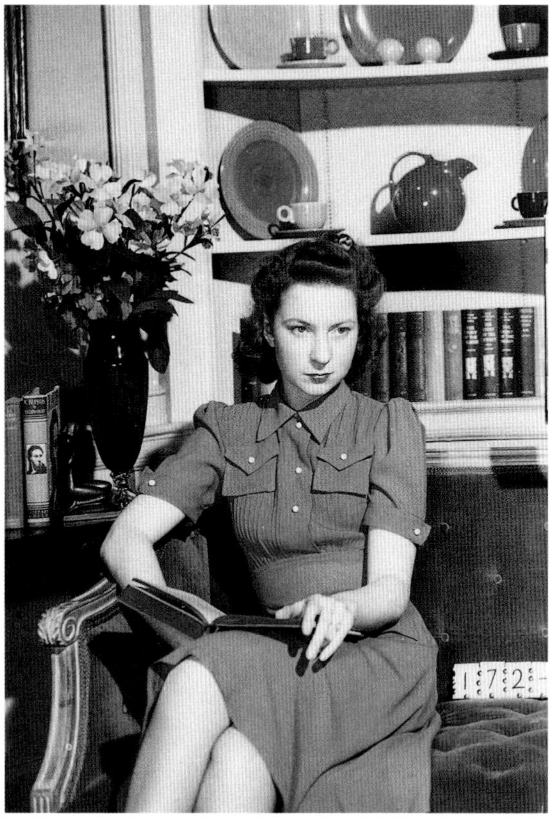

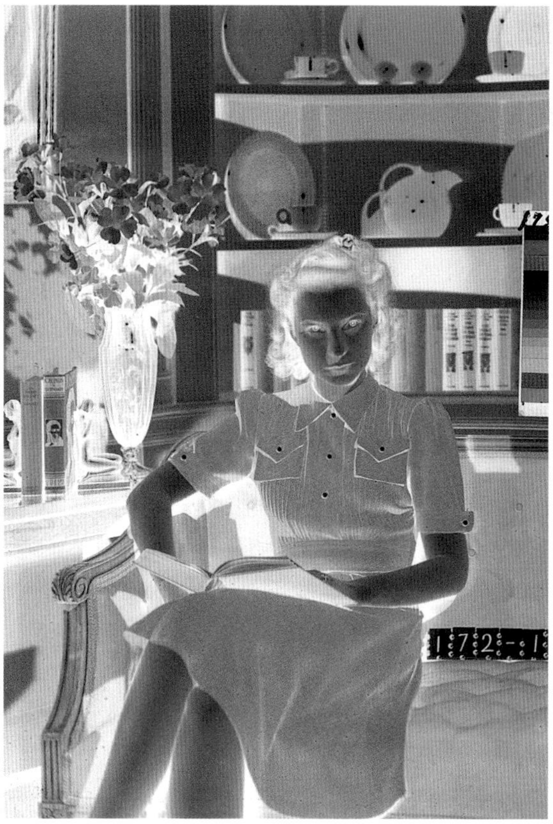

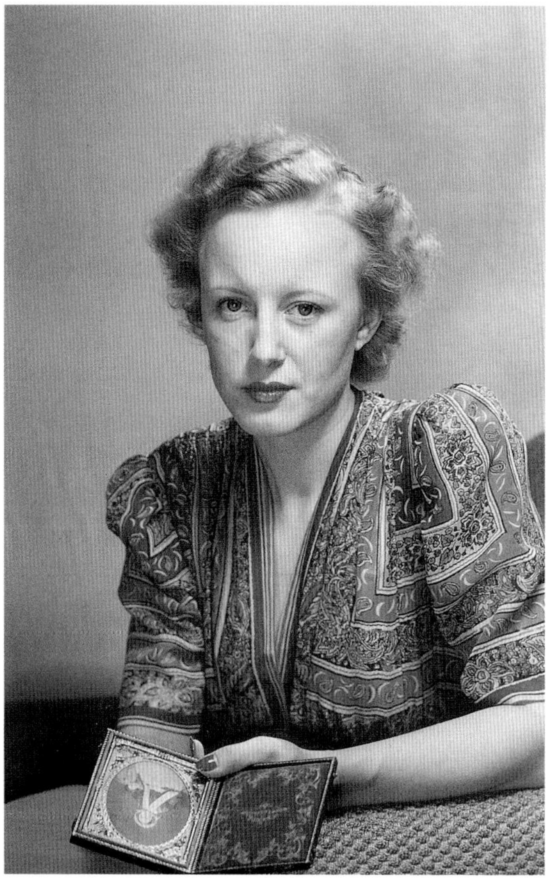

Clockwise from left: Anonymous, Young woman with book, ca. 1942, Kodacolor print, 3" x 4" Kodak test exposure.

Anonymous, Young woman with book, ca. 1942, Kodacolor negative, 4" x 5" Kodak test exposure.

Anonymous, Woman with daguerreotype, 1942, tipped-in Ansco color transparency, 4" x 6", from *The Conquest of Light, 1842–1942*, Agfa Ansco, 1942.

and received high praise. Sanger-Shepherd devised a somewhat similar process in 1899. Ives also used bichromated gelatin in his process of 1911; four years later he introduced the improved Hicro process, using negatives made by the Hess-Ives Corporation. Large commercial models of a camera, called the Hicro, were made for professional use, and a custom model was used by the photographer Elias Goldensky. A Hicro camera for the amateur market was advertised in the magazine *National Geographic* in early 1916, but the Hicro process eventually failed, probably because it was difficult to master and the cameras were priced too low to be profitable.

The Raydex color process, introduced in 1913, was an early successful application of the Carbro, or Ozobrome, method of printing. Sensitized, predyed sheets were contact printed from color-separation negatives. After developing in hot water, they were then temporarily assembled on a support before transfer to the final surface. In the 1920s a number of other color printing processes appeared. In 1935 the Defender Photo Supply Company of America brought out materials for the Chromatone three-color printing process.

The creation of a "tripack," in which all three color-sensitive layers were positioned in sequence, would obviate the need for the reflectors, mirrors, and prisms used in one-shot three-color cameras. Again, Louis Ducos du Hauron deserves credit for early ideas in the field. In an 1895 patent he proposed four separate emulsions, each atop another, which could be separated when it came time for processing and printing. Further advances along this line were made by Dr. J. H. Smith, Frederick E. Ives, and William Tarbin. Tarbin's efforts resulted in the Colorsnap process used by Colour Snapshots Ltd. (1928). While the colors were judged to be "exceedingly pleasing," it was discovered that employees were hand coloring the prints to compensate for their shortcomings. Ultimately, the process failed.

The most desirable tripack process was one in which the elements could be viewed still assembled, with no need for separation. The first to propose such a process, albeit unsuccessfully, was Karl Schnizel of Austria, in 1905. Seven years later, Rudolph Fischer of Germany received a patent for a process along the same lines, but it too fell by the wayside. In the 1930s, the Americans Leopold Mannes and Leo Godowsky Jr. were hired by Eastman Kodak to work on a tripack color process. In 1935 the result of their work, Kodachrome, was launched. This process used a film base coated with three very thin emulsions that were sensitive to red, green, and blue light. Additionally, a yellow filtering layer was placed between the blue and green layers. After a series of repeated developings, bleachings, and re-exposures, the end result was a color transparency that could be viewed by means of transmitted light. The process was so complex it had to be carried out by trained employees in Kodak's plants. The sequence of the commercial release of Kodachrome was: 16 mm movies (April 1935); 8 mm movies (May 1936); and 35 mm film for still cameras (September 1936). An improved Kodachrome process was introduced in 1938. Also that year, Kodachrome sheet films came on the market in sizes up to 11-by-14 inches. In 1951 Kodachrome sheet films were replaced by Ektachrome, which could be processed by users themselves.

In 1936 Germany's Agfa introduced a new Agfacolor film similar to Kodachrome. From the late 1920s until World War II the fortunes of Agfa and the U.S. firm Ansco had been linked; they parted ways when the war broke out. In 1942 Ansco brought out a transparency film of its own, Ansco Color, later called Anscochrome. In the years since World War II, a host of other color transparency films have appeared, among them Sakuracolor, Fujicolor—not the current negative form—Ilford Colour (later Ilfochrome), Gevacolor, and Orwocolor.

Kodacolor, introduced by Eastman Kodak in 1942, was the first negative-positive color process to be made available commercially. Kodacolor has undergone a number of improvements since it first appeared on the market, and today it is just one of many negative-positive color processes available.

Ray Hicks, Woman with flowers, ca. 1947, Kodachrome Type B transparency, 8" x 10".

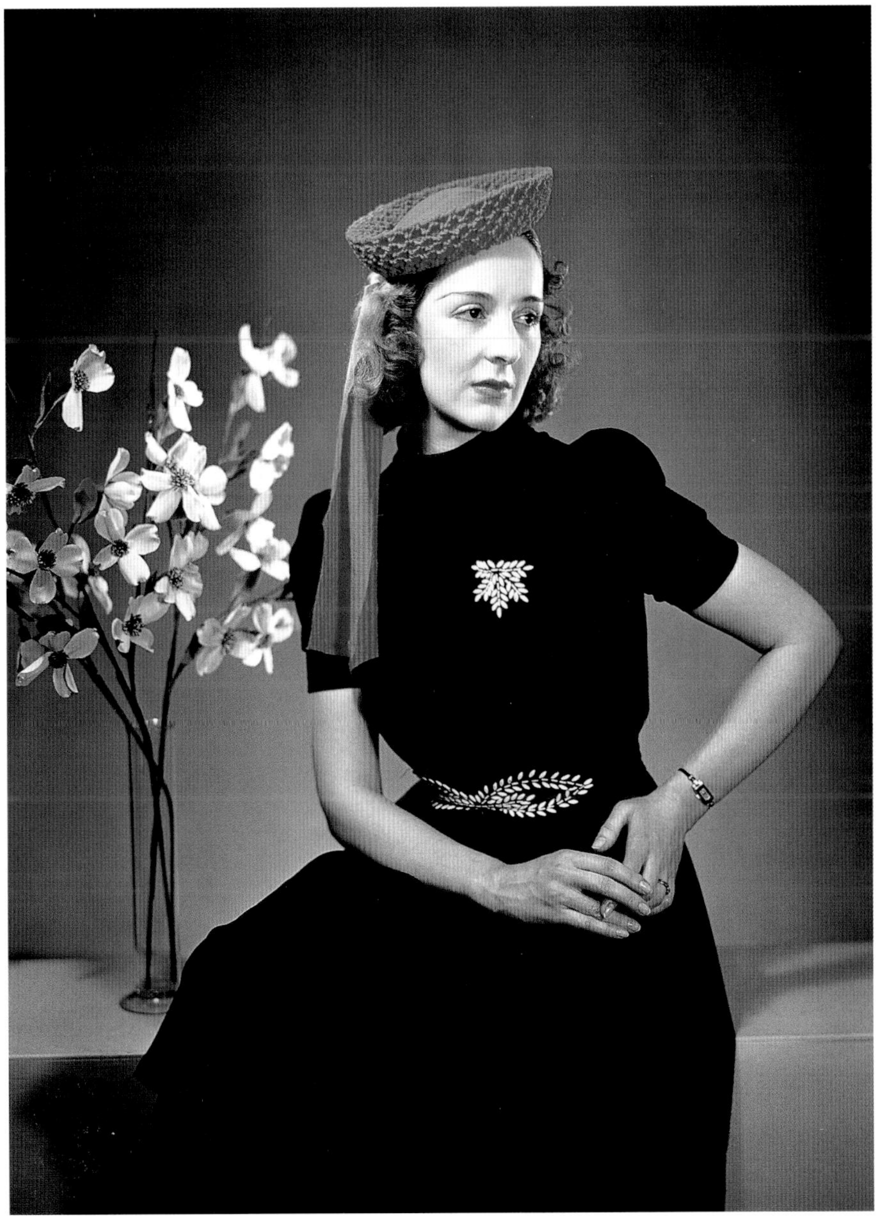

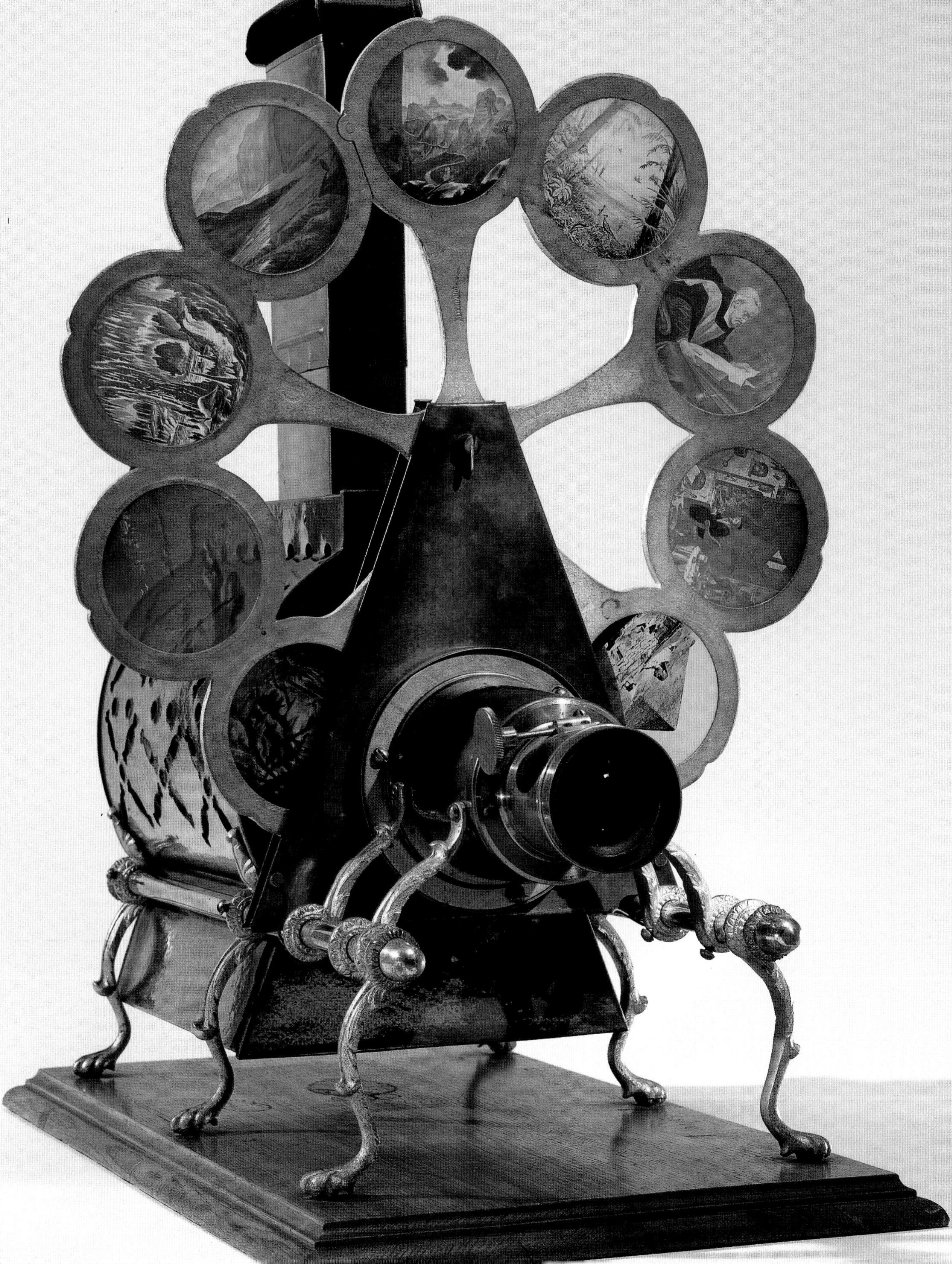

CHAPTER ELEVEN:

THE MOVING IMAGE

Revolving-disc Sciopticon, Pettibone Brothers Manufacturing Co., ca. 1896, 3" slides mounted on 15 ½" aluminum-spoked wheel, four-wick, oil-burning light source.

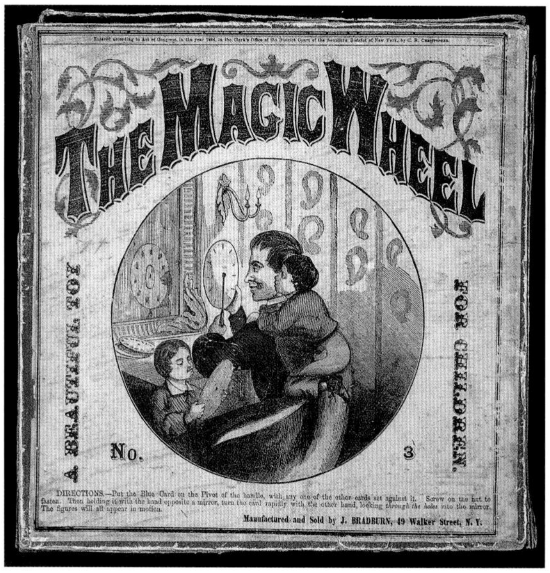

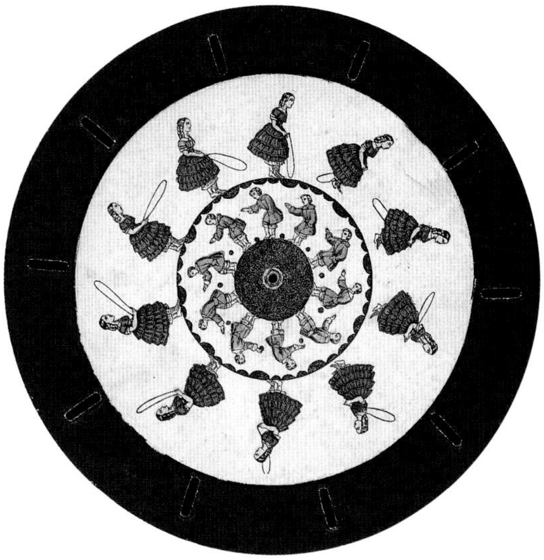

Left: The Magic Wheel No. 3 Phenakistiscope, box cover, J. Bradburn, ca. 1865, 9" x 9 1/4".

Right: Disc for The Magic Wheel No. 3 Phenakistiscope, J. Bradburn, ca. 1865, 6 3/4" diameter, girl jumping rope and boy bouncing ball.

No sooner did mankind solve the riddle of permanently fixing an image onto paper or metal than did the quest to make the image appear to move begin. In fact, the earliest inventions relating to the moving image actually predate the invention of photography, as they do not relate to the photographic aspects of cinematography.

In order to proceed further, an understanding of the neurophysiological phenomenon of "persistence of vision," central to the principles that make cinematic illusion possible, is needed. When an image is interrupted at the input (the eye), an after-image is perceived by the brain for a limited amount of time. If a new image is presented before this after-image has faded, the brain interprets the two as a single, uninterrupted image. Small variations are interpreted by the brain as motion.

In the Victorian era, persistence of vision became a particular obsession amongst scientists and inventors. Thus, some indirect connections exist between the early attempts at simulating motion and photography.

Several of the scientists who first reported on the persistence-of-vision phenomena are familiar to us for their photography-related activities. Among them are David Brewster, best known for his 1815 invention of the Kaleidoscope and pioneering work in the development of stereo photography; John Herschel, whose many chemical discoveries enabled photography; and the well-known physicist and chemist Michael Faraday, who made lasting contributions to many sciences, including photography.

From the late 1830s on, many photographic scientists and inventors added their efforts to persistence-of-vision phenomena, eventually merging the two sciences. In a way it is surprising that, until the 1820s, very little attention had been paid to persistence of vision, while the inventions which are a part of the prehistory of photography date back well before then. One of the earliest recorded observations on persistence of vision was reported in 1824 by Dr. Peter M. Roget (of thesaurus fame), while Brewster, Faraday, and others did not pay serious attention to it until about 1830.

London physician Dr. John Ayrton Paris invented the first persistence-of-vision device, the Thaumatrope, in 1825, although the honor has also been attributed to Charles Babbage, inventor of the mechanical calculator; to John Herschel; and to Dr. William Hyde Wollaston, inventor of the camera lucida.

Dr. Paris described the Thaumatrope in his book *Philosophy in Sport Made Science in Earnest*—originally written to foster a love of science in his children. The classical Thaumatrope consists of a card or a disc with part of an image drawn on one side, with the rest of the image on the other. By quickly rotating the card around its own axis, the two partial images merge. A popular Thaumatrope had on one side a bird, and on the other, a cage—spinning the disc made the bird appear to be inside the cage. Later Thaumatropes were box-shaped, and merged four sequential images rather than just two. Spinning animated the images, creating the illusion of a continued movement.

The Thaumatrope and other primitive persistence-of-vision devices are examples of how the time lag between the formation of an image on the retina of the eye and its reception by the mind can be exploited. Yet, they were not true precursors of the principle used in cinematography, which depends on this time lag in perception to create an illusion of a continuous flow from what is in fact an interrupted succession of stationary images.

A device incorporating such an illusion of a continuous flow followed the Thaumatrope by only seven years, in 1832, and became the basis for most pre-cinema devices until the 1890s. Invented virtually simultaneously by two scientists, the Belgian professor J. A. Plateau and the Austrian professor Simon von Stampfer, the Phenakistiscope rapidly became popular all over Europe and in the United States. It was known variously as Fantascope, and Die Stroboscopische Scheibe (Stroboscope), von Stampfer's term.

The basic Phenakistiscope consists of a cardboard disc with notches around the circumference. Between the notches are drawings of a subject in a number of successively different positions. The disc, attached to a spindle, is spun rapidly in front of a mirror, providing a mirror image of the drawings in motion as seen through the "shutter" action of the notches.

In 1833, a year following the Phenakistiscope's introduction, an Englishman, W. C. Horner of Bristol, invented the Daedelum, or Wheel of Life. This toy, better known as the Zoetrope, is like the Phenakistiscope in that images are viewed through slits on a rotating disc. In the Zoetrope, however, the rotating disc has a wall of several inches along its circumference, making it drum-shaped. The slits are made in this wall, rather than on the base, and the images positioned opposite the slits. Several viewers could use the Zoetrope at the same time, and the images were printed on interchangeable bands of paper. William E. Lincoln, of Providence, Rhode Island, named and manufactured the device in 1867 for the American market. The Zoetrope was made in a large variety of models, some basic and others more elaborate, in some

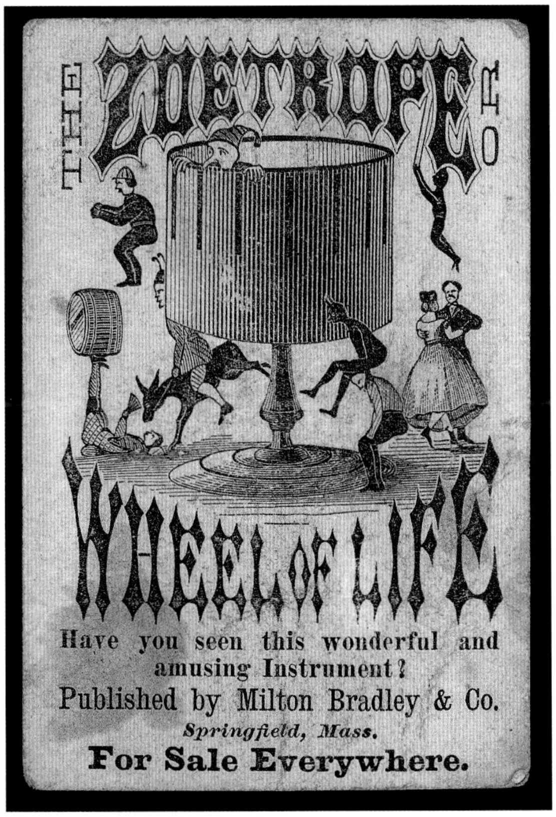

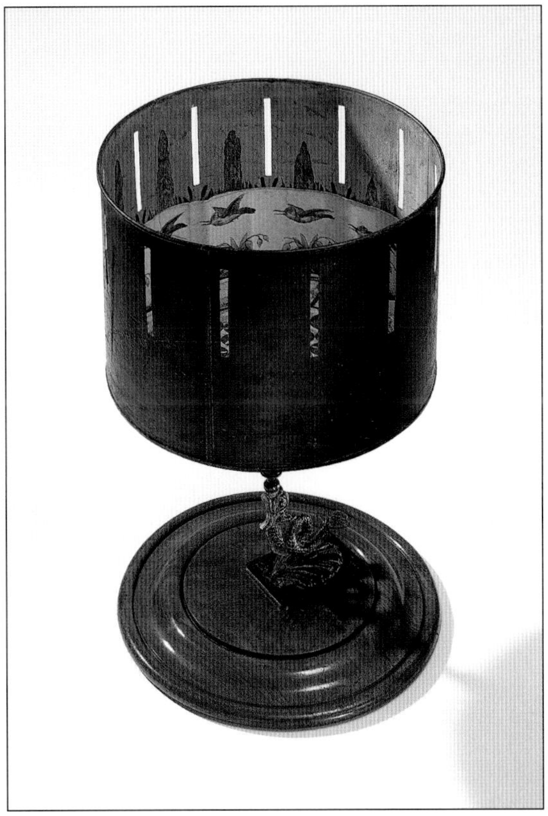

Left: The Zoetrope, or Wheel of Life, advertising trade card, Milton Bradley & Co., ca. 1873, 2 3/8" x 3 1/2".

Right: Zoetrope, English, ca. 1875, 11" drum, pierced with thirteen slots, accommodates 35-inch-long paper strips with figure illustrations.

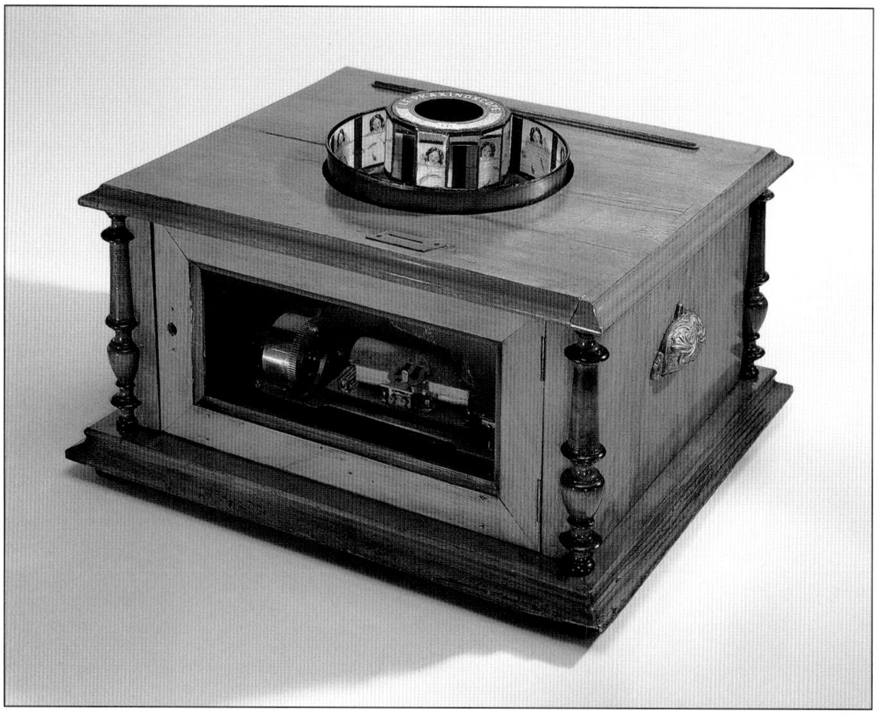

Musical Praxinoscope, ca. 1885. An adaptation of the Praxinoscope, which included a coin-operated, spring-wind music box with thirteen different tunes. A coin dropped into the slot on top of the wooden enclosure activates the music and begins rotation, making this a primitive precursor of sound movies.

instances equipped with hand cranks for smoother turning of the drum.

In 1877, an enterprising Frenchman, Emile Reynaud, invented a device that did away with the slots and allowed the viewer—or any number of viewers—to fix their sights onto mirrors surrounding the inside core of the Praxinoscope, as it was called. The Praxinoscope's simplicity belied its ingenious design. Its mirror-lined cylinder occupied exactly one-half the drum's diameter. Each mirror corresponded to one of the pictures on the strip along the inside of the drum's outer wall and reflected the images nearest the observer. The image, which was bright and clear, appeared to be fixed at the axis of the Praxinoscope's rotation. Consequently, the central lines of all the images would coincide and would not shift their position as a whole. This avoided the distortion inherent in such earlier devices as the Phenakistiscope and the Zoetrope. Reynaud continued to work on his invention for many years, and the Praxinoscope line eventually consisted of dozens of different types, including even some with a projection capability.

A particularly ambitious model was the so-called "Praxinoscope Theatre," in which a moving figure was shown on a stage. A sheet of glass, bearing a painted proscenium, was held at a slight angle between the cutout in the vertically positioned Praxinoscope lid and the Praxinoscope itself. On the interior of the lid, changeable pictures of scenery would reflect in the glass, appearing as if behind the stagefront.

The basic Praxinoscope was manufactured in a variety of sizes; it was copied in several countries and was marketed well into the twentieth century. The American version made by McLaughlin Bros. was called the "Whirligig of Life." Ernst Planck, the famous German toy manufacturer, made a handle-driven version called the "Kinematofor." Even electrically- and steam-engine-operated models of Praxinoscopes were available. The Praxinoscope was the last major optical toy preceding the introduction of motion-picture apparatus.

During the 1880s, photographers such as Eadweard Muybridge, of England, Étienne-Jules Marey, of France, and the Polish-German Ottomar Anschütz dedicated themselves to the perfection of chrono-photography, or the making of rapid, sequential photographs of an action, such as the gallop of a horse or the motion of a hurdler. The relationship between these motion studies and persistence-of-vision devices is reciprocal. In order to demonstrate their work, these photographers used projection devices based on the Phenakistiscope and the Zoetrope. In turn, as their pioneering work created the ability to document motion in a series of photographs, the number of photographic scenarios available for viewing in such devices was greatly expanded.

The era of chrono-photography gave rise to a series of new persistence-of-vision devices. Flick books (also known as flip books), Mutoscopes, Kinoras, and the like all have images printed or drawn on individual cards or the pages of a book. These images are presented to the eye in rapid succession as they escape from under a slowly-drawn-back thumb, or a mechanical device performing the thumb's action.

Flick books themselves actually predate the invention of the movie camera and were based on handmade drawings. However, their popularity grew only when they started employing photographs made by chrono-photography, or reproduced from films taken with motion-picture cameras. In fact, those made during the early days of the motion picture were called "Cinematograph" or "Kinematograph." The 1898 *Harmsworth* magazine, published in England, included contact prints of motion-picture negatives on the top corners of 140 consecutive pages, depicting children dancing and romping. Also referred to as "Cinematograph," this "movie" was credited to the Lumière brothers and to their British agents.

Flick books are still being made today. Their subject matter is varied: advertising, sports, instructional, product-usage demonstrations, and cartoons. Flick books could teach one, for example, how to play the piano, swim, dance, play golf, or how to treat one's store customer correctly. One early example showed a 1906 horse race. Most used photographs, though some of the more contemporary ones use drawings. In the 1940s, a New York manufacturer offered—under the Moviematic name—cameras that gave the user a choice of making Movie Books (flick books), Movies, or Snapshots.

Mutoscopes and Kinoras, mechanized flick books quite popular in penny arcades, had a greater impact on the entertainment industry than did their smaller precursors.

In 1894, Herman Casler invented the Mutoscope. This device moved images, attached to an inner drum, past a viewing aperture. The viewer could control the speed at which the cards were flipped, and could also make the images run in reverse. Mutoscopes, with their sturdy flick-card system, remained popular in penny arcades until the 1940s and competed effectively with motion-picture entertainment devices in showing movie shorts.

Casler also developed a projector, the Biograph, to project Mutoscope cards; later he adapted a Mutoscope, using a mirror, to project motion pictures. This, too, was named the Biograph.

The Kinora was similar to the Mutoscope but designed for home use. Since the flick cards used in Kinoras were much smaller than those used by the Mutoscope, the mechanism required less rigidity, making the unit and picture reels more affordable. Invented in France by the Lumière brothers in

PROFILE: *The Magic Lantern*

Long before the invention of persistence-of-vision devices, another optical instrument, the magic lantern, had been providing entertainment for both children and adults. By the 1860s the magic lantern projector had evolved into quite a sophisticated instrument, incorporating two or even three lenses to create merging or dissolving images, providing a sense of movement. A great variety of motion-producing slides were available; the dancing monkey, a girl skipping rope, or the mouse climbing into the sleeper's mouth are just a few examples of such "motion picture" entertainment.

Because the magic lantern does not employ persistence of vision to create the effect of motion, lantern slides cannot be considered directly pre-cinematic. But some magic lantern shows did simulate a movie effect. As early as 1853, an Austrian army officer, Franz Freiherr von Uchatius, succeeded in projecting Phenakistiscope-like discs in his magic lantern, and he is thus credited with producing the earliest projected motion picture. Also, in 1866, C. S. Beale of Greenwich, England, invented the Choreutoscope, a lantern slide in which the projection of successive images was interrupted by a rising and falling shutter,

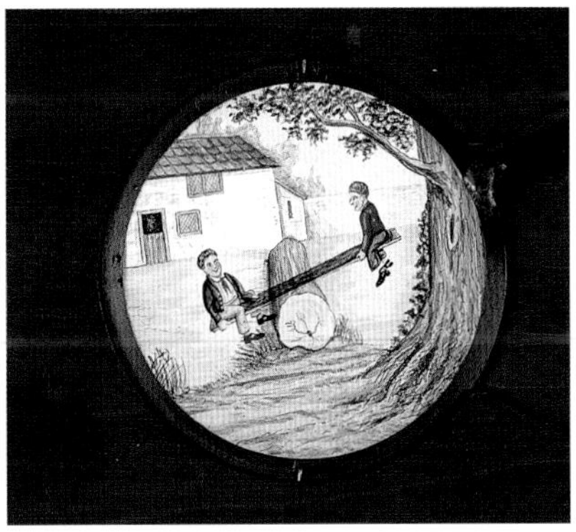

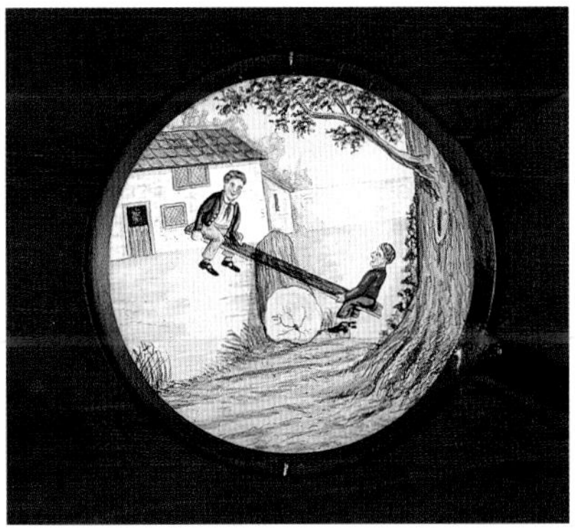

not at all dissimilar from that used in later motion picture apparatus. T. Ross, another Englishman, produced the "Wheel of Life" (not to be confused with the Zoetrope) in 1869. This device created a motion effect based on the principle of the Phenakistiscope, using two discs. The first disc, bearing the painted figures, revolved slowly; at the same time, the second, opaque disc, which had one sector removed, made just one revolution while the transparent disc moved one stage.

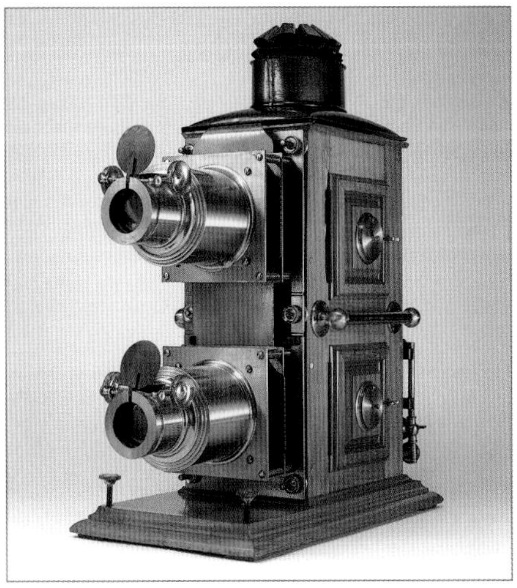

Magic lantern slide, two views of boys on a seesaw, English, ca. 1872, mahogany frame, 4 1/4" x 7", hand-painted.

Right: Biunial magic lantern, "J. W." manufacturer, English, ca. 1895, mahogany construction, flap shutters to facilitate dissolving views.

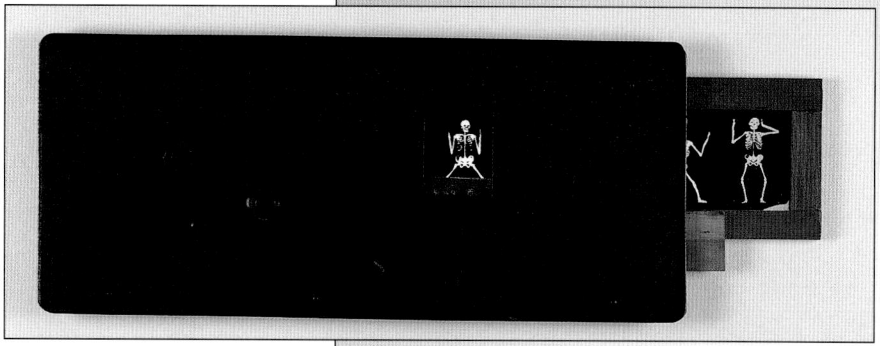

Beale's Choreutoscope, C. Baker, ca. 1866, metal slide 4 1/2" x 10 3/4", containing 2 1/2" x 8" slide with six stages of skeleton removing head.

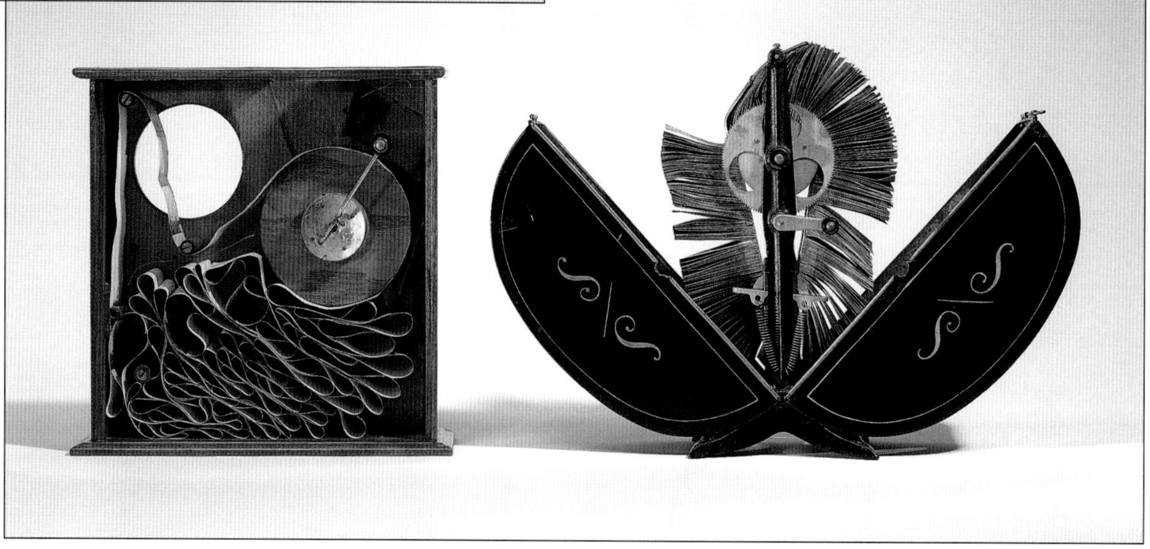

Right: Left: the Parlor Kinetoscope, American, ca. 1898, cherry-wood viewer, side panel removed. Right: the Phantascope, Jenkins Phantascope Co., ca. 1898, approximately 170 halftone photographs on cards, one show on each side, crank-wound.

1896, the British popularized the Kinora by offering a variety of models, ranging from handheld devices to large, ornate Kinoras for multiple viewers.

A different approach to the flick-card principle was taken by C. Francis Jenkins, the American inventor and founder of The Society of Motion Picture Engineers. His Phantascope viewer consisted of an oval metal housing, in which flick cards mounted on a belt were moved by a geared handle turned by the viewer. Very few units of the Phantoscope were sold.

Three components were essential for the production and showing of motion pictures: a suitable camera, a viewer or projector, and a transparent medium on which the images were laid. Most often—though not always—that medium was flexible ribbon film, first available in 1889 with the introduction of Eastman's Transparent Film. This film not only provided the needed medium for motion pictures but also, with the size of film for the No. 1 Kodak, served indirectly to establish the standard width for motion-picture film that was used for over a century.

Early ideas for and attempts at creating motion pictures before Eastman's Transparent Film were few and far between. In 1876 Wordsworth Donisthorpe was issued a provisional British patent for a "Kinematographic apparatus." His invention was a form of magazine camera for dry plates that were "moved forward progressively" for exposure. The plates could then be printed and, as was said in the patent abridgement, "A series of them may be printed on a paper strip to be viewed in a zoetrope or the like." In 1889, in conjunction with W. C. Crofts, Donisthorpe was also granted a patent for a motion-picture camera that used flexible film.

The 1890s saw the first major inventions of cameras and projectors of the type on which we base our modern motion-picture apparatus. The best known of these are probably the Edison Kinetograph and Projecting Kinetoscope and the Lumière Cinématographe combination camera and projector. The number of designs that became available before the turn of the century was substantial, and many inventors and different countries claimed "firsts" in cinematographic equipment.

In the period 1887–1889 Louis Aimé Augustin Le Prince, a Frenchman who lived in England, was experimenting with cinematographic equipment. His first invention, in 1887, was a sixteen-lens combination camera-projector. It recorded sequences of eight images on a pair of paper-film rolls. In 1888 he obtained a patent whose description concerned a separate camera and projector. One of his apparatuses used perforated film and had a "Maltese-cross" gearing. Late in 1889 he tried out a single-lens camera that used celluloid film. In 1890, after boarding a train from Dijon bound for Paris, he disappeared completely and was never heard from again.

In the late 1880s, in the laboratory of the noted inventor Thomas Edison, development was under way of a motion picture camera and viewing device. In 1889, in the same laboratory, the first projection took place, using reliable transparent film, from the Eastman Dry Plate & Film Co. Edison applied for patents for his viewer, the Kinetoscope, and his camera, the Kinetograph. These devices used 35 mm film, made by slitting No. 1 Kodak film lengthwise, which was perforated on four sides of each 18-by-24-mm frame. Positive 35 mm film prints made from the negatives were wound on rollers and moved past the Kinetoscope's electric light source. A full loop ran, at forty-six frames per second, for about fifteen seconds. A magnifier on the outside of the Kinetoscope's cabinet permitted a person—only one—to view the film. The first Kinetoscope show in America was in 1893. In 1894 a Kinetoscope Parlor containing ten machines was opened in New York City.

Left: Pedestal Kinora, English, ca. 1905, mahogany construction with boxwood and ebony stringing and fruitwood banding, three magnifying eyepieces, clockwork mechanism. Pedestal has twenty compartments for reel storage, 57" high.

Right: Table-top Mutoscope, American Mutoscope & Biograph Co., ca. 1900, oak construction, 2" x 2 3/4" silver prints mounted on 10" diameter roll.

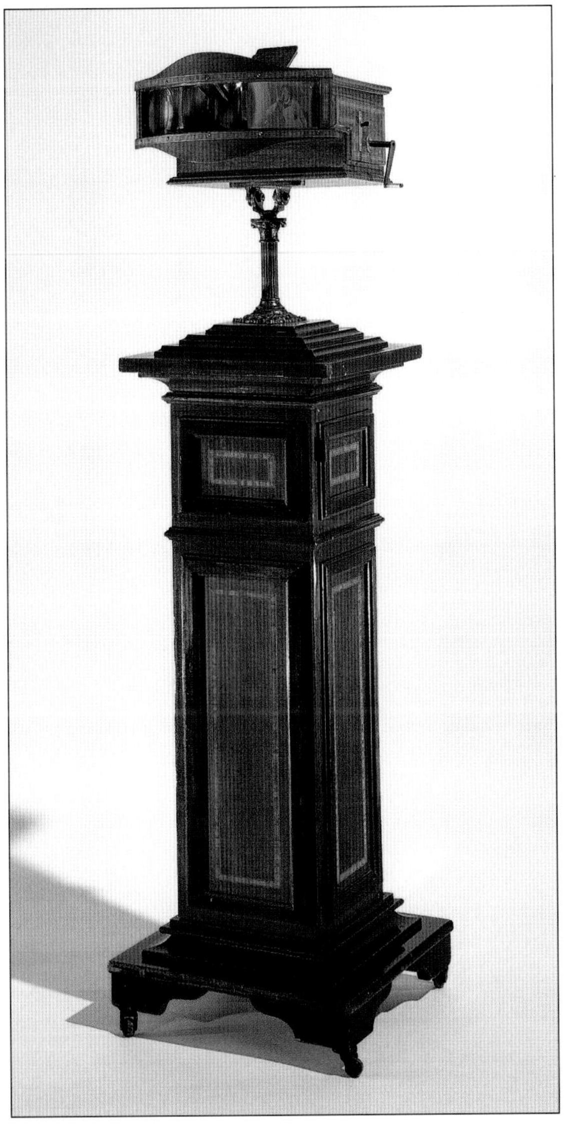

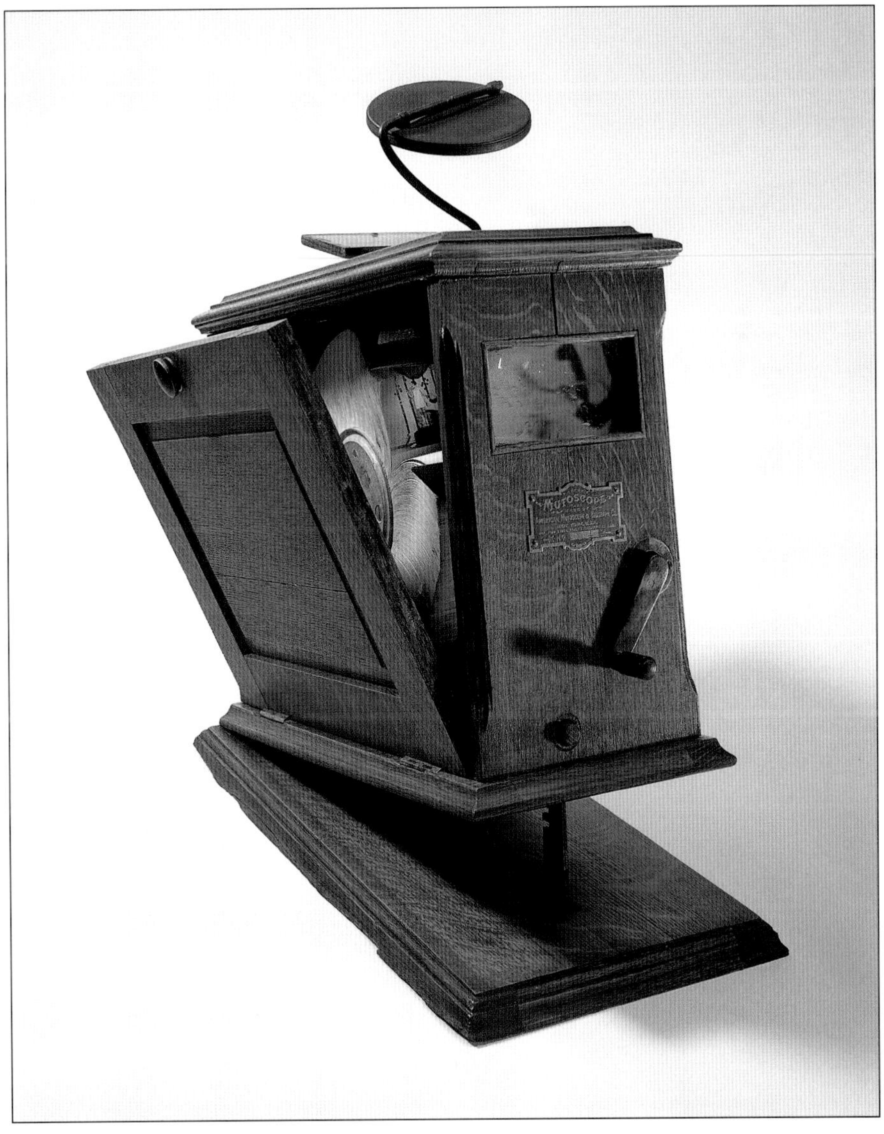

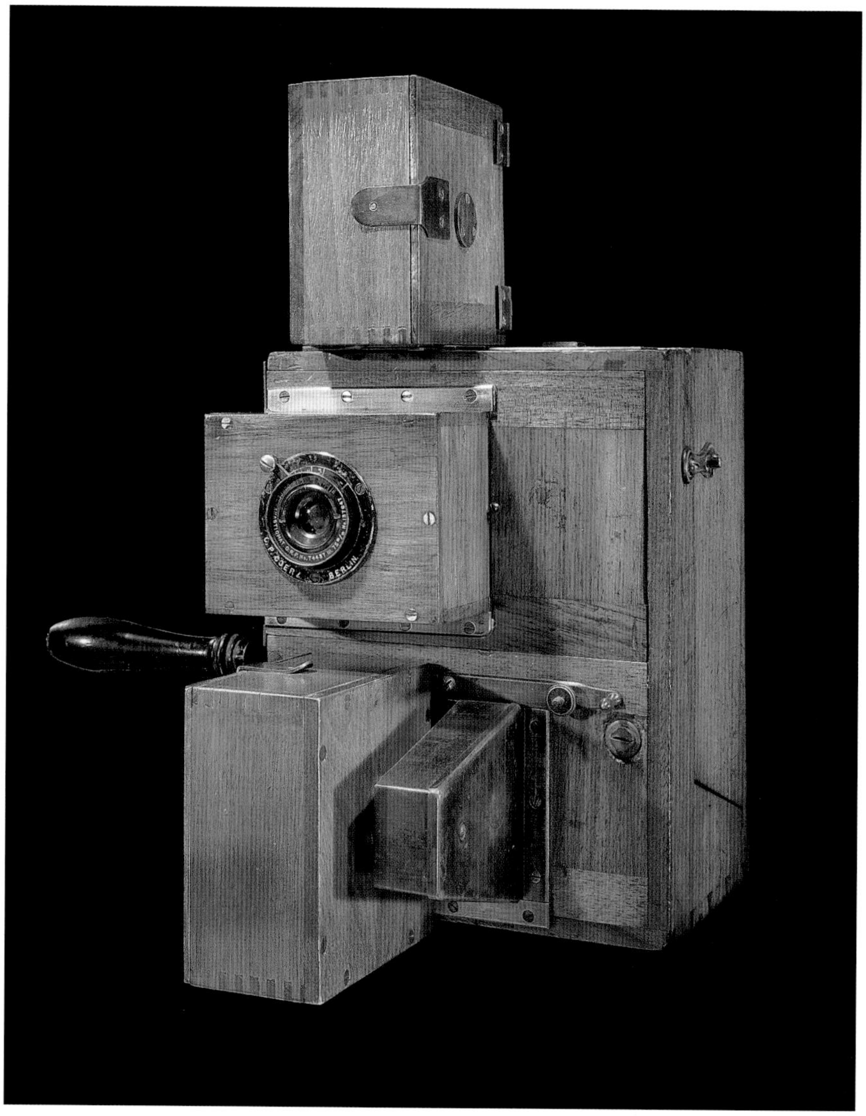

Demeny Chronophotographe, L. Gaumont & Cie., ca. 1899, walnut construction with walnut film magazines, for 35 mm perforated film in lengths of three to five meters, combined camera-projector.

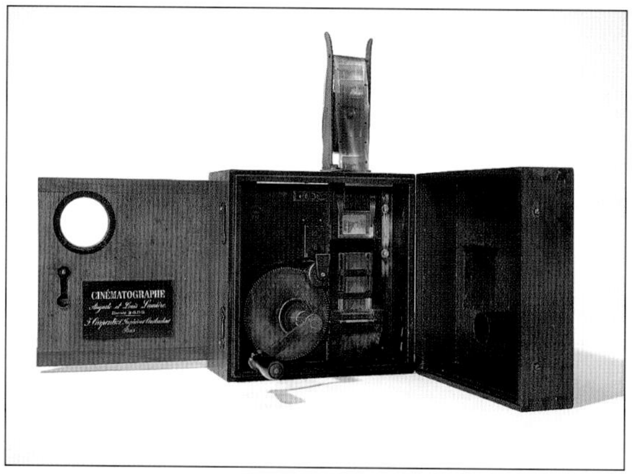

Left: Lumière Cinématographe, Lumière Frères, ca. 1898, for 35 mm perforated film, combined camera-printer-projector. The seventeen meters of film provided about nine hundred frames.

Jean Aimé LeRoy, an American, claimed to have built a motion-picture projector in 1893. It wasn't until February 22, 1895, however, that any evidence of the camera existed. For that date a printed program was issued announcing "LeRoy's Marvelous Cinématographe." This was one week before the public showing of the Lumières' 35 mm projector, and also before the brothers adopted the Cinématographe name for their camera-projector combination. Edison's Kinetoscope, which had its first overseas showing in London in 1894, was patented almost everywhere except in England. There, Robert William Paul manufactured the Kinetoscope. Paul also built, in 1894, a camera using the principle of Marey's Chronophotographic film camera. Working with Birt Acres, Paul also made Edison-size films. Additionally, Paul was manufacturing Kinetoscopes and selling them to Charles Pathé, in France. In February 1896 Paul demonstrated a new camera of his own design, the Paul Theatrograph, which he used for showing films to a paying audience in March of that year. Birt Acres, on the other hand, went on to develop his own motion-picture camera, the Kinetic, in 1895, with which he filmed the Derby at Epsom. He also developed a projector, the Kinetic Lantern, with which he showed films to the Royal Photographic Society, in January 1896.

Two of the major figures in the motion-picture world in the mid-1890s were the brothers Lumière. Louis Jean Lumière and his brother, Auguste Marie Louis Nicholas Lumière, grew up in a photographic family. Their father, Antoine, was a working photographer, and the brothers owned a factory in Lyons that was devoted to the manufacture of photographic products. Louis came up with the idea for a combined motion-picture camera-projector. This was patented in February 1895 and was initially called the Kinetoscope—changed shortly thereafter to Cinématographe. The most important feature of the camera was a claw drive that was driven eccentrically, to move the film. The Lumière devices used 35 mm film, first with a single pair of perforations per frame, and later with four perforations per frame, as in Edison's Kinetoscope. In March 1895 they demonstrated their projector to audiences of specialists, and in late December they gave their first commercial showing.

In 1895 the Latham family, sons Grey and Otway and father Major Woodville, were involved in giving cinematographic shows. Together with W. K. L. Dickson—Edison's key motion-picture

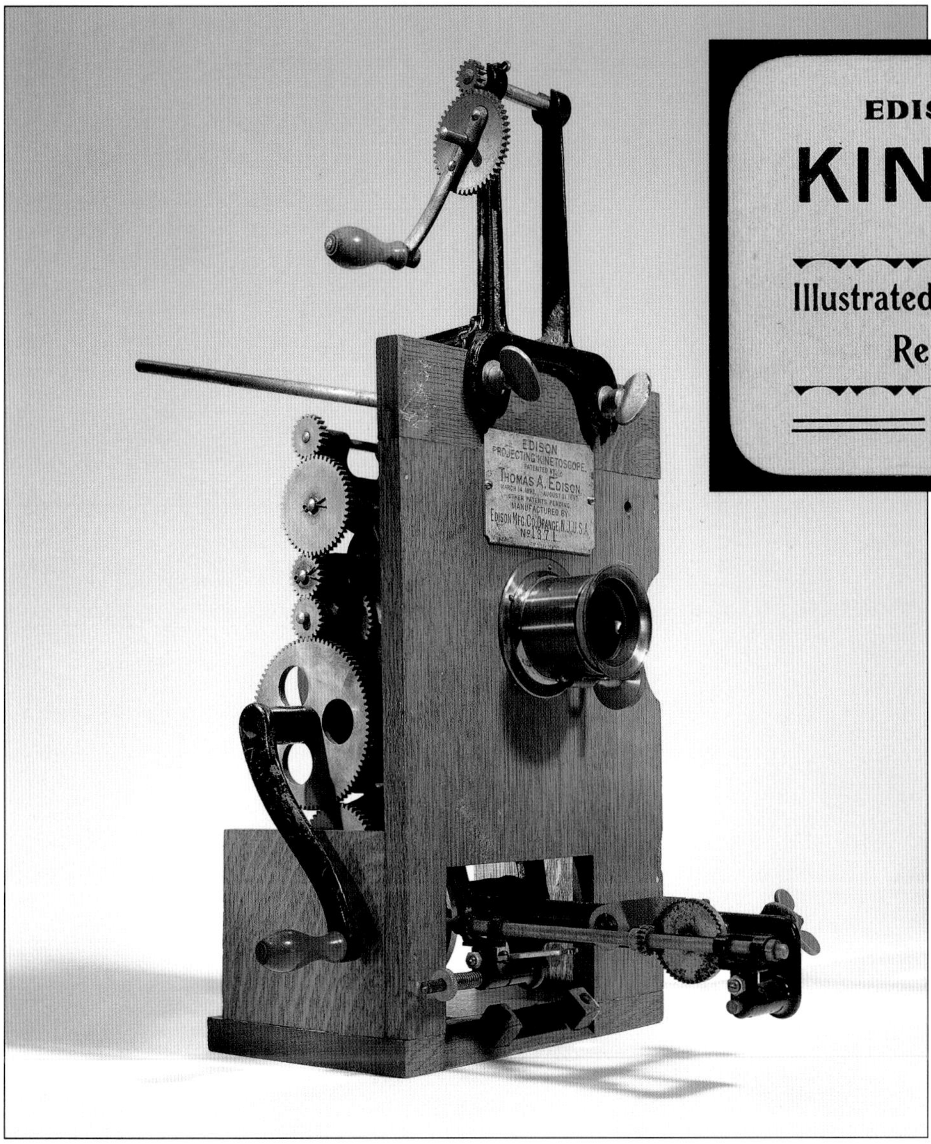

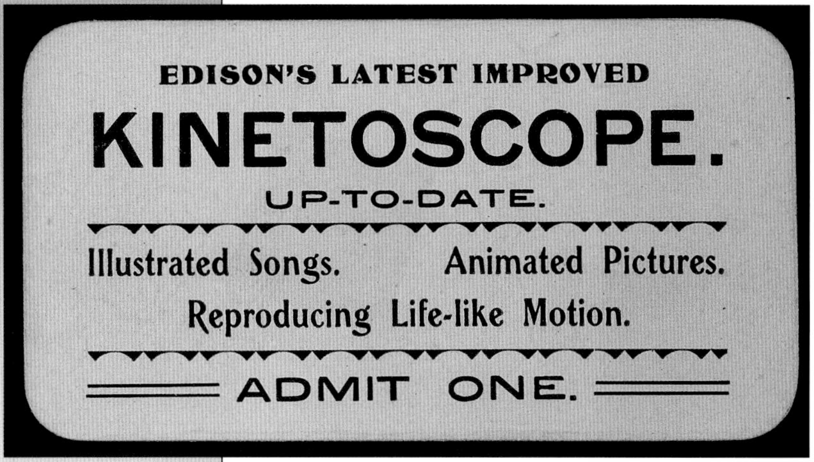

Edison Projecting Kinetoscope—Exhibition Model, Edison Mfg. Co., ca. 1900, for perforated 35 mm cine film, hand-crank operated.

Inset: Kinetoscope ticket, ca. 1898, 1 ³/₄" x 3 ³/₈", for single admission to the Kinetoscope.

man—they produced a projecting Kinetoscope. This differed from the earlier viewing Kinetoscope. The first public showing of films using their machine was on May 22, 1895. The Latham brothers were also inventors of the "Latham loop." Until 1895, the tension on the film in a movie camera as it was pulled into position behind the lens was such that the film often tore or broke. By having a small loop of film on either side of the film gate—which was behind the lens—the tension was reduced and film damage was avoided.

C. Francis Jenkins was granted a patent in January 1894 for a motion-picture camera that he called the Phantoscope, a name he had also applied to his flick-card viewer. It employed continuously moving film, as opposed to the intermittent film motion of most cameras and projectors. A battery of lenses located behind the aperture rotated, with each lens coming into position to expose the film strip, which traveled at the same speed. Jenkins joined forces with Thomas Armat to market the Vitascope, an improved version of the Phantascope projector, in 1896. They showed it to Thomas Edison, who liked it so much that he bought the rights to the projector and sold it under his own name. Vitascope films had their first public showing in early April of 1896, in New York City. Of that showing, the April 7th *New York Herald* commented, "The future of the machine which astonished all who saw last night's views was the almost entire absence of vibration in the pictures as they appeared on the screen, and which has been the hardest obstacle to surmount in perfecting the apparatus." Vitascope projectors became extremely popular. This success was in part due to the projector's use of the Latham loop.

Max and Emil Skladanowsky, of Berlin, worked in the years 1892–1895 to develop their Bioscope projector, which had its first showing in November 1895. This was not a mainstream projector, however, as it used circular loops of film and was not intended for the showing of continuous films.

In 1896 Thomas Armat produced a projector that used both the Latham loop and a Maltese-cross shutter. This combination regularized the rate of opening and closing of the shutter and helped to eliminate the flicker common in many projectors. The presentation of unevenly spaced images behind the lens was the cause of such flicker. Also in 1896, in June, Oscar Messter built a projector that used the Maltese-cross principle to regulate movement of the film. Of course, the ill-fated Le Prince was apparently the first to use the Maltese-cross movement, in 1888–1889. To whomever the credit goes, however, that form of intermittent film movement became the one that was used most throughout the twentieth century.

By the mid-1890s competition in the invention and manufacture of cameras and projectors for the newly-created motion-picture industry intensified, and a variety of apparatus appeared. Dozens of new cameras and projectors were in production by the end of 1896. Obviously there was an increasing need for film stock to feed the voracious appetites of the cameras, projectors, and the public. Although it was not the only option, the 35 mm film width was becoming increasingly popular. In December of 1896 the Eastman Kodak Co. succeeded in negotiating a contract in which it was agreed that they would supply various filmmakers with 300,000 feet of 2 ½-inch (70 mm) film—this would be slit to produce 600,000 feet of 35 mm film—to be taken within six months. Early in 1897 Thomas Edison contracted with Kodak for an additional 35,000 feet of 2 ½-inch film per week.

While most motion-picture cameras and projectors adopted the use of ribbon film—of various widths—"oddball" apparatus were occasionally produced. Leo Kamm's Kammatograph, introduced in 1898, used a 12-inch-diameter circular glass-disc dry plate. One model was advertised as having a disc on which up to 550 6-by-8-mm images could be positioned spirally. On another model 300–350 8-by-12-mm images could be stored. Unfortunately, the total amount of time for a continuous projection was only forty-five seconds. Another motion-picture camera-projector that used a circular film format was the Spirograph, from around 1913. The Olikos was an unusual camera produced in France in 1912. It used eighteen 6.5-by-9-cm dry plates, each of which accommodated eighty-four (twelve rows of seven) 6-by-7-mm exposures. The mechanism enabled the camera to take seven pictures, from left to right, on the top of the plate. The plate was then moved up one row for another sequence of

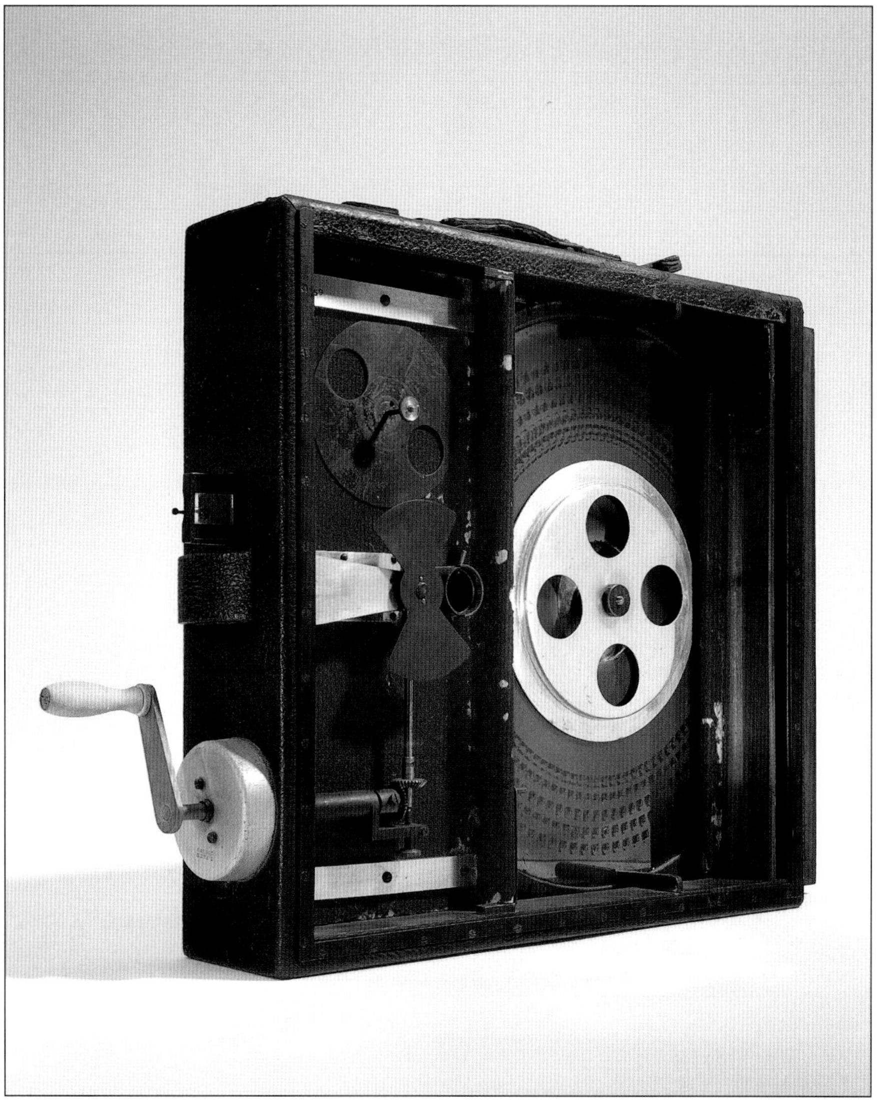

Kammatograph, L. Kamm, ca. 1900, for approximately three hundred 8 x 12 mm exposures on 12" diameter glass plate. When crank is turned, plate on turntable rotates and moves laterally across camera back.

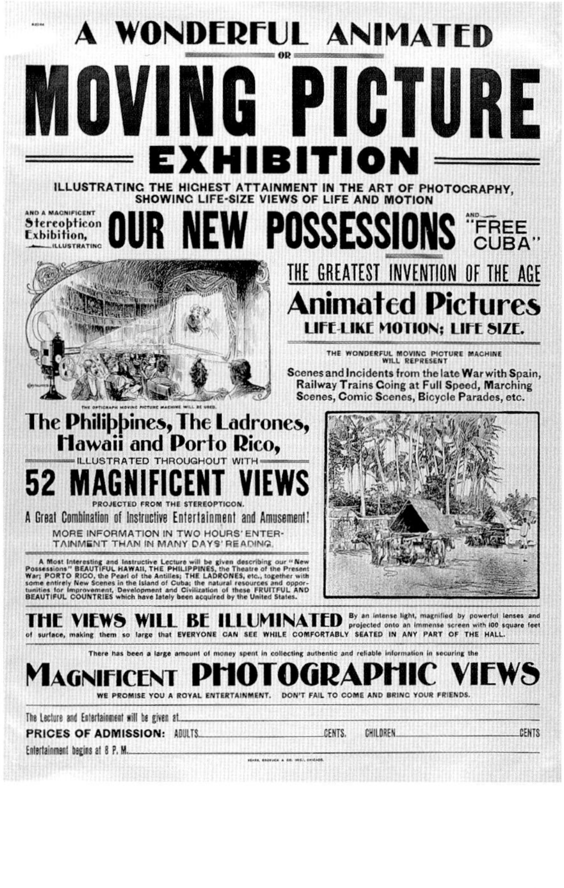

Right: Broadside, Sears, Roebuck & Co., ca. 1900, 21" x 28", for movies shown on the Optigraph Moving Picture Machine, post-Spanish-American War scenes.

seven, taken from right to left, and so on. Once the plate was fully exposed, it was moved to a top storage rack and a new plate was immediately put into position. The eighteen plates produced a ninety-second movie.

By the early 1900s a fair degree of standardization of the mechanical principles of motion picture apparatus existed. The Motion Picture Patents Agreement of 1908—a "trust" comprised of film exchanges, theaters, and the Eastman Kodak Company—brought even further standardization of commercial film. Edison's size and format won out but, as Edison and Eastman were among the principal parties to the agreement, what else could one expect? In 1898, the Eastman Kodak Co. introduced nonflammable "safety" film. There had been a number of terrible theater fires with a number of fatalities as a result of the use of the earlier, nitrocellulose film. Of course, ever bent on sales, Eastman representatives went around convincing municipal governments to enact ordinances banning the use of nitrocellulose film in local theaters. By 1911 the Eastman Kodak Co. was making more than eighty million feet of movie film each year.

Small theaters—called "nickelodeons" because the admission charge was a nickel—showing short movies became very popular in the early 1900s. Thomas Tally opened the first nickelodeon in Los Angeles in 1896. By 1908, around ten thousand nickelodeons had been opened.

A few commercial camera manufacturers came up with novel features. Henry Marvin invented the Biograph camera. This camera used neither film sprockets nor film loops, instead punching holes in the film during its motion through the camera. The Mutograph of 1897 had also employed in-camera film perforation. Joseph Bianchi of Toronto, Canada, devised a "shutterless" motion-picture camera in 1908. It used a moveable second lens in a rotating disc, behind the fixed front lens. The periodic exposure of the film frames was accomplished optically rather than mechanically. The Debrie Parvo, of 1908, was a camera that was quite popular with cinematographers. It combined precise

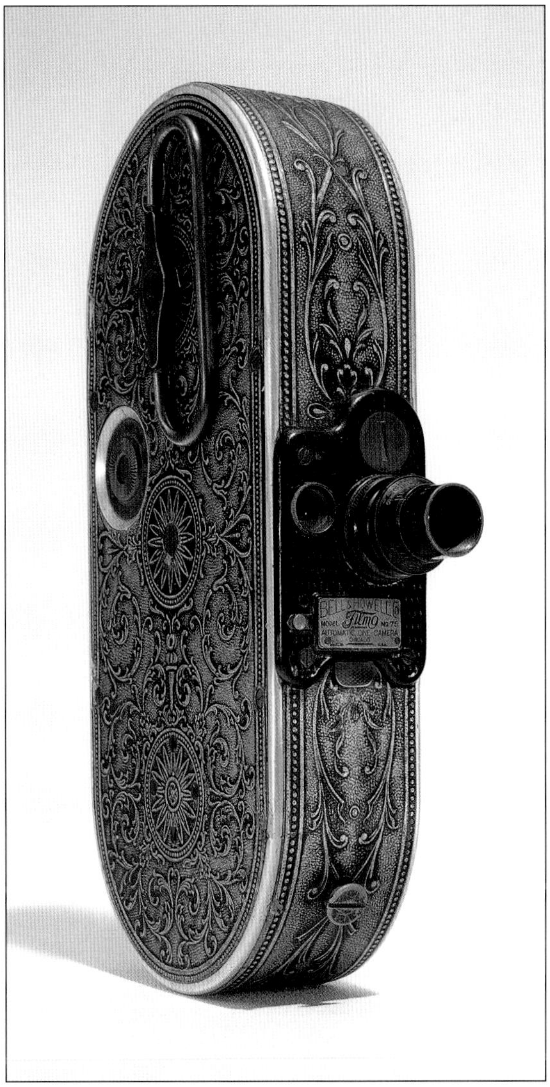

Filmo 75, Bell & Howell, ca. 1928, for hundred-foot spools of 16 mm cine film, spring-wound, lens interchangeable, choice of colors.

machining with a unique film-transport mechanism. The Moy Aerial Camera, of 1912, was designed for filming from balloons. It had an internal gyro-stabilizer, and claimed to be the first electrically-driven movie camera.

From around 1910 on, the most notable motion-picture cameras were those that either introduced some significant feature or that, because of their general utility, were very popular. Among these landmark cameras was the Pathé camera, which was the most universally used motion-picture camera—except in America—prior to World War I. Its mechanism was an improvement on that used by the Lumières' Cinématographe. Pathé had assumed the camera manufacturing business of the Lumières when they abandoned that segment of their operations. The Bell & Howell camera was, up until the 1920s, considered the most outstanding movie camera

FOCUS: *The Spirograph*

In the early part of the last century, two enterprising individuals, Charles Urban and Henry W. Joy, decided to improve on the system of viewing and projecting motion pictures that, at the time, had been in existence for only a few short years. Charles Urban, already well-known in the then infant motion-picture industry for his Bioscope projector, registered the trademark "Spirograph" in England on August 7, 1909, two and a half years before he obtained the American registration, on March 26, 1912. The mark was probably coined to emphasize the spiralling manner in which the images were positioned on the disc the projector used. The Spirograph appeared on the American market before World War I, and was manufactured in "Spiro Park" in Irvington-on-Hudson, a small town slightly north of New York City. The product itself has received minimal attention in the texts on the history of motion-picture apparatus.

Virtually everything else known about the Spirograph and its history and operation is owed to its instruction book—quite an ambitious project in itself—as well as to an examination of the very few examples of the Spirograph which are known to exist. Inspired by a model of an early toy, and despite discouragement from many whom they consulted, Urban and Joy, if their claim is to be believed, worked on the Spirograph project for almost fourteen years before introducing the device to the public. Citing the obvious disadvantages of "ribbon" film, the developers had great confidence in their product. The "film" to be projected was on a safety film base and could never become a "tangled mess of highly inflammable celluloid." There was no rewinding. Moreover, a Spirograph disc would cost only one cent per foot, as compared with eight cents for conventional film. While "ribbon" films could withstand perhaps four hundred projections, the disc could easily take fifteen hundred. Since "still" projection was no problem, the titles on a Spirograph disc did not have to waste the equivalent of a foot of film.

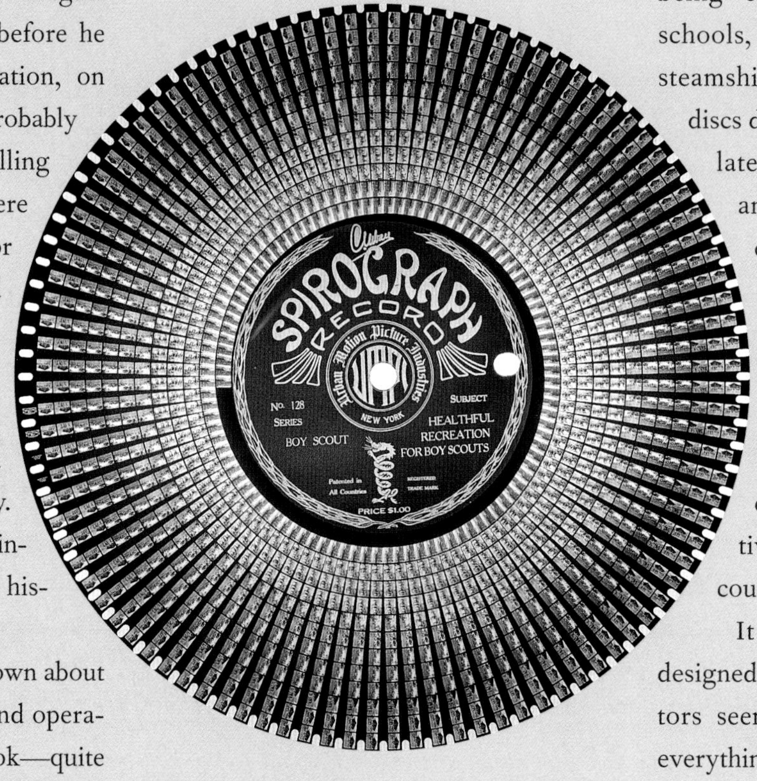

The well-written and well-illustrated manual correctly pointed out that even a young child could operate a Spirograph, that the machine could be stopped at will and started at will, reversed or set forward. Each of the 1,200 images on the disc could be viewed separately, allowing separate study of interesting or important exposures.

The Spirograph disc was 26.5 cm in diameter. The individual images were reduced to five percent of the area of standard 35 mm motion-picture film. The discs were produced from a master negative that, in turn, was obtained by reduction from an ordinary 35 mm motion-picture film. A variety of electric light sources were available for projection; for viewing, daylight was adequate. The instructions covered the proper way of projecting images of 42 inches at 25 feet from the Spirograph, and they even mentioned the possibility of rear projection.

The manufacturers had high hopes for the Spirograph. They envisaged it as being carried by salesmen, used in schools, employed by railways and steamship companies—with Spirograph discs depicting places to visit, to stimulate the resources of their countries and encourage investment. They even promised to add to the Spirograph a simple automatic switchback or repeating device for continuous projection, and to produce an inexpensive moving-picture camera for making ordinary motion-picture negatives, from which Spirograph discs could then be produced as desired.

It is not known why this well-designed, ingenious device, whose inventors seem to have literally thought of everything to make it as versatile and close to perfection as possible, did not catch on. It could have been a lack of reliability, but too few Spirographs have survived to judge this possibility. More likely, as so often in the history of brilliant designs, its total lack of conventionality may have been the Spirograph's undoing. By the time the Spirograph was introduced, the 35 mm motion-picture format and system had already taken a firm hold.

Spirograph disc, C. Urban and H. Joy, ca. 1913, twelve-hundred images per disc, produced from a master negative reduced from standard 35 mm cine film.

Right: Spirograph, C. Urban and H. Joy, ca. 1913, for projection from Spirograph discs, hand crank, electric lamp.

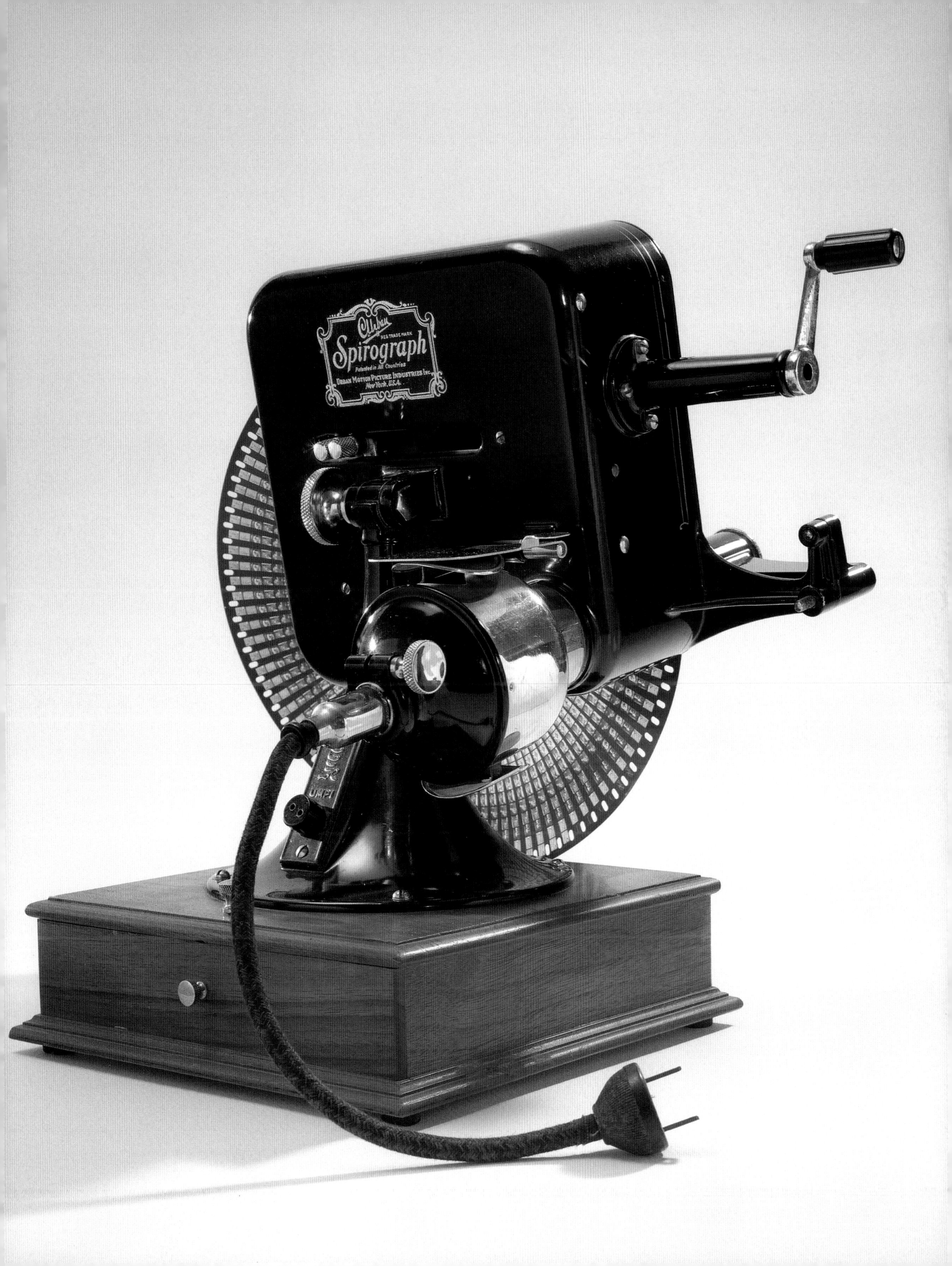
REG. TRADE MARK
Spirograph
Patented in All Countries
URBAN MOTION PICTURE INDUSTRIES Inc.
New York, U.S.A.
UMPI

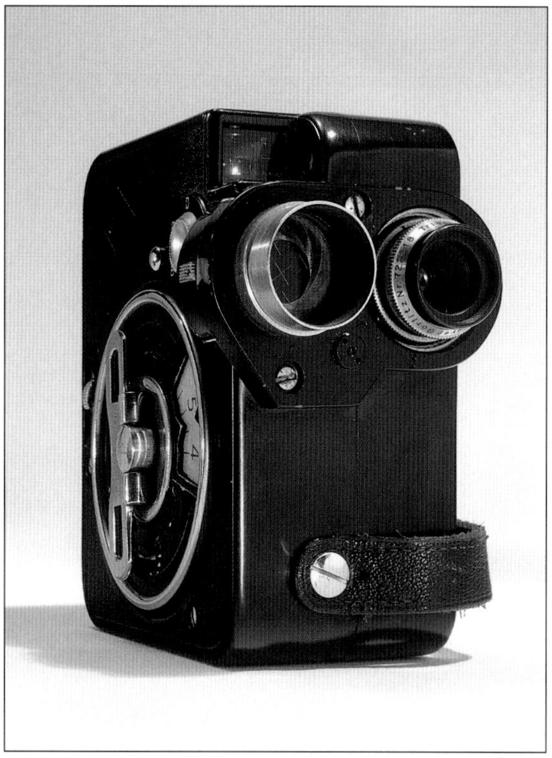

Eumig C39, Eumig, ca. 1939, for 9.5 mm cine film, three speeds, coupled exposure meter.

in the world. Introduced in 1912, it really caught on about 1914–1915, as its high-precision standards and four-lens rotating turret gained in popularity. The Mitchell motion-picture camera, introduced in 1921, also had a multi-lens turret. Dubbed "a Wonder of Efficiency" in the October 1921 issue of *American Cinematographer*, among movie studios it quickly became the standard throughout the world, and remained so until at least the early 1970s. The Éclair 120, of 1932, had a turret that held a total of six lenses, of six different focal lengths.

It was the goal of moviemakers to combine sound with their motion pictures. Over the years a variety of approaches to this coupling have been taken—some with more success than others. The short movies produced in the beginning of the twentieth century were rarely shown without sound. This sound was usually a musical accompaniment from a pianist or an orchestra, sometimes with added sound effects.

One of the first attempts at sound with movies was Edison's Kinetophone, which he invented to provide accompanying music for his Kinetoscope. While looking through the eyepiece of the viewer, the user listened to sound through a pair of rubber ear tubes. In 1900 a mechanical linkage was used to connect a gramophone to a projector, in order to maintain synchronization. The problem was that the projector was the motive force for the sound reproducer and variations in the projector's speed caused unacceptable variations in the sound. In 1908 Captain Couade, Frenchman, devised a system in which an actor sang for a phonograph recording. Following this, the phonograph was mechanically connected to an external electric drive for a camera. The actor then mouthed the singing while the phonograph played and the camera ran. When shown, the phonograph's mechanical propulsion was linked to an electric device that sent current to the projector's motor.

Joseph Poliakoff, a resident of Moscow, is credited with being the first to explain, in 1900, the principle of optically-recorded sound, using selenium cells. Eugene Lauste, who was part of the team that worked on Edison's Kinetoscope, is credited by some as the inventor to whom today's movie-film sound owes a great debt. His sound camera of 1906 had a roll of film, a portion of whose emulsion passed a slit whose width was controlled by an electromagnet. A microphone provided the changes in the current from a battery that was sent to the slit. In 1911, Augustus Rosenberg was granted a patent for recording sound on two separate channels on the camera's film, from two separate microphones. This anticipated the development of stereo sound for motion pictures. In the early 1920s, the Bell Laboratories and Western Electric developed a sound reproduction technique that relied on optics and in 1927, the first sound movie, *The Jazz Singer*, used this technique.

In the field of amateur cinematography, a bifurcation occurred in the early 1900s, with the creation of motion-picture cameras and projectors intended more for the use of amateurs. Among the earliest of these were Ernemann's Kino I (1902) and Kino II (1904). These used 17.5 mm film, a size that could be obtained by slitting 35 mm film in half lengthwise. The Pathé-Baby camera, which was hand cranked, was introduced in 1922 and used 9.5 mm film. This camera and the companion Pathé-

Baby projector helped establish that film width in Europe and the British Empire. Almost all of the film's width was devoted to the image area. The film was a reversal type that the user could process. Later on clockwork motor drives were introduced on both the cameras and the projectors.

In the summer of 1920, the first experimental version of a hand-cranked motion-picture camera that used 16 mm film was produced at Eastman Kodak. Introduced in 1923 as the Cine-Kodak, the camera's release was accompanied by the introduction of the companion Kodascope projector. As with the 9.5 mm Pathé-Baby, when a new film size of movie camera was introduced, it was necessary to produce a companion projector to show the films. Also in 1923, Bell & Howell introduced the first of their 16 mm Filmo amateur movie cameras, a line that lasted until 1979. The Filmo 70-A of 1923 is believed to be the first 16 mm movie camera with a spring-driven motor. The Filmo 70-C, introduced in 1927, was the first 16 mm movie camera to feature a three-lens turret. The Filmo 75 movie camera of 1928 was ornately decorated and was available in three different "rich" colors.

In July 1932 Kodak introduced the Cine-Kodak Eight, Model 20 amateur movie camera. It was the first of a line of Kodak 8 mm movie cameras. Of course a Kodascope Eight projector was introduced at the same time. In 1936 Kodak introduced the Magazine Cine-Kodak, whose 16 mm film was housed in a magazine. The 8 mm equivalent, the Magazine Cine-Kodak Eight, Model 90, was introduced in 1940. In May 1965 Kodak introduced the Super 8 movie film format with the Kodak Instamatic M2. It provided a larger image area on the 8 mm film.

While the Eumig C3 movie camera of 1938—some sources say 1933—was the first 8 mm movie camera to have a photo cell coupled to the lens diaphragm, it was "semi-automatic," that is, the photo cell moved a needle on the diaphragm control. Moving the needle to line it up with a given reference point set the diaphragm. The first fully automatic "electric-eye" 16 mm movie camera was the magazine-loaded Bell & Howell 200EE, introduced in April 1956. The Bell & Howell 290A, which used spool-loaded film, was the first 8 mm fully automatic electric-eye movie camera. It was introduced in July 1957.

A novel piece of apparatus was the Wittnauer Cine-Twin, of 1957. It was spool loaded with 8 mm film. It had an electric-eye exposure meter and its turret held four lenses. After it was used to take the pictures and after the processed pictures were returned, by mounting the camera on a motorized base the camera could be converted to a projector. One of the last—and most novel—innovations in amateur motion-picture cameras and projectors was the Polavision Land system. It used Phototape, a self-developing film, and a player for the developed film cassette. It produced finished color pictures "in minutes." It was a commercial failure.

Wittnauer Cine-Twin, Wittnauer Camera Co., ca. 1957, for spools of 8 mm cine film, battery-powered, converts to projector when mounted on motorized base.

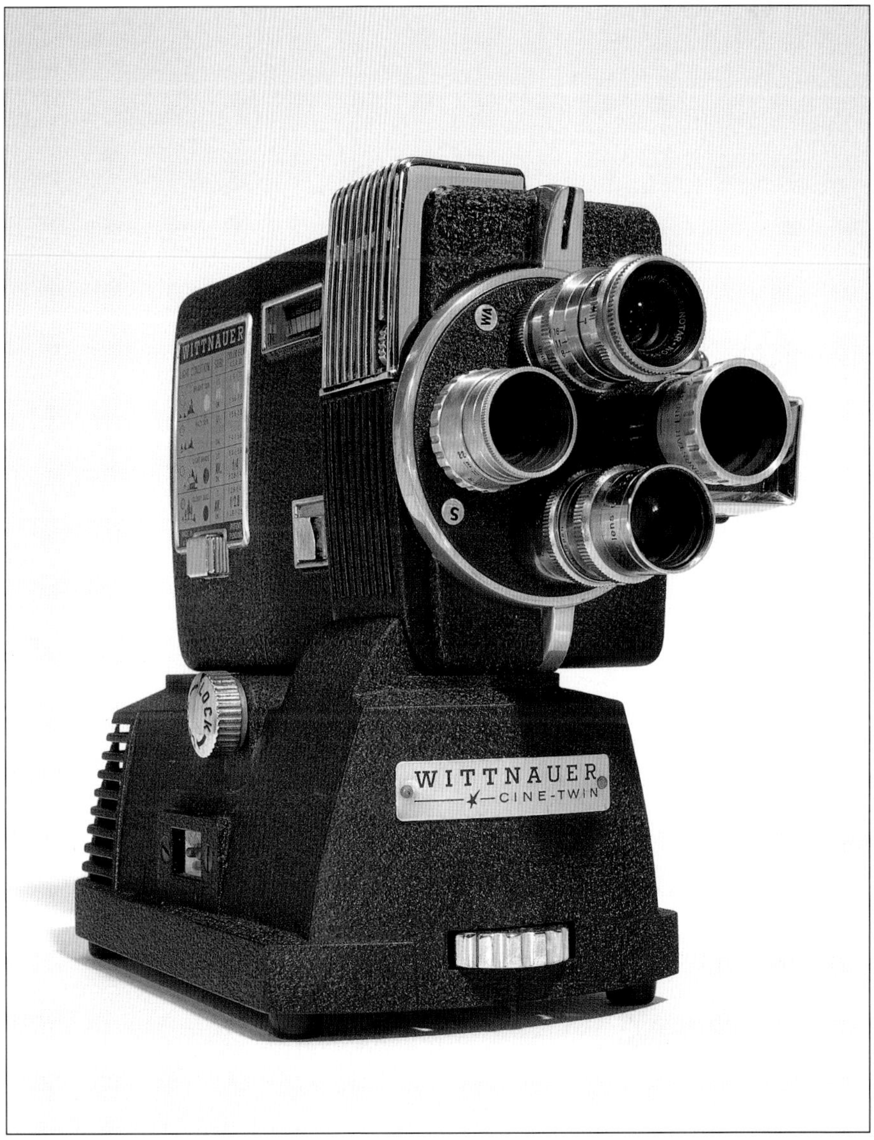

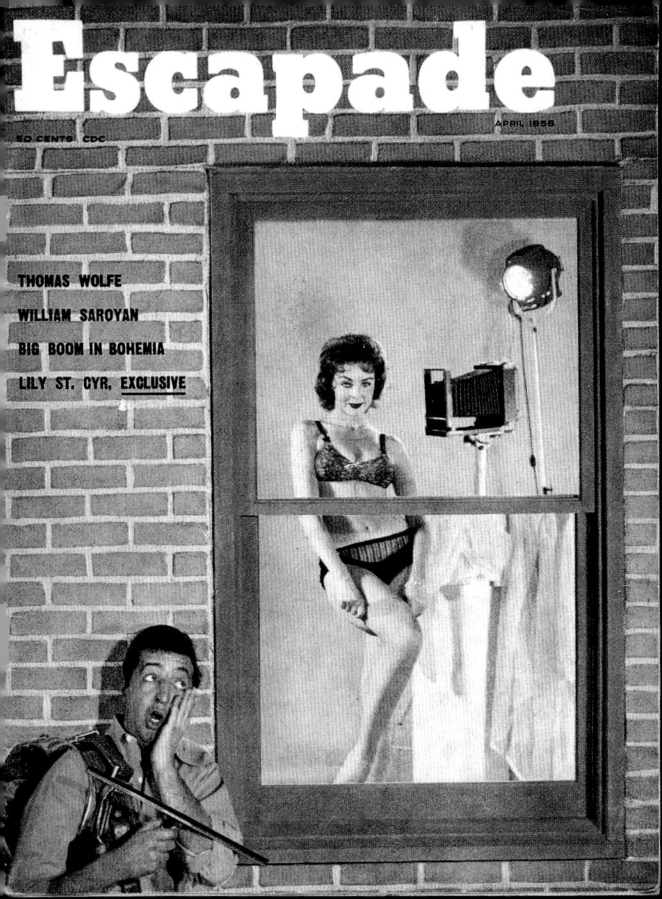
Escapade
50 CENTS
APRIL 1958
THOMAS WOLFE
WILLIAM SAROYAN
BIG BOOM IN BOHEMIA
LILY ST. CYR, EXCLUSIVE

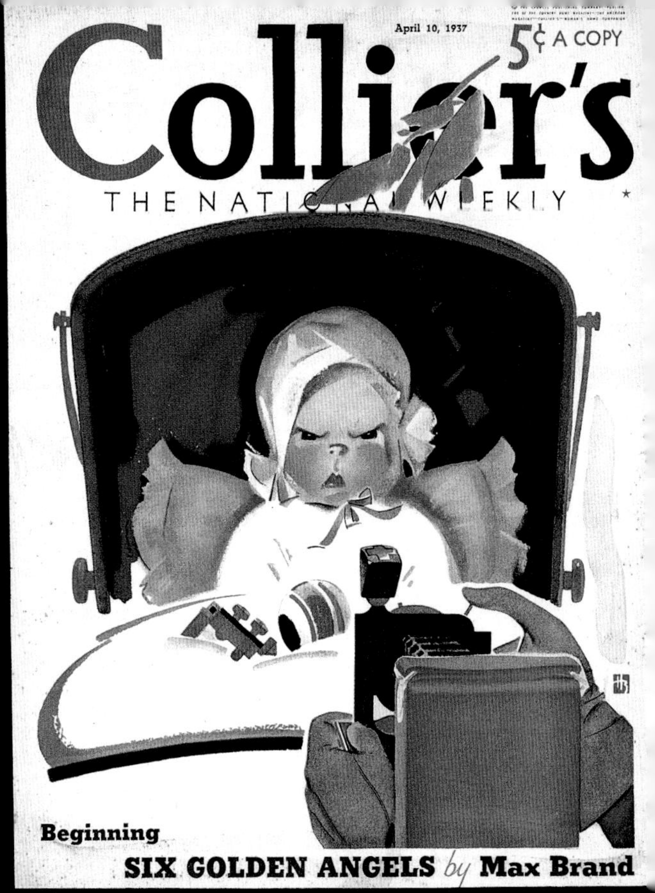
April 10, 1937
5¢ A COPY
Collier's
Beginning
SIX GOLDEN ANGELS by Max Brand

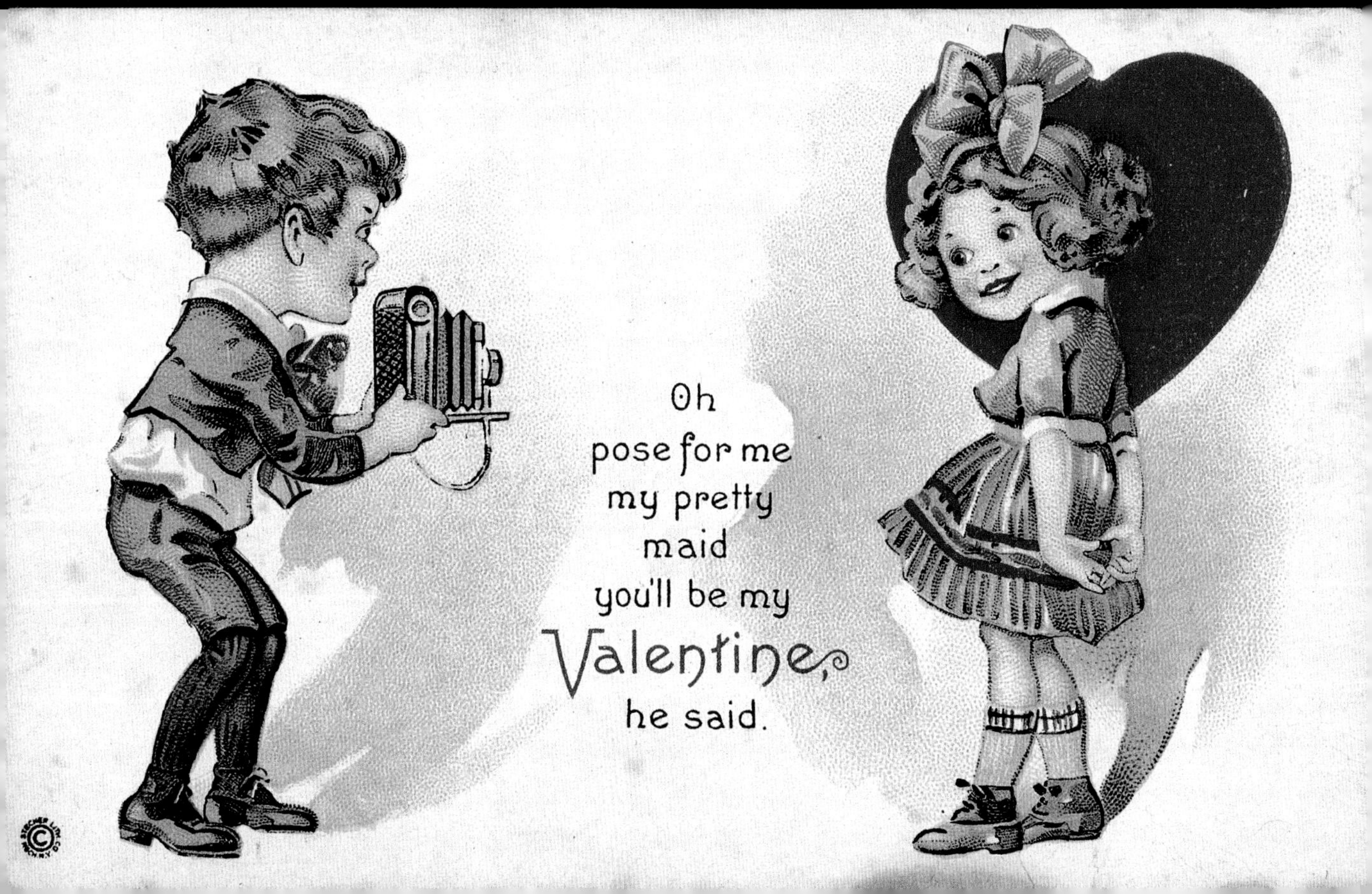
Oh
pose for me
my pretty
maid
you'll be my
Valentine,
he said.

CHAPTER TWELVE:

PHOTOGRAPHY AND HUMOR

Clockwise from top left: Anonymous, cover of *Escapade*, April 1958; Anonymous, cover of *Collier's, The National Weekly*, April 10, 1937, 10" x 13; Valentine postcard, ca. 1909, 3 1/2" x 5 1/2".

Since its beginnings, the function of cartoons and caricature has been to exaggerate and give an opinion on a range of political and social issues, to evaluate and judge, pointing its witty, humorous, and often sharp gaze at the soft underbelly of the times. So it is not surprising that during its boom, photography—and the whole new image of society and set of social interactions it was creating—became a target of caricature.

The first well-known cartoon directed at photography was "Le Daguerreotypomanie," a broadside by Théodore Maurisset, drawn in 1839. This cartoon depicts an urban locale overtaken with a mania for the daguerreotype. Virtually no area of the city is left untouched by this fever for the daguerreotype—the street is thronged with people waiting to have their portrait taken, and the sky is crowded with hot-air balloons containing practitioners of the art in search of a different vantage point for documentation. While this drawing deals in hyperbole, it is surely an accurate portrayal of the way in which artists and intellectuals envisioned the nascent medium irrevocably altering the landscape of the image. The degree to which many became instantly consumed with the daguerreotype was mocked by Maurisset. He also acknowledged the anxiety that accompanied this craze. In his cartoon, engravers lined themselves up in front of a gallows, waiting their turn to execute themselves in the face of this new trend which they predicted would rob them of their livelihood. Perhaps this was a fear that Maurisset himself felt.

Cartoons similar to the one described above were printed in journals or broadsheets devoted to the satirization of the bourgeois class, swelling as a result of the industrial revolution. These journals, which were often issued weekly, were more cheaply produced and less bound by convention than were established newspapers. Among these were the British *Punch*, also known as the *London Charivari*, the American *Puck*, and the French *Le Rire* and *Le Charivari*. These rogue publications often targeted photography's vain and opportunistic face. Caricaturists such as the Reverend Edward Bradley, who used the pseudonym Cuthbert Bede, noted that the whole world surrounding this sudden photographical boom was layered with shallow opulence: the grandiose studios, the ostentatious props and fancy clothes bought only for the occasion—all of this had a considerable impact on public life, and was seen by many as a frenzy of self-conceit and false prestige. Photography gave the middle class access to the portrait, long the provenance of the wealthy. While the upper classes shunned photography as vulgar and cheap, those who saw its revolutionary potential were angered at its trivial applications. For what promised to be an accurate reflector of reality was being used to simulate a fictitious, uniform appearance of wealth among the middle and working classes

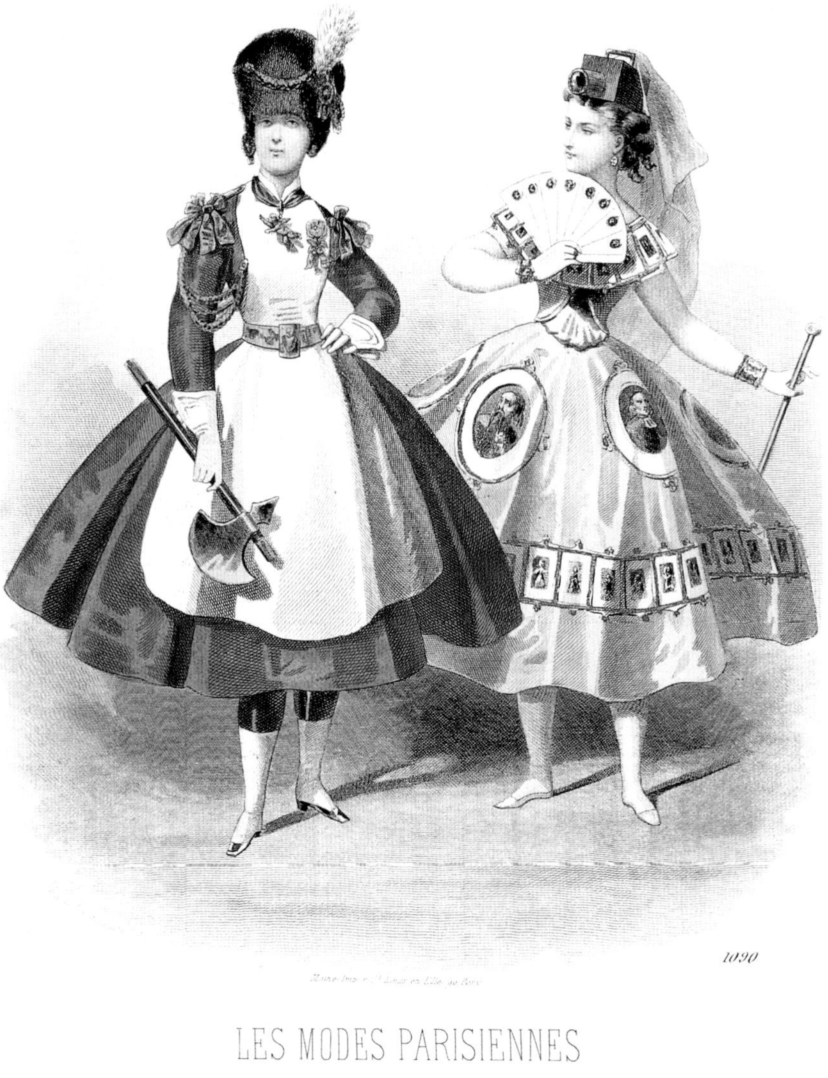

Anonymous, "Les Modes Parisiennes (Paris Fashions)," ca. 1865, a commentary on the popularity of the carte de visite in 1860s Paris.

Opposite: F. Opper, "The Peeping Toms of the Camera," 1891, cover of *Puck*, July 15, 1891. A commentary on the detective-camera craze.

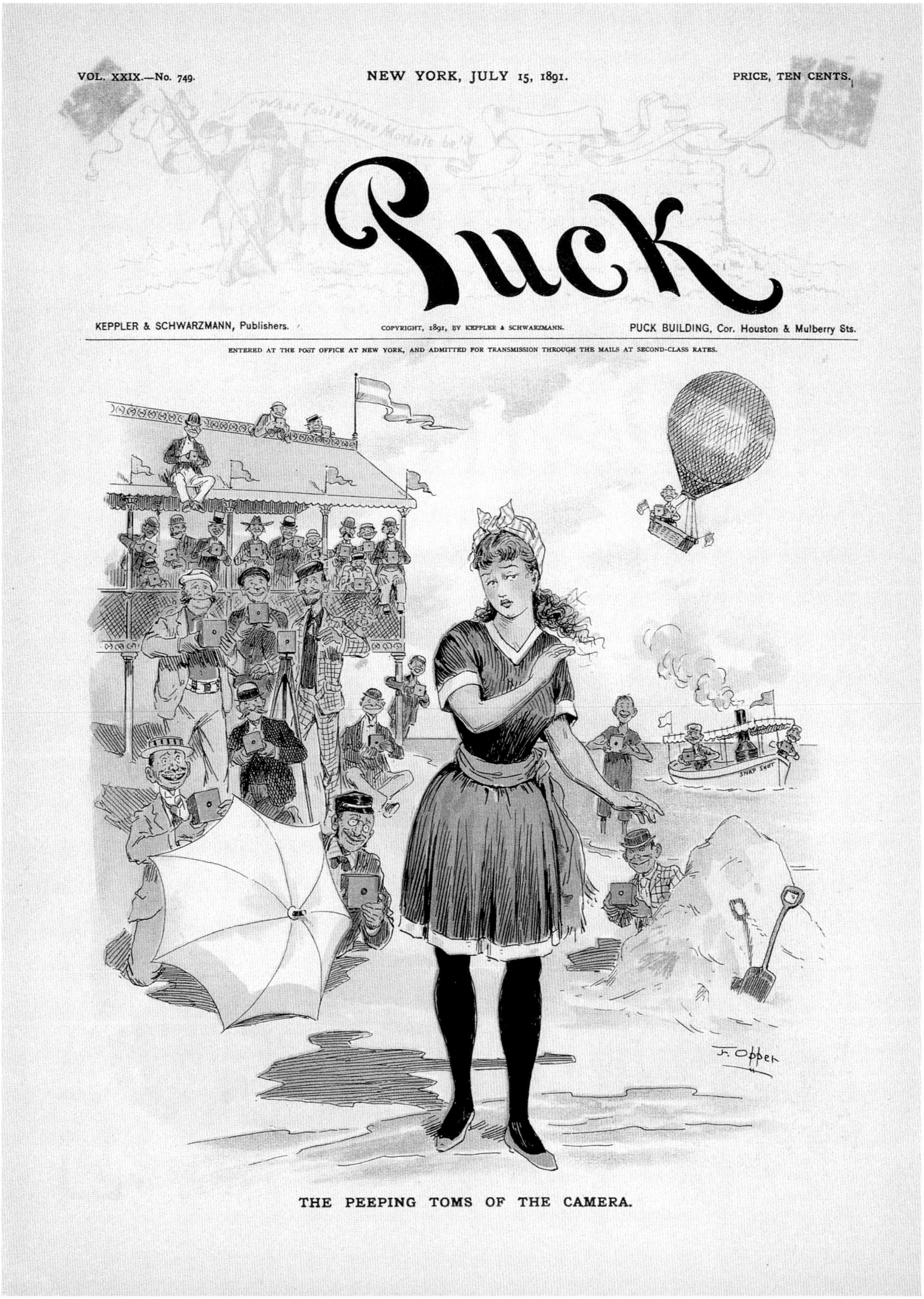

THE PEEPING TOMS OF THE CAMERA.

PROFILE: *The First "Instant" Picture*

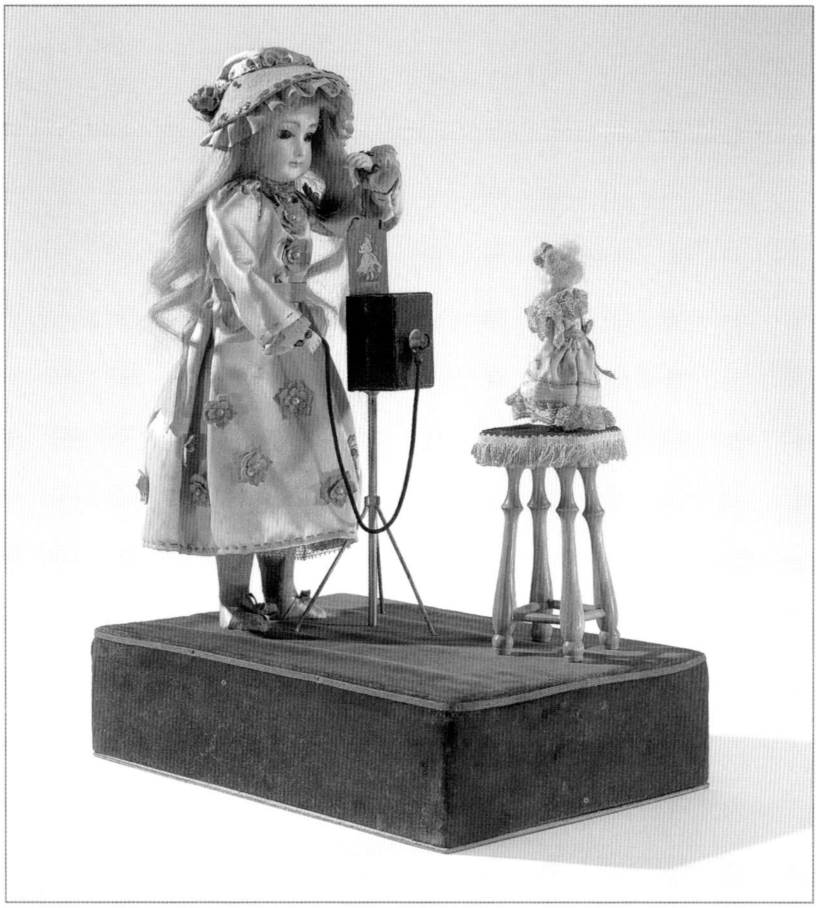

Musical automaton, Renou, France, ca. 1890.

Automatons—self-moving machines that imitate the actions of people or animals—were a popular form of amusement in the nineteenth century. They ranged from singing birds in cages to human figures that performed various, intricate actions. The actions of automatons were often accompanied by music. Coin-operated automatons were common in public places. Others—often more delicate in their construction and/or operation—were sold to the affluent.

One musical automaton with a photographic theme dates from the late 1800s. In it, a young girl, standing on a wooden base, is depicted taking a photograph of a doll standing on a stool. The girl is positioned behind a tripod-mounted camera and holds the shutter's bulb release in her right hand. In her left hand is an unexposed photographic plate. When the automaton is activated, the girl first raises the unexposed plate and then lowers it into the camera. Following that, she moves her right hand, as if counting the length of the exposure. Finally, she raises the finished plate, which now exhibits an image of the doll. All of these actions are accompanied by music. The automaton measures 15 ½ inches in height.

Regardless of one's personal view on the matter, photography's impact on society was indisputable, especially when measuring by the number of illustrations and broadsides devoted to its caricature. Besides focusing on the widespread self-awareness and vanity that accompanied the daguerreotype, cartoonists also played upon the humor inherent in social situations arising from the act of photographing. With photography came an unbridled voyeurism. Whereas before it would have been improper to not avert one's eyes from certain things, photography granted a license to look with impunity. As often noted by the caricaturist, this new freedom played out to its full advantage on the beach or around a woman in a swimsuit.

Photographers themselves were not unaware of the excessive aspects of their medium, and did not hesitate to point their lenses at photography in the same way as the caricaturist. Studio photographers made photographs of posed situations, often for the production of stereo images. Themes addressed in these absurdist photographs include the urge of photographers to document everything, including the mundane and trivial, as though it were of the utmost importance, and various situations hinging upon what "naughty" acts

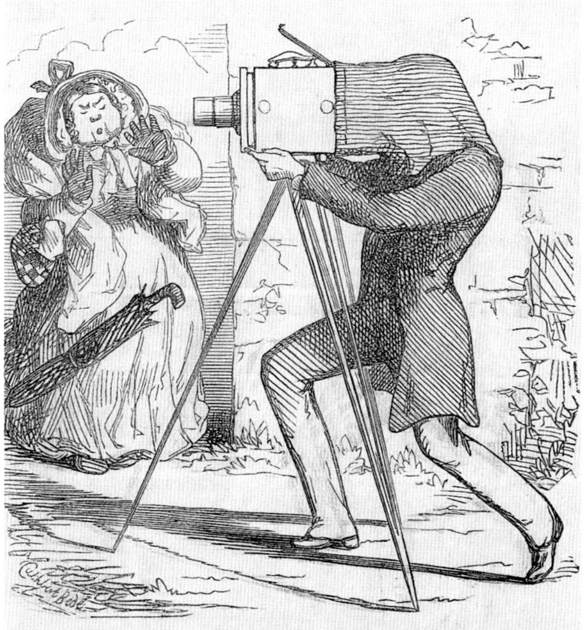

A PHOTOGRAPHIC PICTURE.

Old Lady (who is not used to these new-fangled notions). *"Oh, Sir! Please, Sir! don't, Sir! Don't for goodness' sake Fire, Sir!"*

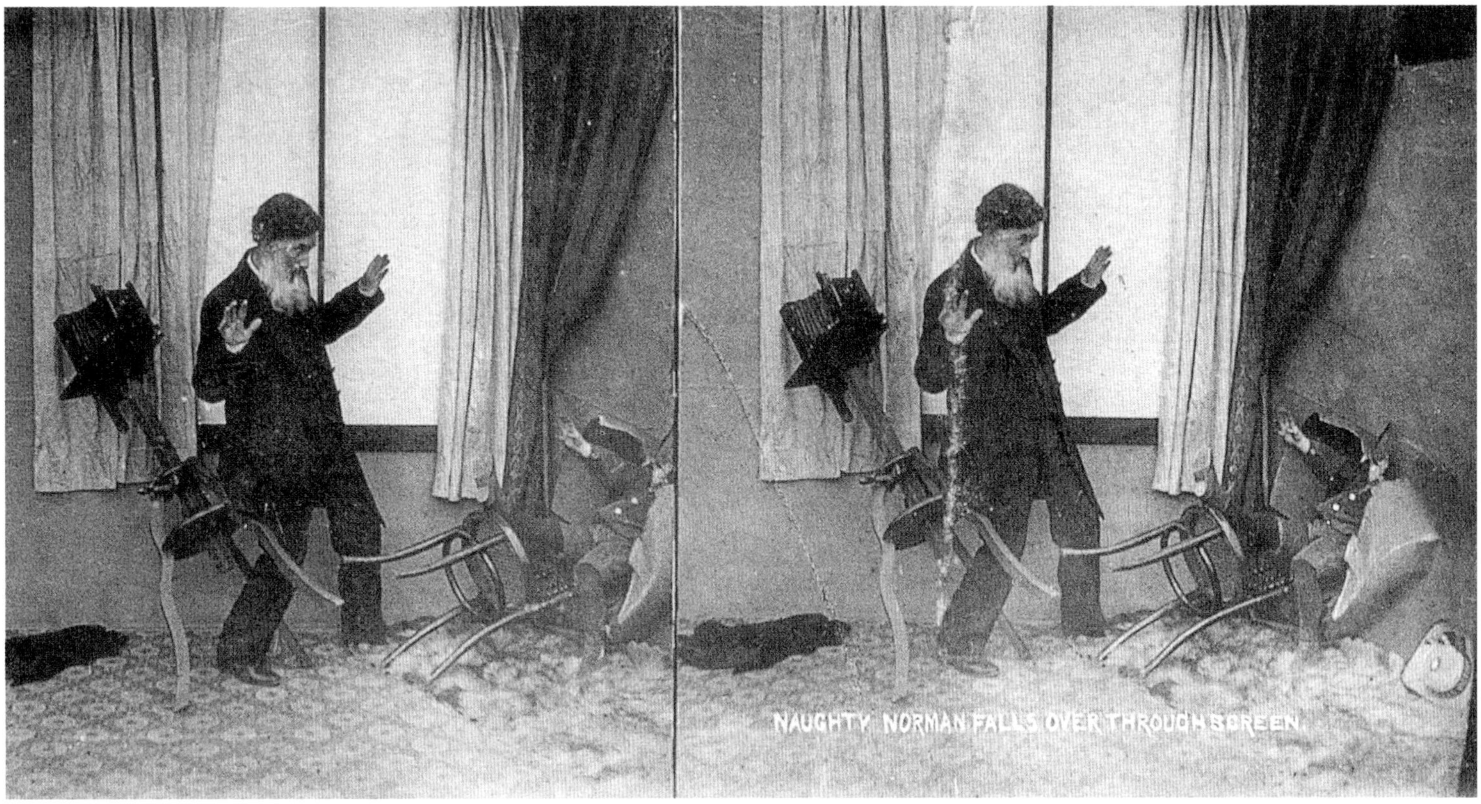

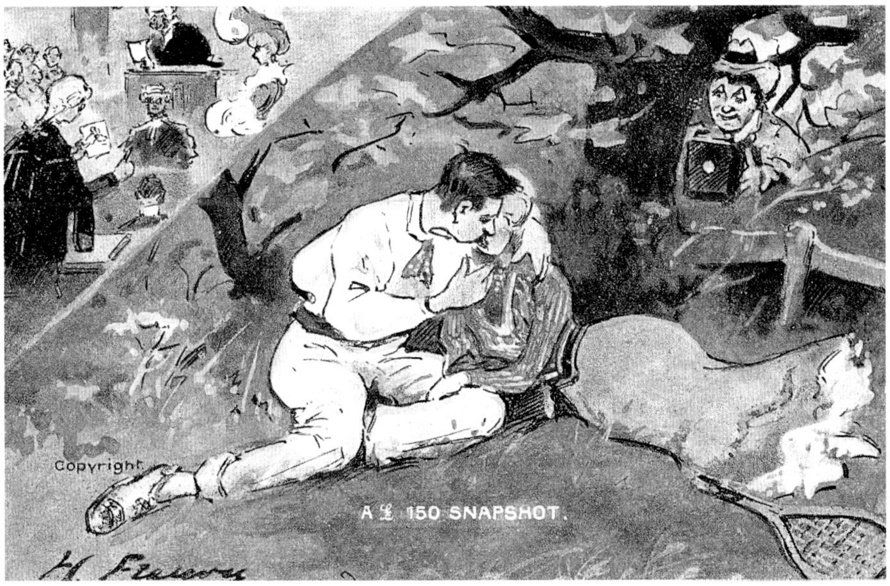

Opposite: Cuthbert Bede (Edward Bradley), "A Photographic Picture," 1853, from *Punch*, or the *London Charivari*, 1853.

Top: Anonymous, "The Photographer and the Unwilling Subject," Albermarle Series, ca. 1900, stereo pair of gelatino-bromide prints on 3 1/2" x 7" card mount.

Bottom: "A £150 snapshot," G. D. & D., Britain (printed in Germany), ca. 1910, postcard, 3 1/2" x 5 1/2". From "Star Series."

may take place in a studio while the photographer dips under his dark cloth, or the plight of the hapless amateur photographer. Often, comic stereo cards were issued in sets, such as the twelve-card Albermarle Series, in which a photographer encounters several hilarious obstacles in his attempt to photograph a rambunctious young boy.

Photography continued to serve as an outlet for self-reflexive humor and satire, especially as photographic technology, including the advent of rapid-film speeds and electronic flash, improved. No longer limited to the staging of humorous situations, street photographers could now capture fleeting moments of comedy. Photographers such as Garry Winogrand, Elliot Erwitt, and Robert Doisneau built their careers by producing street photographs that combined Henri Cartier-Bresson's ability to isolate the exact moment when a composition of disparate elements becomes a photograph with their own, often dark, senses of humor.

The development of wide-angle lenses made possible another brand of droll photography. Just as caricature functions through hyperbole, photography has the ability to distort and exaggerate. Whether it be an unflattering rendering of a subject's visage, or a manipulation of scale such as might make a small child appear to be stepping on a tall building, photography has the ability to present reality in a way that defies expectations, often with humorous results. This ability to manipulate, exaggerate, and distort has only multiplied with the onset of digital photography and digital imaging programs.

From top: Anonymous, "The Headless Man," English, ca. 1875, stereo pair of albumen prints, on 3 1/2" x 7" card mount.

Anonymous, "The Unobservant Stereo Viewer," ca. 1865, stereo pair of albumen prints, on 3 1/2" x 7" card mount.

Anonymous, "A Lover of Art," B. W. Kilburn, 1897, stereo pair of gelatino-bromide prints, on 3 1/2" x 7" card mount.

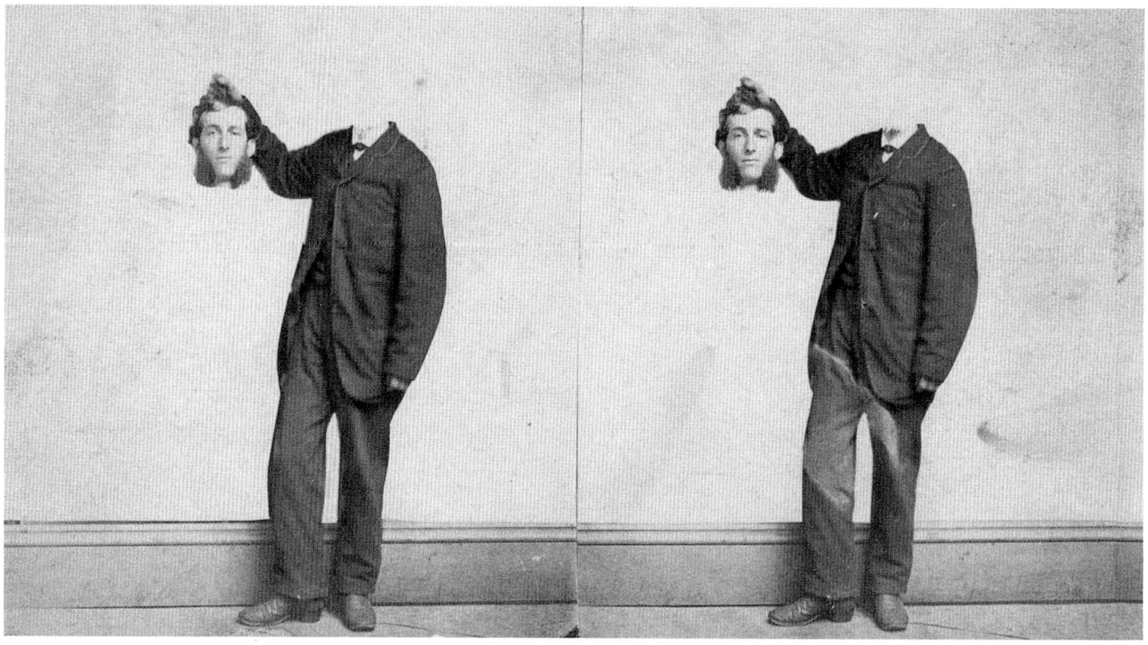

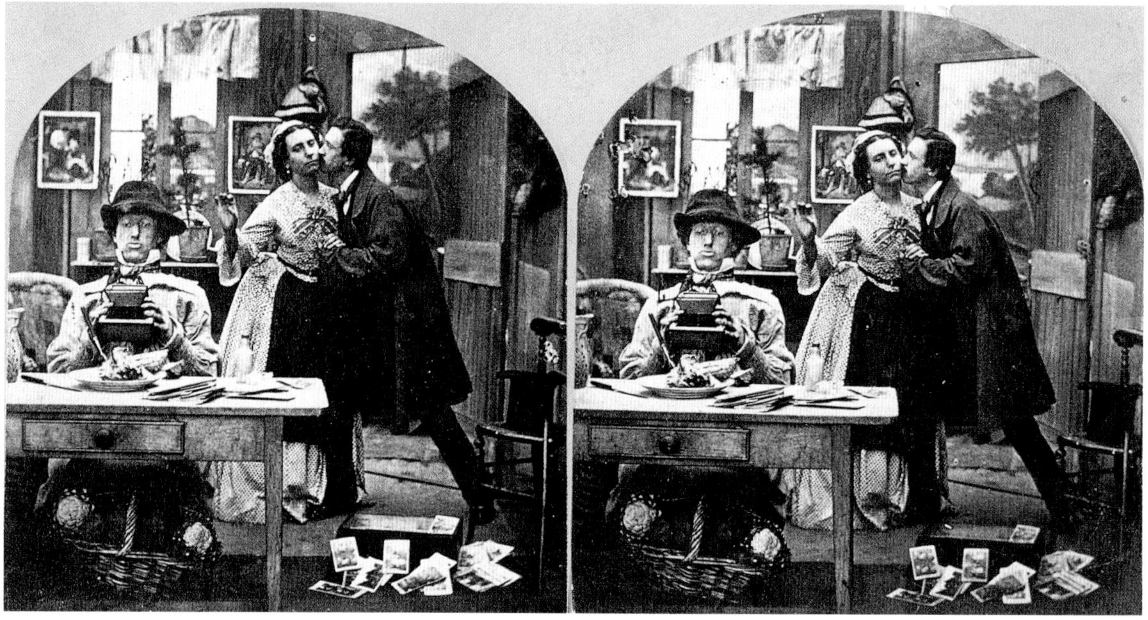

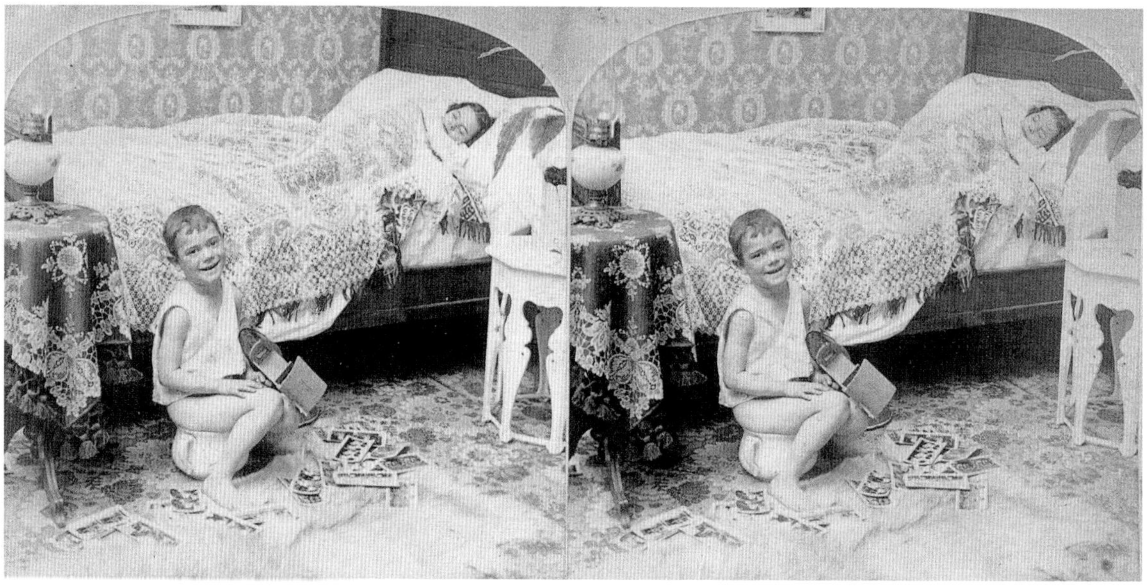

PROFILE: *The Stereo Photosphere*

In 1888 Napoleon Conti was granted a French patent for a camera of an unusual design. The camera, called the Photosphere, was manufactured by the Compagnie Française de la Photographie, Paris, France, and was introduced in 1890. The rear section of the camera was rectangular but the front portion, which housed the shutter, was hemispherical in shape. On the front of that section was a small cylindrical projection that held the lens. The camera could accommodate either double plate holders, for 8-by-9-cm dry plates, or a magazine back that contained twelve plates.

By 1895 the camera had become available in four different models, including a stereoscopic one that used 9-by-18-cm plates. The camera itself had a distinctive design. As the camera's basic pattern had been established prior to its production—with the single-lens version—the Stereo Photosphere was merely an extension of that earlier camera. In the design of the stereo model Conti must have had some awareness of the camera's suggestion of certain female physical attributes. Certainly the cartoonist who drew the cover of the August 31, 1895 issue of *Le Rire* saw that resemblance.

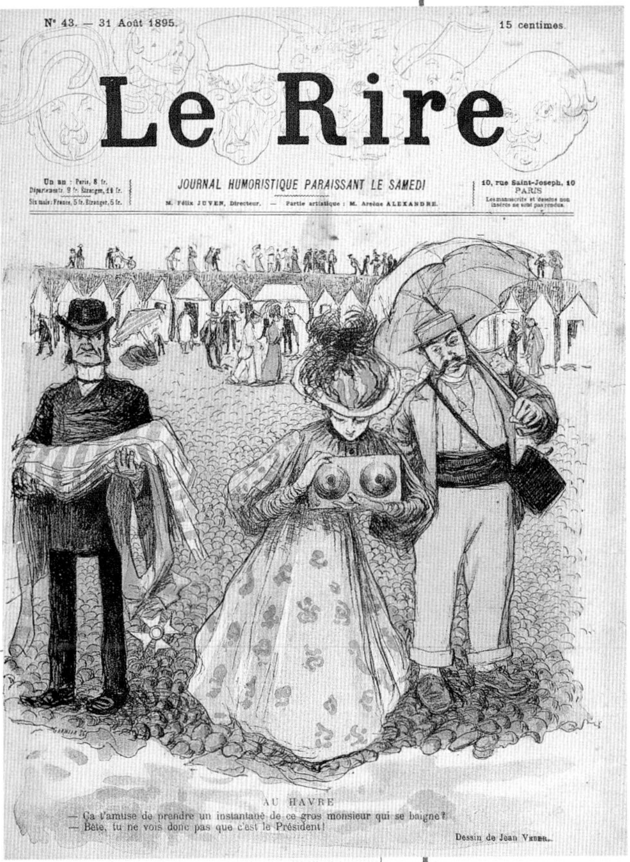

Garnier S. G., "At the Seaside (Harbor)," cover illustration from *Le Rire*, no. 43, August 31, 1895. Caption translates as: Man: "Are you enjoying taking a snapshot of the stout man who's swimming?" Woman: "Stupid, don't you see it's the President!"

Below: Stereo Photosphere, Compagnie Française de la Photographie, ca. 1895, blue-brass body, for paired exposures on 9 x 18 cm dry plates.

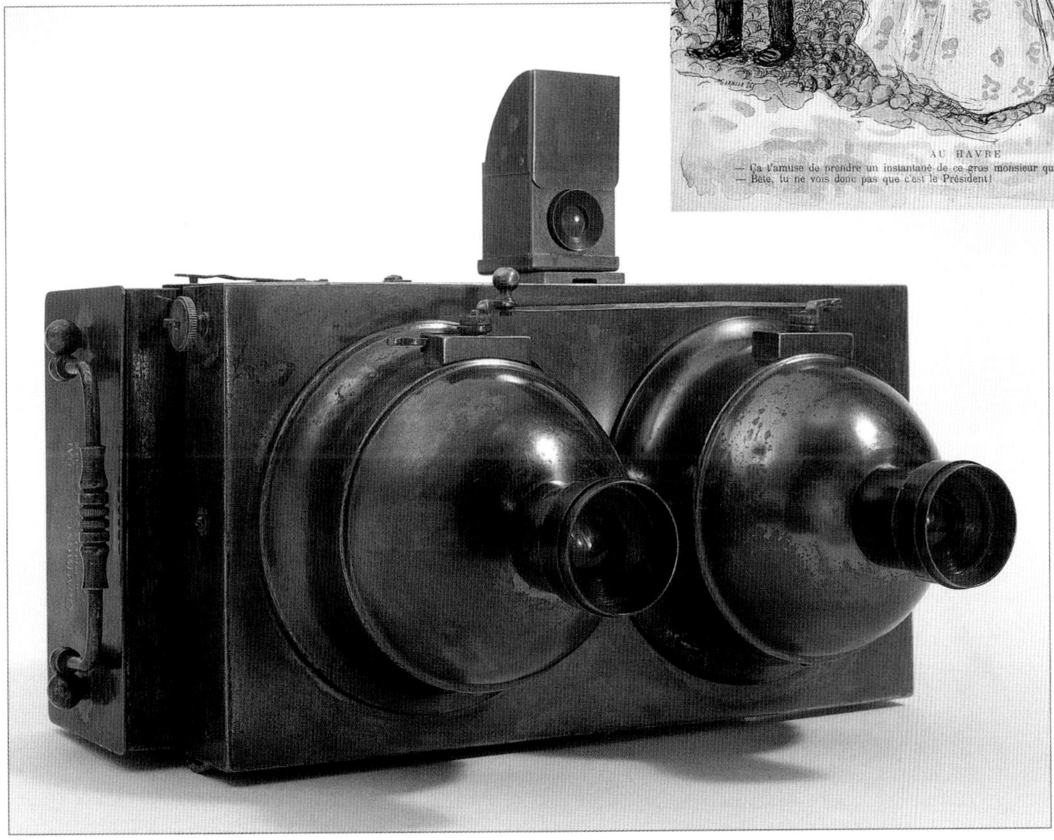

PROFILE: *Novelty Cameras*

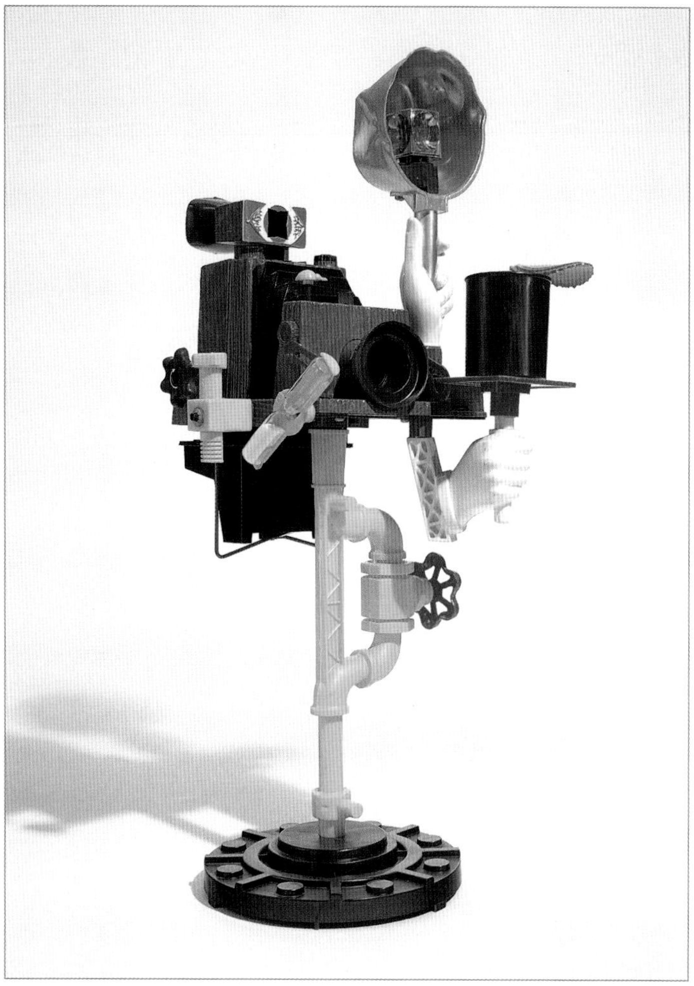

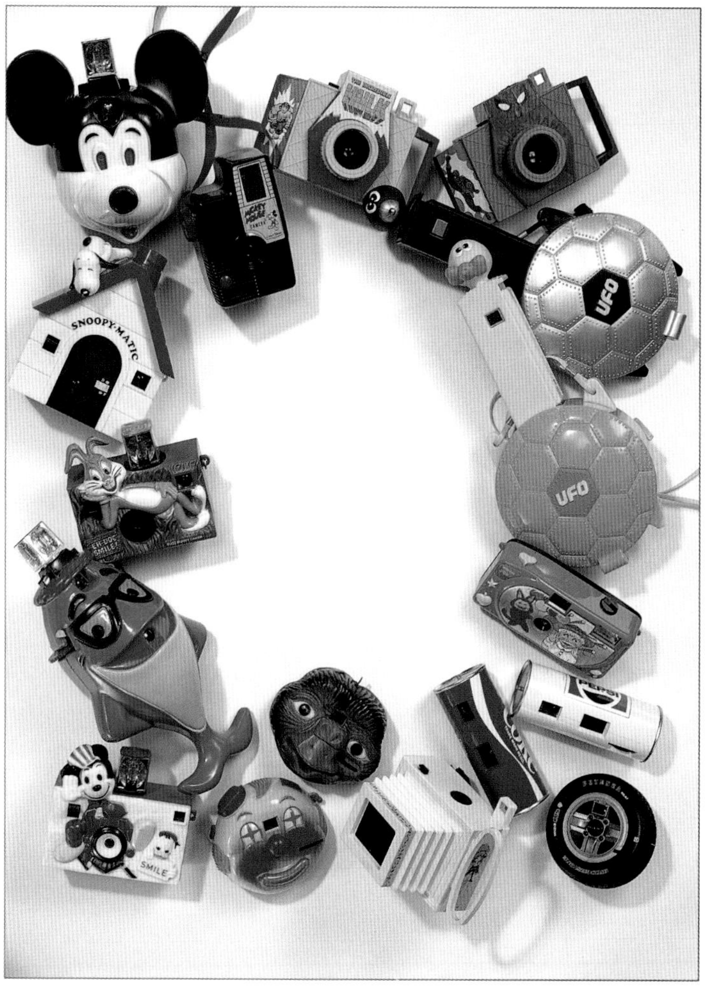

Left: Kookie Camera, Ideal Toy Co., 1968, for 1 $^{3}/_{4}$" x 1 $^{3}/_{4}$" prints on direct positive paper, "instant" developing, with accessory anamorphic lens.

Right: Novelty cameras. Notable examples include: top left, Mick-A-Matic, ca. 1971, for 126 roll film; top right, Amazing Spider Man, ca. 1979, for 126 roll film; lower right corner, Potenza Tire Camera, ca. 1981, for 110 roll film; Coke and Pepsi Can Cameras, ca. 1979, for 110 roll film; left, second from bottom, Charlie Tuna, for 126 roll film; left, second from top: Snoopy-Matic, 1976, for 126 roll film.

Since 1900 a number of cameras have been produced that were tied in with humor, either by their association with a cartoon or comic character, or by their actual appearance. Palmer Cox's Brownies, Mickey Mouse and Bugs Bunny, Charlie Tuna, and Snoopy have all had their likenesses incorporated into the design of a camera. Cameras have even been produced in such shapes as beverage cans, automobiles, automobile tires, cows, and a packet of McDonald's french fries. Even some of the one-time-use cameras available today use comic characters as their themes. The cameras sold at Disneyland and Disneyworld in America, France, and Japan are adorned with images of Mickey, Minnie, Goofy, Donald Duck, and Winnie the Pooh.

Perhaps the strangest of the novelty cameras was the Kookie Camera, manufactured in 1968 by the Ideal Toy Corporation. Measuring almost 21 inches high, including flash—it used Flash Cubes—the camera looked as though it had been designed by the cartoonist Rube Goldberg. Standing on a base, atop a "pipe-fitted" monopod, the pseudo-bellows plastic-bodied camera had a tank mounted below it that provided developing "in minutes." A roll of direct-positive sensitized paper was used in making 1 $^{3}/_{4}$-by-1 $^{3}/_{4}$-inch prints. A built-in film cutter was used to separate the exposures. The Campbell-colored can of "Toymato Soup," held in an extended hand, was actually an accessory anamorphic lens that produced special effects. The camera came complete with "many kookie disguises," to add to the absurdity of it all.

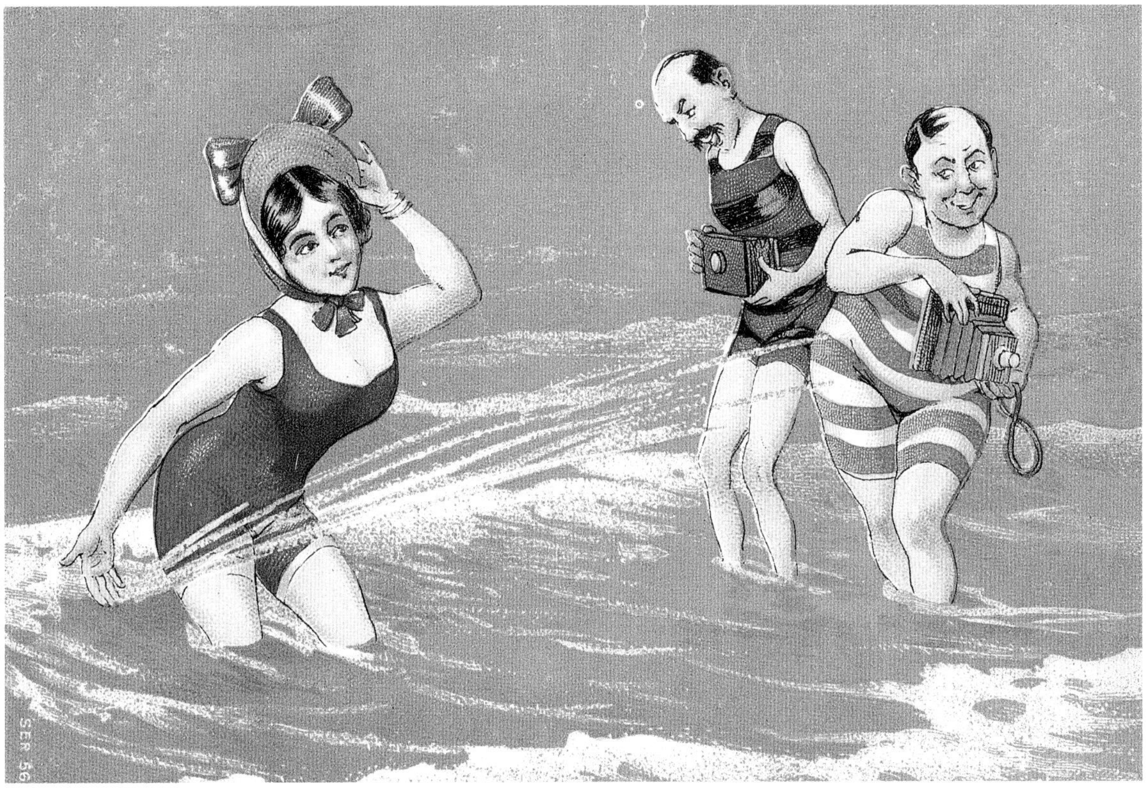

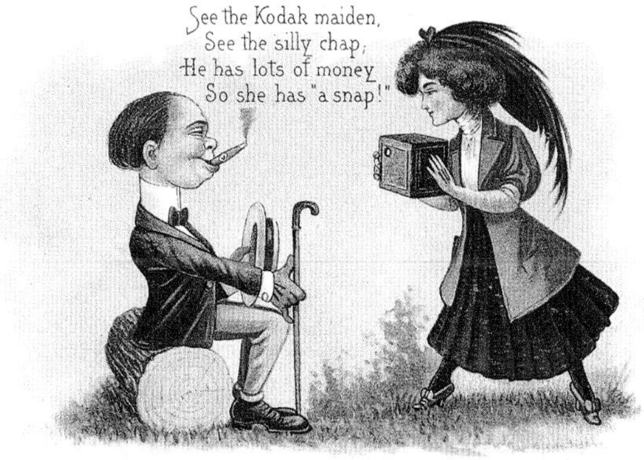

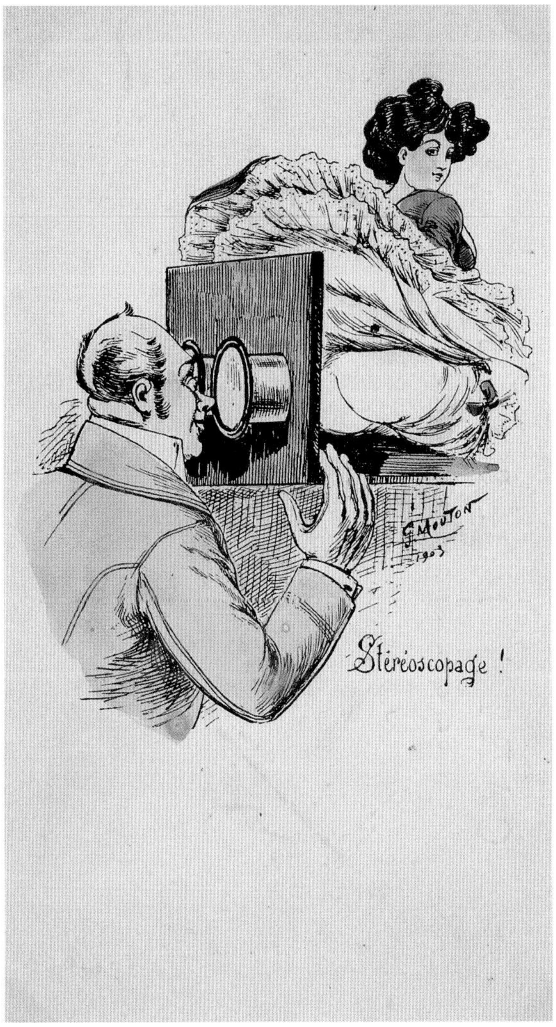

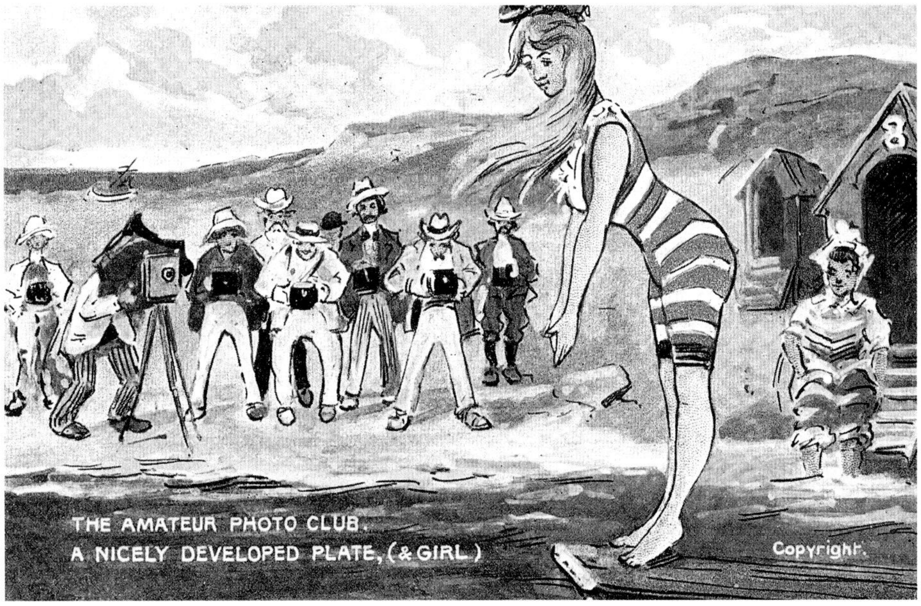

Clockwise from left: Anonymous, "Venturesome Photographers," (probably printed in Germany), ca. 1908, postcard, 3 1/2" x 5 1/2".

A. S. Meeker, "The Kodak Maiden," 1908, postcard, 3 1/2" x 5 1/2". From "Embossed Comics" series.

G. D. & D., "The amateur photo club—a nicely developed plate (& girl)," Britain (printed in Germany), ca. 1910, postcard, 3 1/2" x 5 1/2". From "Star Series."

G. Mouton, "Stéréoscopage," 1903.

CHAPTER THIRTEEN:

FILMLESS CAMERAS

Circuit board assembly of the DCS Pro digital camera, Xirlink, ca. 2000. For different view of camera, see page 213.

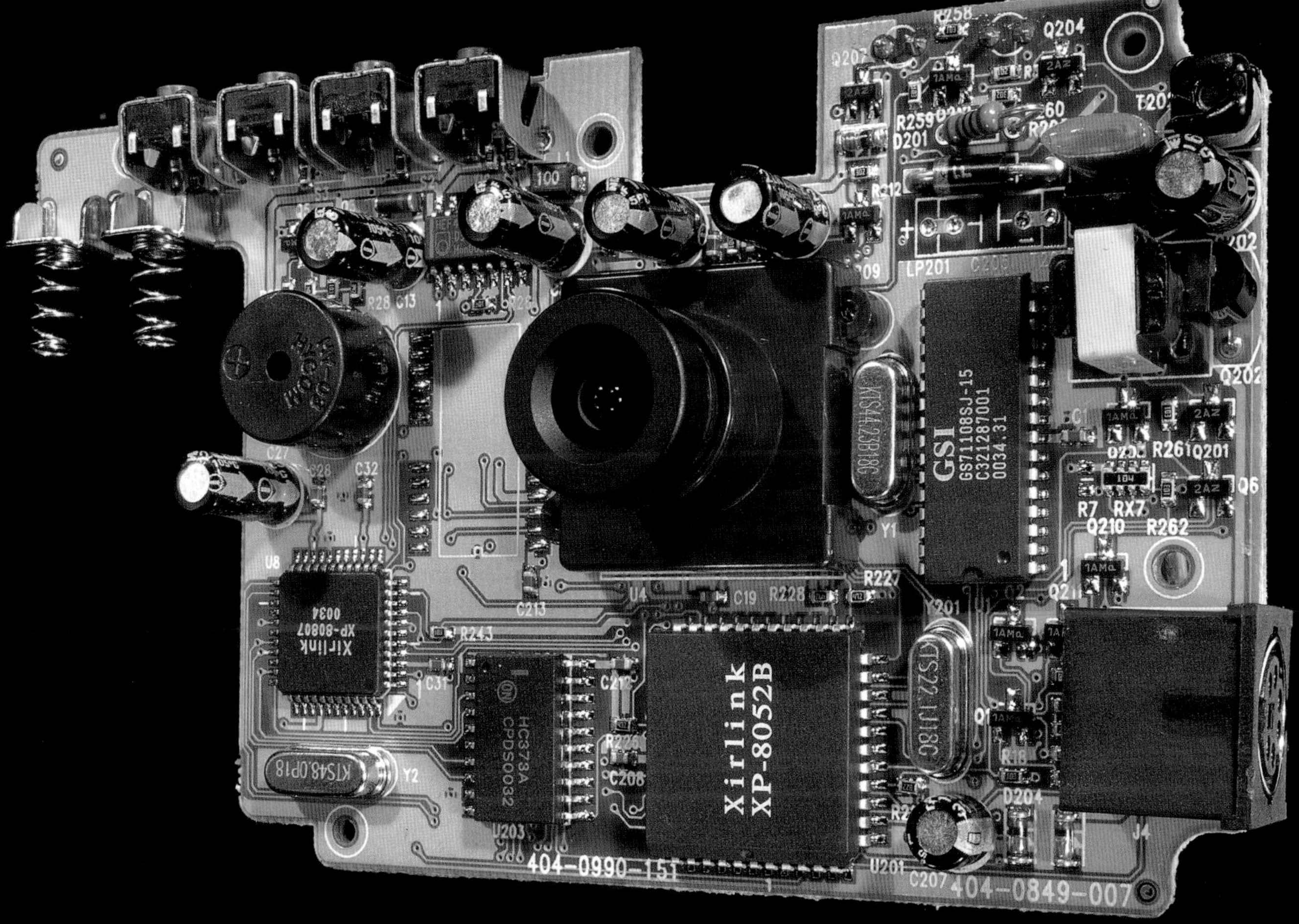
Xirlink
XP-8052B
GSI
GS71108SJ-15
Xirlink
XP-80807
HC3738A
404-0990-151
404-0849-007

TIMELINE

1977
Apple II personal computer launched

Canon developed the first microprocessor-controlled camera, the AE-1

1981
First still-video camera unveiled, the Sony Mavica

First IBM personal computer (PC)

1983
Consortium of seventeen companies met to determine a unified standard for the magnetic disks used in filmless still-video cameras

1984
Canon demonstrated first still-video camera, the Canon RC-701, used at the Summer Olympic Games

Photography experienced perhaps its greatest transformation in the summer of 1981, when Sony unveiled the prototype of its still-video camera, the Mavica (*ma*gnetic *vi*sual *ca*mera). Undoubtedly, the migration from the daguerreotype to wet-plate processes such as the ambrotype in the 1850s, or even the move from wet-plate to dry-plate photography in the 1880s, were of equal import; but in the past the art of photography had far fewer practitioners, and the lack of instantaneous reporting of such discoveries ensured that less debate and discussion ensued. Of course in 1839, at the dawn of the daguerreotype age, Paul Delaroche, one of the most popular and respected French painters of the nineteenth century, is reputed to have said, "From today, painting is dead."

In fact, the information-technology explosion of the late 1990s led to significant growth in the imaging sector, compounded by the proliferation of images on the World Wide Web, in electronic mail, from Mars rovers, satellite photographs, and so on.

Almost immediately upon its introduction, filmless photography (including both still video and digital) was seen by purists as a contradiction. But in reality, photography using what we consider film only became popular in the 1880s. In fact, the word *photography* means nothing more than "light pictures," and even in filmless photography, light strikes the sensor in much the same manner as it does film. The only difference is that in traditional photography, the light comes into direct contact with the surface that serves as the negative or positive, whereas in filmless photography the sensor is a transient medium for the exposure, and the image is electronically stored.

Perhaps to calm the purists and allay industry fears, Sony chairman Akio Morita declared that the Mavica was not intended to replace conventional cameras, but to "provide a new type of video service," similar to a videotape recorder, which records programming for later viewing but is not a substitute for television itself. While Morita described the company's new product as "a revolutionary development in photographic history," it is unlikely that either he or his colleagues envisaged how widespread filmless photography would become, or that individual photographers would one day be placing hundreds of images together for public viewing on the World Wide Web.

Ironically, at the same time that Sony was making its historic announcement, a spokesman for the Eastman Kodak Company predicted that

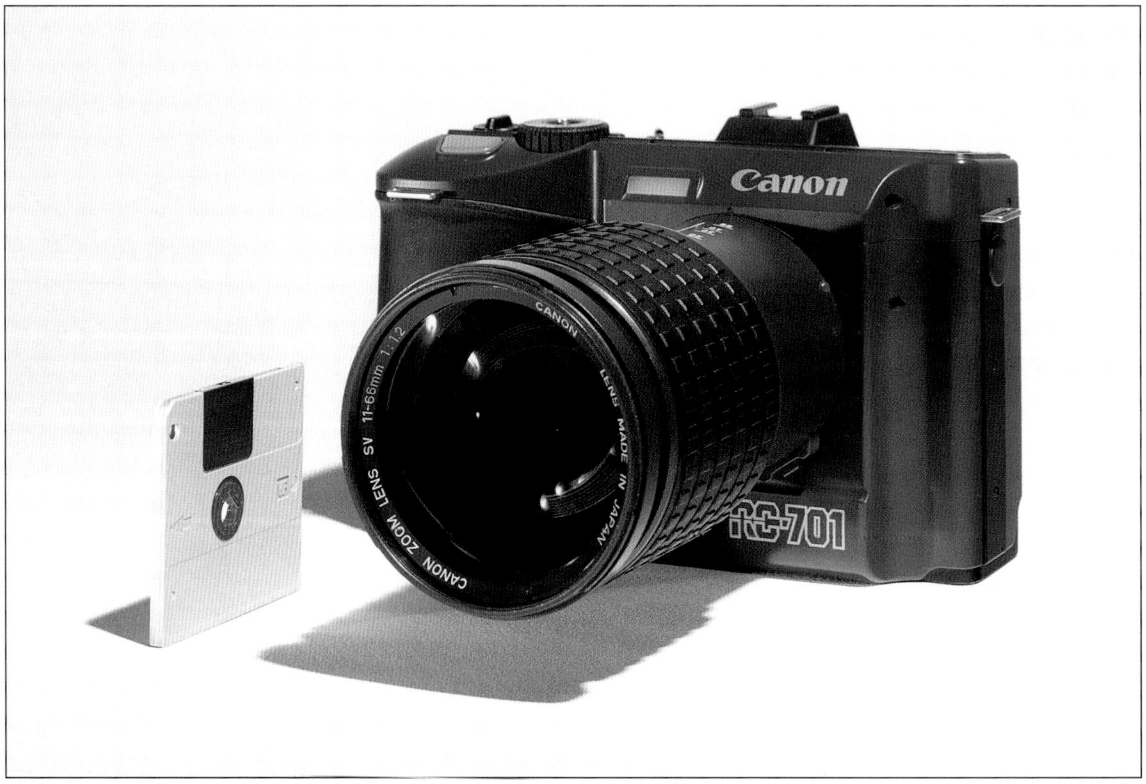

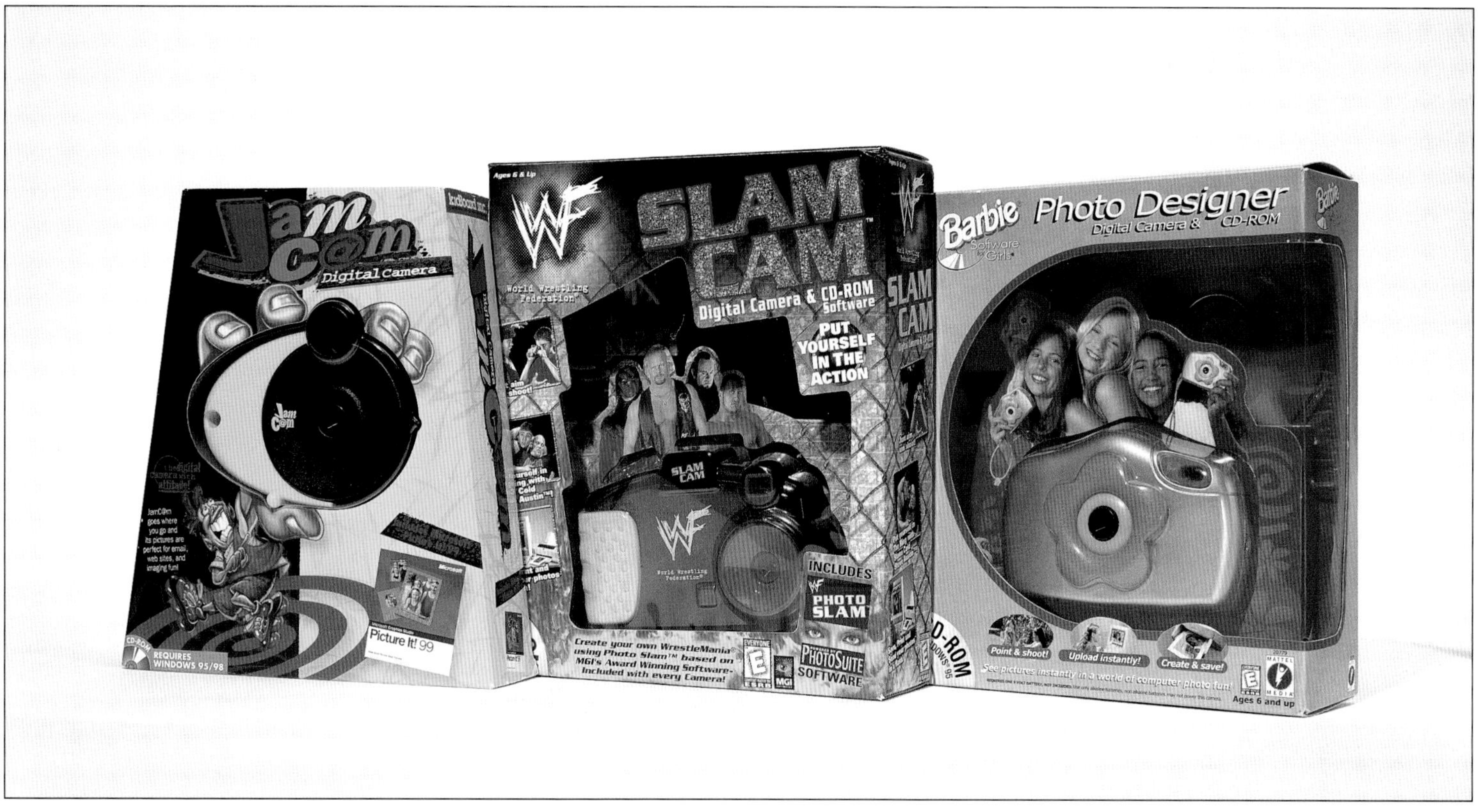

Opposite: RC-701 still-video camera, Canon, ca. 1986. The first filmless camera actually sold, since the original 1981 Sony Mavica was never brought to market. The RC-701 was accompanied by a player-recorder, a transceiver, a color video printer and a laminator (which adds plastic to both sides of the finished print). Shown with Canon VF-50 video floppy disk, used to store and transfer the images.

Above: (from left to right): "JamCam" digital camera, kidBoard, ca. 1999; WWF "Slam Cam" digital camera, Toymax, ca. 1999; Barbie Photo Designer digital camera, Mattel, ca. 2000. Cameras such as these set a new standard for low pricing, selling for as little as $29.95, while producing relatively low-quality images.

silver-based images would remain the dominant form of photography. Kodak's 1981 revenues were $10.3 billion, a good part of which derived from traditional film and film processing.

In 1981, a few days after Sony's announcement, Kodak president Colby Chandler, speaking to financial analysts, revealed that Kodak possessed the technological and manufacturing capability to build an all-electronic camera, but was assessing the camera's place in the amateur market before committing to production.

The concept of taking pictures electronically was first proposed by Alan Archibald Campbell Swinton FRS in 1908, the same year Henry Ford introduced the Model T automobile. Campbell Swinton, in his capacity as president of the Roentgen Society of London, delivered his 1911 presidential address on the subject of "distant electric vision," describing in detail a system resembling today's television, using a type of cathode-ray tube for both the transmitter and the receiver. It took about twenty-five years for his theory to result in the first rudimentary public-television service in England and the U.S.

Television, of course, took its rightful place in the world of imaging. But electronic photography was relegated to the back burner in research-and-development labs until 1981.

Film as a medium held a monopoly over the photographic world from the 1880s through the 1950s, when videotape became the preferred method of recording electronically created images from television cameras.

Along with the Mavica, Sony also previewed the Mavipak magnetic disk, measuring sixty millimeters tall, fifty-four millimeters wide, five millimeters thick, and weighing eight grams. The Mavipak was capable of storing up to fifty color still pictures.

By 1983 seventeen companies had met—among them Sony, Hitachi, Matsushita, Toshiba, Sharp, Canon, Olympus, Nippon Kogaku K.K., Minolta, Asahi, and Fuji—to jointly determine a unified standard for the tiny magnetic disk that would serve as a recording medium for "filmless" cameras. The group agreed to meet once a month, hoping to avoid the problems that had plagued the personal computer industry due to the lack of a standardized format for the compact floppy disks used to record data.

The 1984 Summer Olympic Games were a milestone in filmless photography. At the request

1986
Still-video magnetic disk standard finalized and endorsed by forty-six companies worldwide

1987
Canon launched its RC-760 still-video camera with a 600,000-pixel CCD

Kodak announced a 1.4 megapixel CCD

1988
First popular software program for image manipulation, the PhotoMac, released for the Macintosh

Canon RC-250 introduced

1989
Adobe Photoshop released, for Macintosh only

Sony launched the MVC-5000 Hi-Band camera, with separate CCDs for luminance and chrominance

Toshiba and Fuji Film announced the first digital camera. Toshiba developed the digital recording camera, player and picture filer unit while Fuji invented the display technology. The camera apparently was never marketed.

PROFILE: *The Still-Video Camera*

The still-video camera, similar to the television camera, employs a lens and iris to focus an image onto a charged couple device (CCD), as opposed to the light-sensitive silver halide film used in a conventional film-based camera. The CCD chip uses light falling on its surface to create varying electrical charges that are in turn converted into a video signal comprised of a luminance (black-and-white) portion, detailing the image's brightness levels, and a chrominance (color) portion, which records the color values (at far less detail than luminance). The video signals (in NTSC format) are then recorded onto a magnetic disk. This is an entirely analog process.

In some respects, the Mavica was just another television camera. But rather than capturing twenty-five or thirty frames per second, the Mavica captured single-frame, or "still video," pictures.

A digital camera works in similar fashion, the difference being that the CCD passes the image information onto an analog-to-digital converter, after which the image is digitally compressed and stored.

of the Japanese daily *Yomiuri Shimbun*, Canon configured an experimental still-video system, using the Canon RC-701 (RC stands for "Real-time Camera") to transmit photographs of Olympic events for publication (ultimately via a public telephone, as the car phone intended for use failed to work). In 1986 the RC-701 earned the distinction of being the first filmless camera to hit the market, as the original Sony Mavica never made it past the prototype stage, in part due to its unsatisfactory image quality.

The American press first caught up in 1987, during the Pan-American Games in Indianapolis, where the Canon RC-760 still-video camera was used to feed the wire-photo machines.

By 1986, the still-video standard had been finalized, and was endorsed by forty-six companies worldwide.

Media reports in the 1980s voiced the hope that the consortium would result in the commercialization of still-video photography. But it was clear that the companies involved in film and film processing, most notably Kodak, were deeply anxious about filmless photography. Though recognizing the role of computers in photography, Kodak hoped to

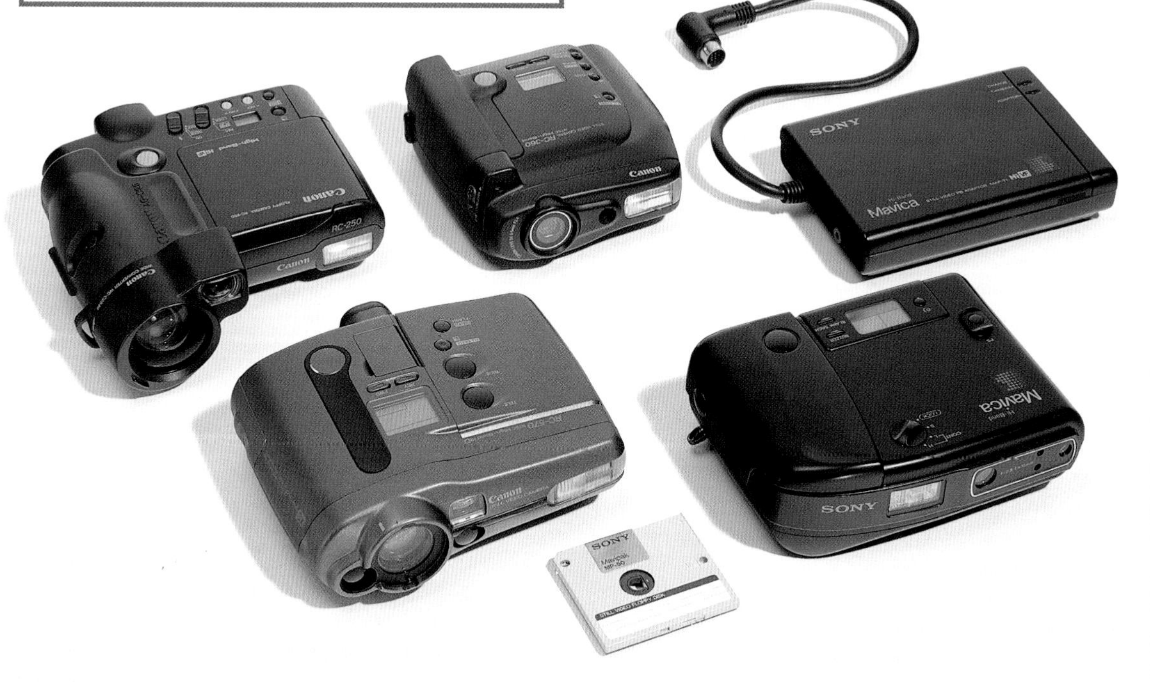

PROFILE: *Floppy-Disk Photography*

A 1985 headline from *Shutterbug Ads Photographic News*: "Here Comes Floppy Disc [sic] Photography." The article, by George Gilbert, noted that the world's first "film" for the "first generation of all-electronic still cameras" had recently been shown at the Photo Marketing Association International Show in Las Vegas. Gilbert went on to comment that the 1.85-inch disk would never be dunked in developer. TDK, one of the world's largest manufacturers of recording tapes and computer disks, called the new medium a "video floppy disk." Konica and Fuji were the first two manufacturers to develop working prototypes, which were displayed at the show.

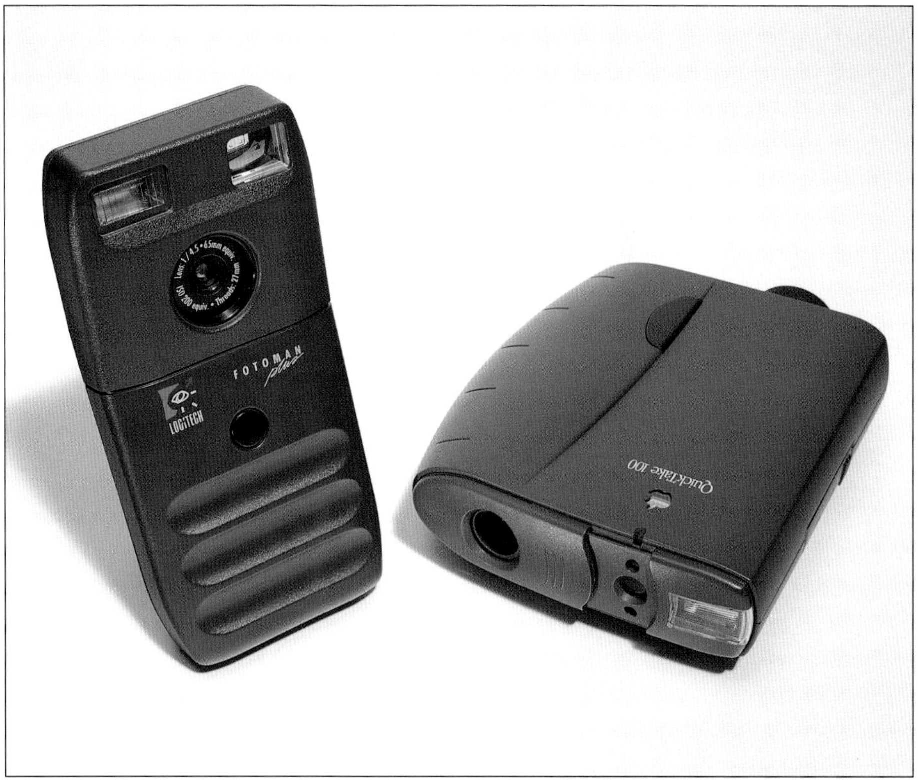

position the new technology as an enabler or supplement, allowing the lucrative film and film-processing businesses to continue undisturbed.

Kodak envisioned and espoused the adoption of a hybrid of film and filmless technology. Pictures, in Kodak's scheme, would be shot on film, then scanned after processing, making messy shoeboxes full of prints a thing of the past, replaced by pictures stored and indexed on videotape.

At the same time, the first software program for image manipulation on an Apple Macintosh computer, PhotoMac, was introduced in 1988. The current market leader, Adobe Photoshop, was actually the second such program introduced, in 1989.

Jason Schneider, editorial director of *Popular Photography*, hedged his bets in an interview with the *Bergen Record* (New Jersey) in 1988, saying "The future of photography is in electronic imaging or a hybrid system of film and electronic transmission."

As late as 1989, the *New York Times* reported Kodak vice president K. Bradley Paxton as saying, "our intention is to supplement people's imaging needs rather than displace conventional photographic systems." Paxton said he saw electronic

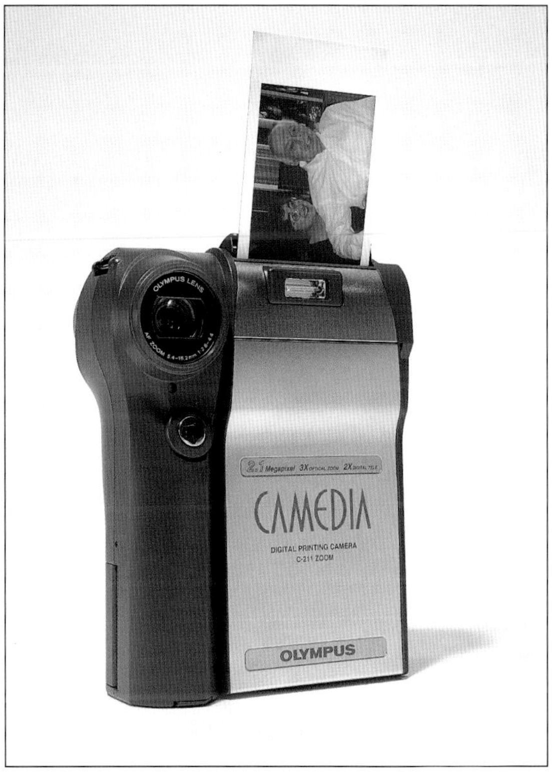

Opposite page: Various early amateur still-video cameras and accessories. Top row: RC-250, Canon, ca. 1988; RC-360, Canon, ca. 1992; Mavica MAP-T1 still-video playback adapter, Sony, ca. 1989. Bottom row: RC-570, Canon, ca. 1992; Mavipak MP-50 still-video floppy disk, Sony, ca. 1989.Hi-Band Mavica, MVC-C1, Sony, ca. 1989.

Above: Left: Fotoman Plus, Logitech, ca. 1994. One of the earliest consumer-grade black-and-white digital cameras; Right: QuickTake 100, Apple, ca. 1993. The first consumer-grade color digital camera.

Left: Camedia C-211 ZOOM digital printing camera, Olympus, 2000. The first digital camera with a built-in Polaroid printer.

photography as something with which to "add value" to film images.

After missing out on the home-video revolution of the 1980s, Kodak decided to take up the fight against filmless photography on two fronts at once. In 1985, the company introduced a still-video floppy-disk system, without camera, for the

Jonathan B. Spira, *Im Französischen Dom von Oben*, 1998. Taken with Olympus D-200L.

Below: D-200L digital camera, Olympus, 1996. One of the first digital cameras from a traditional film camera manufacturer. Unlike many still-video and early digital cameras, the D-200L's form resembles a point-and-shoot camera, a trend that furthered consumer acceptance and continues to date.

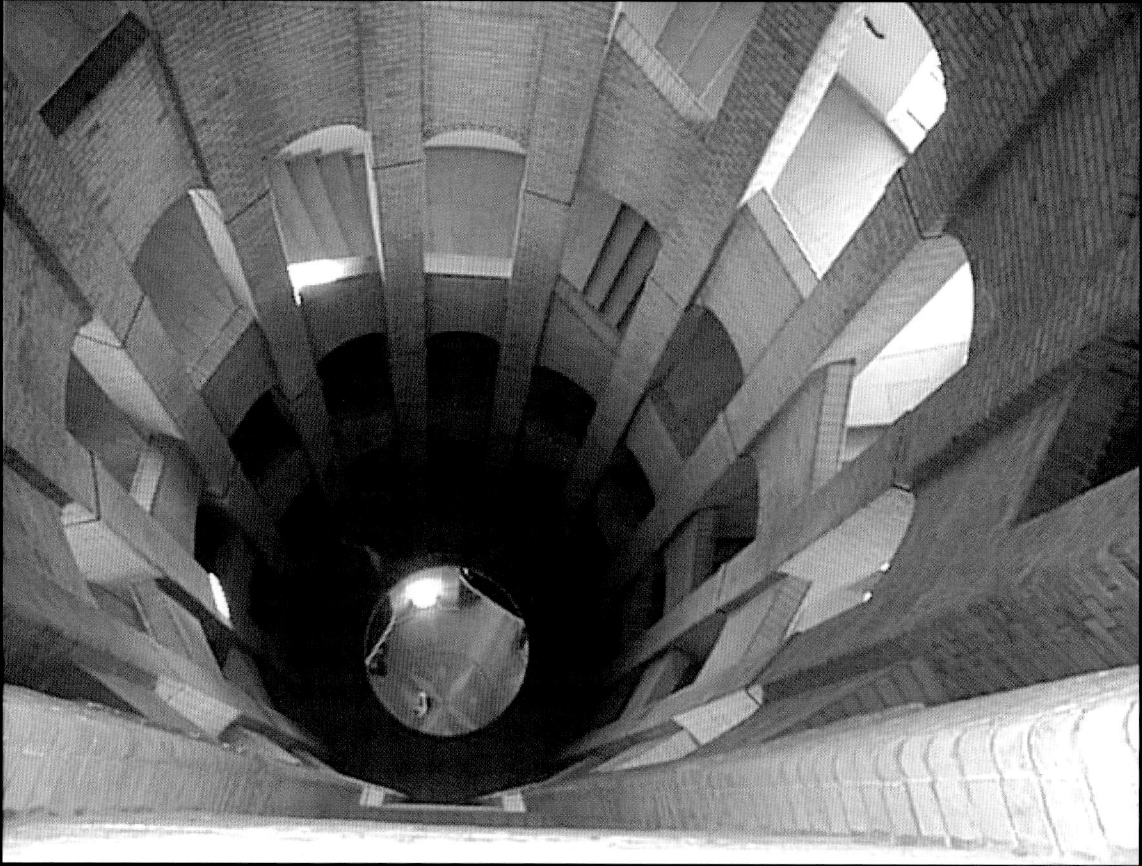

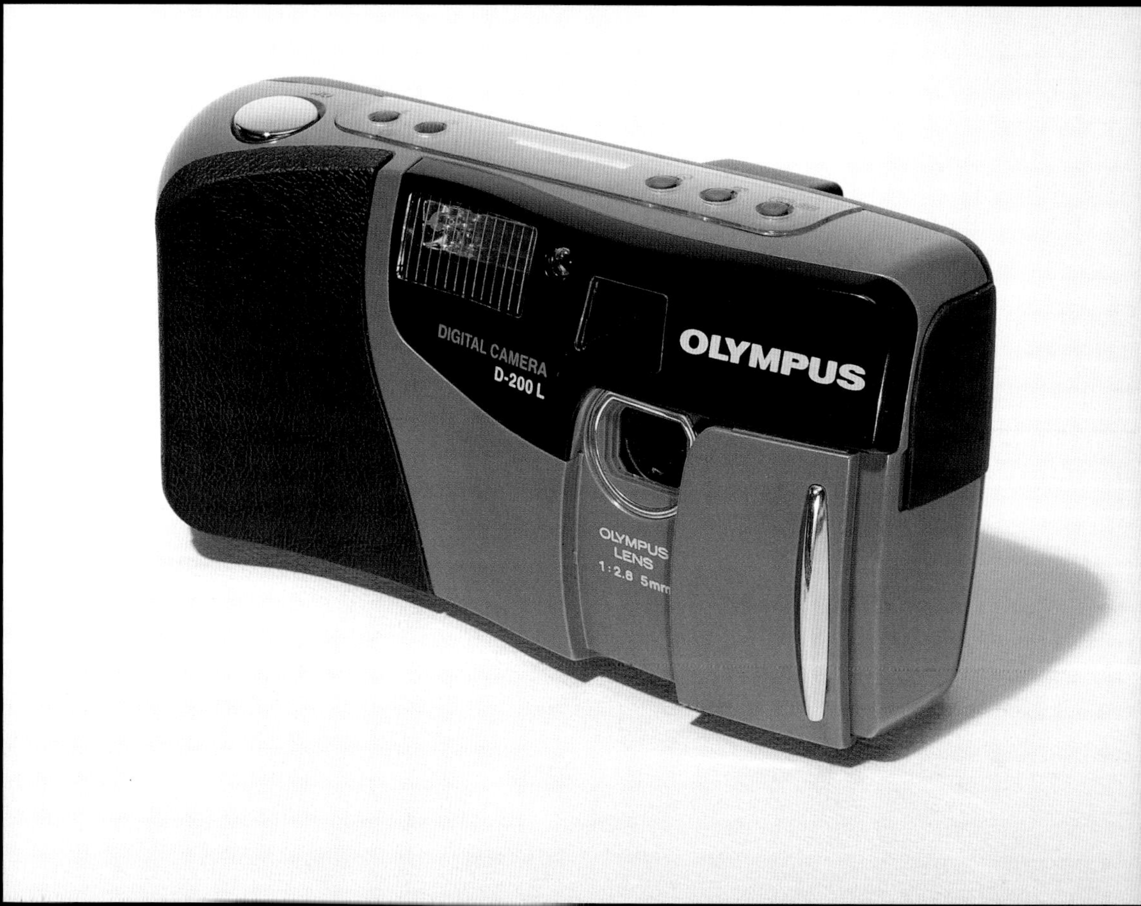

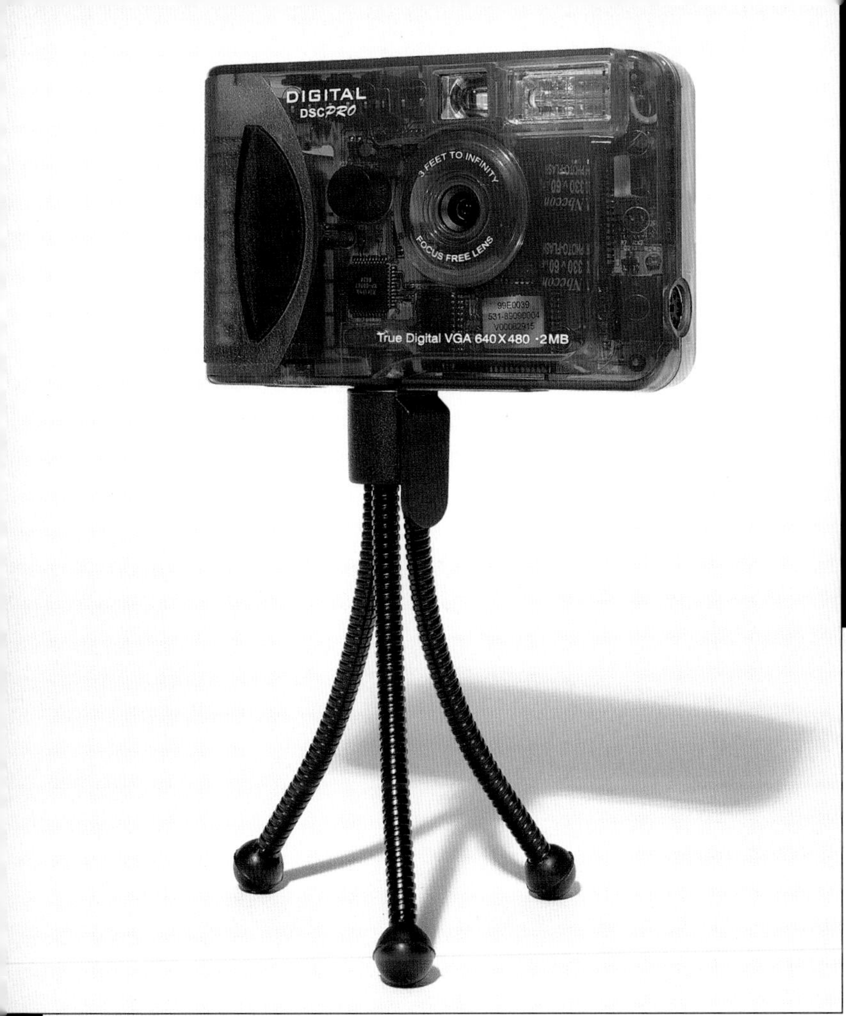

Digital DCS Pro digital camera, Xirlink, ca. 2000. Its unusual clear case emphasizes its digital workings.

Below: Left: PalmPix camera attachment, Kodak, ca. 1999, allows Palm Pilot and IBM WorkPad users to take digital pictures, beam them via infrared link to other users with compatible palm devices, and transfer them to a computer where they can be e-mailed, stored, or printed. Right: Game Boy camera, Nintendo, ca. 2000, slips into Nintendo Game Boy System in the same manner as other Nintendo game cartridges. Camera head or lens can be turned 180 degrees with 7 click-stop positions. User can doodle on images, add stamps, and even send image to another Game Boy camera.

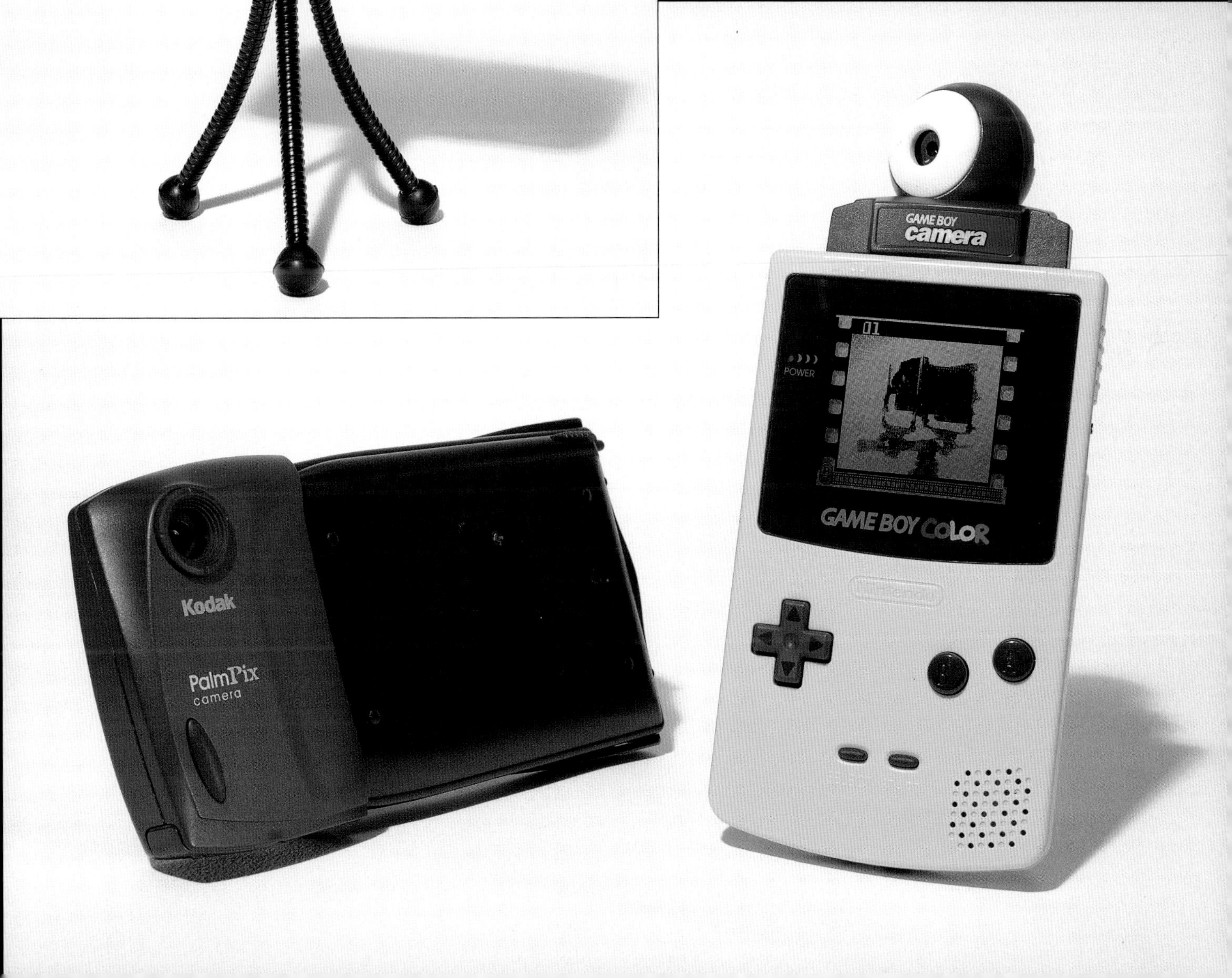

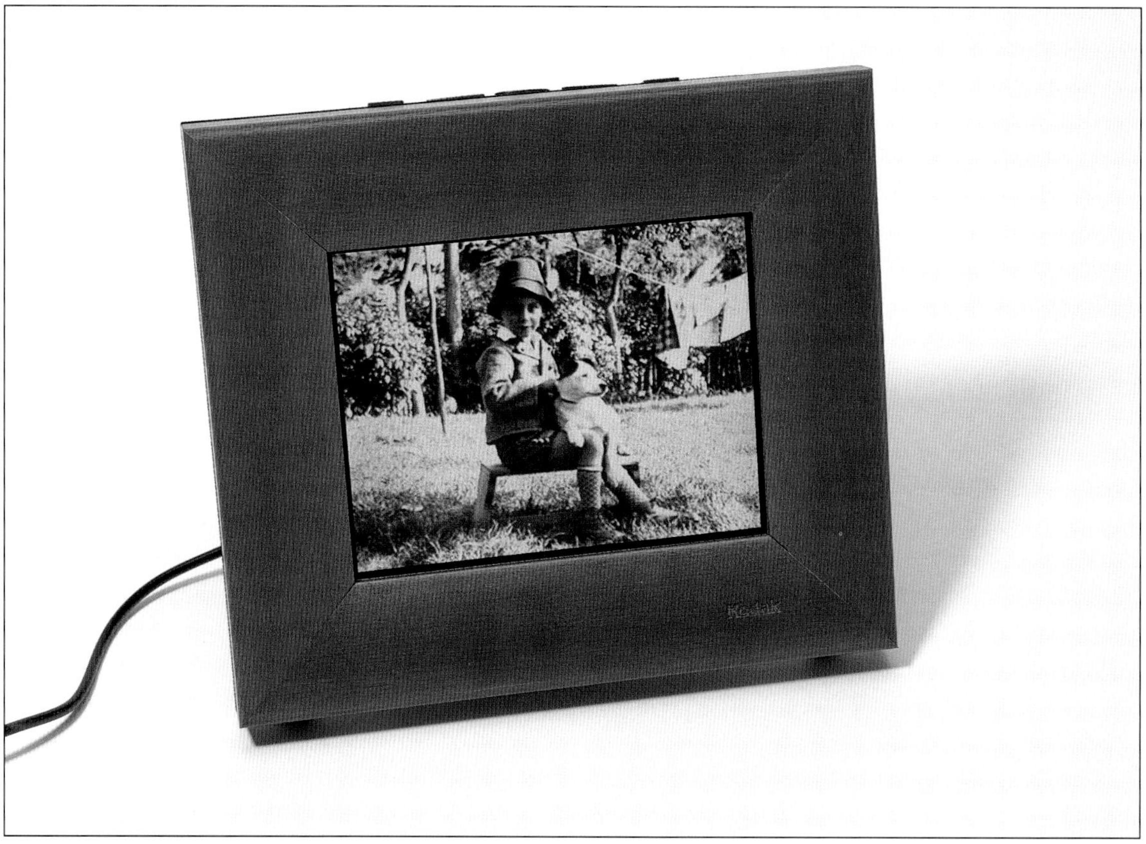

1990
Kodak introduced the Photo CD

First "portable" digital camera: Dycam Model 1, suitable for newspaper-quality halftones up to 5 x 4" and magazine-quality halftones of up to 3 x 2¼"

1991
First professional digital camera, the Kodak DCS, introduced

The World Wide Web (WWW) created by Tim Berners-Lee

1993
Mosaic Web browser introduced for WWW

Nikon, Canon, Leaf Systems, and others announced new digital cameras for photojournalists

Adobe Photoshop for Windows introduced

1994
Apple QuickTake, first consumer-grade color digital camera, introduced

industrial market. This system required images to be taken with film-based cameras, then scanned and transferred onto 2-by-2-inch disks. (Around the same time, in 1982, Kodak unveiled its Disk Camera, as much an attempt to regain the company's dwindling share of the Instamatic-type market as to divert attention away from filmless photography. Due to low quality and poor sales, however, the Disk Camera was quietly discontinued in the late 1980s, while the more competitively priced point-and-shoot 35 mm cameras rose to dominance.)

In 1990, Kodak unveiled the Photo CD, a compact disc formatted to hold one hundred digitally-encoded pictures. Each 35 mm picture was converted into six images of varying resolution, from a 6,144-pixel thumbnail (taking up a miserly 18 kilobytes) to a magnificently detailed 6.3-megapixel image (18.4 megabytes, uncompressed). This format was developed jointly by Kodak and Philips, the key developer of the audio compact disc. Kodak took the opportunity to promise high-resolution, film-based images, in contrast with the decidedly low-resolution electronic image of the still-video camera. Unfortunately, consumers balked at paying four hundred dollars for the CD player required to read the discs. In 1997 Kodak launched the FlashPix CD, which cost twenty-five dollars per unit, required several days for processing, did not allow image manipulation, and captured less than 0.1 percent of all processing orders.

Photo CD's third progeny, the Picture CD, was introduced in 1999, at a price of about nine dollars. Kodak also launched "You've Got Pictures," a partnership with America Online that allowed AOL users to send pictures via e-mail.

Although Kodak never introduced a still-video camera into the market, it did, in 1991, introduce the first professional digital camera, known as the Digital Camera System (DCS). Based on a Nikon F3 body, the camera was connected by cable to a digital storage unit (DSU), a 200-megabyte hard disk with a capacity of 160 images. The DSU also sported a small black-and-white display the photographer could use to check composition and exposure. The Kodak DCS200, based on a Nikon 8008/801 camera body, was completely self-contained and held fifty images on its internal 80-megabyte hard disk. The camera looked like an SLR with motordrive and weighed about the same.

In the early 1990s, three new entrants found a more receptive consumer market: Apple's QuickTake, Dycam's Model 1, and Logitech's Fotoman and Fotoman Plus (identical to Dycam's Model 1 and Model 3, respectively). The reason for this change was the large-scale adoption of the personal computer and, shortly thereafter, the advent of widespread Internet access.

The change in the equation occasioned by the PC was its ability to overcome the poor and expensive color printing that was available, and the fact that images displayed on-screen via a PC (but never printed) could be of far lower resolution.

In 1994 and 1995, *Macworld* tests showed that the Apple digital camera—the first camera sold for under one thousand dollars to offer good color-image quality and relative ease of use—along with the Dycam Model 4 ($795), the Fujix DS-100 ($3,200), and the Canon RC-570 ($3,740), all produced photographs comparable to those taken on film with a twenty-dollar box camera.

Remarkably, ten years after the introduction of the first digital camera in 1991, and despite the fact that forty-six companies had agreed on a standard still-video storage format in the 1980s, there had been little movement toward a common standard for storing digital images. Although several of the first consumer digital cameras used a form of hard disk and floppy disk for this, other early cameras used a variety of methods. The Dycam used RAM chips, which, due to power consumption, were capable of storing images for only a week or so. The Apple QuickTake used EPROMs, which could keep a picture intact in the camera for almost a year.

The excitement of taking digital pictures quickly dulled when it came time to wrest the images from within the camera. Most consumer digital cameras required a slow and tedious download procedure, via a cable between camera and PC, to effect the transfer. And some software packages required images to be "converted" before they were suitable for final viewing.

The year 1996 was pivotal, as Canon, Nikon, and Olympus all introduced their first digital cameras. Easier to use than their predecessors, they also looked more like the popular "point-and-shoot" models so prevalent in the 35 mm world.

Opposite: Smart Picture Frame, Kodak, 2000. Allows downloading of photographs directly to an electronic display without a computer via the Kodak Storybox network.

Left: Digital Camera Coolpix 300, Nikon, ca. 1997. Combining digital image capture, digital audio recording system, and electronic memo using stylus input, the camera evokes turn-of-the-century Kodak Autographic models.

Right: RC-470 still-video camera, Canon, ca. 1988. At that time it was considered to be "high end" at the time of its introduction, with 360,000 pixel resolution.

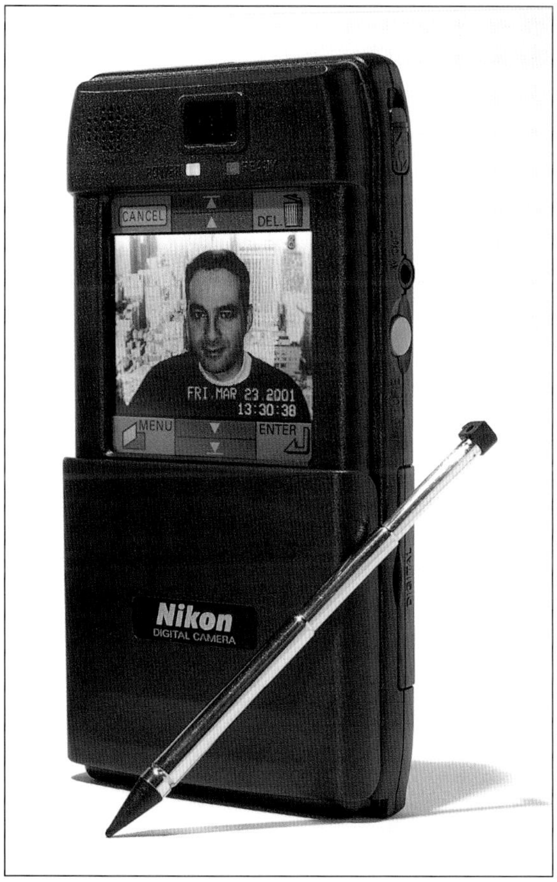

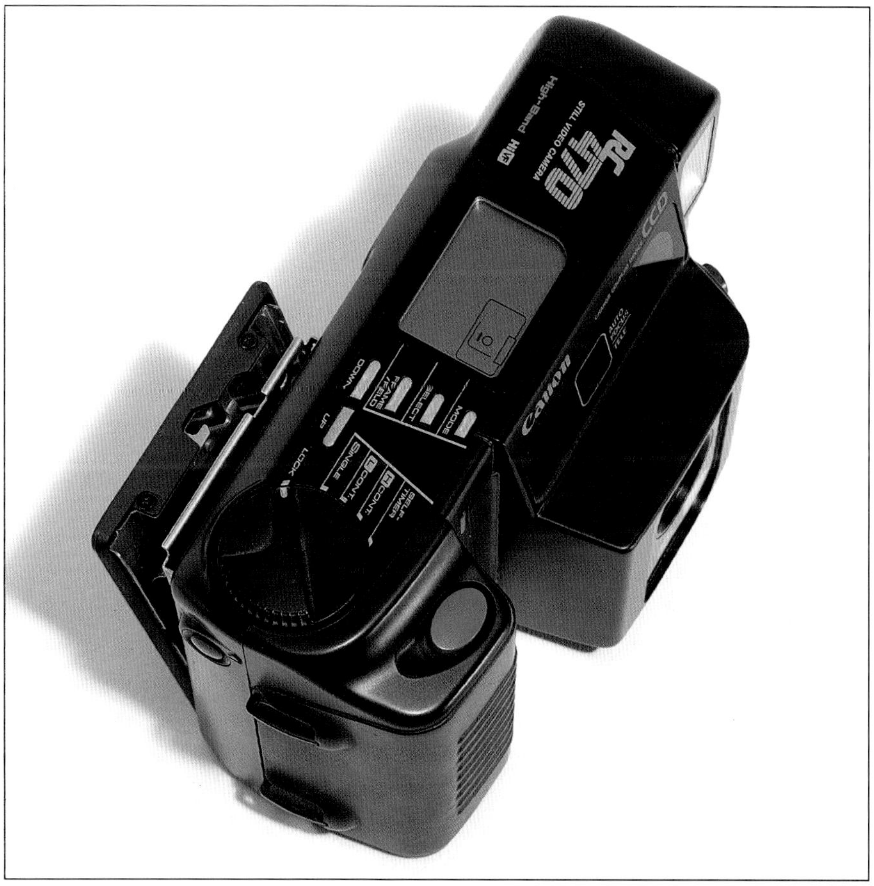

1995
Last still-video camera manufactured

Microsoft released Windows 95

1996
Major camera manufacturers (Canon, Nikon, Olympus) introduced digital cameras

Advanced Photo System (APS) introduced

First consumer-grade photographic printer, the HP PhotoSmart introduced

1997
Megapixel cameras introduced; digital camera resolution improved as a result

Percentage of camera stores selling digital cameras jumped to 67.1 percent (from 42.6 percent in 1996)

2000
Digital cameras available for less than $50

Number of digital cameras sold in U.S. jumped to 4.39 million (from 2.18 million in 1999)

But they were more than just filmless counterparts to traditional cameras. Nikon's Coolpix 300 had an "autograph" feature, not unlike the feature found in many Kodak film cameras of the 1920s, which allowed the photographer to add handwritten and audio notes to an image.

Cameras such as the Olympus D-200L had the "look and feel" of their analog brethren. The Olympus featured an LCD screen for viewing photographs, and included a copy of Adobe PhotoDeluxe software. Prices for this new breed of filmless camera were going down as well, approaching the midrange rather than the high end of the traditional 35 mm camera market.

Other companies in the high-tech arena saw that digital photography was also in their future. Hewlett-Packard, known for its computer printers, introduced the PhotoSmart family of products, which consisted of a low-end digital camera, a high-end scanner suitable for scanning slides and negatives, and the first printer specifically designed for consumers to use to output high-quality digital color photographs.

In 1997, Sony introduced its MVC-FD5 and MVC-FD7 Digital Mavica cameras, notable for the fact that they stored their JPEG images directly onto standard, 3.5-inch floppy disks. Both models came equipped with a 2.5-inch color LCD display and image-editing software, and were capable of storing twenty high-quality or forty standard-quality pictures on a single floppy. The MVC-FD7's higher price tag included a 10:1 optical zoom lens (the lens on the MVC-FD5 had a fixed focal length), a manual focus override, macro capability, and four pre-programmed special-effects modes (monochrome, pastel, negative image, and sepia). The image took only six seconds to load onto the floppy disk (many fixed-media cameras took longer), making it possible to view images instantly on virtually any computer, without lengthy download procedures.

Other manufacturers introduced proprietary removable media, such as Compact Flash, Smart Media, or Memory Sticks, which required a special reader to be attached to the computer. Others (usually of the less-expensive variety) continued

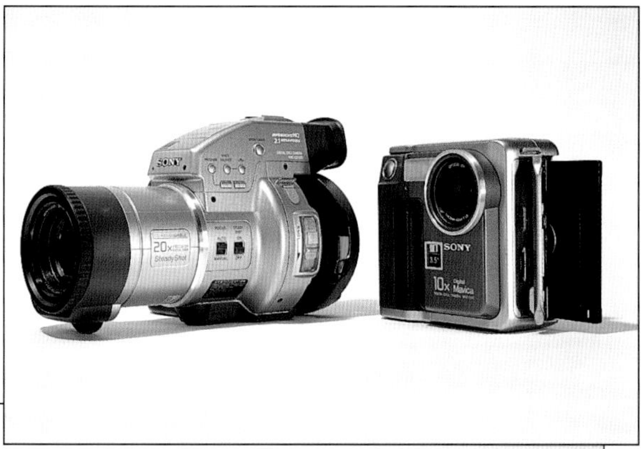

Left: Mavica MVC-CD1000, Sony, 2000. Allowed users to save almost 150 high-resolution photos to a 3" CD-ROM, universally compatible with the CD-ROM drives installed in most personal computers. Right: Digital Mavica MVC-FD7, Sony, ca. 1997. Introduced alongside the more basic MVC-FD5, allowed users to store their images onto a standard 3.5-inch floppy.

Below: From Hewlett-Packard, the first-ever "suite" of digital photography products, included the PhotoSmart digital camera (left), PhotoSmart photo printer (center), and the PhotoSmart photo scanner (right), all ca. 1996.

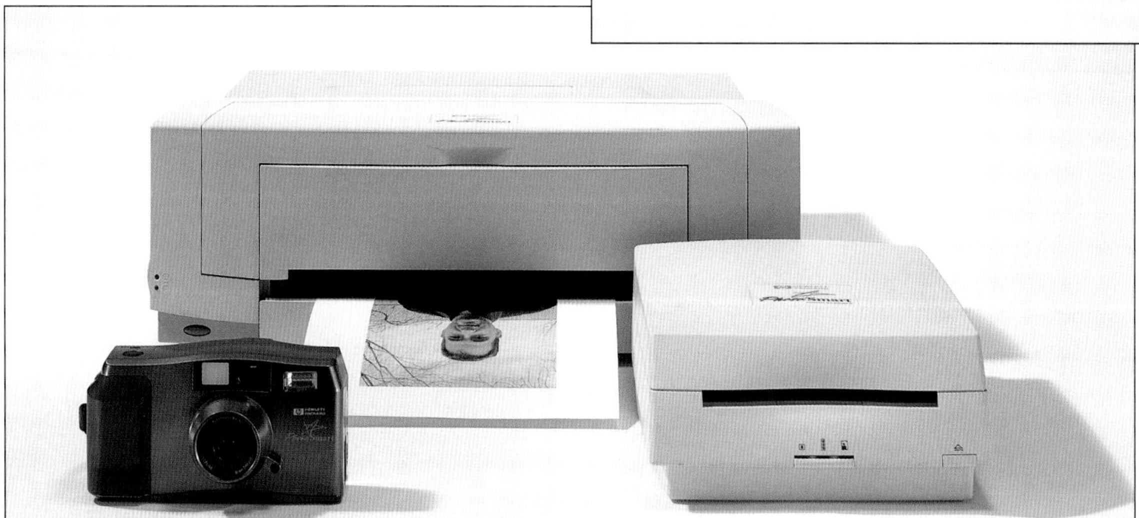

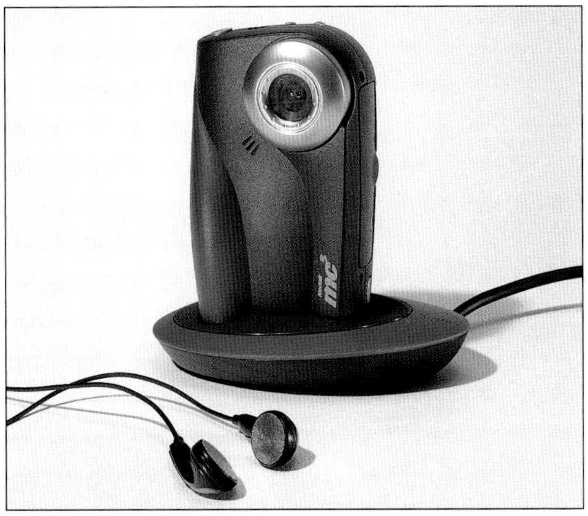

mc3 portable multimedia device, Kodak, ca. 2000. Combines a digital camera (capable of recording video and still pictures) and an MP3 player, designed, according to Kodak, for the "Gen Y" crowd.

with various forms of internal storage, all of which required a cable to download. Olympus used a serial driver with its own Twain; Canon used a parallel interface; Nikon developed a SCSI camera.

By 2000, digital cameras had stratified into three price groups: low, medium, and high. Cameras at the low end, costing as little as $29.95, offered limited storage capacity, no easy way to transfer images, fairly low resolution (640 x 480), and few options (zoom, flash). With their bright-colored plastics and rounded contours, these cameras looked like toys, and given their performance, they may as well have been. With no LCD screen to review snapshots, and cumbersome downloading procedures, low-end digital cameras did little to convince the casual photographer to "go digital."

The next group, with prices in the three- to seven-hundred-dollar range, is where the traditional film-camera marketplace may see the greatest incursions. These digital devices offer resolutions of 2.1 megapixels (2 million pixels per photo), quality optics, with 2x and 3x zoom features, greater storage (8 megabytes or more), removal media (Memory Sticks or, as in the Sony, floppy disks), and LCD displays for reviewing photos.

Finally, the high-end cameras, costing seven hundred dollars and up, offer a level of quality and ease-of-use to rival the best contemporary film cameras. Sporting resolutions of 3.3 megapixels or

PROFILE:

The Compatibility Conundrum

Daguerreotypes taken in 1839 survive today; many photographs taken with early still-video or digital cameras do not, and those that do remain might not last long. Consider a picture taken with a Canon RC-760 in 1988. Unless the photographer has a paper print of the photo, as well as the original camera and a working player for the proprietary floppy disk, the picture may be irretrievably lost. Given the quality of early still-video printing, moreover, the paper print is likely to have deteriorated significantly.

Similar problems may befall the user of a digital camera, for example the Apple QuickTake 100. The QuickTake software for downloading the images came on a 3.5-inch diskette. In order to download a picture, then (and assuming the picture was still stored in the camera), one would need a computer with an operating system that allows the QuickTake software to run. The 3.5-inch diskette will certainly be an historical curiosity within a decade. (In the world of PCs, downward compatibility is never a certainty.)

In 1799, a French engineering officer, stationed at a fort near the Egyptian city of Rosetta, happened upon an ancient basalt slab. Etched into the stone was a priestly decree dating to circa 196 B.C., using Egyptian hieroglyphics, demotic characters, and Greek. In addition to serving as a key to previously undecipherable hieroglyphics, the Rosetta stone was noteworthy for its longevity.

This scenario mirrors media compatibility in the information age. One might presume that the technology revolution of the late twentieth century has increased our ability to preserve our history and cultural artifacts. In actuality, mankind is doing a terrible job. As more information is created and data standards evolve and progress, more and more information is being lost. Digital standards come and go within a few years' time. Already, some of NASA's earliest pictures of Earth are no longer accessible. The operating system and format documentation are long gone.

One solution may be the Rosetta Disc, a three-inch-wide piece of pure nickel, engineered to last ten thousand years. Etched onto the first disc, so finely that a microscope is needed to read it, are the first three chapters of the Book of Genesis in one thousand languages, along with other material that may be of use to scholars thousands of years hence—all in analog form.

Created under the auspices of the San Francisco-based Long Now Foundation, the Rosetta Disc technology, given its analog nature, could provide a means of archiving electronic photographs. Photo historians of the future would then not have to depend on digital system upgrades (or retrogrades) and transitions that took place in the intervening years since the photograph was taken, as the ability to view and retrieve such images will always be available.

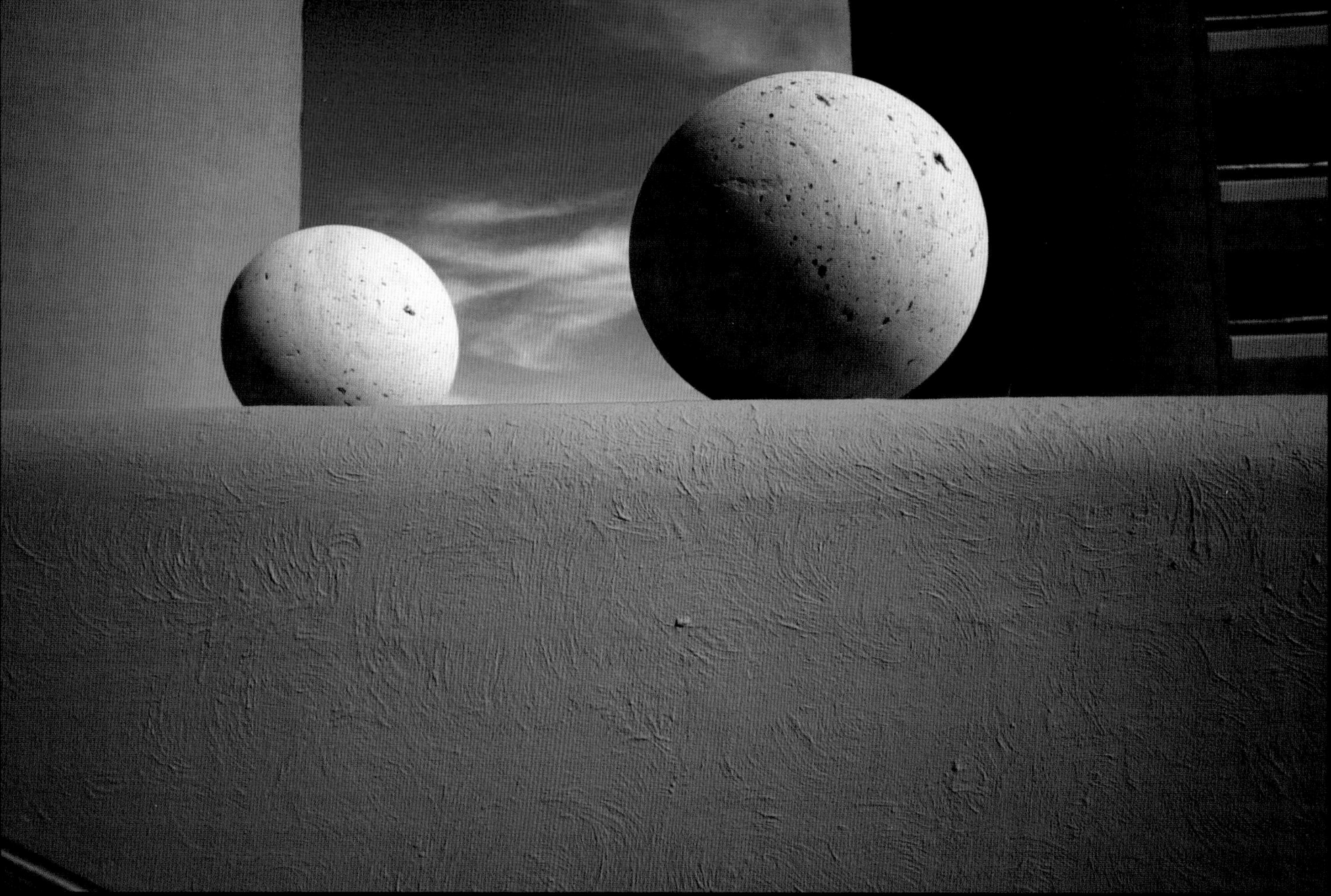

better, with 16 megabytes of storage, some even offer the option of shooting video clips, and one, the Sony MVC-CD1000, has a built-in CD-ROM burner, for storing images.

In 2000, North American digital-camera sales (including toy digital cameras, digital-camera attachments, entry-level, point-and-shoot, and SLRs) reached $1.9 billion, exceeding the revenue generated from traditional film-camera sales by some 10 percent. (The number of film-based cameras sold was actually higher, but digital cameras are more expensive. Single-use film cameras are not included in these figures.)

Digital photography may be viewed as part of a broad cultural change, one in which letters have given way to e-mail, phone conversations to voice-mail messages. The individual user's computing environment has embraced the use of images in the context of ordinary tasks, including e-mail and word processing (previously known as typing). The trend toward instant gratification, perhaps propelled by Federal Express in 1979, has led users to achieve this by printing or e-mailing images immediately, as desired.

The new medium itself is a hybrid of three disciplines: photography, video, and computing. Of course this gives photography the potential to impact far more people than ever before, but it can also lead to an interesting set of uniquely modern problems. An August 1995 article in *Popular Photography* asked "Is this photography?," pointing out that once an image is "scanned in electronically and subsequently enhanced, altered, or combined, using a computer, look out!" It went on to say that "such images no longer represent reality, and capturing reality in pictures is what photography is all about, isn't it?" This article accurately captures the fear of digital-phobes, whose mantra is "Film doesn't lie; computers can be made to." But the veracity of a photograph lies in the trust the viewer has in the photographer, not the medium, and in the connection the photographer is able to make with the viewer through his work.

Filmless photography should be viewed as part of an evolutionary process begun in 1839. Change is always difficult. In some respects, the change from film to "filmlessness" resembles earlier transitions, such as wet-plate to dry-plate, in which the older technology continued but faded, as the newer one built its reputation on superior ease-of-use and convenience.

There will always be some form of recording light images; it is a science that has taken centuries to evolve. What shape it will take in the future has yet to be determined, but each technological advance in photography has served to broaden and deepen its reach.

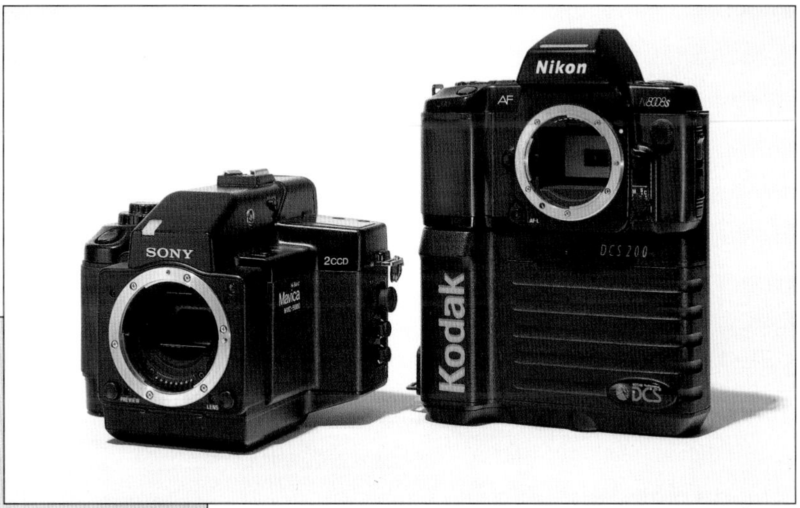

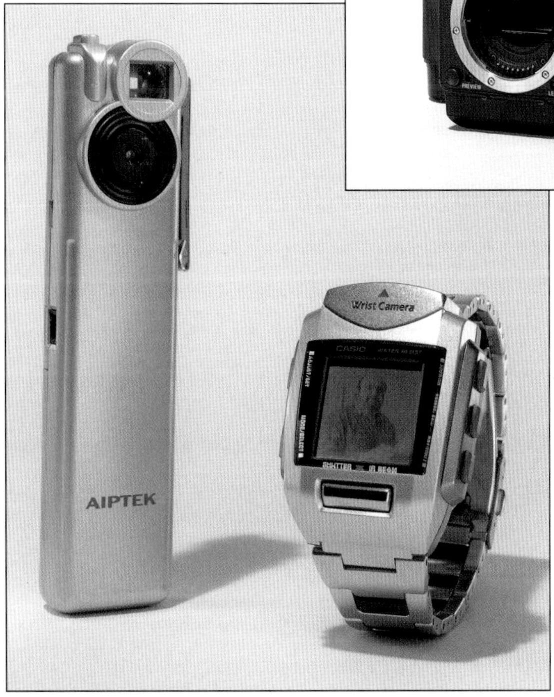

Opposite: Pete Turner, *Mexican Spheres*, 2001, digital photograph taken with a Nikon D1 with a Nikon 14 mm lens.

Left: Left: PenCam Trio digital camera, Aiptek, ca. 2000. True to its name, it functions as a "web cam" for videoconferencing, as a digital still camera and also as a video camera, recording for up to forty seconds in low-resolution mode. But the PenCam does not, as the name implies, actually function as a writing instrument. Right: Wrist Camera, Casio, ca. 2000, water-resistant stainless steel case. Watch, weighing only 32 grams, displays time and date, has alarm and stopwatch functionality, and takes pictures digitally. Images can be viewed on the watch or downloaded to a personal computer, and text may even be added to each image. Images can be transferred from one watch to another via infrared link.

Right: Left: Mavica MVC-5000, Sony, ca. 1989, a professional-grade, still-video, single-lens-reflex camera which operates in either automatic or manual modes; accepts a variety of interchangeable lenses; has a three-frames-per-second sequential picture capability; and features through-the-lens electronic flash. At the time of its introduction it was the only still-video camera with separate CCD chips for managing luminance and chrominance information. Right: Professional DCS 200 digital camera, Kodak, ca. 1993. Kodak's second digital camera, it was based on the Nikon 8008 body. A hard drive is attached to the bottom of the body, giving the impression of a motorwind. In contrast to the Sony, it accepts industry-standard Nikon-mount lenses.

TO MARILYN SPIRA, MY WIFE AND CO-COLLECTOR

—S. F. SPIRA

Contributors

PHOTOGRAPHS BY

STEFAN HAGEN

WITH

CAROLINE LEE

RESEARCH BY

NIGEL H. RUSSELL

AND

BASILIO ALFEROW

Acknowledgements

Eileen Connor
Bernie Danis
Ralph Engel
Steven Morgan Friedman
David M. Goldes
Nicholas Graver
Gayle Hardy
Michael E. Hoffman
Burt Keppler
Yann and Lynn Maillett
Michael Pritchard
Ceil Rosenthal
Jason Schneider
Charles Skop
Phyllis Thompson Reid
Allen Weiner
Harvey Zucker
Members of the various photographica societies

Objects displayed in illustrations in *The History of Photography as Seen Through the Spira Collection* are or were part of The Spira Collection LLC, Photo Historica LLC, and personal collections of S. F. Spira and Marilyn Spira.

"Focus: Stamps and Photography" originally appeared in *History of Photography*, 1979, vol. 3, no. 1, in slightly different form as "Photographica on Postage Stamps." "Focus: The Spirograph" originally appeared in *History of Photography*, 1982, vol . 6, no. 1, in slightly different form as "The Spirograph: The 'Disc' Motion-Picture Viewer and Projector." Both appear courtesy of the journal. Please see www.tandf.co.uk for further information.

Library of Congress Catalog Card Number: 2001092554
Hardcover ISBN: 0-89381-953-0

DESIGN BY MICHELLE DUNN MARSH
Design assistant: Steve McIntyre

Photographs by Stefan Hagen with Caroline Lee

Separations by Bright Arts (HK) Ltd., Hong Kong
Printed and bound by Tien Wah Press (PTE.) Ltd., Singapore

The Staff at Aperture for *The History of Photography as Seen Through the Spira Collection*:
Michael E. Hoffman, Executive Director
Phyllis Thompson Reid, Editor
Eileen Connor, Assistant Editor
Stevan A. Baron, V.P., Production
Lisa A. Farmer, Production Director
Andrew Hiller, Editorial Assistant
Gabriella Gomez-Mont, Editorial Work-Scholar

Aperture Foundation publishes a periodical, books, and portfolios of fine photography and presents world-class exhibitions to communicate with serious photographers and creative people everywhere. A complete catalog is available upon request.

Aperture Customer Service: 20 East 23rd Street, New York, New York 10010. Phone: (212) 598-4205. Fax: (212) 598-4015. Toll-free: (800) 929-2323. E-mail: customerservice@aperture.org

Aperture Foundation, including Book Center and Burden Gallery: 20 East 23rd Street, New York, New York 10010. Phone: (212) 505-5555, ext. 300. Fax: (212) 979-7759. E-mail: info@aperture.org

Aperture Millerton Book Center: 22 Route North, Millerton, New York 12546. Phone: (518) 789-9003.

Visit Aperture's website: www.aperture.org

Aperture Foundation books are distributed internationally through:

CANADA: General/Irwin Publishing Co., Ltd., 325 Humber College Blvd., Etobicoke, Ontario, M9W 7C3. Fax: (416) 213-1917.

UNITED KINGDOM, SCANDINAVIA, AND CONTINENTAL EUROPE: Aperture c/o Robert Hale, Ltd., Clerkenwell House, 45-47 Clerkenwell Green, London, United Kingdom, EC1R OHT. Fax: (44) 171-490-4958.

NETHERLANDS, BELGIUM, LUXEMBURG: Nilsson & Lamm, BV, Pampuslaan 212-214, P.O. Box 195, 1382 JS Weesp, Netherlands. Fax: (31) 29-441-5054.

AUSTRALIA: Tower Books Pty. Ltd., Unit 9/19 Rodborough Road, Frenchs Forest, Sydney, New South Wales, Australia. Fax: (61) 2-9975-5599.

NEW ZEALAND: Southern Publishers Group, 22 Burleigh Street, Grafton, Auckland, New Zealand. Fax: (64) 9-309-6170.

INDIA: TBI Publishers, 46 Housing Project, South Extension Part-I, New Delhi 110049, India. Fax: (91) 11-461-0576.

To subscribe to the periodical *Aperture* write Aperture, P.O. Box 3000, Denville, New Jersey 07834. Toll-free: (800) 783-4903. International subscriptions (973) 627-2427. One year: $40.00. Two years: $66.00. Add $10.00 per year for international orders.

FIRST EDITION
10 9 8 7 6 5 4 3 2 1

VISIT APERTURE'S WEBSITE: WWW.APERTURE.ORG, AND WWW.SPIRA.COM

FOR MORE INFORMATION ON THE HISTORY OF PHOTOGRAPHY